Green Solvents

for Organic Synthesis

Green Solvents

for Organic Synthesis

V.K. Ahluwalia

R.S. Varma

Alpha Science International Ltd.

Oxford, U.K.

Green Solvents
for Organic Synthesis
346 pgs. | 3 figs. | 6 tbs.

V.K. Ahluwalia
B.R. Ambedkar Centre for Biomedical Research
University of Delhi

R.S. Verma
Clean Process Branch
National Risk Management Research Laboratory
U.S. Environmental Protection Agency
Cincinnati, Ohio 45268, USA

Copyright © 2009

ALPHA SCIENCE INTERNATIONAL LTD.
7200 The Quorum, Oxford Business Park North
Garsington Road, Oxford OX4 2JZ, U.K.

www.alphasci.com

ISBN 978-1-84265-520-7

Printed in India

Preface

Green Solvents for Organic Synthesis, is an attempt to discuss some important green solvents available. The primary aim of writing this book is to develop the student's understanding of the green solvents in detail.

In ideal organic synthesis, the objective is to produce the desired product in 100% yield and selectively. Most of the organic solvents that are used as industrial solvents are volatile organic compounds like benzene, chloroform, toluene, carbontetrachloride. The toxic and hazardous properties of many solvents, notably chlorinated hydrocarbons are responsible for serious environmental issues, such as atmosphere emission and thus making there use as prohobitive.

In this book, we have discribed some important green solvents. Part I of the books discribes the use of water as solvent for organic reactions. Organic reactions in super critical water or in near water (RCW) region as well as microwave-assisted organic reactions in water are also described. Besides this, organic synthesis using biocatalysts (which are generally conducted in water) are also incorporated.

Part II of the book discribes organic synthesis in supercritical carbondioxide. Also organic synthesis using carbon dioxide are also incorporated.

Part III of the book deals with organic synthesis in ionic liquids, which are novel replacement for volatile organic compounds used traditionally as industrial solvents and reduce volatility, environmental, and human safety concerns that accompany exposure to organic solvents.

Part IV of the book describes the use of polyethylene glycol and its solutions as green reaction medium of future. The most obvious advantages are the low cost, reduced flammability, reduced toxicity and the most important are reduced environmental risk due to the discharge of various byproducts.

Part V of the book discribes organic synthesis using florous phase techniques.

A large number of synthesis applications of each of the green solvent are described. It may be that we have omitted a number of other applications which other research workers may consider important. In such cases we apologise in advance.

The authors are greatful to Prof. Sukhdev for his valuable advice. The help rendered by Dr. Devendra Kumar, Dr. Uma Shankar, Dr. Mrs. Bindu Orel and Dr. Ms. Chetna are greatfully acknowledged.

Authors

Contents

PART – III

PART – IV

PART – V

PART – I

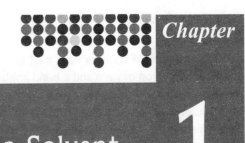

Use of Water as a Solvent for Organic Reaction

Chapter

1

I INTRODUCTION

The use of water - as a solvent for carrying out organic reactions - was not known to people till about the mid of the twentieth century. Solvents which are normally used are extremely harmful. For example, benzene–a commonly used solvent is known to cause or promote cancer in humans and other animals. Certain other aromatic hydrocarbons like toluene can damage the brain and may have adverse effects on speech, vision or cause liver and kidney problems Halogenated solvents commonly used, e.g. methylene chloride, chloroform, polychloroethylene and carbon tetrachloride have been identified as suspected human carcinogens. Besides, the halogenated solvents, being volatile, rise to the stratospheric region, where they get converted into chlorine free radicals by the action of UV light from the sun. The chlorine free radicals are responsible for depletion of ozone layer. Similarly, CFCs (chlorofluorocarbons) used till the twentieth century as cleaning solvents; blowing agents for molded plastics; and for refrigeration are responsible for the depletion of the ozone layer.

In view of the environmental pollutions caused by organic solvents, scientists all over the world are carrying out the experiments in aqueous phase. There are many potential advantages of carrying out reactions using water as a solvent.

- Water is comparatively a cheaper solvent available. Water, can be used as a solvent to make chemical reactions economical.
- Unlike organic solvents, which are inflammable, potentially explosive, mutagenic and/or carcinogenic, water is free of all these disadvantages and is a safe solvent.
- Water-soluble substances can be used directly. This will be particularly useful in carbohydrate, protein and fermentation chemistry.
- In large industrial process, the products can be isolated by simple phase separation. Also, it is easier to control the reaction temperature, since water has one of the largest heat capacities of all substances.
- The use of water as solvent may not cause problems of pollution, which is a major concern in using volatile organic solvents.
- Water can be readily recycled.

The structure of water is very well known. It has two sigma bonds; two lone pair of electrons on oxygen and a bond angle at 104.5°.

Water, as we know exists in three basic forms – vapour, liquid and solid. The relationship between these three forms of water is described by pressure-volume-temperature phase diagram (Fig. 1.1).

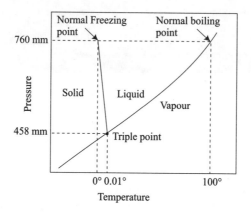

Fig. 1.1 Phase diagram for water

The principal physical properties[1,2] of water are described below:

The peak density of water is at 3.98°C; the density decreases as the temperature falls to 0°C. It is for this reason that ice is lighter than water and floats. This phenomenon insulates the deeper water from the cold temperature and prevents it from freezing. The density of water also decreases when the temperatured exceeds 3.98°C. It reaches the same density of ice at about 70°C.

The viscosity of water also changes with temperature. Infact the decrease in viscosity is inversely proportional to the rise in temperature. This is because the number of hydrogen bonds binding the molecules together decrease when the temperature rises. The viscosity of water affects the movement of solute in water and also the sedimentation rate of suspended solids.

The specific heat of water is highest as compared to other substances. The high value of specific heat of water is due to the great heat capacity of the water mass. This implies that rapid changes of ambient temperatures result in slow changes in water temperature. This effect is important for aquatic organisms. In large-scale industrial processes, this effect is advantageous to control the temperatured both for endo – and – exothermic reactions.

Water has one of the highest surface tension of all liquids. For example, the surface tension of ethanol at 20°C is 22 mN/m, while that of water is 72.75 mN/m. The surface tension of water decreases with temperature. Also the surface tension of water decreases by the addition of surface - active agents (surfactants), such as detergents.

Many substances are soluble in water. However, the solubility is dependent on the temperature. For example, the solubility of gases like oxygen, nitrogen and carbon dioxide in water decreases with rise in temperature. There are, however, some gases like helium in which case the solubility increases with increase in temperature. In case of solids, the solubility of $AgNO_3$ increases with increases in temperature but for NaCl, there is only a slight increase in solubility with rise in temperature. The influences of temperature on the solubility is dependent on heat of solution of a substance, which is the heat emitted or absorbed during the dissolution of one mole of a substance in one liter of water.

Polar compounds and compounds that iosize are readily soluble in water. Such compounds are said to be hydrophilic. On the other hand, hydrophobic substances have very low solubility in water.

Ordinary water behaves very differently under high temperature and high pressure[3]. Thus the electrolytic conductance of aqueas solutions increases with increase in pressure. This effect is more pronounced at lower temperatures. For all other solvents, the electrical conductivity of solutions decreases with increase in pressure. This unusual behaviour of water is due to its peculiar associative properties[4].

Thermal expansion causes liquid water to become less dense as the temperature decreases. Also the liquid vapour density increases as the pressure rises. For example, the density of water varies from 1.0 g/cm^3 at room temperature to 0.7 g/cm^3 at about 300°C. The densities of the two phases become identical at the critrical point. At this point the two phases become a single fluid called supercritical fluid. The water density at this point is only is 0.3 g/cm^3. The phase diagram of water around the super critical regiven is given in Fig. 1.2.

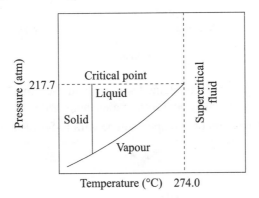

Fig. 1.2

In the chemical reactions given here water is used as a solvent.

2 REACTIONS IN AQUEOUS PHASE

Following are some of the reactions which have been carried out in aqueous medium.

2.1 Pericyclic Reactions

2.1.1 *Diels-Alder Reaction*

Diels-Alder reaction[5] is one of the most important procedures used to form cyclic structures. It is a [4 + 2] cycloaddition reaction between a conjugated diene (4π-electron system) and a compound having a double or triple bond called the dienophile (2π-electron system) to form an adduct. In this reaction, the two components are either heated alone or in an inert solvent (Scheme 1).

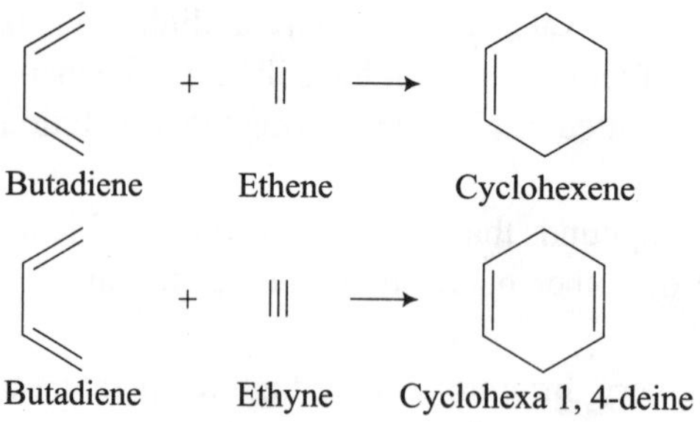

Scheme 1

The Diels-Alder reaction in aquem media was first carried out in the beginning of the nineteeth century[6]. Thus, furan reacted with malieic anhydride in hot water to give the adduct (Scheme 2)

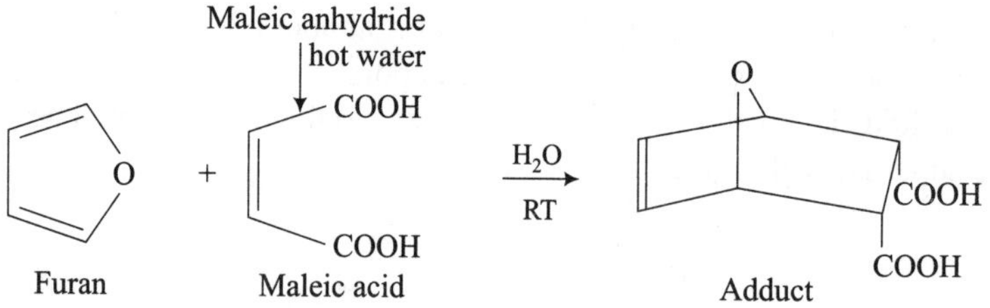

Scheme 2

In the above reaction, the product obtained was a diacid (Scheme 2) showing that the reaction proceeded via the formation of maleic acid from maleic anhydride.

Similarly Diels-Alder reaction of cyclopentadiene with N-Sec. Butyl malemide gave quantitative yield of the adduct (Scheme 3).

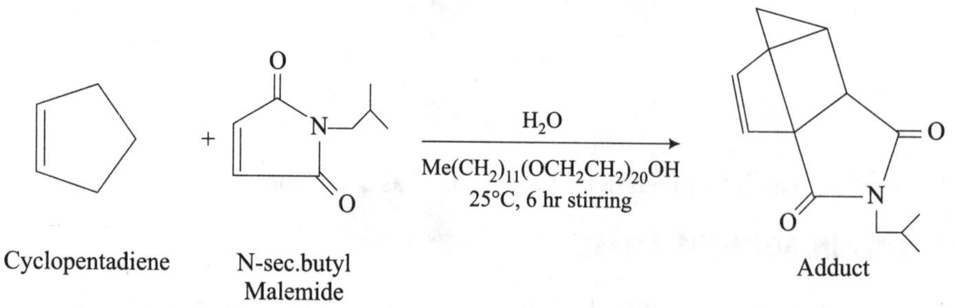

Scheme 3

Using water as a solvent also affected the stercoselectivity of some Diels-Alder reactions[8]. It has been found that at low concentrations, where both the components were completely dissolved, the reaction of cyclopentadiene with butenone gave (Scheme 4) a 21.4 ratio of endo/exo products when they were stirred at 0.15 M concentration in water, compared to only a 3.85 ratio in excess cyclopentadiene and an 8.5 ratio in ethanol as the solvent. An aquenes detergent solution had no effect on the product ratio. The sterochemical changes could be explained by the need to minimize the transition – state surface area in water solution favouring the more compact endo stereochemistry. The results are also in agreement will the effect of polar media on the ratio[9].

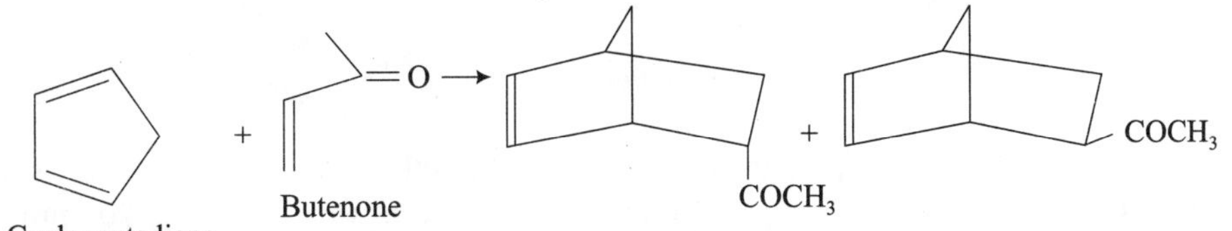

Medium	Endo/exo ratio (25°)
Cyclopentadiene	3.85
Ethanol	8.5
Water	21.4
Water + surfactant	19.5

Data taker from recterence 8

Scheme 4

Water-induced selectivity was also observed[8] in the reaction of cyclopentadiene with dimethyl maleate or methyl acrylate (Scheme 5 and 6). In the above cases, both the diene and dienophile are poorly soluble and are present as a separate phase, the influence of water on the selectivity is marked.

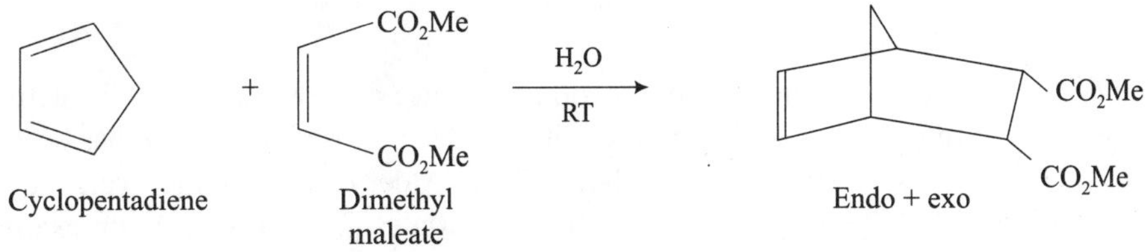

Scheme 5

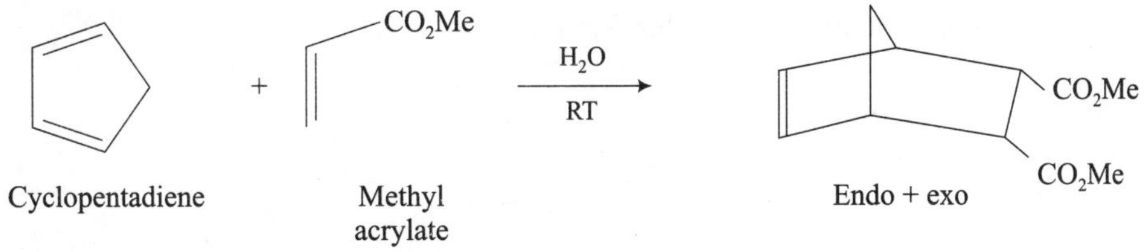

Scheme 6

Diels-Alder reaction of cyclopentadiene with acrylo nitrile proceeded[10] in a similar way (Scheme 7) giving quantitative yield of the adduct.

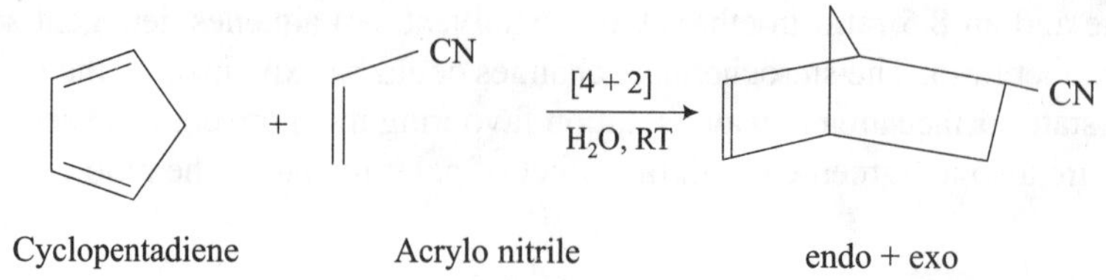

| Cyclopentadiene | Acrylo nitrile | endo + exo |

Scheme 7

The reaction between hydroxymethylanthracene and N-ethyl maleimide was also studied. It was found that in water at 45°, the second order rate constant in water was over 200 times larger than in acetonitrile (Scheme 8). In this case, the β-cyclodextrin became an inhibitor. A slight deactivation was also observed with a salting in salt solution, such as guanidine chloride in aqueous solution.

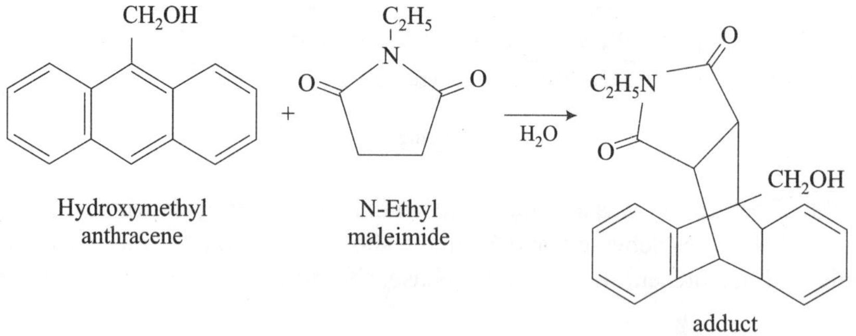

| Hydroxymethyl anthracene | N-Ethyl maleimide | adduct |

Scheme 8

An important feature of the Diels-Alser reaction is the use of Lewis acids for the activation of the substrate. Though most Lewis acids are deactivited or decomposed in water, it has been found[11] that $[Ti(Cp*)_2 (H_2O)_2]^{2+}$ is air stable, water tolerant Diels-Alder catalyst. Other water stable catalysts are[12] scandium triflate $[Sc(OTf)_3]$ and Lanthanide triflates $[Ln(OTf)_3]_2$. As an example, following cyclisation reaction (Scheme – 9) has been reported[13] in an aqueous solution containing 0.010 M $Cu(NO_3)_2$ is 250,000 times faster than in acetonitrile and is 1000 times faster than that in water alone. Other salts such as Co^{2+}, Ni^{2+}, Zn^{2+} also catalyse the reaction, but are not as reactive as Cu^{2+}. The reaction is also catalysed by bovine serum albumin[14].

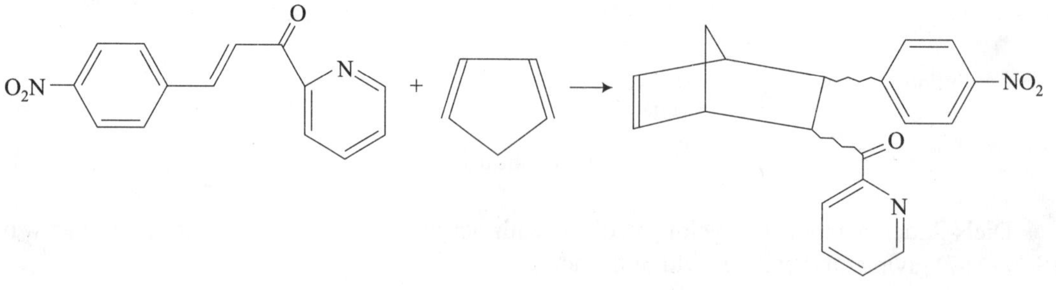

Scheme 9

2.1.1.1 Hetero-Diels-Alder Reactions

Hetero-Diels-Alder reactions with nitrogen or oxygen containing dienophiles are of special interest for the synthesis[15] of hetero cyclic compounds. The first example of Hetero-Diels-Alder reactions with nitrogen-containing dienophiles in aquenes medium was reported[16] in 1985. In this method, simple iminium salts, generated in situ under Mannich – like conditions, reacted with dienes in water to give aza-Diels-Alder reaction products (Scheme-10); this has potential for the synthesis of alkaloids (Table 1)

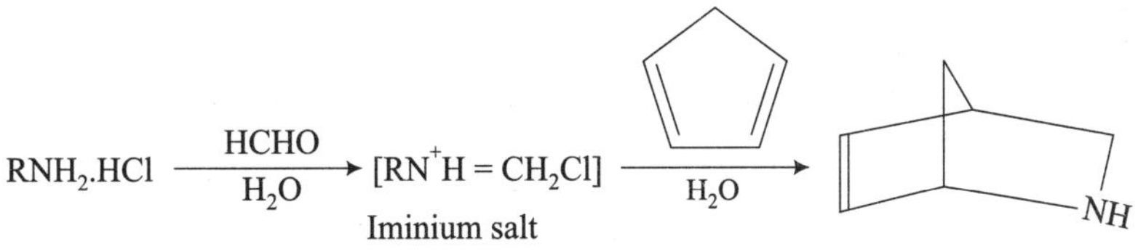

$$RNH_2 \cdot HCl \xrightarrow[\text{H}_2\text{O}]{\text{HCHO}} [RN^+H = CH_2Cl] \xrightarrow{\text{H}_2\text{O}}$$

Iminium salt

Scheme 10

Table 1   Aza-Diels-Alder reactions in aqueous medium

Diene	*Amine + Carbonyl Compound*	*Product*	*Yield (%)*
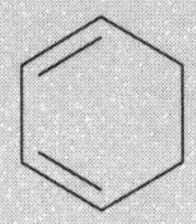	$BnNH_2 \cdot HCl + HCHO$	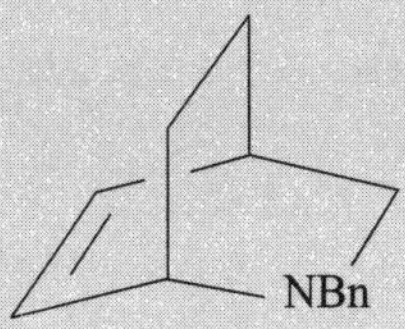	41
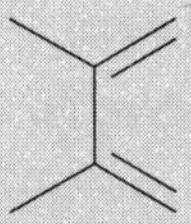	$BnNH_2 \cdot HCl + HCHO$	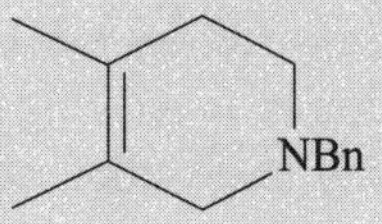	69
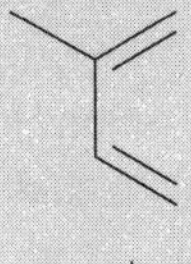	$BnNH_2 \cdot HCl + HCHO$	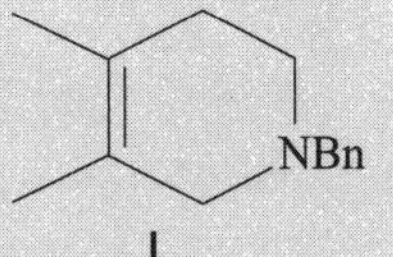	59
	$BnNH_2 \cdot HCl + HCHO$	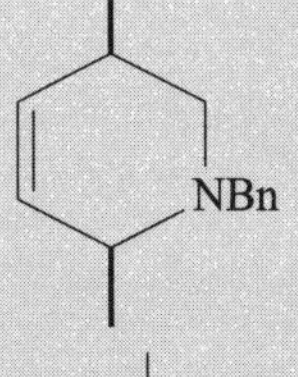	62
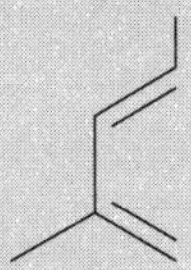	$BnNH_2 \cdot HCl + HCHO$	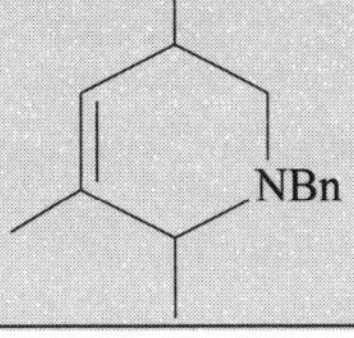	49

Contd.

Contd.

	MeNH$_2$·HCl + HCHO		82
	NH$_4$·HCl + HCHO		44
	NH$_4$·HCl + HCHO		40
	BnNH$_2$·HCl + MeCHO		47

Data taken from reference 16

   The intra molecular Aza-Diels-Alder Reaction occurs[17] similarly in aqueous media. These reactions lead to the formation of fused ring systems (Scheme 11) with bridge head nitrogen; such a structure is characteristics of many alkaloids.

Contd.

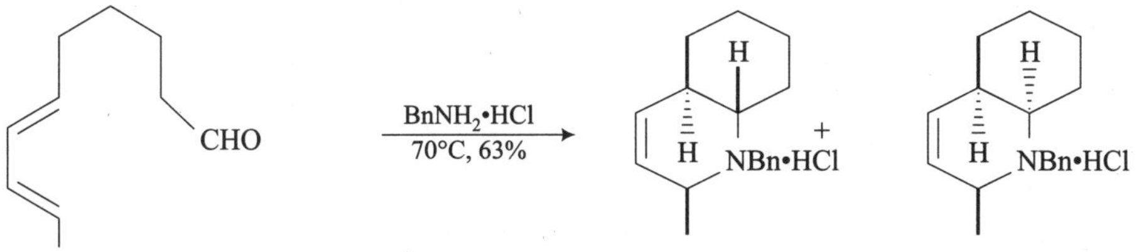

Scheme 11

C-Acyl minimum ions also reactect[18] similarly with cyclopentadienes (Table 2)

Table 2   Aza-Diels-Alder reaction of cyclopentadienes with C-Acyl iminium ions

Substrates	Amine	Product	Yield (%)
C_6H_5COCHO	$CH_3NH_2 \cdot HCl$	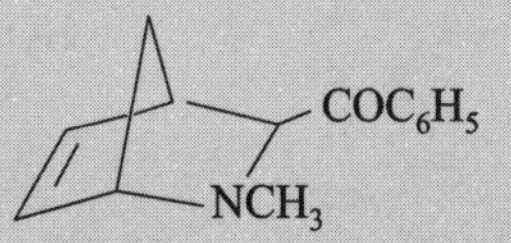	82
CH_3COCHO	NH_4Cl	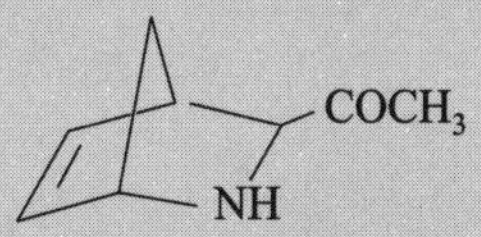	84
CH_3COCHO	$CH_3NH_2 \cdot HCl$	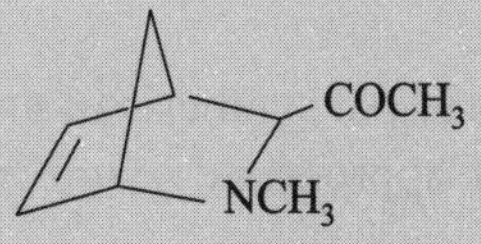	67
CH_3COCHO	$BnNH_2 \cdot HCl$	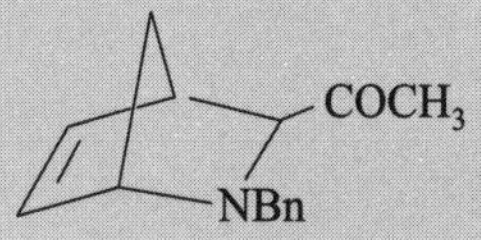	65
$HOOCCHO$	CH_3NH_2	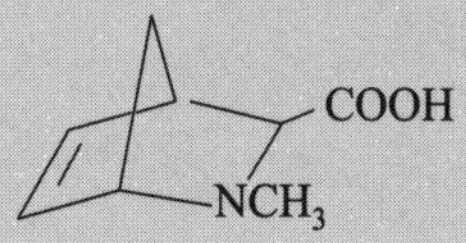	86

Data taken from Ref. 18.

Retro Aza-Diel-Alder Reactions also occurred readily in water[19]. For example 2-azanorbornenes undergo acid-catalysed Retro-Diels-Alder catalysed in water (Scheme 12)

A large number of Retro-Diels-Alter reaction have also been reported[20].

Due to the convenience of conducting Diels-Alder and related reactions in aqueous phase, this methodology has found a number of applications in pharmacentical industry. Some of the interesting applications of Diels-Alder and other cyclisation reactions are given below.

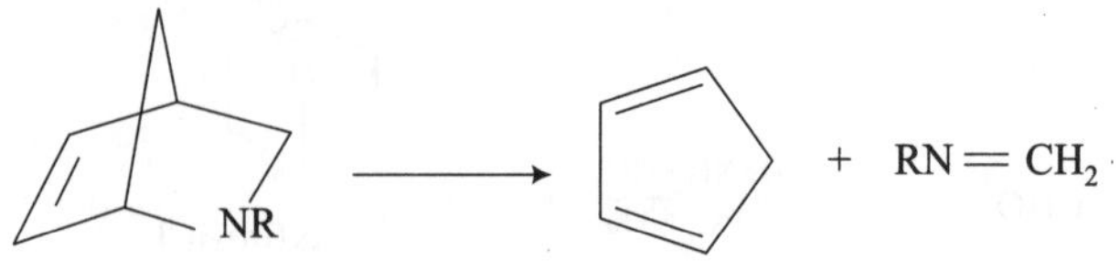

Scheme 12

(i) Synthesis of antifungals based on aqueous Diels-Alder reaction[21].

(ii) Intramolecular version of Diels-Alder reaction with a dienecarboxylate was used in synthetic study of the antibiotic ilicicolin H[22].

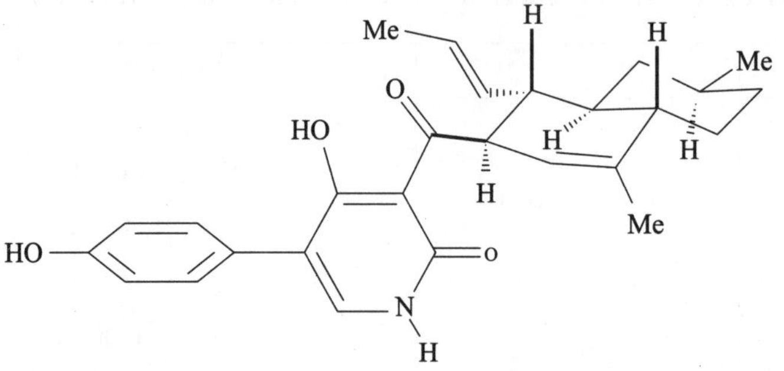

Ilicicolin H

(iii) A convenient one-pot synthesis of a number of different types of heterocyclic products by the reaction of appropriate oxime with NaOCl in H_2O/CH_2Cl_2 (Scheme 13) has been achieved[23].

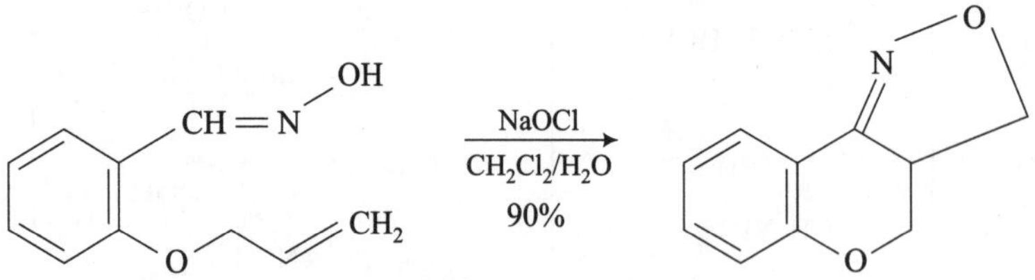

Scheme 13

(iv) An ene-iminium one pot cyclisation (Scheme 14) proceeds smoothly in water- THF mixture. The reaction has been used in the asymmetric synthesis of pipecolic acid derivatives[24].

(v) 1, 3-Dipolar cyclization of nitrile oxide with dipolarophiles generates structurally important heterocycles (Scheme 15). It has been shown[23] that the reaction can be carried out in aqueous-biphase system.

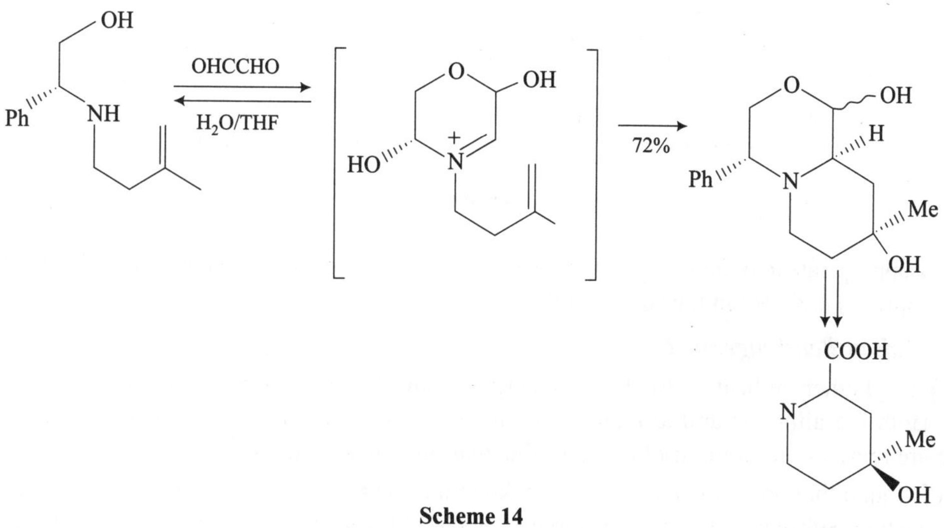

Scheme 14

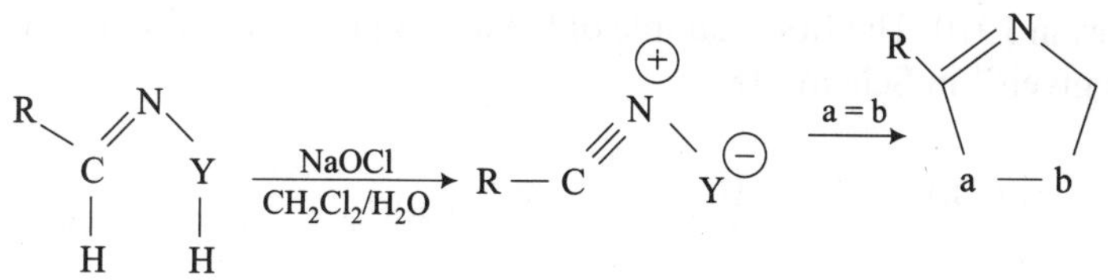

Scheme 15

(vi) The reaction of alkenes by ozone (ozonolysis) to give carbonyl compound is a synthetically useful reaction[25]. Though there is disagreement on the exact mechanism, it is generally accepted that the two heterocyclic intermediates. 1, 2, 3-trioxolane and 1, 2, 4-trioxolane, are involved. The formation of the former could be regarded as a 1, 3-dipolar cyclisation between alkene and ozone and the labter is the result of a retro cleavage followed by a recombination of the fragments (Scheme 16). The 1, 2, 4-trioxolane can be transformed to alcohols, aldehydes (and ketones) or carboxylic acids.

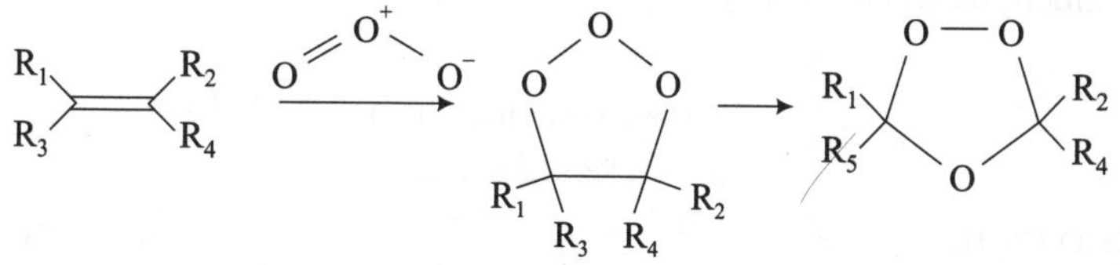

Scheme 16

The ozonelysis is usually performed at low temperature and generally water has been used as a solvent. For example, cyclooctene on ozonolysis in presence of an emulsifier (per oxyethylated lauryl alcohol), with aqueous alkaline hydrogen peroxide gives α, ω-alkanedicarboxylic acid in one pot[26] (Scheme 17).

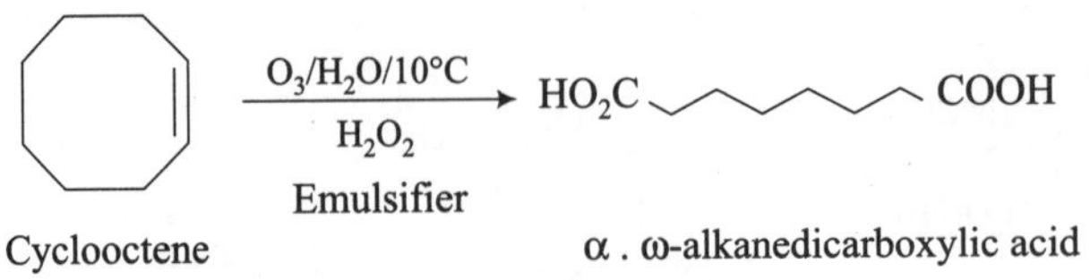

Scheme 17

It is appropriate to mention that Diels-Alder reactions have also been performed in ionic liquids (see Chapter 7) and also in the solid state[26].

2.1.2 Claisen Rearrangement

Allyl phenyl ether on heating to 200°C undergo intramolecular reaction called Claisen rearrangement. Both the aliphatic and aromatic claisen rearrangement involve a 3, 3-sigmatropic shift[27]. There are reviews providing usefulness of this rearrangement reaction[28].

It is found that polar solvents have been known to increase[29] the rate of the claisen rearrangement reaction. Subsequently, it was observed that claisen rearrangement reaction are accelerated on going from non polar to aqueous solvents[30]. The first reported use of water in promoting claisen rearrangement was in 1970. The first example of the use of pure water for claisen rearrangement of chorismic acid is given[31] in Scheme 18.

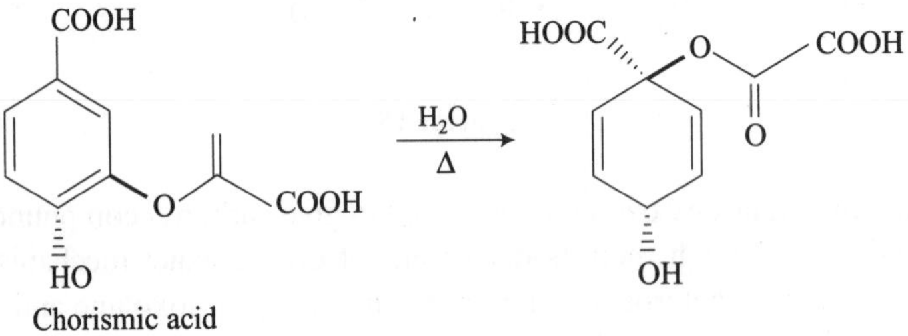

Scheme 18

An aliphatic claisen rearrangement, a [3, 3]-sigmatropic rearrangement of an allyl vinyl ether in water gave[32] the aldehyde (Scheme 19).

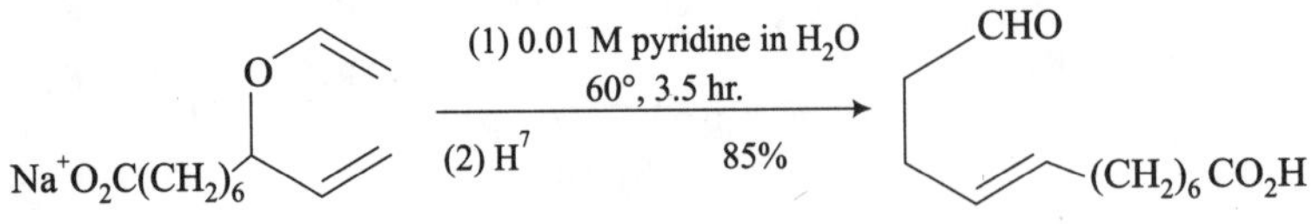

Scheme 19

The corresponding ester also under went similar rearrangement. Similarly, both allyl vinyl ether and 2-hept 3, 5-dienyl-vinyl ether underwent 3, 3-shift. The best results were obtained in 2/1 methanol water; the rates were about 40 times than those in acetone solvent[33].

A feature of the claisen rearrangement in aqueous medium is that it is not necessary to protect the free hydroxyl group (Scheme 20)[34].

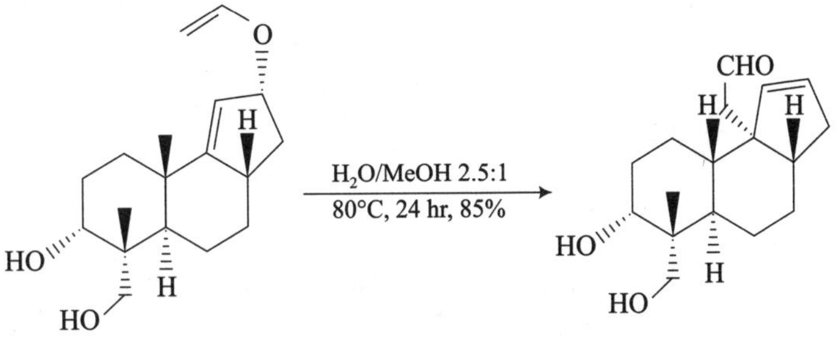

Scheme 20

Following are some of the important applications of claisen rearrangement in aqueous solution.

(i) Synthesis of fenestrene aldehyde having trans rings fusion between two five-membered rings (Scheme 21)[34].

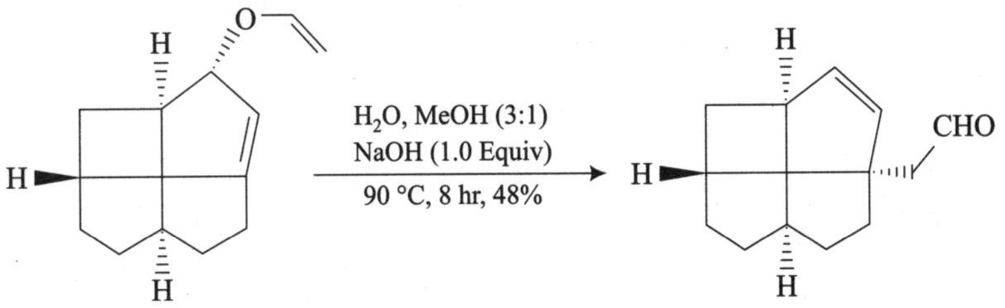

Scheme 21

(ii) The claisen rearrangement of the allyl vinyl ether (Scheme 22) gave the aldehyde in 82 per cent yield[34].

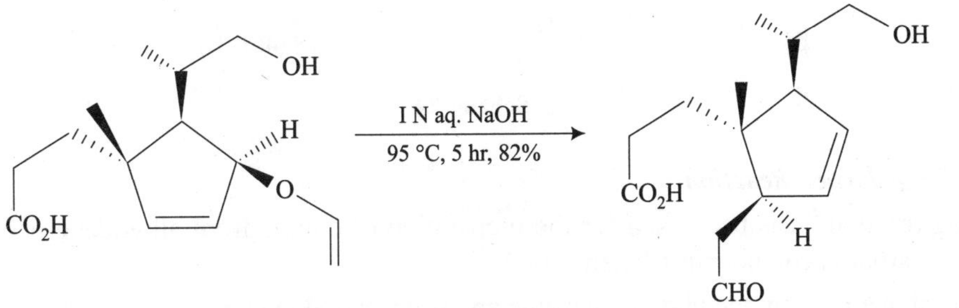

Scheme 22

(iii) The claisen rearrangement of 6-β-glycosyl allylvinyl ether (Scheme 23) and 6-α- glycosyl allylvinyl ether (Scheme 24) has been successful in aqueous medium[35]. In the above reactions NaBH$_4$ was added so that the formed aldehyde gets converted into the corresponding alcohol.

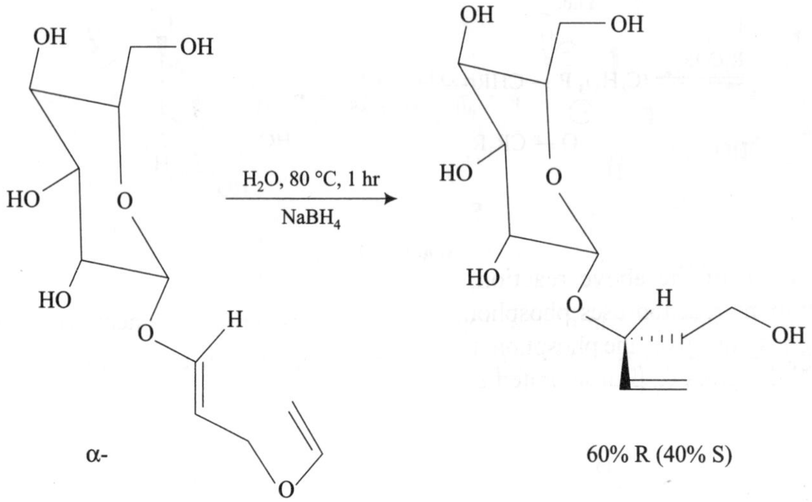

Scheme 23

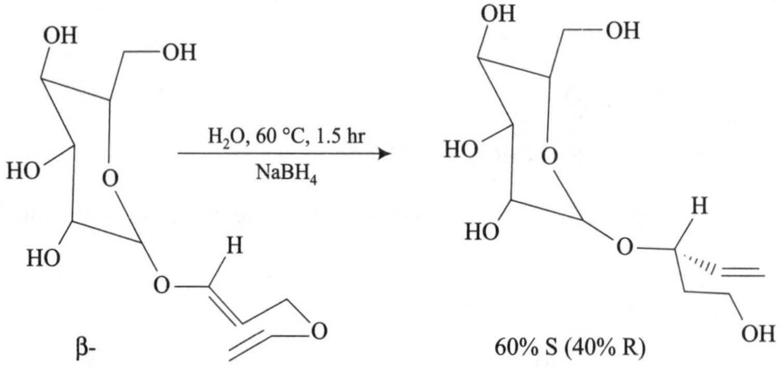

Scheme 24

2.1.3   *Wittig-Horner Reaction*

The wittig reaction[36] has been used for the preparation of olefins from alkylidene phosphoranes (ylids) and carbonyl compounds (Scheme 24a)

In the above reaction the ylide in unstable and is generated in situ.

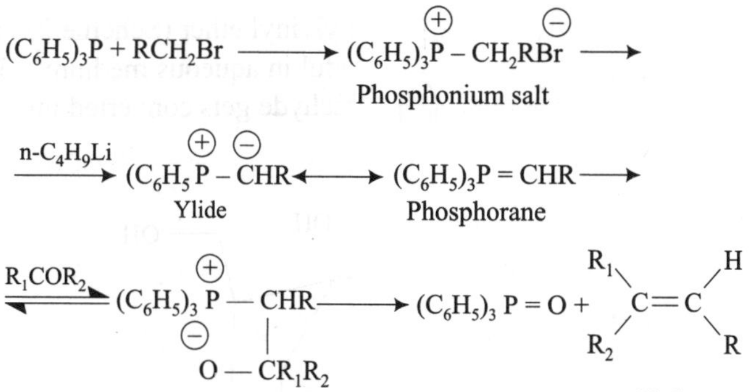

$$(C_6H_5)_3P + RCH_2Br \longrightarrow (C_6H_5)_3\overset{\oplus}{P} - \overset{\ominus}{CH_2RBr} \longrightarrow$$

Phosphonium salt

$$\xrightarrow{n\text{-}C_4H_9Li} (C_6H_5\overset{\oplus}{P} - \overset{\ominus}{CHR} \longleftrightarrow (C_6H_5)_3P = CHR \longrightarrow$$

Ylide   Phosphorane

$$\xrightarrow{R_1COR_2} (C_6H_5)_3 \overset{\oplus}{\underset{\ominus}{P}} - \underset{O - CR_1R_2}{\overset{\mid}{CHR}} \longrightarrow (C_6H_5)_3\,P = O + \overset{R_1}{\underset{R_2}{>}} C = C \overset{H}{\underset{R}{<}}$$

Olefin

Scheme 24a

A modification of the above reaction, known as the Wittig-Horner reaction or Horner-Wadsworth-Emmons reaction uses phosphonate esters. Thus, the reaction of ethyl bromoacetate with triphenylphosphite gives the phosphonate ester, which on reaction with cyclohexanone in presence of base (NaH) gives α, β-unsaturated ester, ethyl cyclohexylidineacetate in 70 per cent yield (Scheme 25)

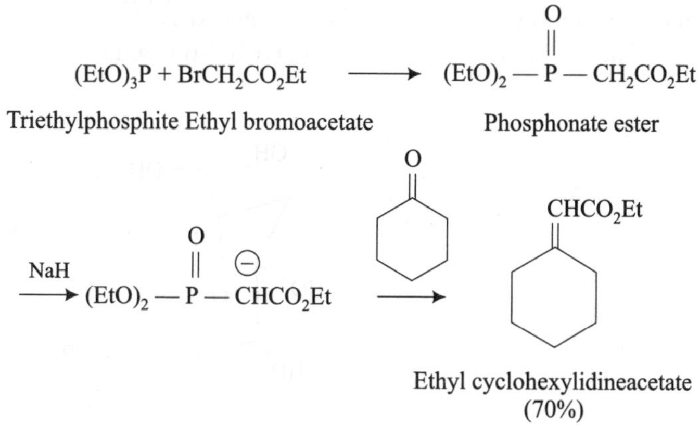

$$(EtO)_3P + BrCH_2CO_2Et \longrightarrow (EtO)_2 \overset{\overset{O}{\|}}{-} P - CH_2CO_2Et$$

Triethylphosphite Ethyl bromoacetate   Phosphonate ester

$$\xrightarrow[\quad]{NaH} (EtO)_2 \overset{\overset{O}{\|}}{-} P \overset{\ominus}{-} CHCO_2Et \longrightarrow$$

Ethyl cyclohexylidineacetate
(70%)

Scheme 25

The above reaction is sometimes performed in an organic/water biphase system[37,38]. In the above reaction (Scheme 25) in place of strong base like NaH, a PTC can be used in aq. NaOH with good results. In the above reaction (Scheme 25) the base used is NaH or any other strong base. It has been found that the reaction proceeds with a much weaker base, such as K_2CO_3 or $KHCO_3$. Even compounds with base and acid sensitive functional groups can be used directly. In a typical example, under such condition β-dimethylhydrazoneacetaldehyde can be obtained efficiently[39].

Recently[39a] water has been demonstrated to be an effective medium for the wittig reaction employing stablized ylides and aldehydes. Inspite of the poor solubility of the reactants good chemical yields ranging from 80 to 98 per cent and high E-selectivites (up to 99%) are achieved. Typical examples of wittig reaction are given below (Scheme-25a).

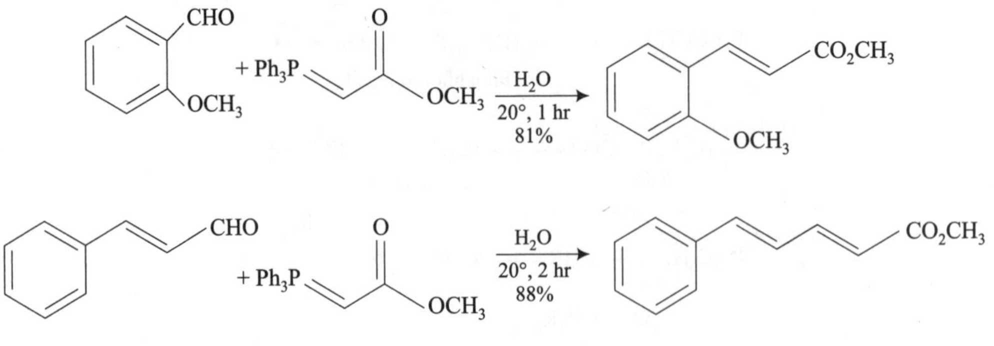

Scheme 25a

2.1.4 Michael Reaction

The reaction[40] between an α, β-unsaturated carbonyl compound and a compound with an active methylene group (e.g. malonic ester, acetoacetic ester, cyanoacetic ester, nitroparaffins, etc.) in presence of a base, e.g. sodium ethoxide or a secondary amine (usually piperidine) is known as Michael Reaction[40].

The first successful report of Michael Reaction in aqueous medium was the reaction of 2-Methylcyclopentane-1, 3-dione with vinyl ketone in water to give adduct without the uses of a basic catalyst (pH > 7). The adduct further cyclises to give a 5-6 fused ring system (Scheme 26)[41].

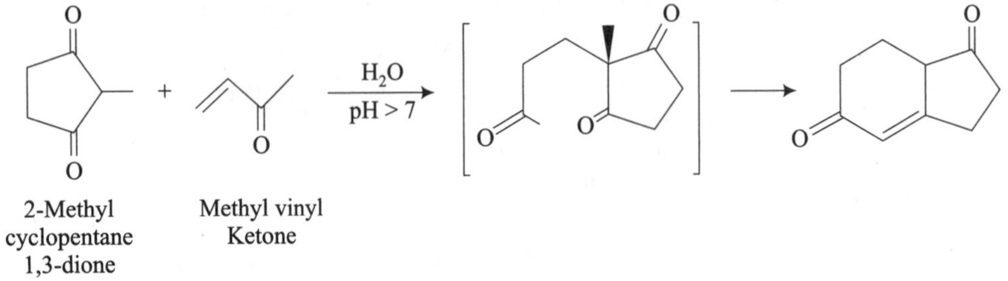

Scheme 26

In this reaction (Scheme 26), use of water as a solvent gave pure compound in better yields compared to reaction with methanol in presence of a base.

Michael Reaction of 2-methyl-cyclohexane-1, 3-dione with methyl vinylketone give optically pure Wieland-Miescher Ketone (Scheme 27) [42].

Use of acrolein in place of methylvinyl ketone in the above reaction gave an adduct (Scheme 28) which was used for the synthesis of 13-α-methyl-14α-hydroxysteroid[43].

The rate of above Michael addition (Scheme-28) was enhanced by the addition of ytterbium triflate [yb(OTf)$_3$].

The Michael addition of nitromethane to methyl vinyl ketone in water (in the absence of a catalyst) gave 4:1 mixture of adducts (A and B) (Scheme 29)[44].

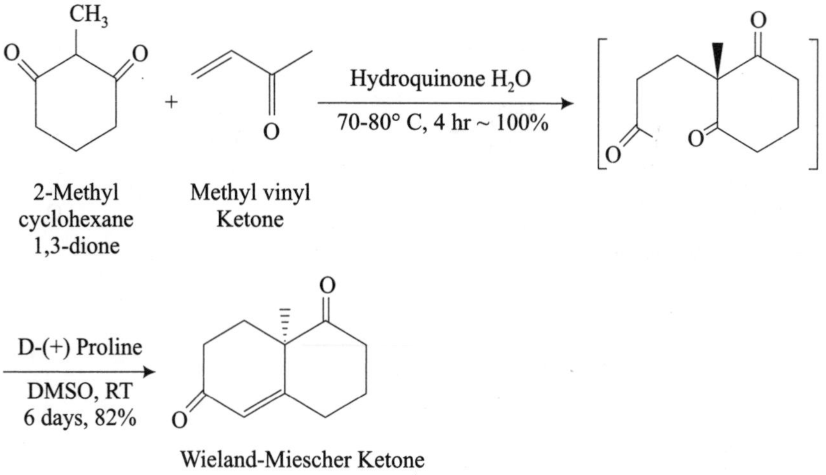

2-Methyl cyclohexane 1,3-dione   **Methyl vinyl Ketone**

Hydroquinone H$_2$O
70-80° C, 4 hr ~ 100%

D-(+) Proline
DMSO, RT
6 days, 82%

Wieland-Miescher Ketone

Scheme 27

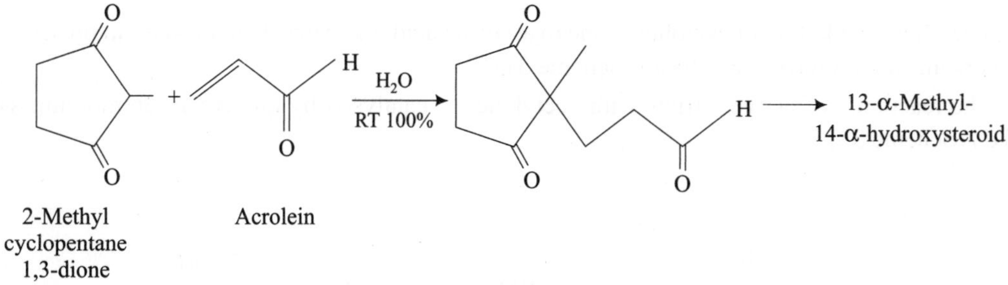

2-Methyl cyclopentane 1,3-dione   **Acrolein**

H$_2$O
RT 100%

13-α-Methyl-14-α-hydroxysteroid

Scheme 28

CH$_3$NO$_2$ +
Nitromethane   **Methyl vinyl ketone**

40°, 32 hr
H$_2$O 100%

O$_2$N

A   B

(4:1)

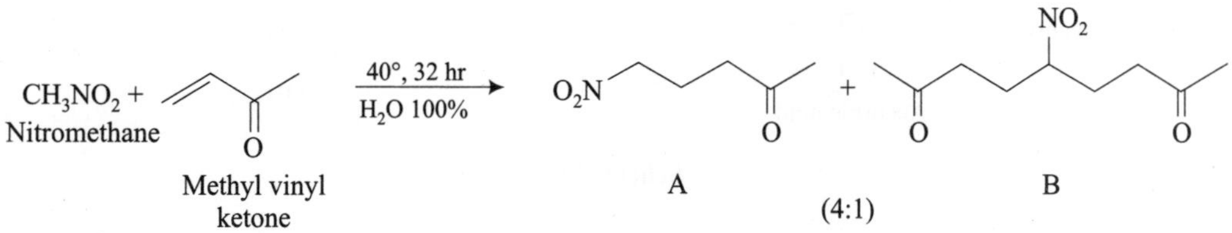

Scheme 29

Use of methyl alcohol as a solvent (in place of H$_2$O) gave 1 : 1 mixture of A and B. The above reaction is unsuccessful in neat condition or in solvents like THF, PhMe etc., in the absence of a catalyst.

A synthesis of allylrethrone, an important component of an insecticidal pyrthroid has been achieved by a combination of michael reaction of 5-nitro-1-pentene and methyl vinyl ketone in presence of Al$_2$O$_3$ followed by an intramolecular aldol type condensation (Scheme 30)[45].

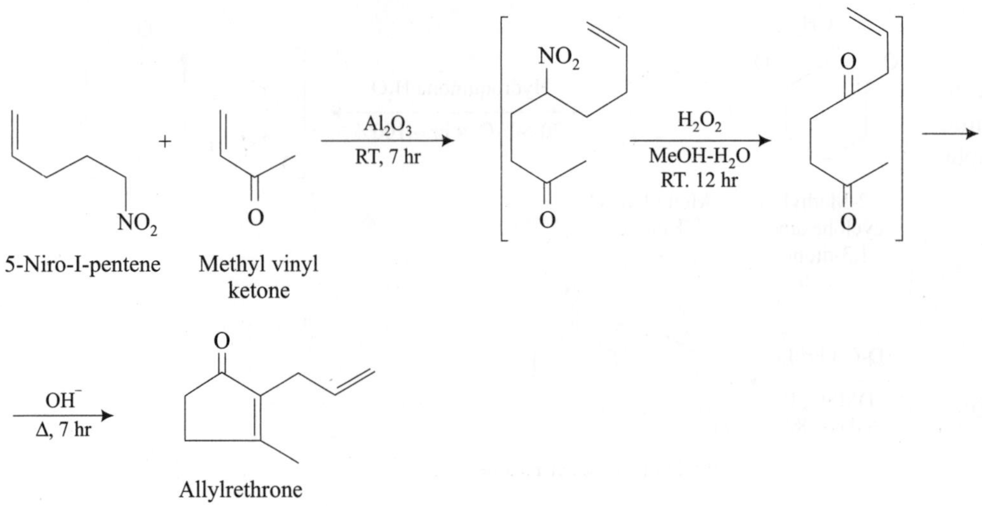

NO2
Al2O3
RT, 7 hr
H2O2
MeOH-H2O
RT. 12 hr
5-Niro-I-pentene
Methyl vinyl ketone
OH⁻
Δ, 7 hr
Allylrethrone

Scheme 30

The Michael addition of cyclohexenone to ascorbic acid was carried out in water in presence of an inorganic acid (rather than a base) (Scheme 31)[46].

The reaction[47] of active nitriles with acetylenes is catalysed by quaternary ammonium salts (PTC) (Scheme 32)

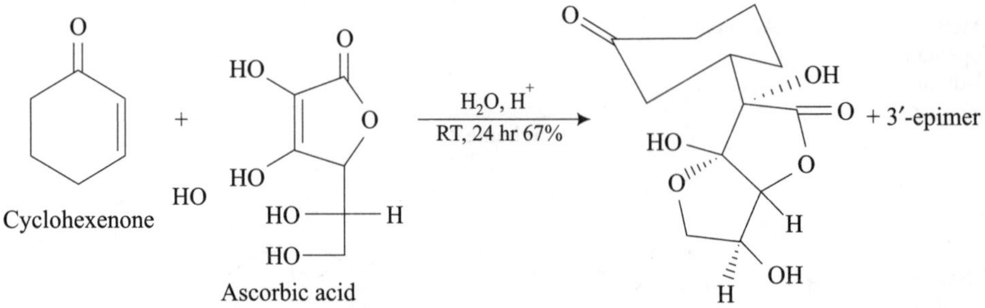

Cyclohexenone
Ascorbic acid
H2O, H+
RT, 24 hr 67%
+ 3′-epimer

Scheme 31

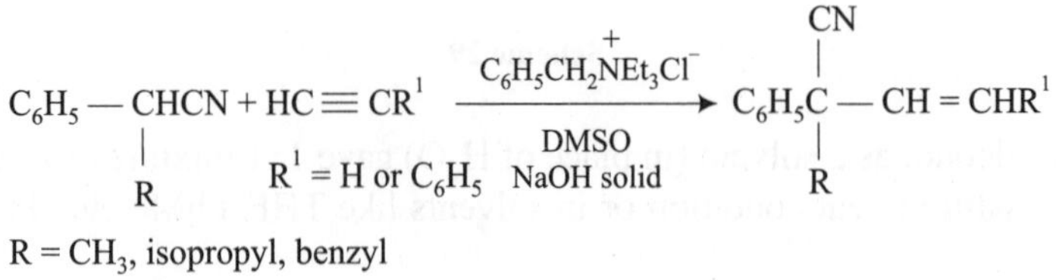

C6H5 — CHCN + HC ≡ CR1
C6H5CH2NEt3Cl⁻
DMSO
NaOH solid
C6H5C — CH = CHR1
CN
R
R1 = H or C6H5
R = CH3, isopropyl, benzyl

Scheme 32

An efficient Michael addition reactions of amines, thiophenol and methyl acetoacetate to chalcone in water suspension have been developed[48]. Thus stirring a suspension of powdered chalcone in a small amount of water containing n-Bu$_2$NH and a surfactant, hexadecyltrimenthylammonium bromide for 2 hr gave the adduct in 98 per cent yield. Similarly adducts were obtained with thiophenol and methyl acetoacetate (Scheme 33).

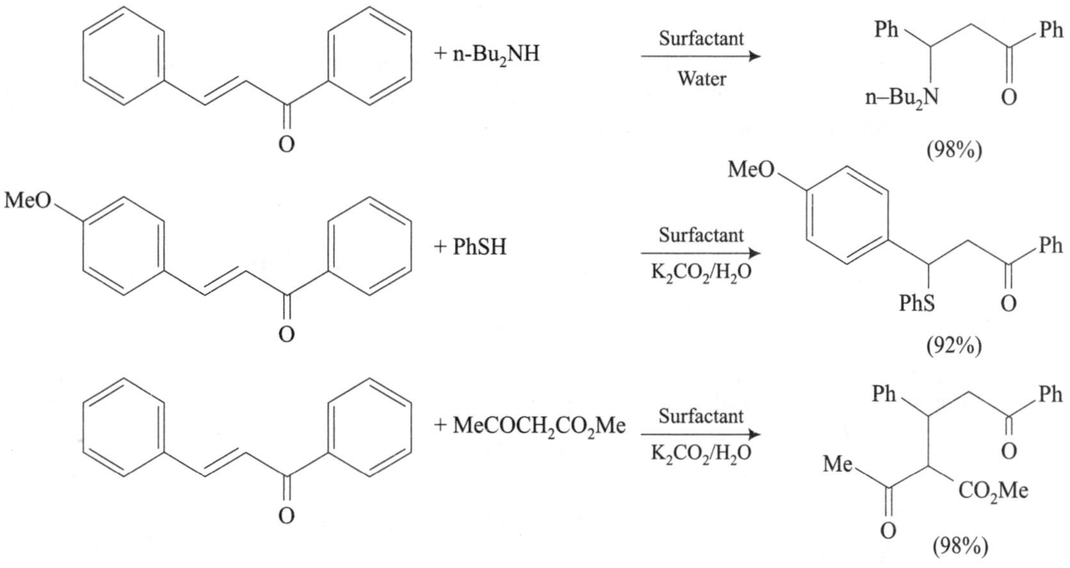

Scheme 33

Asymmetric Michael addition of benzenethiol to 2-cyclohexenone and maleic acid esters proceeds enantioselectively in their crystalline cyclodextrin complexes. The adducts were obtained in 38 per cent and 30 per cent ee respectively. In both cases, the reactions were carried out in aqueous phase (Scheme 34)[49].

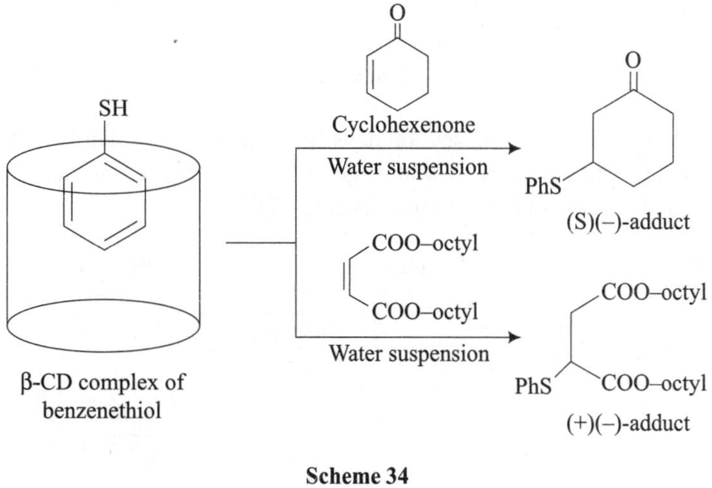

Scheme 34

2.1.5 Aldol Condensation

The aldol condensation is one of the most important carbon-carbon bond forming reactions in organic synthesis. The conventional aldol condensation involve reversible self-addition of aldehydes containing a α-hydrogen atoms; the formed β-hydroxy aldehydes undergo dehydration to give α, β-unsaturated aldehydes. This has been extensively reviewed[50]. The reaction can occur either between two identical or different aldehydes, two identical or different ketones and an aldehyde and a ketone.

Mukaiyama Reaction[51], a stereoselective aldol condensation consists in the reaction of an silyl enol ether of 3-pentanone with an aldehyde (2-methyl-butanal) in presence of $TiCl_4$ to yield an aldol product, Manicone, an alarm pheromone (Scheme 35)[52].

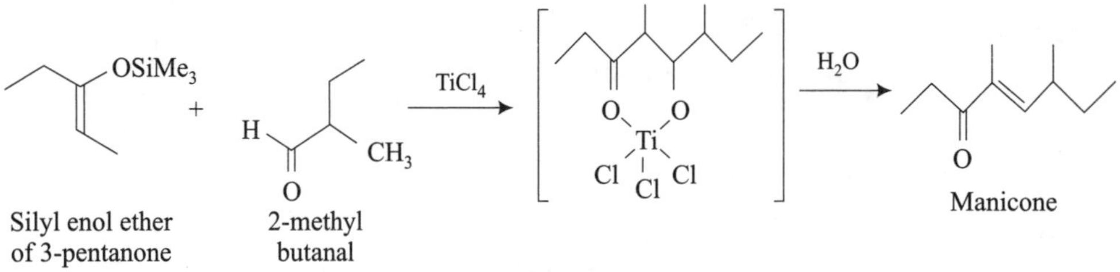

Silyl enol ether of 3-pentanone   2-methyl butanal   Manicone

Scheme 35

The above reactions are carried out in organic solvents.

The first water-promoted aldol reaction of silyl enol ethers with aldehydes was first reported in 1986 (Scheme 36)[53].

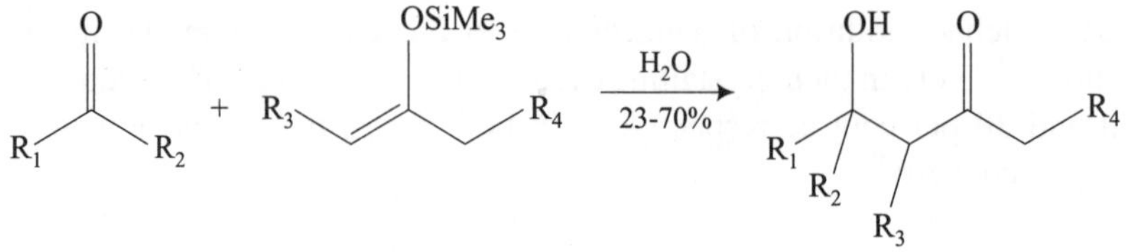

Scheme 36

The above reactions however, took several days for completion, probably because water serves as a weak Lewis acid. The addition of a stronger Lewis acid (e.g. lanthanide triflate) greatly improved the yield and rate of such reactions (Scheme 37)[54].

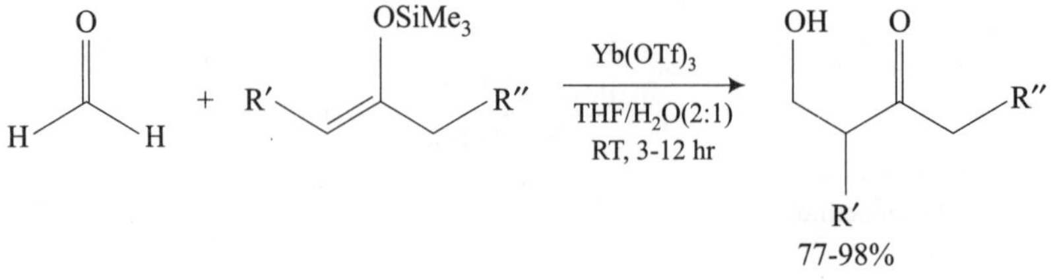

Scheme 37

It has been found that the dehydration of the alcohols can be avoided in presence of complexes of Zn with aminoesters or aminoalcohols[55].

Using the above method, vinyl ketones (Scheme 38) can be obtained by the reaction of 2-alkly-1, 3-diketones with aqueous formaldehyde (formalin) using 6-10 M aqueous potassium carbonate as base followed by the cleavage of the intermediate with base[56].

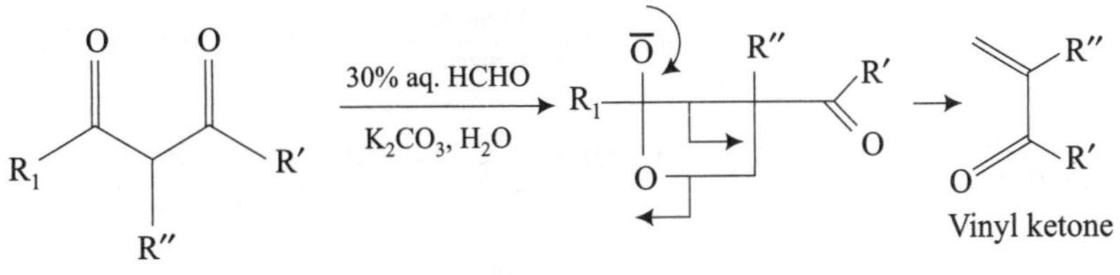

Scheme 38

The reaction of several silyl enol ethers with commercial formaldehyde solution catalysed by yb(OTf)$_3$ gave good yields (80 to 90 per cent) of the products obtained[57,58]. In all the above reactions the catalyst could be recovered and used repetitively. The above methodology has been extensively reviewed[59].

The reaction of isophorone with benzaldehyde in water gives only vinylogous aldol product but with low conversion. However, in presence of CTACl, the condensation product, (E)-benzylideneisophorone, is obtained in 80 per cent yield. Use of tetrabutylammonium chloride (TBACl) gives a mixture of addition and condensation products (Scheme 39)[60].

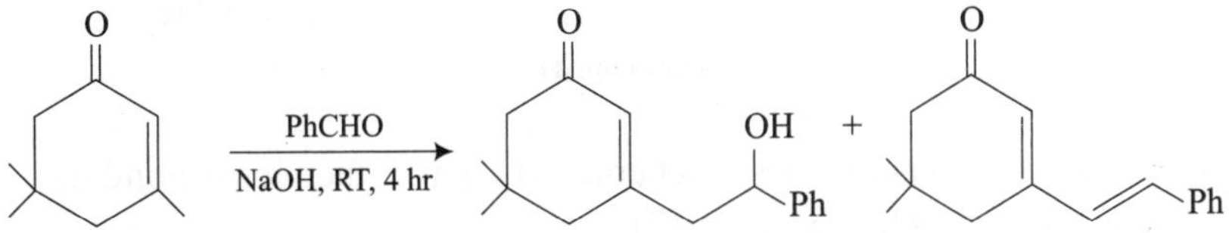

Isophorone		
Water only	24%	—
CTACl	—	80%
TBACl	27%	58%

Scheme 39

2.1.6 Knoevenagel Reaction

It involves the condensation of aldehydes or ketones, with active methylene compounds (especially malonic ester) in presence of a weak base like ammonia or amine (primary or secondary)[61,62]. However, when condensation is carried out in presence of pyridine as a base, decarboxylation usually occurs during the condensation. This is known as Doebner modification[63]. Some examples are given (Scheme 40).

$$CH_3CHO \quad + \quad CH_2(COOH)_2 \xrightarrow{\text{Base}} CH_3CH = C(COOH)_2$$

Acetaldehyde   Malonic acid

$$\downarrow -CO_2$$

$$CH_3CH = CHCOOH$$

Crotonic acid

$$C_6H_5CHO \quad + \quad CH_2(COOC_2H_5)_2 \xrightarrow[\text{Benzene}]{\text{Pyridine}} C_6H_5CH = C(COOC_2H_5)_2$$

$$\xrightarrow[\text{(2) } H_3O^+]{\text{(1) Hydrolysis}} C_6H_5CH = C(COOH)_2 \xrightarrow[-CO_2]{\Delta} C_6H_5CH = CHCOOH$$

Cinnamic acid

Scheme 40

The knoevenagel reaction between o-hydroxy aldehydes and malononitriles in water at room temperature in the heterogeneous aqueous alkaline medium gave α-hydroxybenzylidene malononitriles, which are converted directly to 3-cyanocoumarins by acidification and heating (Scheme 41)[64].

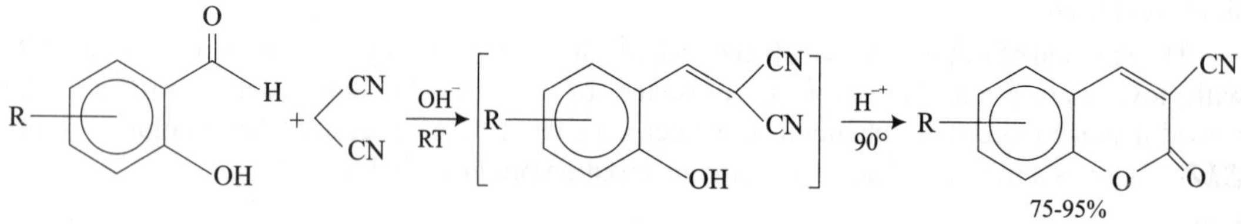

R = H, OH, OMe

Scheme 41

Similarly, substituted acetonitriles (Scheme 41) gave the corresponding 3-substituted coumarins in 66-98 per cent yields (Scheme 42).

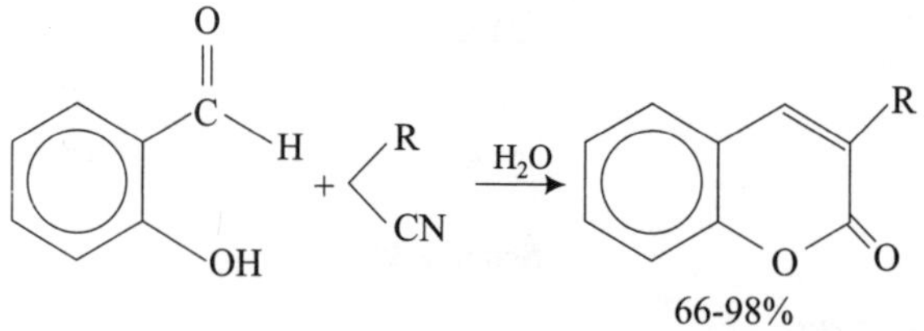

R = CN, CO$_2$Et, NO$_2$, Ph, 2-Py

Scheme 42

In case of phenylacetonitrile, a catalytic amount of CTABr (0.1 mole/equiv) is used. The above reaction gives better yields in aqueous medium compared to in aethanol.

The reaction of benzaldehyde with acetonitrile does not occus in water; however it requires the presence of catalytic amount of CTACl or TBACl to give high yields of the corresponding arylcinnamonitriles (Scheme 43)[61].

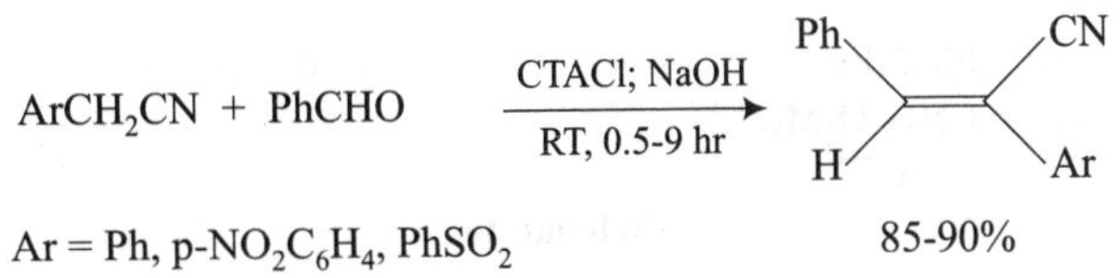

$$ArCH_2CN + PhCHO \xrightarrow[\text{RT, 0.5-9 hr}]{\text{CTACl; NaOH}}$$

Ph, CN / H, Ar

Ar = Ph, p-NO$_2$C$_6$H$_4$, PhSO$_2$

85-90%

Scheme 43

Knoevenagel-type addition product can be obtained by the reaction of acrylic derivatives in presence of a 1, 4-diazabicyclo [2.2.2] octane (DABCO) (Scheme 44)[65].

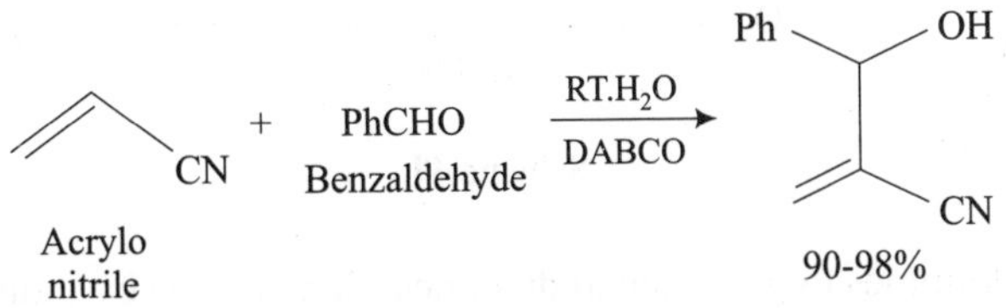

Acrylo nitrile

+ PhCHO
Benzaldehyde

$$\xrightarrow[\text{DABCO}]{\text{RT.H}_2\text{O}}$$

Ph, OH / CN

90-98%

Scheme 44

2.1.7 Pinacol Coupling

Ketones on reaction with Mg/benzene give 1, 2-diols (pinacols). Thus, under these conditions acetone give pinacol (Scheme 45)

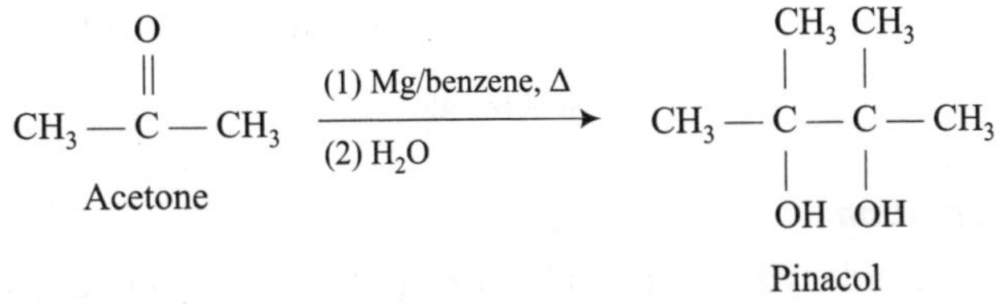

$$CH_3 - \overset{\overset{\displaystyle O}{\|}}{C} - CH_3 \xrightarrow[\text{(2) H}_2\text{O}]{\text{(1) Mg/benzene, }\Delta}$$

Acetone

$$CH_3 - \overset{\overset{\displaystyle CH_3}{|}}{\underset{\underset{\displaystyle OH}{|}}{C}} - \overset{\overset{\displaystyle CH_3}{|}}{\underset{\underset{\displaystyle OH}{|}}{C}} - CH_3$$

Pinacol

Scheme 45

This is known as pinacol coupling. The use of Zn-Cu couple to couple unsaturated aldehydes to pinacols was recorded as early as 1892[66]. Subsequently chromium and vanadium[67] and some ammonical-TiCl$_3$[68] based reducing agents were used.

It has been found[69] that pinacol coupling takes place in aromatic ketones and aldehydes in aqueous media in presence of Ti(III), under basic conditions. However, in presence of acids, only the substrates (aromatic ketones and aldehydes) having electron withdrawing group like CN, CHO, COMe, COOH, COOMe, pyridyl (activating groups) only underwent pinacol coupling[70] (Scheme 46). Excess of the substrate was necessary as solvent to non-activated carbonyl compounds[71].

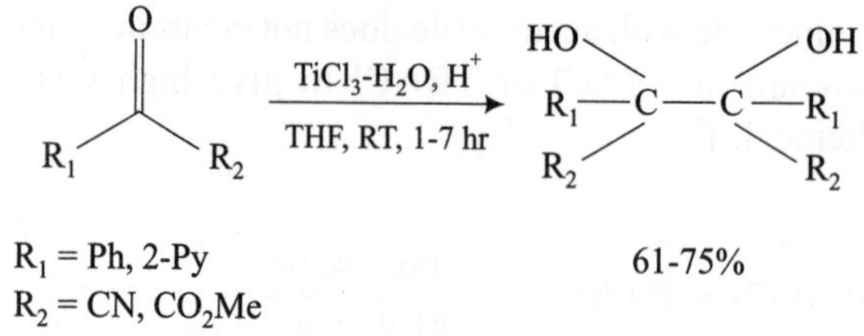

$$R_1 = Ph, 2\text{-}Py$$
$$R_2 = CN, CO_2Me$$

61-75%

Scheme 46

α, β-Unsaturated carbonyl compound and acetone undergo coupling reaction[72] using a Zn-Cu couple and ultrasound in an aqueous acetone suspension (Scheme 47)[72].

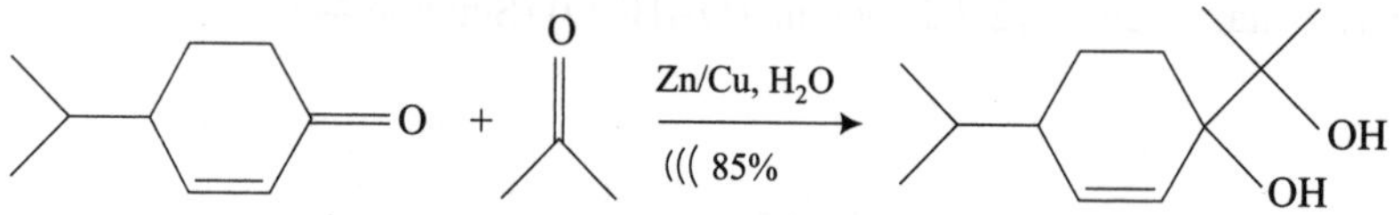

Scheme 47

The coupling of aldimines to give vicinal diamines (Scheme 48) by indium in aqueous ethanol in presence of a small amount of ammonium chloride (which accelerates the reaction)[73] gave the coupled product.

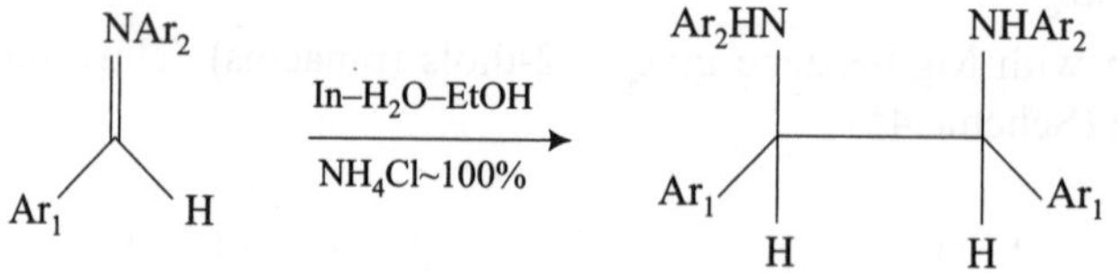

Scheme 48

2.1.8 Benzoin Condensation

The reaction of aromatic aldehydes with sodium or potassium cyanide, usually in an aqueous ethanolic solution give α-hydroxy ketones (benzoins) (Scheme 49)[74]. This reaction is known as Benzoin Condensation.

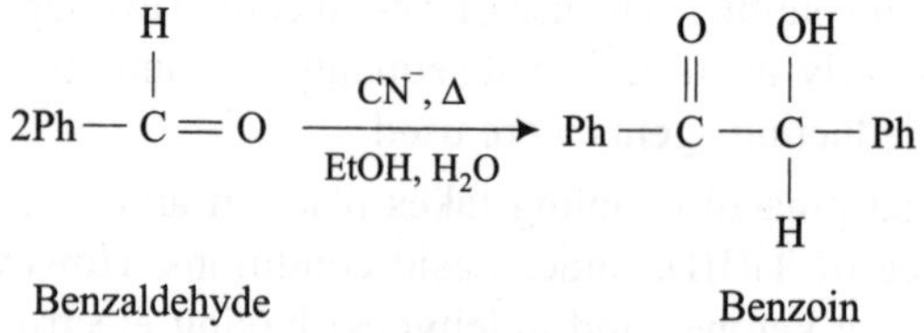

Benzaldehyde   Benzoin

Scheme 49

The mechanism of Benzoin condensation is given as Scheme 50

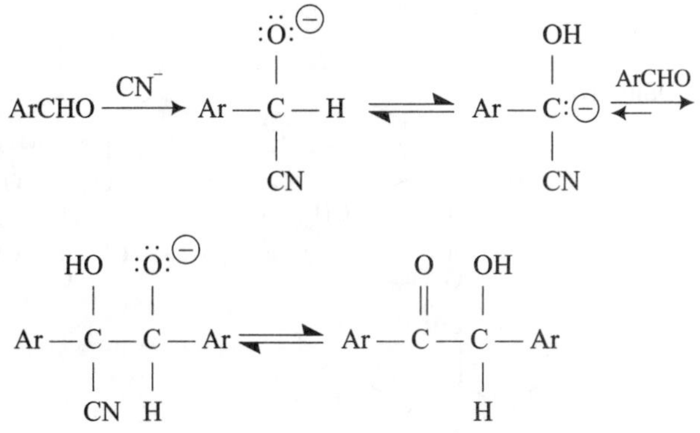

$$ArCHO \xrightarrow{CN^-} Ar-\overset{\displaystyle :\ddot{O}:^{\ominus}}{\underset{\displaystyle CN}{\overset{|}{\underset{|}{C}}}}-H \rightleftharpoons Ar-\overset{\displaystyle OH}{\underset{\displaystyle CN}{\overset{|}{\underset{|}{C}:^{\ominus}}}} \underset{\xrightarrow{\hspace{1cm}}}{\overset{ArCHO}{\rightleftharpoons}}$$

$$Ar-\overset{\displaystyle HO}{\underset{\displaystyle CN}{\overset{|}{\underset{|}{C}}}}-\overset{\displaystyle :\ddot{O}:^{\ominus}}{\underset{\displaystyle H}{\overset{|}{\underset{|}{C}}}}-Ar \rightleftharpoons Ar-\overset{\displaystyle O}{\overset{||}{C}}-\overset{\displaystyle OH}{\underset{\displaystyle H}{\overset{|}{\underset{|}{C}}}}-Ar$$

Scheme 50

The Benzoin condensation of aldehydes are strongly catalysed by a PTC (quaternary ammonium cyanide in a two phase system)[75]. In a similar way, acyloin condensation are easily effected by stirring aliphatic or aromatic aldehydes with a quaternary catalyst (PTC), N-laurylthiazolium bromide in aqueous phosphate buffer at room temperature[76]. The aromatic aldehydes reacted in a short time (about 5 min). However, aliphatic aldehydes require longer time (5-10 hrs) for completion. Mixed α-hydroxyketones are abtained[77] from the benzoin condensation of mixture of aromatic and aliphatic aldehydes.

On the basis of extensive work, Breslow found that the benzoin condensation in aqueous media using inorganic salts (e.g. LiCl) is about 200 times faster than in ethanol (without any salts)[78]. The addition of γ-cyclodextrin also accelerates the reaction, whereas the addition of β-cyclodextrin inhibits the condensation.

2.1.9 *Claisen-Schmidt Condensation*

The condensation of aromatic aldehydes (without α-hydrogen) with an aliphatic aldehyde or ketone (having α-hydrogen) in presence of a relatively strong base (hydroxide or alkoxide) to form α, β- unsaturated aldehyde or a ketone (Scheme 51)[79] is known as Claisen-Schmidt Condensation.

$$C_6H_5CHO + CH_3CHO \xrightarrow{NaOH} C_6H_5CH=CHCHO$$
$$\text{Cinnamaldehyde}$$

$$C_6H_5COCH_3 + C_6H_5CHO \xrightarrow[EtOH]{NaOH} C_6H_5COCH=CHC_6H_5$$
$$\text{Benzalacetophenone}$$
$$\text{(chalcone)}$$

Scheme 51

Mukaiyama reaction[80], a related reaction involves the reaction of silyl enol ether of the ketone with an aldehyde in an organic solvent in presence of $TiCl_4$ (Scheme 52) (see also Scheme 35).

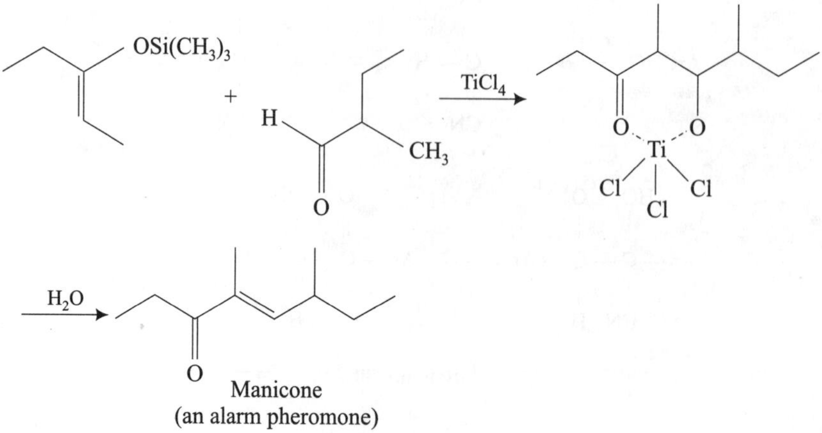

Scheme 52

It has been shown[81] that the trimethyl silyl enol ether of cyclohexanone react with benzaldehyde in water in presence of $TiCl_4$ in heterogeneous phase at room temperature and atmospheric pressure (Scheme 53) to give the products.

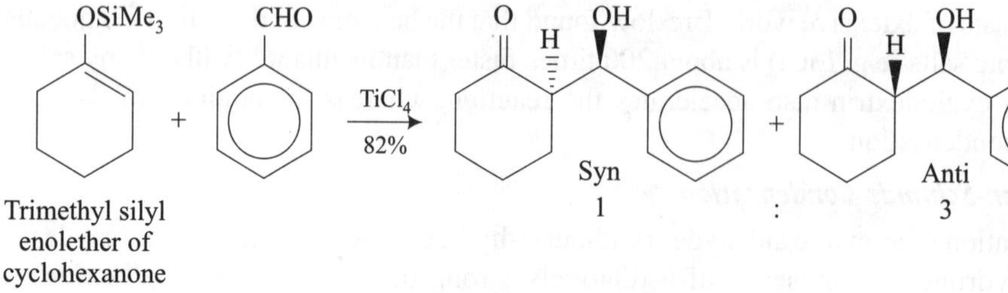

Scheme 53

Better yields are obtained under sonication conditions. The reaction is favoured by an electron-withdrawing subsituent in the pra position of the phenyl ring in benzaldehyde.

Flavanols are obtained by Claisen-Schmidt reaction of acetophenones with aromatic aldehydes in presence of cationic surfactants such as cetylammonium compounds, CTACl, CTABr, $(CTA)_2SO_4$ and CTAOH in mild alkaine conditions give chalcones, which on cyclisation give flavanols (Scheme 54).

The reaction of cyclohexanone with benzaldehyde in water gives high yield of a 1:1 threo-erythro mixture of the ketone. However in presence of CTACl, the bis-condensation product in obtained quantitatively (Scheme 55)[82].

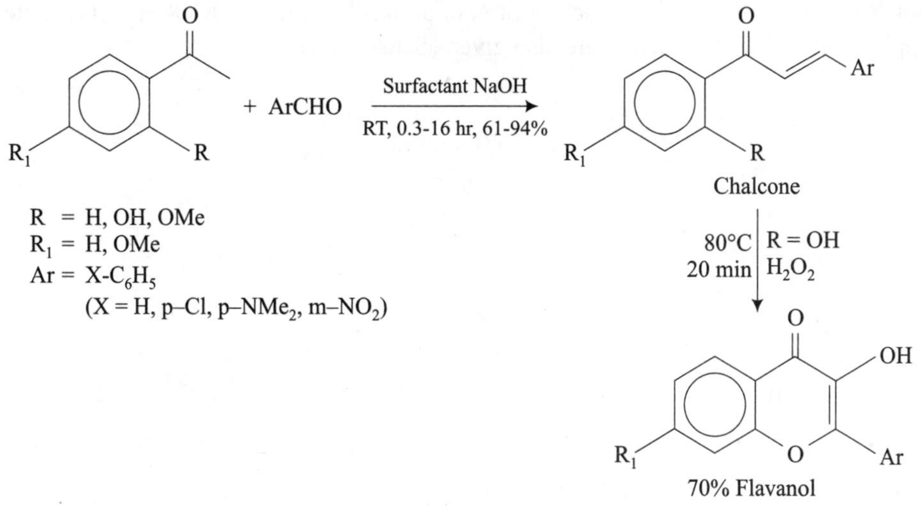

Scheme 54

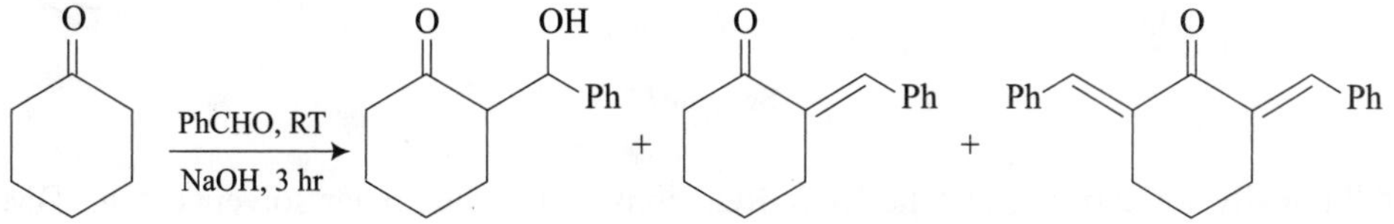

R = H, OH, OMe
R_1 = H, OMe
Ar = X-C$_6$H$_5$
        (X = H, p–Cl, p–NMe$_2$, m–NO$_2$)

Water only	91%	9%	—
with CTACl	—	—	100%

Scheme 55

2.1.10   Heck Reaction

The coupling of an alkene with a halide or triflate in the presence of Pd(O) catalyst to form a new alkene is known as Heck Reaction (Scheme 56).

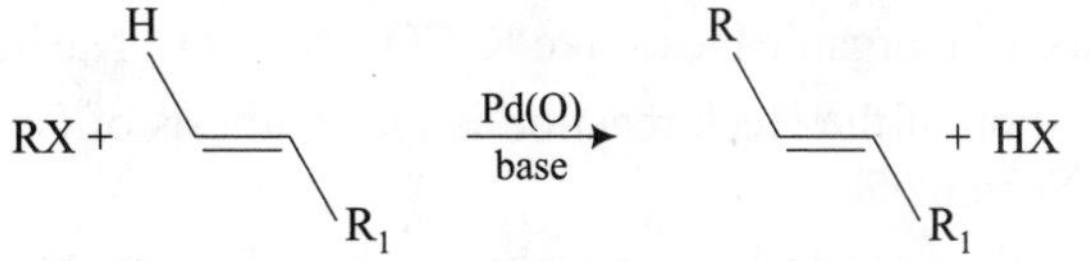

R = aryl, vinyl or alkyl group without β-hydrogens on
        a sp^3 carbon atom
X = halide or triflate (OSO$_2$CF$_3$)

Scheme 56

Heck Reactions uses mild base such as Et_3N or anions like OH^-, $^-OCOCH_3$, CO_3^{2-}, etc. Some other applications of Heck Reaction are also given (Scheme 57).

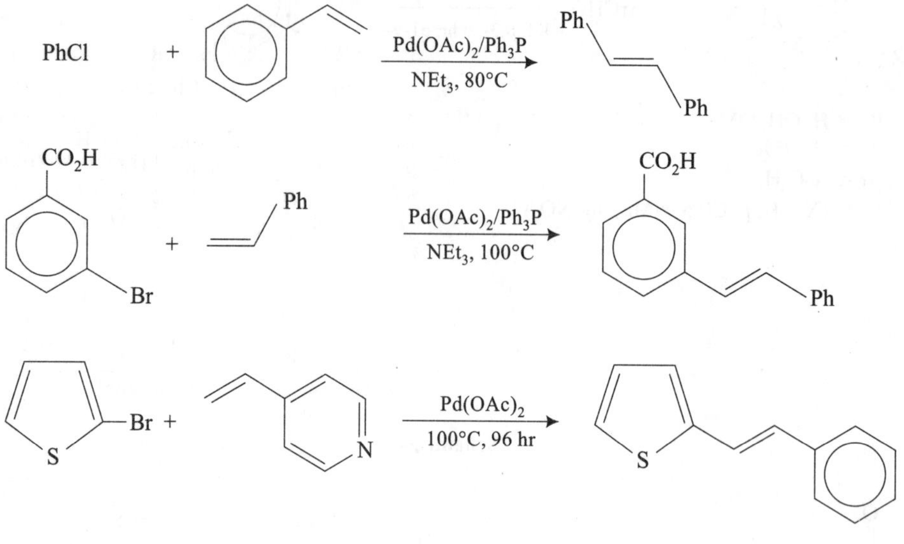

Scheme 57

Traditionally for carrying out the Heck Reactions, anhydrous polar solvents (e.g., DMF and MeCN) and tert, amines as bases are used.

Recently, it has been found that the Heck reaction can proceed very well in aqueous medium. Infact, the role of water in the Heck reaction, as well as in other reactions catalysed by Pd(O) in presence of phosphine ligands is: (i) transformation of catalyst precursor into Pd(O) species and (ii) the generation of zero-valent palladium species capable of oxidative addition by oxidation of phosphine ligands by the Pd(II) catalyst precursor can be affected by water content of the reaction mixture.

It has been found that the Heck reaction can be accomplished under mild conditions using PTC conditions[83] with inorganic carbonates as bases at room temperature. It been shown that the Heck reaction can also be carried out in water and aqueous organic solvents, catalysed by simple palladium salts in presence of inorganic bases like K_2CO_3, Na_2CO_3, $NaHCO_3$, KOH etc.[84]

An interesting application of the Heck reaction is the synthesis of cinnamic acid from of aryl halides and acrylic acid (Scheme 58).

Use of acrylo nitrile in place of acrylic acid in this method (Scheme 58) yield the corresponding cinnamonitriles. The product obtained in Heck reactions are almost exclusively (E) isomers. However, the reaction of acrylonitrile give a mixture of (E) and (Z) isomers with ratio 3 : 1, close to that observed under conventional anhydrous conditions[85].

The Heck reaction can also be performed under milder condition by addition of acetate ion as given in (Scheme 59).

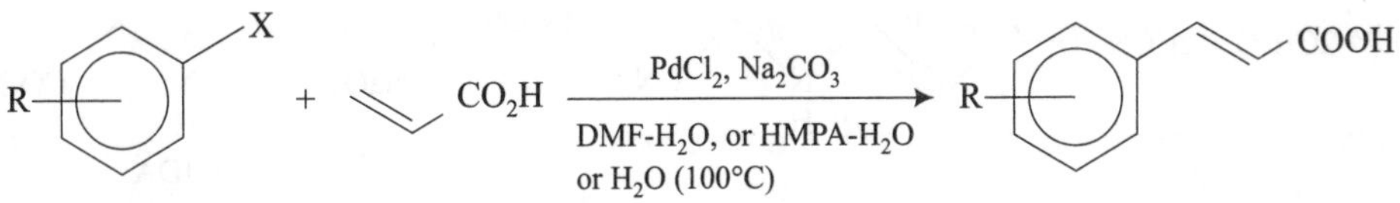

Aryl halide　　Acrylic acid　　Cinnamic acid

X = 1, Br
R = H, p-Cl, p-OMe, p-Me-, p-Ac, p-NO_2, p-CHO, p-OH, m-COOH etc.

Scheme 58

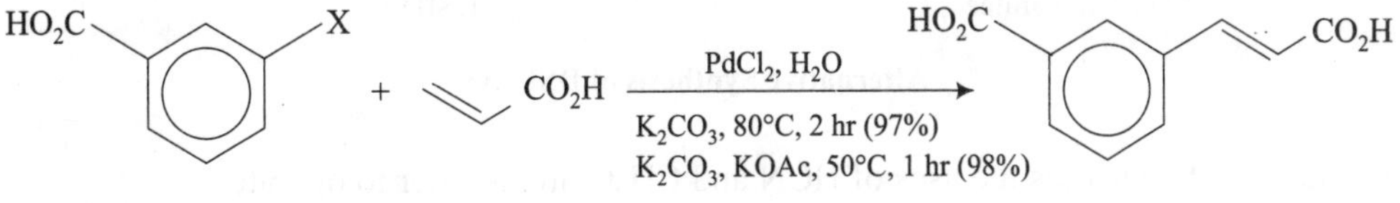

Scheme 59

A large number of other application of the Heck reaction have been described in literature[86].

The Heck reaction has also been performed in ionic liquids (see chapter 7, section 5.7.1)

2.1.11 Strecker Synthesis

The reaction of an aldehyde with ammonia followed by reaction with HCN gives α-aminonitrile intermediates, which on hydrolysis gives α-amino acid. This reaction is known as Strecker Synthesis of amino acids (Scheme 60)[87].

$$PhCH_2CHO \xrightarrow{NH_3/HCN} PhCH_2\underset{}{CH}(NH_2){-}CN \xrightarrow{H_3O^+} PhCH_2CH(NH_2){-}COOH$$

Scheme 60

The α-aminonitrile can also be obtained by the treatment of the aldehyde with HCN followed by reaction of the formed cyanohydrin with ammonia. This method is known as Erlenmeyer modification[88]. A more convenient route is to treat the aldehyde in one step with ammonium chloride and sodium cyanide (this mixture is equivalent to ammonium cyanide, which in turn dissociates into ammonia and HCN). This procedure is referred to as the Zelinsky-Stadnikoff modification[89]. The final step is the hydrolysis of the intermediate α-aminonitrile under acidic or basic conditions.

Using strecker synthesis, disodium iminodiacetate (DSIDA) an intermediate for the manufacture is Monsantos' Roundup (herbicide) was synthesised[90].

In the above procedure hydrogen cyanide, a hazardous chemical is used and this requires special handling to minimise the risk to workers and the environment. An alternative synthesis of DSIDA was developed by Monsanto; this is a green synthesis.

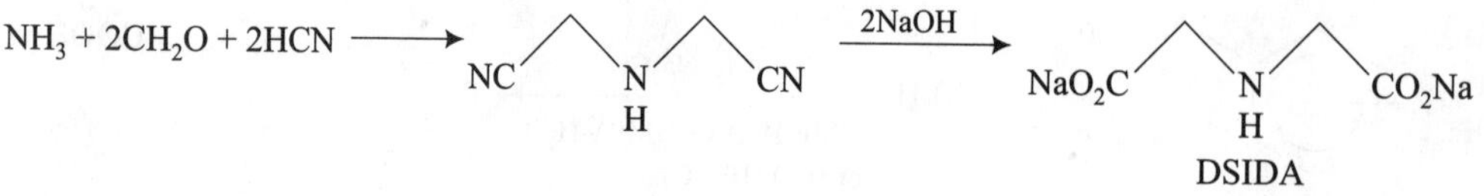
NH3 + 2CH2O + 2HCN
NC
N
H
CN
2NaOH
NaO2C
N
H
CO2Na
DSIDA

Strecker Synthesis of DSIDA

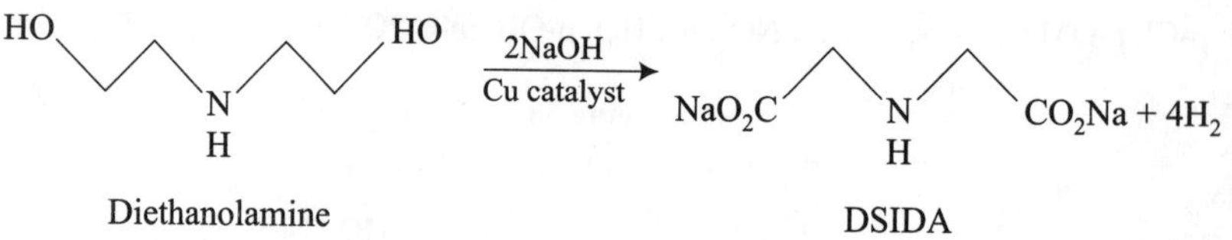
HO
N
H
HO
2NaOH
Cu catalyst
NaO2C
N
H
CO2Na + 4H2
Diethanolamine
DSIDA

Alternative Synthesis of DSIDA

The new method avoids the uses of HCN and CH_2O and is safer to operate.

2.1.12 Wurtz Reaction

Coupling of alkyl halides with sodium in dry ether to give hydrocarbon[91] is known as Wurtz Reaction (Scheme 61).

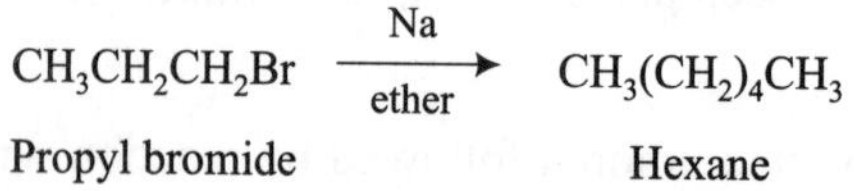
CH3CH2CH2Br
Na
ether
CH3(CH2)4CH3
Propyl bromide
Hexane

Scheme 61

It has been shown[92] that the Wurtz coupling can be achieved by Zn/H_2O (Scheme 62).

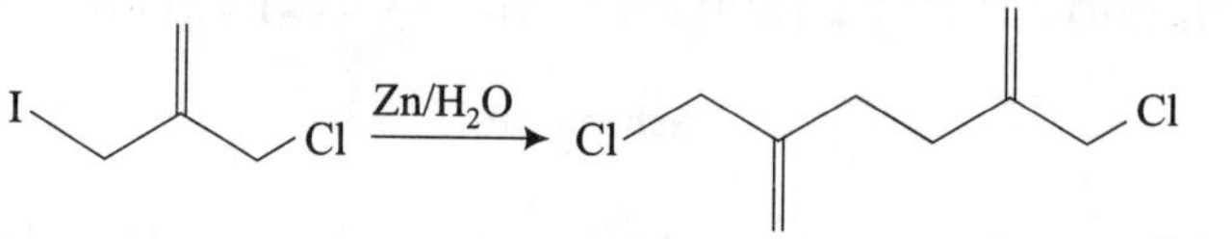
I
Cl
Zn/H2O
Cl
Cl

Scheme 62

2.1.13 Oxidations

It is one of the most widely investigated process in organic chemistry. A large number of reactions involving oxidations are used in laboratory and also in industries. A number of oxidizing agents with different substrates have been described[93].

Oxidations have been known to be carried out in aqueous medium for a very long time. The oxidation of arenes with $KMnO_4$ in aqueous alkaline medium is well known[94]. The yields are however considerably increased by using $KMnO_4$ in presence of a phase transfer catalyst particularly in the oxidation of toluene. Another environment-friendly oxidant is the use of H_2O_2 in water; in this case water is formed as a secondary product.

In the present unit, some recent oxidations by chemical reagents in aqueous media are described as Enzymatic oxidations have also been known to occur in water. However, this subject will be discussed in a separate section. Following are some of the important oxidations in water.

2.1.13.1 Epoxidation

Peracids react with alkenes to give stable three-membered rings containing oxygen atom, called epoxides or oxiranes (Scheme 63).

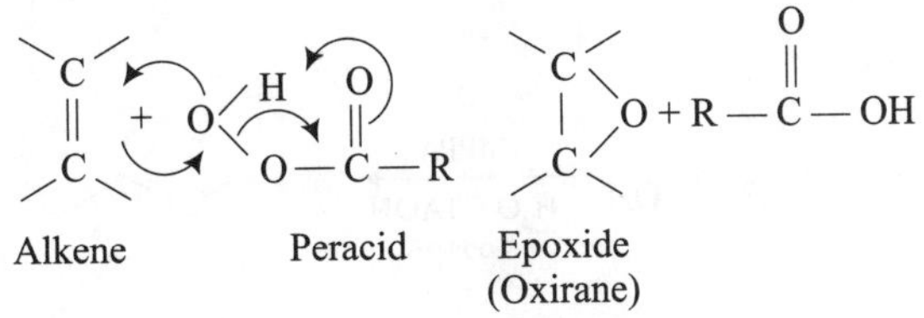

Alkene   Peracid   Epoxide
                                 (Oxirane)

Scheme 63

The reaction takes place in nonpolar solvents such as dichloromethane and benzene. The above epoxidations are stereoselective and takes place by syn addition to the double bond. As the cis alkene gives only cis epoxide and trans alkene gives trans epoxide, the reaction is concerted, i.e. the one-step mechanism retains the stereochemistry of the starting alkenes.

Simple alkenes can be epoxidised[95] with m-chloroperoxybenzoic acid in aqueous $NaHCO_3$ at room temperature to yield epoxides in good yield. A number of alkenes like cyclopentene, cyclohexene, cycloheptene, cyclooctene, methyl cyclohexene and (+)-3-carene have been epoxidized with MCPA at 20° in 30 min to give 90-95 per cent epoxide. Styrene could be epoxidized at 20°C (1 hr), α-Methylstyrene and trans-α-methylstyrene could be epoxidized at 0°C in 1 hr. In aqueous medium, the reaction occurs in heterogeneous phase, but this does not effect the reactivity, which sometimes is higher than in homogenous organic phase.

For direct epoxidation of simple alkenes the peroxide must be activated (Scheme 63a). This is done in buffered aqueous tetrahydrofuran (THF), 50 per cent H_2O_2 activated by stoichiometic amounts of organophosphorus anhydride.

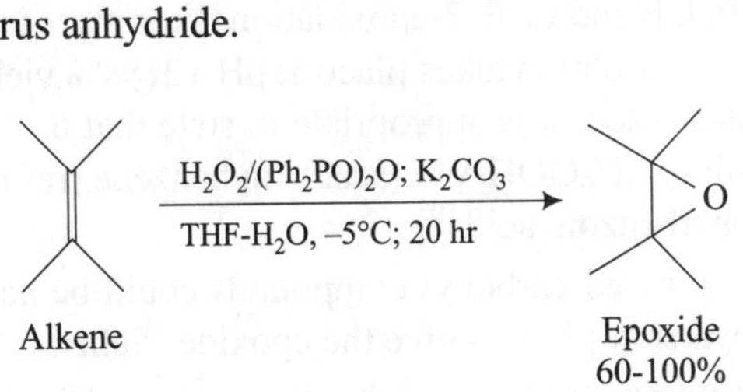

Alkene   Epoxide
                                60-100%

Scheme 63a

Using this procedure a variety of alkenes could be epoxidized[96]. The epoxidation of electron-deficient olefins can be achieved with H_2O_2 in presence of sodium tungstate as a catalyst[97]. The epoxidation of alkene has also been effected with a other oxidizing reagents such as $PhIO_4$, NaClO, O_2, H_2O_2, $KHSO_5$, etc. in aqueous medium in presence of metalloporphyrins[98].

Epoxidation of alkenes on a large scale is generally carried out by using hydrogen peroxide, peracetic acid or t-butyl hydroperoxide (TBHP)[99]. A safe and cheap method for epoxidation has been developed[100]. It consist in using nacent oxygen generated by electrolysis of water at room temperature by using Pd black as an anode. Using this procedure cyclohexene could be epoxidized in good yield. In this illustration, water is used as a reaction medium as well as reagent.

Allyl alcohols could be epoxidised regioselectively in presence of other C = C bonds by using monoperphthalic acid (MPPA) in presence of cetyltrimethyl ammonium hydroxide (CTAOH) (Scheme 64)[101].

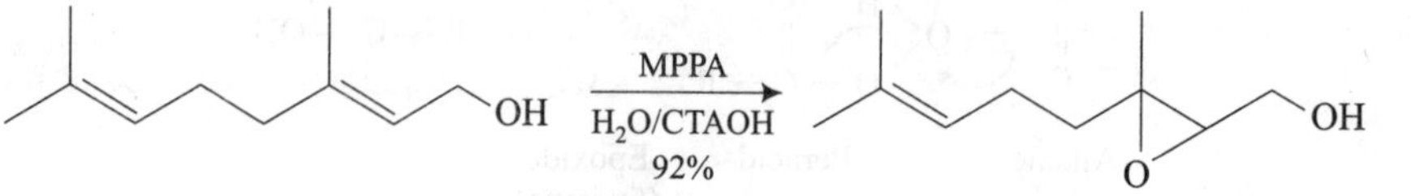

Scheme 64

Epoxidation takes place at different double bonds in the terpenoids, viz., geraniol (I), nerol (II), farnesol (III) and linalool (IV) with MPPA by carrying out the reaction at different pH.

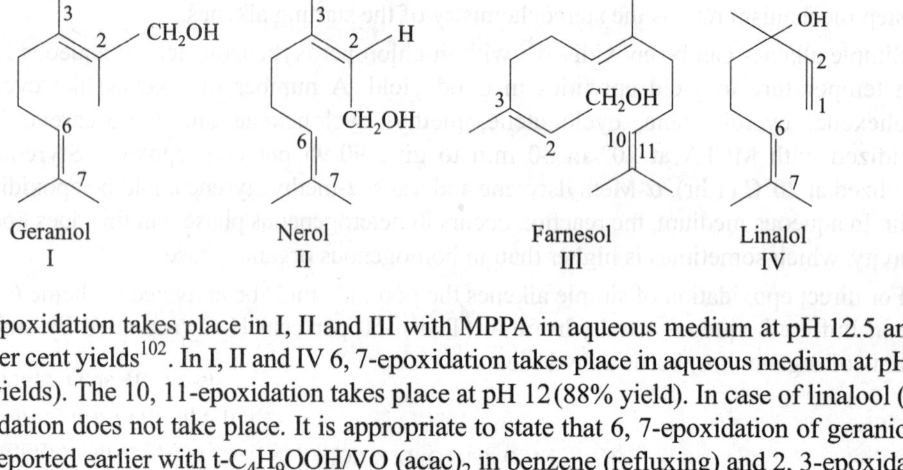

| Geraniol | Nerol | Farnesol | Linalol |
| I | II | III | IV |

2, 3-Epoxidation takes place in I, II and III with MPPA in aqueous medium at pH 12.5 and in about 90 per cent yields[102]. In I, II and IV 6, 7-epoxidation takes place in aqueous medium at pH 8.3 (60-90% yields). The 10, 11-epoxidation takes place at pH 12 (88% yield). In case of linalool (IV), 1, 2-epoxidation does not take place. It is appropriate to state that 6, 7-epoxidation of geraniol (I) has been reported earlier with t-C_4H_9OOH/VO (acac)$_2$ in benzene (refluxing) and 2, 3-epoxidation achieved by using m-chloroperbenzoic acid[103].

Epoxidation of α, β-unsaturated carbonyl compounds could be accomplished[104, 105] by using sodium perborate (SPB) in water at pH 8 to give the epoxide (Scheme 65)

The epoxidation of α, β-unsaturated carbonyl compounds with hydrogen peroxide under basic biphase condition, known as the Weitz-Scheffer epoxidation (Scheme 66)[106] is a convenient and efficient method for producing the epoxides.

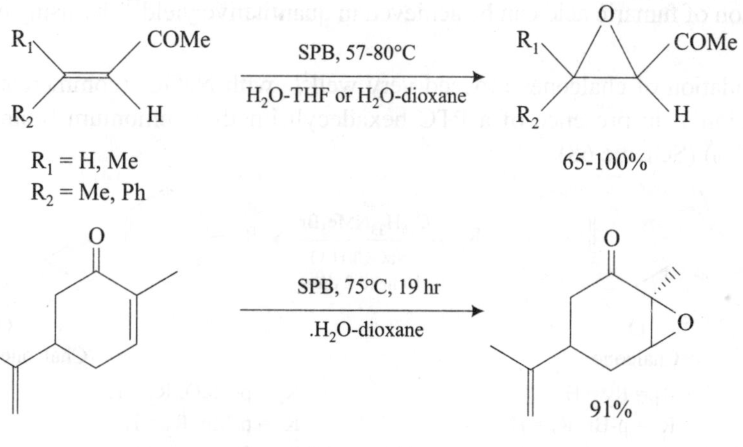

R₁ = H, Me
R₂ = Me, Ph

65-100%

Scheme 65

The new procedure (Scheme 66) has been used for the epoxidation of a number of α, β-unsaturated aldehydes, ketones, nitriles, esters and sulfones, etc.

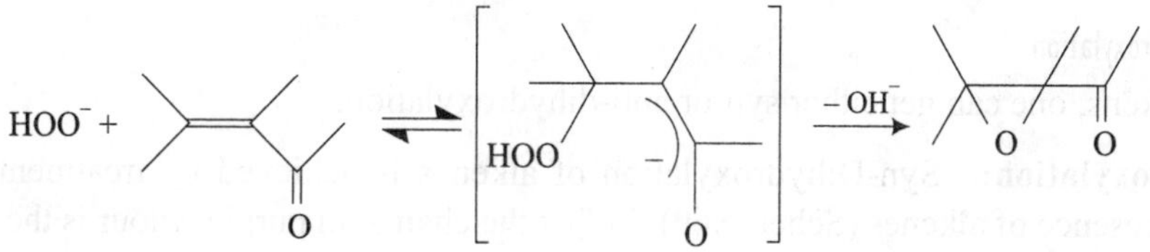

Scheme 66

The epoxidation of α, β-unsaturated carboxylic acid can be achieved with H_2O_2 in presence of Na_2WO_4 at pH 5.8-6.8 (Scheme 67).

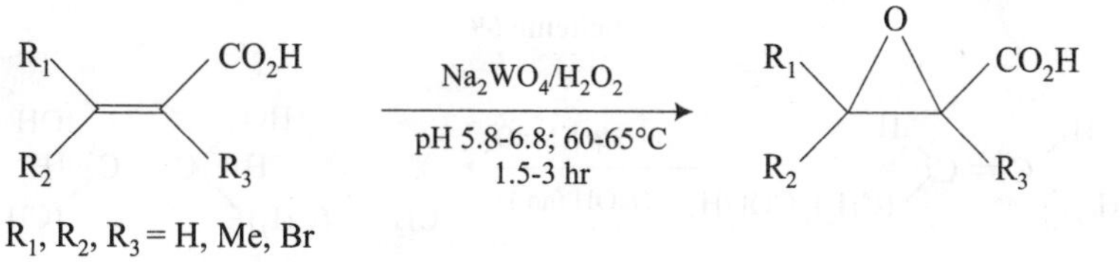

R₁, R₂, R₃ = H, Me, Br

Scheme 67

The above reaction is known as Payne's reaction[107] using the modified procedure of sharpless[108].

The epoxidation of α, β-unsaturated carboxylic acids can also be achieved by using ozone-acetone system and buffering the reaction with $NaHCO_3$[109] in 75-80 per cent yield.

Epoxidation of fumaric acid can be achieved in quantitative yield[110] by using ozone in water at neutral pH.

The epoxidation of chalcones proceed very well[111] with NaOCl (commercially available) in water suspension[111] in presence of a PTC hexadecyltrimethylammonium bromide in excellent yields (50-100%) (Scheme 68).

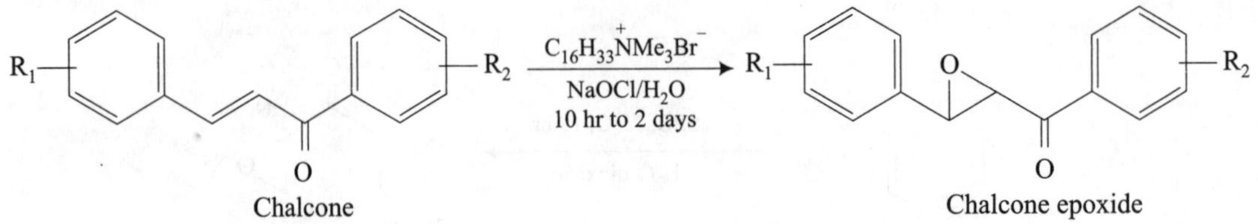

Chalcone

R$_1$ = R$_2$ = H
R$_1$ = p-Br; R$_2$ = H
R$_1$ = H; R$_2$ = p-Br
R$_1$ = m-Me; R$_2$ = H
R$_1$ = p-Cl; R$_2$ = H

Chalcone epoxide

R$_1$ = p-MeO; R$_2$ = H
R$_1$ = p-Me; R$_2$ = H
R$_1$ = H; R$_2$ = p-Me
R$_1$ = R$_2$ = p-Cl
R$_1$ = R$_2$ = p-Me

Scheme 68

2.1.13.2   Dihydroxylation

In case of alkens, one can get either syn-or anti-dihydroxylation.

Syn-Dihydroxylation: Syn-Dihydroxylation of alkenes is achieved by treatment with dilute KMnO$_4$ in presence of alkenes (Scheme 69). In fact the change in purple colour is the basis for the presence of double bond and this is known as Baeyer's test for unsaturation.

This method is used for syn-hydroxylation of oleic acid and norbornene (Scheme 70).

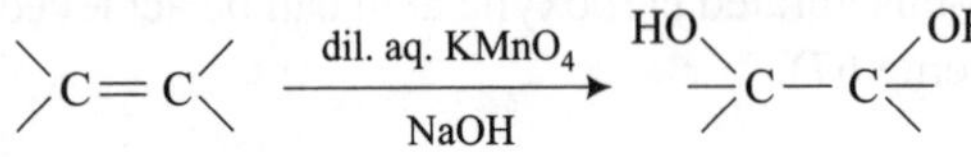

Scheme 69

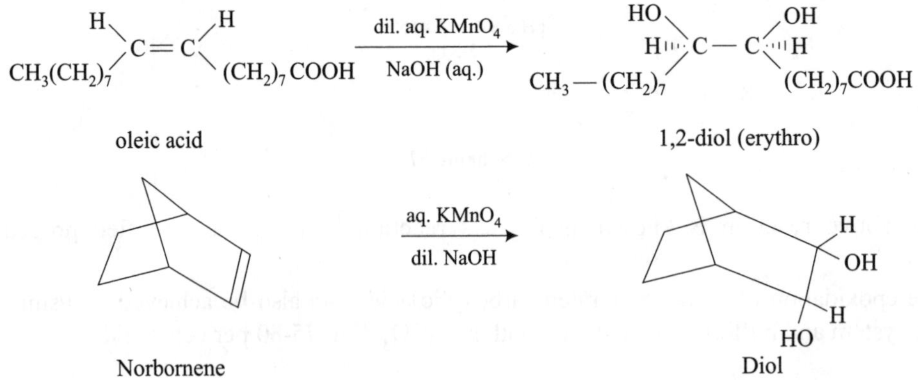

oleic acid

1,2-diol (erythro)

Norbornene

Diol

Scheme 70

A large number of other examples of syn-dihydroxylation of alkenes have been reported in the literature.

Subsequently osmium tetraoxide in dry organic solvents[112] was used for syn-dihydroxylation of alkenes. The reaction is in presence of chlorate salts as the primary oxidant in presence of catalytic amount at OsO_4. The epoxidation is carried out in H_2O-THF solvent (Scheme 71). It is found that Ag or Ba chlorate give better yields.

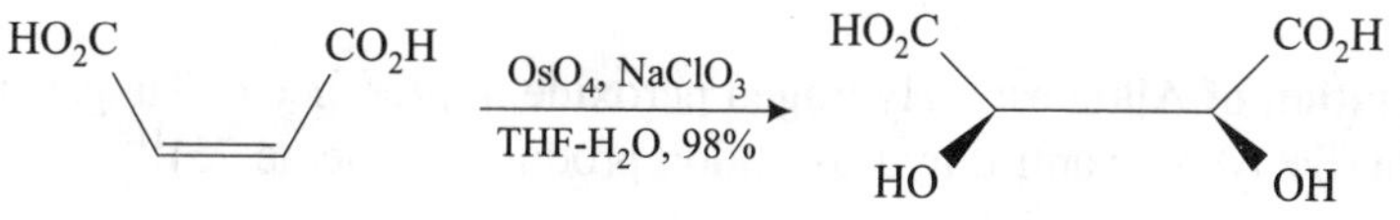

Scheme 71

The syn-dihydroxylation of alkenes can also be carried out by hydrogen peroxide in presence of catalytic amount of OsO_4[113]. By this method allyl alcohol is quantitatively hydroxylated in water (Scheme 72)[114].

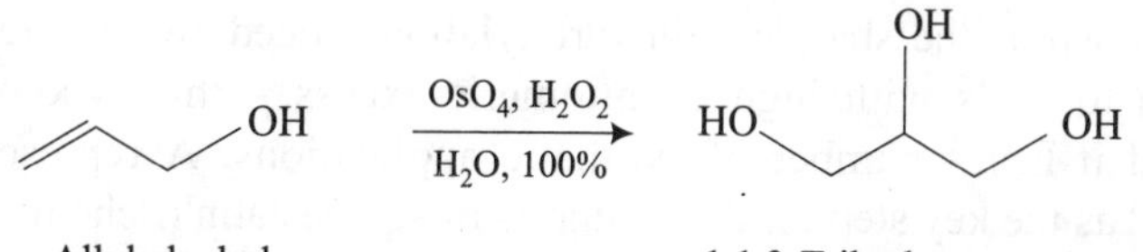

Allyl alcohol

1,1,3-Trihydroxy propane
(glycerol)

Scheme 72

Following are given some other methods used for syn-dihydroxylation of alkenes:
(i) Osmium-tetroxide-tertiary amine N-oxide system[115] has been used in aqueous acetone.
(ii) $K_3Fe(CN)_6$ in presence of K_2CO_3 in aqueous or tertiary butyl alcohol has been used for the osmium-catalysed dihydroxylation of alkenes (Scheme 73)[116]. Using this method even alkene having low reactivity or hindered alkenes could be hydroxylated.

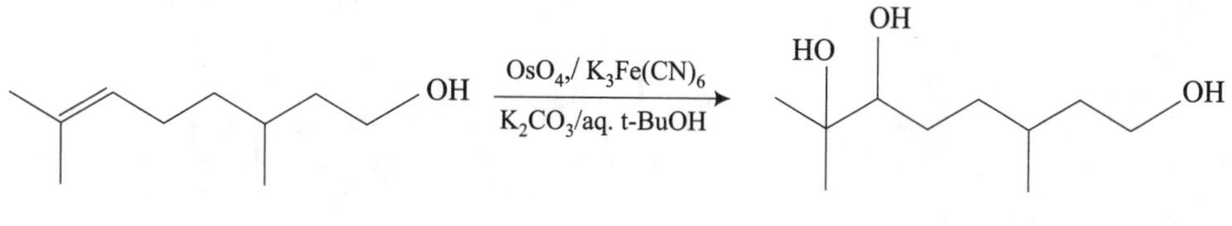

88%

Scheme 73

Syn-hydroxylation of olefins has also been carried out with $KMnO_4$ solution using a PTC catalyst under alkaline conditions. Thus cyclooctene gives[117] 50 per cent yield of cis 1, 2-cyclooctane diol compared to an yield of about 7 per cent by the classical technique (Scheme 74).

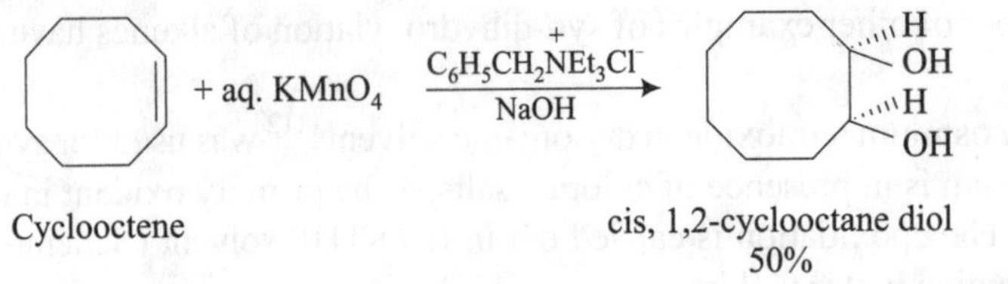

Cyclooctene

cis, 1,2-cyclooctane diol
50%

Scheme 74

Anti Dihydroxylation of Alkenes: Hydrogen peroxide in presence of Tungsten oxide (WO$_3$) or Selenium dioxide (SeO$_2$) give anti-dihydroxylation products (Scheme 75)[118].

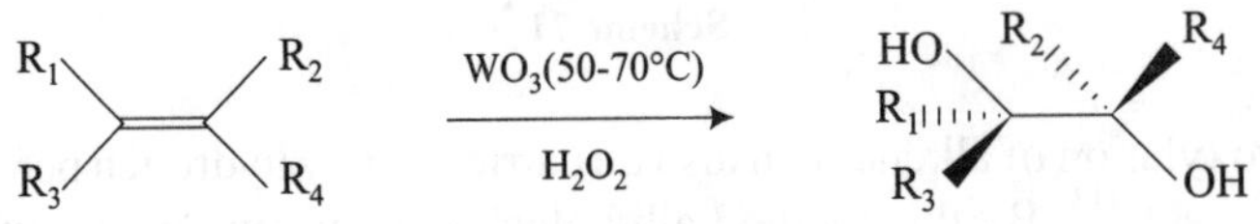

Scheme 75

The above is known as the sharpless dihydroxylation procedure. Different types of alkenes can be transformed to diols with high enantiomeric-excess – this is known as asymmetric dihydroxylation and it has a number of synthetic applications. A representative example is dihydroxylation used as the key step for the synthesis of squalestatin (Scheme 76)[119].

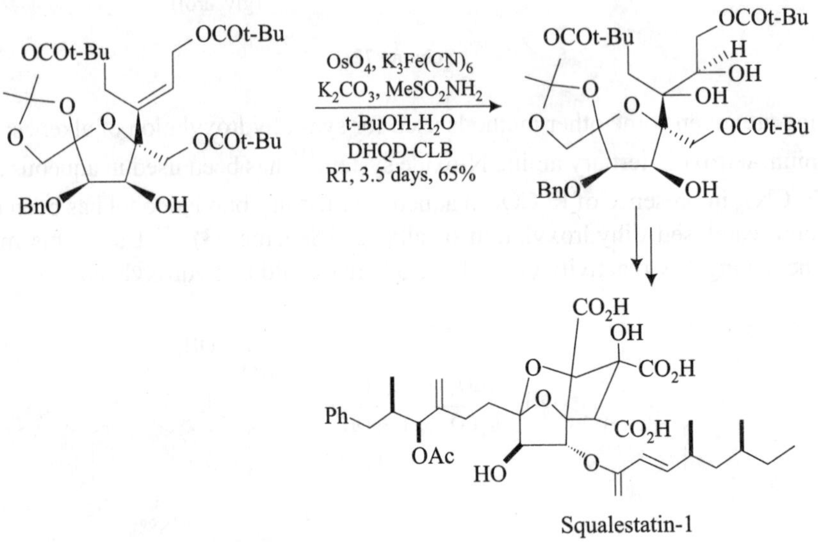

Squalestatin-1

Scheme 76

A one pot procedure for the antihydroxylation of the carbon-carbon double bond can be achieved as shown below (Scheme 77)[120].

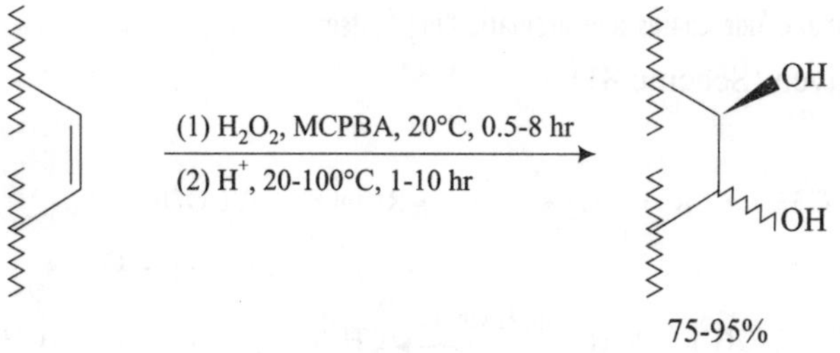

(1) H_2O_2, MCPBA, 20°C, 0.5-8 hr

(2) H^+, 20-100°C, 1-10 hr

OH

OH

75-95%

Scheme 77

Miscellaneous Oxidations in Aqueous Medium

Alkenes

The oxidation of alkenes with aqueous solution of $KMnO_4$ in presence of a phase transfer catalyst (e.g. $CH_3(CH_2)_{15}N^+(CH_3)_3Cl^-$) gives 79 per cent yield of the carboxylic acid. Some examples are given (Scheme 78)

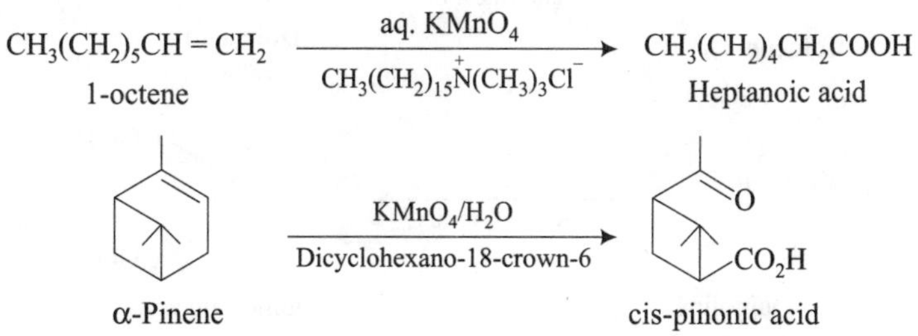

$CH_3(CH_2)_5CH = CH_2$ $\xrightarrow[\text{$CH_3(CH_2)_{15}\overset{+}{N}(CH_3)_3Cl^-$}]{\text{aq. $KMnO_4$}}$ $CH_3(CH_2)_4CH_2COOH$

1-octene   Heptanoic acid

α-Pinene

$\xrightarrow[\text{Dicyclohexano-18-crown-6}]{\text{$KMnO_4$/H_2O}}$

cis-pinonic acid

Scheme 78

Another example is the oxidation of n-octane to 1-octanol (Scheme 79) using Psuedomonas oleovorans[121]. This procedure is used for the industrial production of 1-octanol (>98% pure)[122].

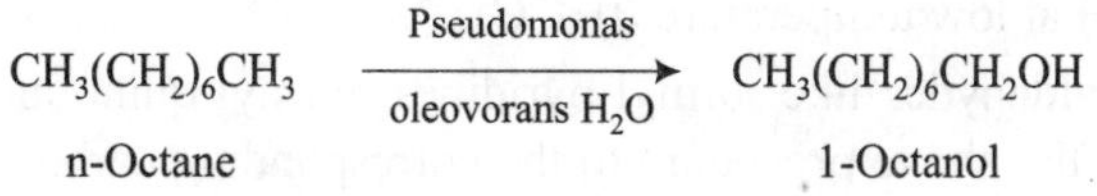

$CH_3(CH_2)_6CH_3$ $\xrightarrow[\text{oleovorans H_2O}]{\text{Pseudomonas}}$ $CH_3(CH_2)_6CH_2OH$

n-Octane   1-Octanol

Scheme 79

Alkynes

Alkynes on oxidation with $KMnO_4$ in aqueous medium give a mixture of carboxylic acids. Some examples are given below (Scheme 80).

2.1.13.3   Oxidation of Aromatic Side Chains and Aromatic Ring System

Some examples are given (Scheme 81).

$$R-C\equiv C-R' + 4[O] \xrightarrow{KMnO_4} RCOOH + R'COOH$$

$$CH_3(CH_2)_7C\equiv C(CH_2)_7COOH \xrightarrow[pH\ 7.5]{aq.\ KMnO_4} CH_3(CH_2)_7 - \overset{O}{\underset{\|}{C}} - \overset{O}{\underset{\|}{C}} - (CH_2)_7 - COOH$$

$$\xrightarrow{alk.\ KMnO_4} CH_3(CH_2)_7COOH + HOOC(CH_2)_7COOH$$

Scheme 80

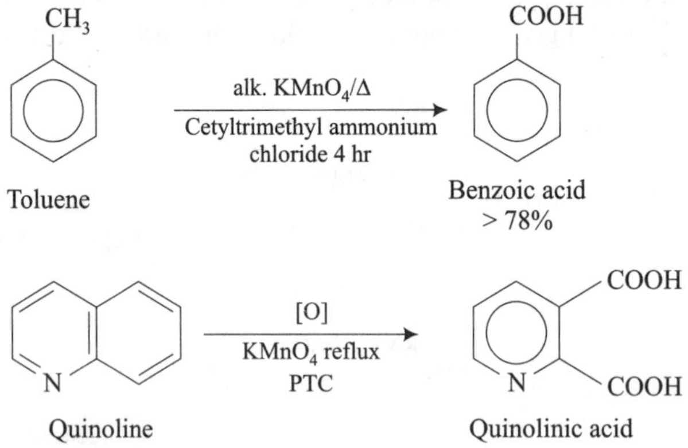

Toluene   Benzoic acid
                            > 78%

alk. KMnO$_4$/Δ
Cetyltrimethyl ammonium
chloride 4 hr

Quinoline   Quinolinic acid

[O]
KMnO$_4$ reflux
PTC

Scheme 81

2.1.13.4   Oxidation of Aldehydes and Ketones

A number of procedures are available for the oxidation of aldehydes to the corresponding carboxylic acids in aqueous and organic media[123].

Aromatic aldehydes can be conveniently oxidized by aqueous performic acid obtained by addition of H$_2$O$_2$ to HCOOH at low temperature (0-4°C)[124].

The hetroaromatic aldehydes like formyl pyridines, formyl quinolines and formylazaindoles can also be oxidised by the above procedure to the corresponding carboxylic acids; in this procedure, the formation of N-oxides is avoided.

Chemoselective oxidation of formyl group in presence of other oxidizable groups can be carried out in aqueous media in presence of a surfactant. Thus, 4-(methylthio) benzaldehyde is quantitatively oxidised to 4-(methylthio) benzoic acid with TBHP in a basic aqueous medium in presence of cetyltrimethyl ammonium sulphate[125].

Aromatic aldehydes having hydroxyl group in ortho or para position to the formyl groups can be oxidised with alkaline H$_2$O$_2$ (Dakin reaction) in low yields[126]. However this reaction has been carried out in high yields using sodium percarbonate (SPC; Na$_2$CO$_3$, 1.5 H$_2$O$_2$) in H$_2$O-THF under ultrasonic irradiation[127]. Using this procedure, following aldehydes have been oxidised in good yields: o-hydroxybenzaldehyde; p-hydroxybenzaldehyde; 2-hydroxy-4-methoxybenzaldehyde, 2-hydroxy-3-methoxybenzaldehyde and 3-methoxy-4-hydroxybenzaldehyde.

The Baeyer-Villiger oxidation[128] is used for the conversion of ketones into the corresponding esters (Scheme 82). Usually the conversion is effected by peracids in organic solvents. This reaction has been carried out satisfactorily in aqueous heterogeneous medium using MCPBA at room temperature[129]. Some examples are given in (Scheme 83).

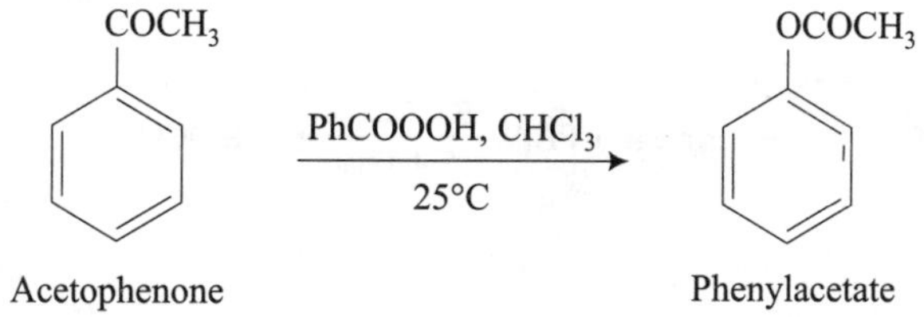

COCH$_3$ $\xrightarrow[\text{25°C}]{\text{PhCOOOH, CHCl}_3}$ OCOCH$_3$

Acetophenone   Phenylacetate

Scheme 82

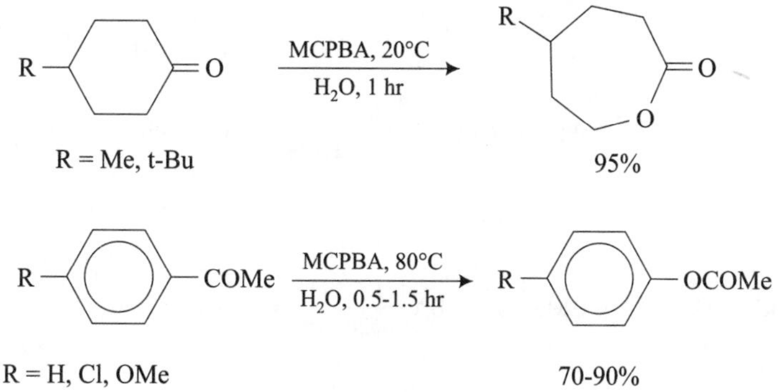

R = Me, t-Bu $\xrightarrow[\text{H}_2\text{O, 1 hr}]{\text{MCPBA, 20°C}}$ 95%

R—⬡—COMe $\xrightarrow[\text{H}_2\text{O, 0.5-1.5 hr}]{\text{MCPBA, 80°C}}$ R—⬡—OCOMe

R = H, Cl, OMe   70-90%

Scheme 83

Using the above procedure even unreactive ketones can also be oxidised (Scheme 84)[130].

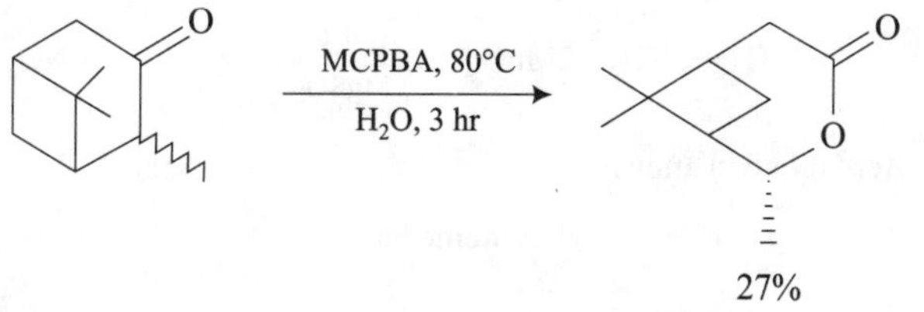

$\xrightarrow[\text{H}_2\text{O, 3 hr}]{\text{MCPBA, 80°C}}$ 27%

Scheme 84

Some Baeyer-Villiger oxidation of ketones with m-chloroperbenzoic acid proceed much faster at room temperature in the solid state[131]. The yields obtained in solid state are much better than in CHCl$_3$. Some representative examples are gives as follows (Scheme 85).

2.1.13.5 Oxidation of Amines into Nitro Compounds

Alkaline $KMnO_4$ oxidises tertiary alkyl amines into nitro compounds (Scheme 86)[132].

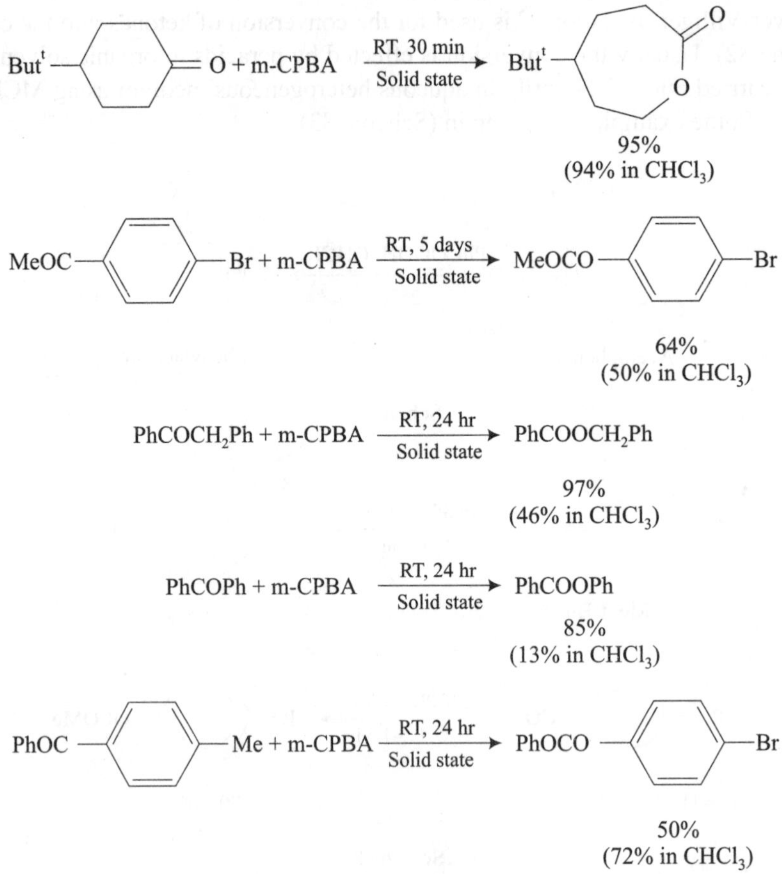

$$But^t\!-\!\!\bigcirc\!\!=\!O + \text{m-CPBA} \xrightarrow[\text{Solid state}]{\text{RT, 30 min}} But^t\!-\!\bigcirc$$

95%
(94% in $CHCl_3$)

$$\text{MeOC}\!-\!\bigcirc\!-\!Br + \text{m-CPBA} \xrightarrow[\text{Solid state}]{\text{RT, 5 days}} \text{MeOCO}\!-\!\bigcirc\!-\!Br$$

64%
(50% in $CHCl_3$)

$$\text{PhCOCH}_2\text{Ph} + \text{m-CPBA} \xrightarrow[\text{Solid state}]{\text{RT, 24 hr}} \text{PhCOOCH}_2\text{Ph}$$

97%
(46% in $CHCl_3$)

$$\text{PhCOPh} + \text{m-CPBA} \xrightarrow[\text{Solid state}]{\text{RT, 24 hr}} \text{PhCOOPh}$$

85%
(13% in $CHCl_3$)

$$\text{PhOC}\!-\!\bigcirc\!-\!Me + \text{m-CPBA} \xrightarrow[\text{Solid state}]{\text{RT, 24 hr}} \text{PhOCO}\!-\!\bigcirc\!-\!Br$$

50%
(72% in $CHCl_3$)

Scheme 85

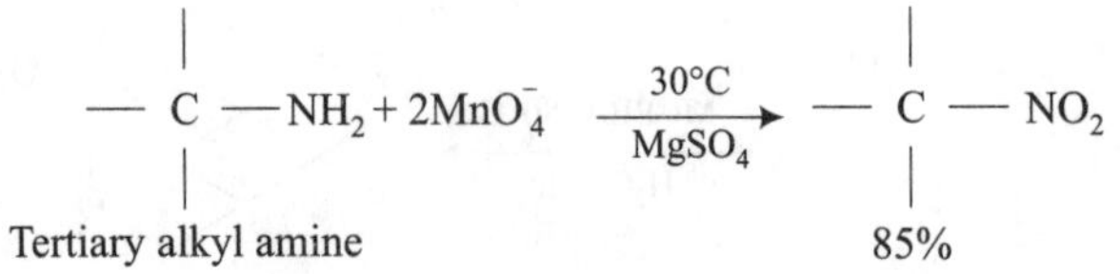

$$-\overset{|}{\underset{|}{C}}\!-\!NH_2 + 2MnO_4^- \xrightarrow[\text{MgSO}_4]{30°C} -\overset{|}{\underset{|}{C}}\!-\!NO_2$$

Tertiary alkyl amine   85%

Scheme 86

Primary and secondary alkyl amines remain uneffected under above conditions.

Aromatic amines containing a carboxylic or alcoholic groups can also be oxidised to nitro compounds by oxone (potassium hydrogen peroxymonosulfate triple salt, $2KHSO_3$, $KHSO_4$, K_2SO_4) in 20-50% aqueous acetone at 18°C in 73-84% yield[133].

Aminopyridine N-oxides are obtained under acidic conditions in organic solvent and usually requires protection of the amino group[134]. It has now been possible to obtain N-oxide in good yield from aminopyridine directly by using oxone in water under neutral or basic conditions at room temperature[135]. The selectivity of the reaction depends on the position of the amino group.

2.1.13.6   Oxidation of Nitro Compounds into Carbonyl Compounds

Primary and secondary nitro compounds can be oxidised into the corresponding carbonyl compounds by alkaline $KMnO_4$ (Scheme 87).

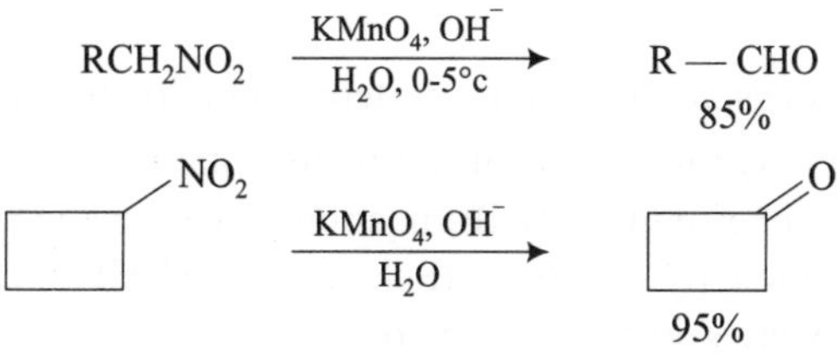

$$RCH_2NO_2 \xrightarrow[\text{H}_2\text{O, 0-5°c}]{\text{KMnO}_4, \text{OH}^-} R-CHO$$
85%

$$\text{NO}_2 \xrightarrow[\text{H}_2\text{O}]{\text{KMnO}_4, \text{OH}^-} \text{O}$$
95%

Scheme 87

2.1.13.7   Oxidation of Nitriles

Oxidation of nitriles into amides was first reported in 1986[136] by heating the nitrile with alcoholic KOH (Scheme 88).

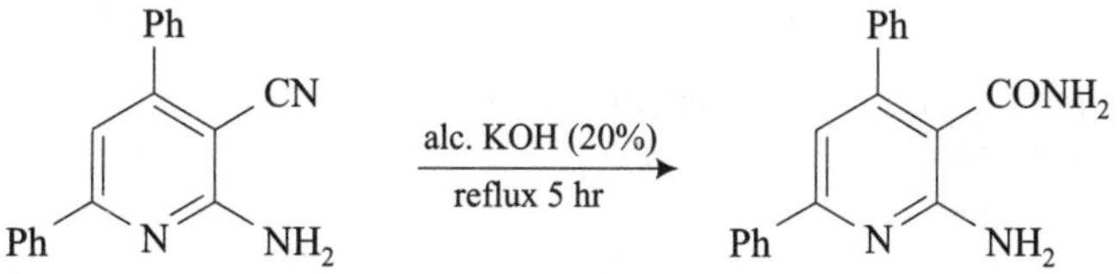

Ph — CN → Ph — CONH₂

2-Amino-3-cycano-
4,6-diphenylpyridine

alc. KOH (20%)
reflux 5 hr

2-Amino-3-carbamoyl-
4,6-diphenylpyridine

Scheme 88

The conversion of nitriles into amides can also be carried out under a variety of conditions in presence of metal catalyst[137].

A convenient method using urea-hydrogen peroxide adduct (UHP, H_2NCONH_2, H_2O_2) in presence of catalystic amount of K_2CO_3 in water-acetone at room temperature (Scheme 89) has been developed[138].

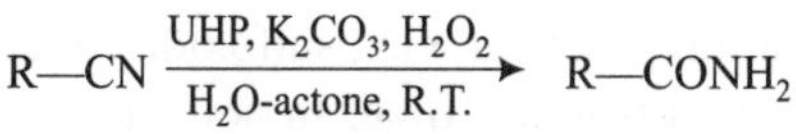

$$R-CN \xrightarrow[\text{H}_2\text{O-actone, R.T.}]{\text{UHP, K}_2\text{CO}_3, \text{H}_2\text{O}_2} R-CONH_2$$

Scheme 89

Using the above procedure following nitriles have been converted into corresponding amides in 85-95% yield: benzonitrile, methyl cyanide and chloromethyl cyanide.

Nitrlies can also be converted into amides by reacting with sodium perborate (SPB; $NaBO_3$, nH_2O, n = 1 to 4) in aqueous media such as H_2O-MeOH[139], H_2O-acetone[140] and H_2O-dioxan[141]. An interesting application of this reaction is the synthesis of quinazolin-4-(3H)-ones[142] (Scheme 90)

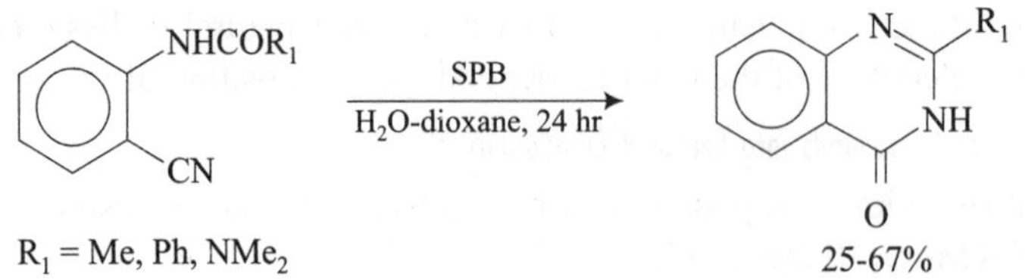

R$_1$ = Me, Ph, NMe$_2$

25-67%

Scheme 90

The quinazolin-4-(3H)-ones are interesting systems to build pharmaceutical compounds.

The CN group of 4-(methylthio) benzonitrile is quantitatively and selectively oxidised[143] to amides by tertiary butyl hydroperoxide (TBHP) in strong alkaline aqueous medium in presence of cetyltrimethyl ammonium sulfate [(CTA)$_2$SO$_4$] (Scheme 91). TBHP does not oxidise the CN group at pH 7 (even at 100°C), however in the absence of (CTA)$_2$SO$_4$, only the methylsulfenyl group is oxidised to methylsulfinyl. But under basic conditions, TBHP converts both groups into amide and sulfonyl groups, respectively (Scheme 91).

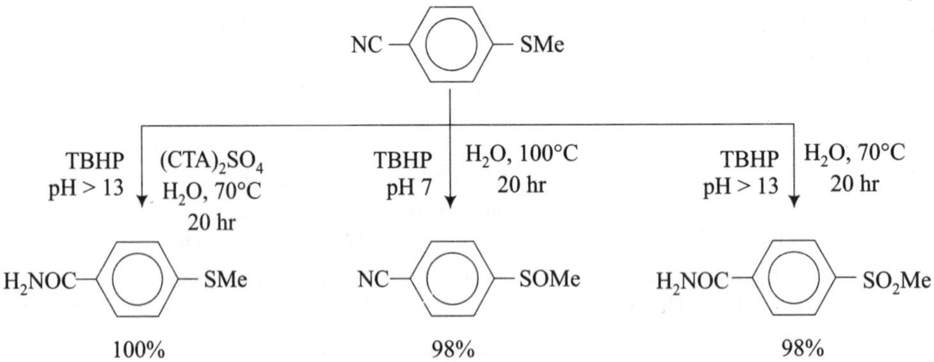

Scheme 91

2.1.13.8 Oxidation of Sulphides

A number of reagents (e.g. H$_2$O$_2$/acetic acid) are available for the oxidation of sulphides to sulfoxides and sulphones. On a large scale, an oxidant like oxone in aqueous acetone, buffered to pH 7.8-8.0 with sodium bicarbonate is used[144]. This procedure is environmentally benin. In this cases, the formation of the oxidation products, viz., sulfoxides or sulphones depend on the equivalent of oxone used, temperature and reaction time. In aqueous medium at pH 6-7 (buffered with phosphate), the reaction is very fast and excellent conversions to sulfoxides and sulphones are obtained[145].

Another cheaply available industrial chemical, sodium perborate (SPB) in aqueous methanolic sodium hydroxide oxidises sulphides to sulphones in very good yield[146]. Sulphide can also be oxidised to sulphoxides exclusively by using commercial 70 per cent aqueous TBHP in water in the heterogeneous phase at 20-70°C[147]. Using this procedure some of the sulphides like Et$_2$S, PhSMe, PhSPh, p-OHC$_6$H$_4$SMe can be oxidised quantitatively into the corresponding sulfoxides at 20°C.

The SMe group of 4-(methylthio) benzaldehyde can be selectively oxidised to the sulfinyl group in water at 70°C at pH 7 with tertiary butyl hydroperoxide (TBHP) (Scheme 92)[148]. Under strong basic conditions both the CHO and SMe groups are oxidised to –COOH and –SO$_2$Me, respectively. By using MCPBA under basic conditions, oxidation of –CHO group is prevented and SMe group is oxidised to SO$_2$Me in good yield.

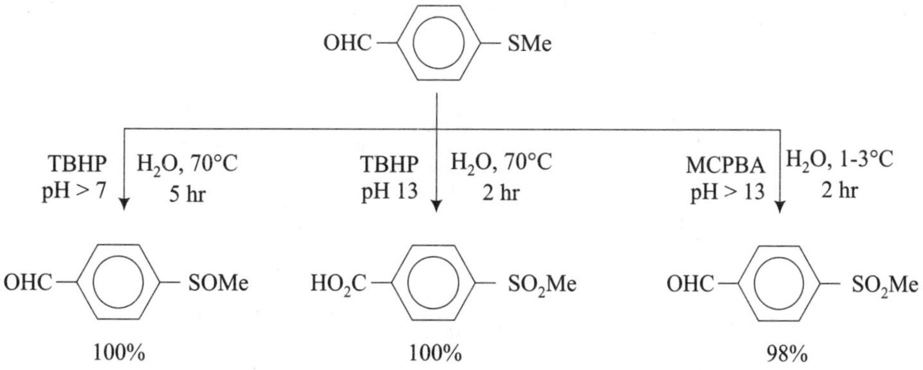

Scheme 92

2.1.13.9 Oxidations with Hypochlorite

Hypochlorite is a well documented oxidizing agent in the haloform reaction for the oxidation of methyl ketones to carboxylic acids. It has been found[149] that the hypochlorite anion can be transferred into organic solutions by PTC (quaternary cations). Some of the applications of this technique are given as follows (Scheme 93).

2.1.13.10 Oxidation with Ferricyanide

1, 2-Disubstituted hydrazines are oxidised by K$_3$Fe(CN)$_6$ in presence 2, 4, 6-triphenyl phenol (TPP) as a PTC in NaOH[150]. The product obtained is 1, 2-disubstituted azo compounds (Scheme 94).

Besides what has been mentioned above, a number of oxidations can be performed in aqueous phase in the presence of a phase transfer catalyst.

2.1.14 *Reductions*

Introduction

Like oxidation, reduction of organic molecules has played an important role in organic synthesis. A number of reducing agents with different substrates have been described[151].

During the last decade there has been considerable progress with respect to the types of bonds which can be reduced and also with respect to regio and stereo-selectivity of the reduction processes. Till some time back the only reducing agent which could be used in aqueous medium is sodium borohydride. From the point of view of industrial application, reduction in aqueous medium is very important. The hydride reductions which at one time seemed impossible to be carried out in

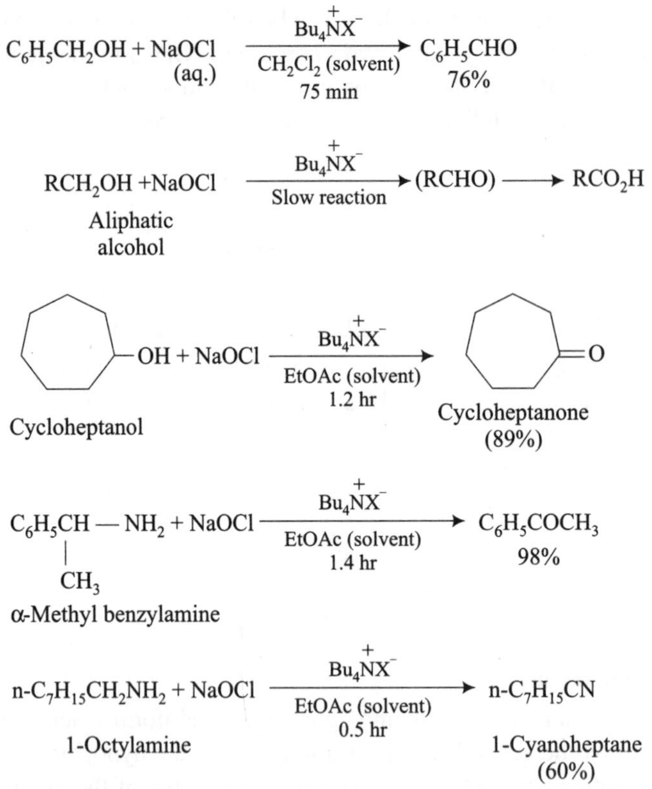

$$C_6H_5CH_2OH + NaOCl \xrightarrow[\substack{CH_2Cl_2 \text{ (solvent)} \\ 75 \text{ min}}]{\overset{+}{Bu_4N}\overset{-}{X}} C_6H_5CHO$$
$$\text{(aq.)} \qquad\qquad\qquad\qquad 76\%$$

$$RCH_2OH + NaOCl \xrightarrow[\text{Slow reaction}]{\overset{+}{Bu_4N}\overset{-}{X}} (RCHO) \longrightarrow RCO_2H$$

Aliphatic
alcohol

Cycloheptanol —OH + NaOCl $\xrightarrow[\substack{EtOAc \text{ (solvent)} \\ 1.2 \text{ hr}}]{\overset{+}{Bu_4N}\overset{-}{X}}$ Cycloheptanone =O (89%)

$$C_6H_5\underset{\underset{CH_3}{|}}{CH} - NH_2 + NaOCl \xrightarrow[\substack{EtOAc \text{ (solvent)} \\ 1.4 \text{ hr}}]{\overset{+}{Bu_4N}\overset{-}{X}} C_6H_5COCH_3$$
$$98\%$$

α-Methyl benzylamine

$$n\text{-}C_7H_{15}CH_2NH_2 + NaOCl \xrightarrow[\substack{EtOAc \text{ (solvent)} \\ 0.5 \text{ hr}}]{\overset{+}{Bu_4N}\overset{-}{X}} n\text{-}C_7H_{15}CN$$

1-Octylamine   1-Cyanoheptane
                              (60%)

Scheme 93

$$RNHNHR + K_3Fe(CN)_6 \xrightarrow[\text{NaOH}]{\text{TPP}} RN=NR$$
$$63\text{-}98\%$$

Scheme 94

aqueous medium have now been accomplished by the development of a number of water-soluble catalysts which give higher yields and selectivities. Even the hydrogenation of aromatic compounds is now possible in aqueous media.

In the present unit, some examples of a few novel reduction performed in aqueous medium are described. Enzymic reduction have also been known to occur in water. However, this subject will be discussed in a separate section. Some important reductions in aqueous media are given as follows:

2.1.14.1   Reductions of Carbon-Carbon Double Bonds

Alkenes can be reduced to the corresponding saturated compounds (e.g. alkanes) by PtO_2/H_2, Pd/H_2 raney Ni/H_2 or diimide.

The reduction of carbon-carbon double bonds by the use of water soluble hydrogenation cata-lyst is possible[152]. Thus, hydrogenation of 2-acetamidoacrylates with hydrogen at room temperature in water in the presence of water soluble chiral Rh(I) and Ru(II) complexes with (R)-BINAP (SO_3Na) [BINAP is 2, 2'-bis (diphenylphosphino-1, 1'-binaphthyl) (Scheme 95)[153].

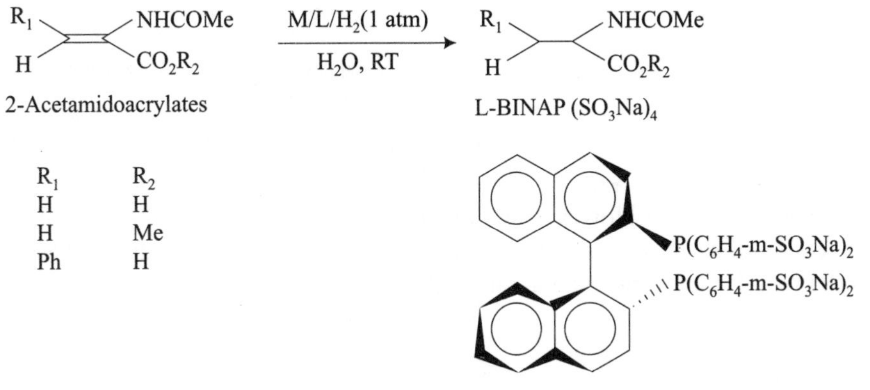

R_1	R_2
H	H
H	Me
Ph	H

Scheme 95

Ruthenium complexes are found to be more stable than the corresponding rhodium analogue; the ee of the final reduced product is found to be 68-88%.

The carbon-carbon double bond of α, β-unsaturated carbonyl compounds can be reduced by using Zn/NiCl$_2$ (9:1) in 2-methoxyethanol (ME)-water system (Scheme 96)[154]. Sonication increases the yield.

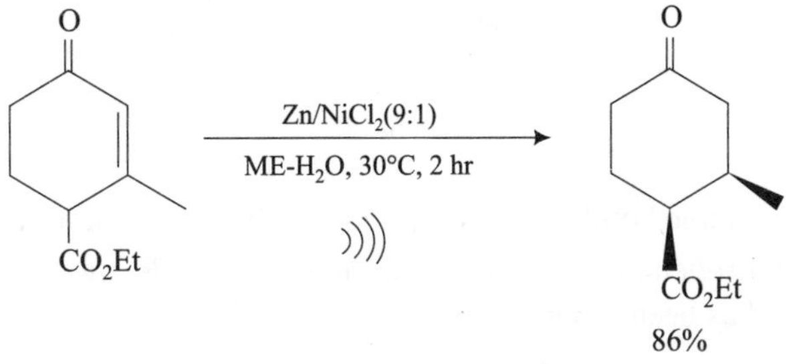

Scheme 96

The above procedure (Scheme 96) has been used to selectively reduce (−) − carvone to (+) dihydrocarvone and carvotanacetone by variation of experimental conditions (Scheme 97)[155].

Carvone was earlier reduced to dihydrocarvone by using homogeneous hydrogenation tech-nique with hydridochlorotris (triphenyl phosphine) ruthenium (Ph$_3$P)$_3$ RuClH[156].

Reduction of 3, 8-nonadienoic acid (a compound containing an terminal as well as an internal double bond) gives different products depending on the reaction conditions[157]. Thus, half hydroge-nation of 3, 8-nonadienoic acid in anhyd. benzene with RhCl[P(p-tolyl)$_3$]$_3$ gives major amount

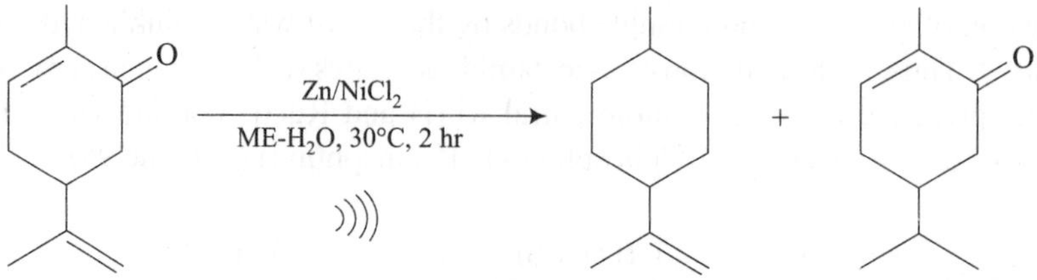

(-)-Carvone — (+)-Dihydro carvone — Carvotanacetone

Scheme 97

(66%)of 3-nonenoic acid (A). However, addition of equal amount of water to the reaction medium gives an inversion of selectivity giving 8-nonenoic acid as the major product (85%). The use of aqueous KOH retards the hydrogenation rate (Scheme 98).

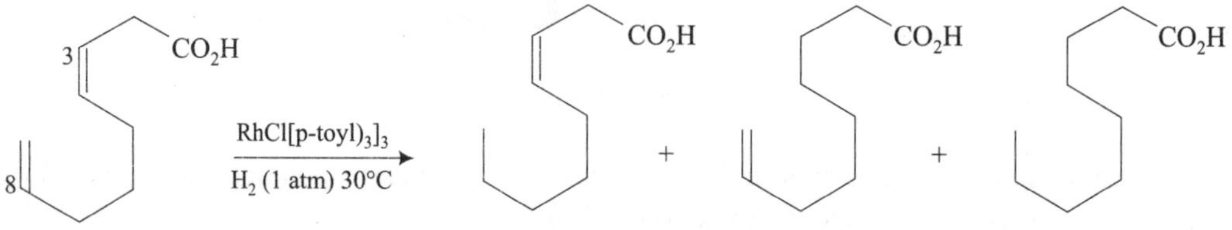

3,8-Nonadienoic acid	A 3-Nonenoic acid	B 8-Nonenoic acid	C Decanoic acie (capric acid)
C_6H_6 (4 hr)	66%	10%	20%
C_6H_6-H_2O (2 hr)	0.7%	85%	8%
C_6H_6-KOH aq. (20 hr)	6%	18%	39%

Scheme 98

The carbon-carbon double bonds can also be reduced by samarium diiodide-H_2O system[158].

Chemoselective hydrogenation of an unsaturated aldehyde by transition metal catlysed process[159] (Scheme 99) has been reported.

2.1.14.2 Reduction of Carbon-Carbon Triple Bonds

The carbon-carbon triple bonds (e.g. alkynes) on catalystic hydrogenation gives the completely reduced product, viz., alkanes. Alkynes can also be reduced partially to give z-alkenes by palladium calcium carbonate catalyst which has been deactivated (partially poisoned) by the addition of lead acetate (Lindlar catalyst) or Pd-$BaSO_4$ deactivated by quinoline. Lindars catalyst is less active and the reduction is more selective. Some examples are given (Scheme 100).

Disubstituted alkynes (which are electron deficient) can be reduced with water soluble monosulfonated and trisulfonated triphenylphosphine (Scheme 101)[160].

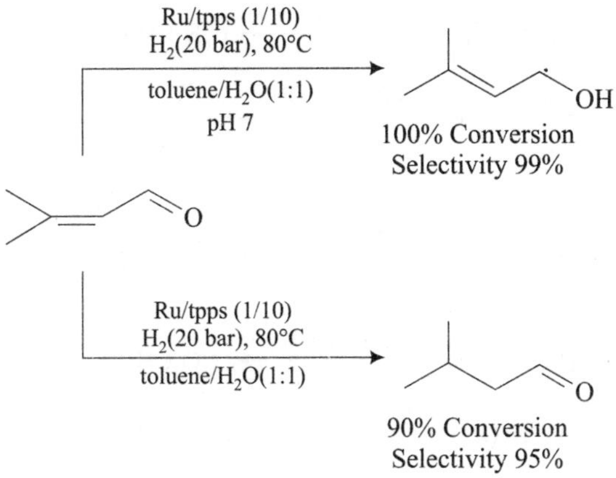

Ru/tpps (1/10)
H$_2$(20 bar), 80°C

toluene/H$_2$O(1:1)
pH 7

100% Conversion
Selectivity 99%

Ru/tpps (1/10)
H$_2$(20 bar), 80°C

toluene/H$_2$O(1:1)

90% Conversion
Selectivity 95%

Scheme 99

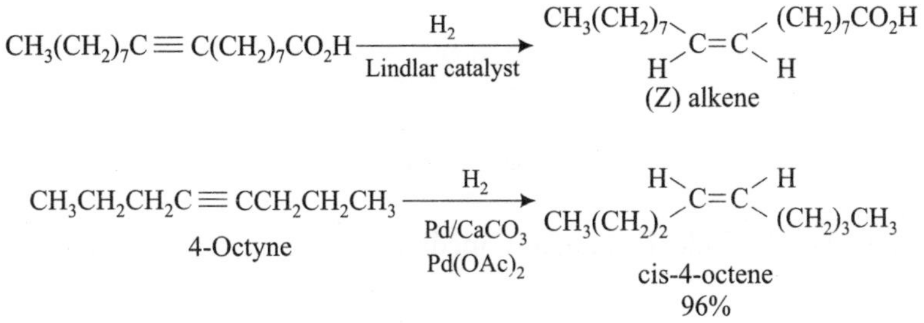

CH$_3$(CH$_2$)$_7$C≡C(CH$_2$)$_7$CO$_2$H $\xrightarrow[\text{Lindlar catalyst}]{\text{H}_2}$

CH$_3$(CH$_2$)$_7$ C=C (CH$_2$)$_7$CO$_2$H
H   H
(Z) alkene

CH$_3$CH$_2$CH$_2$C≡CCH$_2$CH$_2$CH$_3$ $\xrightarrow[\text{Pd(OAc)}_2]{\substack{\text{H}_2 \\ \text{Pd/CaCO}_3}}$ CH$_3$(CH$_2$)$_2$

4-Octyne

H   H
C=C
CH$_3$(CH$_2$)$_2$ (CH$_2$)$_3$CH$_3$
cis-4-octene
96%

Scheme 100

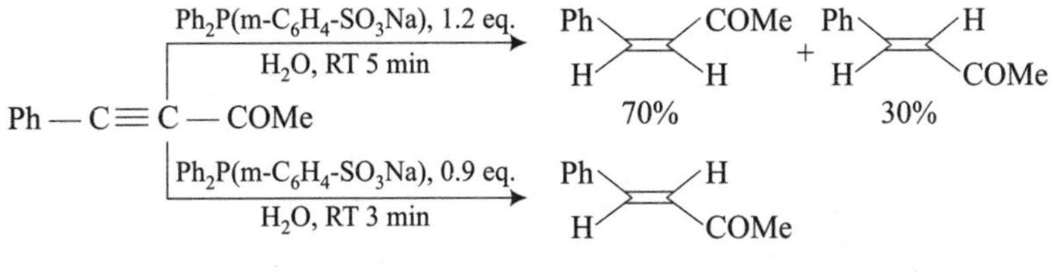

Ph$_2$P(m-C$_6$H$_4$-SO$_3$Na), 1.2 eq.

H$_2$O, RT 5 min

Ph ─ C≡C ─ COMe

Ph   COMe   Ph   H
H   H   + H   COMe
70%   30%

Ph$_2$P(m-C$_6$H$_4$-SO$_3$Na), 0.9 eq.

H$_2$O, RT 3 min

Ph   H
H   COMe

Scheme 101

In the above reaction (Scheme 101), the water acts both as a solvent as well as a reactant, and the amount of phosphine controls the cis/trans ratio of the formed alkenes since it catalyses the cis-trans olefin isomerisation.

2.1.14.3 Reduction of Carbonyl Compounds

Carbonyl compounds can be reduced by a variety of reagents. Some of the common reagents are Na-C$_2$H$_5$OH, PtO$_2$/H$_2$, LAH, NaBH$_4$, Na$_2$BH$_3$CN, HCO$_2$H/EtMgBr, (Et$_2$O)SiH.Me, B$_2$H$_6$[161].

Some of the more common reductions using NaBH$_4$ are given (Scheme 102).

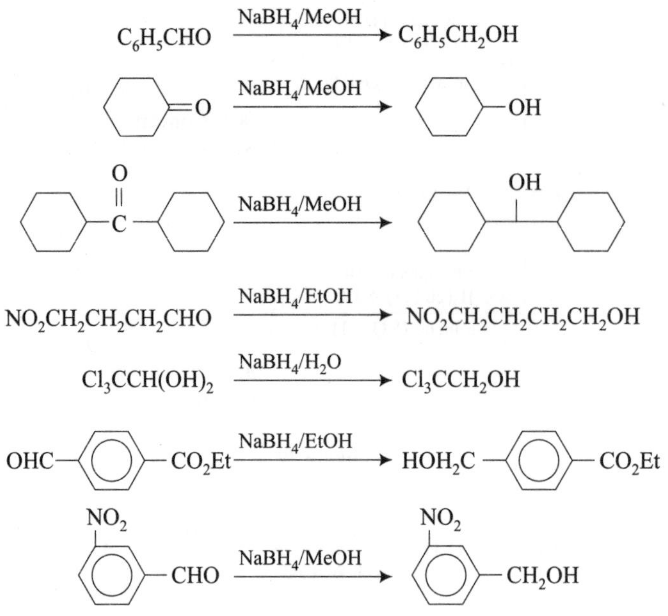

C6H5CHO
NaBH4/MeOH
C6H5CH2OH
NaBH4/MeOH
OH
O
NaBH4/MeOH
OH
NaBH4/EtOH
NO2CH2CH2CH2CHO
NO2CH2CH2CH2CH2OH
NaBH4/H2O
Cl3CCH(OH)2
Cl3CCH2OH
OHC
CO2Et
NaBH4/EtOH
HOH2C
CO2Et
NO2
CHO
NaBH4/MeOH
NO2
CH2OH

Scheme 102

Using sodium borohydride in aqueous medium, 2-alkylresorcinols have been prepared (Scheme 103)[162].

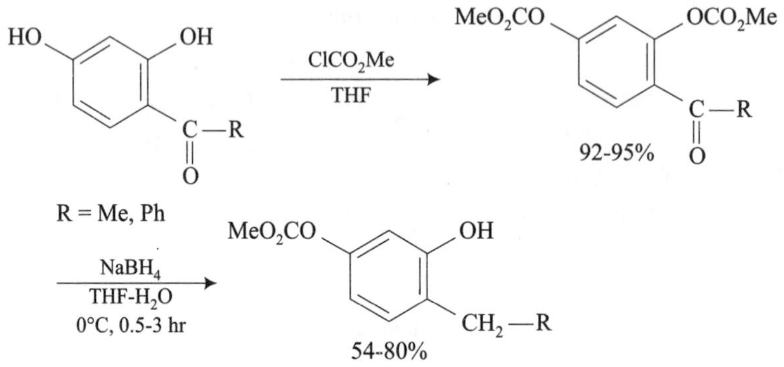

HO
OH
C—R
O
ClCO2Me
THF
MeO2CO
OCO2Me
C—R
O
92-95%
R = Me, Ph
NaBH4
THF-H2O
0°C, 0.5-3 hr
MeO2CO
OH
CH2—R
54-80%

Scheme 103

The reduction of carbonyl compounds in water has been carried out by a number of reagents under mild conditions. The most frequently used reagent is sodium borohydride, which can also be used using phase-transfer catalysts[163] or inverse phase transfer catalyst[164] in a two phase medium in the presence of surfactants.

The carbonyl compounds can be reduced quantitatively regio- and stereo-selectively by $NaBH_4$ at room temperature in aqueous solution containing glycosidic amphiphiles like methyl-β-D-glactoside, dodecanoyl-β-D-maltoside, sucrose, etc[165]. By using this procedure, α, β-unsaturated ketones give 1, 2-reduction product (corresponding allylic alcohols) and cyclohexanones give the more stable alcohol.

Reduction of ketones with $NaBH_4$ also proceeds in the solid state[166]. In this procedure a mixture of powdered ketone and 10-fold molar amount of $NaBH_4$ is kept in a dry box at room temperature with occasional mixing and grinding for five days to give the reduced product. Following ketones were reduced by this procedure (Scheme 104).

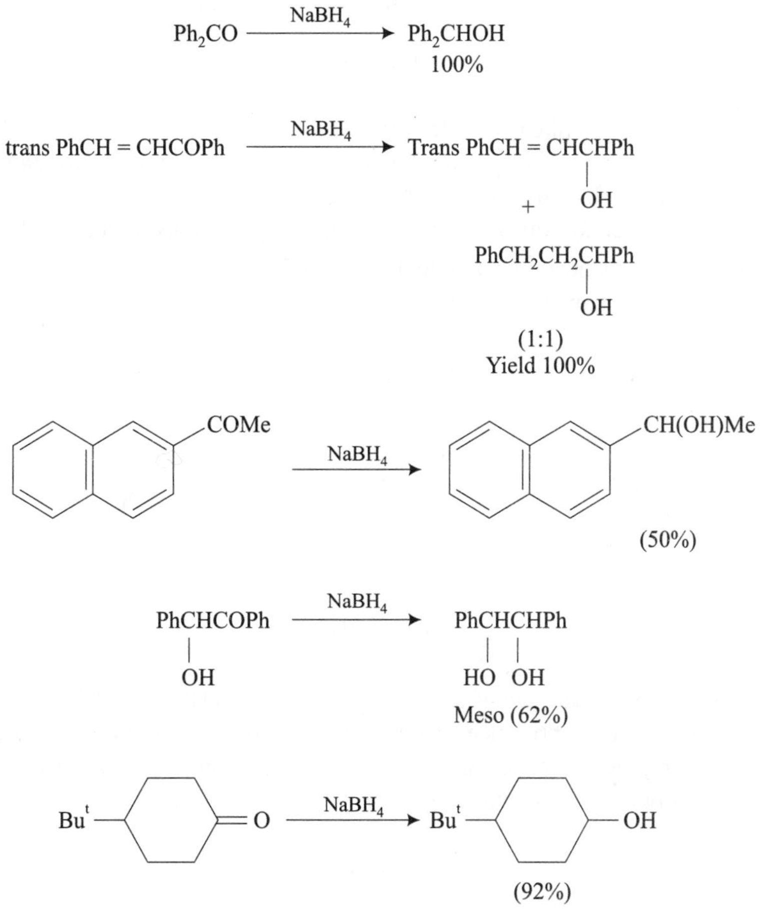

$$Ph_2CO \xrightarrow{NaBH_4} \underset{100\%}{Ph_2CHOH}$$

$$trans\ PhCH = CHCOPh \xrightarrow{NaBH_4} Trans\ PhCH = CHCHPh$$
$$| $$
$$+\quad OH$$

$$PhCH_2CH_2CHPh$$
$$|$$
$$OH$$
$$(1:1)$$
$$Yield\ 100\%$$

$$COMe \xrightarrow{NaBH_4} CH(OH)Me$$
$$(50\%)$$

$$\underset{|}{PhCHCOPh} \xrightarrow{NaBH_4} \underset{|\quad |}{PhCHCHPh}$$
$$OH \qquad\qquad\qquad HO\ OH$$
$$Meso\ (62\%)$$

$$Bu^t-\langle\ \rangle=O \xrightarrow{NaBH_4} Bu^t-\langle\ \rangle-OH$$
$$(92\%)$$

Scheme 104

Enantioselective hydrogenation of β-ketoesters has been carried out by using a ruthenium catalyst derived from (R, R) – 1, 2-bis (trans –2, 5-diisopropylpholano) ethane [(R, R) –i-Pr-PEE-Ru] to give β-hydroxy esters with high conversion and high ee (Scheme 105)[167].

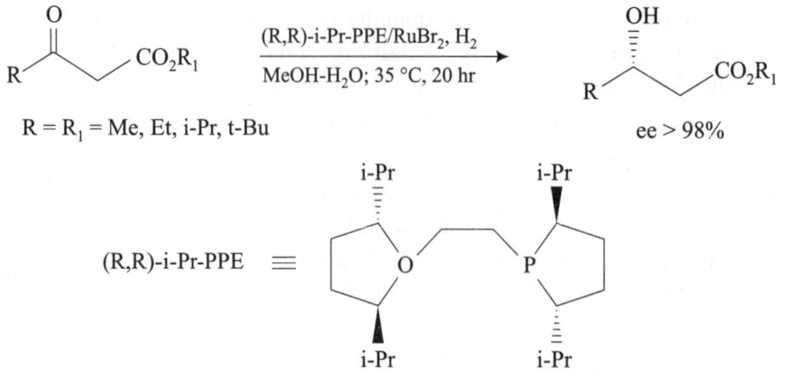

R = R₁ = Me, Et, i-Pr, t-Bu

ee > 98%

(R,R)-i-Pr-PPE ≡

Scheme 105

The reduction of aldehydes like benzaldehyde and p-tolualdehyde with Raney Ni in 10 per cent aqueous NaOH give the corresponding benzyl alcohols in 17-80% yields[168] along with the corresponding carboxylic acids as byproducts, which arise by cannizzaro reaction. However, in aqueous $NaHCO_3$ under sonication conditions give the corresponding alcohols in good yields.

Another interesting reagent used for reduction of carbonyl compounds is cadmium chloride-magnesium in H_2O-THF system (Scheme 106)[169].

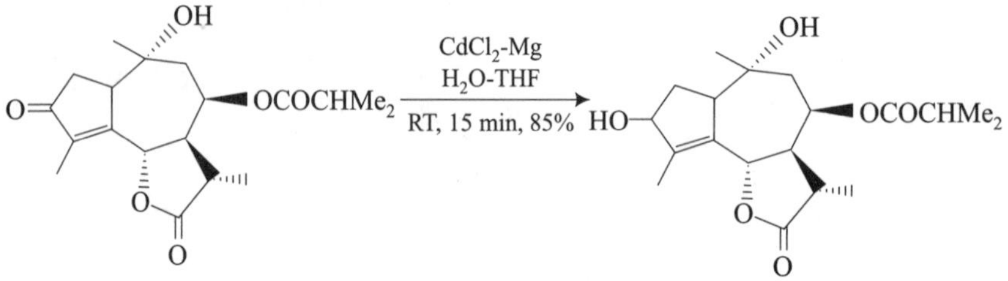

Scheme 106

Certain other reagents include samarium iodide in aqueous THF[170], sodium dithionite in aqueous DMF[171], sodium sulfide in presence of polyethylene glycol[172] and metallic zinc along with nickel chloride[173]. Using the latter reagent ($Zn/NiCl_2$), α, β-unsaturated carbonyl compounds can be very easily reduced under ultrasound conditions[174] (Scheme 107).

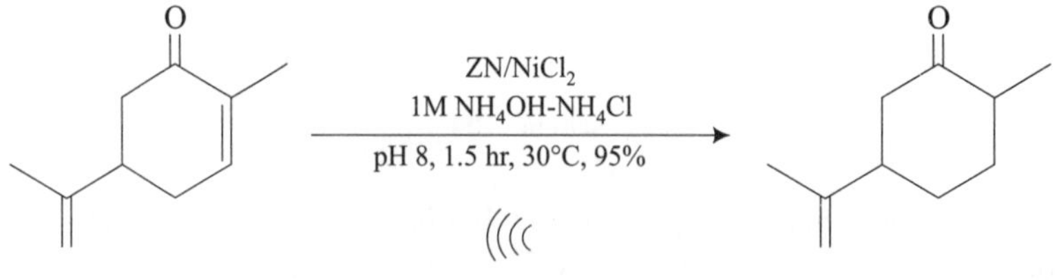

ZN/NiCl₂
1M NH₄OH-NH₄Cl
pH 8, 1.5 hr, 30°C, 95%

Scheme 107

Ketones can also be reduced in an aqueous medium by SmI_2-H_2O[175] (Scheme 108)

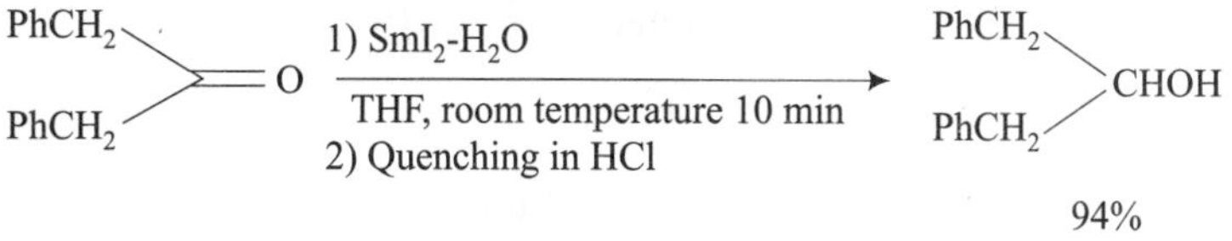

Scheme 108

2.1.14.4 Reduction of Aromatic Ring

The hydrogenation of benzenoids to cyclohexane derivatives is a very useful process. Aromatic hydrocarbons require drastic conditions for reduction (for example PtO_2/H_2/CH_3COOH; Raney Ni/H_2/Pr/Δ, Rh-Al_2O_3/H_2).

It is now possible to effect its reduction of aromatic ring in aqueous medium at 50 atm of H_2 and at room temperature with ruthenium trichloride stabilised by trioctylamine ($RuCl_3$/TOA)[176]. One such example is given (Scheme 109).

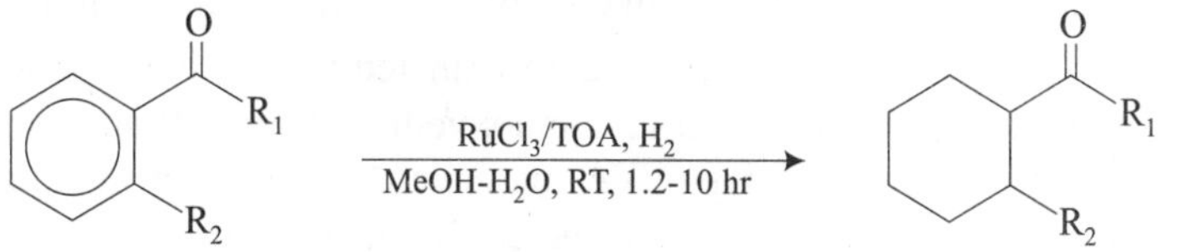

R_1 = OMe, CO_2Me
R_2 = H, Me, NH_2

80-90%
cis-trans 6:15

Scheme 109

In the given procedure (Scheme 109) the rate of the reaction is 10–12 times the rate in organic solvents and in the aqueous medium, in comparision to cis, the trans isomer is the major product.

The hetercyclic compounds, like pyridine, 2-phenylpyridine and 3-methylpyridine can be reduced to the corresponding hexahydro product by Sm-20 per cent HCl in 90-95% yields[177]. However in the reduction of 4-aminopyridine by the above procedure, the 4-amino group is eliminated giving piperidine as the major product (60%). The heterocyclic compounds can also be reduced in 70-94 per cent yield by SmI_2-H_2O system at 0°C for 2.5 hr[178]. Using this method 2-amino–, 2-chloro–, and 2-cyano-pyridine on reduction give piperidine, the substituent groups are eliminated.

2.1.14.5 Miscellanous Reactions

  (i) Reductive removal of halogen from α-halocarbonyl compounds in aqueous medium can be effected by using sodium dithionite[179], zinc[180], chromous sulfate[181] and sodium iodide[182].

 (ii) 2, 3-Epoxyallyl halides can be transformed readily into allylic alcohol (Scheme 110) using zinc-copper couple in H_2O under sonication.

(iii) Reductive dehalogenation in aryl halides can be effected in aqueous alkaline media in presence of $PdCl_2$ with NaH_2PO_2 as a hydrogen source (Scheme 111)[183].

Scheme 110

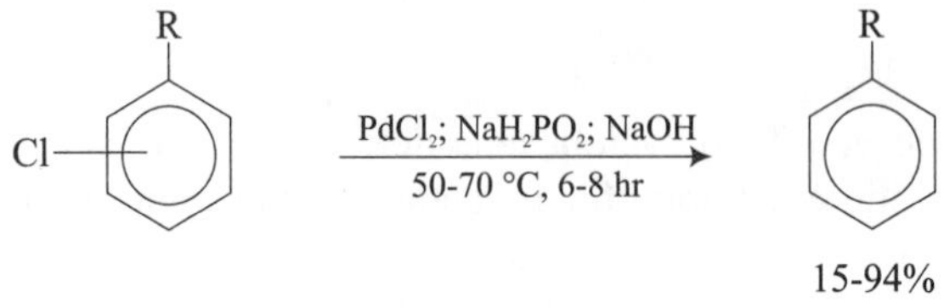

Scheme 111

The above procedure (Scheme 111) does not work in case of nitrogen containing heterocylic compounds and the yield in case of m-substituted aryl halides is low.

However, m-bromobenzoic acid can be debrominated to give benzoic acid in 90 per cent yield by using water soluble tris [3-(2-methoxyethoxy) propyl] stannane in presence of 4, 4′-azobis (4-cyanovaleric acid)(ACVA) or sunlamp as initiator in aqueous $NaHCO_3$[184]. Above debromination can also be effected by using [bis (potassium propanoate)$_n$ (hydroxystannate)], which in presence of $NaBH_4$ and ACVA affords reductions and free radical cyclisation of aryl and alkenyl bromides (Scheme 112).

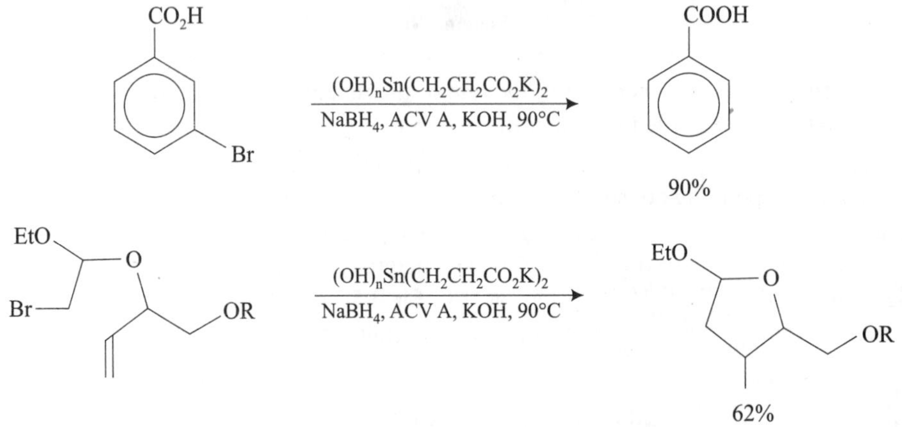

Scheme 112

The hydrogenolysis of halopyridines can be effected with 15 per cent aqueous $TiCl_4$ in presence of acetic acid[185]. Aqueous titanium trichloride quantitatively removes cyano group from cyanopyridines. Reductive dehalogenation is also catalysed by SmI_2.

(iv) Groups like azide, sulfoxide, disulphide, activated C = C bond and nitroxide can be reduced by using sodium hydrogen telluride (NaTeH) (Prepared in situ by the reaction of tellurium powder with aqueous ethanolic solution of NaBH₄)[186].

(v) Groups like aldehydes, ketones, olefins, nitroxides and azides are reduced by sodium hypophosphite buffer solution[187].

(vi) Vinyl sulphones are stereospecifically reduced to the corresponding olefins with sodium dithionite in aqueous medium (Scheme 113)[188].

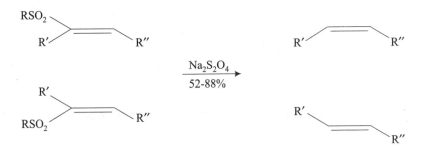

Scheme 113

(vii) Diarly and dialkyl sulphides can be reduced by triphenylphosphine in aqueous solvents (Scheme 114)[189].

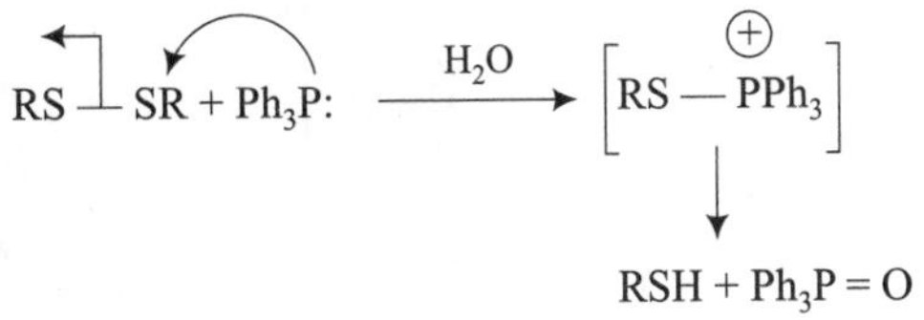

$$RS - SR + Ph_3P: \xrightarrow{H_2O} \left[RS - \overset{\oplus}{PPh_3} \right]$$

$$RSH + Ph_3P = O$$

Scheme 114

2.1.15 *Polymerisation Reactions*

Polymers

It is known that most of the polymers are not biodegradable. This problem can be approached in two ways. One way is to recycle the polymer and the other way is to convert it again into the monomers and recycle them again. However, the best way is to make polymers which are biodegradable.

Recycling of Polymers: Let us now consider recycling, taking the example of the polyester, polyethyleneterephthalate (PET). We know that PET is obtained by the polymerisation of dimethylterephthalate and ethylene glycol and is used in different products like beverages and food containers, non food containers, trays, luggage, boat parts, tapes, etc. Fibers of PET are also used in clothing, carpets, blankets, cord, ropes, etc. The recycled PET cannot be reused for food containers, as the impurities present are not sanitized at the temperature used in the melt process. Some of the products made of PET are mixtures with other polymers and contain dyes and other materials.

These have to be disposed off by only incineration or land-filled. Also, during incineration the products obtained cause atmospheric pollution.

2.1.15.1 Conversion of PET Materials into Monomers

The process for the conversion of scrap PET into monomers is known as the Petrette process[190]. The details of the Petrette process for the recovery of monomers from PET scrap is given (Scheme 115)

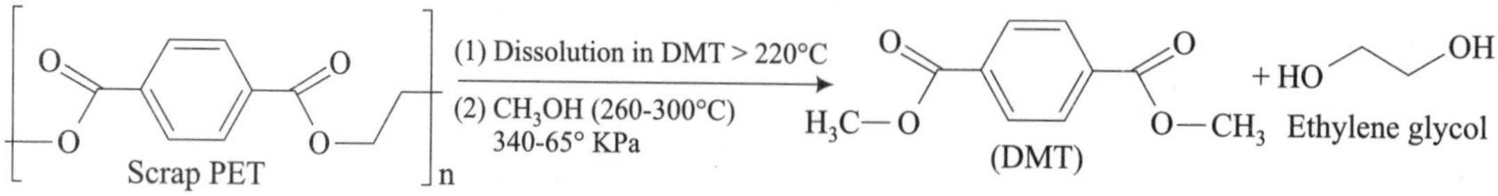

Scheme 115

The monomers (DMT and ethylene glycol) are purified and again polymerised to give PET.

2.1.15.2 To Make Polymers which are Biodegradable

One of the commonly used biodegradable polymer is Thermal Polyasparatate polymer (TPA). Before the synthesis of TPA, polyacrylate polymer (PAC) was used as scale inhibitor in water handling processes. If not inhibited, the scale formation lead to loss of energy, non-functioning of pumps, boilers and candensers.

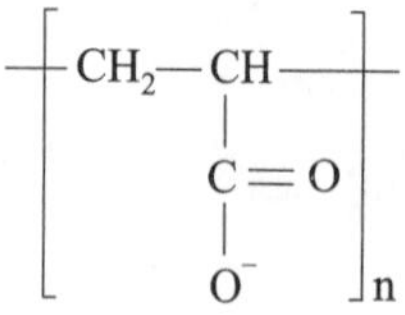

PAC

Though PAC is relatively non-toxic and environmentally benign. However, being non biodegradable, it causes a disposal problem in waste water treatment facilities, where the PAC must be removed and land filled. The problem for its disposal has been solved by Donlar Corporation, which has developed a method for the production of TPA, a biodegradable alternative to PAC[191]. The Donlar's synthesis consists of heating the aspartic acid followed by hydrolysing the formed succinimide polymer with aqueous base (Scheme 116).

The above synthesis is 'green' because it uses no organic solvents, produces little or no waste and the yield is better than 97 per cent.

2.1.15.3 Manufacture of Polycarbonates

Polycarbonates were earlier prepared by the polymerisation of phenols (e.g. bisphenol-A) using phosgene and methylene chloride. A novel process has been developed by Asahi Chemical Industries using solid state polymerisation[193] for producing polycarbonate without phosgene and methylene chloride[194].

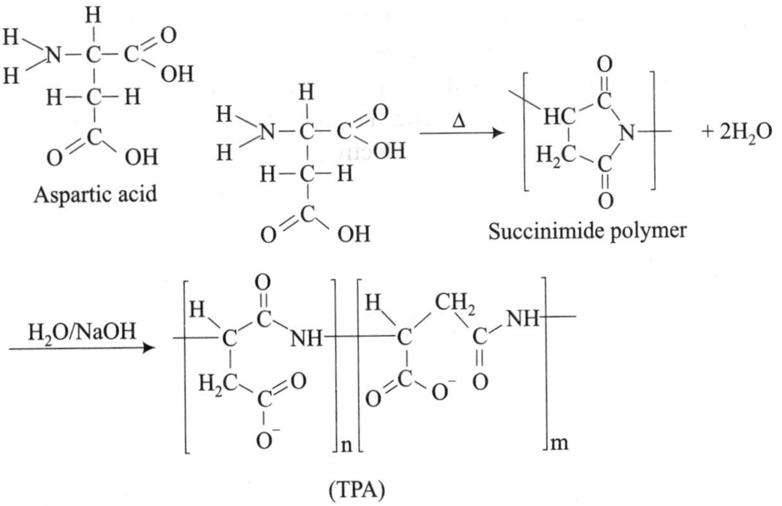

Scheme 116

In this process bisphenol-A and diphenyl carbonate directly give low molecular weight prepolymers, which are converted into high molecular weight polymers by crystallisation followed by further polymerization (Scheme 117).

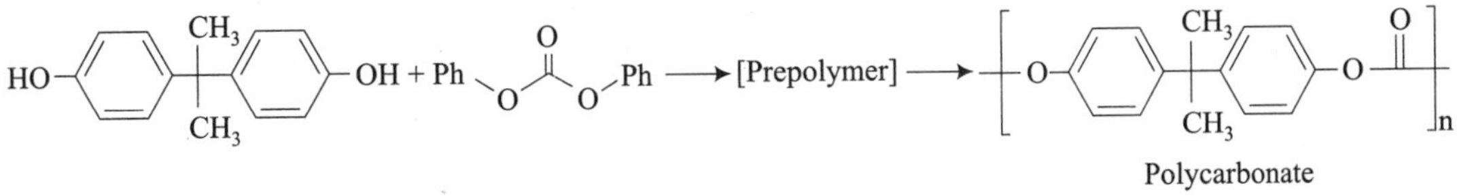

Scheme 117

2.1.15.4 Emulsion Polymerisation

Emulsion polymerisation of norbornenes in aqueous sodium hydroxide using iridium complexes as catalysts gave only 10 per cent yield[194]. However, it was subsequently found that 7-oxaborane derivatives could be rapidly polymerised in aqueous solution in presence of air using some group VIII coordination complexes as catalysts giving a quantitative yield of a ring-opening metathesis polymerisa-tion product (Scheme 118)[195].

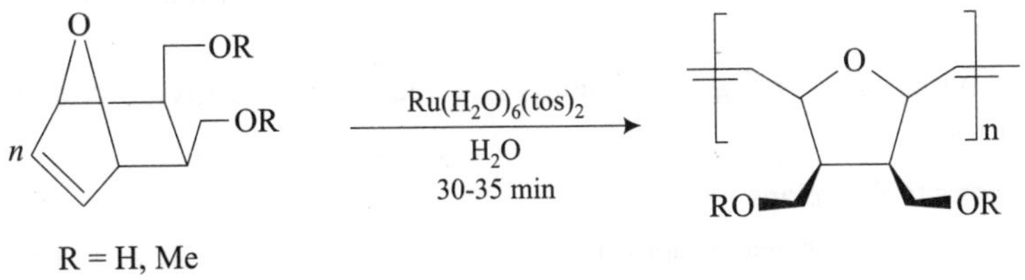

Scheme 118

Using the above procedure norbornene could also be polymerisation[196,197]. The ruthenium catalyst required for the above polymerisation are obtained by the procedure of Berhard-Ludi[198]. The aqueous catalyst solution can be reused. Another Ru(IV) catalyst[199] can also be used for emulsion ring-opening polymerisation of norbornene. The polymers obtained by the later catalysts had very high molecular weight and had high cis-selectivity. Using this procedure neogytcopolymers were synthesised (Scheme 119).

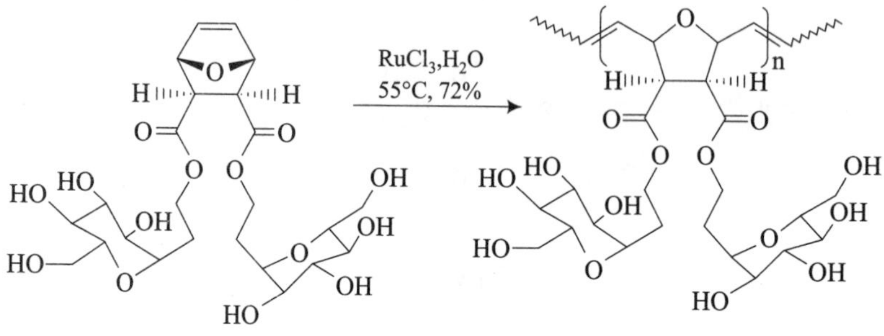

Scheme 119

A non-metallic conducting polymer is synthesised (Scheme 120)[200].

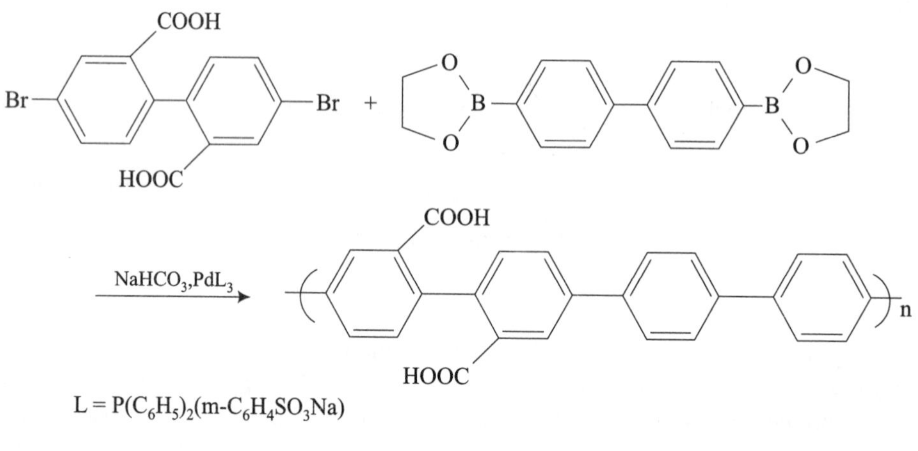

$L = P(C_6H_5)_2(m\text{-}C_6H_4SO_3Na)$

Scheme 120

A helical polymer is prepared bu using palladium-catalysed coupling between aryl halides with acetylene gas (Scheme 121)[201].

Solid state polymerisation of α-amino acids has been achieved giving rise to high molecular weight polypeptides.

2.1.16 Photochemical Reactions

The importance of photochemical reactions can hardly be overemphasized. The earliest known photochemical reaction is the photosynthesis of sugars by plants using sunlight, CO_2 and H_2O in presence of chlorophyll. Some of the common examples of photochemical reactions are as follows.

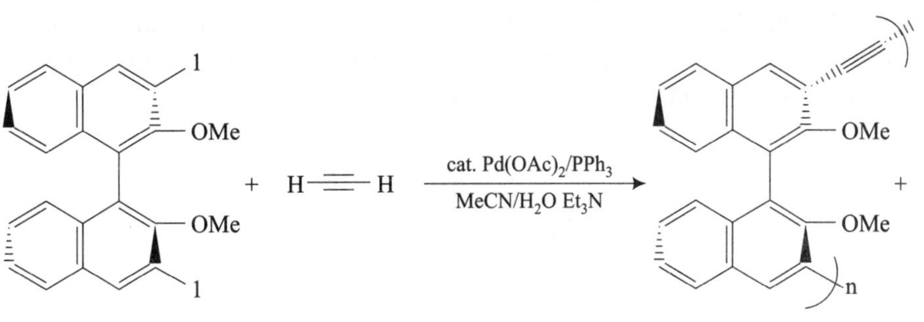

Scheme 121

(i) Photochemical cycloaddition of carbonyl compounds and olefins (Paterno-Buchi reaction) give four membered ether rings (Scheme 122)[202].

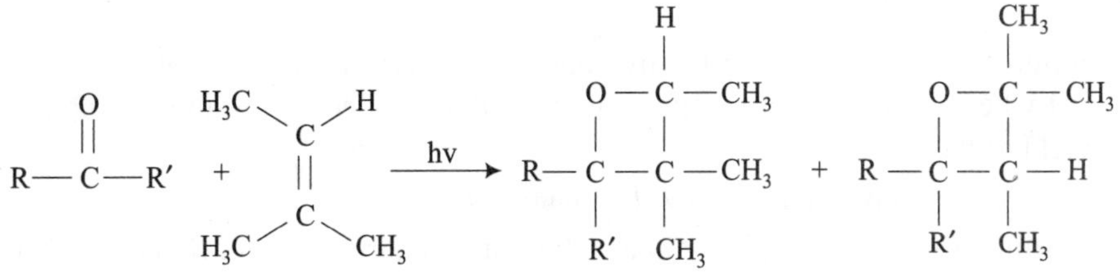

Scheme 122

(ii) Photo fries rearrangements. The phenolic esters in solution on photolysis give a mixture of o- and p-acylphenols[203].

Most of the photochemical reaction are carried out in solvents like benzene. In view of the scare of the medium dependence of photochemical reactions, attempts were made for carrying out the reactions in water as a solvent[204].

It has been found that the photochemical reactions can be conveniently carried out in aqueous phase. Thus, the photodimerisation of thymine, uracil and their derivatives could be carried out in water giving considerably better yields than in other organic solvents (Scheme 123)[205].

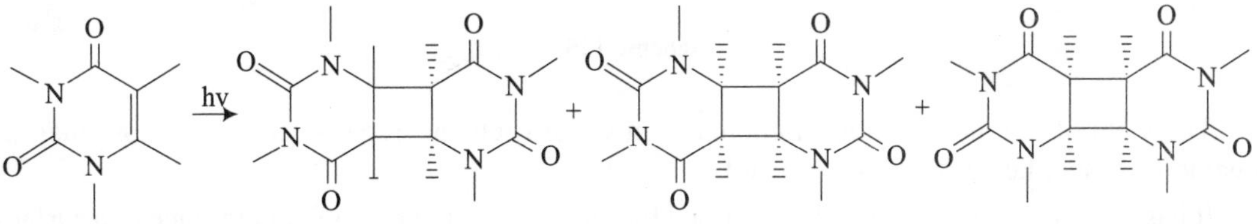

Water	27.8%	63.1%	9.1%	$\emptyset = 0.015$
Acetonitrile	24.9%	68.2%	6.7%	$\emptyset = 0.0047$
Methanol	31.4%	68.6%	–	$\emptyset = 0.004$

Scheme 123   Data taken from Reference 205

Organic substrates having poor solubility in water (e.g. stilbenes and alkyl cinnamates) also photodimerize in water (Scheme 124). The same reactions in organic solvents such as benzene gives mainly cis-trans isomers[206].

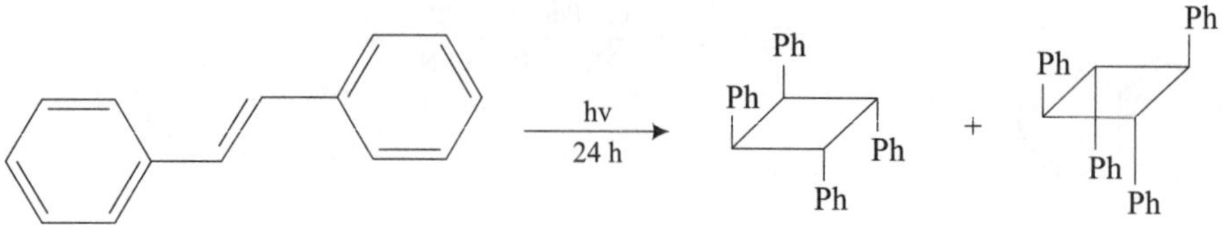

Benzene	0%	0%
Water	12%	10%
Water + LiCl	25%	17%
Water + guanidinium chloride	8%	6%

Scheme 124   Data taken from reference 206

The addition of LiCl (decreasing the hydrophobic effect) increases the yield of dimerisation (Scheme 124) whereas the addition of guanidinum chloride (decreasing the hydrophobic effect) lowers the yield of the product.

Similar results were obtained with alkyl cinnamates[207].

An interesting example is the photodimerisation of coumarin in water (Scheme 125).

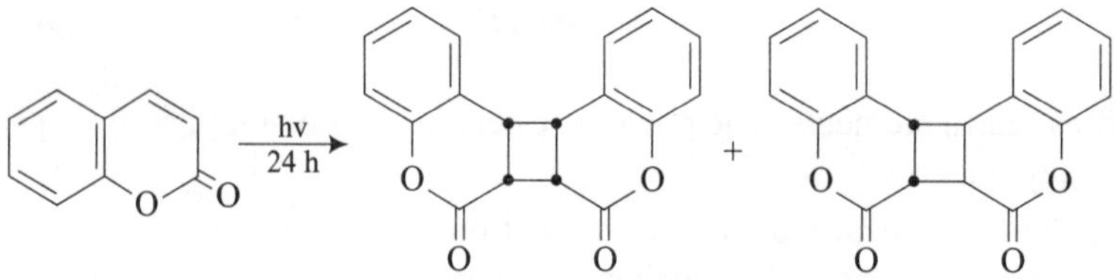

Solvent	Quantum Yield
Benzene	$< 10^{-5}$
Methanol	$< 10^{-5}$
Water	2×10^{-5}

Scheme 125

The yield of the dimerisation of coumarin in water (Scheme 125) is 100 times more than in organic solvents like benzene or methanol.

It has been found that the micelles (formed by carrying out the reaction in presence of a surfactant/water) have a pronounced effect on regio- and stereo-selectivity of photochemical reactions.

Thus, the photodimerisation of anthracene-2-sulphonate in water gives four products A, B, C, D (Scheme 126). However, if the reaction is carried out in presence of β-cyclodextrin, only the isomer A is obtained[208]. Some other examples of photochemical reactions are:

(i) Photoirradaition of dibenzoyl diazomethane in CH_3CN-H_2O in presence of an amino acid derivative gave the addition product (Scheme 127) via the formation of a carbene[209].

(ii) The photoirridation of o-fluoroanisole in KCN-H_2O gave o-substitution product (catechol monomethyl ether) as the major product along with o-cyanoanisole as the minor product. Similar photoirradiation reaction with p-fluoroanisole gave p-cyanoanisole as the major product along with amount minor of hydroquinol monomethyl ether (Scheme 128)[210].

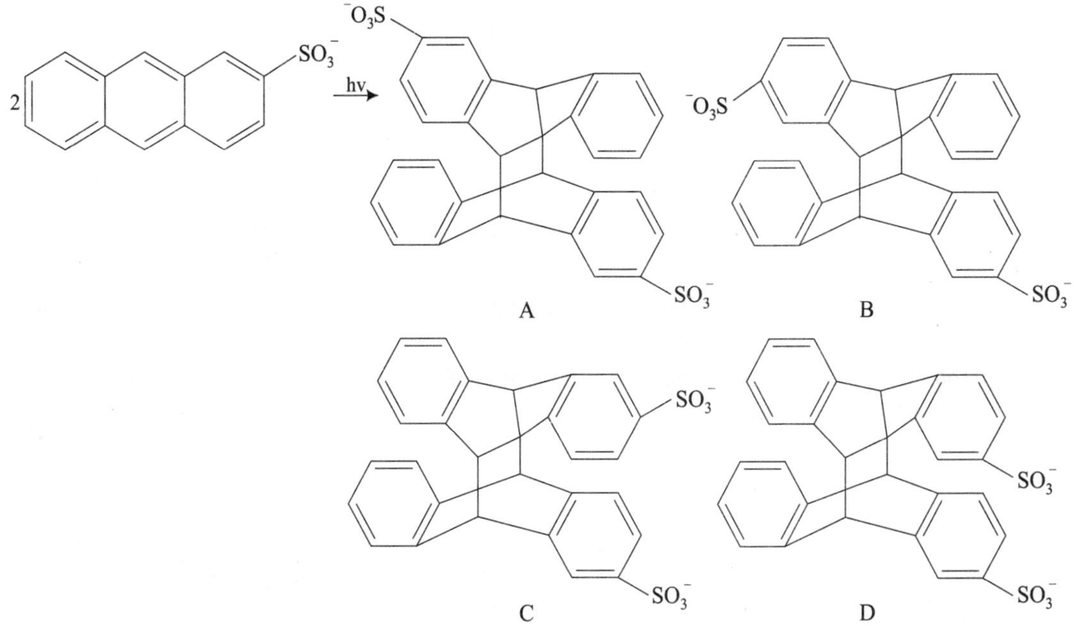

A

B

C

D

Medium

Water

Water + β-CD

Product (A : B : C : D)

1 : 0.8 : 0.4 : 0.05

A only

Scheme 126   Data taken from reference 205

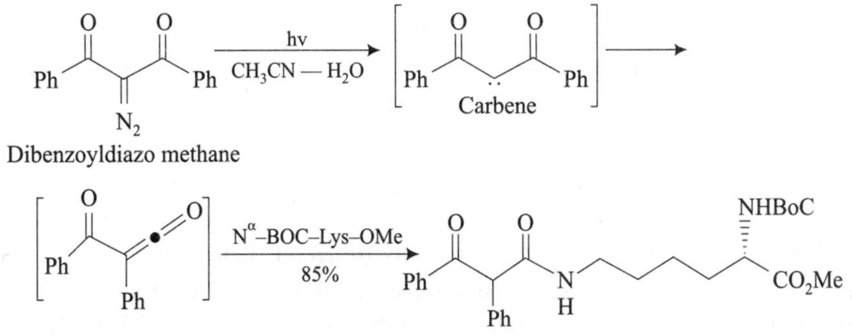

Dibenzoyldiazo methane

Scheme 127

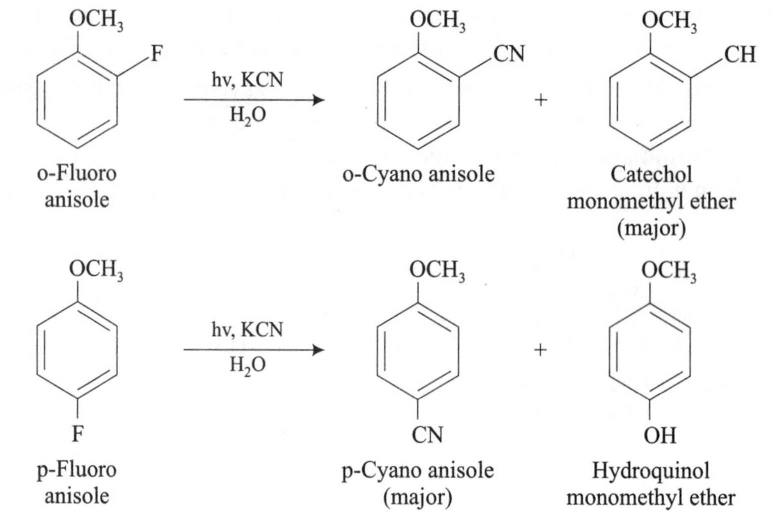

Scheme 128

(iii) Photochemical oxidative dimerisation of capasacin in aqueous ethanol gave dimer in 60 per cent yield (Scheme 129)[211].

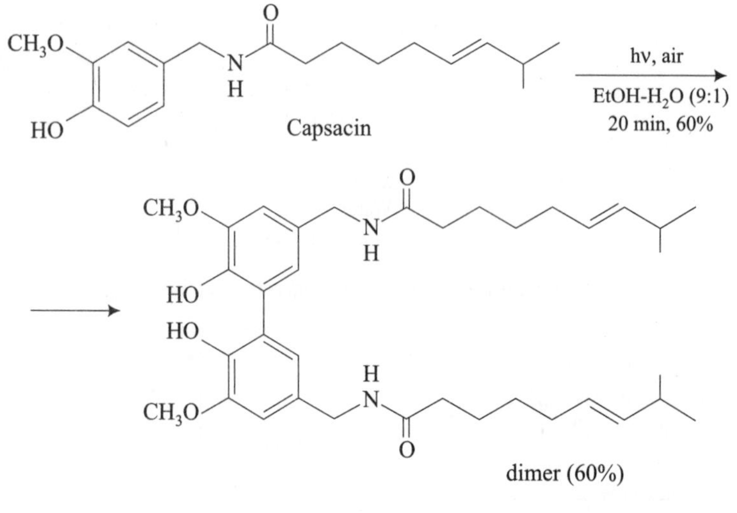

Scheme 129

(iv) Photooxidation of phenol is of interest in enviromental chemistry[212].

Photochemical reactions have also been studied in solid state. Thus the photodimerisation of cinnamic acid to truxillic acid has been achieved in the solid state (Scheme 130)[213].

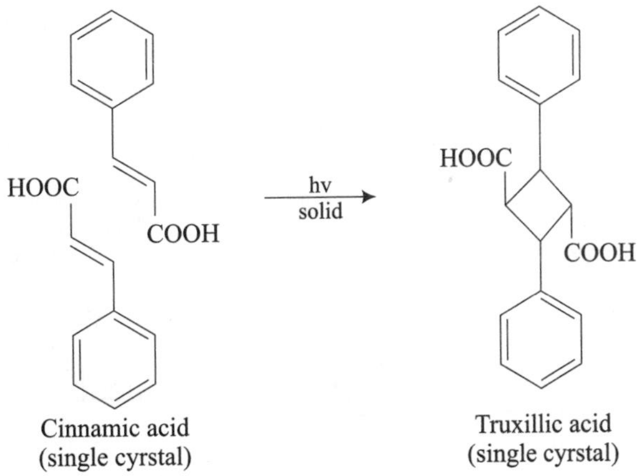

Cinnamic acid
(single cyrstal)

Truxillic acid
(single cyrstal)

Scheme 130

The photodimerisation of cinnamic acid can be controlled by irradiation of its double salts with certain diamines in the solid state. Thus, the double salt crystal of cinnamic acid and o-diaminocyclohexane gave upon irradiation in the solid state, β-truxinic acid as the major product (Scheme 131)[214].

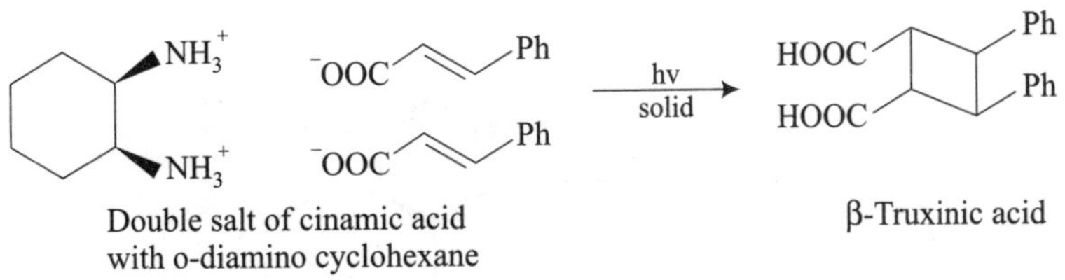

Double salt of cinamic acid
with o-diamino cyclohexane

β-Truxinic acid

Scheme 131

Similarly irradiation of naphthoic acid-derived cinnamic acid (A) in solid state on irradiation for 20-50 hr afforded a single cyclobutane derivation in 100 per cent yield (Scheme 132)[215].

The photocyclisation of coumarin and its derivative in the solid state gave[216] a mixture of A, B and C in 20 per cent yield after 48 hr. However, irradiation of an aqueous solution of coumarin for 22 hr affords only the syn-head to head dimer (D) in 20 per cent yield (Scheme 133).

Benzopinacol can be obtained quantitatively on photoirradiation of 4, 4'-dimethyl benzophenone in isopropylalcohol. However, in the solid state photoirradiation gives the dimeric compound (Scheme 134)[217]. Besides the representative example of photochemical reactions in solid phase a large number of illustrations are available[218].

2.1.17 Electrochemical Synthesis

Introduction

The well known Kolbe reactions involving the oxidation of carboxylic acids to give decarboxylated coupling products (alkanes) is the earlist electrochemical synthesis. At present, the electrochemical synthesis has become an independent discipline. A large number of organic reactions (synthesis)

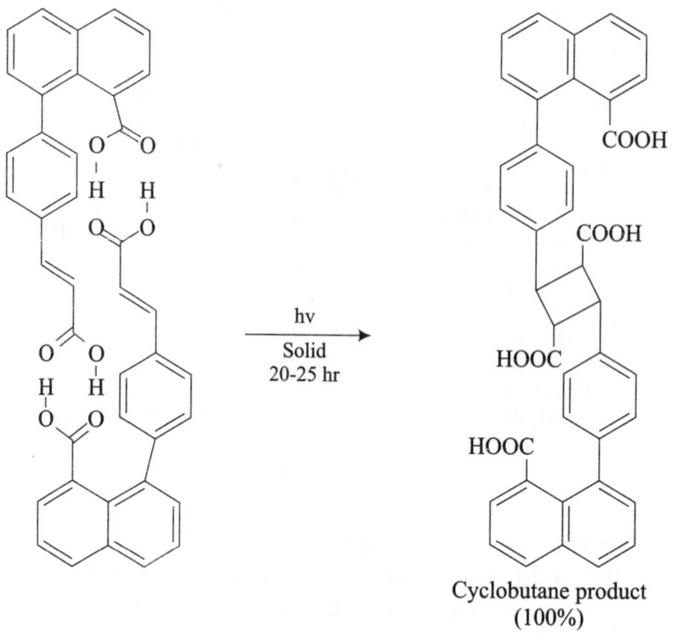

Scheme 132

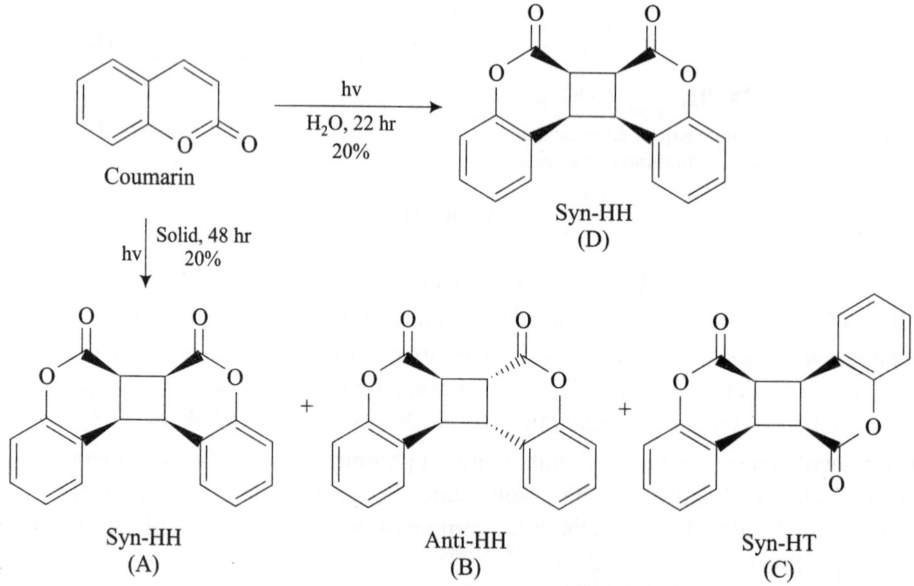

Scheme 133

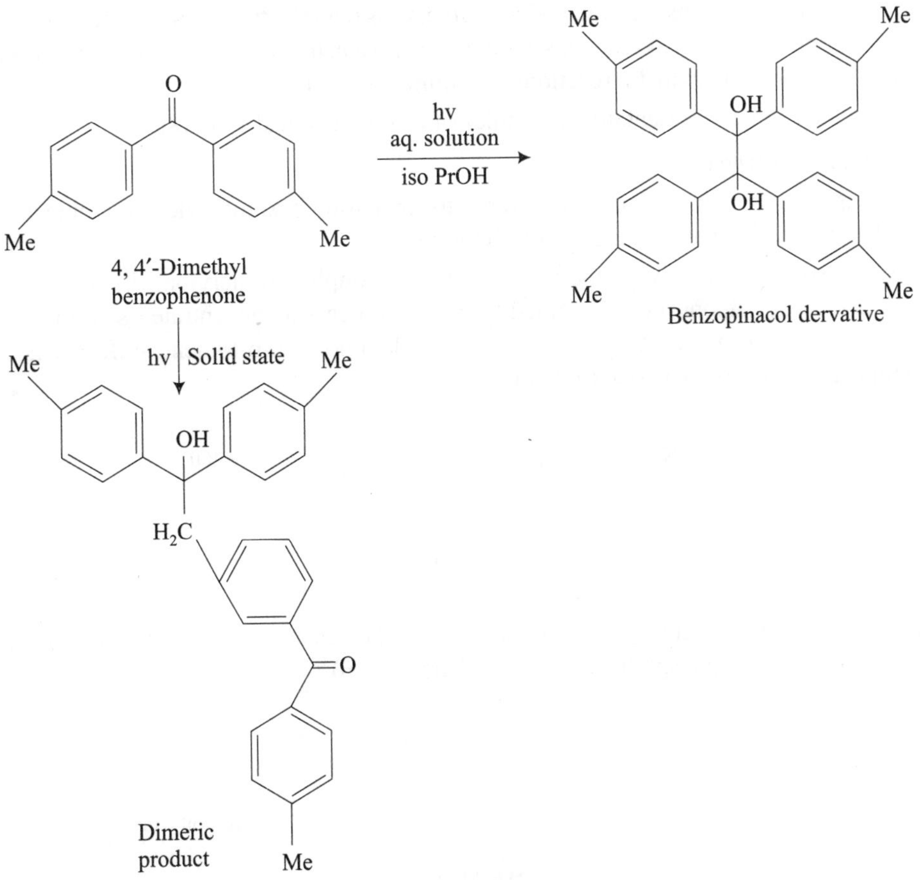

4, 4′-Dimethyl benzophenone

hv
aq. solution
iso PrOH

Benzopinacol dervative

hv | Solid state

Dimeric product

Scheme 134

have been achieved by this technique used solvent is water, though organic solvents have also been used. However, there is a distinct advantage in using aqueous solutions over organic solvents[219].

The electrochemical synthesis are of two types: anodic oxidative processes and cathodic reductive processes. During anodic oxidative processes, the organic compounds are oxidised. The nature of the product of anodic oxidation depends on the solvent used, pH of the medium and oxidation potential.

In cathodic reductive processes, the cathode of electrolysis provide an electron source for the reduction of organic compounds. Generally the rate of reduction increase with the acidity of the medium. Electroreduction of unsaturated compounds in water or aqueous-organic mixtures give reduced products-this process in equivalent to catalytic hydrogenation.

An electrochemical process uses a anode made of metal that resists oxidation, such as lead, nickel or most frequently platinum. The anode is usually in the shape of a cylinder made of a wire guage. The usual electrolytes are dilute sulphuric acid or sodium methoxide prepared in situ from methanol and sodium. The direct current voltage is 3-100 V, the current density is 10-20 A/dm^3, and the temperature of the medium is 20-80°C.

Electrochemical reactions are practically as diverse as non-electrochemical reactions. Thus, the combination of electrochemical reactions with catalysts (electrochemical catalytic process), enzymatic chemistry (electroenzymatic reactions) are quite common.

Following are some representative examples of electrochemical synthesis:

2.1.17.1   Synthesis of Adiponitrile

Adiponitrile is used as an important raw material for preparing hexamethylene diamine and adipic acid, which are used for the manufacture of Nylon-66.

It is obtained commercially by the electroreductive coupling of acrylonitrile. By this process about 90 per cent of adiponitrile is obtained[220]. In this process a concentrated solution of certain quaternary ammonium salts (QASs), such as tetraethylammonium-p-toluene sulfonate is used together with lead or mercury cathode (Scheme 135).

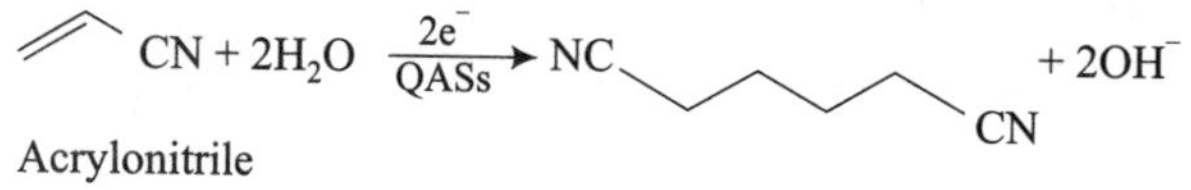

Acrylonitrile

Scheme 135

Another route for its preparation of adiponitrile is the selective hydrocyanation of butadiene catalysed by Ni(O)/triarylphosphite complexes (Scheme 136)[221].

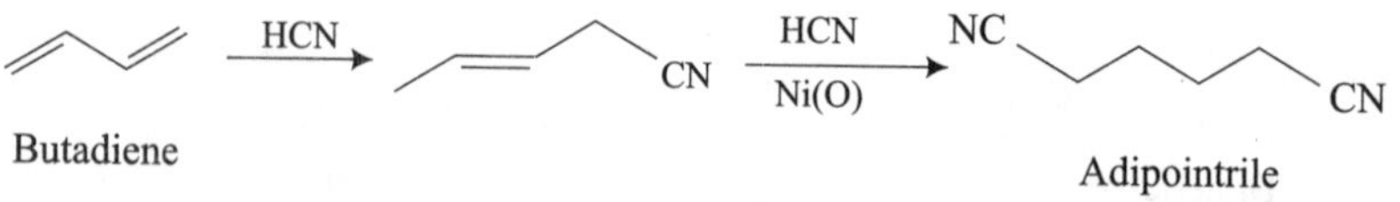

Butadiene   Adipointrile

Scheme 136

2.1.17.2   Synthesis of Sebacic Acid

Sebacic acid is an important intermediate in the manufacture of polymide resins. It was obtained earlier on a large scale by saponification of castor oil[222]. It is now obtained by electrochemical process involving the following three steps (Scheme 137)

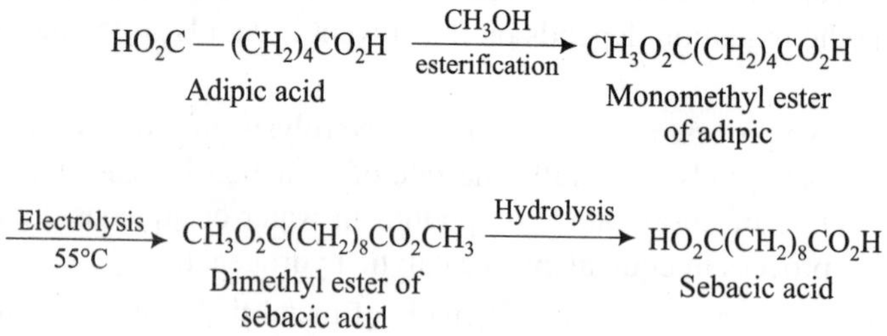

$$HO_2C - (CH_2)_4CO_2H \xrightarrow[\text{esterification}]{CH_3OH} CH_3O_2C(CH_2)_4CO_2H$$

Adipic acid   Monomethyl ester
                                                    of adipic

$$\xrightarrow[55°C]{\text{Electrolysis}} CH_3O_2C(CH_2)_8CO_2CH_3 \xrightarrow{\text{Hydrolysis}} HO_2C(CH_2)_8CO_2H$$

Dimethyl ester of   Sebacic acid
sebacic acid

Scheme 137

In the above process, anodic coupling of the monomethyl ester of adipic acid takes place. The electrolyte is a 20 per cent aqueous solution of monomethyl adipate, neutralised with sodium hydroxide. The anode is platinum-plated with titanium and cathode is of steel[223].

2.1.17.3 Miscellaneous Electrochemical Reactions

(i) Reduction of glucose for the manufacture of sorbitol and mannitol[224].

(ii) Reduction of phthalic acid to the corresponding dihydrophthalic acid[225].

(iii) Coupling of acetone to yield pinacol[226].

(iv) Oxidation of 1, 4-butynediol to acetylene dicarboxylic acid[227].

(v) Oxidation of furfural to maltol[228].

(vi) Epoxidation of alkenes[229].

(vii) Conversion of alkenes into ketones[230].

(viii) Oxidation of aromatic rings and side chains to carboxylic acids[231].

(ix) Oxidation of primary alcohols to carboxylic acids[232].

(x) Oxidation of secondary alcohols to ketones[233].

(xi) Oxidation of vicinal diols to carboxylic acids[234].

(xii) Hydroxylation or dehydrogenative coupling of phenols[235].

(xiii) Kolbe synthesis of hydrocarbons[236].

2.1.18 Miscellaneous Reactions in Aqueous Phase

2.1.18.1 Isomerisation of Alkenes

Alkenes isomerise in presence of transition metal complexes. It is found that isomerisation of allylic alcohols (or ethers) can be performed in aqueous media in presence of Ru(II)(H$_2$O)$_6$(tos)$_2$ (tos = p-toluene sulfonate) (Scheme 138)[237].

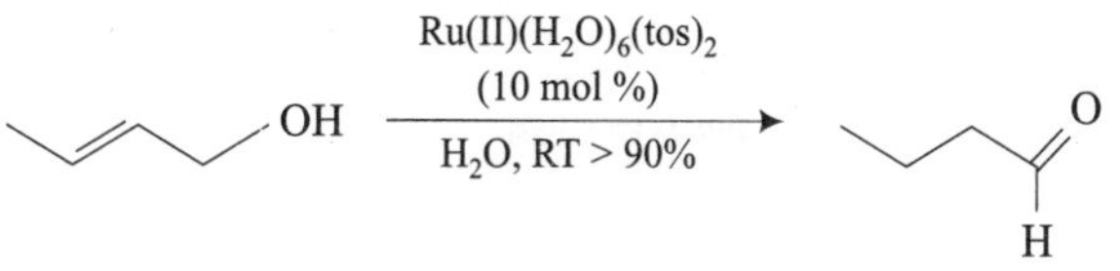

Scheme 138

In the above reaction the initially formed enols and enolethers are unstable and are hydrolysed instaneously to give the corresponding carbonyl compounds.

Some other examples are given as follows (Scheme 139)[238].

In both the given examples (Scheme 139) the substrates undergo structural reorganisation involving reshuffling of both the hydroxyl group and the olefin in water. These reactions can be considered as olefin migration followed by an allylic rearrangement.

2.1.18.2 Carbonylation

Carbonylation is a very important process[239] for the preparation of carboxylic acids (and their derivatives), aldehydes and ketones.

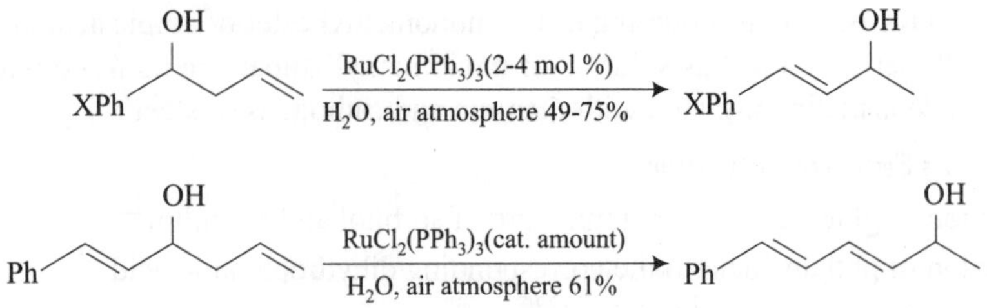

Scheme 139

The aryl halides can be converted into the corresponding carboxylic acid by carbonylation in presence of water using a PTC[240]. Carbonylation of organic halides using various types of phase transfer techniques has been extensively reviewed[241].

Aryl halides can be carbonylated to give the corresponding carboxylic acids (Scheme 140) under mild conditions in presence of inorganic bases (like alkaline metal hydroxides, carbonates, acetates etc.) and certain palladium catalysts (like $Pd(OAc)_2$, K_2PdCl, $Pd(NH_3)_4Cl$, $PdCl_2(PPh_3)_2$ etc.). Best results are obtained with simple palladium salt using K_2CO_3 as base (Scheme 140).

$$ArX \xrightarrow[\text{DMF-H}_2O(2:1)\ 25\text{-}50°C]{Pd(OAc)_2\ (1\ \text{mole}\ \%),\ CO,\ K_2CO_3} ArCOOH$$

$$Ar = p\text{-}ZC_6H_4(Z = NO_2,\ Cl,\ CN,\ Me,\ NH_2\ \text{etc.})$$

Scheme 140

Water soluble aryl iodides can be carbonylated in aqueous medium in presence of soluble palladium salt or complexes and K_2CO_3 as base at 25-50°C (Scheme 141).

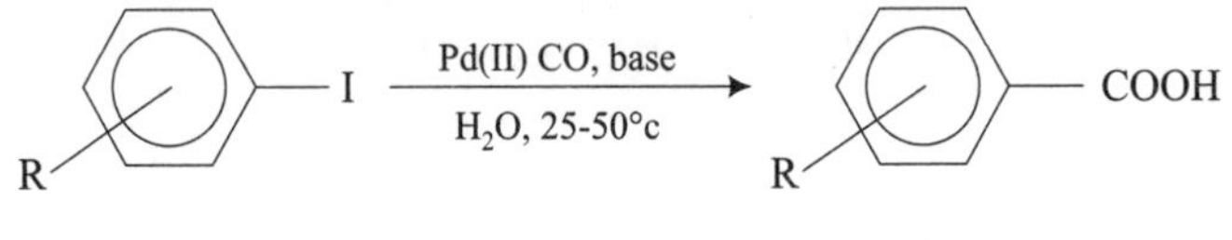

$$R = m\text{-},\ p\text{-}COOH$$
$$o\text{-},\ m\text{-},\ p\text{-}OH$$

Scheme 141

Ortho-iodobenzoic acid cannot be carbonylated under the above conditions (Scheme 141). It, can, however be carbonylated in presence of excess iodide ion to give phthalic acid (Scheme 142).

In case of water insoluble aryl iodides, the iodine atom is first oxidized to the iodyl group by $NaClO_3$, the formed iodyl derivative are readily carbonylated to give carboxylic acids (Scheme 143)[242].

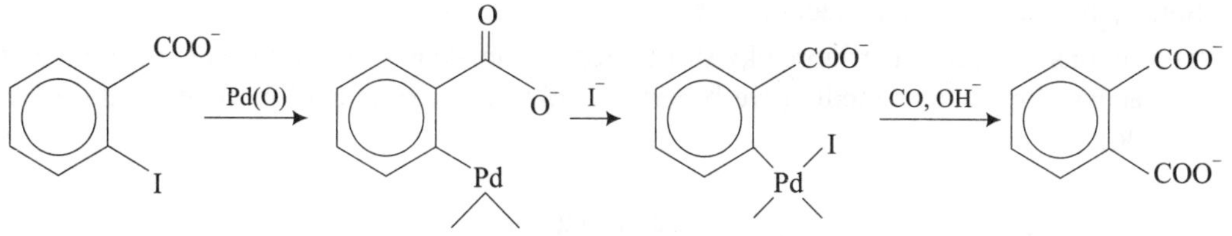

Scheme 142

$$ArI \xrightarrow{\text{NaClO}_3} ArIO_2 \xrightarrow[\text{CO (1 atm), H}_2\text{O, 40-50°C}]{\text{Na}_3\text{PdCl}_4,\ \text{NaOH}} ArCOOH$$

Scheme 143

Carbonylation of allylic and benzylic chlorides was earlier carried out by transition-metals (as catalysis) to give β, γ-unsaturated acids[243] in low yields. It is found that carbonylation of benzyl bromide and chloride could be carried out by stirring with an aqueous sodium hydroxide and an organic solvent using a PTC and a cobalt catalyst. Even benzylic mercaptan could be carbonylated to give esters under high pressure and temperature (Scheme 144)[244].

$$PhCH_2X \xrightarrow[\text{PTC}]{\text{Co[CO]}_4^-\ \text{aq. NaOH}} PhCH_2CO_2Na$$

X = Cl or Br

$$ArCH_2SH + CO + R'OH \xrightarrow[\substack{850\text{-}900\ \text{psi (1b/in}^2) \\ 190°C,\ 24hr,\ 25\text{-}83\%}]{\text{Co}_2(\text{CO})_8,\ \text{H}_2\text{O}} ArCH_2COOR'$$

Scheme 144

Carbonylation of allyl bromides and chlorides has also been carried out in presence of a nickel catalyst in aqueous NaOH at atmospheric pressure[245]. Subsequently it is found that Palladium-catalysed carbonylation of allyl chloride proceeded smoothly in two-phase aqueous NaOH/benzene under atmospheric pressure at room temperature (Scheme 145)[246].

$$CH_2 = CHCH_2Cl + CO + ROH \xrightarrow[\text{19-98\%}]{\text{Pd}} CH_2 = CHCH_2COOR$$

R = H, CH₃, CH₂H₅ etc.

$R = H, CH_3, CH_2H_5$ etc.

Scheme 145

In the above method addition of surfactants (e.g. n-$C_7H_{15}SO_3Na$ or n-$C_7H_{15}CO_2Na$) accelerate the carbonylation[247].

Some other carbonylation reactions are:

(i) Carbonylation of 1-perfluoroalky substituted 2-iodoalkanes in presence of transition metal catalysts in aqueous media give β-perfluoroalkyl carboxylic acid in good yield (Scheme 146)[248].

$$R_f - CH_2CHR'I + CO + H_2O \xrightarrow[\text{base}]{\text{Pd, Co, or Rh cat.}} R_f - CH_2CHR'COOH$$

R_f = perfluoroalkyl group

Scheme 146

(ii) γ-Lactones can be obtained by the carbonylation of terminal alkynes in water in presence of rhodium carbonyl (Scheme 147)[249].

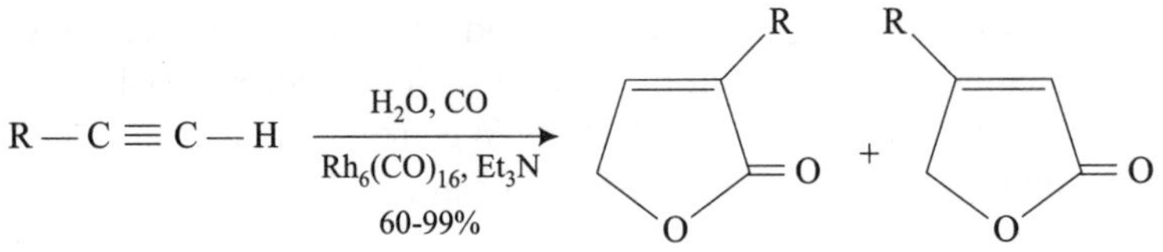

$$R - C \equiv C - H \xrightarrow[\substack{Rh_6(CO)_{16}, Et_3N \\ 60\text{-}99\%}]{H_2O, CO}$$

Scheme 147

(iii) The reaction of styrene oxide with carbon monoxide is catalysed by a cobalt complex in presence of methyl iodide to give enol (Scheme 148)[250].

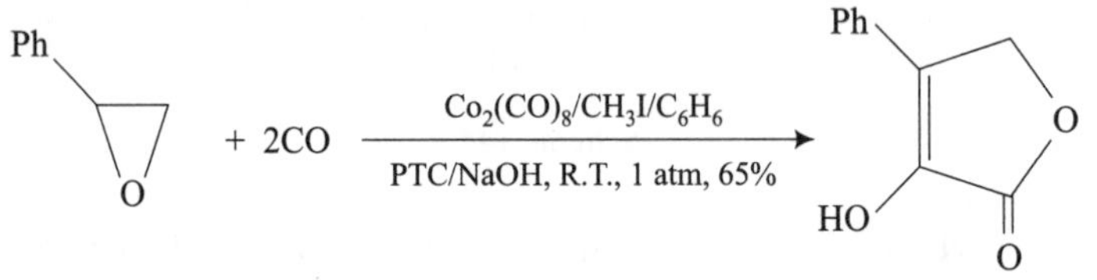

Scheme 148

(iv) Carbonylation of methane under acidic conditions by oxygen and CO in water, catalysed by palladium, platinum or rhodium catalysts gives acetic acid[251].

(v) 5-Hydroxymethyl furfural can be selectively carbonylated to the corresponding acid by using water soluble palladium catalysts (Scheme 149)[252].

(vi) Carbonylation of 1-(4-isobutylphenyl) ethanol gives ibuprofen (Scheme 150)[253].

2.1.18.3 Hydroformylation of Olefins

Aldehydes and alcohols can be manufactured by Hydroformylation of olefins by reaction with CO and H_2 in presence of a catalysts[254].

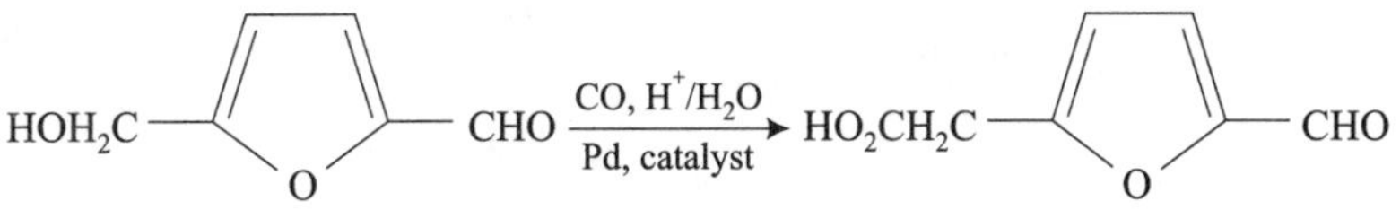

Scheme 149

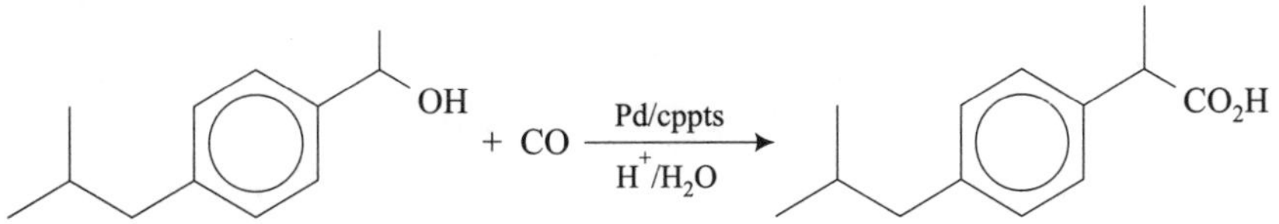

Ibuprofen

Scheme 150

Carbon monixide and hydrogen are used for the manufacture of methyl alcohol. Also, the first product to be manufactured by the hydroformylation of propene is butyraldehyde (Scheme 151)[255].

$$CO + H_2 \xrightarrow[300°C,]{ZnO, CrO_3,} CH_3OH$$
Methyl alcohol

$$CH_3CH{=}CH_2 + CO + H_2 \xrightarrow[\text{Catalyst}]{\text{Rhodium}} CH_3CH_2CH_2CHO$$
Propene   Butyraldehyde

Scheme 151

A number of catalysts were tried for the hydroformylation of olefins. Main among these are:

(i) Rhodium combined with phosphorus ligand.

(ii) Attachment of a normally soluble catalyst to an insoluble polymer support.

Finally a variety of 1-alkenes were hydroformylated with water soluble tris-sulphonate ligand, $P(m - PhSO_3Na)$[256]. Some more effective catalysts involve the use of other sulphonated phosphine ligands[257].

A unique approach is the concept of support aqueous phase (SAP) catalysis[258]. In this approach, a thin, aqueous film containing a water soluble catalyst adheres to silica gel with a high surface area; the reaction occurs at the liquid-liquid interface. Using this method, hydroformylation of alkenes like octene, discyclopentadiene is possible. Through SAP approach, hydroformylation of acrylic acid derivatives is of industrial applications (Scheme 152)[259].

The major product obtained (Scheme 152) is formylpropionic acids, which are precursors of methacrylate monomers and can be used for a number of important pharmaceuticals. A number of other application of hydroformylation have been reviewed[260].

2.1.18.4 Homologation of 1, 3-dihydroxyacetone

The homologation of 1, 3-dihydroxyacetone with formaldehyde in presence of base gives the homologated derivatives A and B (Scheme 153)[261].

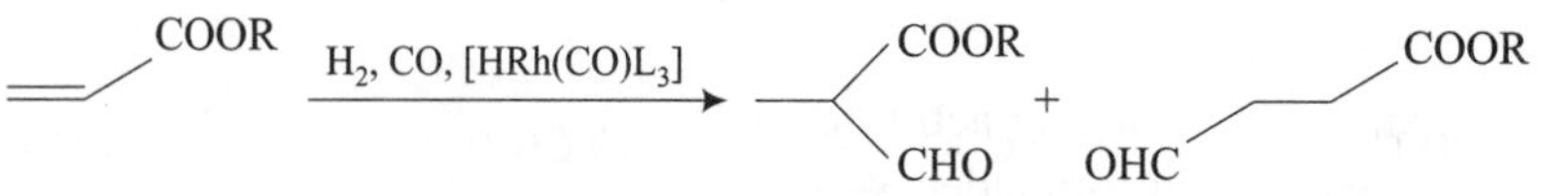

Scheme 152

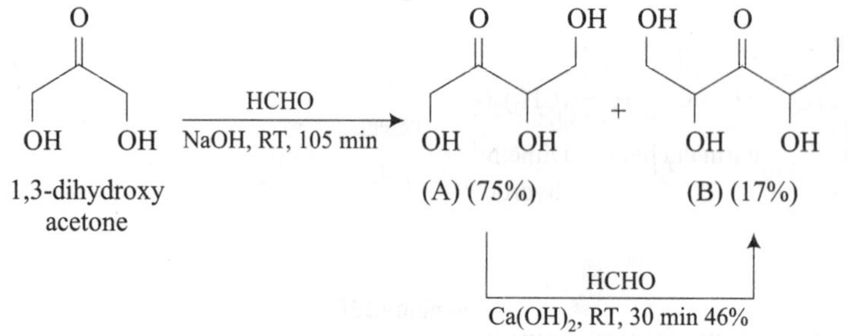

1,3-dihydroxy
acetone   (A) (75%)   (B) (17%)

HCHO
Ca(OH)$_2$, RT, 30 min 46%

Scheme 153

2.1.18.5   Weiss-Cook Reaction

The reaction of dimethyl 3-oxoglutarate with glyoxal in aqueous acidic solution gives [3.3.0] octane, 3, 7-dione-2, 4, 6, 8-tetracarboxylate; which on acid catalysed hydrolysis followed by decarboxylation gives cis-bicyclo [3.3.0] octane-3, 7-dione (Scheme 154)[262]. The reaction is believed to involve a double Knoevenagal reaction.

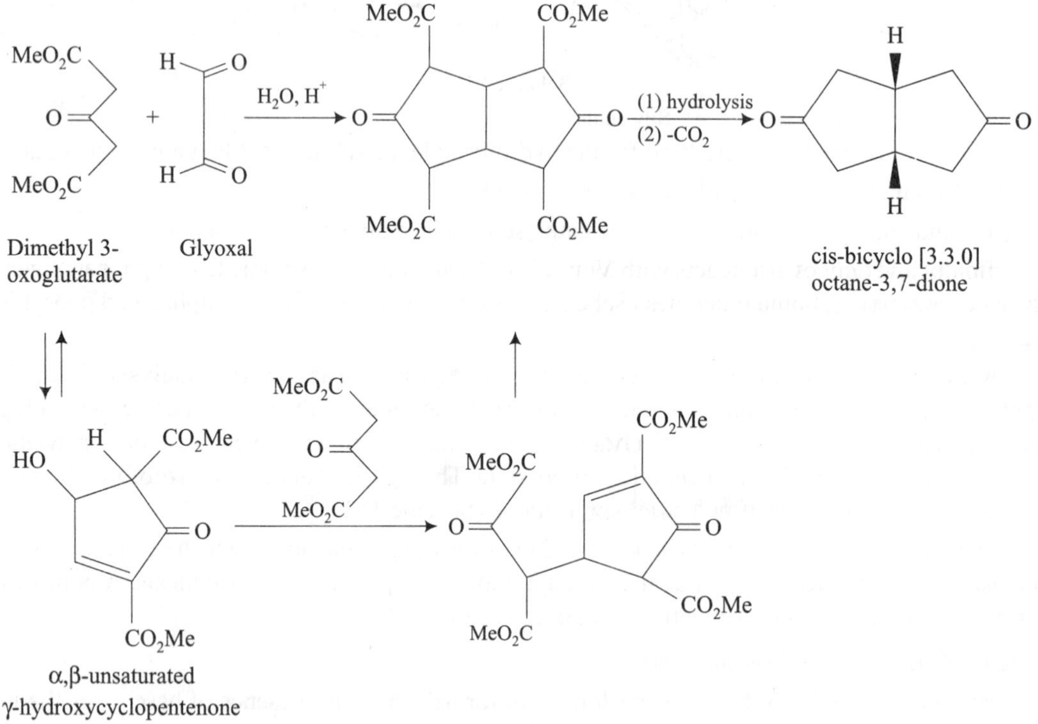

Dimethyl 3-
oxoglutarate   Glyoxal

cis-bicyclo [3.3.0]
octane-3,7-dione

α,β-unsaturated
γ-hydroxycyclopentenone

Scheme 154

2.1.18.6 Mannich Type Reactions

Compounds containing at least one active hydrogen atom (ketones, nitroalkanes, β-ketoesters, β-cyano ester) condenses with formaldehyde and 1° or 2° amine or ammonia (in the form of HCl salt) to give the product known as mannich base (Scheme 155)[263].

$$\underset{\text{Acetophenone}}{C_6H_5-\overset{\overset{\displaystyle O}{\|}}{C}-CH_3} + \underset{\text{Formaldehyde}}{H-\overset{\overset{\displaystyle O}{\|}}{C}-H} + \underset{\substack{\text{Dimethylamine}\\\text{hydrochloride}}}{(CH_3)_2\overset{+}{N}H_2Cl^-} \longrightarrow \underset{\substack{\text{β-N, N-Dimethylamino ketone}\\\text{(HCl salt)}}}{C_6H_5-\overset{\overset{\displaystyle O}{\|}}{C}-CH_2\,CH_2\,\overset{+}{N}H(CH_3)_2\,Cl^-} + H_2O$$

Scheme 155

Modification using preformed iminium salts and imines has been developed. The imines react with enolate (especially trimethylsilyl ethers) to give β-amino ketones[264]. The general Scheme for the synthesis of β-aminoketones is given in Scheme 156.

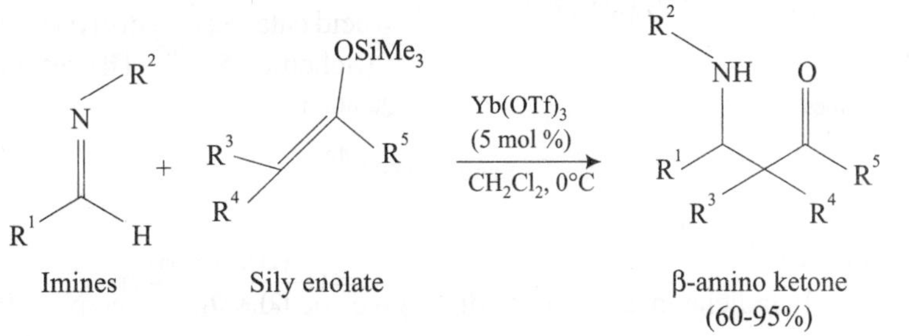

Imines   Sily enolate   β-amino ketone
(60-95%)

Scheme 156

Imines and amines also reacts with Vinyl ethers in presence of catalytic amount of Yb(OTf)₃ to give corresponding β-amino ketones (Scheme 157)[265].

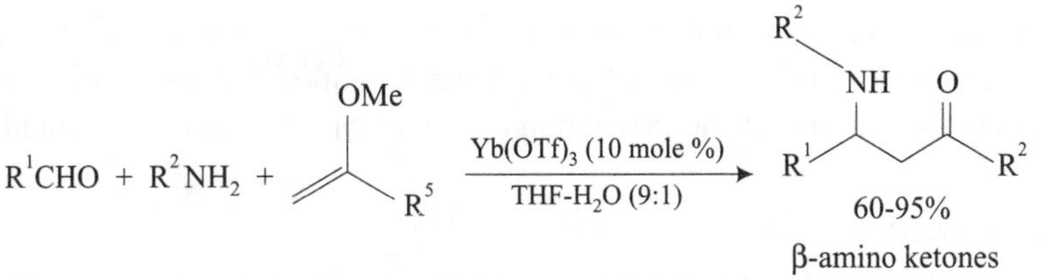

β-amino ketones

Scheme 157

The above reaction was also used for the synthesis of β-amino esters from aldehydes using Yb(OTf)₃ as catayst (Scheme 158)[266].

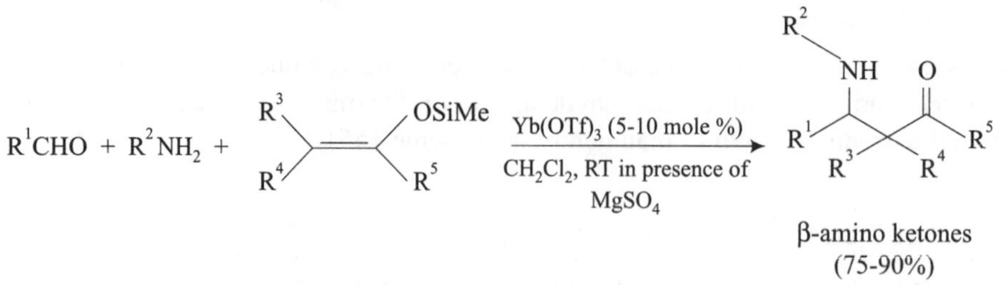

Scheme 158

2.1.18.7 Conversion of o-nitrochalcones into Quinolines and Indoles

Reduction of o-nitrochalcone under WGSR conditions[267] followed by the cyclisation give the formation of quinolines and indoles (Scheme 159)[268].

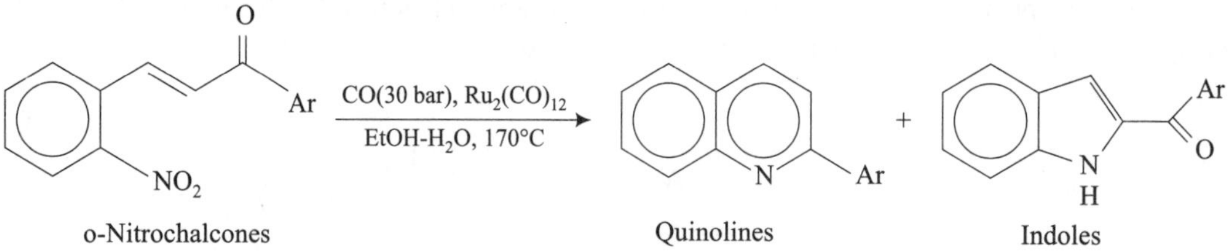

Scheme 159

2.1.18.8 Synthesis of Octadienols

The isomerisation of butadiene in aqueous medium gives octadienols (Scheme 160)[269].

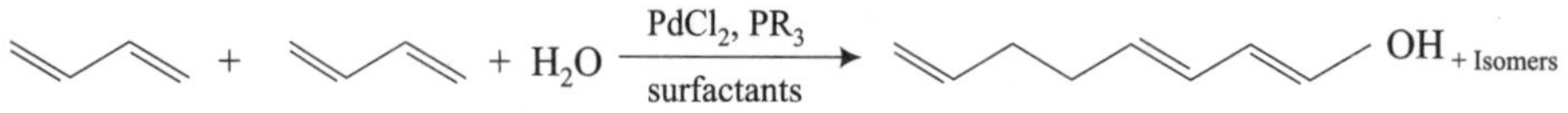

Scheme 160

2.1.19 Carbon-Carbon Bond Formations in Aqueous Media

Carbon-Carbon bond formations and functional group transformation are the two basic types of reactions for organic synthesis[270]. Carbon-Carbon bond formation is the essence of organic synthesis. It provides the foundation for the generation of complicated organic compounds from simple molecules.

2.1.19.1 Reactions of Alkanes

Alkanes are generally considered unreactive in conventional organic chemistry. However, under drastic conditions, alkanes are known to react. It has now been possible to carry out some reactions of alkanes in aqueous conditions[271]. Thus it is possible to couple methane with CO to generate acetic and in aqueous conditions using several catalysis[272] (Scheme 161).

$$CH_4 + CO \xrightarrow[\substack{\text{aq. soln. pH 7.3} \\ \text{5-25 hr.}}]{\text{air, NaVO}_3, 80°} CH_3COOH + CH_3OH + CH_2O$$

$$\qquad\qquad\qquad\qquad\qquad\qquad\quad \text{major} \qquad \text{Minor} \qquad \text{Trace}$$

Scheme 161

Direct alkynylation of an Sp^3-hybridized C-H bond adjacent to nitrogen could be effected by tert.butylhydroperoxide in presence of copper catalyst (Scheme 162)[273].

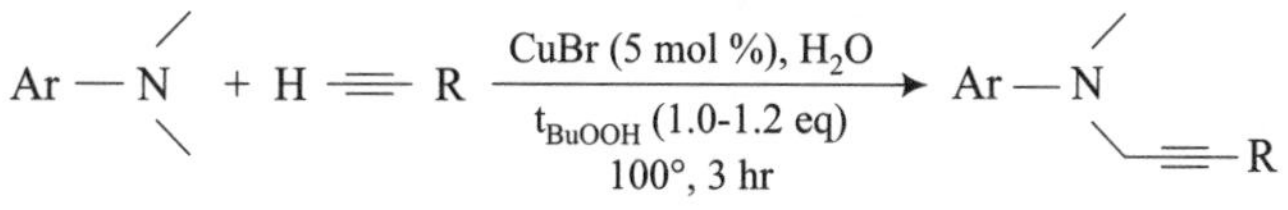

$$Ar - N + H \equiv\!\!\!-\, R \xrightarrow[\substack{t_{\text{BuOOH}} \ (1.0\text{-}1.2 \ eq) \\ 100°, \ 3 \ hr}]{\text{CuBr (5 mol \%), H}_2\text{O}} Ar - N \diagdown\!\!\!\equiv\!\!-R$$

Scheme 162

Carbon-Carbon bond formation via carbene insertion into an alkane C-H bond is possible in aqueous media under photolytic conditions[274].

2.1.19.2   Reactions of Alkenes

Alkenes and its derivatives are known to undergo catonic polymerisation in aqueous media[275]. Also, the reaction of simple oletins with aldehydes in the presence of acid catalyst is known as 'Prins reaction'[276]; in this reaction a mixture of carbon-carbon bond formation product is obtained[277]. A direct formation of tetrahydropyranol derivative has been reported[278] in water using a cerium-salt catalysed cyclization in aqueous ionic liquids (Scheme 163).

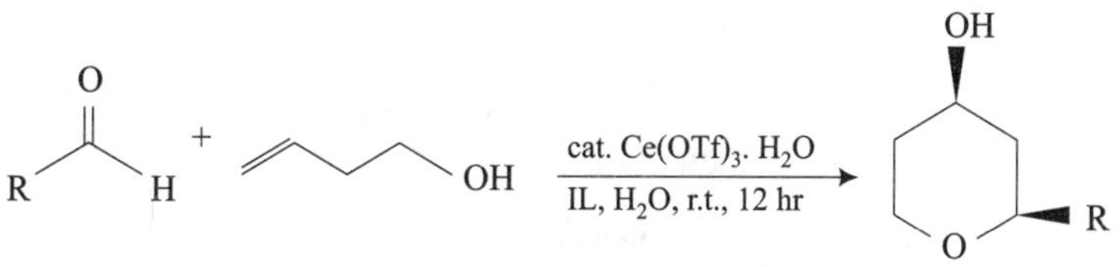

Scheme 163

The yield of the tetrahydropyranol (Scheme 163) improved[279] by using the Amberlite 1R-120 plus resin. A related reaction involving alkene-imine coupling proceeds well in water-THF. This reaction is used in the asymmetric synthesis of pipecolic acid derivatives[280] (Scheme 164).

The radical addition of 2-iodoalkanamide or 2-iodoalkanoic acid to alkenols using water soluble radical intator yielded γ-lactones[281] (Scheme 165).

The reaction of ethyl diazoacetate and olefins proceeded well in aqueous media using Rh(II) carboxylates. This is a convenient procedure for cyclopropanation. In situ generation of ethyl diazoacetate and cydopropanation also proceeded well[282] (Scheme 166).

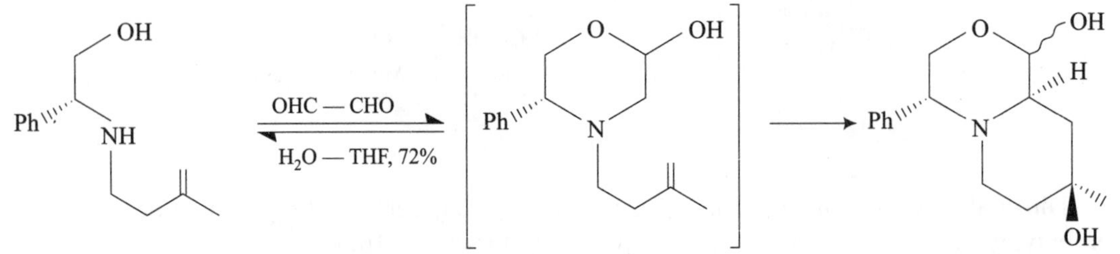

Scheme 164

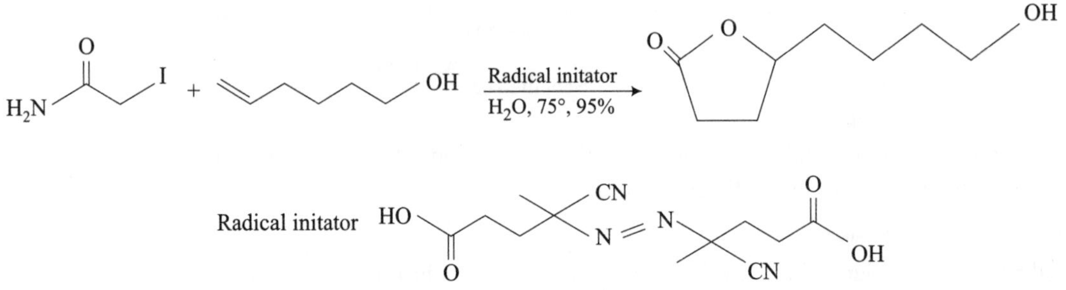

Scheme 165

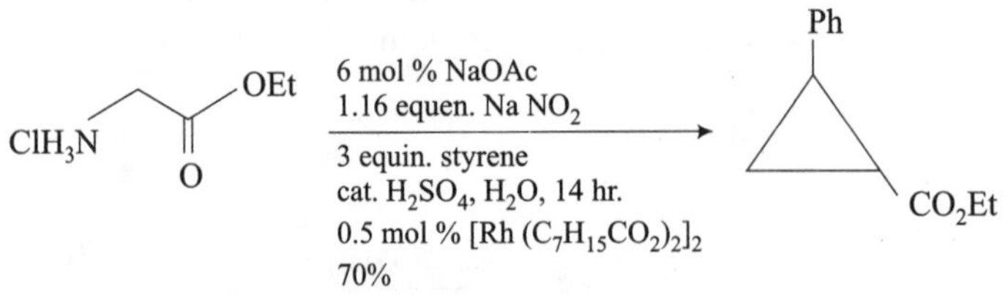

Scheme 166

The addition of activated alkenes to unactivated alkynes resulted in Alder-ene products using a ruthenium catalyst[283] (Scheme 167).

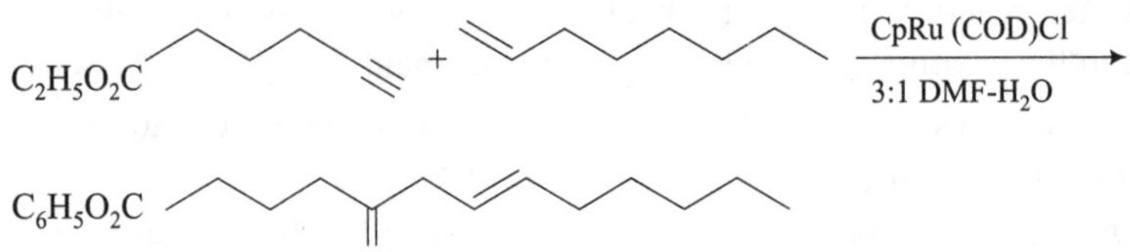

Scheme 167

2.1.19.3   Reactions of Alkynes

Terminal alkenes could be dimerised to give mixture of diynes in moderate yield[284] (Scheme 168). Although such coupling are mainly catalysed by copper, other transition metal catalysts also work.

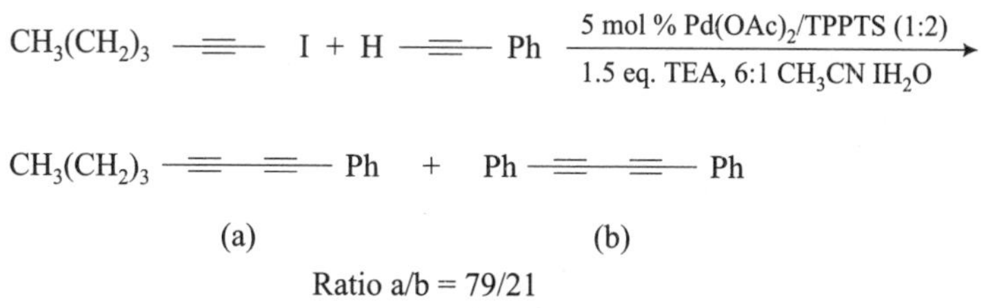

$$CH_3(CH_2)_3 \equiv\!\!\!-\!\!\!I + H \equiv\!\!\!-\!\!\!Ph \xrightarrow[\text{1.5 eq. TEA, 6:1 } CH_3CN \, IH_2O]{\text{5 mol \% } Pd(OAc)_2/TPPTS \, (1:2)}$$

$$CH_3(CH_2)_3 \equiv\!\!\!=\!\!\!-\!\!\!Ph \quad + \quad Ph \equiv\!\!\!=\!\!\!-\!\!\!Ph$$

(a)   (b)

Ratio a/b = 79/21

Scheme 168

Such dimenisation of terminal alkynes is known as the Glasar coupling or the Eglinton coupling. It was found that using a catalytic amount of Pd(OAc)$_2$ and triphenylphosphine in dichloroethane resulted in a high yield of homocoupling of terminal alkynes[285].

Terminal alkynes coupled with 2-iodoaniline or 2-iodophenol to give the corresponding indoles or benzofurans in good yield[286] (Scheme 169).

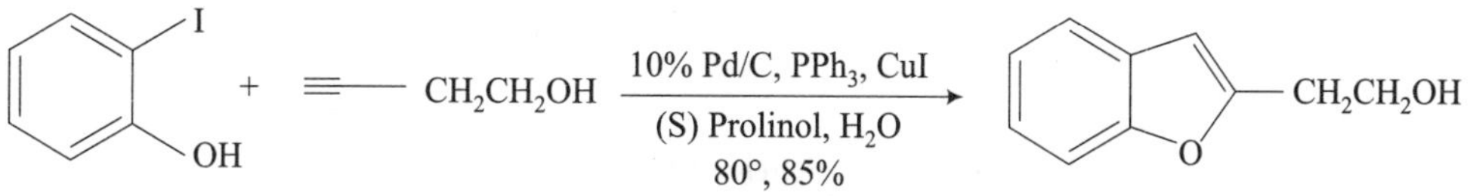

Scheme 169

An efficient coupling of acetylene with aryl halides in a mixture of acetonitrile and water (Scheme 170) has been reported[287].

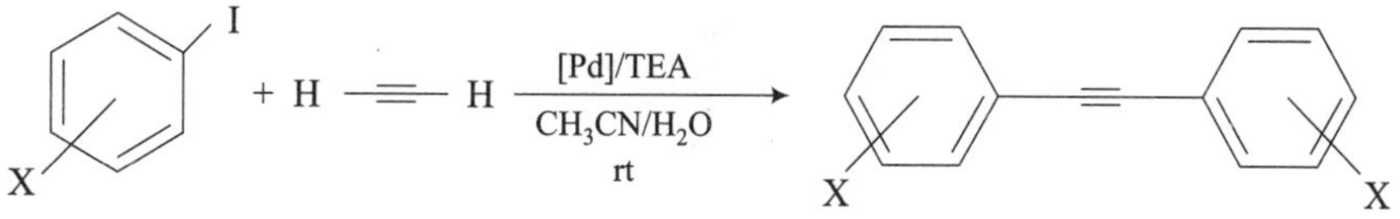

Scheme 170

Terminal alkynes have been reported to couple with acid chlorides; the reaction is catalytic by PdCl$_2$(PPh$_3$)$_2$/CuI along with a catalytic amount of sodium lauryl sulfate as the surfactant and K$_2$CO$_3$ as the base; the coupled product are ynones (Scheme 170)[288].

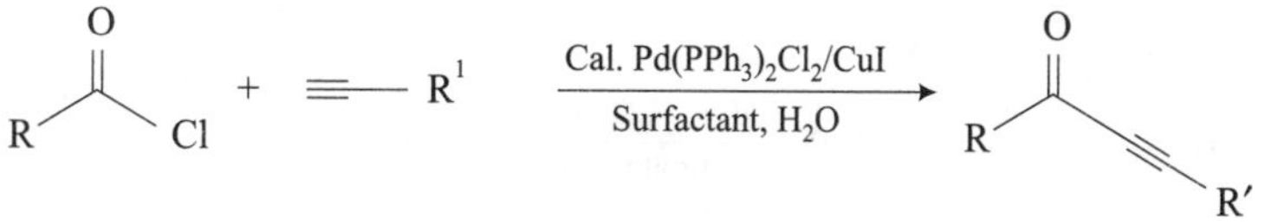

Scheme 170a

A direct addition of terminal alkynes to aldehydes in water by using a ruthenium – indium bicatalyst system has been reported[289] (Scheme 171).

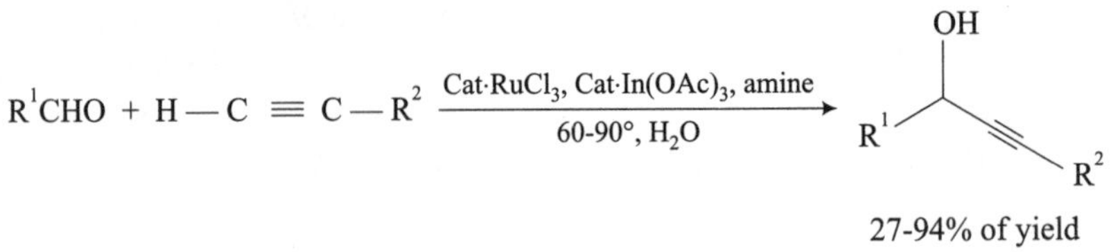

$$R^1CHO + H-C \equiv C-R^2 \xrightarrow[\text{60-90°, H}_2\text{O}]{\text{Cat·RuCl}_3,\ \text{Cat·In(OAc)}_3,\ \text{amine}}$$

R¹ (with OH group and C≡C–R²)

27-94% of yield

Scheme 171

Terminal alkynes reacted with aldehydes and amines under suitable conditions to give[290] propargylamines (Scheme 172).

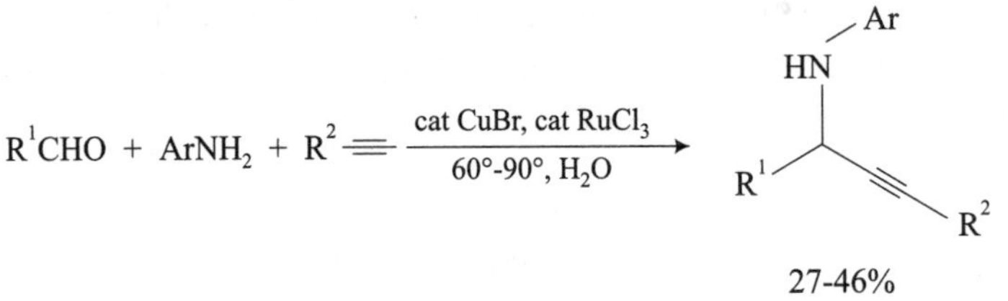

$$R^1CHO + ArNH_2 + R^2 \equiv \xrightarrow[\text{60°-90°, H}_2\text{O}]{\text{cat CuBr, cat RuCl}_3}$$

R¹ (with HN–Ar group and C≡C–R²)

27-46%

Scheme 172

Terminal alkynes could be added to activated alkynes in water without the competition of the homocoupling of the terminal alkynes[291] (Scheme 173).

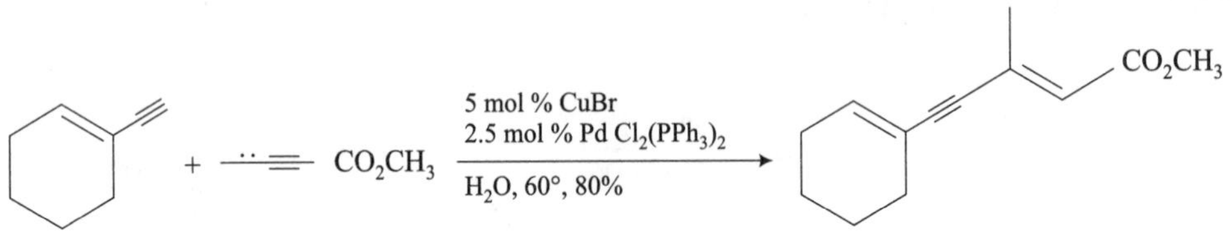

$$+ \quad \text{---}\!\!\equiv\!\! \text{CO}_2\text{CH}_3 \xrightarrow[\text{H}_2\text{O, 60°, 80\%}]{\substack{\text{5 mol \% CuBr} \\ \text{2.5 mol \% Pd Cl}_2(\text{PPh}_3)_2}}$$

CO₂CH₃

Scheme 173

A simple and highly efficient Pd-catalysed addition of a terminal alkynes to a C = C double bond such as a conjugated enone, either in water or in acetone in air (Scheme 174) has also been reported[291].

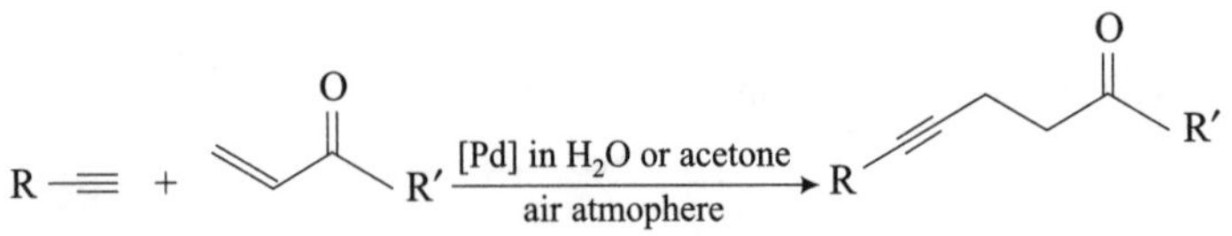

$$R-\!\!\equiv + \quad \underset{\text{R'}}{\overset{\text{O}}{\parallel}} \xrightarrow[\text{air atmophere}]{\text{[Pd] in H}_2\text{O or acetone}} R \quad \underset{\text{R'}}{\overset{\text{O}}{\parallel}}$$

Scheme 174

Hydration of terminal alkynes is catalysed by Ru(II) complexes in presence of phosphine ligands to yield the anti-markovnikov addition of water. In this reaction aldehydes with only a small amount of ketone are obtained[292] (Scheme 175).

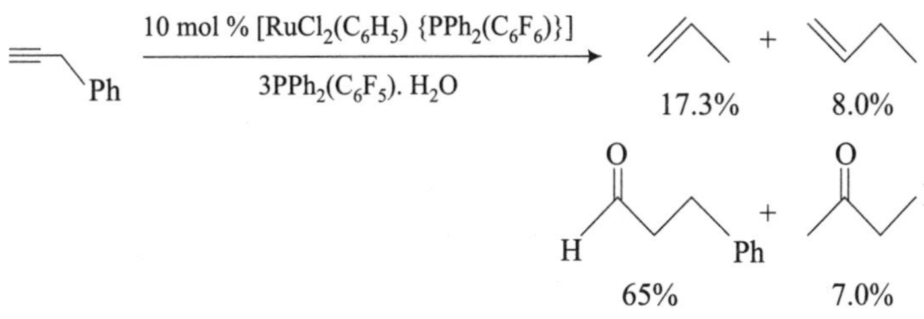

$$\equiv\!\!-\!\!Ph \xrightarrow[\substack{3PPh_2(C_6F_5).\ H_2O}]{10\ mol\ \%\ [RuCl_2(C_6H_5)\ \{PPh_2(C_6F_6)\}]}$$

17.3%   8.0%

65%   7.0%

Scheme 175

Nucleophitic addition of H_2O to alkynes is found to take place in presence of Au(I) catalysed procedure, to form the corresponding carbonyl compounds in high yields[293] (Scheme 176).

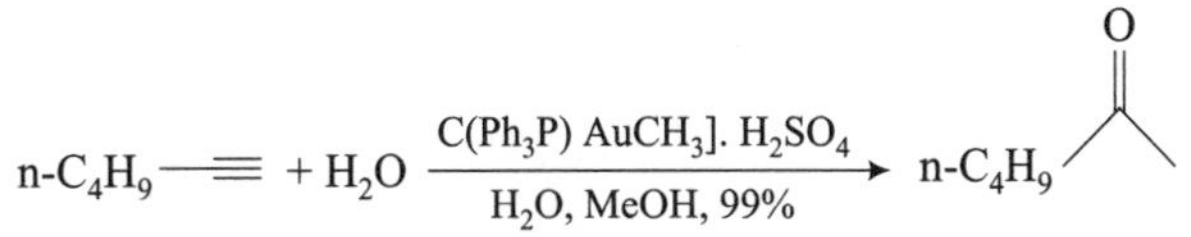

$$n\text{-}C_4H_9\!\!-\!\!\equiv\ +\ H_2O \xrightarrow[\substack{H_2O,\ MeOH,\ 99\%}]{C(Ph_3P)\ AuCH_3].\ H_2SO_4} n\text{-}C_4H_9$$

Scheme 176

The above procedure is a valuable alternative to the Wacker oxidation.

Alkynes are hydrocarboxylated with HCO_2H in presence of $Pd(OAc)_2$ and a phosphine ligand (100-110°, 120 psi of CO gas pressure) to give the corresponding unsaturated carboxylic acids (Scheme 177)[294]

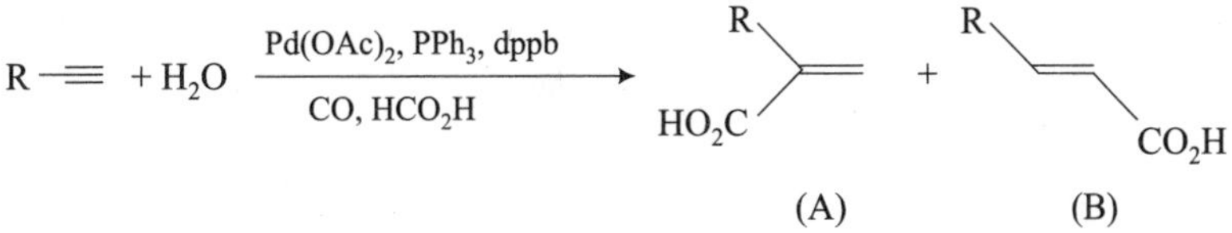

$$R\!\!-\!\!\equiv\ +\ H_2O \xrightarrow[\substack{CO,\ HCO_2H}]{Pd(OAc)_2,\ PPh_3,\ dppb}$$

(A)   (B)

Scheme 177

In the above hydrocarboxylation reaction, the regioselectivity is approximately 90:10 in favour of (A) (when R is Ph or a straight chain alkyl). However, when R is tert-butyl, (B) is favoured and is the exclusive product when R is Me_3Si.

Reductive carbonylation of alkynes can be effected[295] in presence of palladium iodide catalyst along with KI and H_2O (Scheme 178); the products obtained are 3-alkyl- or 3-aryl substituted furan $-2(5H)$ – ones.

Carbonylation of terminal acetylens in water in presence rhodium carbonyl gives[296] γ-lactones (Scheme 179).

An efficient and steroselective hydrosilation of terminal alkynes was developed using ambient conditions of air, water and room temperature by using Pt(DVDS)-P as catalyst[297] (Scheme 180).

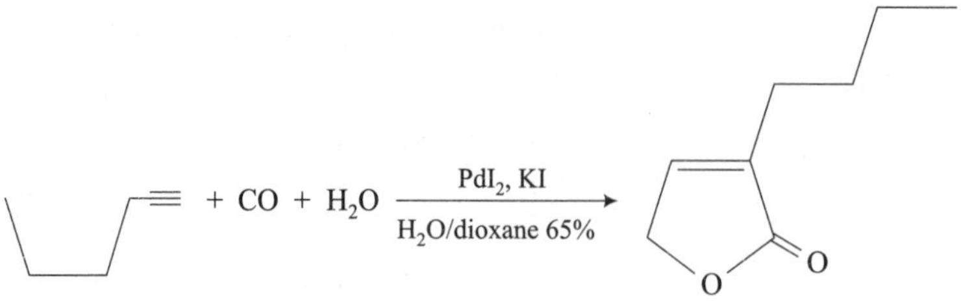

Scheme 178

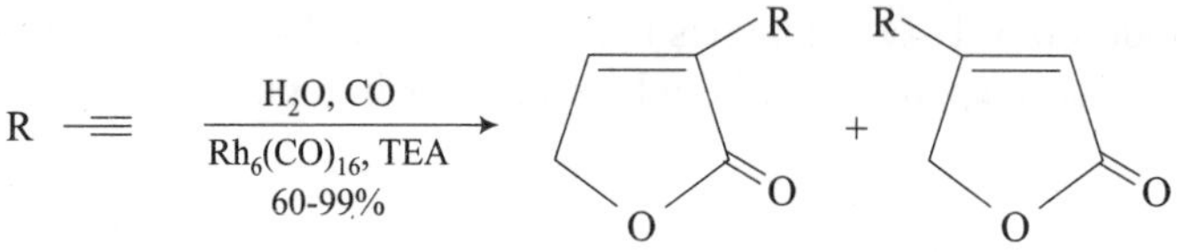

Scheme 179

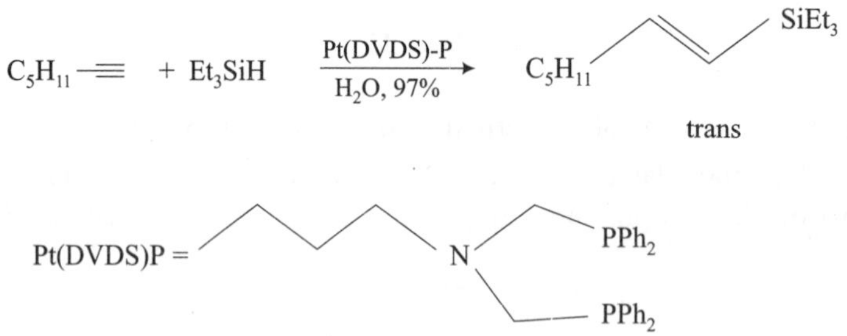

Scheme 180

The above hydrosilation proceeds much faster in water than under neat conditions[298].

Cyclopentenone derivatives are obtained by the Pauson-Khand reaction; the reaction was conducted in aqueous media and promoted by a small amount of 1, 2-dimethyloxyethene or water[299]. An intramolecular Pauson-Khand reaction in water was carried out in water using aqueous colloidal cobalt-nanoparticles as catalyst[300] (Scheme 181).

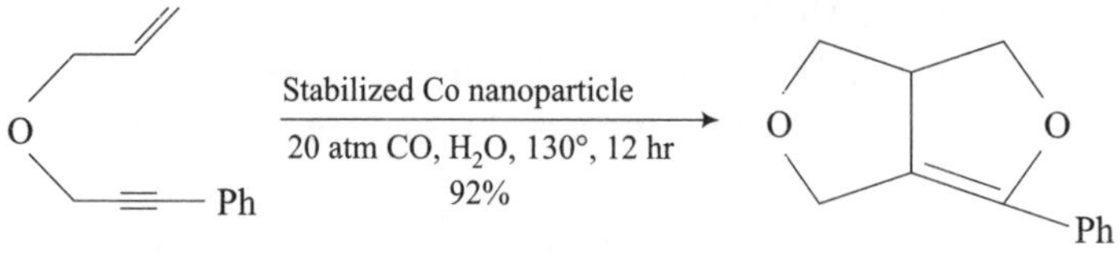

Scheme 181

Some other cyclisation reactions of terminal alkynes have also been described[271].

2.1.19.4   Reactions of Aromatic Compounds

Carbon-Carbon bond formation via the electrophilic substitution of aromatic hydrogens proceeded under aqueous conditions. The well known example is the Friedel-Crafts-type reactions. Thus, various indole derivatives reacted with equimolar amounts of 3 per cent aqueous CH_2O and 33 per cent aqueous Me_2NH at 70-75° in 96 per cent ethanol to give Mannich-type products[301]. A lanthanide catalised reaction of indole with benzaldehyde was reported in ethanol-water system[302] (Scheme 182).

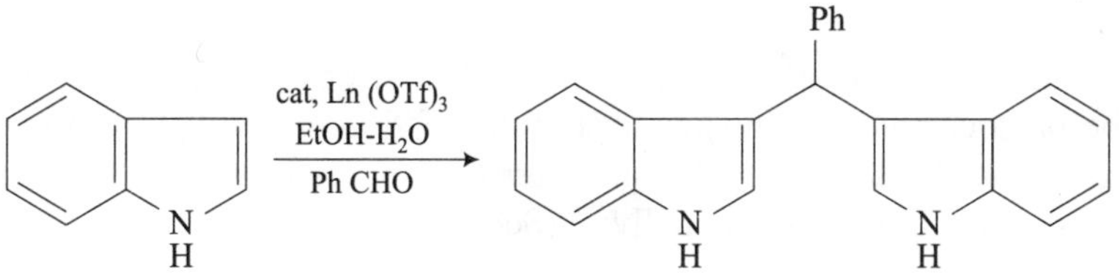

Scheme 182

The reaction of N-methylindole and N-methylpyrole via Friedel-Crafts reaction with $OCHCO_2Et$ in aqueous medium yielded substituted indoles and pyrroles; it was not necessary to use any metal catalyst[303] (Scheme 183).

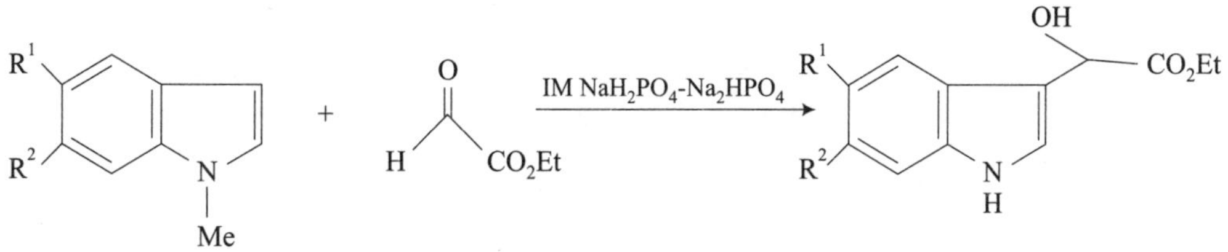

Scheme 183

Friedel-Crafts reaction of aromatic compounds with methyl trifluoropyruvate in water yielded[304] various α-hydroxy esters (Scheme 184).

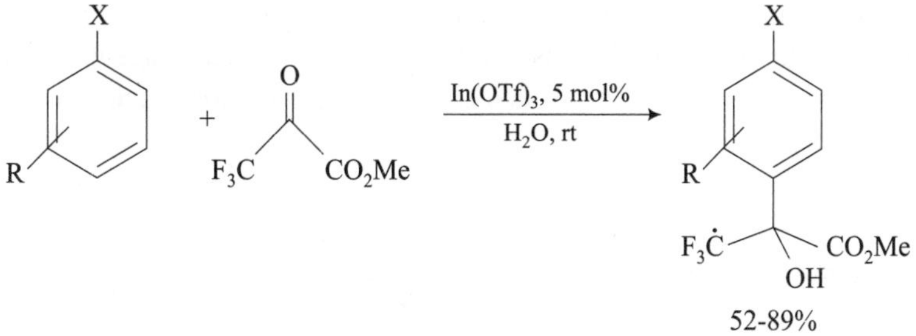

Scheme 184

Benzene can be oxidised by Pd(OAc)$_2$/molydo phosphoric acid/AcOH-H$_2$O(2:1) to give[305] biphenyl by oxidative dimerisation with 100 per cent selectivity and 19 per cent yield under the conditions of 130°, 10 atom and 4 hr (Scheme 185)

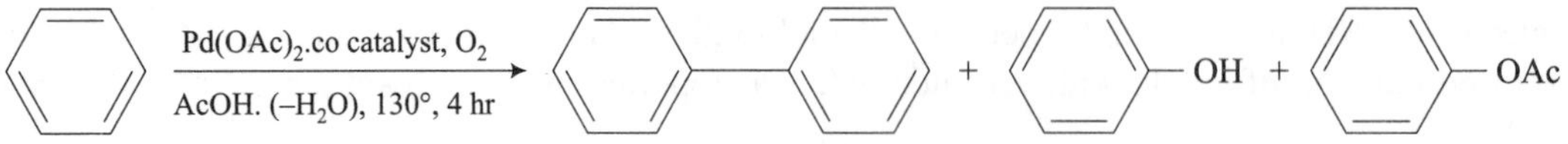

Scheme 185

The use of water as solvent influences the chemoselectivity in photochemical substitution reactions. Thus, the photochemical aromatic substitution of fluorine by the cyano group in ortho-fluoroanisole gives mainly the hydroxylation product; the same reaction with para fluoroanisole generates the cyanation product preferentially[306] (Scheme 186).

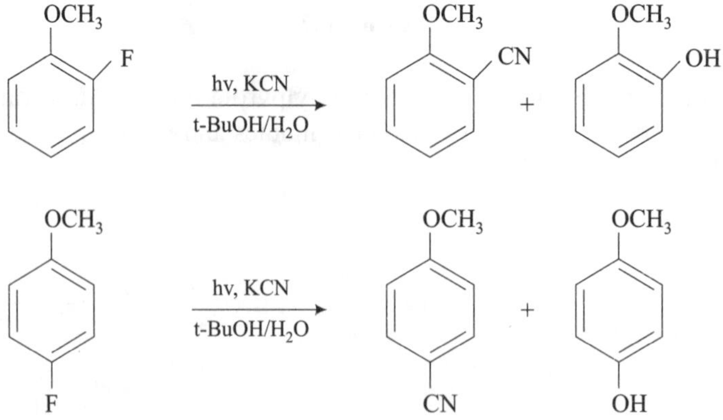

Scheme 186

2.1.19.5 Reactions of Carbonyl Compounds

Some of the common reactions of carboxyl compounds which have already been discussed are Aldol condensation (Scetion 2.1.5), knoevenagel Reaction (Section 2.1.6), Pinacol Coupling (Section 2.1.7) and Benzoin condensation (Section 2.1.8). Besides these Reformatsky-type reactions have been conducted in aqueous phase. Thus, aromatic aldehydes reacted with an α-bromo ester in water mediated by zinc in low yields[307]. Also, the reaction of bromoacetates is greatly enhanced by catalytic amounts benzoyl peroxide or per acids and give satisfactory yields with aromatic aldehydes (Scheme 187).

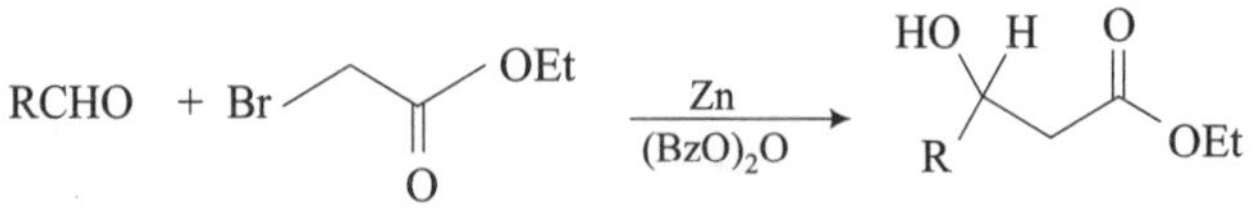

Scheme 187

A radical chain mechanism indicated by electron abstraction from organometallic Retormatsky reagent has been proposed[308].

The reaction of aldehydes or ketones with allyl bromide in presence of stirred slurry of activated Zinc dust in 95 per cent ethanol at 78° give[309] the allylation product. The reaction can also be conducted in aqueous medium[310] (Scheme 188).

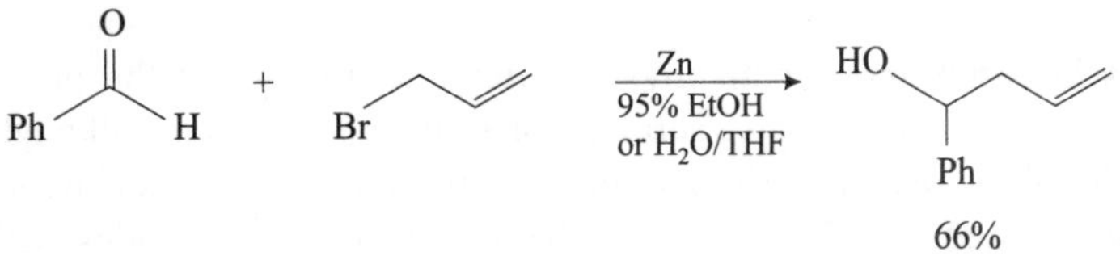

Scheme 188

The above reaction could also be mediated by other metals like Sn, In, B, Si, Ga, Mg, Mn, Bi, etc.

2.1.19.6 Reactions of α, β-unsaturated Carbonyl Compounds

A typical reaction of α, β-unsaturated carbonyl compounds is the well known Michael addition (See Section 2.1.4).

The reaction between activated olefins (e.g. $CH_2 = CH – CN$) with aldehydes in presence of tertiary amines generates useful compounds[311] (Scheme 189); the reaction is known as Baylis-Hillman Reaction.

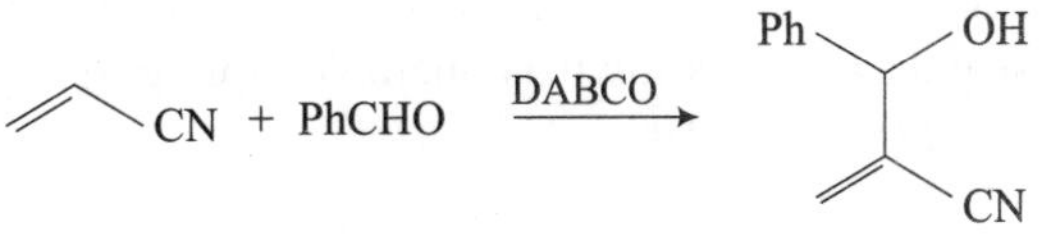

Scheme 189

A significant increase in the reactivity has been observed[312] when the reaction is conducted in water. The addition of lithium or sodium chloride increases the reactivity.

An important reaction of acrylonitrile is its electro reductive coupling to adiponitrile. The reaction was conducted[313] in the presence of certain quaternary ammonium salts (QAS), such as tetraethylammonium-p-toluenesulfonate, with lead or mercury cathodes (Scheme 190).

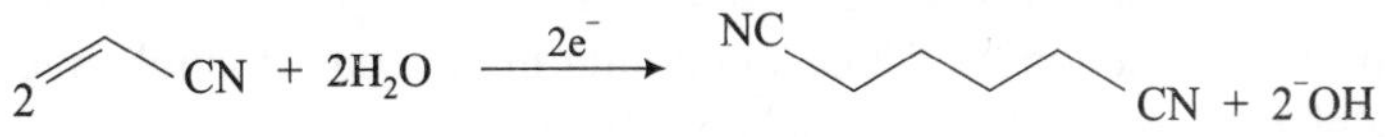

Scheme 190

2.1.19.7 Reactions of Organic Halides

The most important reaction of organic halides are the coupling reactions. These include Wurtz-type coupling (See section 2.1.12) and Ullmann-type coupling[314] (Scheme 191).

$$2ArX \xrightarrow[\text{H}_2\text{O-me OH}]{\text{H}_2, \text{ cat. PdCl}_2, \text{K}_2\text{CO}_3} Ar — Ar$$

X = I, Br; -
Ar = p-MePh, p-Cl Ph, m-CF$_3$-Ph

Scheme 191

The reactions between aryl (or alkenyl) halides and alkenes in the presence of catalytic amount of a palladium compound to give substitution of the halides by the alkenyl group is referred to as the Heck Coupling reaction. Both inter and intramolecular Heck Reactions have been performed in aqueous media[315]. Palladium catalysed reactions aryl halides with acrylic acid or acrylonitrile yielded the corresponding coupled product in high yield in presence of a base in water[316] (Scheme 192).

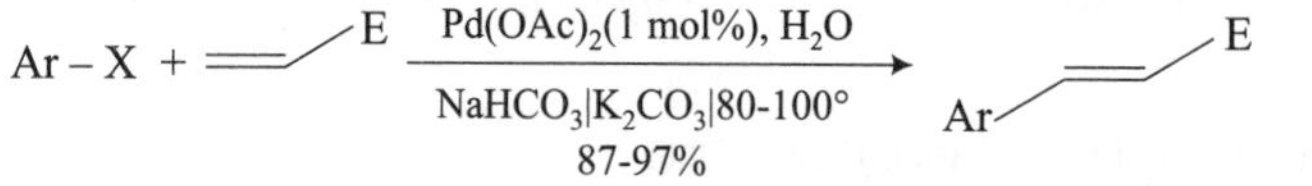

$$Ar – X + \text{\hspace{-0.3cm}}\diagup\!\!\!\!=\!\!\!\diagdown_E \xrightarrow[\substack{\text{NaHCO}_3|\text{K}_2\text{CO}_3|80\text{-}100° \\ 87\text{-}97\%}]{\text{Pd(OAc)}_2(1 \text{ mol\%}), \text{H}_2\text{O}} Ar\!\diagup\!\!\!=\!\!\!\diagup^E$$

E = COOH or CN

Scheme 192

The above procedure (Scheme 192) provides a convenient method for the synthesis of substituted cinnamic acids and cinnamonitriles.

The cross-coupling reaction of alkenyl and aryl halides with organo borane derivatives in presence of a palladium catalyst and a base is known as Suzuki coupling. It is generally carried out in an organic/aqueous mixed solvent (Scheme 193)[317].

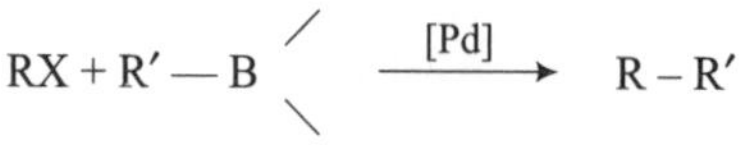

$$RX + R' — B \diagup_{\diagdown} \xrightarrow{[Pd]} R – R'$$

R = 1-alkenyl or aryl
R' = aryl or alkyl
X = Br or I

Scheme 193

The coupling of alkenyl and arylhalides with organostannanes in presence of a palladium catalyst is known as the Stille reaction[318]. Thus, a coupling in aqueous ethanol gave high yield of the coupled product, which hydrolysed in situ (Scheme 194).

Biaryls are obtained in good yield by reaction of diphenyldifluorosilane or diphenyldiethoxysilane with aryl halides in aqueous DMF at 120° in presence of KF and catalyst amount PdCl$_2$ (Scheme 195)[320].

Besides what has been stated above the reactions of C = N, C – N and C ≡ N compounds are also useful for carbon-carbon bond formation[271].

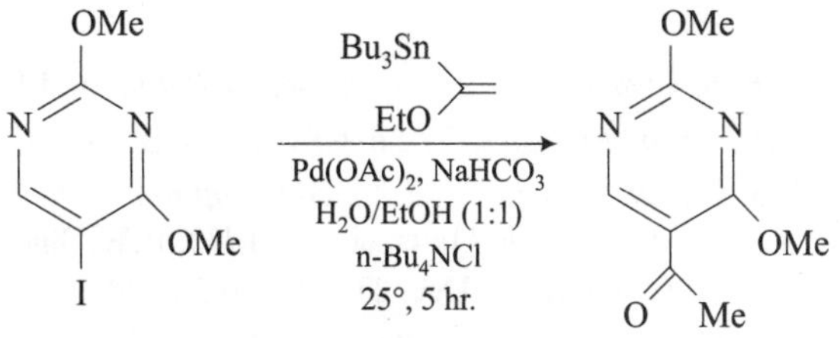

Scheme 194

$$\text{Ar Br} + \text{Ph}_2\text{SiF}_2 \xrightarrow[\substack{\text{DMF-H}_2\text{O, 120°} \\ \text{KF}}]{2 \text{ mol\% PdCl}_2} \text{Ar-Ph} + [\text{PhSiF}_3]$$

Scheme 195

2.1.20 Coupling of Indoles with 1, 4-benzoquinones in water

An efficient direct coupling of indole compounds with 1, 4-benzoquinones in water in the absence of any catalyst, organic. co solvents or additives gave[321] the corresponding products in excellent yield (Scheme 196).

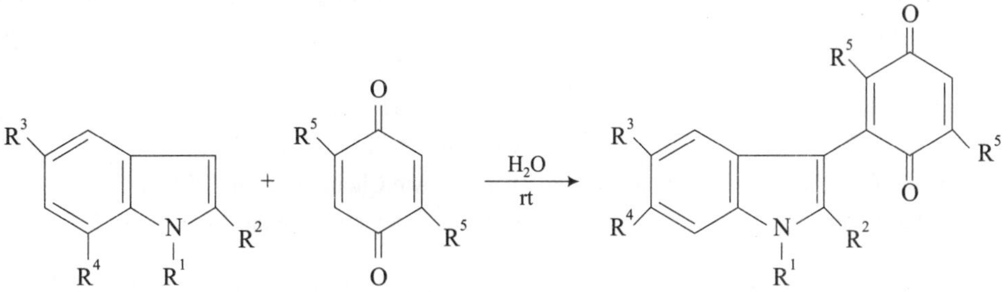

Scheme 196

3 CONCLUSION

Due to the environmental concerns caused by pollution of volatile organic solvents, attempts have been made to use alternative solvents which may be environmentally benin. Of the various solvents which can be used as alternative solvents, water is the best choice. The advantage of using water as a solvent is its cost, safety (it is non-inflammable and is devoid of any carcinogenic effect) and simple operation. Water is being recognised as a medium for promoting old and new reactions. In fact a large numbers of organic reactions, which have been conventially performed using volatile organic solvents can be performed in water. Most importantly, completely new reactiones have been discovered by using water as a solvent. A special advantage is that organic synthesis in water can significantly reduce the number of steps when designed properly. The use water as a medium for organic reactions will provide economical, health and environmental benefits.

According to C & EN news (Sept 3, 2007), *'When organics fail, try water'*

References

1. J.R. Dojilido and Y.A. *Best, Chemistry of Water and Water Pollution,* Ells Horwood, 1993.
2. *CRC Handbook of Chemistry and Physics,* 75 e.d. CRC Press, Boca Ration, 1994.
3. S.B. Brummer and A.B. Ganey, in *Water and Aqueous Solution: structure, Thermodynamics, and transport processes,* R.A. Horne ed. Wiley Interscience, 1972; R.W. Shaw, T.B. Brill, A.A. Clifford, C.A. Eckert and E.U. Frank, C. and E. N., Dec. 23. 1991, p.26.
4. J.L. Kavanau, *Water and Solute-water Interactions*, Holden-Day, San Francisco, 1964.
5. R. Breslow, Acc. Chem. Res. 1991, **24**, 159; P.A. Grieco, Aldrichim. Acta, 1991, **24**, 59.
6. O. Diels and K. Alder, Liebigs, Ann, 1931, **490**, 243, 1948, **70**, 1161.
7. H. Hopff and C.W. Rautenstrauch, U.S. patent, 2, 262, 002, chem. Abstr, 1942, **36**, 1046.
8. R. Breslow, U. Maitra and D. Rideout, Tetrahedron Lett, 1983, **24**, 1901; R. Breslow and U. Martra, Tetrahedron Lelt., 1984, **25**, 1239.
9. J.A. Berson, Z. Hamlet and W.A. Muller, J.Am.Chem.Soc, 1962, **84**, 297; A.A.Z. Samil, A. Desavignac, I. Rico and A. Lattes, Tetrahedron, 1985, **41**, 3683.
10. D.C. Rideout and R. Breslow, J.Am.Chem.Soc, 1980, **102**, 7816.
11. T.K. Hollis, N.P. Robinson and B. Bosnich, J.Am.Chem.Soc 1992, **114**, 5464.
12. S. Kobayashi, I. Hachiya, M. Araki and M. Ishilani, Tetrahedron Lett, 1993, **34**, 3755.
13. S. Otto, J.B.F.N. Engberis, Tetrahedron Lett, 1995, **36**, 2645.
14. S. Colonna, A. Manfredi and R. Annuziata, Tetrahedron Lett, 1988, **29**, 3347.
15. D. Boger and S. Weireb, Hetro-Diels-Alder Methodology in Organic synthesis, Academrc press, Orlando, 1987.
16. P.A. Grieco and S.D. Larsen, J.Am.Chem.Soc, 1985, **107**, 1768.
17. W. Oppolzer, Angew. Chem. Int. Ed. Engl, 1972, **11**, 1031.
18. P. Grieco, S.D. Larsen and W.F. Fobare, Tetrahedron Lett, 1986, **27**, 1975.
19. P. Grieco, D.T. Parker, W.F. Fobane and R. Ruckle, J.Am.Chem.Soc, 1987, **109**, 5859.
20. Chao-Jun Li and Tak-Hang Chan, Organic Reaclions in aqueous media, John, Wiliy & Sons and the reterences cited there in.
21. A.K. Saksena, V.M. Yirijavallabhan, Y.T. Chen, E. Joe, R.E. Pike, J.A. Desai, D. Rane and A.K. Ganguly, Heterocycles, 1993, **35**, 129.
22. D.R. Williams, K.D. Gastan and I.B. Horton, Tetrahedron Lelt, 1985, **26**, 1391.
23. G.A. Lee, Synthesis, 1982, 508.
24. C. Agami, F. Couty, M. Poursoulis and J. Vaissermann, Tetrahedren, 1992, **48**, 431.
25. For general revievs, see P.S. Bailey, Chem. Rev, 1958, **58**, 925; R. Criegee, Rec. Chem. Progr., 1957, **18**, 111.
26. V.K. Ahluwalia and M. Kidwai, *New Trends in Green Chemistry*, Anamaya Publishers, 2006, Page 113.
27. R.B. Woodward and R.B. Hoffmann, Angew. Chem. Int. Ed. Engl; 1969, **8**, 781.
28. P. Wipf, *Comprehensive Organic synthesis*; B.M. Trost, I. Felming and L.A. Paquelle Eds., Pergman Press, New York, 1991, Vols 5, P. 827; F.E. Zieglar, Chem. Rev., 1988, **88**, 1423; S.T. Rhoads and N.R. Raulins, Org. React., 1975, **22**, 1.
29. W.N. White and E. F. Wolfarth, J. Org. Chem, 1870, **35**, 2196, 3585.
30. A.A. Ponaras, J. Org. Chem, 1983, **48**, 3866; R.M. Coates, B.D. Rogers, S.J. Hobbs, D.R. Peck and D.P. Curran, J. Am. Chem. Soc., 1987, **109**, 1160; J.J. Gajewski, J. Jurayj; D.R. Kimbrough, M.E. Gande, B. Ganem and B.K. Carpenter, J. Am. Chem. Soc., 1987, **109**, 1170.

31. S.D. Copley and J. Knowles, J. Am. Chem. Soc., 1987, **109**, 5008.

32. E. Brandes, P.A. Grieco and J. J. Gajewski, J. Org. Chem. 1989, **54**, 515.

33. J.J. Gajewski, J. Jurayj, D.R. Kimbrough, M.E. Gande, B. Ganem and B.K. Carpenter, J. Am. Chem. Soc., 1987, **109**, 1170.

34. P.A. Grieco, F.B. Brandes, S. McCann and I.D. Clark, J. Org. Chem., 1989, **54**, 5849.

35. A. Lubineau, J. Auge, N. Bellanger and S. Caillebourdin, J. Chem. Soc. Perkin Trans I, 1992, **13**, 163.

36. G. Wittig, U. Schollkopf, Ber., 1954, **87**, 1318; G. Wittig and W. Hang, Ber., 1955, **88**, 1654; U. Schollkopf, Angew. Chem. 1959, **71**, 20; S. Trippet, Quart. Rev., 1963, **17**, 406.

37. C. Piechucki, Synthesis, 1976, 187.

38. M. Milolajczk, S. Grzejszezk, W. Midura and A. Zatoria, Synthesis, 1976, 397.

39. M. Schimtt, J.J. Bourguignon and C.G. Wermith, Tetrahedron Lett, 1990, **31**, 2145.

39a. A. El – Batta, C. Jiang, W. Zhao, R. Anness, A.L. Cooksy and M. Bergdahl, J. Org. Chem, 207, **72**, 5244.

40. A. Michael, J. Prak. Chem, 1887, **35(2)**, 349; E.D. Bergmann, D. Ginsburg and R. Pappo, Org. Reactions, 1959, **10**, 179.

41. Z.G. Hajos and D.R. Parrish, J. Org. Chem. 1974, **39**, 1612; U. Elder, G. Sauer and R. Wiechert, Angew. Chem. Int. Edn. Engl., 1971, **10**, 496.

42. N. Harada, T. Sugioka, U. Uda and T. Kurili, Synthesis, 1990, 53.

43. J.F. Lavelle and P. Deslongchamps, Tetrahedron Lett, 1988, **29**, 6033.

44. A. Lubineau and J. Auge, Tetrahedrm Lett, 1992, **33**, 8073.

45. R. Ballini, synthesis, 1993, 687.

46. K. Sussang Karn, G. Fodor, I. Karle and C. George, Tetrahedron, 1988, **44**, 7047.

47. M. Makosza, Tetrahedron Lett., 1966, 5489.

48. F. Toda, H. Takumi, M. Nagami and K. Tanaka, Heterocycles, 1988, **47**, 469.

49. H. Sakuraba, Y. Tanaka and F. Toda, J. Incl. Phenom, 1991, **11**, 195.

50. A.T. Neilsen and W.J. Houliban, Org. Reactions, 1968, 16, 1; W. Foerst, Ed., Newer methods of preparative Organic chemistry, 1971, **6**, 48.

51. T. Mukaiyama, K. Narasaka and K. Banno, Chem. Lett, 1973, 1011; T. Mukaiyama, K. Banno and N. Narasaka J. Am. Chem. Soc. 1974, **96**, 7503; T. Mukaiyama, Org. React.; 1982, **28**, 203.

52. K. Banno and T. Mukaiyama, Chem. Lett., 1976, 279.

53. A. Lubineau, J. Org. Chem., 1986, **51**, 2142; A. Lubineau, E. Meyer, Tetrahedron, 1988, **44**, 6065.

54. S. Kobayashi and I. Hachiya, J. Org. Chem. 1994, **59**, 3590; For a review on lanthanides catalysed organic reactions in aqueous media see Kobayashi, Synlett, 1994, 589.

55. P.T. Baurona, K.G. Rosauer and L. Dai, Tetrahedron Lett; 1995, **26**, 4009.

56. T. B. Ayed and H. Amri, Synth. Commun. 1995, **25**, 3813.

57. S. Kobayashi, Chem. Lett; 1991, 2187.

58. S. Kobayashi and I. Hachiya, Tetrahedron Lett; 1992, 1625.

59. S. Kobayaski, Water stable rare earth Lewis-acid catalysis in aqueous and organic solvents in Organic synthesis in water, Paul A. Grieco, Ed, Blackie Academic and Professional 1998, Past 262-302.

60. F. Fringuelli, G. Pani, O. Piematti and F. Pizzo, Tetrahedron, 1994, **50**, 1149.

61. F. Knoevenagel, Ber, 1898, **31**, 2596.

62. A.R. Johnson, Org. Reactions, 1942, **1**, 210.

63. O. Doebner, Ber. 1900, **33**, 2140.

64. Y. Nakono, S. Nik, S. Kinouchi, H. Miyamae and M. Igarashi, Bull. Chem. Soc. Japan, 1992, **65**, 2934.

65. A. Auge, M. Lubin and A. Lubineau, Tetrahedran Lett; 1994, **35**, 7947.

66. Grinder, Ann. Chem. Phys; 1982, **26**, 369.

67. J.B. Conant and H.B. Cutter, J. Am. Chem. Soc., 1926, **48**, 1016.

68. P. Karrer, Y, Yen and A. Reichstein, Helv. Chem. Acta, 1993, 13, 308.

69. A. Clerici and O. Porta, Tetrahedron Lett. 1982, **23**, 3517.

70. A. Clerici and O. Porta, J. Org. Chem. 1982, **47**, 2852; A. Clarici, O. Porta and M. Riva, Tetrahedron Lett, 1981, **22**, 1043.

71. A. Clarici and O. Porta, J. Org. Chem., 1983, **48**, 1690; Tetrahedron, 1983, **39**, 1239; A. Clerici, O. Porta and P. Zaga, Tetrahedron, 1986, **42**, 561; A. Clerici and O. Porta, J. Org. Chem., 1989, **54**, 3872.

72. P. Deliar and J.L. Luchl, J. Chem. Soc. Chem. Commun., 1989, 398.

73. K. Kalyanam and V.G. Rao, Tetrahedron Lett., 1993, **34**, 1647.

74. A.J. Lapworth, J. Chem. Soc., 1903, **83**, 995; 1904, **85**, 1206; J. S. Buck, Organic Reactions, 1948, **IV**, 269.

75. J. Solodar, Tetrahedron Lett, 1971, 287.

76. W. Tagaki and H. Hara, J. Chem. Soc. Chem. Commun., 1973, 891.

77. H. Stetter and G. Dambkes, Synthesis, 1977, 403.

78. E.T. Kool and R. Breslow, J. Am. Chem. Soc. 1988, **110**, 1596.

79. L. Claisen and A. Claparede, Ber, 1981, **14**, 2460; J.G. Schmidt, Ber., 1881, **14**, 1459.

80. T. Mukaiyama, K. Banno and K. Narasaka, J. Am. Chem. Soc., 1974, **96**, 7503; T. Mukaiyama, Chem. Lett.; 1982, 353; J. Am. Chem. Soc., 1973, **95**, 967; Chem. Lett., 1986, 187; K. Banno and T. Mukaiyama, Chem. Lett., 1976, 279; Organic reactions, 1982, **82**, 187.

81. A. Lubineau, J. Org. Chem, 1986, **51**, 2142; A. Lubineau and E. Meyer, Tetrahedron, 1988, **44**, 6065.

82. F. Fringueli, G. Pani, O. Piemattic and F. Pizzo, Life Chem. Rep., 1995, **13**, 133.

83. T. Jeffery, Chem. Commun, 1984, 1287.

84. N.A. Bumagin, P.G. More and I.P. Beletskaya, J. Organometallic Chem. 1989, 371, 397.

85. N.A. Bumagin, N.P. Andryukhova and I.P. Beletskaya, Dolk. Akad. Nauk, SSSR, 1900, **313**, 107.

86. N.A. Bumagin, L.I. Sakhomlinova, A.N. Vanchikov, T.P. Tolstaya and I.P. Beletskaya, Bull Russ. Acad. Sci. Div. Chem. Sci., 1992, **41**, 2130 N.N. Demik, M.M. Rabachnik, M.M. Novikova and I.P. Beletskaya, Zh. Org. Khim, 1995, **31**, 64; T. Jeffery, Tetrahedron Lett., 1994, **35**, 3051; S. Lemaine – Audoire, M. Savignac, C. Dupuis and J.P. Genet, Tetrahedon Lett, 1996, **37**, 3003; J. Diminnie, S. Metts and E.J. Parson, Organometallics, 1995, **14**, 4023; P. Reardon, S. Metts, C. Crittendon, P. Daugherity and E.J. Parsons, Organometallics, 1995, **14**, 3810.

87. A. Strecker, Ann; 1850, **75**, 27; 1954, **91**, 345; D.T. Moury, Chem. Rev; 1948, **42**, 236.

88. D.T. Moury, Chem. Rev. 1948, **42**, 189.

89. K. Weinges, Chem. Ber., 1971, **104**, 3594.

90. T. Paul Anastas and John C. Warner, Green Chemistry Theory and Practice, Oxford University Press, 1998, pp. 98-99.

91. A. Wurtz, Ann. Chem. Phys., 1855, **44(3)**, 275; Ann, 1855, **96**, 364; R.E. Buntrock, Chem. Rev., 1968, **68**, 209.

92. C.J. Li and T.H. Chan, Organometallics, 1991, **10**, 2548.

93. M. Hudlicky, *Oxidations in Organic Chemistry*, ACS Monograph 186, American Chemical Society, Washington DC, 1990. V.K. Ahluwalia and R.K. Parashar, *Organic Reaction Mechanisms*, Narosa Publishing House-New Delhi, 2002, PP 137-219.

94. A.I. Vogel, *Textbook of Practical Organic Chemistry Including Qualitative Analysis*, Longmans, London, 1988.

95. F. Fringuelli, R. Germani, F. Pizzo and G. Savelli, Tetrahedron Lett. 1989, **30**, 1427.

96. A.S. Kende, P. Delair, B.E. Blass, Tetrahedron Lett. 1994, 44, 8123.

97. K.S. Kirshenbaum and K.B. Sharpless, J. Org. Chem; 1985, 50, 1979.

98. B. Meunier, Chem. Rev; 1992, **92**, 1414.

99. B. Notari, stud. Surf. Sci, Catal, 1991, **67**, 243; R.A. Sheldon, J. Mol. Catal; 1980, **7**, 107.

100. K. Otsuka, M. Yoshinaka and I. Yamanaka, J. Chem. Soc. Chem. Commun; 1993, 611.

101. G. Bertic in topics in sterochemistry, N.L. Allinger and E.L. Eliel, Eds, Vol. 7, p. 97, John Wiley, 1967.

102. E. Fringuelli, R. Germani, F. Pizzo, F. Santinelli and G. Savelli, J. Org. Chem; 1992, **57**, 1198; F. Fringuelli, F. Pizzo and K. Germani, Synlelt, 1991, 475.

103. K.B. Sharpless and R.C. Michaelson, J. Am. Chem. Soc., 1923, **95**, 6136; B.E. Rossiter, T.R. Verhoeven and K.B. Sharpless, Tet. Lett, 1997, 4733.

104. M. Hudlicky, Oxidation in Organic Chemistry, ACS Monograph 186, American Chemical society, Washington DC, 1990.

105. J. Muzart, Synthesis, 1995, 1325; K.L. Reed, J.T. Gupton and T.L. Solarz, Synth, Commun., 1989, 19, 3579.

106. G. Beri, *Topics in stereochemistry*, N.L. Allinger, E.L. Eliel, Eds, Vol 7, p – 93, John Wiley, 1967.

107. G.B. Payne and P.H. Williams, J. Org. Chem., 1959, **24**, 54.

108. K. Kirshenbaum and K.B. Sharpless, J. Org. Chem., 1985, **50**, 1979.

109. R. Curci, M. Fiarentino, L. Troisi, J. O. Edwards and R. H. Pater, J. Org. Chem., 1986, **51**, 1925.

110. T.C. Zheng and D.E. Richandson, Tetrahedron Lett., 1991, 56, 1253.

111. F. Toda, H. Takumi, M. Nagami and K. Tanaka, Hetrocycles, 1998, 47, 469.

112. K.A. Hofmann, Ber; 1912, **45**, 3329; P. Grieco, Y. Ohfume, Y. Yokoyama and W.J. Owens, J. Am. Chem. Soc., 1979, 101, 4749.

113. N.A. Milas and S. Sussman, J. Am. Chem. Soc., 1936, **58**, 1302; R. Daniels and J. L. Fischer, J. Org. Chem. 1963, 28, 320.

114. M. Mugdan and D. P. Young, J. Chem. Soc., 1949, 2988.

115. K.B. Sharpless and K. Akashi, J. Am. Chem. Soc., 1976, 98, 1986.

116. M. Mimato, K. Yamamoto and J. Tsuji, J. Org. Chem; 1900, **55**, 766.

117. W.B. Webber and J.P. Shephard, Tetrahedron Lett. 1972, 4907.

118. M. Mugdan and D.P. Young, J. Chem. Soc. 1949, 2988.

119. H. Abedel-Rahman, J.P. Adams, A.L. Boyes, M.J. Kelly, D.P. Mansfield, P.A. Procupiou, S.M. Roberts, D.H. Slee, P.J. Sidebottom, V. Silk and N.S. Watson, J. Chem. Soc. Commun, 1993, 1841.

120. F. Fringuelli, F. Germani, F. Pizzo and G. Savelli, Synth. Commun., 1989, **19**, 1939.

121. R.G. Mathys, A. Schmid and B. Witholt, Biotechnol, Biology; 1999, **64**, 459.

122. R.G. Mathys, O.M. Kuts and B. Witholt, J. Chem. Tech. Bioeng; 1998, **71**, 315.

123. M.A. Olgioruso and J.F. Wolfe, *Synthesis of Carboxylic Acids and their Derivatives*, S. Patai and Z. Rappoporol Eds, Wiley, New York, 1991.

124. R.H. Dodd and M. LeHyaric, Synthesis, 1993, 295.

125. F. Fringuelli, R. Pellegrino, O. Piermatti and F. Pizzo, Synth. Commun; 1994, **24**, 2665.

126. H.D. Dakin, OS, 1941, **1**, 149; J.E. Lettler, Chem. Rev; 1949, **45**, 385; H.D. Dakin, J. Am. Chem. Soc; 1909, **42**, 477.

127. G.W. Kabalka, N.K. Reddy and C. Narayana, Tetrahedron Lett., 1992, **33**, 865.

128. A.V. Baeyer and V. Villiger, Ber; 1899, **32**, 3625.

129. F. Fringuelli, R. Germani, F. Pizzo and G. Savelli, Gazz. Chem. Ital, 1989, **119**, 249.

130. A.E. Thomas and F. Ray, Tetrahedron, 1992, **48**, 1927.

131. K. Tanaka and F. Toda, Chem. Rev. 2000, **100**, 1028-29.

132. N. Karnblum and W.J. Jones, Org. Synthesis, 1963, **43**, 187.

133. K.S. Webb and V. Seneviratrie, Tetrahedron Lett. 1995, **36**, 2377.

134. A. Albini and S. Pietra, Hetrocyclic N – Oxides, CRC Press, Boca Raton, Fl. 1991; A. Albini, Synthesis, 1993, 263.

135. G.D. Robke and E. Behrman, J. Chem. Res.(S), 1993, 412.

136. A. Sakurai and M. Midorikawa, Bull. Chem. Soc. Japan, 1968, **41**, 430.

137. R. Balicki and L. Kaczmarek, Synth. Commun., 1993, **23**, 3149.

138. H. Heaney, Aldrichim. Acta, 1993, **26**, 35.

139. A. Mckillop and D. Kemp, Tetrahedron, 1989, **45**, 3299.

140. G.W. Kabalka, S.M. Deshpande, P.P. Wadgankar and N. Chatla, Synth, Commun., 1990, 20, 1445.

141. K.L. Reed, J.T. Gupton and T.L. Solarz, Synth. Commun., 1990, 20, 563.

142. B. Baudoin, Y. Ribeill and N. Vicker, Synth. Commun., 1993, **23**, 2833.

143. F. Fringuelli, R. Pellogrino, O. Piematti and F. Pizzo, Synth. Commun., 1994, **24**, 2665.

144. K.S. Webb, Tetrahedron Lett., 1994, 35, 3457.

145. T.C. Zheng and P.E. Richardson, Tetrahedron Lett., 1995, **36**, 833.

146. A. Mckillop and J.A. Tarbin, Tetrahedron; 1987, **43**, 1753.

147. F. Fringuelli, R. Pellegino and F. Pizzo, Synth. Commun., 1993, **23**, 3157.

148. F. Fringuelli, R. Pellegrino, O. Piermattic and F. Pizzo, Synth. Commun. 1994, **24**, 2665.

149. G.A. Lee and H.H. Freedman, Tetrahedron Lett., 1976, 3985.

150. K. Dimroth and W. Tuncher, Synthesis, 1977, 339.

151. Michael B. Smith, Organic Synthesis, Mc-Graw Hill, New York, 1994, PP. 343-484; V.K. Ahluwalia and R.K. Parashar, Organic Reaction Mechanism, Narosa Publishing House, New Delhi, 2002, PP 221-263 and the references cited there in.

152. K. Kalack and F. Monteil, Adv. Organomet. Chem., 1992, **134**, 219.

153. K. Wan and M.E. Davis, *Tetrahedron Asymmetry*, 1993, 4, 2461; K. Wan and M.L. Davis, J. Chem. Soc. Chem. Commun., 1993, 1262.

154. C. Petrier and J.L. Luche, *Tetrahedron Lett.*, 1987, **28**, 1234.

155. C. Petrier and J.L. Luche, Tetrahedron Lett., 1987, **28**, 2351.

156. R.E. Harman, S.K. Gupta and D.J. Brown, Chem. Rev., 1973, **73**, 21.

157. T. Okano, M. Kaji, S. Isotani and J. Kiji, Tetrahedron Lett; 1992, **33**, 5547; The Application and Chemistry of Catalyst by Soluble Transition Metal Complex, Wiley, London, 1980.

158. G.A. Molander, Chem. Rev. 1992, **92**, 26; J.A. Soderquist, Aldrichim Acta, 1991, **24**, 15.

159. G. Papadogianakas, Specialist Periodical Reports Catalysts, J.J. Spivey(Ed). The Royal Society Of Chemistry, 1997, Vol 13, PP. 114-193.

160. C. Larpent and G. Meignan, *Tetrehedron Lett.*, 1993, **34**, 4331.

161. V.K. Ahluwalia and R.K. Parashar, *Organic Reaction Mechanism*, Narosa Publishing House, New Delhi, 2002, PP. 221-263.

162. D. Mitchell, C.W. Doecke, L.A. Hay, T.M. Koening and D.D. Wirth, Tetrahedron Lett., 1995, **36**, 5335.

163. G. Lamaty, M.H. Reviere and J.P. Roque Bull, Soc. Chem. Fr, 1983, 33.

164. B. Boyer, J.F. Betzer, G. Lamaty, A. Leydet and J.P. Roque, New J. Chem; 1995, **19**, 807.

165. C. Denis, B. Laignel, D. Plusquellec, J.Y. Le Marouille and A. Botrel, *Tetrahedron Lett.*, 1996, **37**, 53.

166. F. Toda, R. Kiyoshige and M. Yagi, Angew. Chem. Int. Ed. Engl, 1989, **28**, 320.

167. M.J. Burk, T.G.P. Harper and C.S. Kalberg, J. Am. Chem. Soc., 1995, **117**, 4423.

168. T. Tsukinok, K. Ishimoto, H – Tsuzuki, S. Mataka and M. Tashiro, Bull. Chem. Soc., Japan, 1993, **66**, 3419.

169. M. Mordolol, *Tetrahedron Lett.*, 1993, **34**, 1681.

170. A.K. Singh, R.K. Bakshi and E.J. Corey, J. Am. Chem. Soc., 1987, **109**, 6187; E. Hasegawa and D.P. Curran, J. Org. Chem; 1993, **58**, 5008.

171. A.P. Krapcho and D.A. Seidman, Tetrahedron, Lett., 1981, **22**, 179.

172. V. Stagopan and S.B. Chandalia, Synth. Commun., 1989, **19**, 1217.

173. C. Petrier and J. L. Luck, Tetrahedron Lett., 1987, 33, 5417; R. N. Baruah, Tetrahedron Lett., 1992, **33**, 5417.

174. C. Petrier, I.L. Lavaitte and C. Morat, J. Org. Chem; 1989, **54**, 5313.

175. C. Hasegawa and D.P. Curran, J. Org. Chem; 1993, **58**, 5008.

176. F. Fache, S. Lehueds and M. Lemaine, Tetrahedron Lett., 1995, **36**, 885.

177. Y. Kamochi and T. Kudo, Chem. Pharm, Bull; 1995, **43**, 1422.

178. S. Hanessian and C. Girard, Synlett., 1994, 861.

179. S.K. Chug and Q.Y. Hu. Synth. Commun; 1982, **12**, 261.

180. C.J. Rizzo, N.K. Dunlap and A.B. Smith, J. Org. Chem., 1987, **52**, 5280.

181. C.E. Castro and W.C. Kray, Jr, J. Am. Chem. Soc., 1963, **85**, 2768

182. A. Ono, E. Fujimoto and M. Ueno, Synthesis, 1986, 570.

183. D.V. Davydov and I.P. Belotskaya, Russ. Chem. Bull., 1993, **42**, 572.

184. J. Light and R. Breslow, Tetrahedron Lett., 1990, 31, 2957; J. Light and R. Breslow, Org. Synth; 1993, **72**, 199.

185. A. Clerici and O. Porta, Tetrahedron, 1982, **38**, 1293.

186. N. Petragnani and J.V. Comasseto, Synthesis, 1986, 1.

187. S.K. Boyer, J. Bach, J. Mc Kenna and E. Jagdmann, Jr, J. Org. Chem., 1985, **50**, 3409.

188. J. Bressner, M. Julia, M. Launay and J. P. Stacino., Tetrahedron Lett., 1982, **23**, 3265.

189. A. Schonberg and M. Z. Barakat, J. Chem. Soc., 1989, 892; L. E. Overman and E. M. O'Connor, J. Am. Chem. Soc., 1976, **98**, 771.

190. R.E. Michel, Recovery of methyl esters of aromatic acids and glycols from thermoplastic polyster scrap using methanol vapour, Eur. Patent, 484, 963, May 13, 1992; R.R. Hepner, R.E. Michel, Process for separation of Glycerols from Dimethyl Terphthalate, U.S. Patent, 5, 391, 263, Feb 21, 1995; R E. Michel, Recovery of Demethyl Terphthalate from polymer waste, U.S. Patent 5, 504, 122, April 2, 1996.

191. K.W. Hater, Environmental Compatible scale Industry, Corrosion, 1998, 213.

192. K.C. Low, A.P. Wheeler and L.P. Koskan, Advances in Chemical Series 248; American Chemical Society, Washington DC, 1996.

193. K.K. Komiya, S. Kuluoka, M. Aminaka, K. Hasegawa, H. Hachiya, H. Okamoto, T. Watanabe, H. Yoneda, I. Fukawa and T. Dozone, 'New Process for producing polycarbonate without phosphene and methylene chloride', In Green Chemistry Designating Chemistry for the environment, P.T. Anastas and T. C. Williamson, Eds, American Chemical Society symposium series No. 626 (ed) American Chemical Society, 1996, PP 1-7.

194. R.F. Rhinehard and H.P. Smith, Polym. Lett., 1965, **3**, 1049.

195. B.M. Norak and R.H. Grubbs, J. Am. Chem. Soc. 1988, **110**, 7542.

196. S.B.T. Nguyen, L.K. Johnson, R.H. Grubbs and J.W.A. Ziller, J. Am. Chem. Soc., 1992, **114**, 3974.

197. S.T. Nguyen and R.H. Grubbs, J. Am. Chem. Soc; 1993, **115**, 9858; C. Fraser and R.H. Grubbs, Macromolecules; 1995, **28**, 7248.

198. P. Bernhard, H. Lehmann and A. Ludi; J. Chem. Soc. Chem. Commun., 1981, 1216; P. Bernhard, M. Biner and A. Ludi, Polyhedron, 1990, **9**, 1095.

199. S. Wache, J. Organometallic Chem. 1995, **494**, 235.

200. T.I. Wallow and B.M. Novak, J. Am. Chem. Soc., 1991, **113**, 7411.

201. C.J. Li, D. Wang and W.T. Slaven, Tetrahedron Lett., 1996, **37**, 4459.

202. E. Paterno and G. Chieffi, Gazz. Chem. Ital, 1909, **39**, 341; G. Buck, C.G. Inman and E.S. Lipinsky, J. Am. Chem. Soc., 1954, **76**, 4327; G.C. Lang, Tetrahedron Lett., 1971, **12**, 712.

203. D. Bellus et al, Chem. Rev. 1967, 599; J.C. Anderson and C.B. Reese, Proc. Chem. Soc; 1960, 217.

204. A.G. Griesbeck, K. Kramer and M. Oelgemöller, Green Chem., 1999, **1**, 205.

205. For a review of Organic Photochemistry in organic solvents as well as in aqueous solvent see R. Ramamurthy, Tetrahedron Lett., 1986, **42**, 5753.

206. M.S. Sayamala and V. Ramamurthy, J. Org. Chem. 1986, **51**, 3712.

207. Y. Ito, T. Karita, K. Kunimoto and T. Matsuura, J. Org. Chem., 1989, **54**, 587.

208. T. Tamaki, Chem, Lett., 1984, 53; T. Tamaki and T. Kokuba, Inclusim Phenom., 1984, **2**, 815.

209. K. Nakatani, J. Shiral, R. Tamaki and I. Saito, Tetrahedron Lett., 1995, **36**, 5363.

210. J.H. Liu and R.G. Weiss, J. Org. Chem; 1985, **50**, 3655.

211. H. Tateba and S. Mihara. Agric. Biol, chem; 1991, **55**, 873.

212. P.G. Tratnyek and J.J. Hoigne, Photochem. Phtobiol A. Chem., 1994, **84**, 153 and the references cited therein.

213. V. Ramamurthy, Ed. Photochemistry of organized and constraint media, VCH, Weinheimn, German; 1991; CRC Handbook of organic photochemistry and photobiology, W.H. Horspool, Ed., CRC Press, Boca Ratan, Fl, 1995.

214. Y. Ito, B. Borecka, J. Trotter and J.R. Scheffer, Tetrahedron Lett., 1995, **36**, 6083; Y. Ito, B. Borecka, G. Olovsson, J. Trotter and J.R. Scheffer, Tetrahedron Lett., 1995, **36**, 6087; Y. Ito, B. Olovasson, J. Chem. Soc, Perkin Trans I, 1997, 127.

215. K.S. Feldmann and R.F. Compbell, J. Org. Chem., 1995, **60**, 1924.

216. R. Ganaguru, K. Ramsubbu, K. Venkatesan and V. Ramamurty, J. Org. Chem., 1985, **50**, 2337; J.N. Moorty, K. Venkatesan and R.G. Weiss, J. Org. Chem., 1992, **57**, 3292; K. Venkatisan, T.N. Guru Row and K.J. Venkatasan, J. Chem. Soc. Perkin Trans 2, 1996, 1475; K. Vishnumurthy, T. N. Guru Row and K.J. Venkatesan, J. Chem. Soc., Perkin Trans 2, 1997, 615.

217. Y. Ito, T. Matsuura, K. Tabata and M. Ji – Ben, Tetrahedron Lett., 1987, **43**, 1307.

218. K. Tanaka and F. Toda, Chem. Rev. 2000, 100, 1044-1066.

219. P.M. Bersier, L. Carlsson and J. Bersier, in Topics in Chemistry, J.D. Bunitz, S. Hafter, J.M. Ito, J.M. Lehn, K.N. Raymond, C.W. Rees and J.T.F., eds, Springer –Verlag, 1994, **Vol. 70.**

220. D.E. Danly and C.J.H. King, in Organic Electrchemistry, 3rd ed, H. Lund and M. M. Baizer, eds, Marcel Dekker, New York, 1991; M.M. Baizer and D.E. Danly, Chemtech, 1980, **10(3)**, 161.

221. W.C. Drinkard and R.V. lindsay, U.S. Patent 3, 496, 215 (1970) to DuPont.

222. Tropchiev, Pavlov, Chem. Abstr, 1953, **47**, 8002h; Domingue et al, J. Chem. Ed, 1952, **29**, 446.

223. T. Isoya, R. Kakuta and C. Kawamura, U.S. Patent 3, 896, 611 (1975) – Asahi Kasu.

224. R.L. Taylor, Chem. Met. Eng., 1973, 44, 588.

225. H. Nohe, Chem. Ing. Tech, 1974, 46, 594.

226. T.T. Sugano, B.A. Schenber, J.A. Walburg and N. Shuster, U.S. Patent 3, 992, 269 (1976) to Diamond Snamrock Corpn.

227. D. Degner, in Techniques of Electroorganic Synthesis, Part III, J. N. Walburg and B.V. Tilak, eds, Wiley, New York, 1982.

228. M. Taniquchi, in Recent Advances in Electroorganic Synthesis, S. Tori, ed. Elsevier, Amsterdam, 1987.

229. J. Yoshida, J. Hashmoto and N. Kawabata, J. Org. Chem., 1982, **47**, 3575.

230. J. Tsuji and M. Minato. Tetrahedron Lett, 1987, **28**, 3683.

231. M. Kulka, J. Am. Chem. Soc., 1946, **68**, 2472.

232. J. Kaulen and H.J. Schafer, Synthesis, 1979, 513.

233. T. Shono, Y. Matsumura, J. Hayashi and M. Mizoguchi, Tetrahedron Lell, 1979, 165.

234. H. Ruholi and H.J. Schafer, Synthesis, 1988, 54.

235. F. Fichier and F. Ackermann, Helv. Chim. Acta, 1919, **2**, 583.

236. F.L.M. Pattison, J.B. Stothers and A.G. Woolford, J. Am. Chem. Soc., 1956, **78**, 2255.

237. D.V. McGrath and R.H. Grubbs, Organometallic, 1994, **13**, 224.

238. C.J. Li, D. Wang and D.L. Chem. J. Am. Chem. Soc., 1995, 117, 12867.

239. For a review, see M.M.T. Khan, Platinum Metals Rev, 1991, **35(2)**, 70.

240. D.J. Colquhoun, H.M. Thomson and M.V. Twigg. Carbonylation: Direct Synthesis of Carbonyl Compounds, Plenum Press, New York, 1991.

241. H. Alper, J. Orgnometallic Chem., 1986, **300**, 1.

242. V.V. Grushin and H. Alper, J. Org. Chem. 1993, **58**, 4794.

243. R.F. Heck, Palladium Reagents in Organic Synthesis, Academic Press, London, 1985.

244. H. Alper, J. Organomet. Chem., 1986, **300**, 1 and the references cited therein.

245. F. Joo and H. Alper, Organometallics, 1985, **4**, 1775.

246. N.A. Bumagin, K.V. Nikitin and I.P. Beletskaya, J. Organomet Chem. 1988, **358**, 563.

247. T. Okano, T. Hayashi and J. Kiji, J. Bull. Chem. Soc. Japan, 1994, **67**, 2339.

248. H. Urata, O. Kosukegawa, Y. Tshil, H. Yugari and T. Fuchikami, Tetrahedron Lett. 1989, **30**, 4403.

249. T. Joh. K. Doyama, K. Onituska, T. Shichara and S. Takahashi, Organometallic, 1991, **10**, 2493; T. Joh, H. Nagata and S. Takahashi, Chem. Lett, 1992, 1305.

250. H. Alper, H. Arzoumanian, J. F. Petrignani and M. Saldana Maldonado, J. Chem. Soc. Chem. Commun., 1985, 340.

251. M. Lin and A. Sen, J. Am. Chem. Soc., 1992, **114**, 7307; Nature, 194, **368**, 613.

252. H. Alper, J.A. Currie, H.J. des Abbayes, J. Chem. Soc. Chem. Commun., 1978, 311; V. Galamb, M. Gopal and H. Alper, J. Chem. Soc. Chem. Commun., 1983, 1154.

253. G. Papadogianakis, L. Maat and R.A. Sheldon, J. Chem. Technol, Biotechnol, 1997, 70, 83.

254. B. Cornits, Hydroformylation, Oxo Synthesis, Roelen Reaction: New Sythesis with carbon monoxide, Spinger-Verlag, Berlin, 1980.

255. B. Cornits and E.G. Kuntz, J. Orgometallic Chem; 1995, **502**, 177.

256. E. Kuntz, U.S. Patent 4, 248, 802, Rhone – Pouline Ind., 1981; Chem. Abstr., 1977, **87**, 101944n; J. Jenck, Fr.Patent 2,478,078 to Rhone – Poulence Industries (03-12-1980); E. Kuntz, Fr. Patent 2,349,562 to Rhono – Poulence Industries (04-24-1976).

257. W.A. Hermann, C.W. Kohlpainter, R.B. Manetsberger and H.Bahrmann (Hoechst AG), DE – B 4220,267A, 1992.

258. J.P. Archancet, M.E. Davis, J.S. Merola, B.E. Hansan, Nature, 1989, **339**, 454; J. Haggin, Chem. Eng. News, 1992, **70(17)**, 40.

259. G. Frenny, Y. Castanet, R. Grzybek, E. Monflier, A. Mortreux, A.M. Trzeciak and J.J. Ziolkowski, J. Organomet. Chem., 1995, 505, 11.

260. I.P. Beletskaya and C.V. Cheprakov, Aqueous transition-metal catalysis, in organic synthesis in water, Paul A. Grieco, ed, Blackie Academic and Professional, 1998, PP. 196-205.

261. Y. Shigemasa, K. Yokoyama, H. Sashiwa and H. Saimoto, Tetrahedron Lett, 1994, **35**, 1263.

262. U. Weiss and J.M. Edwards, Tetrahedron Lett., 1968, 4885.

263. C. Mannich and W. Krosche, Arch. Pharm., 1912, **250**, 647; F.E. Blike, Org. Reactions, 1942, **1**, 303.

264. I. Ojima, S – I. Inaba and K. Yoshida, Tetrahedron Lell, 1977, 3643.

265. S. Kobayashi and H. Ishitani, J. Chem. Soc. Chem. Commun. 1995, 1379.

266. S. Kobayashi, M. Araki and M. Yasuda, Tetrahedron Lett., 1995, **36**, 5773.

267. R.M. Iaini and E.J. CrawFord, J. Mol. Catal., 1988, **44**, 357.

268. S. Tollari, M. Fedele, E. Bettethine and S. Cenimi, J. Mol. Catal. A. Chem., 1996, **111**, 37.

269. D.M. Roundhill and S. Ganguly, Organometallics, 1993, **12**, 4825; E. Monflier, P. Bourdauducq, J.L. Courturier, J. Kervennel and A. Mortreux, Appl. Catal. A – Gen., 1995, **131**, 167.

270. E.J. Corey and X.M. Cheng, The logic of Chemical Synthesis, John Willy & Sons, New York, 1989

271. C.J. Li, Chem. Rev., 2005, 3095 and the refrences cited therein.

272. M. lin and A. Sen. Nature, 1994, 368, 613; G.V. Nizova, G.B. Shulpin, G.V. Suss – Fink and S. Stanislas, Chem. Commun., 1998, 1885; M. Asadullah, Y. Taniguchi, T. Kitamura and Y. Fujiwara, Appl. organomet. Chem. 1998, 12, 277.

273. Z.P. Li, and C. Li, J. Am Chem. Soc. 2004, **126**, 1181; Z. P. Li and C. Li, Org, Lett., 2004, **6**, 4997. For a review, see, S. Doye – Angew. Chem. Int. Ed. 2001, **40**, 3351.

274. U.H. Brinker, R. Buchkremer, M. Kolodzierjczyk, R. Kupler, M. Rosenberg, M.D. Poliks, M. Orlando and M.L. Gross, Angew. Chem. Int. Ed. Engl. 1993, **32**, 1344; S.A. Keibaugh, Biochemistry, 1983, **22**, 5063.

275. For a review, see, V. B. Kazansky, Catal. Today, 202, **73**, 127.

276. H.J. Prins, Chem. Weekbl; 1919, **16**, 1072. For a review see D.R. Adams and S.P. Bhatnagar, Synthesis, 1977, 661.

277. P.R. Stapp, J. Org. Chem., 1970, **35**, 2419.

278. C.C.K. Keh, V.V. Namboodri, R.S. Varma and C.J. Li, Tetrahedron Lett., 2002, **43**, 4993.

279. C.C.K. Keh and C.J. Li, Green Chem., 2003, **5**, 80.

280. C. Agami, F. Couty, M. Poursoulis and J. Vaissermann, Tetrahedron, 1992, **48**, 431.

281. H. Yorimitsu, K. Wakabayashi, H. Shinokubo and K. Oshima, Tetrahedron Lett; 1999, **40**, 519.

282. S. Iwasa, F. Takezawa, Y. Tuchiya and H. Nishiyama, Chem. Commun., 2001, 59; R.P. Wurtz and A.B. Charette, Org. Lett., 2002, **4**, 4531.

283. B.M. Trost, A.F. Indolese, T.J.J. Mullar and B. Treptow, J. Am. Chem. Soc. 1995, **117**, 615.

284. C. Amatore, E. Blart, J.P. Genet, A. Jutand, S. Lemaire-Andoire and M. Savignac, J. Org. Chem., 1995, **60**, 6829.

285. B.M. Trost, C. Chan and G. Ruhter, J. Am. Chem. Soc., 1987, **109**, 3486.

286. M. Pal, V. Subramanian and K.R. Yeleswarapu, Tetrahedron Lett; 2003, **44**, 8221; Y. Uozumi and Y. Kobayasi, Hetrocycles, 2003, **59**, 71; B. Liang, M. Dai, J. Chen. and Z. Yang, Org. Chem; 2005, **70**, 391.

287. C.J. Li, D.L. Chen and C.W. Costello. Org. Res. Process Dev; 1997, **I**, 315.

288. L. Chen and C.J. Li. Org. Lett., 2004, **6**, 3151.

289. C. M. Wci and C.J. Li, Green chem, 2002, **4**, 39.

290. C.J. Li and C.M. Wei, Chem. Commun., 2002, 268.

291. L. Chen and C.J. Li, Tetrahedron Lett., 204, **45**, 2771.

292. M. Tokumaga and Y, Wakatsuki, Angew. Chem. Int. Edn. 1998, **37**, 2867.

293. E. Mizushima, K. Sato, T. Hayashi and M. Tanka. Angew. Chem. Int. Ed; 2002, **41**, 4563.

294. D. Zargarian and H, Alper, Organometallics, 1993, **12**, 712.

295. R. Gabriele, G. Salerno, M. Costa and G.P. Chiusoli, Tetrahedron Lett; 1999, **40**, 989.

296. T. Joh, H. Nagata and S. Takahashi. Chem. Lett; 1992, 1305.

297. W. Wu and C.J. Li. Chem. Commun; 2003, 1668.

298. H. Kinoshita, T. Nakamura, H. Kakiya, H. Shinokubo, S. Matsubara and K. Oshima, Organic Lett; 2001, **3**, 2521.

299. T. Sugihara and T.M. Yamaguchi, Synlett, 1998, 1384; T, Sugihara, M. Yamaguchi and M. Nishizawa, Chemistry, 2001, **7**, 1589.

300. S.U. Son, S.I. Lee, Y.K. Chung, S.W. Kim and T. Hyeon, Organic Lett; 2002, **4**, 277.

301. J. Thesing and P. Binger, Chem. Ber; 1957, **90**, 1419.

302. D. Chen, L. Yu and P.G, Wang, Tetrahedron Lett; 1996, **37**, 4467.

303. W. Zhuang and K.A. Jorgensen, Chem. Commun; 2002, 1336.

304. R. Ding, H.B. Zhang, Y.J. Chen, L. Liu, D. Wang and C. – J. Li, Synlett, 2004, 555.

305. M. Okamoto, M. Watanabe and T, Yamaji, Organomet. Chem., 2002, **664**, 59; H.A. Burton and I.V. Kozhevnikov, Mol. Catal A: Chem. 2002, 185, 285; T. Jintou, H. Taniguchi and Y. Fujeward, Chem. Lett; 1987, 1865.

306. J.H. Liu and R.G. Weiss, J. Org. Chem; 1985, **50**, 3655.

307. T.H. Chan, C.J. Li, M.C. Lee and Z.Y. Wci, Can. J. Chem; 1994, **72**, 1181.

308. L.W. Bieber, I.M. Malvestiti and E.C. Stroch, J. Org. Chem; 1997, **62**, 9061.

309. T.A. Killinger, N.A. Boughton, T.A. Runge and J.J. Wolinsky, J. Organometallic Chem., 1977, **124**, 131.

310. C. Petricr and J.L. Luche, J. Org. Chem. 1985, **50**, 910; C. Einhorn and J. L. Luche, J. Organomet. Chem., 1987, **322**, 177; C. Petrier, J. Einhorn and J.L. Luchi, Tetrahedron Lett., 1985, **26**, **1449**.

311. For a review, see, D. Basavaiah, P.D. Rao and R.S. Hyman, Tetrahedron, 1996, **52**, 8001.

312. J. Auge, N. Lubin and A. Lubineau, Tetrahedron Lett; 1994, **35**, 7947.

313. M.M. Baizer and D.E. Danly, Chem. Tech; 1980, **10(3)**, 161.

314. D.V. Davydov and I.P. Beletskaya, Russ. Chem. Bull; 1995, **44**, 1139.

315. For a review, see, R.F. heck, Acc. Chem. Res.; 1979, **12**, 146.

316. N.A. Bumagin, P. More and I.P. Beletskaya, J. Organomet. Chem; 1989, **371**, 397; N. A. Bumagin, V.V. Bykov, L.I. Sukhomlinova, T.P. Tolstaya and I.P. Beletskaya, J. Organomet. Chem. 1995, **486**, 259.

317. For a review, see N. Miyaura and A. Suzuk, Chem. Rev, 1995, **95**, 2451; T.A. Bryson, J.M. Gibson, J.J. Stewart, H. Voegtle, A. Tiwari, J.H. Dawson, W. Marley and B. Harmon, Green Chem, 2003, **5**, 177.

318. A. Herrbach, A. Marinetti, O. Baudoin, D. Guenard and F. Gueritte, J. Org. Chem; 2003, **68**, 4897.

319. H. Zhang and D. Davis, Organometallics, 1993, **12**, 1499.

320. A.I. Roshchin, N.A. Bumagin and I.P. Beletskaya, Dokl, Chem; 1994, **334**, 47.

321. H.-B. Zhang, L, Liu, Y.-J. Chen, D, Wang and C.-j. Li, Eur. J. Org. Chem; 2006, 869.

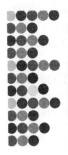

Organic Reactions in Super Critical Water or in Near Water (NCW) Region

2

I INTRODUCTION

Super critical water (ScH_2O), the critical temperature of which are 374°C and 22.1 MPa has been attracting attention of synthetic organic chemists because of its unique physical and chemical properties that are quite different from those of ambient water[1]. For example, because the dielectric constant of ScH_2O is much lower, a number of organic compounds are soluble in it. Also, the ion dissociation constant of water initially increases with the rise in temperature. However, at the critical point under constant pressure conditions, the ion dissociation constant drops considerably. In $Sc – H_2O$, the persistence of hydrogen bonds are also diminished. Due to this, high temperature water behaves like many organic solvents in which several organic compounds are soluble.

The near critical water region is described as 250-300°C at pressures 100-80 bar[2,3]. As in the case of $Sc – H_2O$, water near its critical point (NCW) also process properties very different from those of ambient water. For the sake of convenience, some typical organic reaction have been described separately in $Sc – H_2O$ and near critical water (NCW).

2 ORGANIC REACTIONS IN SC – H₂O

It has already been stated that water near critical point can serve as an environmentally benign solvent. In addition it can also serve as a reactant and a catalyst in organic chemical reactions. These special properties of $SC – H_2O$ have been utilised for conducting chemical synthesis. Following are given some of the important reaction in $Sc – H_2O$.

1. Cyclohexane, Cyclohexene and cyclohexanol in $Sc – H_2O$ in presence of PtO_2 catalyst yielded[4] benzene as the major product.
2. Dibenzothiophene in $Sc – H_2O$ on treatment with the catalyst $NiMo/Al_2O_3$ resulted[5] in desulphurisation. Higher yields were obtained in $CO – Sc – H_2O$ and $HCOOH – Sc – H_2O$ than in $H_2 – Sc – H_2O$. This showed that hydrosulfurization could be achieved without the addition of expensive H_2 gas as is the normal practice in industry.
3. Heck-coupling reaction could be conducted[6,7] in $Sc – H_2O$.
4. Friedel-crafts alkylation reactions have been accomplished[8,9] in high temperature water.

5. Phenol and p-cresol could be alkylated in $Sc - H_2O$ with tert. butyl alcohol and 2-propanol at 275° in the absence of any added catalyst to produce sterically hindered phenols[9].

6. Diels-Alder cycloaddition reactions have also been conducted[10] in $Sc - H_2O$. A number of different diene/dienophiles have been used.

7. Aldol condensation reactions can be accomplished in high temperature water. Though, 2, 5-hexanedione is unreactive in pure water, but it undergoes intramolecular aldol condensation in presence of small amount of base (NaOH) to form 3-methylcyclopent-2-enone in 81% yield[11].

8. 2, 5-Dimenthyl furan on treatment with $Sc - H_2O$ at 250° produced quantatively 2, 5-hexanedione[12].

9. Pinacol could to be arranged[13] to pinacolone in $Sc - H_2O$ at 275°.

10. Cyclohexene on treatment with $Sc - H_2O$ rearranged to methyl cyclopentene[4] in presence of mineral acid or acidic melal salts.

11. Claisen, Rupe and Meyer-Schuster rearrangements have also been reported[11] in $Sc - H_2O$ at elevated temperature.

12. Dehydration of tert. butyl alcohol to isobutylene in $Sc - H_2O$ at 250° was reported[14,15] in the absence of any added catalyst. However addition of acid or base did accelerate the reaction rate.

13. The dehydration of alcohols such as cyclohexanol[4,12], 2-methylcyclohexanol[12] and 2-phenylethanol[7] have also been reported in $Sc - H_2O$.

14. Carboxylic acids, eg, formic acid[16], citric acid and itaconic acids[17] and cinnamic acid and indole 2-carboxylic acid[11] undergo facile decarboxylation in $Sc - H_2O$.

15. Esters undergo hydrolysis in $Sc - H_2O$ to form carboxylic acds and alcohols; the acid produced catalyses the hydrolysis. This is referred to as autocatalysis[8,11] Nitriles also undergo hydrolysis to form the corresponding amide and then get further hydrolysed to the corresponding acid.

16. The action of $Sc - H_2O$ has been examined[18] on a large number of other compounds like hydrocarbons, 1-nitrobutane, butyronitrile, nitroanilines, benzyl sulfide, a large number of oxygen containing compounds and chlorine and fluroine containing compounns. The results obtained are still in explarotary stage.

17. A facite carbon-silicon bond cleavase of organoilicon compounds in $Sc - H_2O$ has been reported[19] (Scheme 1)

$$R - Si\ Me_2X \xrightarrow{\ Sc - H_2O\ } R - H$$

R = aryl, allkenyl, allyl and alkyl
X = OH, Cl, OEt, OSi R'_3, $SiMe_3$, Me

Scheme 1

The reaction of arylsilanes in $Sc - H_2O$ at 390° also underwent $C - Si$ bond cleavage giving benzene derivatives in high yields[19] (Scheme 2).

$$p\text{--R } C_6H_4 \text{ --- Si Me}_3 \xrightarrow[\substack{390°, 27 \text{ MPd} \\ 300 \text{ mm}}]{\text{Sc --- } H_2O} p \text{ --- R } C_6H_4\text{---H}$$

R = H, Bu   72 --- 91% yield

Scheme 2

If the above reaction was conducted in Sc – D_2O, the benzene derivative obtained contained deuterium (>95% D); in this case, as expected D occupied the position previously occupied by $SiMe_3$, group. The reaction of alkenyl silane in Sc – H_2O (390°, 5 min) gave[19] a mixture of dodecene in 67% yield. The initially formed desilation product (1-dodicane) is believed to isomerize into thermodynamically more stable inner alkenes under the reaction conditions (Scheme 3).

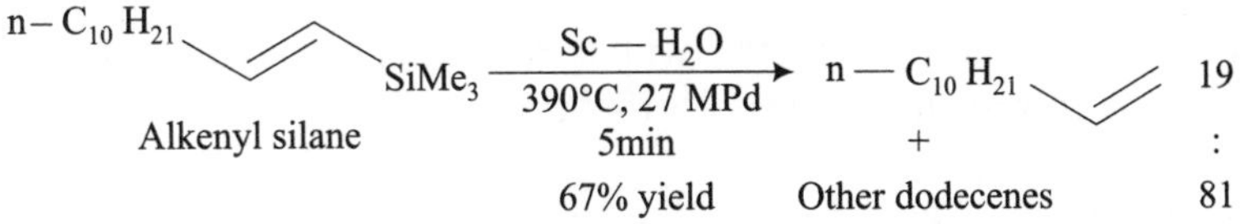

$$n\text{--} C_{10} H_{21} \diagdown\diagup SiMe_3 \xrightarrow[\substack{390°C, 27 \text{ MPd} \\ 5\text{min} \\ 67\% \text{ yield}}]{\text{Sc --- } H_2O} \begin{array}{cc} n\text{---} C_{10} H_{21} \diagdown\diagup & 19 \\ + & : \\ \text{Other dodecenes} & 81 \end{array}$$

Alkenyl silane

Scheme 3

Similarly, the following allylic silane underwent rapid desilylation in Sc – H_2O (Scheme 4)

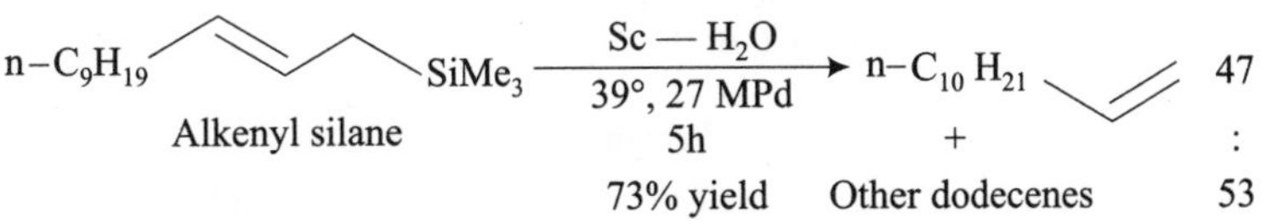

$$n\text{--}C_9H_{19}\diagup\diagdown SiMe_3 \xrightarrow[\substack{39°, 27 \text{ MPd} \\ 5\text{h} \\ 73\% \text{ yield}}]{\text{Sc --- } H_2O} \begin{array}{cc} n\text{--}C_{10} H_{21} \diagdown\diagup & 47 \\ + & : \\ \text{Other dodecenes} & 53 \end{array}$$

Alkenyl silane

Scheme 4

However, in the case alkylsilances, which are known to be much less reactive towards C – Si bond cleavage than the organosilanes mentioned above, the addition of either HCl or NaOH had a beneficial effect on the C – Si bond cleavage (Scheme 5).

$$n\text{--}C_{12} H_{25} \text{ --- } SiMe_2X \xrightarrow[390 - 410°]{\text{Sc --- } H_2O} n\text{--}C_{12} H_{25}\text{-H}$$

x = OH, Cl, OEt, $OSiMe_2 C_{12} M_{25}$ and $SiMe_3$

Scheme 5

18. The conversion of ε-caprolactone into ε-caprolactam in 79.2 per cent yield using ammonia in supercritical H_2O at 380° (and a water density of 0.5g/cm³) was reported[20]. It was believed[20] that the amide bond in ε-caprolactam was formed by the intramolecular dehydration between the hydroxyl group and the amide group in 6-hydroxyhexamide.

19. The amidation of 1-n-hexanol with acetamide as the amidation agent occured in Sc – H_2O^{21}. It was assumed[19] that the N – n-hexylacetamide was formed by the intermolecular dehydration between the hydroxyl group in 1-n-hexanol and the amide group in acetamide. The reaction pathway for the above reaction was subsequently studied[22].

3   ORGANIC REACTIONS IN NEAR-CRITICAL WATER (NCW) REGION

The organic reactions described in this section were conducted in specially designed microwave oven, in which temperature between 200 and 300° with higher pressure limits (80 – 100 bars) could be achieved. Following are given some of the reactions which have been conducted in water in the near critical water (NCW) region. This can also be equivalent to reactions conducted in high temperature water

3.1   Conversion of Aryl Halides into Phenols

The reaction of aryl halides in water at 300° with L-proline and sodium hydroxide in presence of CuI (catalyst) gave the corresponding phenol[23] (Scheme 6)

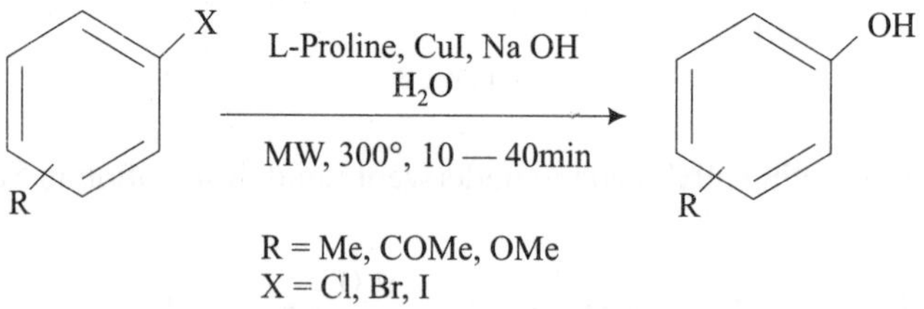

$$\text{L-Proline, CuI, Na OH}$$
$$H_2O$$
$$\text{MW, 300°, 10 — 40min}$$

R = Me, COMe, OMe
X = Cl, Br, I

Scheme 6

Higher yields are obtained in case of aryl bromides and chlorides, higher (10-40%) are possible when the reactions are conducted at 300°.

3.2   Claisen Rearrangement

The claisen rearrangement of allyl phenyl ether to 2-allyl phenol was performed in near critical water at 240° in a MW oven to give 84% yield. However, at 200° only 10% yield was obtained[24, 25]. It was also shown[26] that by increasing the reaction temperature to 250° and time to 1 hr, a cyclic product, dihydrobenzofuran was produced in 72% yield (Scheme 7)

3.3   Pinacol-pinacolone Rearrangement

Pinacol on heating with water in MW oven at 270° gave pinacolone[27] in 76% yield. Pinacolone was isolated by converting it into the 2, 4-dinitrophenyl hydrazone. Pinacole-pinacolone rearrangement generally proceeds in presence of acid catalyst. It was therefore assumed[27] that here NCW acts as an acid catalyst itself (Scheme 8)

3.4   Hydration of Alkenes: Synthesis of Carvacrol from Carvone

Carvone [(+)–isomer] on heating with water in MW oven at 210° for 10 min give (S) – (+) – 8 – hydroxy-p-6-menthen 2 one as an intermediate (isolated in 20% yield), which isomerises quantitatively (95% yield) to carvacrol (Scheme 9)

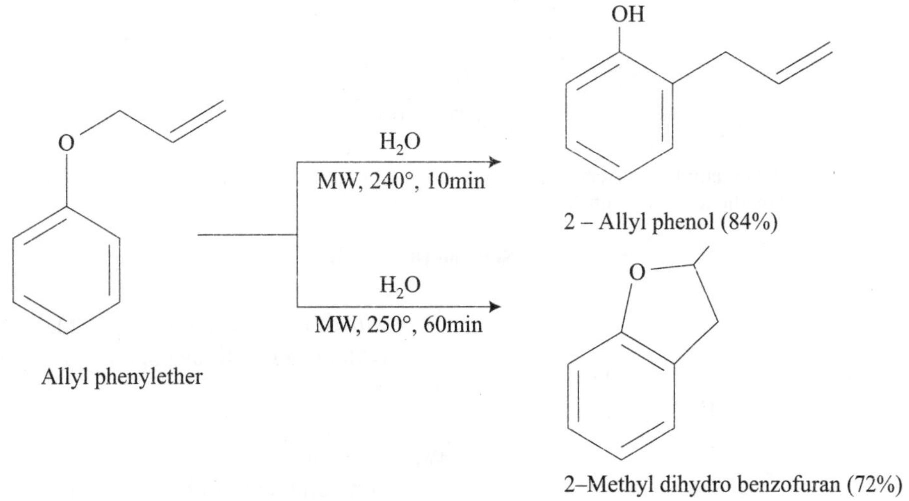

OH

2 – Allyl phenol (84%)

H_2O

MW, 240°, 10min

H_2O

MW, 250°, 60min

Allyl phenylether

2–Methyl dihydro benzofuran (72%)

Scheme 7

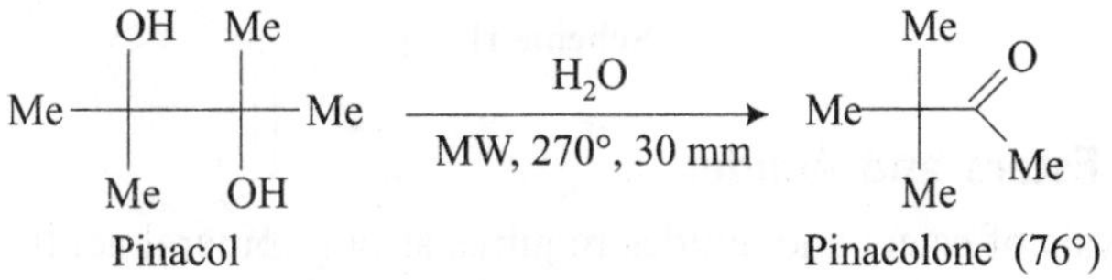

OH   Me

Me —|—|— Me

Me   OH

Pinacol

H_2O

MW, 270°, 30 mm

Me   O

Me —|— Me

Me

Pinacolone (76°)

Scheme 8

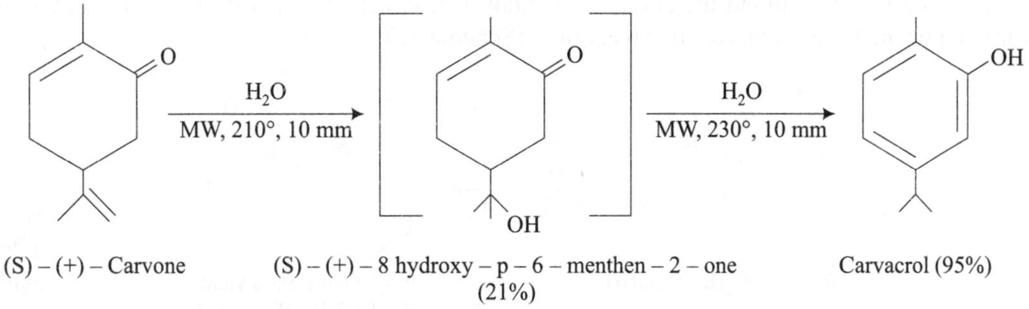

H_2O

MW, 210°, 10 mm

H_2O

MW, 230°, 10 mm

OH

(S) – (+) – Carvone

(S) – (+) – 8 hydroxy – p – 6 – menthen – 2 – one
(21%)

Carvacrol (95%)

Scheme 9

3.5   Diels-Alder Cycloaddition Reaction

A simple Diels-Alder Cycloaddition reaction was reported[27] by reacting 2, 3-dimethyl butadiene and acrylonitrile by heating with water in a MW oven at 295° for 20 min (using microwave generated NCW) (Scheme 10)

3.6   Fischer Indole Synthesis

The reaction of phenylhydrazine with ethyl methyl ketone by heating with water in a microwave oven at 270° for 30 min gave[28, 29] 64% yield of the indole derivative (Scheme 11)

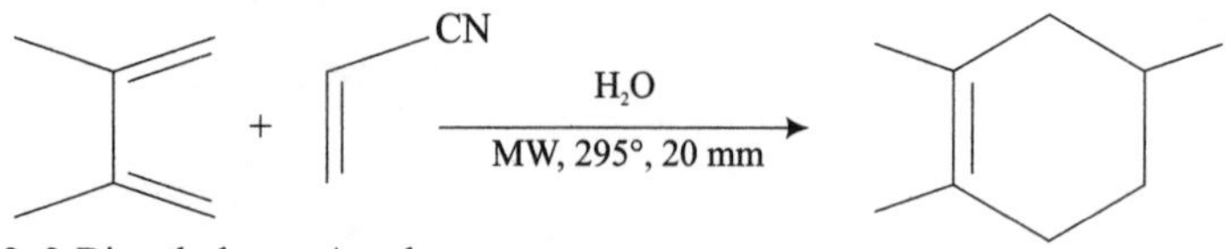

Scheme 10

2, 3-Dimethyl
butadiene

Acrylo
nitrile

65%

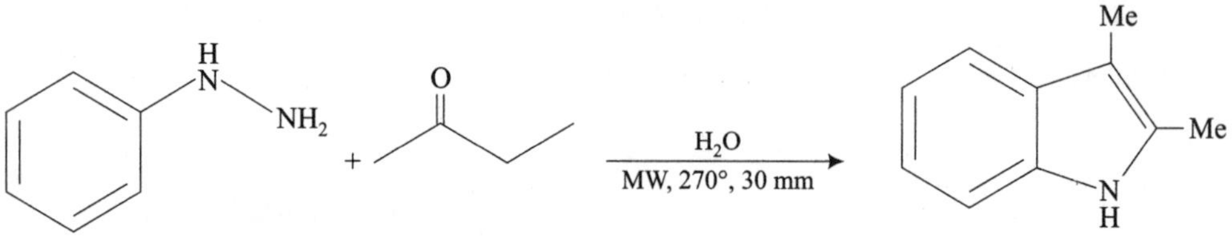

Phenylhydrazine

Ethylmethyl
ketone

2, 3-Dimethyl indole
(64%)

Scheme 11

3.7 Hydrolysis of Esters and Amides

Normally, the hydrolysis of esters and amides requires strong mineral acids or bases. However, in the NCW region no addition of any catalyst is necessary. Ethyl benzoate hydrolysed to benzoic acid in MW at 295° for 2 hr. In case of benzamide, complete hydrolysis under NCW conditions (295°) was achieved in 4 hr without the addition of catalyst. It is believed that in this case ammonium hydroxide formed acetocatalyzes this reaction[27] (Scheme 12)

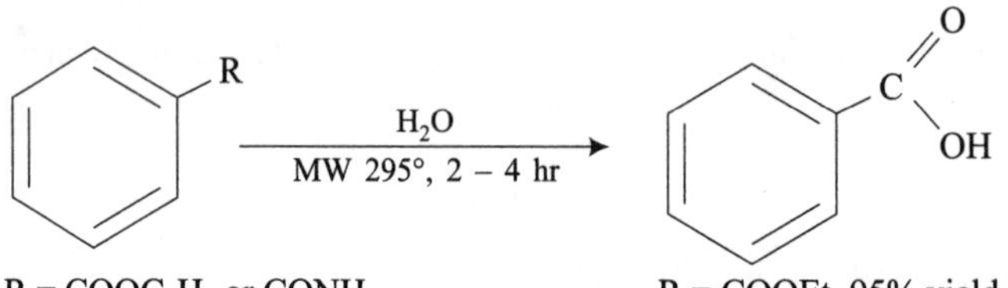

R = COOC$_2$H$_5$ or CONH$_2$

R = COOEt, 95% yield
R = CONH$_2$, 92% yield

Scheme 12

3.8 Decarboxylation

Indole-2-carboxylic acid could be decarboxylated[25] to give indole. This decarboxylation was quantitative in 20 min at 255° in near critical region (Scheme 13)

2-Carbethoxy indole on similar hydrolysis gave[25] only 20% yield of the decarboxylated product. This problem could be overcome by heating with 0.2 M aqueous NaOH solution; in the latter case the ester group is first deesterified to the acid, which undergoes decarboxylation to give indole (Scheme 14)

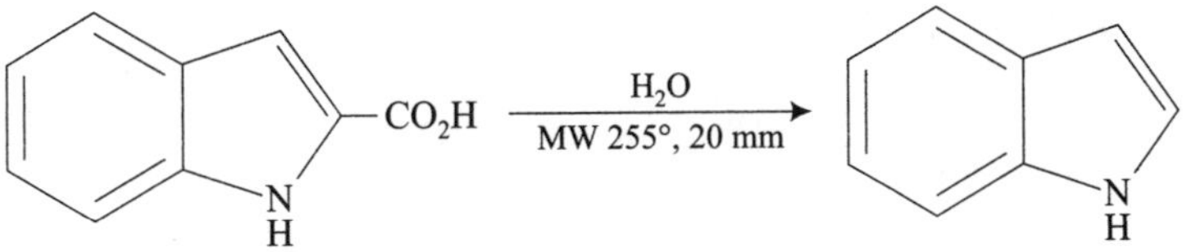

Indole 2-carboxylic acid   Indole (100%)

Scheme 13

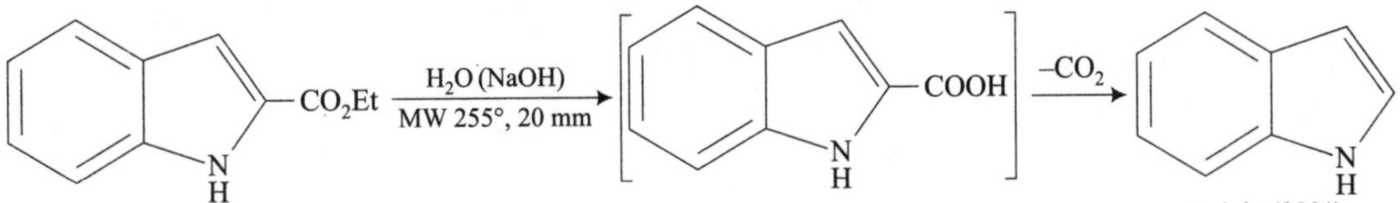

2-Carbethoxyindole   Indole (93%)

Scheme 14

9   Autocatalysis

The reactivity (for example hydrolysis) of some organic compounds in near critical region or in high temperature water is enhanced[30] by some water-soluble compounds. For example, carboxylic acids produced by the hydrolysis of esters, aldehydes and amines and mineral acids (HX, HNO_3) produced by the hydrolysis of halogen and nitrogen compounds can acts as acid catalyst. In a similar way, ammonia produced by the hydrolysis of amines, amides and nitriles acts as a base catalyst. This is referred to as autocatalyses. Following are given the expected products obtained[30] by the hydrolysis of ethers, esters, amides, amines, nitroalkanes and alkyl halides (Scheme 15).

R — O — R' ethers	$\xrightarrow{\text{HTW}}$	ROH + R'OH
R — COOR' esters	$\xrightarrow{\text{HTW}}$	RCOOH + R'OH
RCONH$_2$ Amides	$\xrightarrow{\text{HTW}}$	RCOOH + NH$_3$
RNH$_2$ 1° Amines	$\xrightarrow{\text{HTW}}$	ROH + NH$_3$
RNHR' 2° Amines	$\xrightarrow{\text{HTW}}$	ROH + R'NH$_2$
RR'NR'' 3° Amines	$\xrightarrow{\text{HTW}}$	ROH + R'OH + R''NH$_2$
RCNO$_2$ 1° Nitroalkanes	$\xrightarrow{\text{HTW}}$	RCHO + HNO$_3$
RCNO$_2$R' 2° Nitroalkanes	$\xrightarrow{\text{HTW}}$	RCOR' + HNO$_3$
R – X Alkyl halide	$\xrightarrow{\text{HTW}}$	ROH + HX

Contd.

$$RCX_2H \xrightarrow{\text{HTW}} RCHO + 2HX$$
1° gem-dihalides

$$RCX_2R' \xrightarrow{\text{HTW}} RCOR' + 2HX$$
2° gem dihalides

Scheme 15

4 MISCELLANEOUS REACTIONS

Following are given some other reactions which have been performed at high temperature either in water on in presence of acid or alkali[28] (Scheme 16)

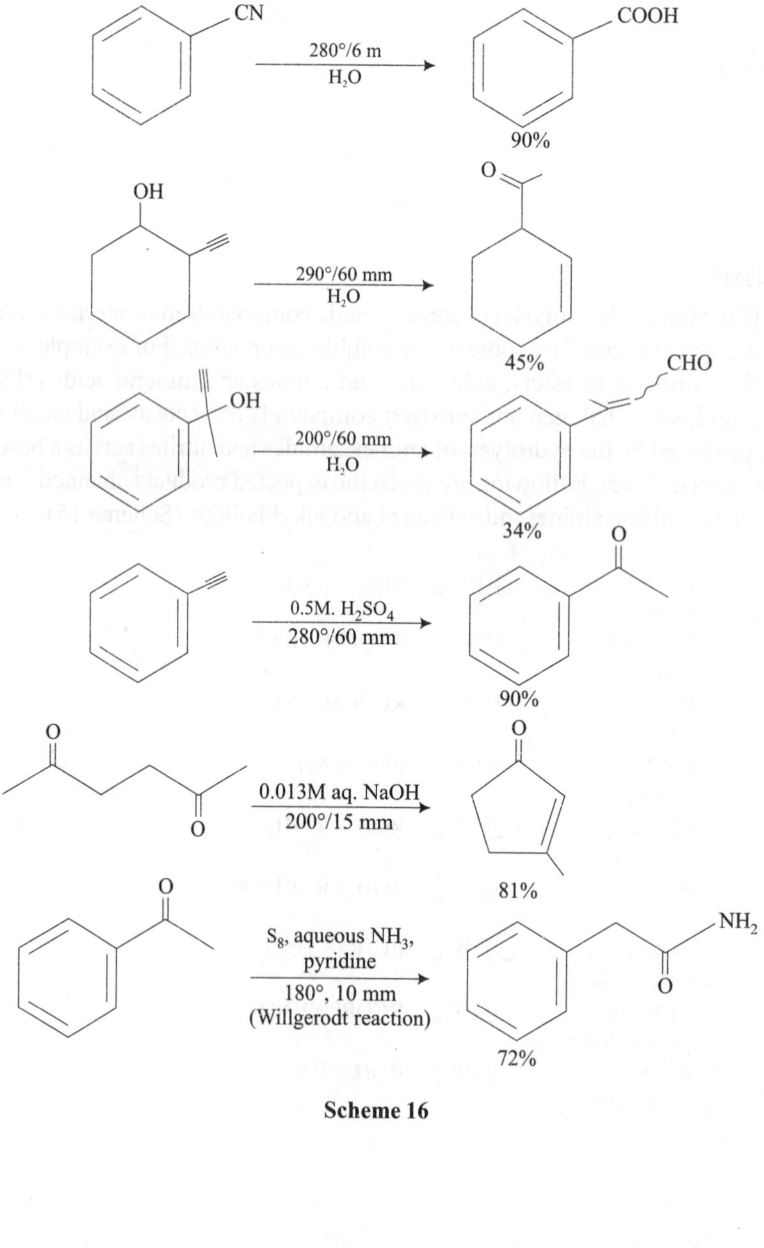

Scheme 16

5 CONCLUSION

Super critical water or high temperature water is a good medium for organic chemical reaction. In addition, it can serve as a reactant and catalyst. These properties have been utilised for conducting chemical synthesis.

References

1. O. Kajmoto, Chem. Rev., 1999, 99, 355; P.E. Savage, Chem. Rev., 1999, 99, 603; D. Broli, C. Kaul, A. Kramer, P. Krammer, T. Richter, M. Jung, H. Vogel and P. Zehner, Angew. Chem. Int. Ed., 1999, **38**, 2998; M. Siskin and M. Katrinzky, Chem. Rev., 2001, **101**, 825.

2. A. Stadler, B.H. Yousfi, D. Dallinger, P. Walla, E. Vander Eycken, N. Kaval and C.O. Kappe, Org. Precess Res. Dev., 2003, **7**, 707.

3. K.D. Raner, C.R. Strauss and R.W. Trainer, J. Org. Chem., 1995, **60**, 2456.

4. R. C. Crittendon and E.J. Parsons, Organometallics., 1994, **13(7)**, 2587.

5. T. Adschiri, R. Shibata, T. Sato, M. Watanabe and K. Arai, Ind. Eng. Chem. Res., 1998, **37**, 2634.

6. P. Reardon, S. Metts, C. Critttendon, P. Daugherity and E.J. Parsons, Organometallics, 1995, **14(8)**, 3810.

7. J. Diminnie, S. Metts and E.J. Parsons, Organometallics, 1995, **14(8)**, 4023.

8. A.R. Katritzky, S.M. Allin and M. Siskin, Acc. Chem. Res., 1996, **29(8)**, 399.

9. K. Chandler, F. Deng, A.K. Dillow, C.L. Liotta and C.A. Eckert, Ind. Eng. Chem. Res., 1997, **36(12)**, 5173.

10. M.B. Korzenski and J.W. Kolis, Tetrahedron Lett., 1997, **38**, 5611.

11. J. An, L. Bagnell, T. Cablewski, C.R. Strauss and R.W. Trainer, J. Org. Chem., 1997, **62(8)**, 2505.

12. B. Kuhlmann, E.M. Arnett and M. Siskin, J. Org. Chem., 94, **59**, 3098.

13. B. Kuhlmann, E.M. Arnett and M. Siskin, J. Org. Chem., 1994, **59**, 5377.

14. X. Xu and M.J. Antal, Alch E.J., 1994, **40**, 1524.

15. X. Xu and M.J. Antal, Ind. Eng. Chem. Res., 1997, **36**, 23.

16. J. Yu and P.E. Savage, Ind. Eng. Chem. Res. 1998, **37**, 2.

17. M. Carlsson, C. Habenicht, L. C. Kam, M. Antal, N. Bian, R. J. Cunningham and M. Jones, Ind. Eng. Chem. Res., 1994, **33**, 1989.

18. P.E. Savage, Chem. Rev., 1999, **99**, 603, and the references cited therein

19. K. Itami, K. Terakawa, J – i Yoshida and O. Kajimoto, J. Am. Chem. Soc., 2003, **125**, 6058.

20. H. Ito, J. Nishiyama, T. Adschiri and K. Arai, Kobunshi Robunshu, 2001, **58**, 679.

21. M. Sasaki, J. Nishiyama, M. Uchida, K. Goto, K. Tajima, T. Adschiri and K. Arai, Green Chem., 2003, **5**, 95.

22. K. Tajima, M. Uchida, K. Minami, M. Osada, K. Sue, T. Nonaka, H. Hattori and A. K. Arai, Environ. Sci, Technol, 2005, **39**, 9721.

23. C.M. Kormos and N.E. Leadbeater, Tetrahedron Lett., 2006, **62**, 4728.

24. K.D. Raner, C.R. Strauss and R.W. Trainor, J. Org. Chem., 1995, **60**, 2456.

25. J. An. L. Bagnell, T. Cablewski, C.R. Strauss and R. W. Trainor, J. Org. Chem., 1997, **62**, 2505.

26. L. Bagnell, T. Cablewski, C. R. Strauss and K.W. Trainor, J. Org. Chem., 1996, **61**, 7355.

27. J.M. Kremsner and C.O. Kappe, Eur, J. Org. Chem., 2005, 3672.

28. C.R. Strauss and K.W. Trainor, Aust. J. Chem., 1995, **48**, 1665 and the references cited therein.

29. C.R. Strauss, Aust. J. Chem., 1999, **52**, 83.

30. N. Akiya and P. E. Savage, Chem. Rev., 2002, **107**, 2725 and the references cited therein.

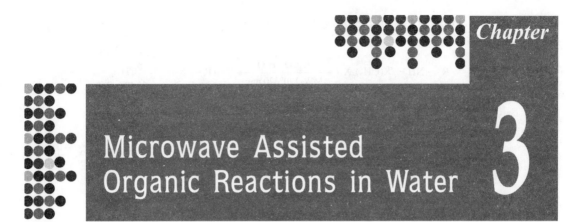

I INTRODUCTION

The main problem in using water as a solvent is that a larger number of organic substrates are insoluble in water. This makes the reaction mixture heterogeneous. We can overcome this by using phase transfer catalysts. However, this makes the process more expensive. In addition, the isolation of products from aqueous medium is another concern. The only option available is the evaporation of water from the reaction mixture, but this is not an energy-efficient process. However a solution to all this is the usage of microwave (MW) heating technique for the reaction in aqueous medium.

Microwave assisted organic reactions are based on the efficiency of the interaction of the substrate constituents (substrates, catalyst and solvent) with electromagnetic waves generally by a microwave dielectric effect. This process basically depends on the specific polarity of molecules. Since water is polar in nature, it has excellent potential to absorb MW radiation and convert it to heat energy and this is the reason why MW promotes as well as accelerates reactions in an aqueous medium compared to results obtained with conventional heating[1].

Following are some of the microwave assisted organic reactions in water.

2 SYNTHESIS OF HETEROCYCLES

Heterocyclic compounds are especially important as pharmaceutical products – both natural products and synthetic compounds[2,3]. Nitrogen containing hetrocycles are abundant in nature and are of considerable significance to life since their structural subunits exist in many natural products like vitamins, hormones, antibiotics and alkaloids as well as pharmaceuticals, herbicides and dyes[2].

Nitrogen-containing heterocycles such as substituted azetidines, pyrrolidines, azepanes, N-substituted 2, 3-dihydro-1H-isoindoles, 4, 5-dihydro pyrazoles, pyrazolidines and 1, 2-dihydrophthalazines have been synthesised in a basic aqueous medium using MWs. The reactions proceed via double N-alkylation of primary amines and hydrazine derivatives (Scheme 1) with readily available alkyl dihalides (or ditosylates). This protocol provided a facile entry to important class of building blocks in natural products and pharmaceuticals[4-6].

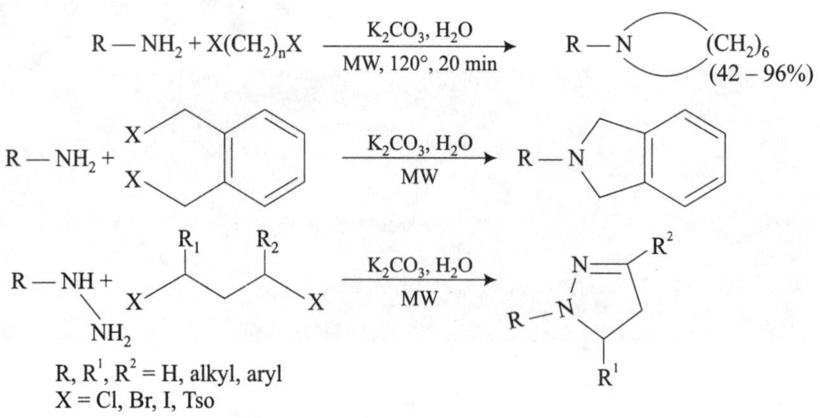

Scheme 1

The above reaction (Scheme 1) is not a single phase system as neither reactant is soluble in aqueous alkaline reaction medium. It is believed that the selective absorption of microwaves by polar molecules and intermediates in a multiphase system could substitute as a phase transfer catalyst without using any phase transfer reagent, thereby providing the observed acceleration as had been observed for ultrasonic radiation[7].

A variety of nitrogen hetrocycles have been synthesized by the condensation of hydrazine, hydrazide and diamines with diketones and β-ketoesters respectively (Scheme 2)[8].

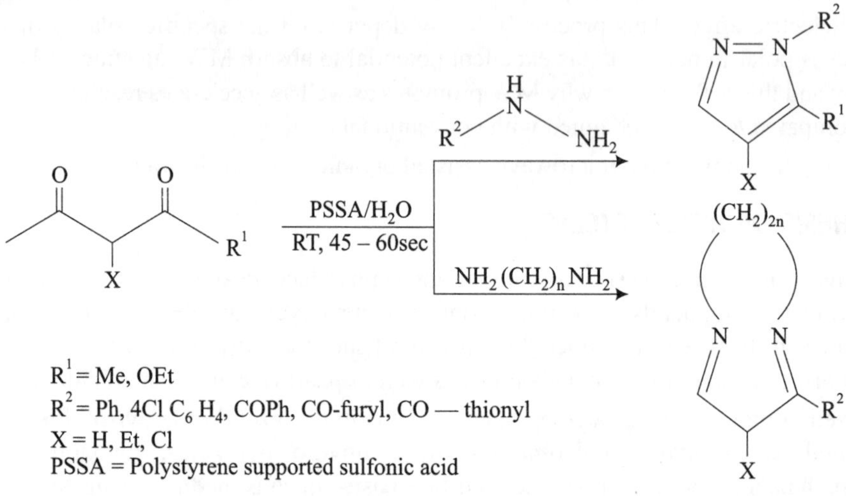

R^1 = Me, OEt
R^2 = Ph, 4Cl $C_6 H_4$, COPh, CO-furyl, CO — thionyl
X = H, Et, Cl
PSSA = Polystyrene supported sulfonic acid

Scheme 2

3   N-ALKYLATION OF NITROGEN HETEROCYCLES

N-Alkylation of nitrogen heterocycles has been achieved in aqueous media under MW irradiation conditions (Scheme 3)[9].

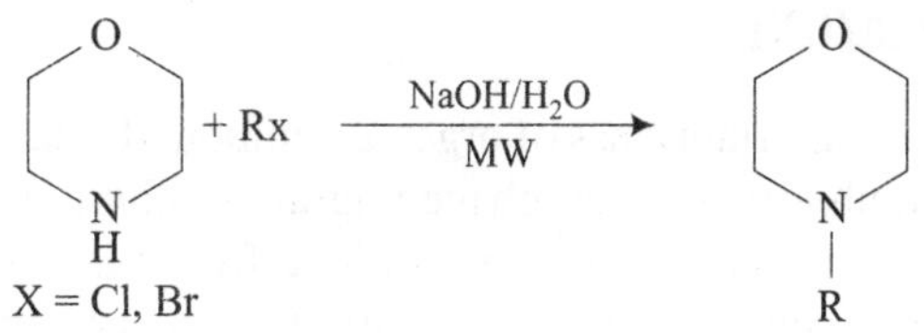

Scheme 3

4 BIGINELLI REACTION

Dihydropyrimidones, important class of organic compounds, which show prominent biological activity, were symthisised under solvent free conditions[10] or by an environmentally benign Biginelli reaction using PSSA as a catalpt (Scheme 4)[11]. The latter procedure using microwave proceeds efficiently in water without the use of any organic solvent.

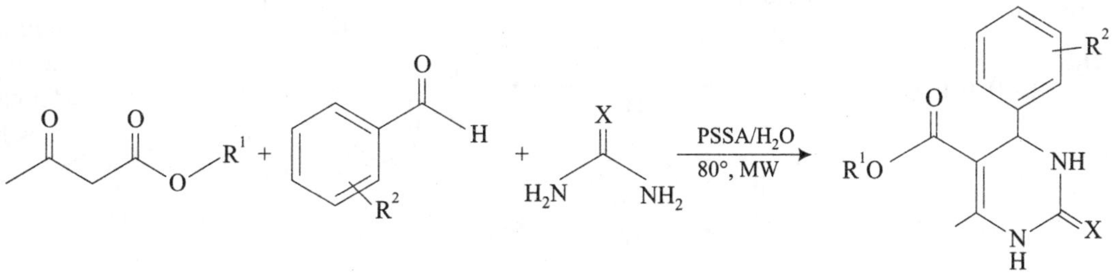

Scheme 4

5 I, 3-DIOXANES

Dioxanes rings are common structural motifs in numerous bioactive molecules. Such 1, 3-dioxanes have been synthesized in aqueous media via tandem bis-aldol reaction of ketones with paraformaldehyde catalysed by PSSA under MW irradiation condition (Scheme-5)[12].

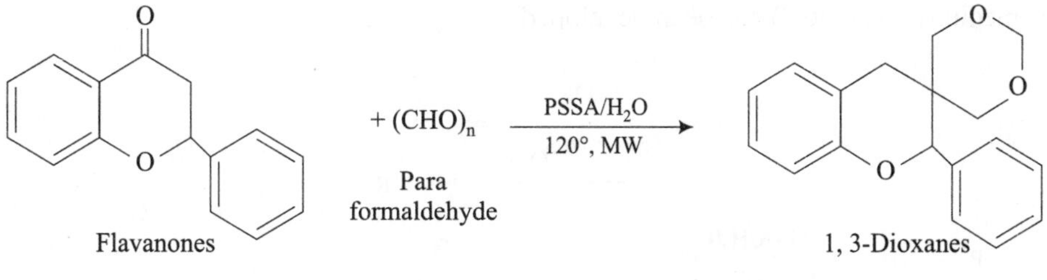

Scheme 5

6 HETEROCYCLIC HYDRAZONES

Heterocyclic hydrazones, an important class of organic compounds, have been found to be useful as anti-malaria drugs and as inhibitors of macrophage migration inhibitory factor (MIF) taurtomerase activity[13]. These were earlier synthsised[14] in solvent free and catalytic environment using heteroaro-matic hydrazones under microwave irradiation conditions[8]. These hetercyclic hydrazones have been synthesized using PSSA as a catalyst. The reaction proceeds efficiently in water in the absence of any organic solvent under MW irradiation. The formed hydrazones are isolated by simple filtration (Scheme 6)[15].

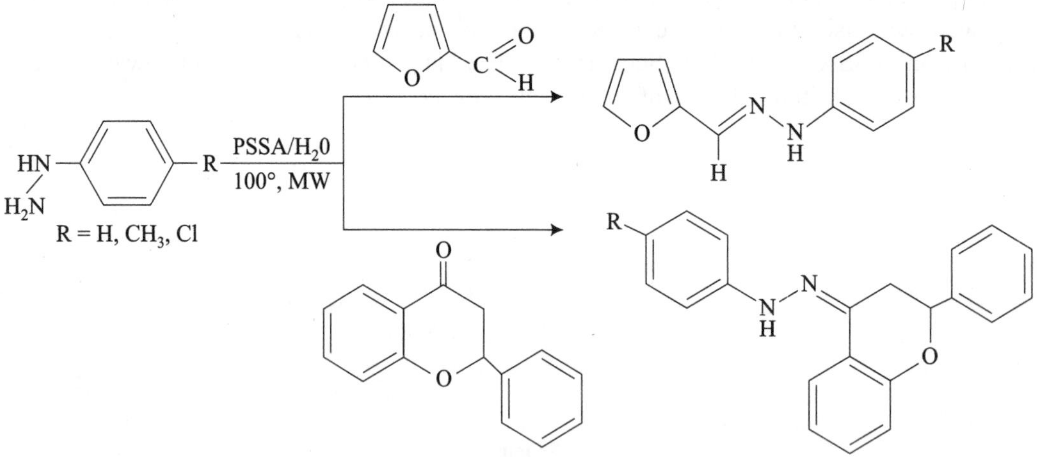

Scheme 6

7 AZA-MICHAEL REACTION

Aza-Michael addition in an important class of carbon-nitrogen bond-forming reaction and is a powerful tool in organic chemistry. An efficient aza-Michael addition of amines catalyzed by PSSA in aqueous medium (Scheme 7) has been developed[16].

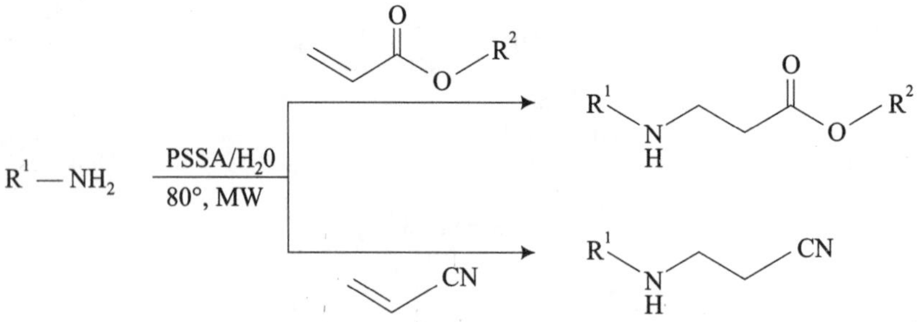

Scheme 7

Bis-aza-Michael addition reaction of alkyl diammes with methyl acrylate and acrylonitrile (Scheme 8) has also been reported[16].

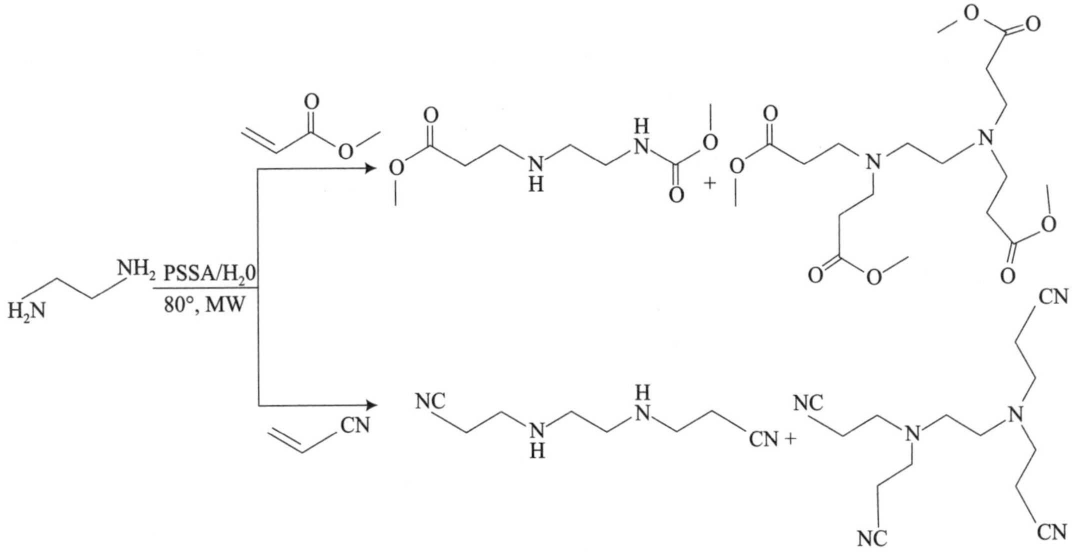

Scheme 8

8 TROST'S γ-ADDITION

Complementary to Michael reaction Trost developed[17] the 'γ-addition' of nucleophiles to 2-alkynoates catalyzed by a phosphine. In these reactions a nucleophilic tertiary phosphine is first added to the triple bond of an electron-deficient alkyne and finally gets eliminated from the reaction product after a series at transformations. In this reaction tertiary phosphinc plays the role of the catalyst. Subsequently, a recyclable and efficient polymer-supported triphenyl phosphate-catalysed 'atom economical' Trost's addition of nucleophiles to alkynoate in aqueous media (Scheme 9) has been reported[18].

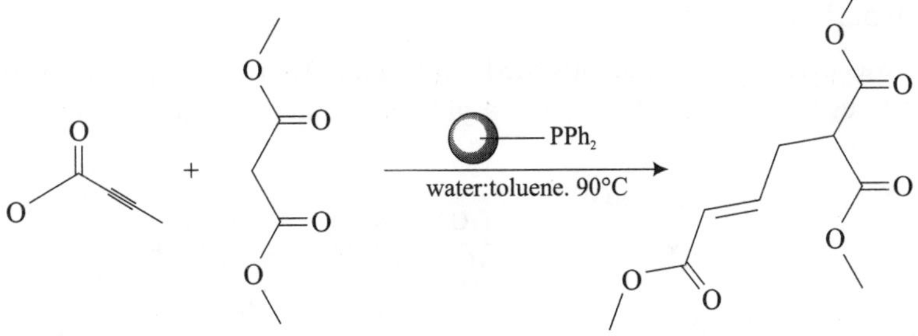

Scheme 9

9 SYNTHESIS OF AZIDES, THIOCYANATES AND SULFONES

An efficient and rapid MW promoted synthesis of various azides, thiocyantes and sulfones has been developed in aqueous medium (Scheme-10)[19].

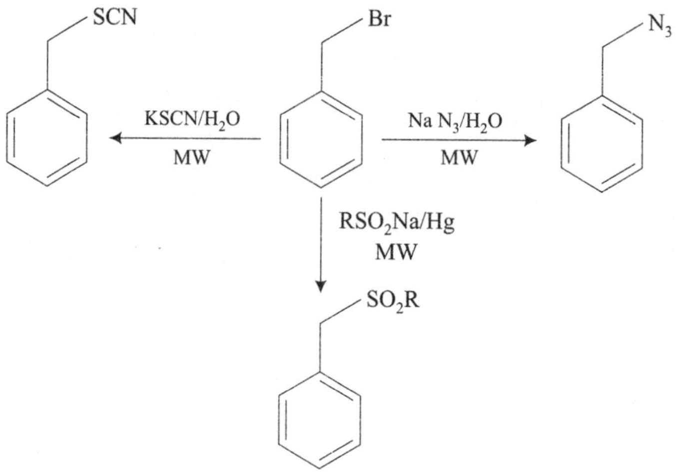

Scheme 10

In the above reaction (Scheme 10), various functional groups such as ester, carboxylic acid, carbonyl and hydroxyl were uneffected under the mild reaction conditions involved[19].

10 COUPLING REACTIONS

The suzuki[20] and Heck[21] reaction are the most important carbon cross coupling reactions in organic chemistry. These reactions are generally catalyzed by soluble palladium (Pd) complexes with various ligands. The main problem in these reactions are the efficient separation and subsequent cyclisation of the homogeneous transition metal catalysts. Heterogeneous Pd catalyst systems were found to be highly effective to overcome some of these issues[22]. However, MW-assisted coupling reactions (as discussed below) in aqueous medium is the recent choice of chemicals.

10.1 Suzuki Reaction

Suzuki reaction was performed in aqueous medium using MW irradiation. By this procedure various biaryl derivatives were prepared[23,24] from aryl halides and phenylboronic acid (Scheme 11).

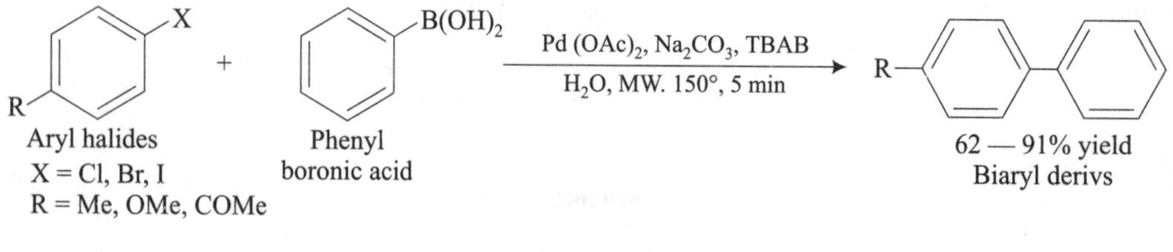

Scheme 11

It was found that in case of aryl chloride, the yield was poor as compared to other halides. This was overcome by carrying out the reaction of aryl chloride and phenyl boronic acid catalysed by Pd/C in aqueous medium using simultaneous cooling technique in conjction with MW heating[25]. By this technique it was found that the life time of aryl chloride was prolonged resulting in increased yields of biaryls. Suzuki reaction of heterocycle imidazo [1,2-a] pyridines with a number of aryl boronic acid was performed in aqueous medium under MW irradiation [Scheme 12]. This is an excellent procedure as compound to conventional conditions[26].

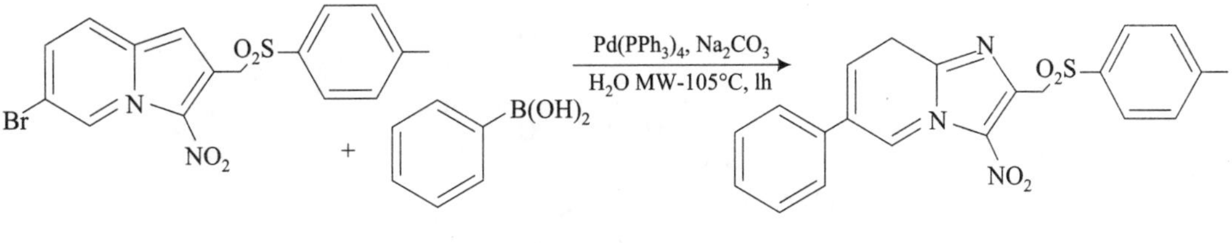

Scheme 12

Suzuki reaction was also used for the synthesis at 5-aryltriazole acyclonucleosides[27] (with various aromatic groups in the triazole ring). (Scheme 13). Such compounds are potential candidates for combating various viruses.

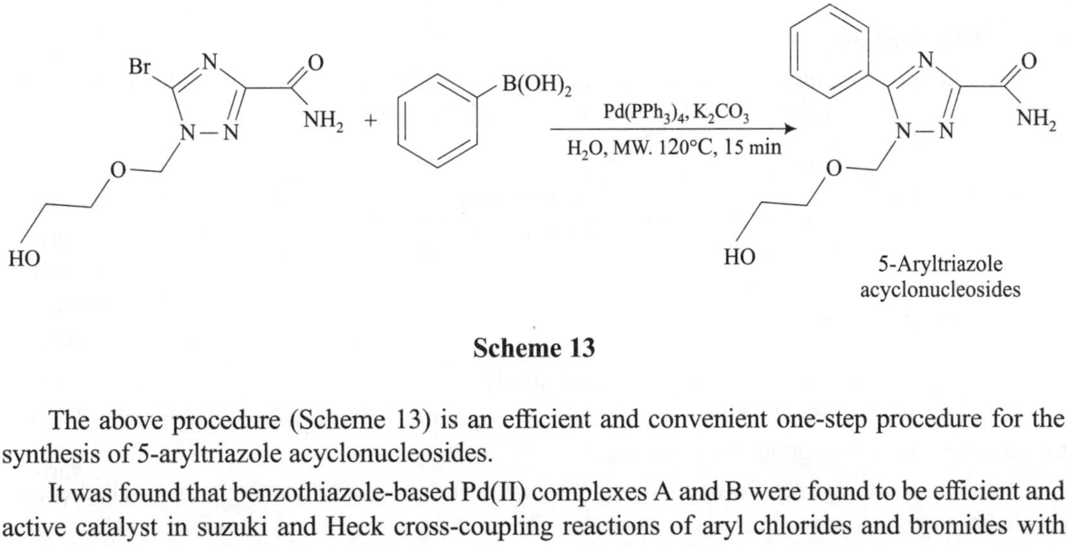

5-Aryltriazole
acyclonucleosides

Scheme 13

The above procedure (Scheme 13) is an efficient and convenient one-step procedure for the synthesis of 5-aryltriazole acyclonucleosides.

It was found that benzothiazole-based Pd(II) complexes A and B were found to be efficient and active catalyst in suzuki and Heck cross-coupling reactions of aryl chlorides and bromides with olefins and arylboronic acids under MW irradiation conditions in water. The deactivated aryl bromides were found to be more efficient for both C-C cross-coupling than their chloride analogs. The immobilized catalyst B was found to have high durability compared with its mobilized catalyst A. The high turnover number associated with the catalytic activity of these catalysts is highly important for the mass production on industrial scale (Scheme 14)[28].

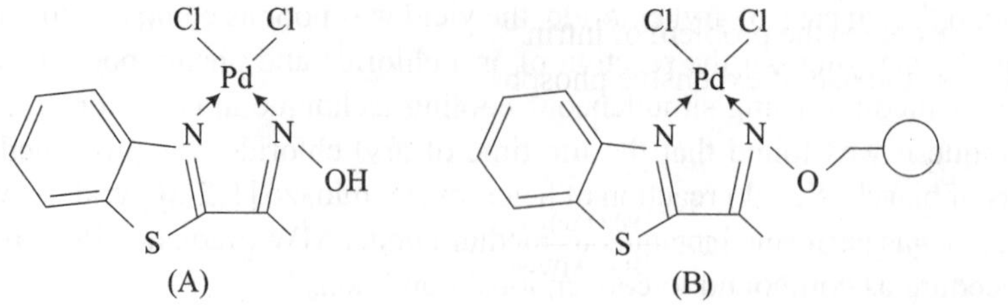

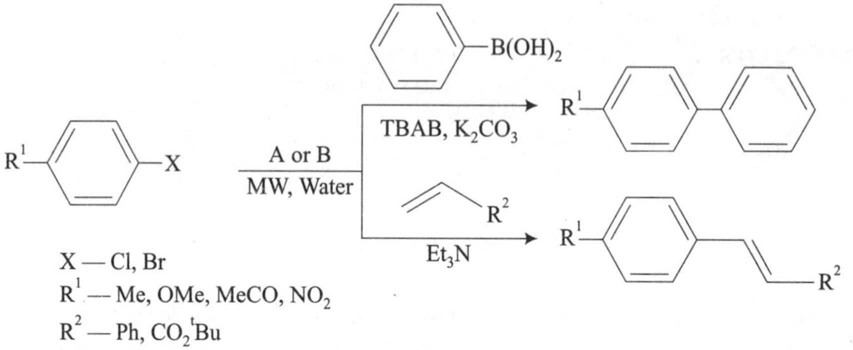

Scheme 14

10.2   Heck Reaction

Heck reaction, like suzuki reaction is also versatile in its applications[21]. Heck coupling reaction in water using MW heating (Scheme 15) give the coupled products[29].

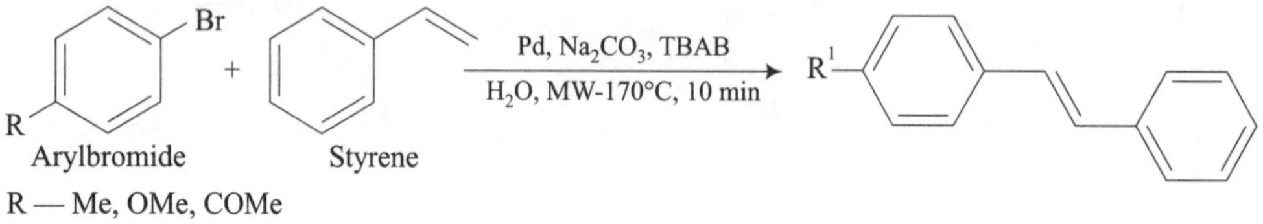

Scheme 15

It was found[29] that in Heck reaction Pd-catalyst concentration as low as 500 ppb was sufficient for these reactions with good product yield.

Regio-selective and fast Pd(0) catalyzed internal R-arylation of ethylene glycol vinyl ether and aryl halides in aqueous medium was reported[30]. The reaction was referred to as internal Heck reaction (Scheme 16)

10.3   Sonogashira Reaction

Cross-coupling reaction of terminal acetylenes with aryl or vinyl halides is another convenient method for the reaction of carbon-carbon bonds[31]. In this reaction, known as sonogashira reaction, coupling is done in aqueous medium under MW irradiations (Scheme 17). The reaction proceeds in water as the sole solvent, without the need for copper (I) or any transition metal-phosphane complex[32]. This overcomes the problem of intrinsic toxicity and air sensitivity of transition–metal complexes as well as the use of expensive phosphane ligands.

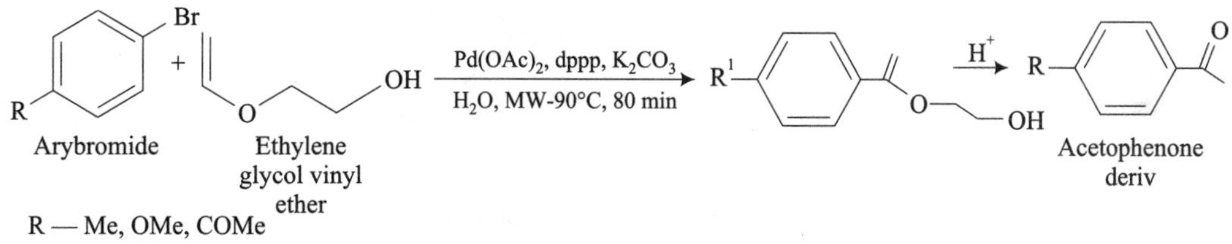

R — Me, OMe, COMe

Scheme 16

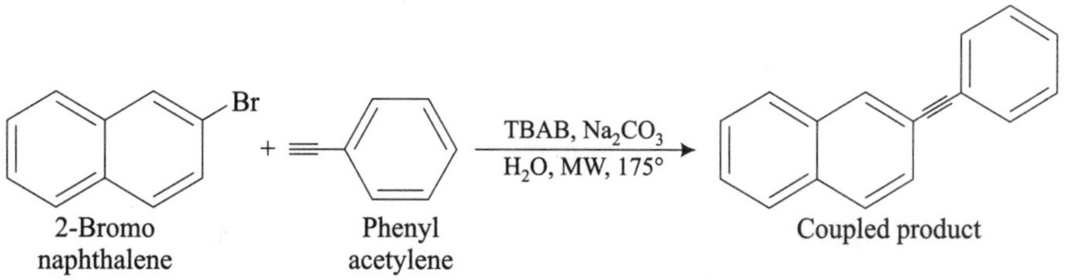

Scheme 17

10.4 Hiyama Reaction

It is convient to effect the cross-coupling reaction of organosilanes and aryl halides. Organo silanes are effective agents and are environmentally benign and stable to many reaction condition[33]. This reaction is known as Hiyama cross-coupling reaction which takes place between vinylalkoxysilanes and aryl halides and is promoted by aqueous sodium hydroxide (under fluoride free conditions) under MW irradiation in aqueous medium (Scheme 18). These reactions are catalysed by palladium(II) acetate or a 4-hydroxy acetophenone oxime derived palladacycle at 120° with low catalyst loading in the presence of TBAB as additive[34].

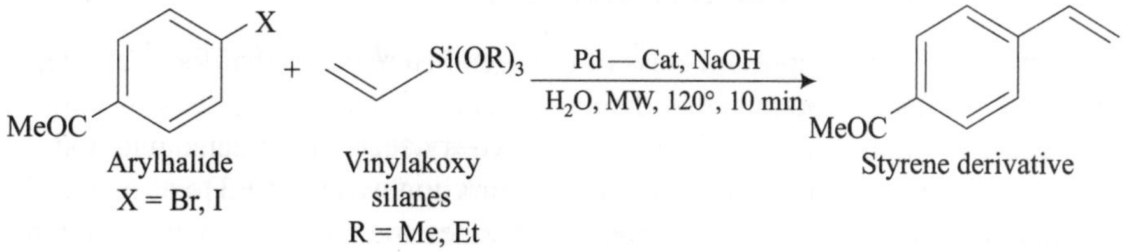

Scheme 18

II SYNTHESIS OF SPIRO 2, 5-DIKETOPIPERAZINES

Spiro amino acids incorporated into bioactive peptides are useful to both restrict the flexibility of the peptide and to provide information on the topographical requirements of peptide receptors[35].

An efficient method for the synthesis of spiro-2, 5-dikelopiperazines was developed by the cyclisation of Boc-protected dipeptides containing spiro-amino acids using MW heating in water (Scheme 19)[35].

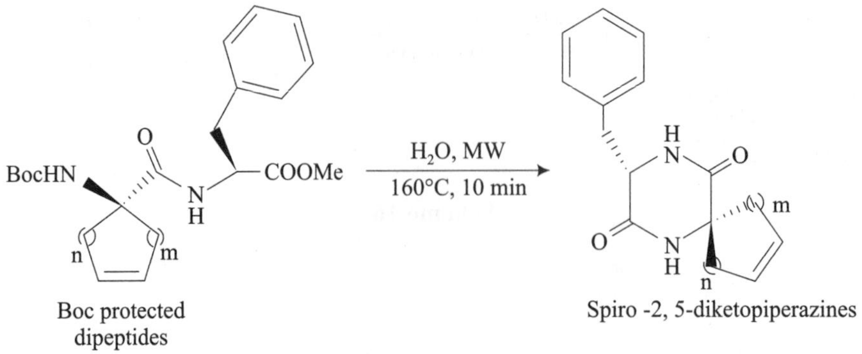

Boc protected
dipeptides

Spiro -2, 5-diketopiperazines

Scheme 19

I2   SYNTHESIS OF DIAZEPINES

A number of diazepines were synthesized by the condensation of diamines with diketones (Scheme 20)[36].

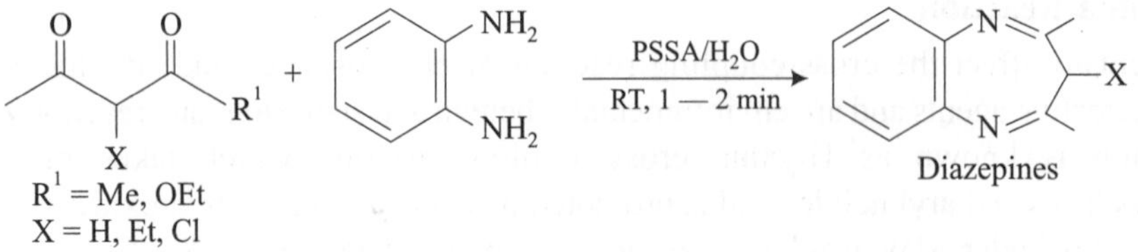

R^1 = Me, OEt
X = H, Et, Cl

Diazepines

Scheme 20

I3   SYNTHESIS OF TRIZINES AND TETRAZOLES

Trizines and Tetrazoles are an important class of nitrogen heterocycles that form an integral part of therapeutically interesting compounds that display diverse biological activities. A number heterocycles were prepared form primary alcohols and aldehydes which were treated with iodine in aqueous ammonia under MW irradiation to yield nitriles which underwent [2 + 3] cycloaddition reaction with dicyanodiamide and sodium azide to produce triazines and tetrazoles with high optical purity (Scheme 21)[37].

I4   AMINOCARBONYLATION REACTION

Aryl bromides can be readily converted into the corresponding secondary and tertiary benzamide by reaction with various amines in water using $Mo(CO)_6$ as the source at carbon monoxide and using MW heating (Scheme 22)[38]

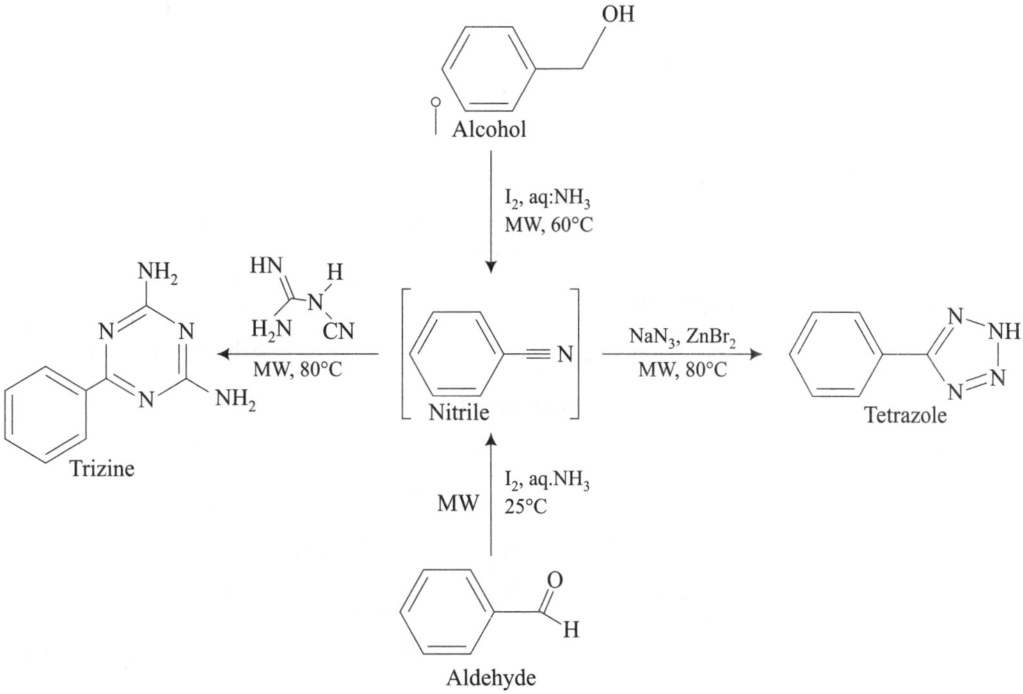

Scheme 21

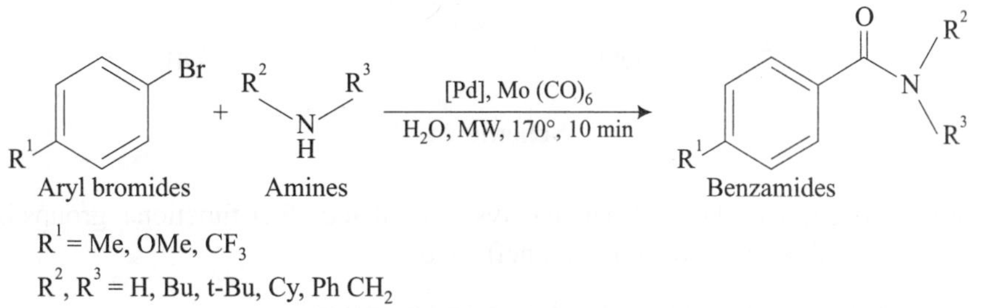

Aryl bromides   Amines

R^1 = Me, OMe, CF_3

R^2, R^3 = H, Bu, t-Bu, Cy, Ph CH_2

Scheme 22

15 KRÖHNKE REACTION

Substrituted pyridines were synthesised[39] by a one-pot condensation at aromatic ketones with aromatic aldehydes and ammonium acetate in water under MW irradiation (Scheme 23).

16 DEPROTECTION OF ACETALS AND KETALS

Acetals and Ketals are frequently used to protect carbonyl function during complex synthetic processes. A variety of methods have been developed for their deprotection. A convienient procedure of MW-assisted clevage of acetals and Ketals in pure water has been accomplished[40] (Scheme 24).

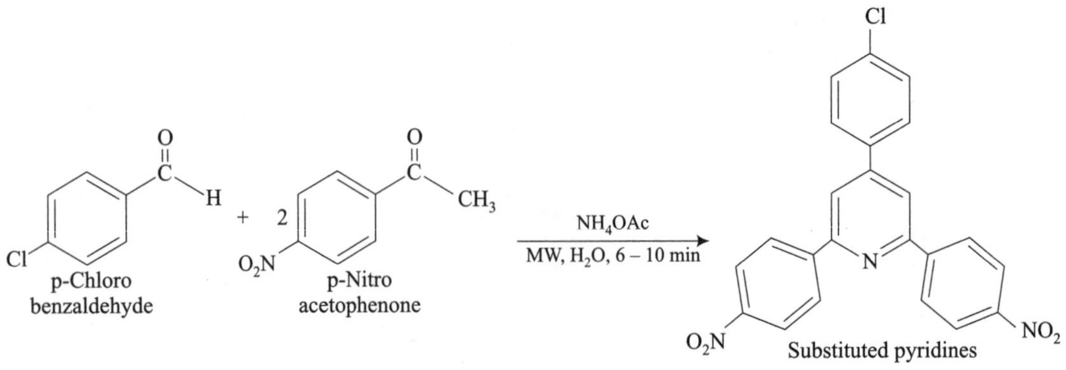

Scheme 23

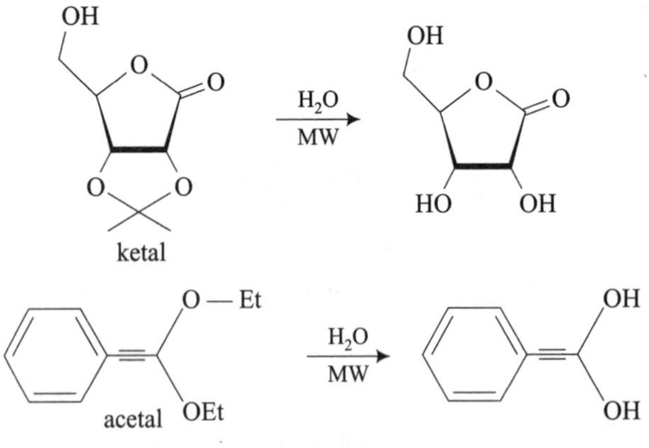

Scheme 24

In the above procedure (Scheme 24) no catalyst is used and other functional groups like carbonyl, triple bond and hydroxyl groups remain uneffected.

17 NUCLEOPHILIC SUBSTITUTION OF 6-CHLOROPURINE

Nucleosides play vital roles in various biological processes. Many nucleoside analogues with modification in the heterocyclic bases have been investigated for their antiviral and anticancer activities. A rapid nucleophilic substitution reaction of 6-chloropurine has been developed in aqueous medium under MW irradiation (Scheme 25)[41].

18 STILLE REACTION

Only few examples are known of MW-assisted Stille reaction involving organotin as coupling partners[42-44]. An aqueous MW-assisted Stille reaction has been reported[45] in the 2(H) pyrazinone divertive at the C-3 position (Scheme 26).

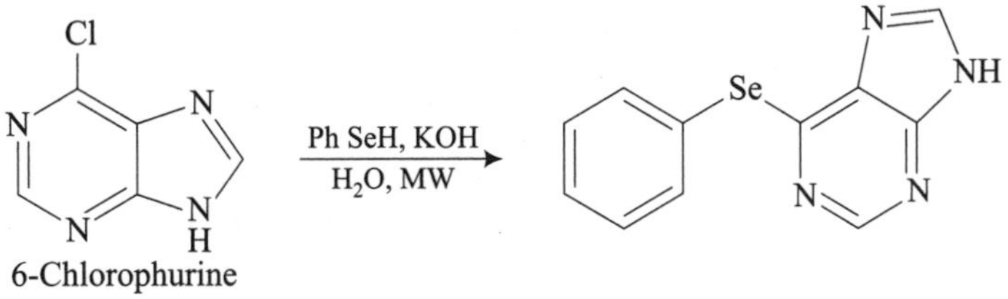

6-Chlorophurine

Scheme 25

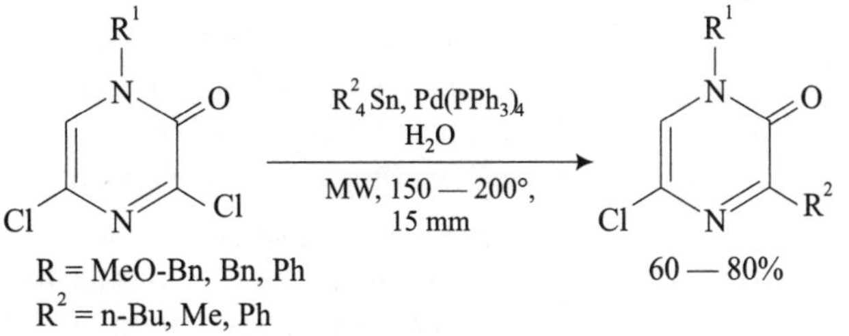

R = MeO-Bn, Bn, Ph
R^2 = n-Bu, Me, Ph

60 — 80%

Scheme 26

For tetraphenyl tin a higher temperture (200°) had been applied for full conversions.

19 CYANATION REACTIONS

Aryl iodides could be converted into aryl nitriles using CuCN, in presence of a PTC (TBAB), using aqueous MW irradiation (Scheme 27)[46].

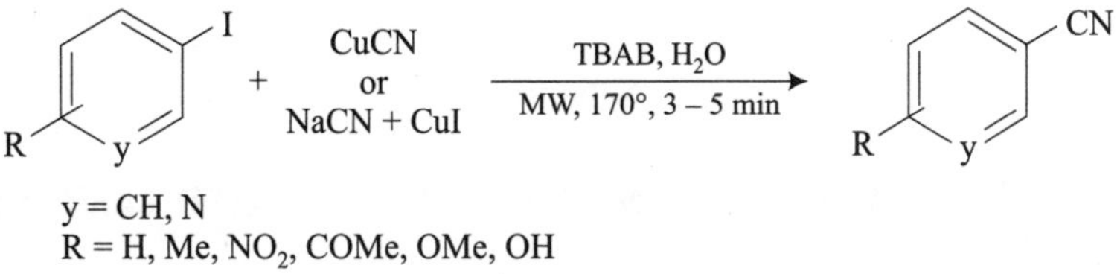

y = CH, N
R = H, Me, NO_2, COMe, OMe, OH

Scheme 27

In the above reaction (Scheme 27) high concentration of cyanide resulting from a 1:2 ratio of aryl halide/CuCN gave best results. Conventional heating under identical conditions gave no products. Even activated aryl bromides did not show any conversion. The reaction could also be performed by using less expensive NaCN in combination with CuI(forming CuCN in situ).

20 SYNTHESIS OF KETONES FROM AMINES

The Pd/C synthesis of ketones from amines via a retro-reductive amination pathway using water as an oxygen source was accomplished[47] (Scheme 28).

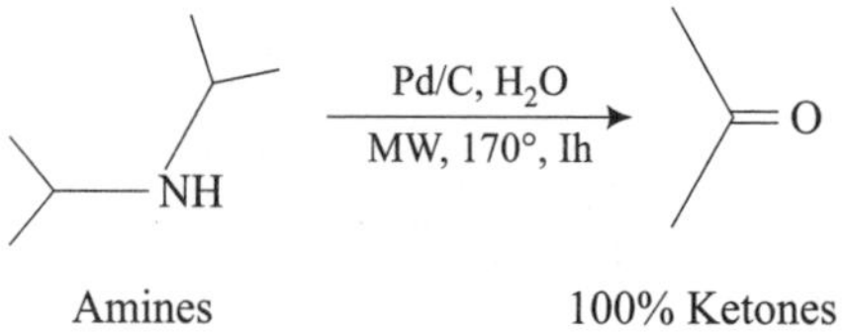

Scheme 28

The reaction depended on the number of hydrogen atoms on the α-carbon of the amine. Only amines possessing one hydrogen (mono-or di-sec-alkylamines) could be converted to the corresponding ketones. However amins with two alpha hydrogen atoms (e.g. n-butylamine) gave the corresponding imines and secondary alkyl amines. The reactions were conducted at constant microwave power which resulted in a maximum temperature of 170°. Conventional heating or microwave heating under reflux conditions were less efficient regarding conversion.

Using the above procedure, primary armies could be converted into secondary amines[48]. In this conversion Pd/C catalyst worked very well giving secondary amine as the main producet along with imine and tertiary amine (Scheme 29). It was found that the addition of aluminium powder to the reaction mixture prevented the formation imine; this is because hydrogen produced with water reduced imine to amine.

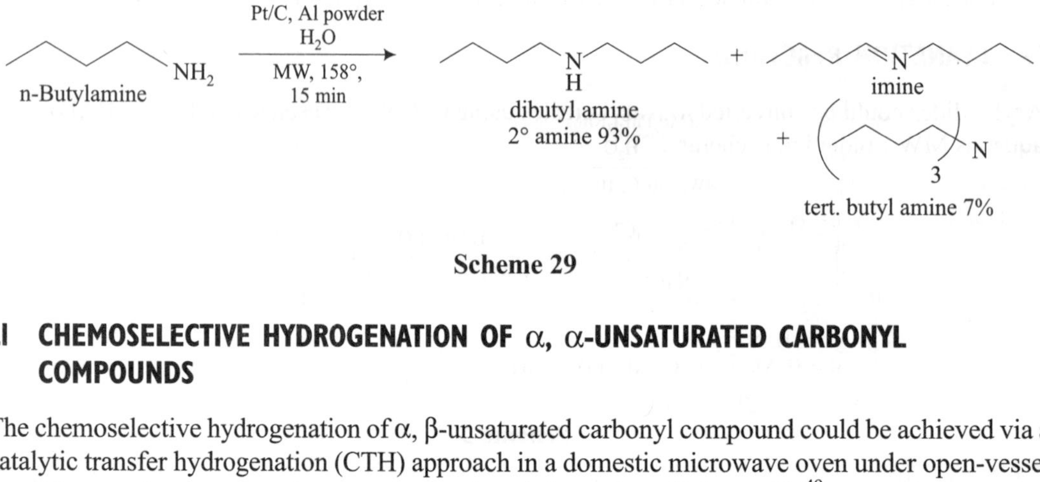

Scheme 29

21 CHEMOSELECTIVE HYDROGENATION OF α, α-UNSATURATED CARBONYL COMPOUNDS

The chemoselective hydrogenation of α, β-unsaturated carbonyl compound could be achieved via a catalytic transfer hydrogenation (CTH) approach in a domestic microwave oven under open-vessel conditions to the corresponding saturated carbonyl derivatives (Scheme 30)[49].

For best result the α, β-unsat'd ketones were treated under heterogeneous conditions using silica-supported Pd Cl$_2$ as catalyst and a 1:2:3 mixture of MeOH/HCOOH/H$_2$O as hydrogen source. In this reaction, use of water plays an important role since it causes rapid release of hydrogen gas from HCOOH. This makes the reaction proceed faster and in better yields. Interestingly under conventional heating both the unsat'd carbonyl compound and its corresponding alcohol were obtained under the same CTH conditions. The catalyst (Silica supported Pd) can be reused at least five times with virtually no loss of activity.

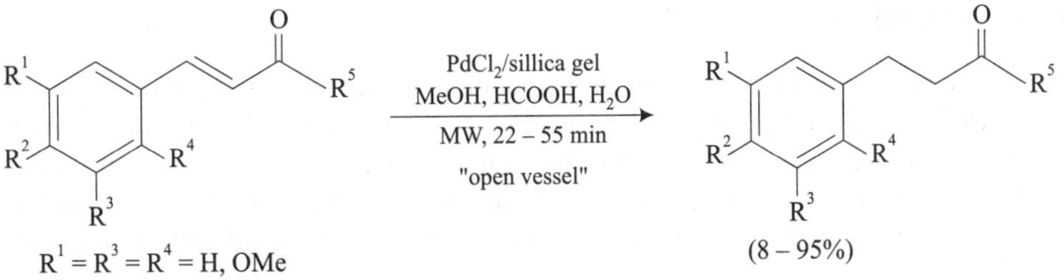

$$R^1 = R^3 = R^4 = H, OMe$$
$$R^2 = H, OH, OMe, HO_2, F$$
$$R^5 = H, Me, OH, OEt, aryl$$

Scheme 30

22 HYDROPHOSPHINYLATIONS OF PROPARGYL ALCOHOLS AND ETHYNYL STEROIDS

Hydrophosphinylations of propargyl alcohols and ethynyl steroids has been reported[50]. The reaction of simple propargyl alcohols generated mixtures of addition and elimination products. However addition of P(0)-H bonds to ethynyl steroids (e.g., ethisterone, see Scheme 31) furnished the addition products A or B, respectively. The special feature is that the reactions in aqueous media employing ethynyl steroids showed very high tolerance to oxygen and so the reaction can be carried out under an atmosphere of air without removal of oxygen.

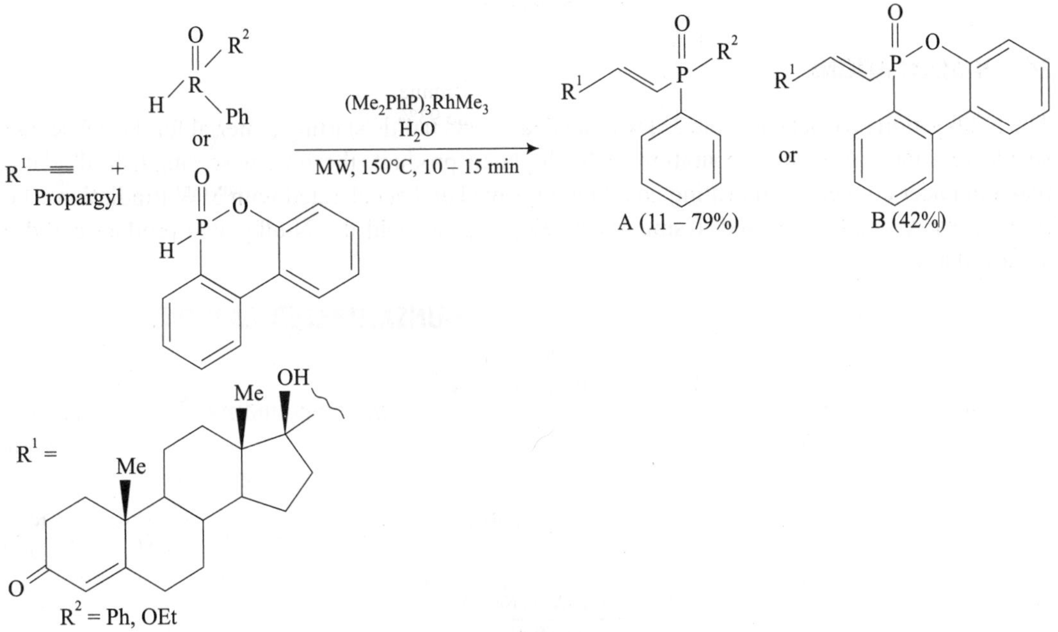

A (11 – 79%)   or   B (42%)

$$R^2 = Ph, OEt$$

Scheme 31

23 N-ACYLATIONS

The microwave heating in aqueous media proved to be very efficient (Scheme 32)[57] in the transformation of fused succinic anhydrides with hydrazines to the fused N-aminosuccinimide derivatives of bicyclo [2.2.2.] oct. 7-enes. Compared to the conventional heating, the reaction time could be reduced from several hours to 13-90 min, less hydrazine was required (2.2-2.4 vs 10 equiv.). Most important is that cleaner conversions were possible giving high yield (80-94 per cent) of the product.

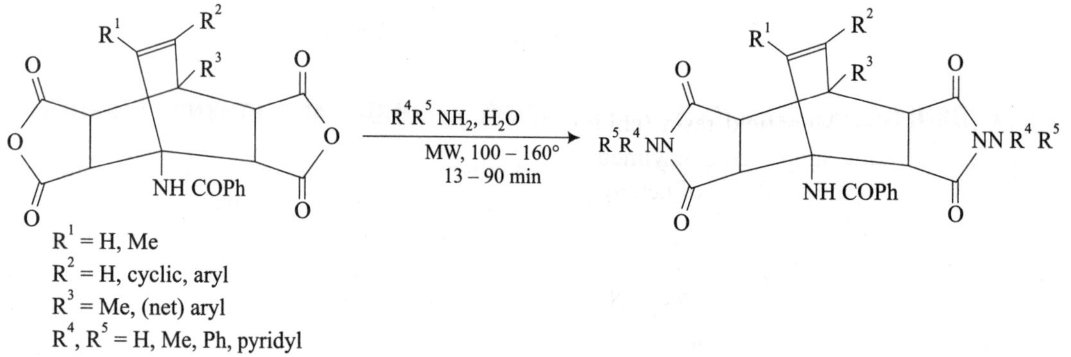

R^1 = H, Me
R^2 = H, cyclic, aryl
R^3 = Me, (net) aryl
R^4, R^5 = H, Me, Ph, pyridyl

Scheme 32

24 N-ALKYLATIONS

The N-alkyation product (Scheme 33) was needed as aryl halide starting material for the subsequent suzuki reaction[52]. For the preparation of N-alkylated product, the otherwise sluggish alkylation reaction under conventional heating could be improved and accelerated with MW irradiation when protic polar solvent were used. Using water, 99 per cent yield the N-alkylated product could be achieved at 160°.

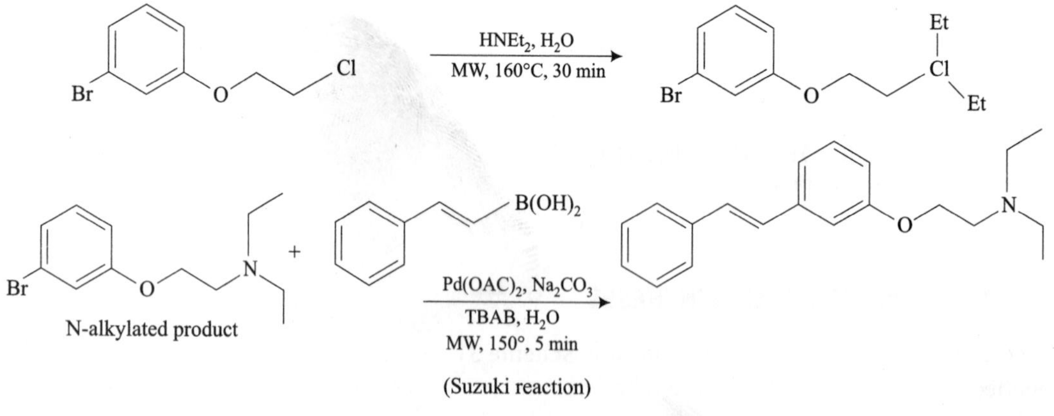

N-alkylated product

(Suzuki reaction)

Scheme 33

N-Alkylation of primary and secondary amines (aromatic, cyclic and non cyclic) with alkyl halides gave tertiary amines (Scheme 34)[53]. Using MW heating (open vessel, 45-100°), the reaction time could be reduced from 12 hr to 20-30 min; the formation of side products, mainly secondary amines could be suppressed.

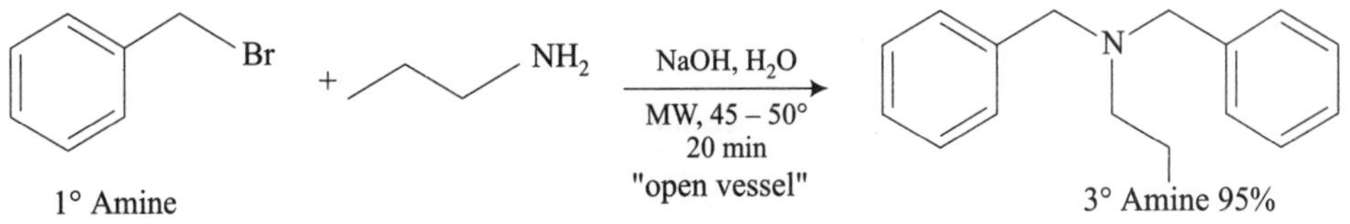

Scheme 34

The reaction of Merrifield resin (chloromethylated polystyrene resin) with aqueous methyl amine gave the solid supported benzylmethylamine produced (Scheme 35)[54] in 86 per cent yield, which was used for the synthesis of heterocycles.

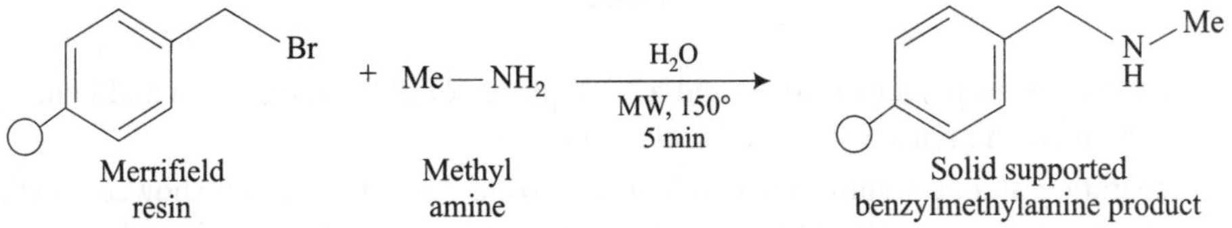

Scheme 35

25 N-ARYLATIONS

A base free inter and intramolecular N-arylation promoted by active copper has been achieved[55]. Thus, the reaction of aryl halides with amines, amides, (Scheme 36 a) and β-lactams (Scheme 36 b) proceeded under very mild conditions. The intramolecular N-arylations of β-lactams in the absence of base in the reason for success, since base decomposes the starting material.

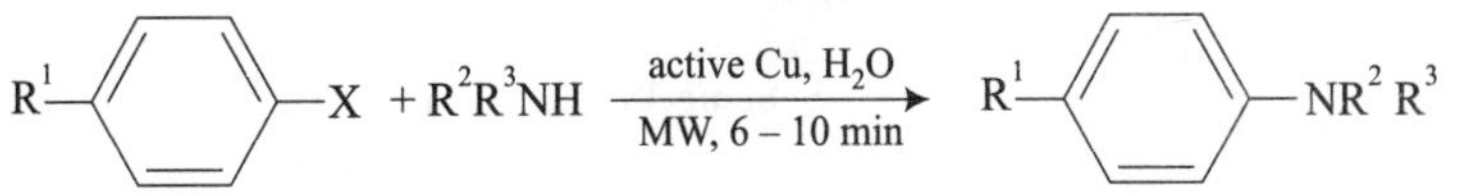

$R^1 = Me$
$R^2, R^3 = H$, alkyl, cyclic, aryl, COMe
$X = Cl, Br, I$

$(71 - 91\%)$

Scheme 36a

26 WILLIAMSONS ETHER SYNTHESES

In an especially designed instrument, a combined microwave and ultra sound procedure was reported[56] for Williamson's ether synthesis by the reaction of phenol and aryl or alkyl chlorides (Scheme-37). This rather uncomman combination gave higher yield in much shorter time compared to only MW heating or sonication[57].

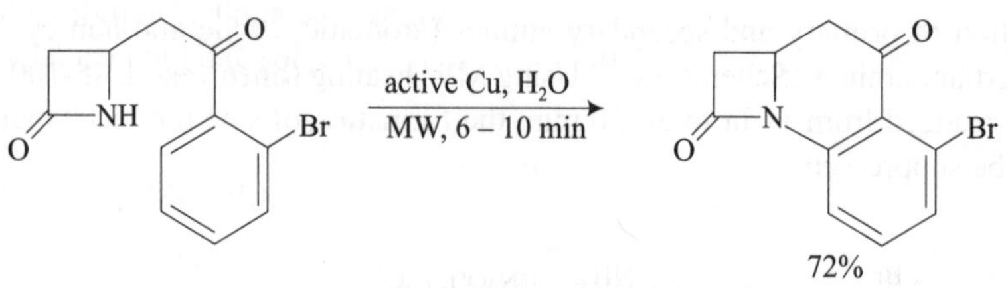

Scheme 36b

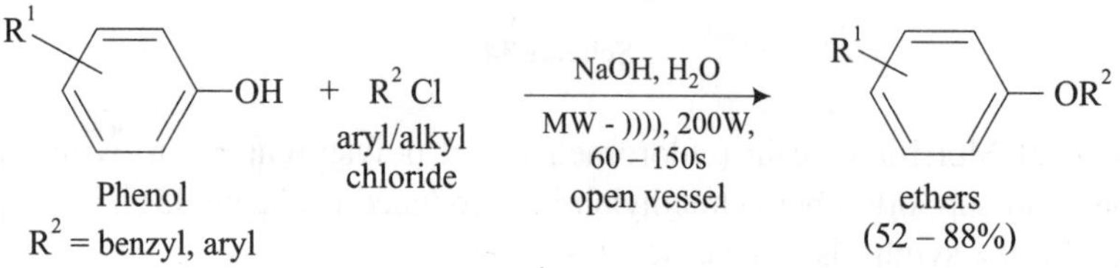

Scheme 37

With an ultra sound power of 50 W and a MW power of 200 W, diphenyl and benzylphenyl ethers were obtained[56] in reasonably good yield in 60-150 s.

The preparation at a new sulfonylmethylbenzothiazole derivative which showed considerable cytotoxic activity was reported[58]. The procedure involves aqueous S–alkylation of sodium salt of differently substituted sulfinic acids with 2-chloromethyl-6 nitrobenzothiazole (Scheme 38).

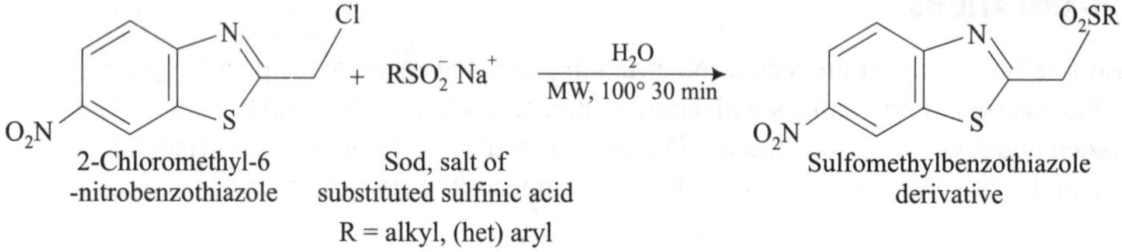

Scheme 38

27 SYNTHESES OF HETEROCYCLES

The synthesis of some nitrogen containing heterocycles was reported earlier (see Schemes 1 and 2). The present section deals with the synthesis of five membered N-heterocycles, six membered O-heterocycles, six-membered N-heterocycles and six-membered N, S-heterocycles.

27.1 Five-membered N-heterocycles

One pot synthesis of fused pyrazoles was reported[59] by the reaction of cyclic 1, 3 diketones with N, N-dimethylformamide dimethyl acetal (DMFDMA) and a hydrazine derivative under MW irradiation in presence of acid catalyst and water (Scheme 39).

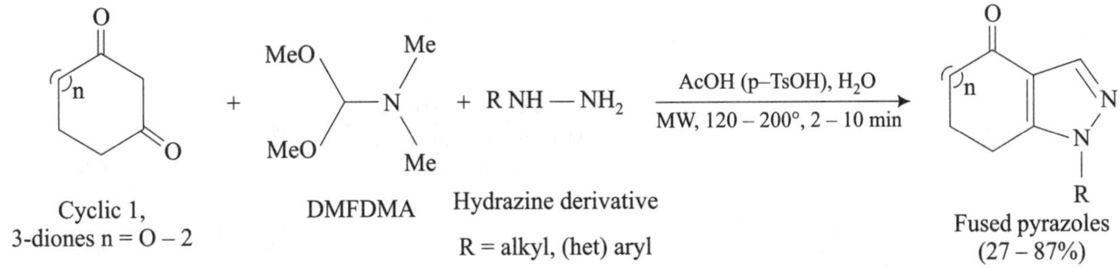

Scheme 39

The above reaction (Scheme 39) proceeds via the initial formation of an enaminoketone in situ followed by a tandem addition-elimination/cyclodehyration step. Normally 2.6 equivalent of acetic acid is necessary for complete conversion at 200° within 2min. However for 1, 3-cyclopentanedione (n = 0), p-totuene sulfonic acid is used in place of acetic acid at lower temperature but longer irradiation time (120°, 10 mim) to afford the corresponding pyrazole in 27 per cent yield. Using amidines and hydroxylamine in place of hydrazine derivates in the above procedure, other heterocyclic compounds like pyrimidines and isoxazoles could be synthesised

The synthesis of benzimidazoles as potential HIV-1 integrase inhibitors were synthesised[60] by the condensation of α-hydroxy cinnamic acids with 1, 2-phenylenediamine in water and MW irradiation (Scheme 40).

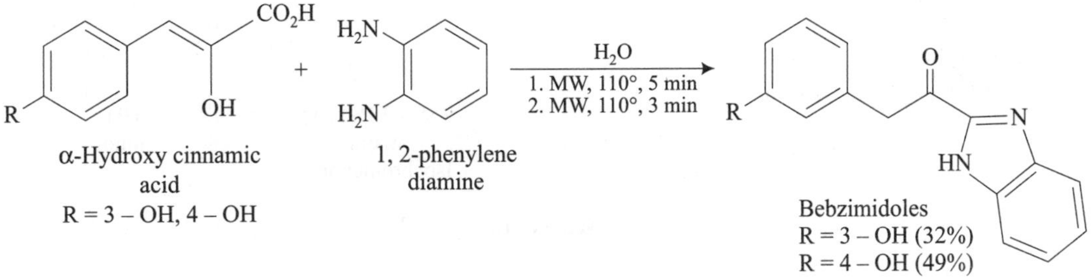

Scheme 40

Benzimidazole (R = 3-OH was found[61] to prevent the cytophatic effect of HIV-I III$_B$ with an EC$_{50}$ of 27, μm but did not inhibit the HIV-1 integrase enzymatic activity.

The synthesis of 4-H- pyrano[2, 3-c] pyrazoles was reported[57,62] using combind microwave and ultrasound irradiations (CMuI) (as in the case of Willamsons ether syntheses – see Scheme 37) in aqueous media. Thus the reaction of pyran derivative with hydrazine monohydrate and a catalytic amount of piperazine using CMUI approach gave 100 per cent yield of the pyrano pyrazole in 1 min (Scheme 41). Use of only microwave irradiation gave 48 per cent yield in 20 mim. and the combination of both heating and ultrasound irradiation gave 99 per cent yield in 20 mim. The rate enhancement by ultrasound could be that a passivation coating on the surface of the substrate particles, which occurred due to poor solubility of the products in water is removed by sonication. This is a general method for the synthesis of pyranopyrazoles in excellent yields.

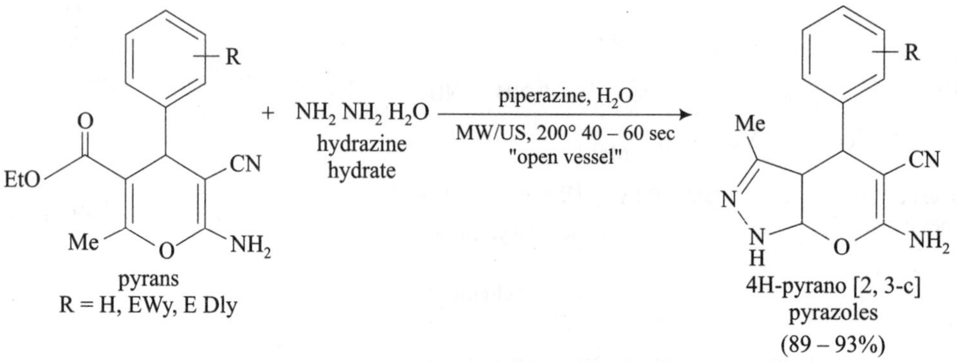

Scheme 41

27.2 Six-membered O-heterocycles

Isochrome derivatves were obtained[63] by aromatic substitution by activated methylene compounds (1, 3–diketones) with base and stoichiometric amount of a copper (I) catalyst (Scheme 42).

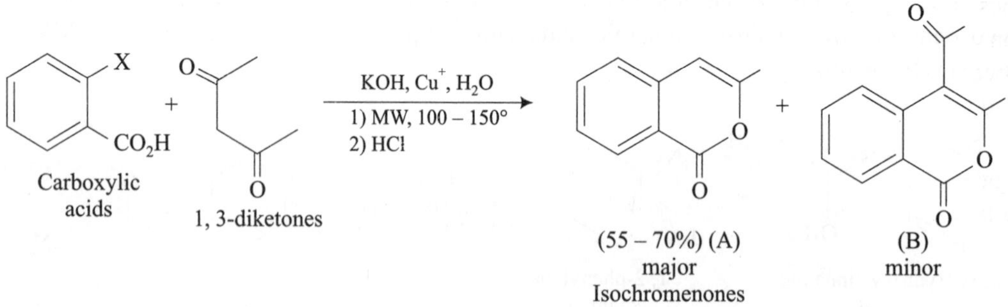

Scheme 42

Under normal reflux condition (NaH, Cu⁺) in THF isochromene (B) is obtained as the main product after acidification. However under MW irradiation (KOH, Cu⁺) in water at 100 – 150° (3-14 bar) the acetyl group gets knocked out giving the isochromene(A) as the major product.

2-Amino-4H-chromenes were oblaned[64] by one pot reaction of an aldehyde, malononitrile and resorcinol under MW irradiation in presence of H_2O and K_2CO_3 (Scheme 43).

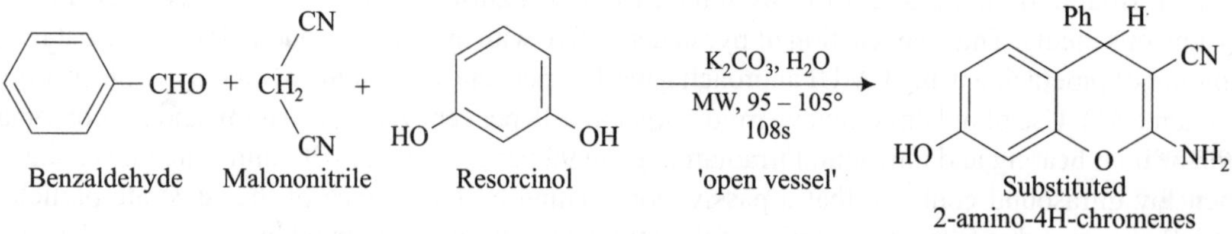

Scheme 43

27.3   Six-membered N-Heterocycles

Dihydropyridines (DHP) were prepared by Hantzsch reaction by a one-pot reaction involving condensation of an aldehyde, β-keloester and aqueous ammonium hydroxide (which servet as both reagent and solvent) (Scheme 44)[65]. Best yield were obtained by MW irradiation at 140–150° for 10–15 mim.

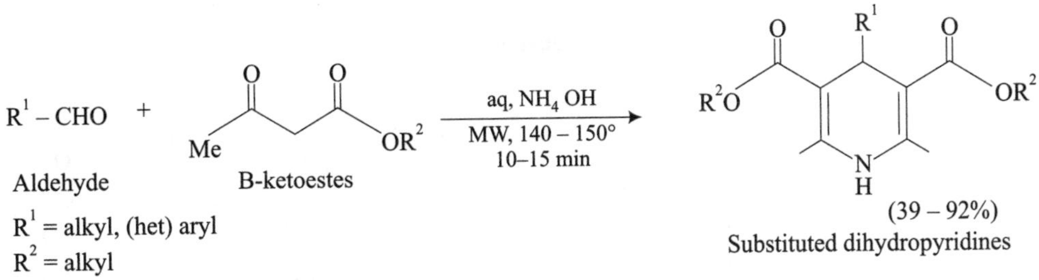

R[1] = alkyl, (het) aryl
R[2] = alkyl

Scheme 44

A number at related dihydropyridines were subsequently prepared by the same procedure[66]. These DHPS could further be aromatised in only 1 mim at 100° against MW irradiation, by oxidation with MnO_2 to generate the corresponding pyridines in excellent yields (91-99%). In a modified procedure[67] aqueous ammonium acetate instead of ammonium hydroxide and TBAB as PTC were used to prepare DHPS in 77.92 per cent yield.

N-substituted acridine derivatives were synthesises by one pot Hantzsch type reaction involving the condensation of an aldehyde, 2 equiv. of 1, 3 cydohexanedione and methylamine under open vessel reflux conditions in domestic MW oven[68] (Scheme 45). When 1, 3-cydohexanedione is used (Scheme 45) water was used as solvent. However the reaction with dimedone (scheme-46) only proceeded in glycol with good yields.

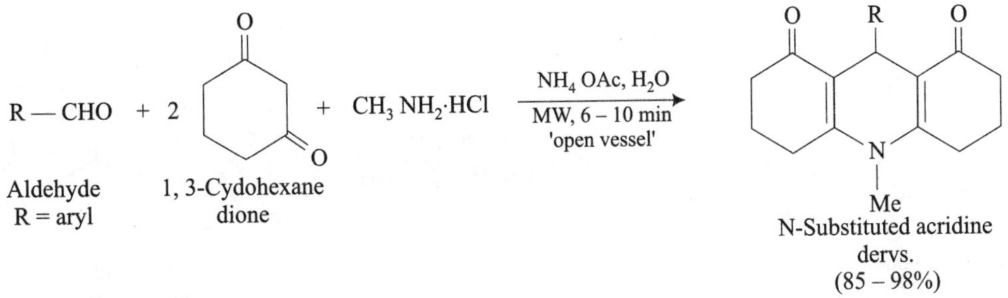

Scheme 45

4-Aza-podophyllotoxin derivatives (A and B) were prepared[69] by the reaction of an aldehyde, aromatic amine and tetronic acid or 1, 3 indanedione respectively (Scheme 47).

Substituted indeno [1, 2-b] quinolines were prepared[70] in one-pot synthesis by the reaction of 1, 3-indanedione, (het) aryl or aryl aldehydes and various substituted enaminones using p-toluene sulfonic acid as catalyst (Scheme 48).

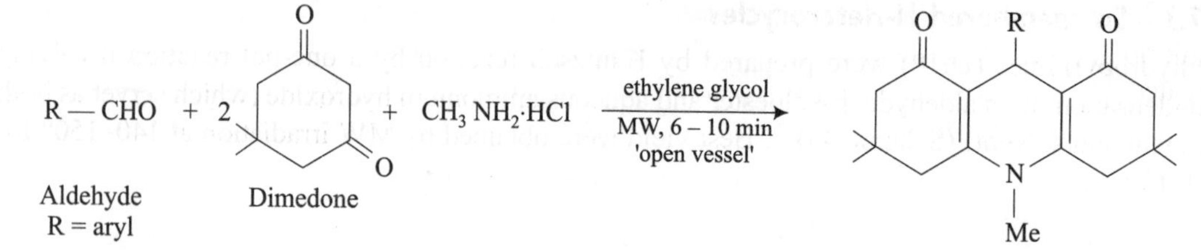

R—CHO + 2 [Dimedone] + CH₃NH₂·HCl $\xrightarrow[\text{MW, 6 – 10 min}]{\text{ethylene glycol}}$ 'open vessel'

Aldehyde
R = aryl

Dimedone

Scheme 46

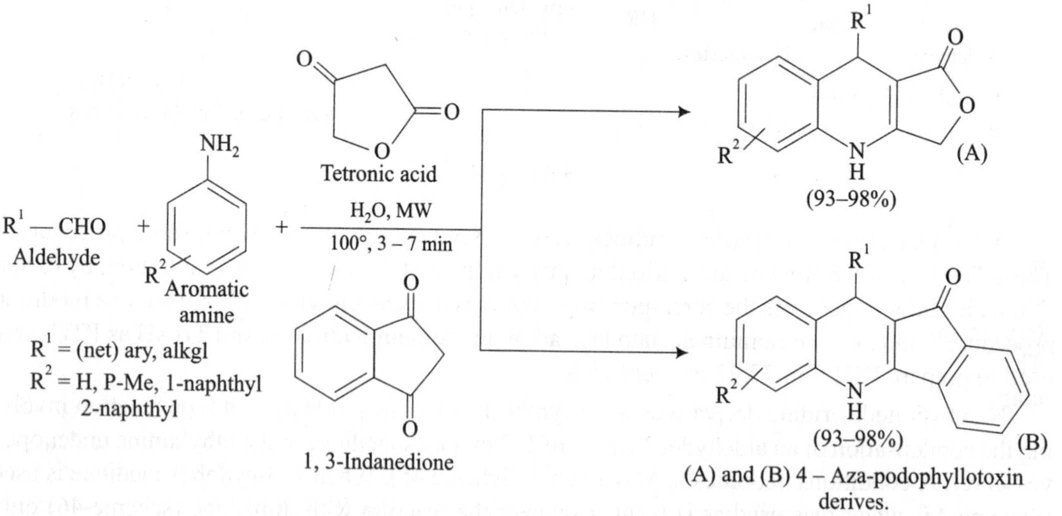

R¹—CHO + [Aromatic amine] + [Tetronic acid / 1,3-Indanedione] $\xrightarrow[\text{100°, 3 – 7 min}]{\text{H}_2\text{O, MW}}$

Aldehyde

Aromatic amine

R¹ = (net) ary, alkgl
R² = H, P-Me, 1-naphthyl
   2-naphthyl

Tetronic acid

1, 3-Indanedione

(A)
(93–98%)

(B)
(93–98%)

(A) and (B) 4 – Aza-podophyllotoxin
derives.

Scheme 47

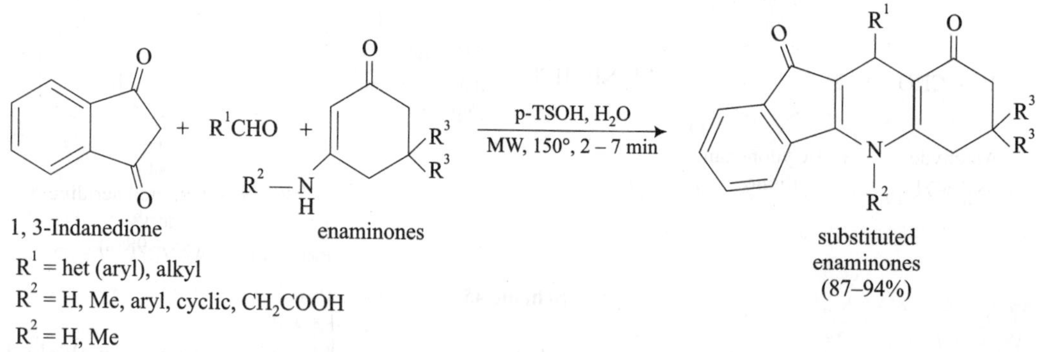

[1,3-Indanedione] + R¹CHO + [enaminones] $\xrightarrow[\text{MW, 150°, 2 – 7 min}]{\text{p-TSOH, H}_2\text{O}}$

1, 3-Indanedione

R¹ = het (aryl), alkyl
R² = H, Me, aryl, cyclic, CH₂COOH
R² = H, Me

enaminones

substituted
enaminones
(87–94%)

Scheme 48

It was found in the above reaction (Scheme 48) that aryl halides with electron withdrawing groups reacted within 2-3 mim. However aryl halides with electron donating substituent had a decreased reactivity requiring about double the reaction time.

2, 5-Dikelopiperazines were synthesised[71] starting with dipeptide methyl esters as their hydrochloride salt, (obtained by the removed of the BOC protecting group with HCl/MeOH) which were heated in MW at 140° for 10 mim. with triethylamine and water (Scheme 49).

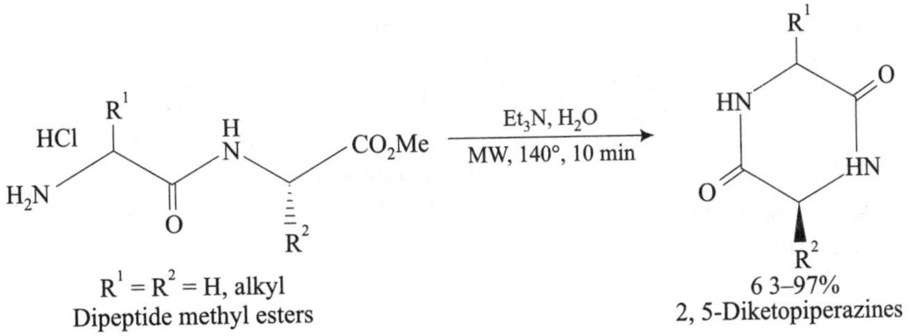

R¹ = R² = H, alkyl
Dipeptide methyl esters

6 3–97%
2, 5-Diketopiperazines

Scheme 49

The above synthesis (Scheme 49) is in fact a two-step process. The first step is the removal of the BOC protecting groups followed by step two as given in Scheme 49. The two steps could be combined in one step by heating BOC protected dipeptide methyl ester in water under MW irradiation at 150° for 15 mim. The 2,5-diketopiperazine was obtarred in 75 per cent yield (Scheme 50)[72]. The 2, 5 diketopiperazine in the starting material for the synthesis of schollkopf bis-lactim ether chiral auxilary (A).

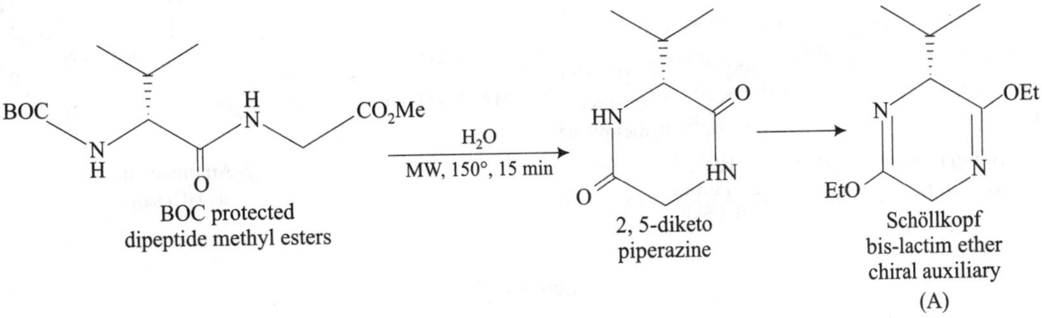

BOC protected
dipeptide methyl esters

2, 5-diketo
piperazine

Schöllkopf
bis-lactim ether
chiral auxiliary
(A)

Scheme 50

Synthesis of spiro –2, 5-driketopiperazines has been disussed earlier (see Schme 19).

27.4 Six-membered N, S-hetrocycles

Novel 10 H-phenothiazines were synthesised[73] (Scheme 51) by an iodine catalysed reaction of diarylamines with sulphur in doubly distilled water at 190° within 20 min of MW irradiation. Further alkylation at the NH and subsequent animation (MW, 100°, 40 mim) yielded scaffolds, which contain an aliphatic amine functionality at the side chain and were screened for binding to HIV-I TAR RNA.

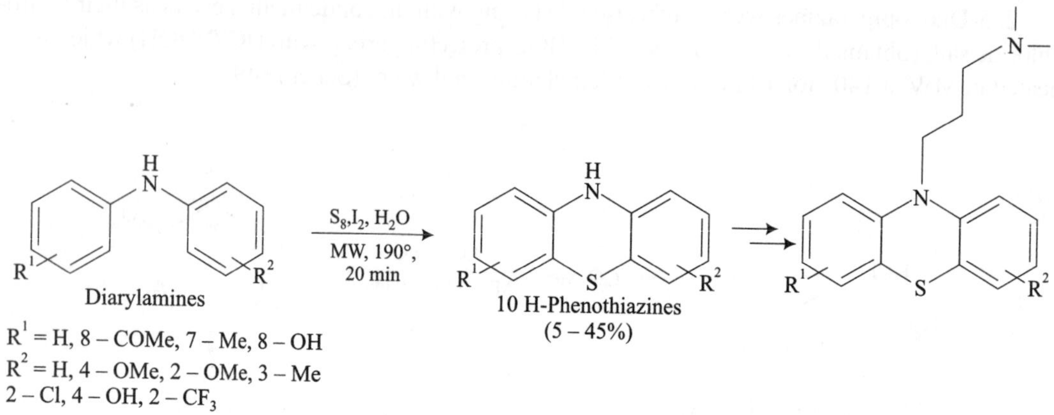

R^1 = H, 8 – COMe, 7 – Me, 8 – OH
R^2 = H, 4 – OMe, 2 – OMe, 3 – Me
2 – Cl, 4 – OH, 2 – CF$_3$

Scheme 51

28 MANNICH REACTION

Mannich Reaction is a very useful reaction for the synthesis of β-aminoketones. The original reaction needs drastic conditions, long reaction times and low yields. An aqueous MW-assisted Mannich reactions has been reported[74] by the reaction of acetophenones, secondary amines in the form of their hydrochloride salts and trioxymethylene as a sources of formaldehyde (Scheme 52).

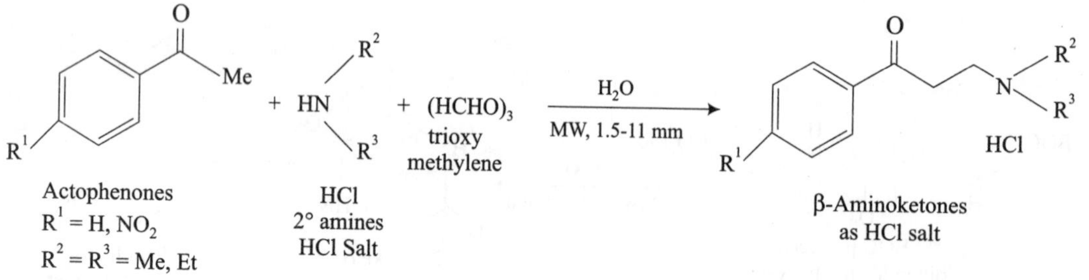

Actophenones
R^1 = H, NO$_2$
R^2 = R^3 = Me, Et

HCl
2° amines
HCl Salt

β-Aminoketones
as HCl salt

Scheme 52

The above reaction (Scheme 52) could be performed to give higher yields in shorter reaction times (20 – 50s) by using combined microwave and Ultra sound conditions[57].

A novel type of Mannich Reaction involving the condensation of an aldehyde, a primary or secondary amine and a terminal alkyne in presence of Cu (I) iodide, which promotes activation of the C-H bond of alkyne was reported (Scheme 53)[75].

Using (S) proline methyl ester as chiral amine an asymmetric synthesis of propargylamines was developed with high distereoselectivity (95:5 for R^1 = R^4 = Ph).

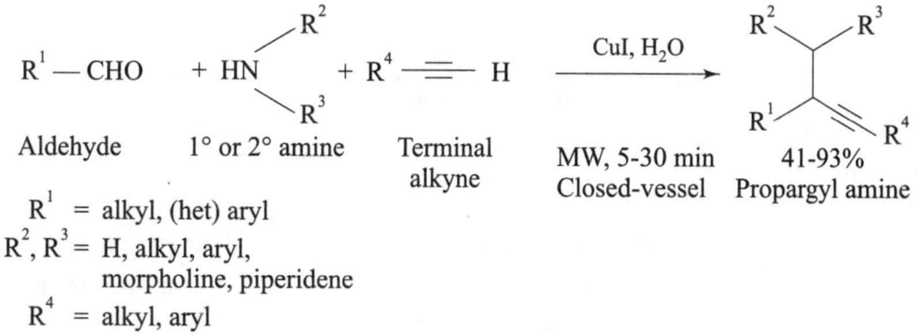

$$R^1 - CHO \quad + \quad HN\begin{smallmatrix}R^2\\\\R^3\end{smallmatrix} \quad + \quad R^4 \!\!\equiv\!\! H \quad \xrightarrow[\text{MW, 5-30 min}]{\text{CuI, H}_2\text{O}}$$

Aldehyde	1° or 2° amine	Terminal alkyne

MW, 5-30 min   41-93%
Closed-vessel Propargyl amine

R^1 = alkyl, (het) aryl
R^2, R^3 = H, alkyl, aryl,
        morpholine, piperidene
R^4 = alkyl, aryl

Scheme 53

29 NUCLEOPHILIC AROMATIC SUBSTITUTIONS

Normally, nucleophilic substitution reactions conducted under conventional heating are difficult to perform requiring high temperture and long reaction times. Also the aryl component, which in reacted with various nuclcophiles like amines or alcohols must contain an electron withdrawing group. Thus 2, 4-dinitrofluorobenzene (Sangers reagent) on reaction with amino acids afforded N-aryl-α-amino acid derivatives in good yield in about 35 seconds (Scheme 54)[76].

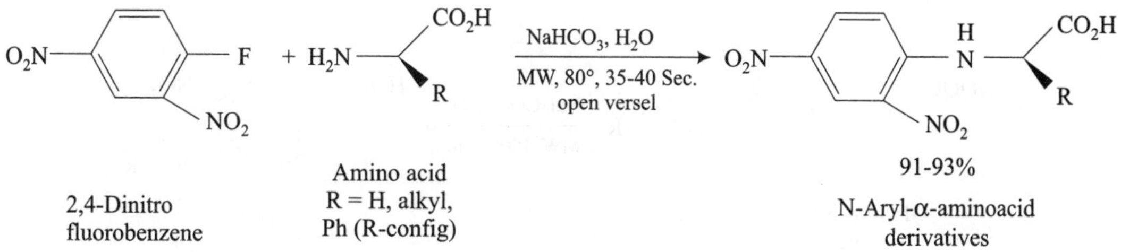

2,4-Dinitro fluorobenzene	Amino acid R = H, alkyl, Ph (R-config)	N-Aryl-α-aminoacid derivatives 91-93%

Scheme 54

In the above reaction (Scheme 54) the nucleophilicity of the amino acid is increased by using 2 equivalent of NaHCO$_3$. In conventional heating at 95°, no product was detected within 1 min. The bromo and chloro derivatives of 2, 4-dinitrobenzene reacted slowly and gave low yields (6-15 mim, 48-64%).

Nucleophilic substitution o-fluoro benzaldehyde with pyrrolidine at 130° for 3 mim. gave an intermediate (A) which on further heating at 210° in presence of potassium carbonate-water for 50 mim gave the pyrrolobenzoxazine (B). The intermediate (A) on reaction with malononitrile (Knoevenagle condensation) and subsequent cyclisation gave tricyclic pyrido fused product (C) in 50 per cent yield (Scheme 54a)[77].

NI-Alkyl benzotriazole –5-carboxylic acids were prepared[78] by the reaction of 4-fluoro –3-nitrobenzoic acid with diversely substituted amines via nucleophilic substitution under MW conditions (Scheme 55). The product obtained (A) was converted into N1-alkyl benzotriazole –5-carboxylic acid (B) by a two-step reaction.

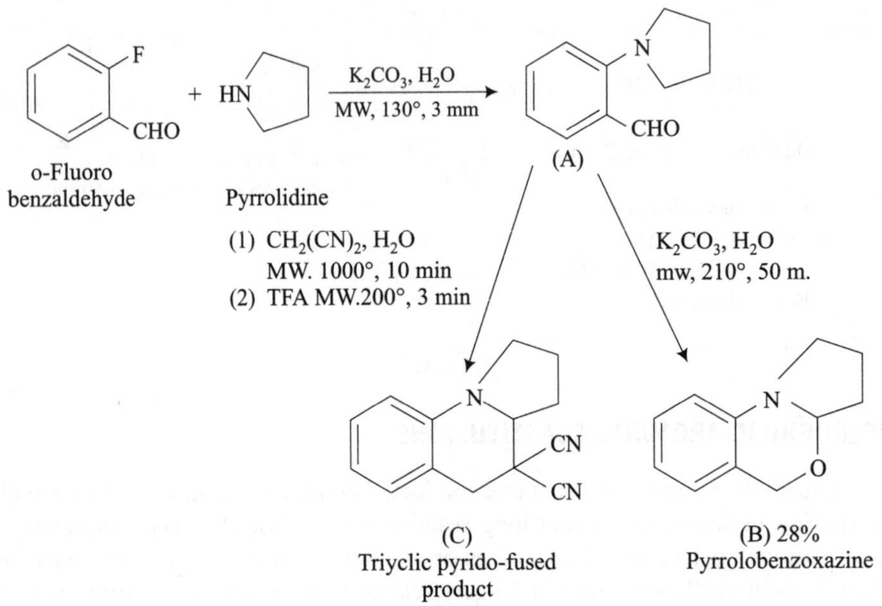

o-Fluoro benzaldehyde

Pyrrolidine

K$_2$CO$_3$, H$_2$O
MW, 130°, 3 mm

(A)

(1) CH$_2$(CN)$_2$, H$_2$O
   MW. 1000°, 10 min
(2) TFA MW.200°, 3 min

K$_2$CO$_3$, H$_2$O
mw, 210°, 50 m.

(C)
Triyclic pyrido-fused product

(B) 28%
Pyrrolobenzoxazine

Scheme 54a

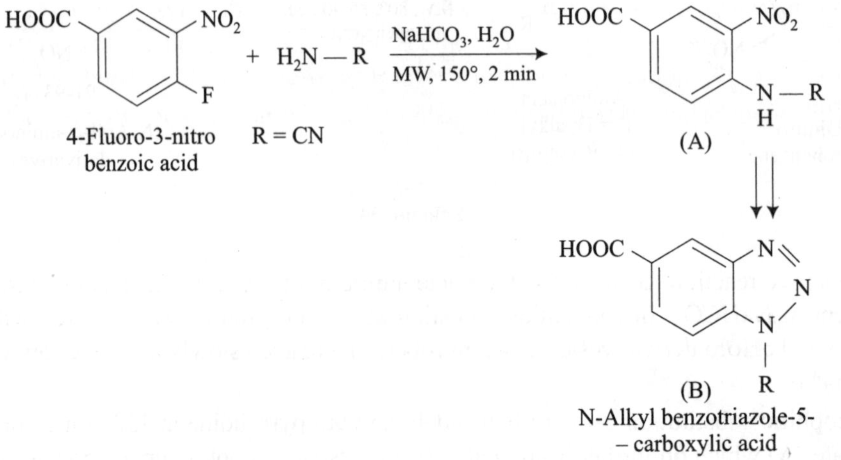

4-Fluoro-3-nitro benzoic acid

R = CN

NaHCO$_3$, H$_2$O
MW, 150°, 2 min

(A)

(B)   R
N-Alkyl benzotriazole-5-
– carboxylic acid ,

Scheme 55

1-Isopropyl-benzotriazole –5-terozole was synthesised[78] by the reaction of 4-Fluoro –3-nitrobenzonitrile with isopropylamine by using the procedure used in (Scheme 55). The formed produced (C) was converted into 1-isopropyl-benzotriazole-5-tetrazole as shown below (Scheme 56).

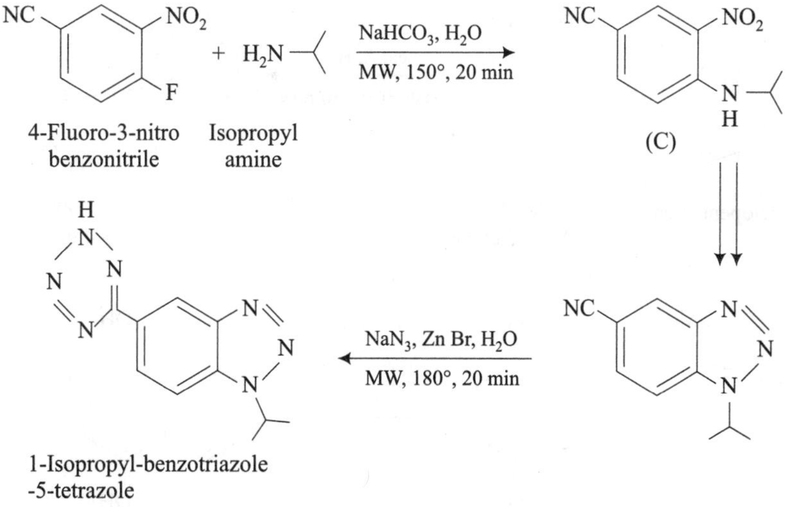
NC
NO2
F
+ H2N
NaHCO3, H2O
MW, 150°, 20 min
NC
NO2
N
H
4-Fluoro-3-nitro benzonitrile
Isopropyl amine
(C)
H
N
N
N
N
N
N
N
NaN3, Zn Br, H2O
MW, 180°, 20 min
NC
N
N
N
1-Isopropyl-benzotriazole -5-tetrazole

Scheme 56

30 EPOXIDE RING-OPENING REACTION

β-Hydoxy sulfides were synthesised[79] via the aqueous thiolysis of epoxies with thiophenol in presence of a catalytic amount at NaOH (Scheme 57). The ring opening was found to be completely anti steroselective and the trans products were obtained in excellent yields (85-98%). In addition to the above a one-pot procedure was developed[79] for the synthesis of β-hydroxysulfoxide. Addition of two equivalent of tert-butyl hydroperoxide to the reaction mixture which already contained β-hydxysulphide and subsequent irradition at 100° generated the oxidised produced (β-hydroxysulfoxide) in 89 per cent yield as a 25:27 mixture of diasteromers (Scheme 57).

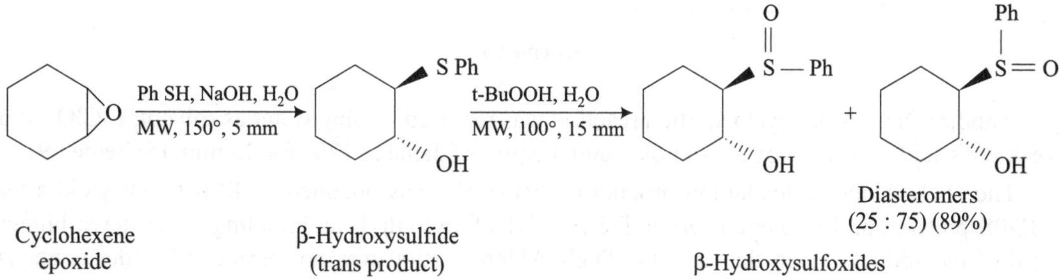
O
Ph SH, NaOH, H2O
MW, 150°, 5 mm
S Ph
OH
t-BuOOH, H2O
MW, 100°, 15 mm
O
S — Ph
OH
+
Ph
S = O
OH
Diasteromers
(25 : 75) (89%)
Cyclohexene epoxide
β-Hydroxysulfide (trans product)
β-Hydroxysulfoxides

Scheme 57

31 DIELS-ALDER CYLOADDETIONS

In Diels-Alder cycloaddition, considerable rate acceleration was observed[80] due to combined effect of a water soluble organotungston lews acid catalyst (A), water as solvent and MW heating. The reaction could be completed in less them 1 mim at 50° employing 3 mol % of the lewis acid catalyst (Scheme 58)

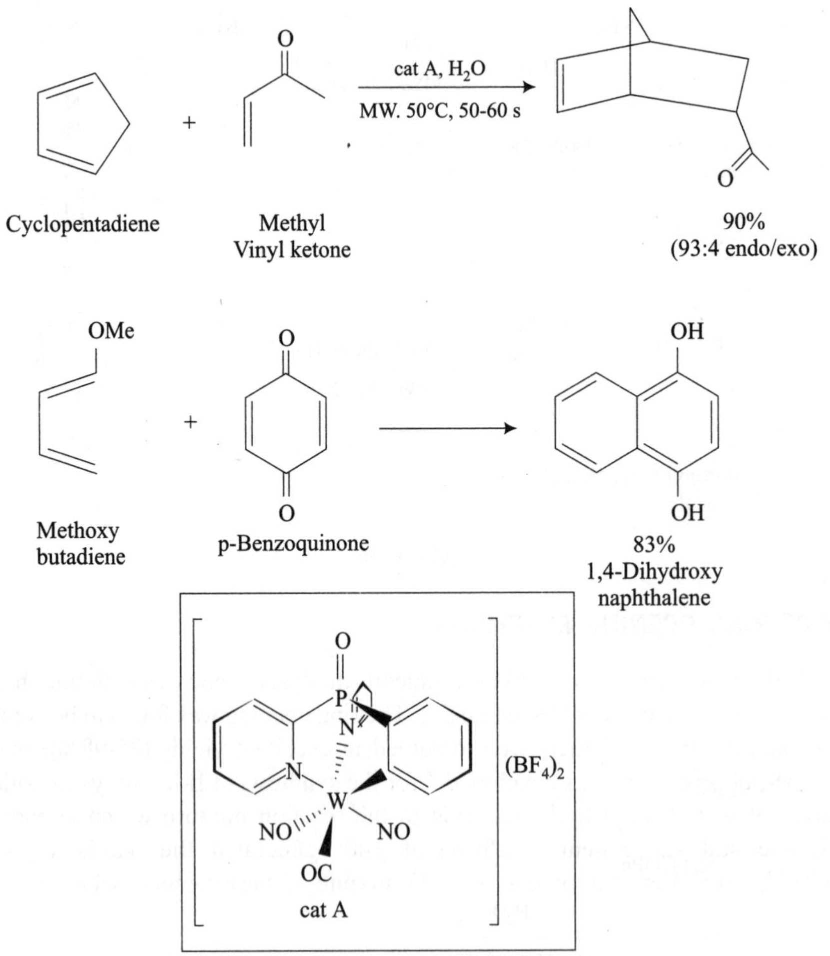
O
cat A, H_2O
MW. 50°C, 50-60 s
+
O
Cyclopentadiene
Methyl
Vinyl ketone
90%
(93:4 endo/exo)
OMe
O
OH
+
O
OH
Methoxy
butadiene
p-Benzoquinone
83%
1,4-Dihydroxy
naphthalene
O
P
N
N
W
NO
NO
OC
cat A
$(BF_4)_2$

Scheme 58

Another Diels-Alder cycloaddition reaction was reported[81] using water as solvent, $LiClO_4$ as a weak lews acid, 0.6 equiv of 2, 6-lutidine and 3 equiv of diene at 170° for 45 mim (Scheme 59)

The Diels-Alder cycloaddition product (Scheme 59) was obtained in 48 per cent yield after TBDPS protection. The diene bearing Tse (p-tolylsufonyl ethyl) as proteting group gave higher yield of the adduct, but in this case the Diels-Alder reaction was not performed under aqueous conditions.

The Diels-Alder cycloadditon reaction was used for the preparation of bicyclo [2. 2. 2.] octenes by the reaction 2 H-pyran-2 ones and maleimides (Scheme 60)[82]. This reaction procceded in water without any additive. For conventional heating longer reaction times (1.5-2 hr) and higher temperature (refluxing decalin, 190°) were needed with water as solvent under reflux conditions (2 hr), a decrease of 30 per cent yield was observed.

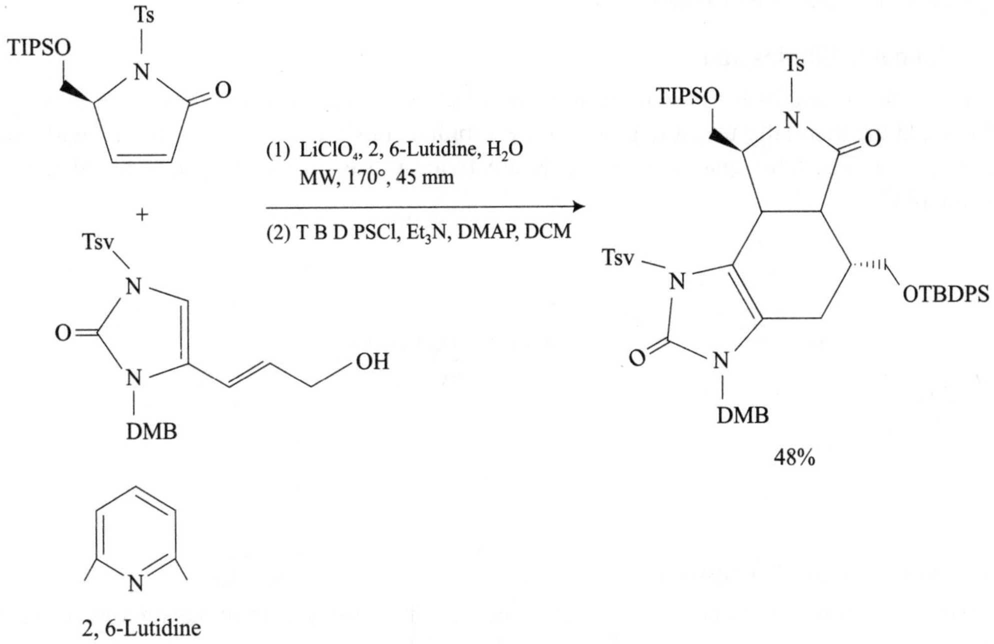

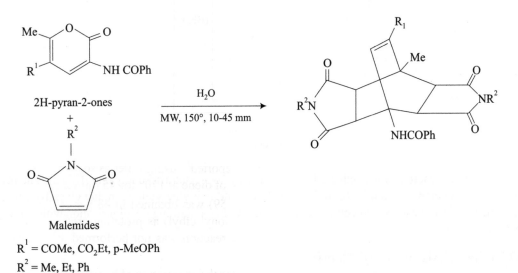

TIPSO
Ts
N
O
+
Tsv
N
O
N
DMB
OH
(1) LiClO4, 2, 6-Lutidine, H2O
MW, 170°, 45 mm
(2) T B D PSCl, Et3N, DMAP, DCM
TIPSO
Ts
N
O
Tsv
N
OTBDPS
O
N
DMB
48%
N
2, 6-Lutidine

Scheme 59

Me
O
O
R1
NH COPh
2H-pyran-2-ones
+
R2
N
O
O
Malemides
R1 = COMe, CO2Et, p-MeOPh
R2 = Me, Et, Ph
H2O
MW, 150°, 10-45 mm
R1
Me
O
O
R2N
NR2
O
NHCOPh
O

Scheme 60

32 MISCELLANEOUS APPLICATIONS

32.1 Hofmann Elimination

This procedure is useful for preparing aryl vinyl ketones. The reaction takes place in aqueous medium and the thermally unstable products are simultaneously extracted and diluted with cooler organic phase. The near quantitative yields are twice those obtained by traditional methods (Scheme 61)[83].

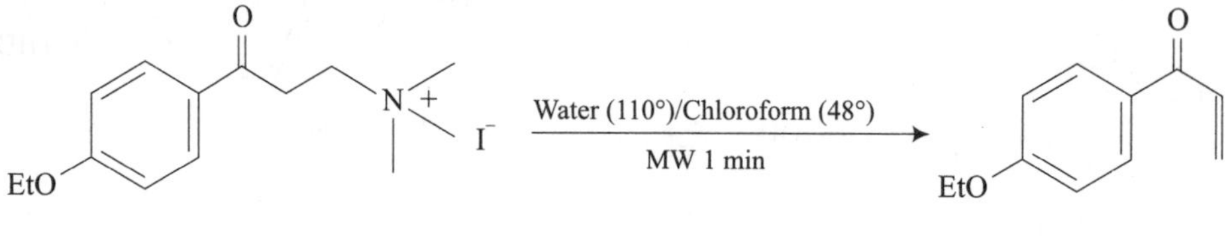

Scheme 61

32.2 Synthesis of Deferiprone

Treatment of maltol with 25 per cent aqueouse methylamime using continuous microwave reactor (CMR) gives[84] 3-hydroxy –1, 2-dimethyl-4-pyridone (deferiprone)(Scheme 62).

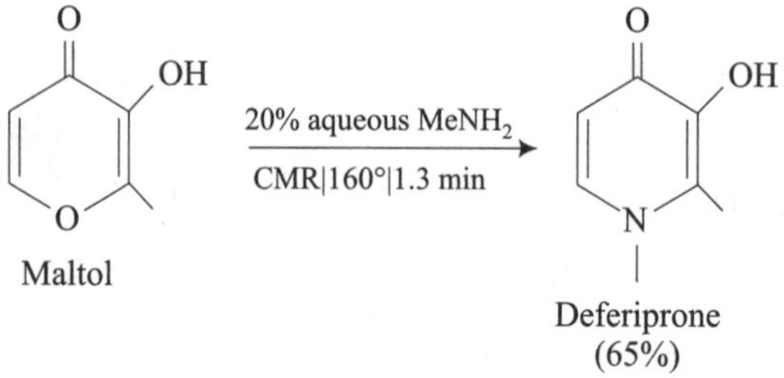

Scheme 62

The above reaction was conducted in container from polytetrafl010uroethylene (PTEE). The reaction was completed within minutes rather than hours and in higher yield than that given by a literature method[85]. In the above procedure (Scheme 62) waste-generating decolourisation with charcoal was also avoided.

32.3 Hydrolysis of Benzyl Chloride

Hydrolysis of benzyl chloride with water in microwave oven gives[86] 97 per cent yield of benzyl alcohol in 2 min (Scheme 63). The usual hydrolysin by usual heating takes about 35 min.

32.4 Hydroloysis of Benzamide

The usual hydrolysis of benzamide take about 1 hr. However, under microwave, the hydrolysis is completed[87] in 7 min. giving 99 per cent yield benzoic acid (Scheme 64).

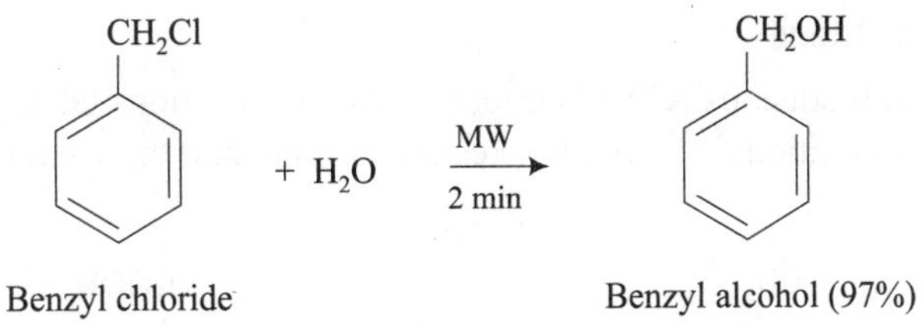

CH$_2$Cl + H$_2$O $\xrightarrow[\text{2 min}]{\text{MW}}$ CH$_2$OH

Benzyl chloride   Benzyl alcohol (97%)

Scheme 63

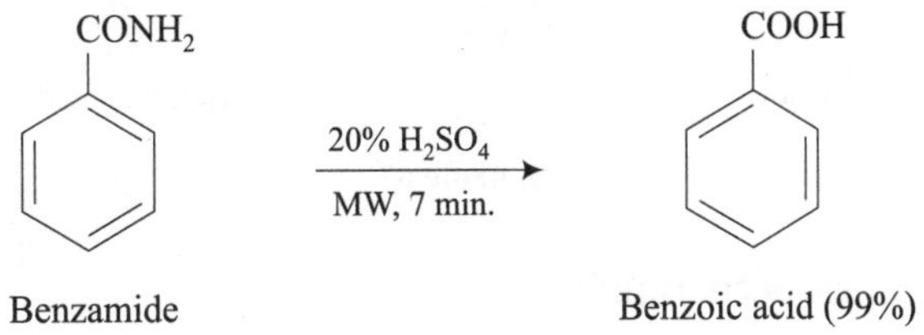

CONH$_2$ $\xrightarrow[\text{MW, 7 min.}]{\text{20\% H}_2\text{SO}_4}$ COOH

Benzamide   Benzoic acid (99%)

Scheme 64

32.5 Hydrolysis of N-phenyl Benzamide

N-Phenyl benzamide on heating with 20 per cent H$_2$SO$_4$ in a microwave for over 12 min. gives[88] 74 per cent yield of benzoic acid (Scheme 65). The conventional heating procedure take 18 hours.

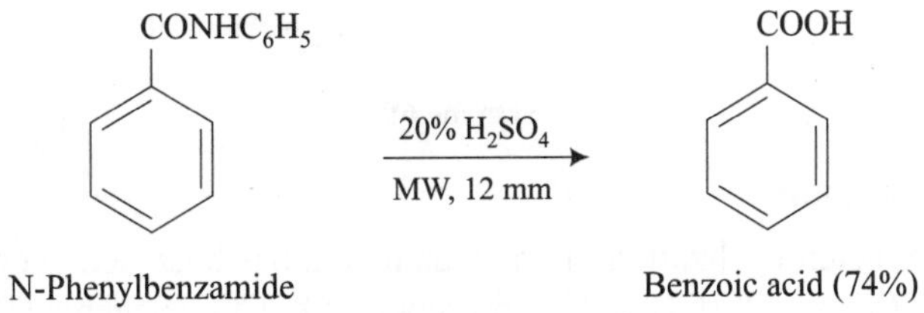

CONHC$_6$H$_5$ $\xrightarrow[\text{MW, 12 mm}]{\text{20\% H}_2\text{SO}_4}$ COOH

N-Phenylbenzamide   Benzoic acid (74%)

Scheme 65

32.6 Hydrolysis of Methyl Benzoate to Benzoic Acid (Saponification)

Saponification of methyl benzoate in aqueous sodium hydroxide under microwave irradiation (2.5 min) gives[88] 84 per cent yield of benzoic acid (Scheme 66).

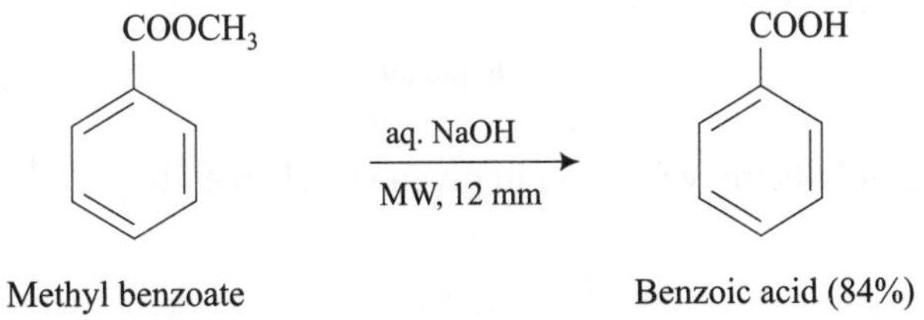

COOCH$_3$ $\xrightarrow[\text{MW, 12 mm}]{\text{aq. NaOH}}$ COOH

Methyl benzoate   Benzoic acid (84%)

Scheme 66

32.7 Oxidation of Toluene

Oxidation of toluene with aqueous $KMnO_4$ under normal condititions takes 10-12 hr compared to reaction in microwave conditions[87,88] which takes only 5 min. and the yield is 40 per cent (Scheme 67).

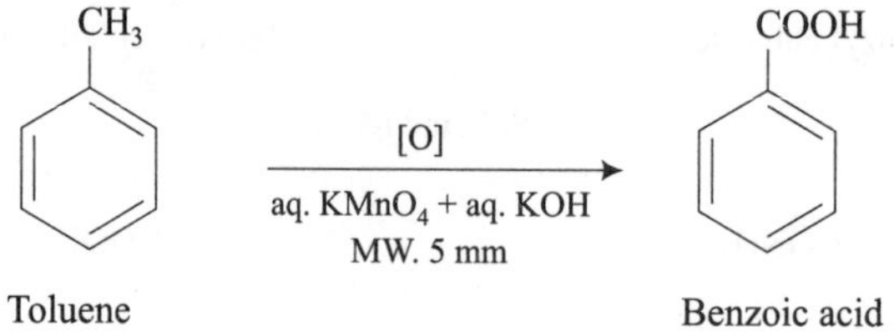

Scheme 67

32.8 Coupling of Amines with Halides

Amines on heating in microwave with alkyl halide with $NaOH/H_2O$ gives[89] the corresponding N-alkyl derivatives (Scheme 68).

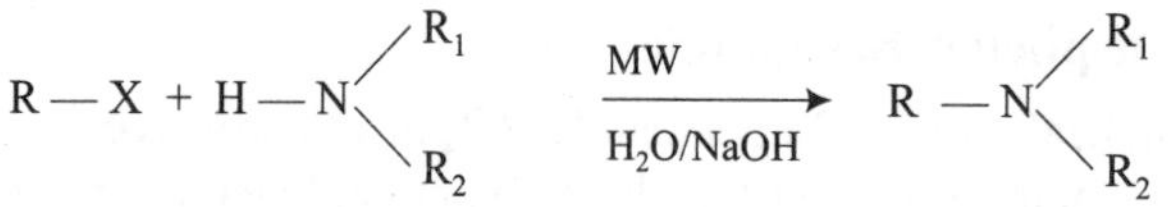

$$X = Cl, Br, I$$

$$R_1 = H, alkyl, aryl$$
$$R_2 = Alkyl, allyl$$

Scheme 68

32.9 N-Heterocyclisations

Microwave assisted N-heterocyclization in aqueous media has been achieved[90] using an aromatic amine and dihalide of the type $X (CH_2)_n X$ in presence of K_2CO_3 (Scheme 69).

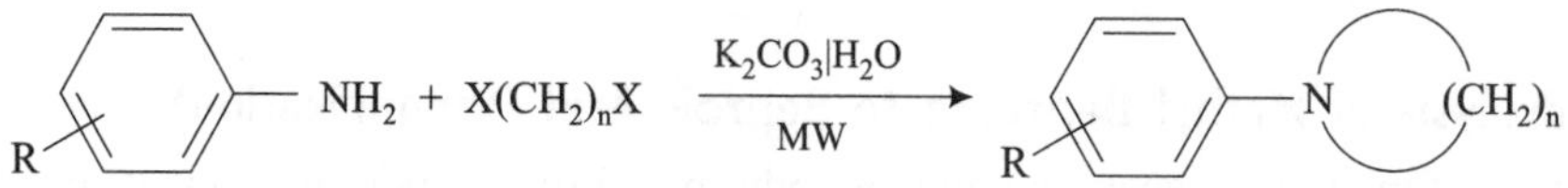

$R = H, CH_3, CH_2CH_3, Br, COCH_3, COOCH_2CH_3$
$X = Br, I, OTs; n = 3,4,5,6$

Scheme 69

A typical example of N-hetrocyclization in given in Scheme 70.

33 CONCLUSION

The combined use of microwave irradiation as a healthy source and water as a solvent for a large number of organic transformations has been achieved. These are environmentally benign processes which is the goal of Green Chemistry.

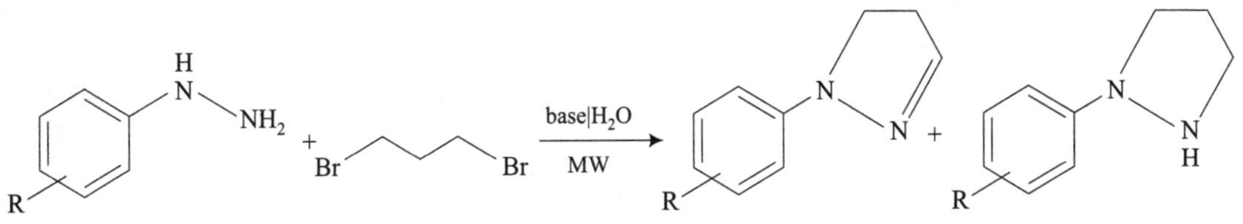

Scheme 70

References

1. A Loupy and R.S. Varma, Chimica Oggi, 2006, **24**, 36.
2. L. Garutic, M. Roberti and D. Pizzirani, Mini Rev. Med. Chem., 2007, **7**, 481.
3. J.B. Sperry and D.L. Wrigaht, Curr. Opin. Drug. Dis. Dev. 2005, **8**, 723.
4. Y. Ju and R.S. Varma, Tetrahedron Lett. 2005, **46**, 6011.
5. Y. Tu and R.S. Varma, Org. Lett, 2005, **7**, 2409.
6. Y. Ju and R.S. Varma, J. Org. Chem. 2006, **71**, 135.
7. R.S. Varma, K.P. Naricker and D. Kumar, J. Mol. Cat. A. Chemical, 1999, **149**, 153.
8. V. Polshettiwar and R.S. Varma, Tetrahedron Lett, 2008, **49**, 397.
9. Y. Ju and R.S. Varma, Green Chem, 2004, **6**, 219.
10. C.O. Kappe, D. Kumar and R.S. Varma, Synthesis , 1999, 1799.
11. V. Polshettiwar and R.S. Varma, Tetrahedron Lett, 2007, **48**, 7443.
12. V. Polshettiwar and R.S. Varma, J. Org. Chem., 2007, **72**, 7420.
13. D.R. Dabideen, K.F. Cheng B. Aljabari, E.J. Miller, V.A. Pavlov and Y. Al–bed, J. Med. Chem. 2007, **50**, 1993.
14. M. Jeselnik, R.S. Varma, S. Polanc and M. Kocevar, Chem. commun. 2001, 1716.
15. V. Polshettiwar and R.S. Varma, Tetrahedron Lett, 2007, **48**, 5649.
16. V. Polshettiwar and R.S. Varma, Tetrahedron Lett, 2007, **48**, 8735.
17. V. Polshettiwar and R.S. Varma, Accounts Chemical Res, 2008 in press.
18. R. Skouta, R.S. Varma and C.J. Li. Green Chem., 2005, **7**, 571.
19. Y. Ju, D. Kumar and R.S. Varma, J. Org. Chem., 2006, **71**, 6697.
20. N. Miyaura, K. Yamada and A. Suzuki, Tetrahedron Lett, 1979, **36**, 3437.
21. R.F. Heck and J.P. Nolly, J. Org. Chem., 1972, **37**, 2320.
22. V. Polshettiwar and A. Molnar, Tetrahedron, 2007, **63**, 6949.
23. N.E. Leadbeater and M. Marco, J. Org. Chem., 2003, **68**, 888.
24. L. Bai, J.X Wang and Y. Zhang, Green Chem., 2003, **5**, 615.
25. R.K. Arvela and N.E. Leadbeater, Org. Lett. 2005, **7**, 2101.
26. M.D. Crozet, C. Castera – Ducros and P. Vanclle, Tetrahedron Lett, 2006, **47**, 7061.
27. R. Zhu, F. Qu, G. Quéléverb and L. Peng, Tetrahedron Lett, 2007, **48**, 2389.
28. K.M. Dawood, Tetrahedron, 2007, **63**, 9642.
29. R.K. Arvela and N. E. Leadbeater, J. Org. Chem., 2005, **70**, 1786.
30. R.K. Arvela, S. Pasquini and M. Larhed, J. Org. Chem., 2007, **72**, 6390.
31. R. Chinchilla and C. Najera, Chem. Rev., 2007, **107**, 874.

32. P. Appukkuttam, W. Dehaen and E.V. der Eycken, Eur. J. Org. Chem. 2003, 4713.

33. S.E. Denmark, J.M. Kallimeyn, J. Am. Chem. Soc, 2006, **128**, 15958.

34. E. Alacida and C. Najera, Adv. Synth. Catal. 2006, **348**, 2085.

35. F. Jam, M. Tullberg, K. Luthman and M. Grotle, Tetrahedron, 2007, **63**, 9881.

36. V. Polshettiwar and R.S. Varma, Tetrahedron Lett, 2008, **49**, 397.

37. J.-J. Shie and J.M. Fang, J. Org. Chem., 2007, **72**, 3141.

38. X. Wu and M. Larhed, Org. Lett. 2005, **7**, 3327.

39. S. Tu, R. Jia, B. Jiang, J. Zhang, Y, Zhang, C. Yaoa and S. Jib, Tetrahedron, 2007, **63**, 381.

40. A. Procopio, M. Gaspari, M. Nardi, M. Oliverio, A. Tagarelleib and G. Sindina, Tetrahedron Lett, 2007, **48**, 8623.

41. L.-K. Huang, Y.-C. Cherng, Y.-R. Chen, J.-P. Jang Y.L. Chao and Y.-J. Cherng, Tetrahedron, 2007, **63**, 5323

42. Microwave Enhanced chemistry, Fundamentals, sample preparation and applications; H.M. Kingston and S.J. Haswell, Eds; American Chemical Society, Washington, DC 1997; Microwave in Organic Synthesis, A. Loupy, Ed, Wiley – VCH. Weinheim, 2002; B.L. Hayes, Microwave Synthesis : Chemistry at speed of light; CEM Publishing: Matthews. N.C, 2002; Microwave assisted Organic Synthesis, P. Lidstrom, J.P. Tierney, Eds.; Blackwell Publishing, Oxford, 2005, C.O Kappe, A. Sladler, Microwave in Organic and Medicinal Chemistry; Wiley – VCH; Weinheim, 2005, Microwaves in Organic Synthesis, 2nd Ed; A Loupy Ed; Wiley VCH. Weinham 2006; Microwave method in Organic Synthesis, M. Larhed, K. Olofsson, Eds, Springer, Berlin, 2006.

43. C.O. Kappe, Angew chem. Int. Ed, 2004, **43**, 6250; B.L. Hayes, Aldrichim. Atca, 2004, **37**, 66.

44. A. De La Hoz, A. Diaz – Ortiz and A. Moreno, Chem. Soc. Rev., 2005, **34**, 164; L. Perreux and A. Loupy, Tetrahedron, 2001, **57**, 9199; N. Kuhnert, Angew. Chem. Int Ed. 2002, **41**, 1863, C.R. Strauss, Angew. Chem. Int Ed. 2002, **41**, 3589.

45. N. Kaval, K. Bisztray, W. Deharen, C.O. Kappe, E. Van der Eycken, Mol. Diversity, 2003, **7**, 125.

46. R.K. Arvela, N.E. Leadbeater, H.M. Torenius and H. Tye, Org. Biomol. Chem. 2003, **I**, 1119.

47. A. Miyazawa, K. Tanaka, T. Sakakura, M. Tashiro, G.K.S. Prakash and G.A. Olah, Chem. Commum, 2005, 2104.

48. A. Miyazawa, K. Soitou, K. Tanaka, T.M. Gadda, M. Tashiro, G.K.S. Prakash and G.A. Olah, Tetrahedron Lett, 2006, **47**, 1437.

49. A. Sharma, V. Kumar and A.K. Sinha, Adv. Synth. Catal. 2006, **348**, 354.

50. R.A. Stockland, A.J. Lipman, J.A. Bawiec, R.E. Morrison. I.A. Guzei, P.M. Findeis and J.F. Tamblin, Organometallic Chem, 2006, **691**, 4042.

51. M. Martelane, K. Kranjc, S. Polonc and M. Kočevar Green Chem., 2005, **7**, 737.

52. R.K. Arvela and N.E. Leadbeater, Org Lett, 2005, **7**, 2101.

53. Y. Ju and R.S. Varma, J. Org. Chem., 2006, **71**, 135;
    Y. Ju and R.S. Varma, Tetrahedron Lett, 2005, **46**, 6011;
    Y. Ju and R.S. Varma, Org. Lett, 2005, **7**, 2409.

54. J. Westman and R. Lundin, Synthesis 2003, 1025.

55. L.D.S. Yadav, B.S. Yadav and V.K. Rai, Synthesis, 2006, 1868.

56. Y. Peng and G. Song, Green Chem. 2002, **4**, 349.

57. Y. Peng and G. Song, Green Chem., 2001, **3**, 302.

58. A. Gellis, N. Boufatah and P. Vanelle, Green Chem., 2006, **8**, 483.

59. V. Molteni, M.M. Hamilton, L. Mao, C.M. Crane, A. Termim, D.M. Wilson, Synthesis , 2002, 1669.

60. S. Ferro, A. Rao. M. Zappala, A. Chrmirri, M. L. Barreca, M. Witvrouw, Z. Debyser and P. Monforte, Hetrocycles, 2004, **63**, 2727.

61. D. Dallinger and C.O. Kappe, Chem. Rev. 2007, **107**, 2563 and the reference cited therein.

62. Y. Peng, G. Song and R. Dou, Green Chem. 2006, **8**, 573.

63. T.A. Bryson, J.J. Stewart, J.M. Gibson, P.S. Thomas, J.K. Berch. Green Chem. 2003, **5**, 174.

64. M. Kidwai, S. Saxena, M.K.R. Khan and S.S. Thukral, Bioorg Med. Chem. Lett. 2005, **15**, 4295.

65. L. Öhberg and J. Westman, Synlett, 2001, 1296.

66. M.C. Bagley and M.C. Lubinu, Synthesis, 2006, 1283.

67. H. Salehi and Q. X. Guo, Synth. Commun, 2004, **34**, 4349.

68. G.P. Hua, S.J. Tu, X.T. Zhu, X.J. Zhang, J.N. Xu, J.P. Zhang, F. Shi, Q. Wang and S.J. Ji, Chin. J. Chem, 2005, **23**, 1646.

69. S. Tu, Y. Zhang, J. Zhang, B. Jiang. R. Jia, J. Zhang, and S. Ji, Synlett, 2006, 2785.

70. S.J. Tu, B. Jiang, J.Y. Zhang, R.H. Jia, Y. Zhang and C.S. Yao, Org. Biomol. Chem, 2006, **4**, 3980.

71. M. Tullberg, M. Grotli and K. Luthman, Tetrahedron, 2006, **62**, 7484.

72. A. C. Carlesson F. Jam, M. Tullerg, A. Pilotti, P. Ioannidis, K. Luthman and M. Grøtli, Tetrahedron Lett, 2006, **47**, 5199.

73. M. Mayer, P.T. Lang, S. Gerber, P.B. Madrial, I. Gómez Pinto, R.K. Guy and T.L. James, Chem. Biol, 2006, **13**, 993.

74. Y. Peng, R. Dou, G. Song and J. Jiang, Synlett, 2005, 2245.

75. L. Shi, Y.Q. Tu, M. Wang, F.M. Zhang and C.A. Fan, Org. Lett, 2004, **6**, 1001.

76. Y.J. Cherg, Tetrahedron, 2000, **56**, 8287.

77. N. Kaval, W. Dehaen, P. Mátyus and E. Vander Eycken, Green. Chem. 2004, **6**, 125.

78. G. Semple, P.J. Skinner, M.C. Cherrier, P.J. Webb, C.R. Sage, S.Y. Tamura, R. Chen, J.G. Richman and D.T. Connolly, Med. Chem. 2006, **49**, 1227.

79. V. Pirotic and S. Colonna, Green Chem., 2005, **7**, 43.

80. I.H. Chen, J.N. Young and S.J. Yu, Tetrahedron, 2004, **60**, 11903.

81. P. Dransfield, A.S. Dilley, S. Wang D. Romo, Tetrahedron, 2006, **62**, 5223.

82. K. Kranjc, K. Koćevar, F. Lusif, S.M. Coman, V.I. Pavulescu, E. Genin, J.P. Genét and V. Michelet, Synlett, 2006, 1075.

83. C.R. Strauss, K.D. Raner, R.W. Trainor and J.S. Thorn, Aust. Pat. 677876 (1977)

84. T. Cablewiski, A.F. Faux and C.R. Strauss, J. Org. Chem. 1194, **59**, 3404.

85. G.T. Kontoghiorghes and L. Sheppard, Inorg. Chem. Acta, 1987, **136**, L11.

86. R.N. Gedye, W. Rank and K.C. Westaway, Can. J. Chem. 1991, **69**, 706.

87. R.N. Gedye, F.E. Smith and K.C. Westaway. Can. J. Chem, 1988, **66**, 17.

88. R.N. Gedye, W. Rank and K. C. Westaway, Can. J. Chem, 1988, **66**, 700.

89. Y. Ju and R.S. Varma, Green Chem., 2004, **6**, 219.

90. Y. Ju. and R.S. Varma, Org. Lett, 2005, **7**, 2409, Y. Ju and R.S. Varma, Tetrahedron Lett, 2005, **46**, 6011; Y. Ju and R.S. Varma J. Org. Chem., 2006, **71**, 135.

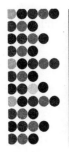

Organic Synthesis using Biocatalysts

4

I   INTRODUCTION

Enzymes are proteins that act as biological catalysts, i.e. these alter the rates of biochemical reactions without undergoing any permanent change in themselves. These have a high degree of specificity besides high efficiency on rates of reactions. In nature, enzymes help million of chemical reactions to occur at extraordinary speeds and under moderate conditions. In the absence of enzymes most chemical reactions that maintain a living organism would occur only under very drastic conditions, e.g. at a temperature of the order of 100° or above which would 'kill' the fragile cell. At normal body temperatures, these reactions would often proceed at an extremely slow rate. For example, the dissociation of carbonic acid into CO_2 and H_2O takes place in the lungs, proceeds only at a rate of about 10^7 mol dm^{-3} S^{-1} at room temperature in a test tube. On the other hand, in the cells, the enzyme carbonic anhydrase accelerates the reaction by more than a million times.

$$H_2CO_3 \xrightarrow{\text{Carbonic anhydrase}} CO_2 + H_2O$$

In a similar way, a single molecule of enzyme, catalyses the decomposition of about 10^7 molecules of H_2O_2, a toxic byproduct of metabolism, in one second. A comparison of the rates of the catalysed and uncatalysed reactions give an idea of the capability of the enzymes. For example:

$$2H_2O_2 \xrightarrow{\text{Catalyst}} 2H_2O + O_2 \qquad K_{295} = 3.5 \times 10^7$$

$$2H_2O_2 \xrightarrow{Fe^{2+}} 2H_2O + O_2 \qquad K_{295} = 5.6$$

The most important conversions in the context of green chemistry is with the help of enzymes. Enzymes are also referred to as biocatalyst and the transformation are referred to as biocatalytic conversion. Enzymes are now easily available and are an important tool in organic synthesis. The earliest biocatalytic conversion known to mankind is the manufacture of ethyl alcohol from molasses, the mother liquor left after the crystallisation of cane sugar from concentrated cane juice. This transformation is brought about by the enzyme 'invertase' which converts sucrose into glucose and fructose and finally by the enzyme zymase which converts glucose and fructose into ethyl alcohol. It is well known that most of the antibiotics have been prepared using enzymes (enzymatic fermentation).

The biocatalytic conversions have many advantages in relevance to green chemistry. Some of these are given below:

- Most of the reactions are performed in aqueous medium at ambient temperature and pressure.
- The biocatalytic conversions normally involve only one step.
- Protection and deprotection of functional groups is not necessary.
- The reactions are fast reactions.
- The conversions are stereospecific.

One of the most common examples is the biocatalytic conversions of Penicillin into 6-APA by the enzyme 'Penacylase' (one step process). However, the chemical conversion requires a number of steps (Scheme 1).

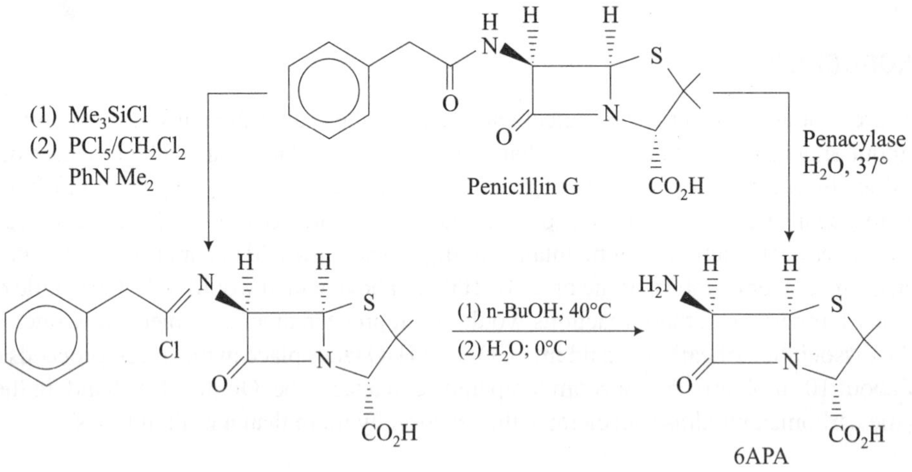

Scheme 1

A special advantage of the biochemical reactions is that they are chemoselective, regioselective and stereoselective. Also, some of the biochemical conversions are generally not possible by conventional chemical means. Two such examples in heterocyclic compounds are given in (Scheme 2)[1].

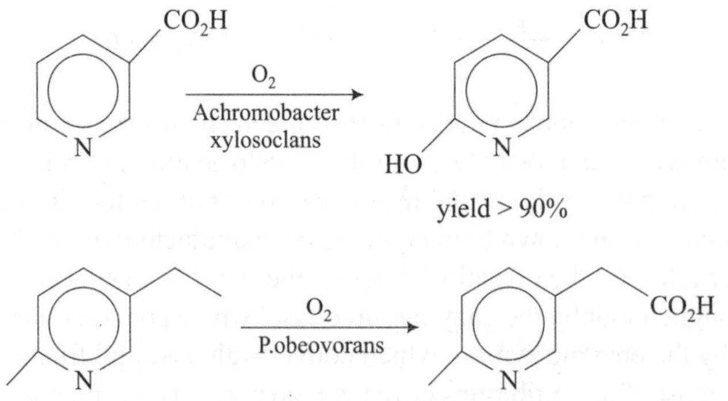

Scheme 2

A number of diverse reactions are possible by biocatalytic processes, which are catalysed by enzymes. The major six classes of enzymes and the type of reactions they catalyse are discussed below:

1. **Oxidoreductases:** These enzymes catalyse oxidation-reduction reactions. This class includes oxidases (direct oxidation with molecular oxygen) and dehydrogenases (which catalyse the removal of hydrogen from one substrate and pass it on to a second substrate).

2. **Transferases:** These enzymes catalyse the transfer of various functional groups, e.g. transaminase.

3. **Hydrolases:** This group of enzymes catalyse hydrolytic reactions, e.g. penteases (proteins), esterases (esters), etc.

4. **Lyases:** These are of two types, one which catalyses addition to double bond and the other which catalyses removal of groups and leaves double bond. Both addition and eliminations of small molecules are on sp^3-hybridized carbon.

5. **Isomerases:** These catalyse various types of isomerisation, e.g. racemases, epimerases, etc.

6. **Ligases:** These catalyse the formation or cleavage of sp^3-hybridized carbon.

As already stated, the enzymes are specific in their action. This specificity of enzymes may be manifested in one of the three ways:

(i) An enzymes may catalyse a particular type of reaction, e.g. esterases hydrolyses only esters. Such enzymes are called reaction specific. Alternatively, an enzyme may be specific for a particular class of compounds. These enzymes are referred to as substrate specific, e.g. urease hydrolyse only urea and phosphatases hydrolyse only phosphate esters.

(ii) An enzyme may exhibit kinetic specificity. For example, esterases hydrolyse all esters but at different rates.

(iii) An enzymes may be stereospecific. For example, maltase hydrolyses α-glycosides but not β-glycosides. On the other hand emulsin hydrolyses the β-glycosides but not the α-glycosides.

It should be noted that a given enzyme could exhibit more than one specificites.

2   BIOCHEMICAL (MICROBIAL) OXIDATIONS

The oxidations accomplished by enzymes or microorganisms excel in regiospecificity, stereospecificity and enantioselectivity. The optical purity (enantiomeric excess) is usually very high nearing 100 per cent. An unbelievable large number of enzymatic (or microbial) oxidations have been accomplished.

Two important enzymatic oxidations have been very well known since early times. One is the conversion of alcohol into acetic acid by bacterium acetic in presence of air (the process is now known as quick-vinegar process) (Scheme 3) and the second one is the conversion of sucrose into ethyl alcohol by yeast (Scheme 4) (this process is used for the manufacture of ethyl alcohol).

In a similar way, lactose can be converted into lactic acid (Scheme 5). The above enzymatic oxidations are referred to as fermentation.

$$CH_3CH_2OH + O_2 \xrightarrow{\text{Bacterium acetic}} CH_3COOH + H_2O$$

Ethyl alcohol   Acetic acid

Scheme 3

$$C_{12}H_{22}O_{11} + H_2O \xrightarrow[\text{yeast}]{\text{Invertase}} 2C_6H_{12}O_6$$

Sucrose   Glucose & fructose

$$C_6H_{12}O_6 \xrightarrow[\text{yeast}]{\text{Invertase}} 2C_2H_5OH + 2CO_2$$

Ethyl alcohol

Scheme 4

$$C_{12}H_{22}O_{11} + H_2O \xrightarrow[\text{yeast}]{\text{Invertase}} 4CH_3CH(OH)COOH$$

Lactose   Lactic acid

Scheme 5

Microbial oxidations occur under mild conditions, usually around 70°C and in dilute solution. They are slow and often take days.

Considerable amount of work has been reported in the hydroxylation of aromatic rings. Thus, benzene on oxidation with Pseudomonas putida in presence of oxygen gives the cis-diol (Scheme-6)[2]. The cis-diol obtained could be converted by four steps into 1, 2, 3, 4-tetrahydroxy compound, conduritol-F[3] and by five steps into the hexahydroxy compound, pinitol, an antidiabetic agent (Scheme 6)[4].

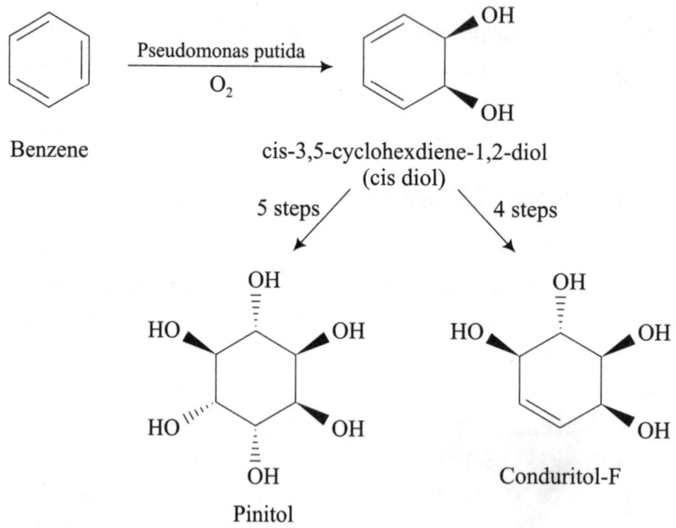

Benzene   cis-3,5-cyclohexdiene-1,2-diol
                            (cis diol)

Pinitol   Conduritol-F

Scheme 6

However, Micrococuus spheroids like organism converts benzene into trans, trans-muconic acid (Scheme 7)[5].

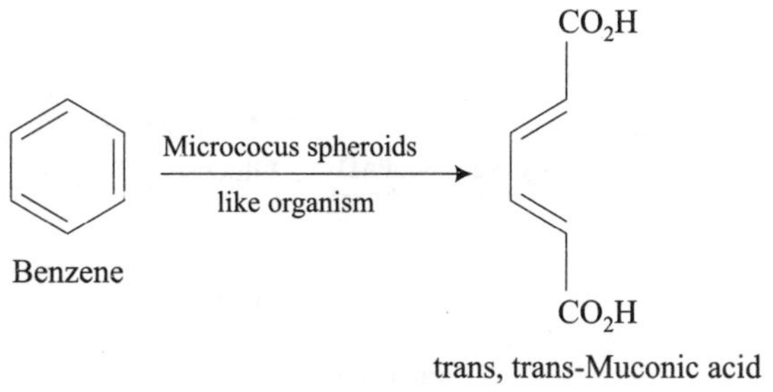

Scheme 7

In a similar way, toluene, halogensubstituted benzenes, halogensubstituted toluene gave the corresponding cis diols (Scheme 8)[6].

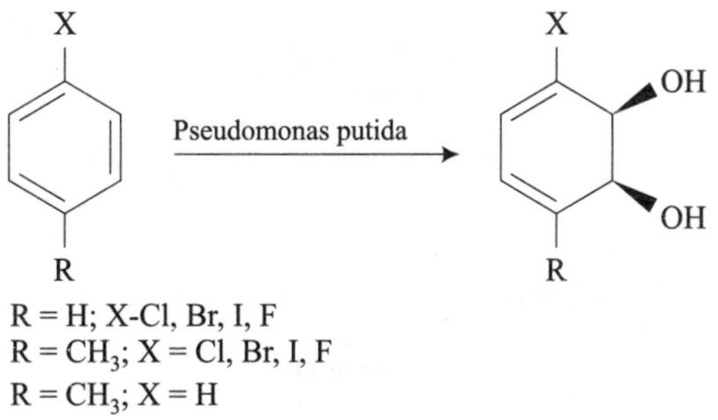

R = H; X-Cl, Br, I, F
R = CH$_3$; X = Cl, Br, I, F
R = CH$_3$; X = H

Scheme 8

The cis-diol obtained from chlorobenzene is converted into 2, 3-isopropylidene – L-ribose-γ-lactone in four steps (Scheme 9)[7].

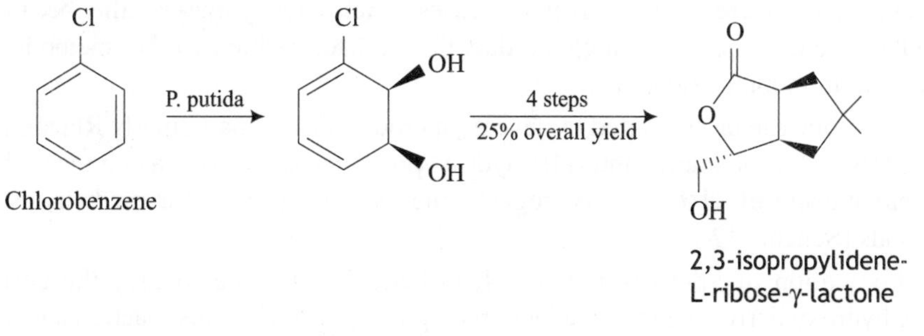

2,3-isopropylidene-
L-ribose-γ-lactone

Scheme 9

Enzymatic conversion of ketones to esters is commonly encountered in microbial degradation[8]. A typical transformation in the enzymatic Baeyer-Villiger oxidation, which converts cyclohexanone into the lactone (Scheme 10) using a purified cyclohexanone oxygenase enzyme[9,10].

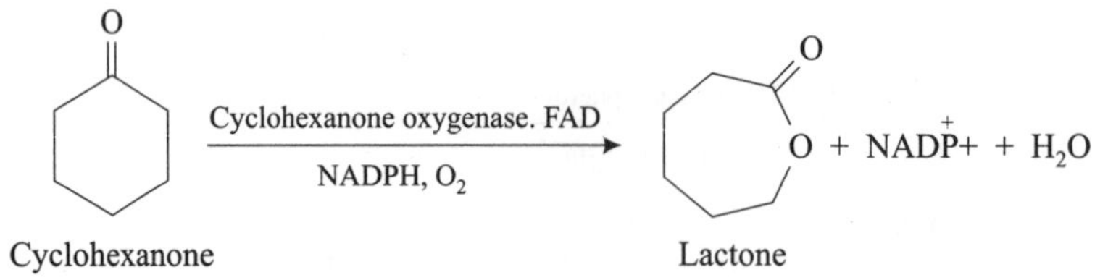

Cyclohexanone   Cyclohexanone oxygenase. FAD / NADPH, O_2 Lactone + NADP+ + H_2O

Scheme 10

This enzymes also converts phenylactaldehyde into phenylacetic acid in 65% yield.

Similarly, 4-methylcyclohexanone can be converted into the corresponding lactone (Scheme 11) in 80% yield[11] with > 98% ee with cyclohexanone oxygenase, obtained from Acineto bacter.

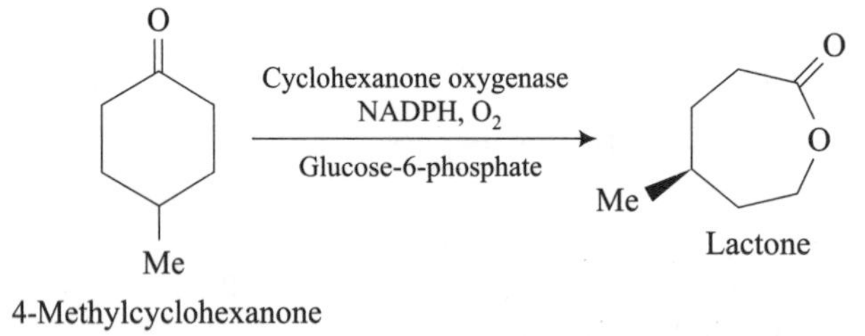

4-Methylcyclohexanone   Cyclohexanone oxygenase NADPH, O_2 / Glucose-6-phosphate   Lactone

Scheme 11

In case of steroids, many different positions can be hydroxylated by different microorganisms, and usually, only one diastereomer is formed. From achiral molecules, optically active compounds are generated.

A number of microbial reagents have been used for successful oxidation of steroids, isoprenoids, alkaloids, hydrocarbons and other type of molecules. A number of reviews and monographs are available[12]. Here we have given few cases which offer synthetic utility because they can afford excellent yield or they give single product that is inaccessible by other methods. Following are some typical microbial oxidations:

(1) Progestesone can be converted by several microorganism[13] particularly Rhizopus nigrioans and Aspergillus ochraceus into 11α-hydroxyprogesterone. This is a commercial method of manufacturing of 11α-hydroxyprogesterone as raw material for medicinally important steriods (Scheme 12).

(2) Hydroxylation of 9β-10α-pregna – 4, 6-diene-3, 20-dione to give the corresponding 16α-hydroxy derivative by Sepedonuim ampullosporium[14]. This reaction has been carried out in 81 per cent yield on a kilogram scale (Scheme 13).

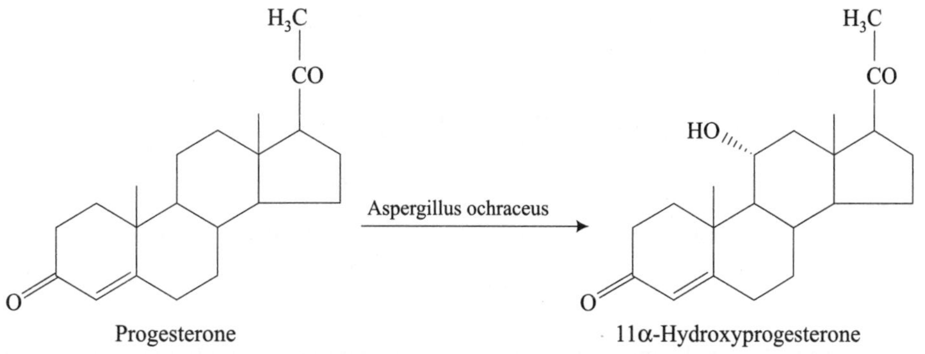
H3C
CO
HO
O
Aspergillus ochraceus
Progesterone
11α-Hydroxyprogesterone

Scheme 12

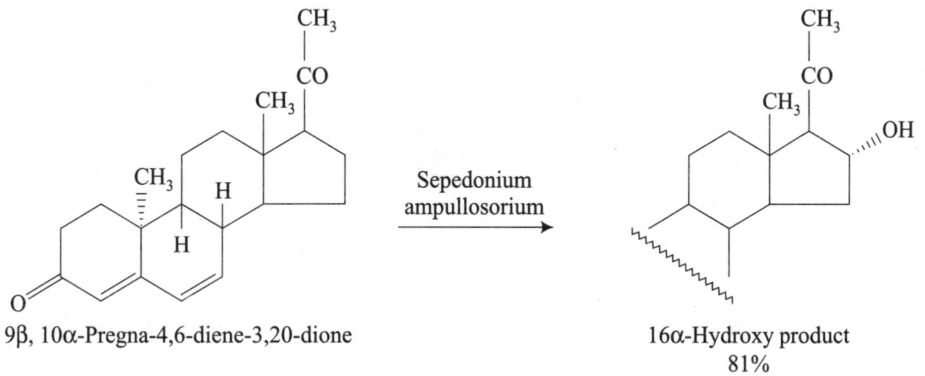
CH3
CO
CH3
H
O
Sepedonium ampullosorium
OH
9β, 10α-Pregna-4,6-diene-3,20-dione
16α-Hydroxy product
81%

Scheme 13

(3) Oxidation of oesterone by Gibberella fujikuroi gives[15] 75 per cent yield of 15α-hydroxy-oesterone (Scheme 14).

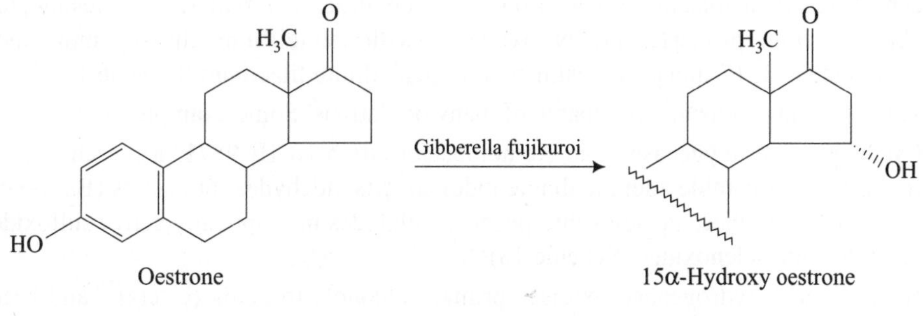
O
H3C
HO
Gibberella fujikuroi
OH
Oestrone
15α-Hydroxy oestrone

Scheme 14

(4) Hydroxylation of the cholesterol by Mycobacterium sp. gives[16] cholest – 4 – en – 3 – one (Scheme 15).

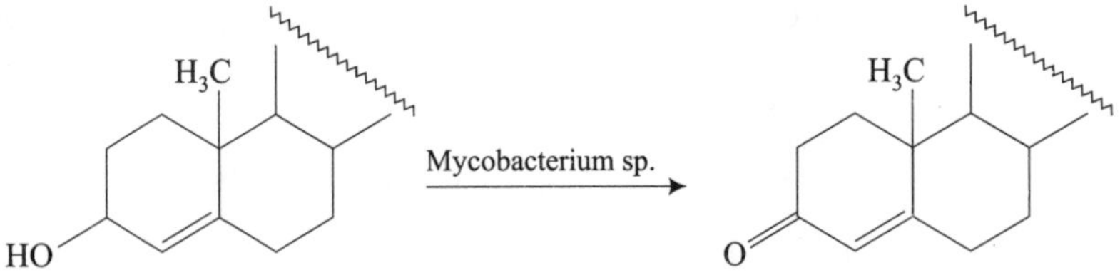

Cholesterol   Cholest-4-en-3-one

Scheme 15

(5) Allylic oxidation of 17-methyltestosterone by Gibberalla saubinetti gives[17] the corresponding 6β-hydroxy product (Scheme 16).

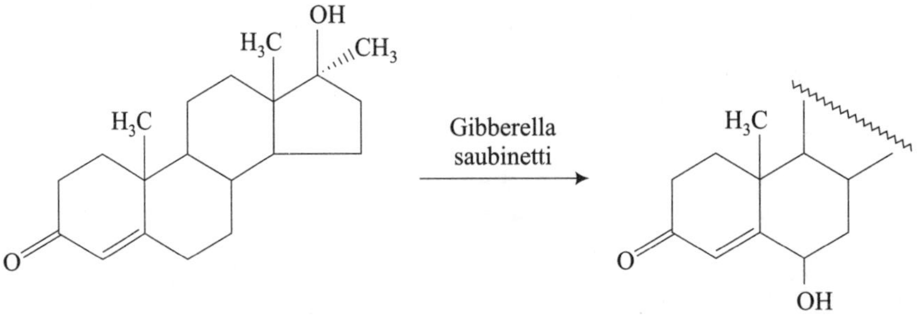

17-Methyltestosterone   6β-Hydroxy-17-methyl
                               testosterone

Scheme 16

(6) Baeyer-Villiger oxidations of steroids are accomplished biochemically. Thus, 19-Nortestosterone on treatment with Aspergilus tamarii gives 70 per cent yield of 19-Nortestolo-lactone[18]. Progresterone and testosterone are converted into Δ^1-dehydrotestololactone by fermentation with cyclindrocarpon radicicola[19]. Testololactone is obtained from progesterone by oxidation with Penicillium chrysogenum and from 4-androstene-3, 17-dione by treatment with penicillium lilacinum (Scheme 17)[20].

Sometimes, a single enzyme is capable of many oxidations. Some examples are:

(i) Cyclohexanone oxygenase from Acinotobactor strain NCIB 9871 in presence of NADH (reduced nicotinamide adenine dinuleotide) coverts aldehydes into esters (Baeyer-Villiger reaction); phenylboronic acids into phenols; sulphides into optically active sulfoxides; and selenides into selenoxides (Scheme 18)[21].

(ii) Horse liver dehydrogenase oxidises primary alcohols to acids (esters)[22] and secondary alcohols to ketones[23] (Scheme 19).

(iii) Horseradish peroxidase catalyses dehydrogenative coupling[24] and oxidation of phenol to quinones[25] (Scheme 20).

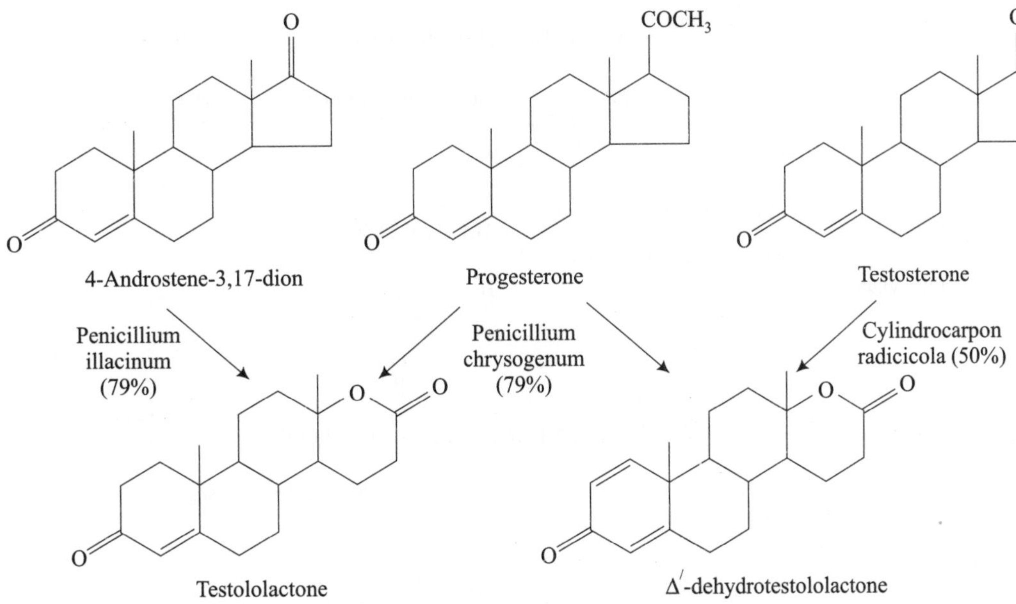

O

COCH₃

OH

4-Androstene-3,17-dion   Progesterone   Testosterone

Penicillium illacinum (79%)   Penicillium chrysogenum (79%)   Cylindrocarpon radicicola (50%)

Testololactone   Δ'-dehydrotestololactone

Scheme 17

(iv) Mushroom polyphenol oxidase hydroxylates phenols and oxidizes them to quinones[26] (Scheme 21).

Besides the above, there are a number of other examples involving the use of enzymes in oxidations[27].

(v) Some important transformations (oxidations) of diols with horse liver alcohol – dehydrogenase (LHADH) using NAD are given in Table 1.

3   BIOCHEMICAL (MICROBIAL) REDUCTIONS

Like enzymatic oxidations, the enzymatic reductions are straightforward and highly stereoselective. Prelog was the first to study the reduction of carbonyl compounds with a number of enzymatic systems. For example, reduction of ketones with curvularia fulcata gave predictable stereochemical induction based on the groups present (large and small) in the keto group. This is known as Prelog's rule[31]. According to this rule, if the steric difference between large (L) and small (S) groups attached to the carbonyl group is large enough, the enzymes deliver hydrogen from the less hindered face to give the corresponding alcohol.

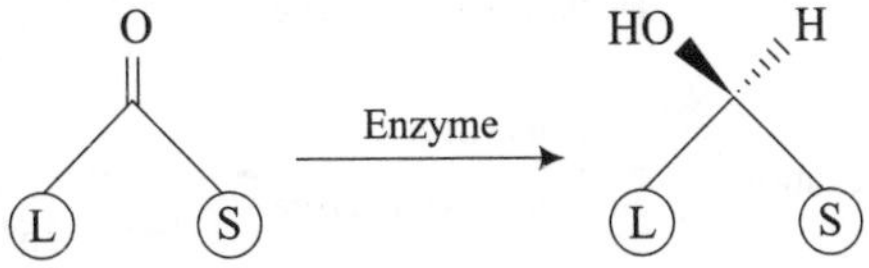

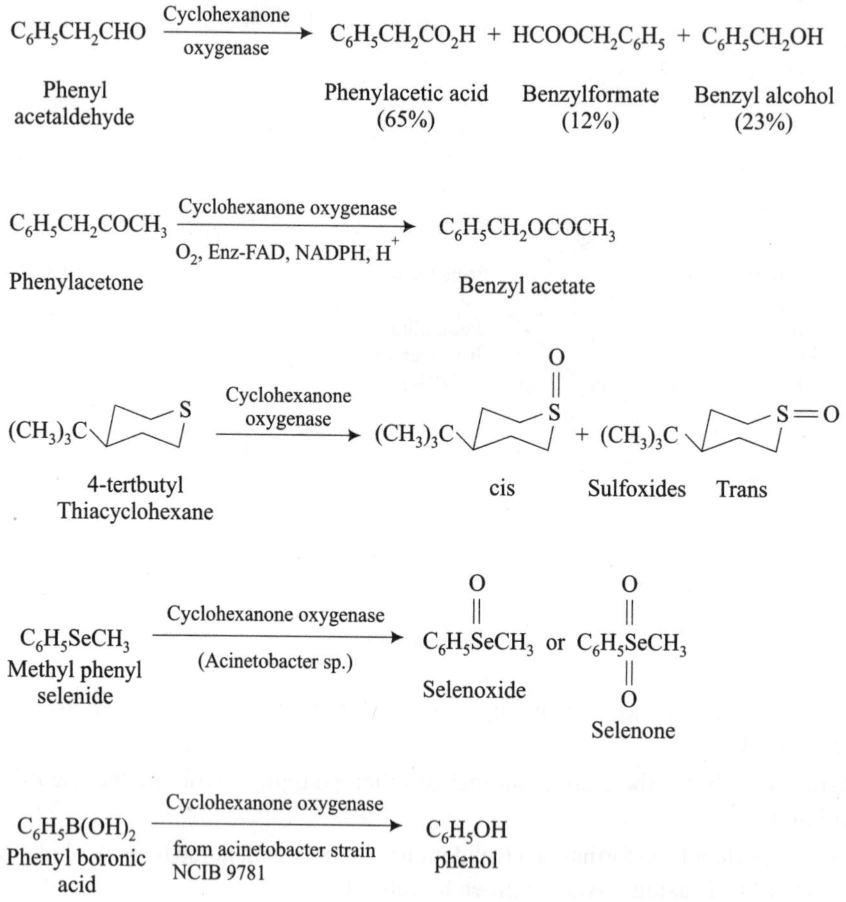

$$C_6H_5CH_2CHO \xrightarrow[\text{oxygenase}]{\text{Cyclohexanone}} C_6H_5CH_2CO_2H + HCOOCH_2C_6H_5 + C_6H_5CH_2OH$$

| Phenyl acetaldehyde | Phenylacetic acid (65%) | Benzylformate (12%) | Benzyl alcohol (23%) |

$$C_6H_5CH_2COCH_3 \xrightarrow[\text{O}_2\text{, Enz-FAD, NADPH, H}^+]{\text{Cyclohexanone oxygenase}} C_6H_5CH_2OCOCH_3$$

Phenylacetone   Benzyl acetate

4-tertbutyl
Thiacyclohexane   cis   Sulfoxides   Trans

$$C_6H_5SeCH_3 \xrightarrow[\text{(Acinetobacter sp.)}]{\text{Cyclohexanone oxygenase}} \underset{\text{Selenoxide}}{C_6H_5SeCH_3} \text{ or } \underset{\text{Selenone}}{C_6H_5SeCH_3}$$

Methyl phenyl
selenide

$$C_6H_5B(OH)_2 \xrightarrow[\substack{\text{from acinetobacter strain} \\ \text{NCIB 9781}}]{\text{Cyclohexanone oxygenase}} \underset{\text{phenol}}{C_6H_5OH}$$

Phenyl boronic
acid

Scheme 18

72-77%

$$(\pm)\text{-trans-3-methycyclohexanol} \xrightarrow[\text{alcohol dehydrogenate}]{\text{Horse liver}} \underset{\substack{50\% \text{ yield ee } 100\%}}{(-)-(S)-3-\text{methylcyclohexanone}}$$

$$(\pm)\text{-cis-3-methycyclohexanol} \xrightarrow[\text{alcohol dehydrogenate}]{\text{Horse liver}} \underset{\substack{55\% \text{ yield ee } 96\%}}{(+)-(S)-3-\text{methylcyclopentanone}}$$

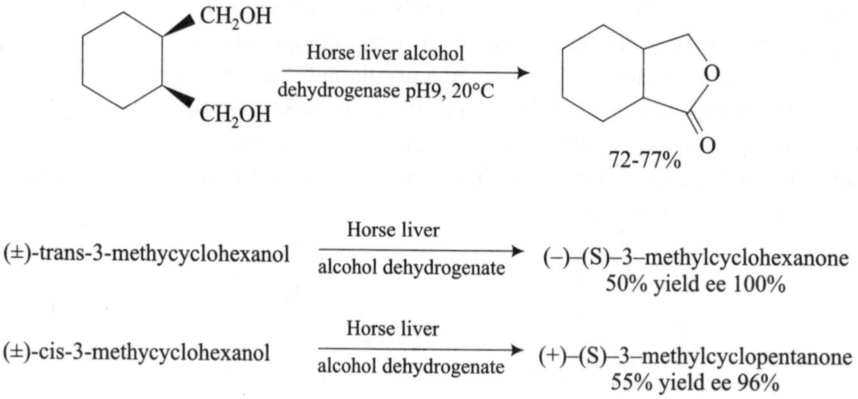

Scheme 19

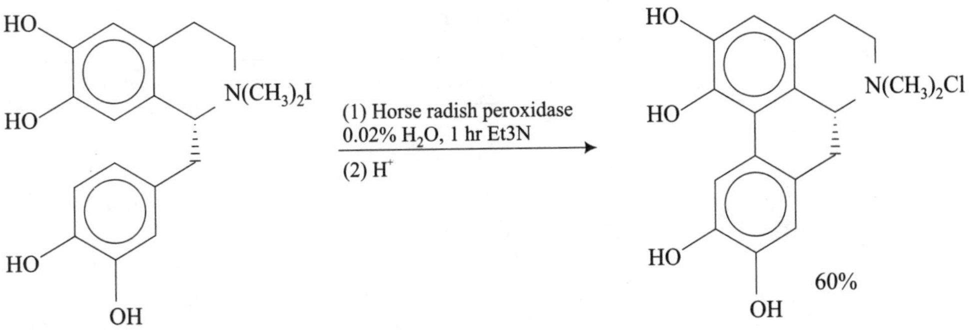

Laudanosline
methiodide

(1) Horse radish peroxidase
0.02% H₂O, 1 hr Et3N

(2) H⁺

Apomorphine
methochloride

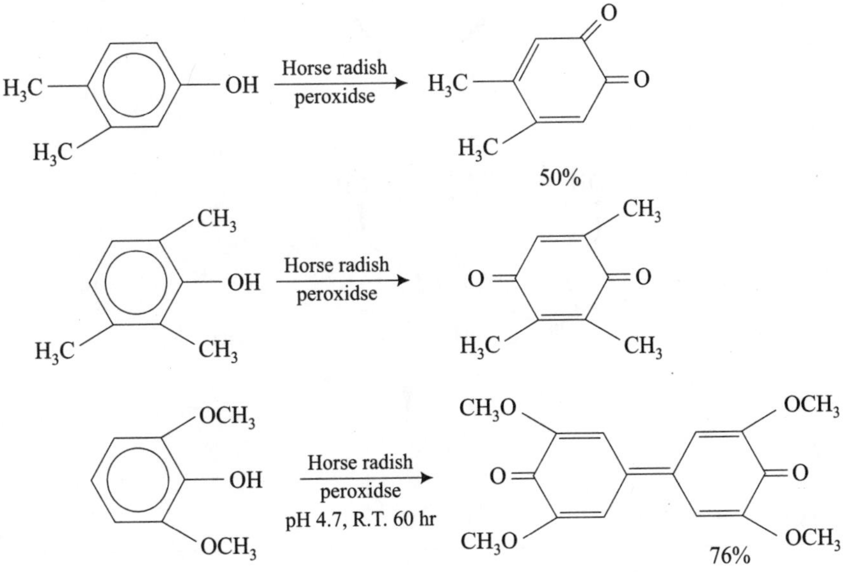

60%

Horse radish
peroxidse

50%

Horse radish
peroxidse

Horse radish
peroxidse
pH 4.7, R.T. 60 hr

76%

Scheme 20

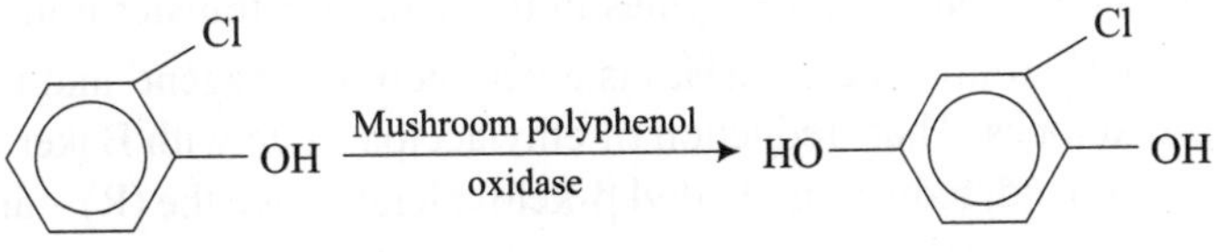

o-Chlorophenol

Mushroom polyphenol
oxidase

62%

Scheme 21

Table 1

Substrate	Product	ee(%)	Ref.
		100	28
		100	28
		100	28
		100	29
		96	30

Two most common enzymatic systems are yeast alcohol dehydrogenase (YAD) and horse liver alcohol dehydrogenase (HLADH). The selectivity observed with these enzymes is determined by non-bonded interaction of subtrate and enzymes in the hydrogen transfer transition state[31].

Baker's yeast (Saccharomyces cerevisiae) is a very comon 'reagent' and it selectively reduces β-ketoesters and β-diketones. Thus, reduction of ethylacetoacetate with Baker's yeast gave the (S) – alcohol. On the other hand, reduction of ethyl β-ketovalerate gave the (R) – alcohol (Scheme 22).

It was shown that the selectivity of reduction changed from (S) selectivity with small chain esters to (R) selectivity with long chain esters[32].

The (S)-alcohol obtained above (Scheme 22) is used in the Mori's synthesis of (S) – (+) – sulcatol[33].

The selectivity of reduction is illustrated by the observation that 2-butanone is reduced by Thermoanaerobium brockii which gave the (R)-alcohol (2-butanol) in 12 per cent yield and 48 per cent ee, but the large kenotes are reduced to the (S)-alcohol (85 per cent yield and 96 per cent ee, S)[34], (Scheme 23).

The above examples illustrate the enantioselectivity of the reduction and that selectivity depends on the size and nature of the groups around carbonyl.

The (S)-alcohol obtained above (Scheme 23) is used in the Mori's synthesis of (S)–(+) sulcatol[33].

There are a number of synthesis applications of the use of Baker's yeast. Thus, reduction of the β-ketoester (Scheme 24) gave 71 per cent yield of the alcohol, which was used in the Hoffmann's synthesis of the cigarette beetle[34a].

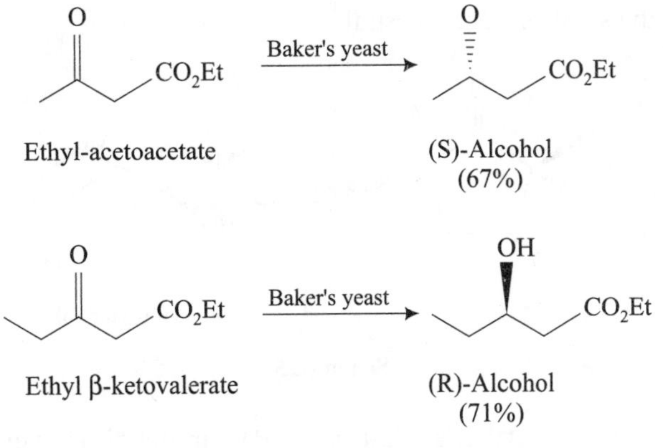
Baker's yeast
Ethyl-acetoacetate
(S)-Alcohol
(67%)
Baker's yeast
Ethyl β-ketovalerate
(R)-Alcohol
(71%)

Scheme 22

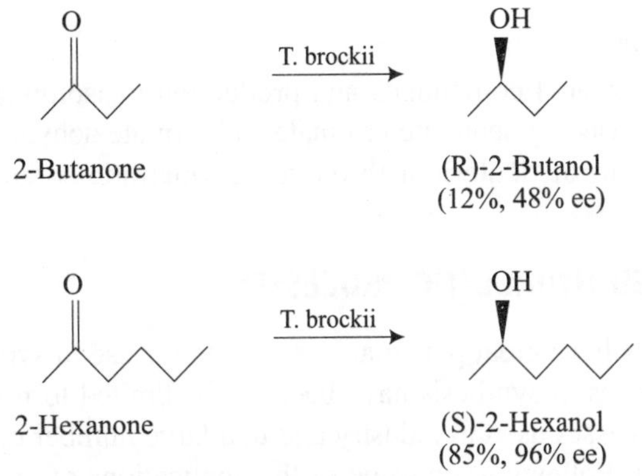
T. brockii
2-Butanone
(R)-2-Butanol
(12%, 48% ee)
T. brockii
2-Hexanone
(S)-2-Hexanol
(85%, 96% ee)

Scheme 23

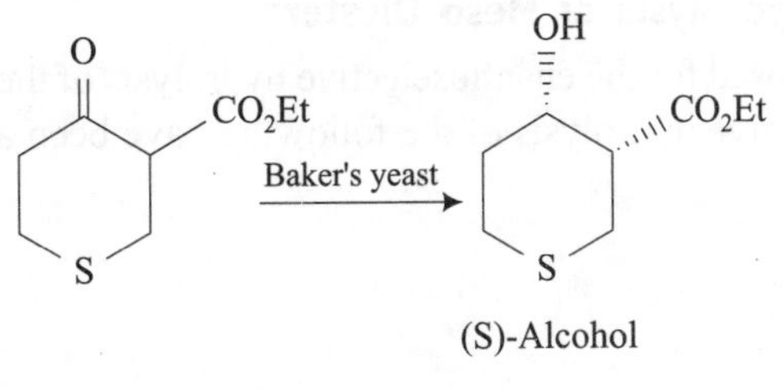
Baker's yeast
(S)-Alcohol

Scheme 24

The selectively of all these reactions is in consistent with the (S)-selectivity as predicted by Prelog's rule. It is found that 1, 3 – diketones are normally reduced to β-ketoalcohol. Thus, 2, 4-hexanedione gave quantitatively (S)-5-hydroxy-3-hexanone (90% ee)[35].

The reduction of ethyl acetoacetate with Aspergillus niger gives 98 per cent of a 75:21 mixtures favouring (R)-alcohol. This is an contrast to the formation of (S)-alcohol with Baker's yeast or geotrichum candidum[36].

Baker's yeast reduces simple ketones[37] as shown by the selective reduction of the ketonic moiety on the side cahin of the cyclopentadione to the (R)-alcohol (Scheme 25). The formed (R)-alcohol is used in the synthesis is norgestral[38].

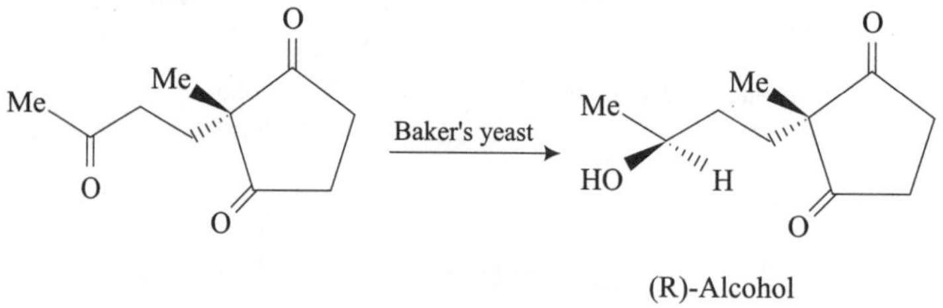

Scheme 25

Geranial on reduction with Baker's yeast gave (R)-citronellol. However reduction of the Z isomer (neral) gave a 6:4 R:S mixture probably due to isomerisation of the double bond in neral prior to the delivery of hydrogen[39].

Miscellaneous Reductions

Asymetric reduction of carbonyl compounds and production of isotopically labelled species has been achieved. A system based on deuterated formate and formate dehydrogenase provides the best system for the introduction of deuterium through nicotinamide-cofactor catalysed process [40] (Table 2).

4   ENZYMES CATALYSED HYDROLYTIC PROCESSES

As already stated enzymes have great potential as catalysts for use in synthetic organic chemistry. The applications of enzymes in synthesis have been so far limited to relatively small number of large scale hydrolytic processes used in industry and to a large number of small scale synthesis of products used in research. Following are some of the applications of enzymes in hydrolytic processes.

4.1   Enantioselective Hydrolysis of Meso Diesters

Pig liver esterase has been used for the enantioselective hydrolysis of the following meso substrates (Table 3). The enantioselective hydrolysis of the following have been achieved by hog pancreatic lipase (Scheme 26)[51].

Table 2

Substrate	Enzyme (cofactor)	Product (ee%)	Ref.
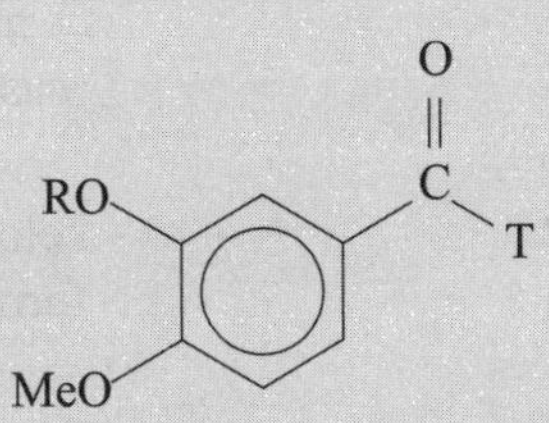	HLADH (NADH)	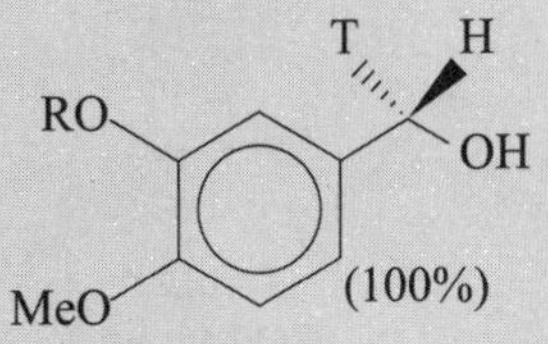 (100%)	41
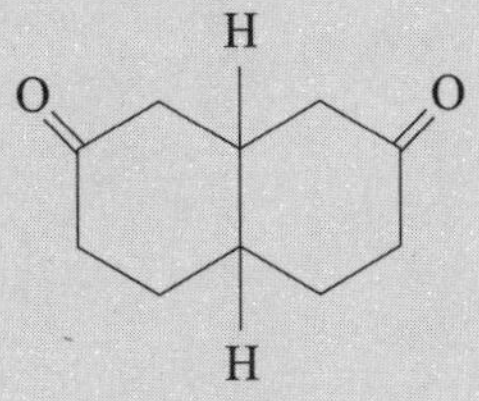	HLADH (NADH)	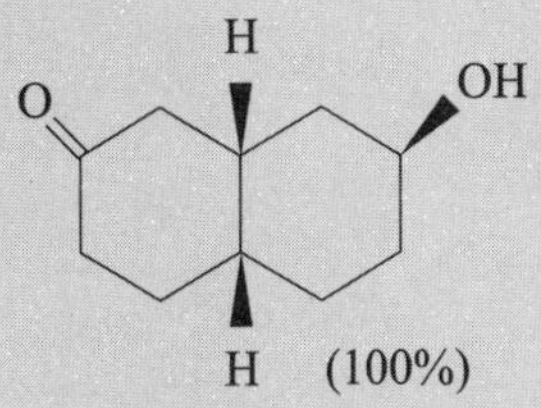 (100%)	42
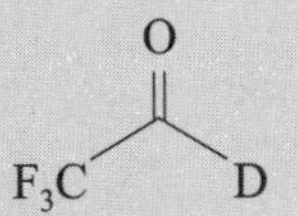	HLADH (NADH)	 (>97%)	43
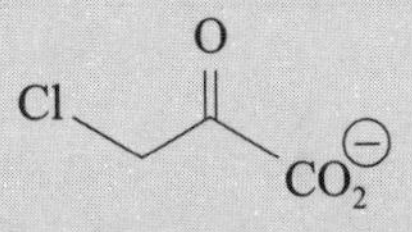	L-LDH (NaDH)	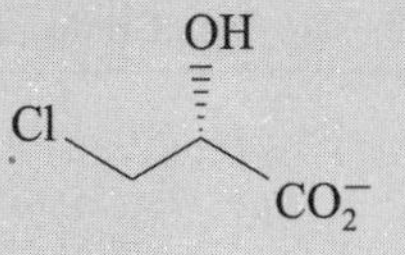 (98%)	44

HLADH = Horse liver alcohol dehydrogenase
L-LDH = L-lactic dehydrogenase

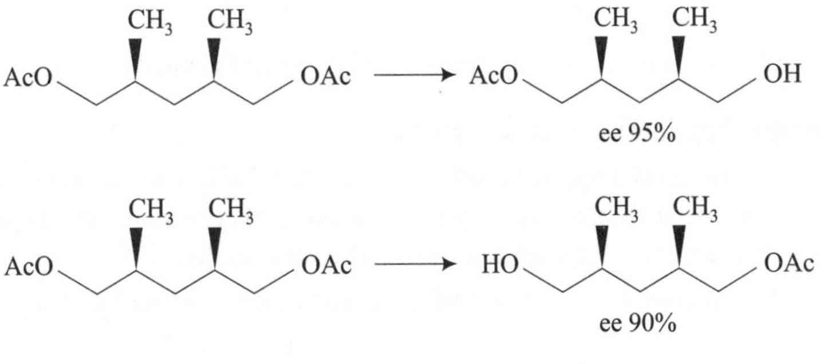

Scheme 26

4.2 Hydrolysis of N-acylamino Acids

The hydrolytic enzymes 'amidases' are useful for the hydrolysis of N-acylamino acids for the synthesis of amino acids and in the formation of amino bonds in polypeptides and proteins. In facts, this method is used in is the resolution of amino acids[52] (Scheme-27).

Table 3

Substrate	Product	ee(%)	Ref.
CO_2Me CO_2Me	CO_2H CO_2Me	77	45
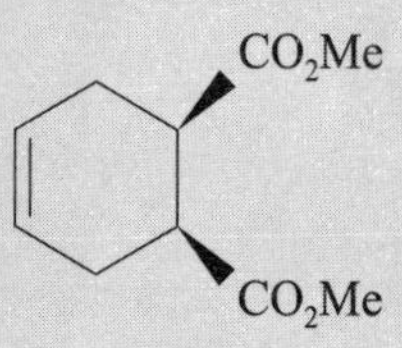 CO_2Me CO_2Me	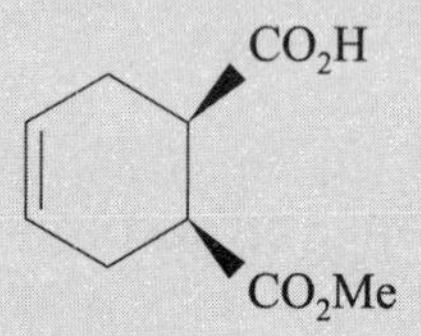 CO_2H CO_2Me	96	46, 47
R^1 R^2 MeO_2C CO_2Me	R^1 R^2 MeO_2C CO_2H	100	48, 49, 50

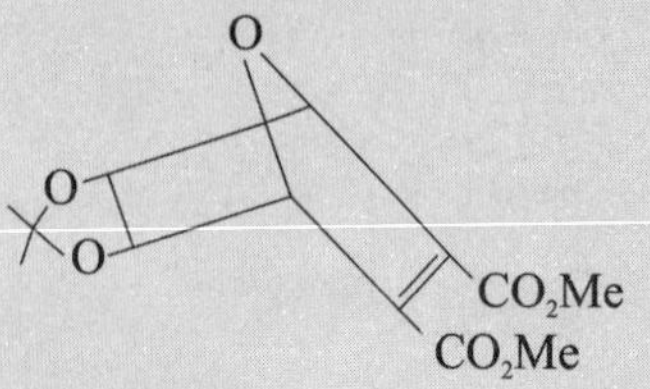

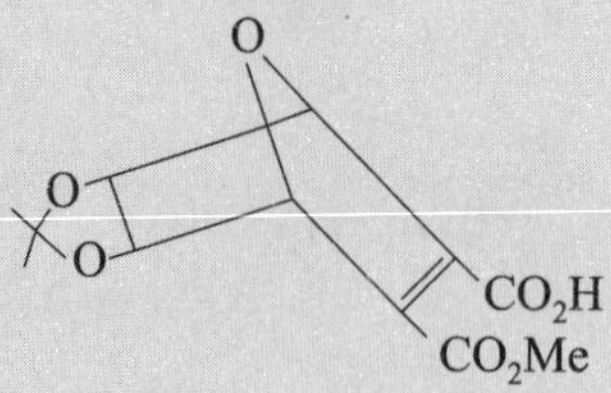

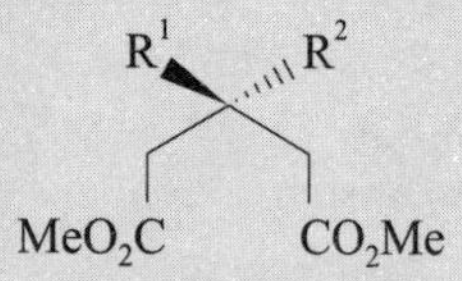

R^1 = OH, CH_3, H, $PhCH_2OCONH$
R^2 = CH_3, H, CH_2Ph, NO_2, C_6H_5, $CHMe_2$, cyclohexyl

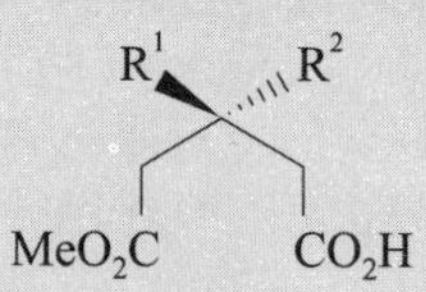

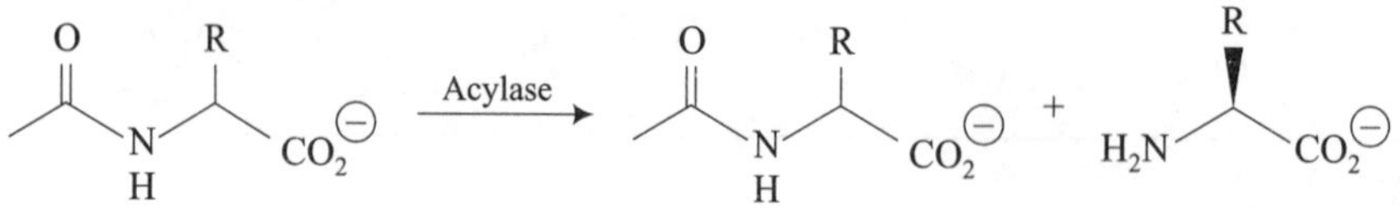

Scheme 27

Some other applications in use of amidases are also given (Table 4):

4.3   Miscellaneous Applications of Enzymes

(a) A number of commercial applications of Isomerases and Lyases are recorded. For example, glycosidases are used in large quantity in conversion of corn starch to glucose[56] and glucose isomerase catalyses the equilibration of glucose and fructose[57].

(b) Aspartic acid is prepared by addition of ammonia to fumaric acid in a reaction catalysed by aspartase[58].

(c) Malic acid is obtained by hydration of fumaric acid by the enzyme fumarase[59].

(d) Enantioselective condensation of HCN with aldehydes is catalysed by cyanohydrolases from several sources[60].

Table 4

Substrate	Ref.

(e) S-adenosylhomocysteine (or analogues) can be synthesised from homocysteine and adenosine (or analogues) by adenosylhomocysteine hydrolase[61].

(f) Ester groups at $Sn-1$ and $Sn-2$ positions of glycerol moiety can be hydrolysed by phospholipases A_1 and A_2 respectively[62].

(g) L-Phenylalanine synthesised by addition of isotopivally labelled ammonia to cinnamic acid cataysed by phenylalanine ammonia lyase[63].

(h) Using hydrolytic deaminations, L-citraline, L-arginine has been prepared on a large scale[64].

(i) Acrylamine has been synthesised from acrylonitrile by nitrile hydratases[65].

(j) D–, L– and mesotartaric acids have been synthesised by using epoxidehydrolases as shown as follow[66] (Scheme 28).

(k) The synthesis of 5-phospho – D-ribosyl – 1-pyrophosphate, a key intermediate in the biosynthesis of nucleotide has been achieved[67].

(l) A large number of biocatalytic transformation have been conducted in super critical CO_2 and also in ionic liquids. For details see chapter 5 and chapter 7.

E₁ = D-tartarate epoxidase

E_1 = D-tartarate epoxidase
E_2 = L = tartarate epoxidase
E_3 = epoxide hydrolysate from rabit liver microsomes

5 CONCLUSION

The most important conversions in the context of green chemistry is with the help of enzymes. Most of the enzymatic reactions are conducted in aqueous medium at ambient temperature and pressure. Generally the biocatalytic conversion involves only one step. The reactions are fast and the conversions and stereospecific.

References

1. A. Kiener, CHEMTECH, September 1995, pp. 31-35.
2. L.M. Shirley and S.C. Taylor, J. Chem. Soc. Chem. Commun., 1983, 954.
3. S.V. Ley and A.J. Redgrave, J. Synlett., 1990, 393.
4. S.V. Ley, F. Sternferd and S. Taylor, Tetrahedron Lett., 1987, **28**, 225.
5. A. Kleinzeller and Z. Fenel, Chem. Listy, 1952, **46**, 300; Chem. Abstr., 1953, **47**, 4290.
6. D.T. Gibson, J.R. Koch, C.L. Schuld and R.E. Kallio, Biochemistry, 1968, **7**, 3795; D.T. Gibson, M. Hansley, H. Yoshioka and T.J. Mabry, Biochemistry, 1970, **9**, 1626.
7. T. Hudlicky and J.D. Price, Synlett, 1990, 159; T. Hudlicky, H. Lund, J.D. Price and F. Rulin, Tetrahedron Lett., 1989, **30**, 4053.
8. C.J. Sih and J.P. Rosazza in Applications of Biochemical Systems in Organic Chemistry; J.B. Jones, C.J. Sih and D. Perlman, Eds, Wiley, New York, 1976; Part II, pp. 100-102; G.S. Fanken and R.A. Johnson, Chemical Oxidations with Microorganisms, Marcel Dekker, New York, 1972, pp. 157-164.

9. C.C. Ryerson, D.P. Ballou and C. Walsh, Biochemistry, 1982, **21**, 2644; N.A. Donoghu, D.B. Norris and P.W. Trudgill, Eur, J. Biochem., 1976, **63**, 175.

10. B.P. Branchand and C.T. Walsh, J. Am. Chem. Soc., 1985, **107**, 2153.

11. J.D. Blck and M.J. Taschner, J. Am. Chem. Soc., 1988, **110**, 6892.

12. Ch. Tamm, Angew. Chem., 1962, **74**, 225; Angew. Chem. Int., Ed 1962, **1**, 78; D. Perlan (ed.), Fermentation Advances, Academic, New York, 1969; K. Kieslich, Synthesis, 1969, 120; W. Charney and H.L. Herzog, Microbial Transformations of Steroids, Academic, New York 1967; A. Capek, O. Hanc and M. Tadra, Microbial Transformations of Steroids, Academia, Prague, 1966; M. Raynaud, Ph. Daste, F. Grossin, J.F. Biellmann and R. Wennig. Ann. Inst., Pasteur, 1960, **115**, 731; H. Tizuka and A. Naqito, Microbial Transformation of Steroids and Alkaloids, University Park Press, State College, Pennsylvania, 1967; J.B. Davis, Petroleum Microbiology, Elsevier, Amsterdam, 1967; C. Ralledge, Chem. Ind., 1970, 843; L. Wallen, F.H. Stodola and R.W. Jacksom, Type Reactions in Fermentation Chemistry, U.S. Department of Agriculture, 1959, pp, 185-189; D.W. Ribbins, Ann, Rept. Chem. Soc., London, 1965, **62**, 445; W.C. Evans, Ann. Rept. Chem. Soc., London, 1956, **53**, 279; O. Hayashi and M. Noyaki, Science, 1969, **164**, 338; D.T. Gibson, Science, 1968, **161**, 1093; Grunther S. Fonken and Roy A. Johnson, Chemical Oxidations with Microorganism, Mercel Dekker, New York, 1972.

13. D.H. Peterson and H.C. Murray, J. Am. Chem. Soc., 1952, **174**, 1871; H.C. Murray and D.H. Peterson, U.S. Patent, 2, 602, 769 (July 8, 1952).

14. W.F. Vander Waard, D. Vander Sijde and J. de Flines, Trans. Chim., 1966, **85**, 712.

15. P. Crabbe and C. Cassas Campillo, U.S. Patent, 3, 375, 175 (March 26, 1968).

16. I.I. Zaretskaya, L.M. Kogan, O.B. Tikhomirova, Jr., D. Sis, N.S. Wulfon, V.I. Zareksu, V.G. Zaikin, G.K. Skrybin and I.V. Torgov, Tetrahedron Lett., 1968, **24**, 1595.

17. J. Ureaht, E. Vischer and A. Wettstein, Helv. Chim. Acta, 1996, 43, 1077.

18. J.T. McCurdy and R.D. Garrett, J. Org. Chem., 1968, **33**, 660.

19. F.J. Fried, R.W. Thoma and A. Klingsberg, J. Am. Chem., 1953, **75**, 5764.

20. R.L. Prairie and P. Talalay, Biochemistry, 1963, **2**, 203.

21. B.P. Branchaud and C.T. Walsh, J. Am. Chem. Soc., 1985, **107**, 2153.

22. J.B. Jones and I.J. Jokovac, Org. Synth., 1984, **63**, 10.

23. J. Grunwald, B. Wirz, M.P. Scollar and A.M. Klibanov, J. Am. Chem. Soc., 1986, **108**, 6732.

24. A. Brossi, A. Ramel, J. O'Brien and S. Teitel, Chem. Pharm. Bull., 1973, **21**, 1839.

25. B.C. Saunders and B.P. Stark, Tetrahedron, 1967, **23**, 1867.

26. R.Z. Kazandjian and A.M. Klibanov, J. Am. Chem. Soc., 1985, **107**, 5448.

27. Milos Hudlicky, Oxidations in Organic Chemistry, ACS Monograph 186, American Chemical Society, Washington DC, 1990.

28. G.S.Y. Ng., L.C. Yuan, I.J. Jakovac and J.B. Jones, Tetrahedron, 1984, **40**, 1235.

29. J.B. Jones and I.J. Jakovac, Can. J. Chem., 1982, **60**, 19.

30. J.B. Jones, Methods Enzymol, 1976, **44**, 831.

31. V. Prelog, Pure Appl. Chem., 1964, **9**, 119.

32. B. Zhou, A.S. Gopalan, F. van Middlesworth, W.R. Shiej and C.J. Sih, J. Am. Chem. Soc., 1983, **105**, 5925.

33. K. Mori, Tetrahedron, 1981, **37**, 1314.

34. E. Kienam, E.K. Hafeli, K.K. Seth and R. Lamed, J. Am. Chem. Soc., 1986, **108**, 162.

34a. R.W. Hoffman, W. Helbig and W. Landner, Tetrahedron Letters, 1982, **23**, 3479.

35. J. Bolte, J.G. Gourey and H. Veschambre, Tetrahedron Lett., 1986, **27**, 4051.

36. R. Bernardi, R. Cardillo and D. Ghiringhelli, J. Chem. Soc. Chem. Commun., 1984, 460.

37. J.K. Lieser, Synth. Commun., 1982, **13**, 765.

38. W.H. Zhou, D.Z. Hung, O.C. Deng, Z.P. Zhuang and Z.O. Wang, Nat. Prd. Proc. Sino-Am. Symp., 1980, 299; Chem. Abstr., 1983, **88**, 198545w.

39. M. Bostmembrum-Desrut, G. Dauphin, A. Kergomard, M.F. Renard and H. Veschambre, Tetrahedron., 1985, **41**, 3679.

40. C.H. Wong and G.M. Whitesides, J. Am. Chem. Soc., 1983, **105**, 5012.

41. A.R. Battershy, P.W. Sheldrake, J. Staunton and D.C. Williams, J. Chem. Soc. Perkin Trans., 1976, **1**, 1056

42. D.R. Dodds and J.B. Jones. J. Chem. Soc. Chem. Commun., 1982, 1080.

43. C.H. Wong and G.M. Whitesides, J. Am. Chem. Soc., 1983, **105**, 5012.

44. B.C. Hirschbein and G.M. Whitesides, J. Am. Chem. Soc. 1982, **104**, 4458.

45. Y. Ito., T. Shibata, M. Arita, H. Sawai and M. Ohno., J. Am. Chem. Soc., 1981, **103**, 6739.

46. H.J. Gais and K.L. Lukas, Angew. Chem., 1984, **96**, 140; Angew. Chem. Int. Ed. Engl., 1984, **23**, 142.

47. S. Kobayashi, K. Kamiyama, T. Limori and M. Ohno, Tetrahedron Lett., 1984, **23**, 2557.

48. F.C. Huang, L.F.H. Lee, R.S.D. Mittal, P.R. Ravi Kumar, J.A. Chan and C.J. Sih, J. Am. Chem. Soc., 1975, **97**, 4144; C.H. Chervenka and P.E. Wilson, J. Biol. Chem., 1956, **222**, 635.

49. Y.F. Wang, T. Izawa, S. Kabayski and M. Ohno., J. Am. Chem. Soc., 1982, **104**, 6465.

50. C.J. Francis, J.B. Jones, J. Chem. Soc. Chem. Commun., 1984, 579.

51. Y.F. Wang, C.S. Chen, G. Girdaukas and C.J. Sih., J. Am. Chem. Soc., 1984, **106**, 3695.

52. I. Chibata, Immobilized Enzymes – Research and Development, Halsted Press, New York, 1978; Y. Izumi, I. Chibata and T. Itoh, Angew. Chem., 1978, **90**, 187; Angew. Chem. Int. Ed., Engl., 1978, **17**, 176.

53. H.D. Jakubki, P. Kuhl and A. Konnecke, Angew. Chem., 1985(97); Angew Chem. Int. Ed. Engl., 1985, **24**, 85.

54. B.J. Abbott, Adv. Appl. Microbiol, 1976, **20**, 203.

55. D.L. Regan, M.D. Dunnill and M.D. Lilly, Biotechnol. Bioeng., 1974, **16**, 333.

56. H.M. Walton, J.E. Eastman and A.E. Staly, Biotechnol. Bioeng., 1973, 447; J.H. Wilson and M.D. Lilly, Biotechnol. Biology, 1969, **11**, 349; J.J. Marshall and W.J. Whelan, Chem. Ind., London, 1971, **25**, 701; C. Gruesbeck and H. F. Rase, Ind. End. Chem. Proc. Res. Dev., 1972, **11**, 74.

57. H.H. Weetall, Process Biochem, 1975, **10**, 3; H.H. Weetall, W.P. Vann, W.H. Pitcher, Jr., D.D. Lee, Y. Y. Lee et al, Methods Enzymol, 1976, **44**, 776; G.W. Strandberg and K.L. Similey. Appl. Microbiol., 1971, **21**, 588; N.B. Havewala and W.H. Pitcher, Ir., Enzyme Engg., 1974, **2**, 315; N.H. Mermelstein, Food Technol, Chicago, 1975, **29**, 20.

58. T. Tosa, T. Sato, T. Mori, Y. Matuo and I. Chibata, Biotechnol. Biology, 1973, **15**, 69.

59. K. Yamamoto, T. Tosa, K. Yamashita and I. Chibata, Eur. J. Appl. Microbiol, 1976, **3**, 169.

60. W. Becker and E. Pteil, J. Am. Chem. Soc., 1966, **88**, 4299.

61. B. Chabannes, A. Garib, L. Cronenberger and H. Pacheco, Prep, Biochem., 1983, **12**, 395; R.C. Knudsen and I. Yall, J. Bacteriol, 1972, **112**, 569; S.K. Shapiro and D.J. Ehninger, Anal. Biochem., 1966, **15**, 323

62. G. Rao, H.O.O. Schmid, K.R. Reddy and J.G. White, Biochem. Biphys. Acta., 1982, **715**, 205; H. Eibi, Angew. Chem. Int. Ed. Eng., 1984, **23** 257 (a review).

63. A. R. Battersby, Chem. Ber., 1984, **20**, 611.

64. Y. Izumi, I. Chibata and T. Itoh, Ang. Chem. Int. Ed. Engl., 1978, **17**, 176.

65. Y. Asano, T. Yasunda, Y. Tani and H. Yamada, Agric. Biol. Chem., 1982, **46**, 1183.

66. M. Ohno, Ferment, Ind. Tokyo, 1979, **37**, 836; H. Sato, Jap. Patent 75 140 684, Japan Kokai; Chem Abstr., 1975, **84**, 149212; R.H. Allen, W.B. Jakoby, J. Biol. Chem., 1969, **244**, 2078.

67. A. Gross, O. Abril, J.M. Lewis, S. Geresh and G.M. Whitesides J. Am. Chem. Soc., 1983, **205**, 7428.

PART – II

Organic Synthesis in Super Critical Carbon Dioxide

I HISTORICAL DEVELOPMENT

Till the early sixteenth century Carbon dioxide CO_2 was not known to people. It was in 1823 when Faraday introduced the existence of various liquefied gases including CO_2. Gore[1] in 1961 gave the process of preparing liquid CO_2. However, most work on using carbon dioxide as a solvent for extraction of natural products dates from 1960.

Properties of Carbon Dioxide

Carbon dioxide can exist as a solid, liquid or gas. The gas phase is very familiar and needs no further comment. The solid phase is frequently used for cooling applications and is sold as 'Dry-Ice'. At atmospheric temperature and pressure, the solid transforms directly to the gas without passing through the liquid phase. However under certain conditions (e.g. compression of the gas or heating of solid CO_2 under pressure), liquid carbon dioxide can be formed. At the triple point all three phases are in equilibrium. The critical point is of considerable interest for CO_2 as the critical temperature (31°C) lies close to ambient temperature.

The critical temperature for a substance is that temperature above which it is impossible to liquify the gas no matter what pressure is applied. Hence 31°C is the upper limit for extraction using liquid carbon dioxide. The lower limit is theorically –56° but there are problems with running an extractor at such low temperatures.

Phase Diagram for Carbon Dioxide

As already stated CO_2 can exist in different states depending on the temperature and pressure of its surroundings. A phase diagram provides a graphic representation to the states of matter for CO_2 under various pressures and temperatures (Fig. 1).

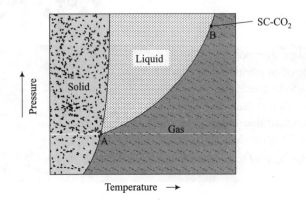

Phase diagram of CO$_2$ (Figure in not to scale)

However, if we increase pressure, CO$_2$ becomes liqiud; at this point (–56°C and 5.1 atm), CO$_2$ exists as gas, liquid and solid simultaneously. At point *B* (31°C and 73 atm) CO$_2$ exists as super critical fluid. In the supercritical state, CO$_2$ has a viscosity similar to that of a gas and density similar to that of a liquid.

The present discussion on the uses and applications of supercritical carbon dioxide is divided into following three heads.

(1) Use of supercritical carbon dioxide for extracting natural products.

(2) Use of supercritical carbon dioxide for dry cleaning.

(3) Use of supercritical carbon dioxide as solvent for organic reactions

2 USE OF SUPER CRITICAL CARBON DIOXIDE (SC CO$_2$) FOR EXTRACTING NATURAL PRODUCTS

The two common methods used for extraction of natural products are

(i) Steam Distillation

(ii) Classical Solvent Extraction

The quality of the product isolated is the principal measure of the value and efficiency of an extraction procedure. It is of course, expected that the native chemical composition of the compound should remain unchanged.

(i) Steam Distillation

This is the oldest and most important method for obtaining essential oils, i.e. the characteristic smelling of volatile oils contained in plant material. These relatively-volatile oils with boiling range 150 – 250° are separated from other materials with the help of the carrier steam.

In steam distillation, the starting material is heated to 100°. This causes alteration of the essential oil constituents which are often thermolabile. Also, water can bring about chemical changes in the oils. Many steam distillations are accompanied by hydrogen sulphide, ammonia, acetaldehycle, or acetic acid. These being water-soluble also enter the oil and render subsequent refining necessary.

(ii) Classical Solvent Extraction

Extraction of natural products with classical organic solvents is an important procedure for obtaining 'Lippophilic' plant components. The material obtained using this technique contain a large amount and number of impurities which are difficult to separate and purification procedures like chromatography has to be used. The classical solvents, as we know display poor selectivity; thus the desired components often contain interfering side products. The crude product obtained by solvent extraction has an undesirable colour. Also, the solvent extracts have often a viscous wax like contency. Thus refining procedures have to be used.

The choice of the solvent to be used for extraction is very important. Following are the criteria for solvents selection:

1. Energy Required	• Lowest Latest heat
	• Low specific heat
	• Low boiling pant
2. Capacity	• Should have high dissolving capacity per kg of solvent.
3. Stability	• Highly stable
4. Hazards	• Non combustible
	• Very high flash point if at all combustible
	• Explosivity range should be very narrow.
5. Viscosity	• Lowest
6. Surface tension	• Should not foam
7. Corrosion	• Very low
8. Environmentally Friendly	

It is on record that the most common organic solvents which have been used for the extraction of natural products are alcohol (methyl and ethyl alcohol), benzene, chloroform, methylene chloride, ether and petroluem ether. We find that some of the solvents are carcinogenic (particularly benzene) and a large number are volatile solvents and are harmful for the environment. The halogenated solvents like chloroform, methylene chloride once released in the atmosphere, rise to the stratospheric region and are responsible for the destruction of the ozone layer. In view of this attempts have been made by various scientists to find a solvent which besides having solvent properties should be environmentally benign. One such solvent is super critical carbon dioxide (SCC). A detailed account of the historical development of super critical carbon dioxide has already been given.

The advantages of using SC CO_2 over conventional solvent extracts are:

(1) No thermal degradation product

(2) No hydrolysis as occus in steam distillation

(3) No loss of volatile components

(4) High concentration of valuable ingredients

(5) No solvent residue

(6) Free of inorganic salts or heavy metals (these are insoluble in SCC)

(7) Free of any microbacterial life.

(8) Meets legal requirement of being environmentally benign.

(9) High extraction yields.

(10) High solubility towards lipophilic miolecules, hydrocarbons, ethers, esters, ketones, lactones, alcohols (mono and sesquiterpenes).

(11) Polar substances like sugars, glycosides, amino acids and tannins are insoluble in SCC.

Applications

Following are some of the applications of using SCC for extraction of natural products:

(i) Essential oils from crushed/prepared Ajowan, Turmeric, Ginger and Caraway have been isolated.

(ii) A number of food products including spices like pepper, ginger, cumin, cardamon, cloves and decaffeination of coffee and Tea, oils from ground nuts, rice bran, wheat germ etc. have been isolated.

(iii) Essential oils from Acorus calamus, Angelica sp., Costus sp., Turmeric, coriander and bottle brush have been extracted with SCC.

(iv) Vegetable Tannin materials, which find extensive applications in leather processing, ink manufacture, engraving and in the preparation of formulation of drugs have been isolated using SCC extraction procedure .

(v) Pyrethrin – a naturally occurring insecticide found in flowers of a variety of chrysanthemum can be a product at lower capital and operating costs than by conventional organic solvent molecules.

In fact, over the last decade, SC CO_2 extraction technology has emerged as a superior alternative to conventional techniques of extraction of natural products.

3 USE OF SUPER CRITICAL CARBON DIOXIDE (SC CO_2) FOR DRY CLEANING

Articles of clothing made from fabrics cannot be washed in water and require a dry – cleaning process. In fact, the term dry cleaning is somewhat misleading, because a liquid solvent is actually used for removing dirt and stains. Most of the drycleaners use the solvent perchloroethylene, or PERC.

Perchloroethylene

Disposal of perchloroethylene, a suspected carcinogen, can contaminate ground water. Besides this, PERC when released into the atmosphere rises to the stratosphere region, where it gets decomposed into chlorine radical by the action of UV rays of the sun. The chlorine radicals, as we know are responsible for depleting the ozone layer.

$$PERC \xrightarrow{\text{uv rays}} \overset{\bullet}{C}l$$

$$O_3 + \overset{\bullet}{C}l \longrightarrow O_2 + Cl\overset{\bullet}{O}$$

$$Cl\overset{\bullet}{O} + O \longrightarrow \overset{\bullet}{C}l + O_2$$

Net result $O_3 + O \longrightarrow 2O_2$

The environmental problems associated with drycleaning clothes and the rising costs of complying with environmental laws have encouraged search for alternative methods. One such approach uses liquid or super critical carbon dioxide (CO_2) as the cleaning solvent.

Joseph M. De Simone of the universals of North carolina and North carolina state university and cofounder of Micell Technologies has developed polymers that acts as surfactants so that liquid CO_2 can be used more effectively as a drycleaning solvent.

Though carbon dioxide (a non polar molecule) dissolves non-polar substances – most greases and oils (from cloths) turn out to be very insoluble in CO_2. However, the new surfactants increase the solubility of oils and grease in CO_2, in much the same way that soaps increase the solubility of non-polar substances in water. This makes CO_2 a more effective cleaning agent.

The surfactant developed by De Simone is a polymer composed of 'CO_2 – philic' segments (which are attracted to CO_2) and 'CO_2 – phobic' segments (which are not attracted to CO_2)

"CO_2-phobic"   "CO_2-phibic"
chain segment   chain section

The 'CO_2 – phobic' segment can be made lipophilic (attracted to fats, oils and grease) or hydrophilic (attracted to water). When this polymer is placed in a medium of supercsitical or liquid CO_2, it assembles into a micelle structure. The "CO_2 – philic" segments surrounds or encase the "CO_2 – phoblic" segments.

The miscelle structure can encase materials such as greases and oil in the inner "CO_2 – phoblic" area of the miscille structure and allow them to be washed away by the CO_2 solvent.

The Micell Technologies have produced dry – cleaning machines that use liquid CO_2 and a surfactant to dry – clean clothes, potentially replacing the environmentally harmful PERC.

[For more details on use pf liquid CO_2 for dry – cleaning see *Introduction to Green Chemistry*, American Chemical Society (2002)].

4 USE OF SUPERCRITICAL CARBON DIOXIDE (SC CO_2) AS SOLVENT FOR ORGANIC REACTIONS

There are a number of advantages associated with the use of supercritical carbon dioxide (SC – CO_2) as a solvent for organic reactions.

- CO_2 is non – toxic and environmentally benign[2].
- Solvent properties of SC – CO_2 (e.g., dielectric constant, solubility parameter, viscosity and density) can be dramatically altered or changed is a manner not possible with conventional solvents – via manipulation of temperature and pressure[3, 4].
- The properties of SC – CO_2 are intermediate between that of a liquid and gas.

Some of the important application on the use of super critical carbon dioxide are given. We apologize in advance to anyone who believes their contributions have been omitted.

4.1 Asymmetric Catalyst Using Super Critical Carbon Dioxide

It has been found[4a] that asymmetric catalytic reductions, particularly hydrogenations and hydrogen transfer reactions can be carried out in super critical carbon dioxide with selectivities comparable or superior to those observed in conventional organic solvent (Scheme 1)

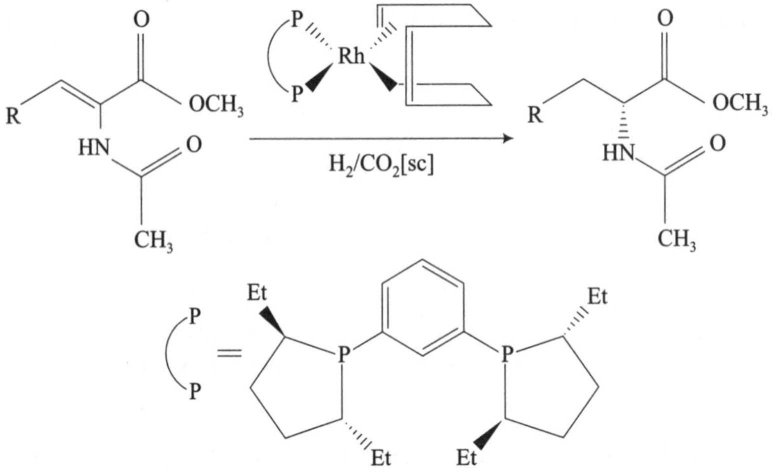

Scheme 1

It has been found[4] that asymmetric hydrogen transfer reductions of enamides using ruthenium catalysts proceeds with enantioselectivities that exceed those in conventional solvents. The success of the asymmetric catalytic reductions in CO_2 is due to the several unique properties of CO_2 including tunable solvent strength, gas miscibility, high diffusivity and ease of separation. The problem arising due to insolubility of salts has been overcome by using lipophilic anions, particularly tetrakis [3, 5-bis (trifluoromethyl) – phenyl] borate (BARF). This discovery has been useful for the synthesis of wide range of speciality chemicals like pharmaceuticals and agrochemicals.

4.2 Supercritical Polymerisations

Supercritical CO_2 has been used in place of less acceptable organic chemicals[5] for polymerisations. As has already been stated, supercritical CO_2 is mixed with a surfactant in order to enhance the solubility for large, hydrocarbon-based molecules. One such polymerisation is described below (Scheme 2).

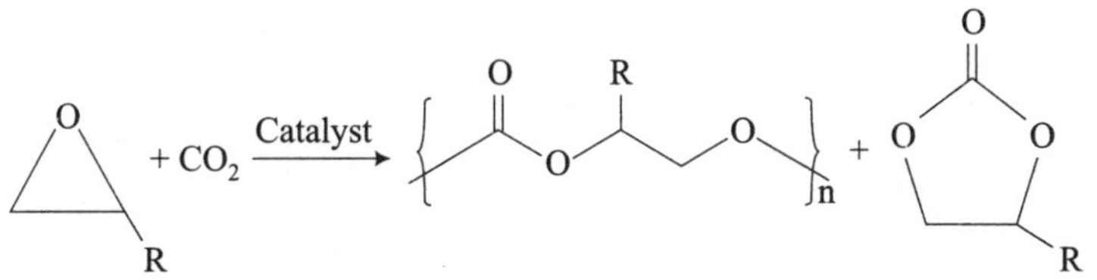

Scheme 2

This supercritical CO_2 containing a surfactant has been described as 'Soapy CO_2'.

Various types of polymers have been synthesised[5a] using SC – CO_2.

4.3 Free Radical Bromination

Free radical bromination can be performed[6] in supercritical CO_2, where selectivity and yield are not compromised. Thus free radical bromination of toluene in super critical CO_2 using bromine as a brominating agent gives a mixture of benzyl bromide (>70%) and 4 – bromotoluene. However when N – bromosuccinimide was used in super critical CO_2 quantitative yield of benzylbromide was obtained (Scheme 3).

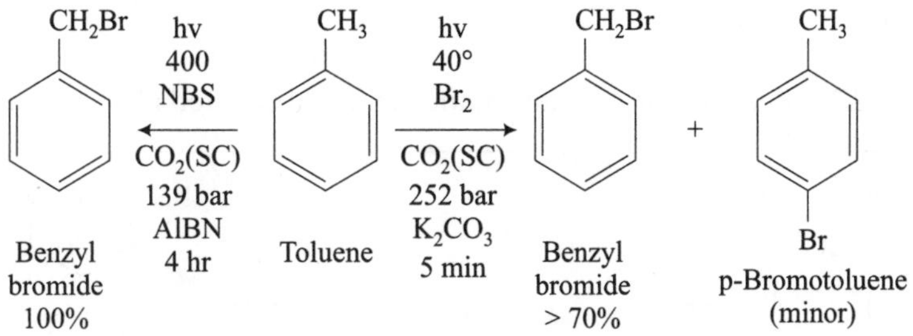

Scheme 3

Some other radical reactions in SC – CO_2 have been discussed subsequently in a separate section.

4.4 Hydrocarbon Functionalization

As already stated supercritical CO_2 is proving to be a suitable solvent for free radical reactions. Towards this end, a new chemical process has been developed[6] which results in concomitant hydrocarbon functionalisation.

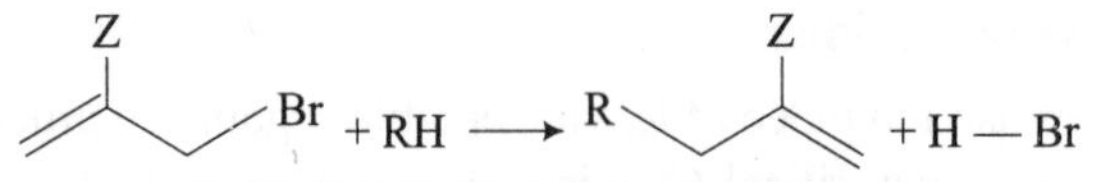

$Z = H, P, CO_2$ Et, CN; R = H, CH$_3$

The suggested mechanism[6] of this reaction is the free radical chain process (Scheme 4)

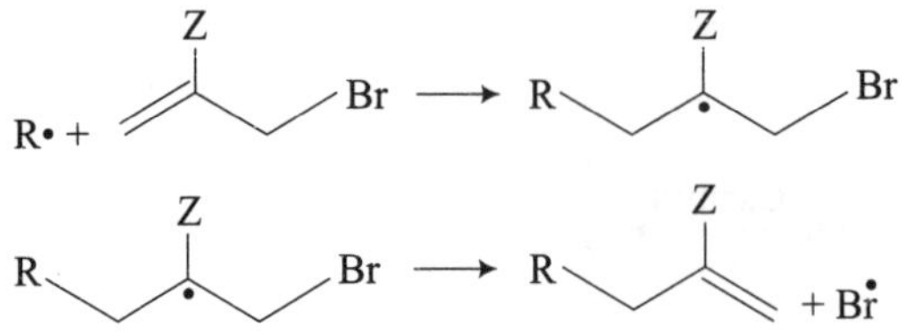

Scheme 4

As seen, the key intermediate in this process is bromine atom, which abstracts (with high selectivity) a hydrogen atom from a hydrocarbon (typically an alkylaromatic such as toluene or cumene). The resulting benzyl radical subsequently adds to a double bond of an allyl bromide $(CH_2 = C(Z))$ CH_2Br; where z = Ph, CO_2R or (N). The resulting radical adduct completes the chain by undergoing β – cleavage to eliminate bromine atom. The reaction requires a free radical initiator such as benzoyl peroxide or di-t-butyl peroxide.

This reaction achieves hydrocarbon functionalization and C – C bond formation, while avoiding the use of strong bases. Since Br is the chain carrier, hydrogen abstraction proceeds with high selectivity (i.e. only the weakest C – H bond in the hydrocarbon is susceptible to attack). This reaction can be carried out in SC – CO_2 as a reaction solvent. Overall yields in this reaction are excellent (Table 4.1).

Table 4.1 Reaction of Alkylaromatics with substituted allyl bromides

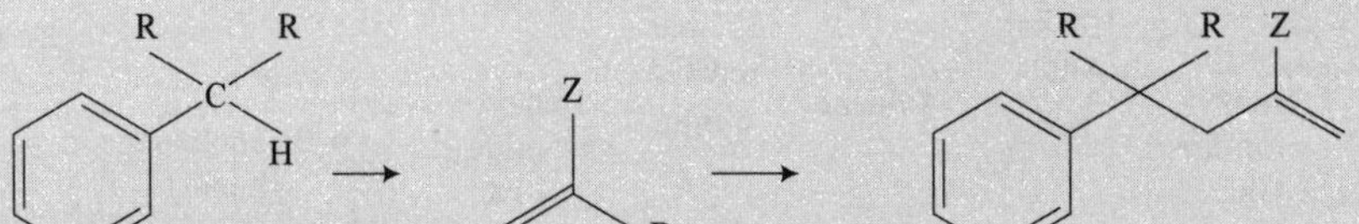

R	Z	Yield (%)
H	H	33
H	Ph	82
CH$_3$	Ph	100
H	CO$_2$Et	47
CH$_3$	CO$_2$Et	48
H	CN	66
CH$_3$	CN	80

Data taken from Ref. 7

4.5 Diels-Alder Reaction

A typical reaction for carbon–carbon bond formation is the well-known Diels–Alder reaction. Following Diels-Alder reactions have been reported[8].

(a) Diels-Alder reaction of isoprene and methylacrylate to produce para and meta isomers (Scheme 5)

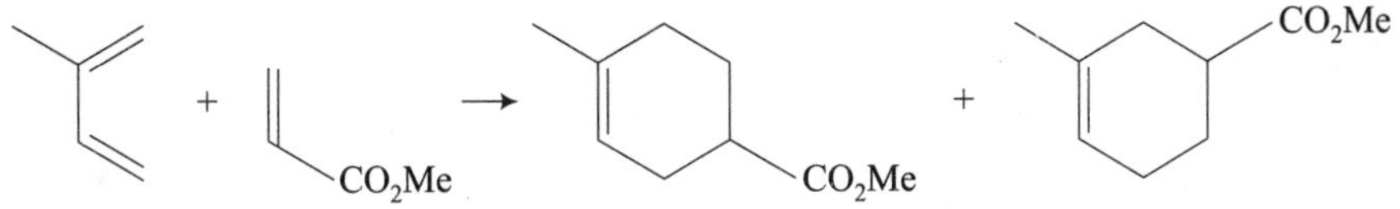

| Isoprene | Methyl acrylate | (1) Para isomer | (2) Meta isomer |

Scheme 5

Following Table gives the ratio of para and meta isomer along with the total yield obtained in conventional solvent (toluene) and super critical CO_2.

Condition	Yield (%)^a	Ratio^b 1 : 2
PhCH$_3$, 145°, 15hr	78	71 : 29 (71 : 29)
PhCH$_3$, 50°, 3d	(7)	69 : 31 (72 : 28)
CO$_2$, 49.5 bar, 50°, 4d	(11)	69 : 31 (73 : 27)
CO$_2$, 74.5 bar, 50°, 4d	(5)	67 : 33 (73 : 27)
CO$_2$, 95.2 bar, 50°, 7d	(4)	71 : 19 (73 : 27)
CO$_2$, 117 bar, 50°, 3d	(3)	70 : 30 (72 : 28)

a isolated yield (estimated by ^{1}H NMR)
b Ratio of isomers determined by ^{1}H HMR and GC analysis
Data taken from Ref. 8

The above Diels-Alder reaction was also examined by other workers[9-11] but the ratio of the products obtained were different. It was believed[8] that the experiments[9-11] were conducted in a two phase region rather than in a homogenous supercritical phase.

(b) Diels-Alder reaction of 2-t-butyl-1, 3-butadiene and methyl acrylate to produce[8] para and meta products (Scheme 6)

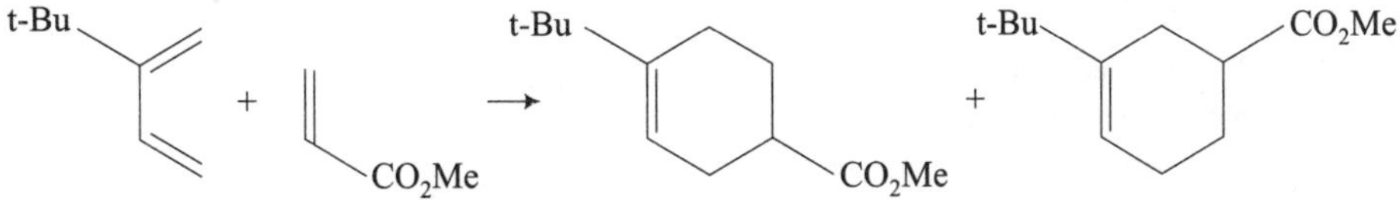

| 2-t-butyl 1,3-butadiene | Methyl acrylate | (1) | (2) |

Scheme 6

Following table gives the ratio of para (1) and meta (2) isomers along with the total yield obtained in conventional procedure and super critical CO_2.

Conditions	Yield[a]	Ratio[b] (1 : 2)
neat, 185°, 16h	78	63 : 37 (63 : 37)
PhCH$_3$, 50°, 3d	(19)	69 : 31 (68 : 32)
CO$_2$, 87 bar, 50°, 3d	(5)	71 : 29 (68 : 32)
CO$_2$, 117 bar, 50°, 3d	(4)	69 : 31 (69 : 31)
CO$_2$, 117 bar, 150°, 24h	54	65 : 35 (64 : 36)

a Isolated yield (estimated by ^{1}H NMR)

b Ratio of isomers determined by ^{1}H NMR and G C analysis

Data taken from Ref. 8

(c) Diels-Alder reaction of 2-trmethylsiloxybutadiene with methyl acrylate to give para and meta products (Scheme 7)

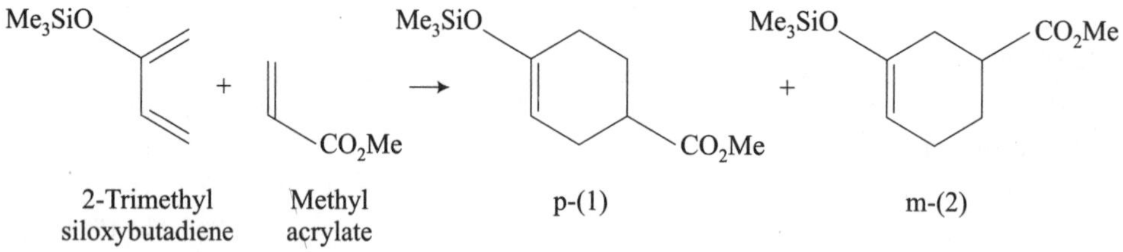

2-Trimethyl siloxybutadiene	Methyl acrylate	p-(1)		m-(2)

Scheme 7

Following table gives the ratio of para (1) and meta (2) products along with total yield obtained in conventional procedure.

Conditions	Yield %[a]	Ratio[b] (1 : 2)
PhCH$_3$, 110°, 45h	48	87 : 13
CO$_2$, 90 bar, 50°, 3d	trace[c]	
CO$_2$, 117 bar, 50°, 3d	(<1)	92 : 8[d]
CO$_2$, 117 bar, 150°, 24h	(31)	85 : 15

a Isolated yields (estimated by ^{1}H NMR)

b Ratio of isomers determined by ^{1}HNMR and G C analysis

c Ratio could not be determined

d Approximate ratio due to low conversion.

In the above reaction little variation in regioselectivity was observed relative to normal Diels-Alder synthesis.

(d) Diels-Alder reaction of isoprene and nitroethylene to give[8] para and meta products (Scheme 9).

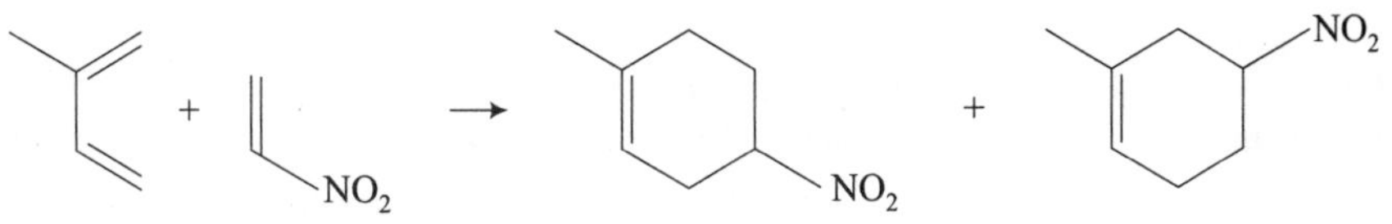

Isoprene   Nitro ethylene   p-isomer   m-isomer

Scheme 9

Following table gives the ratio of para (1) and meta (2) products along with the total yield ontained in conventional procedure.

Conditions	Yield[a]%	Ratio[b] (1:2)
PhH, BHT, 60°, 5h	77	81 : 19 (81 : 19)
CO_2, 86 bar, 50°, 3d	(31)	84 : 16 (84 : 16)
CO_2, 117 bar, 50°, 3d	(14)	84 : 16 (84 : 16)

a Isolated yields (estimated by ^{1}H NMR)
b Ratio of isomers determined by ^{1}H NMR and G C analysis
Data taken from Ref. 8

(e) Diels-Alder reaction of cyclopentadiene and ethyl acrylate derivative to produce[12] endo-exo isomer product (Scheme 10).

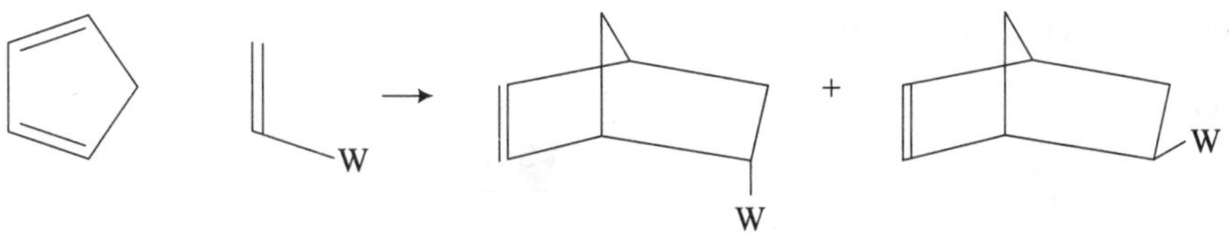

Cyclopentadine   W = COMe,   endo   exo
                  CN or CO_2Me   (1)   (2)

Scheme 10

Following table gives the yield of the product obtained along with endo and exo isomer ratio.

Conditions	Promolar	yield %	Endo : Exo (1 : 2)
W = COMe			
CO_2, 50°, 4h	none	29	82 : 18
CO_2, 50°, 4hr	0.5 g SiO_2	82	92 : 8
W = CN			
CO_2, 50°, 4h	none	5	57 : 43
CO_2, 50°, 4hr	0.5 g SiO_2	14	59 : 41
W = CO_2Me			
CO_2, 50°, 4hr	none	5	72 : 28
CO_2, 50°, 4hr	0.5 g SiO_2	21	85 : 15

Data taken from Ref. 12

In Diel-Alder reactions, the most important results have been recorded in presence of Lewis acid catalyst such as Scandium trifluoromethane sulfonate, optimium selectivity (endo/exo ratio) was observed around the critical point of the reaction mixture (Scheme 10a)[12a].

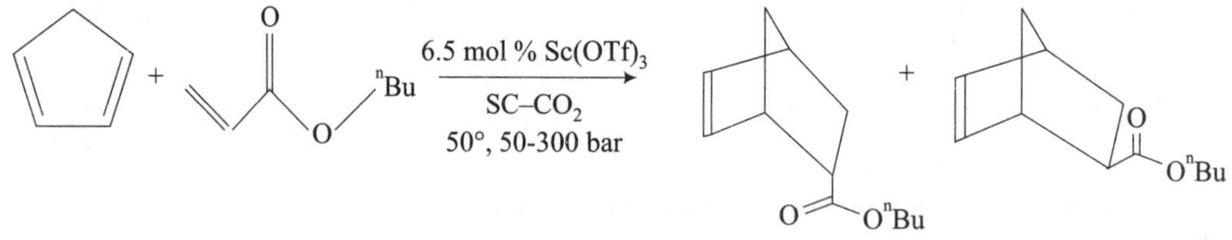

Scheme 10a

An aza-Diels-Alder reaction of Danishefsky's diene with an imine in presence of scandium perfluoroalkanesulfonate $[Se(OSO_2C_8F_{17})_3]$ in $SC-CO_2$ gave the aza-Diels-Alder adduct in 99% yield (Scheme 10b)[12b]. Silica gel has also been reported[12c] to be an efficient catalyst for Diel- Alder reaction in $SC-CO_2$ (Scheme 10b).

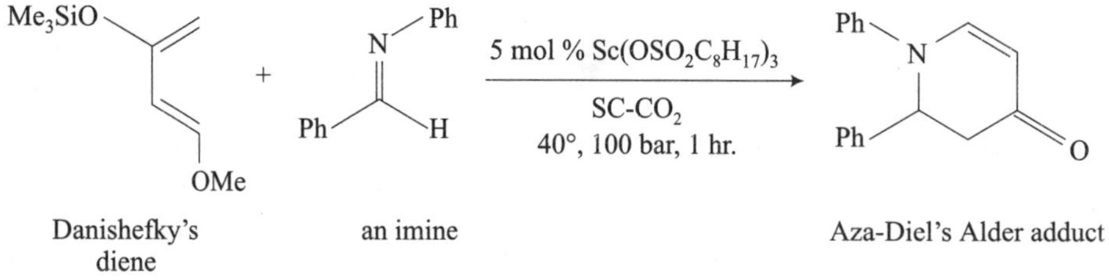

| Danishefky's diene | an imine | Aza-Diel's Alder adduct |

Scheme 10b

4.6 Kolbe-Schmitt Synthesis

This is a direct carboxylation reaction in super critical CO_2[13,14]. One of the isomers (o-hydroxy benzoic acid) leads to the production of aspirin. The ortho-and para selectivity between isomers of hydroxy benzoic acids are of particular interest (Scheme 11).

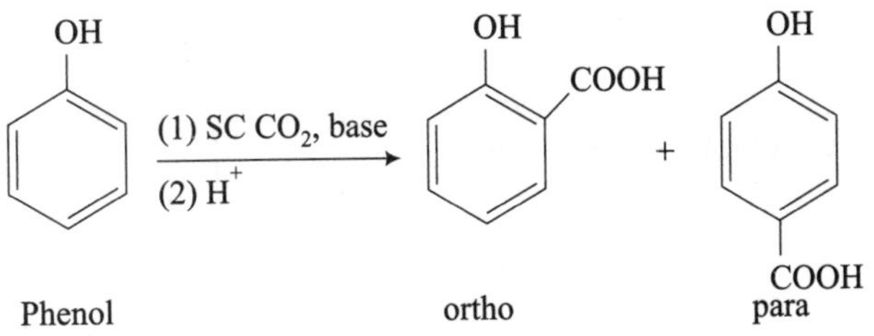

Scheme 11

4.7   Bromination: Displacement of a Chlorinated Aromatics

Phase transfer catalysed reaction of benzyl chloride with potassium bromide in presence of PTC catalyst in super critical CO_2 gives[15,16] benzyl bromide (Scheme 12).

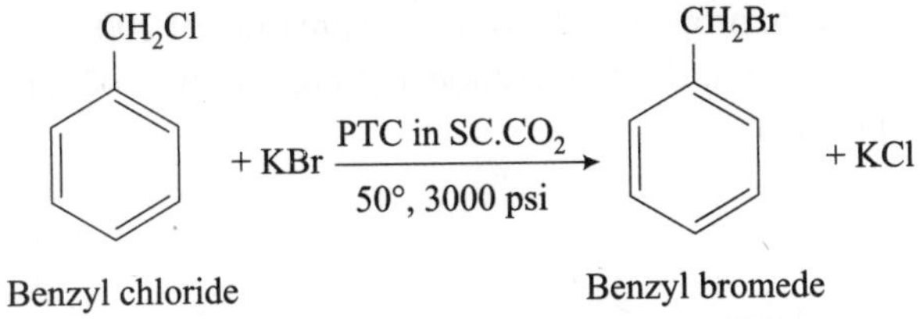

PTC is tetra-n-heptammonium bromide or 18-crown-6

Scheme 12

4.7A   Polymerisations

A disadvantage in using super critical CO_2 as a replacement solvent in the low solubilities of many common reagents and reactants in CO_2. The solvating ability of high density CO_2 (Super critical or liquid) is often compared to that of non-polar organic solvents such as hexane. It has been found[17] that use of water in super critical CO_2 considerably enhances the solubility of organics. Thus the following polymerisation has been achieved[18] (Scheme 13).

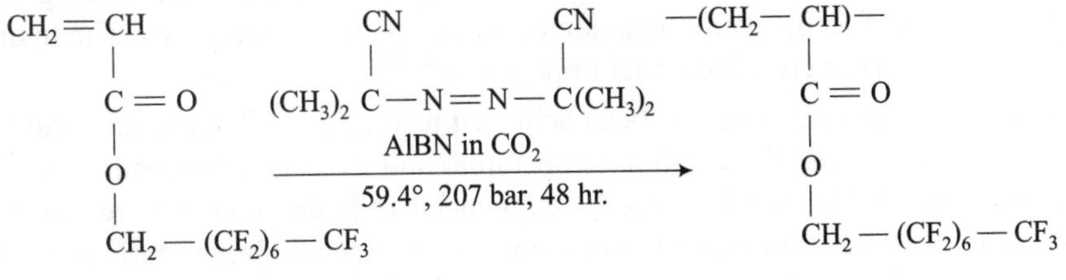

Scheme 13

4.8   Freidel-Crafts Reaction

Using Friedal-Crafts reaction following transformation has been achieved[19] in SC – CO_2. (Scheme 14).

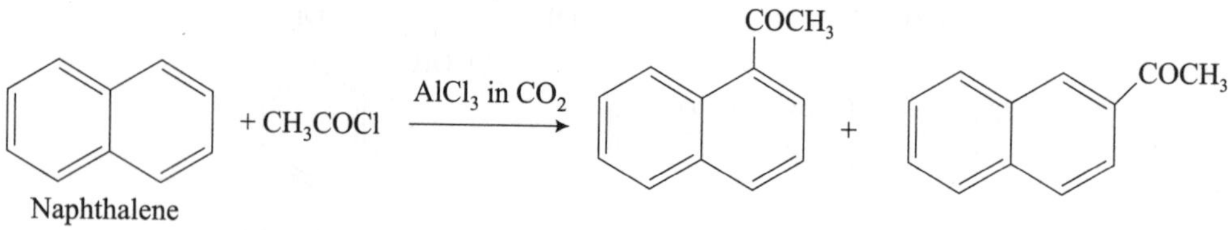

Scheme 14

Freidel-Crafts alkylation of aromatics has been performed in super critical fluids (SCF) media [19a]. Thus, alkylation of mesitylene in SC – propane (Tc = 91.9°, Pc = 46.0 bar), which acted both as solvent and alkylating agent (Scheme – 14a). A mixture of three products, vis. mono –, di and trialkylated products was obtained in 25 per cent, 6 per cent, minor respectively. The selectivity is much improved if SC – CO_2 is used as the reaction medium with propan-2-ol as alkylating agent. At a molar ratio of mesitylene to propane – 2 – ol 2 : 1, a pressure of 200 bar, catalyst temperature of 250° and a flow rate of 0.60g/min, the mono alkylated product was obtained as the only product with a conversion of 42 per cent.

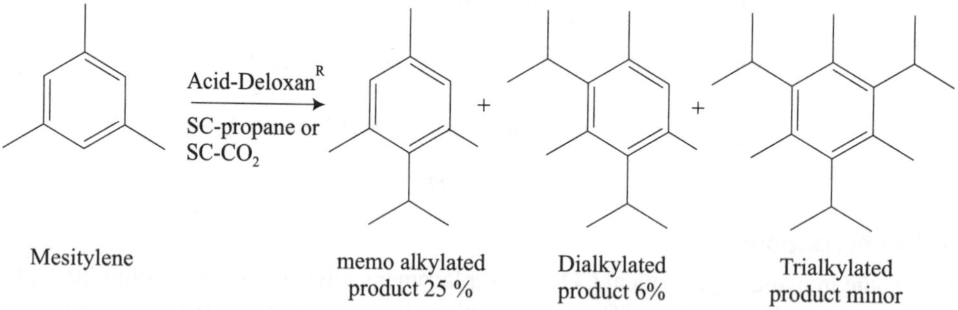

Mesitylene	memo alkylated product 25 %	Dialkylated product 6%	Trialkylated product minor

Scheme 14a

4.10   Hydrogenation in SC – CO_2

Hydrogen is soluble in SC – CO_2. The ability of SC – CO_2 is to bring together hydrogen substrates and catalysts in a single homogenation reactions over conventional processes. The hydrogenation of alkenes in SC – CO_2 is of great industrial importance [20, 21].

Hydrogenation of acetophenone has been achieved using a polysiloxane supported palladium catalyst [22]. In fact by adjusting the reaction temperature and hydrogen concentration, the product obtained can be adjusted. Thus at 90° using 2 – equivalents of hydrogen the corresponding alcohol (15.1) is produced in 90 per cent yield. However at 300° and the hydrogen ratio of 6 : 1 the fully saturated product (Ethyl cyclohexane, 15.2) is produced with >95% yields. At intermediate temperature of 200°, product (15.3) and (15.4) are obtained, the actual ratio depends on the concentration of hydrogen used (Scheme 15).

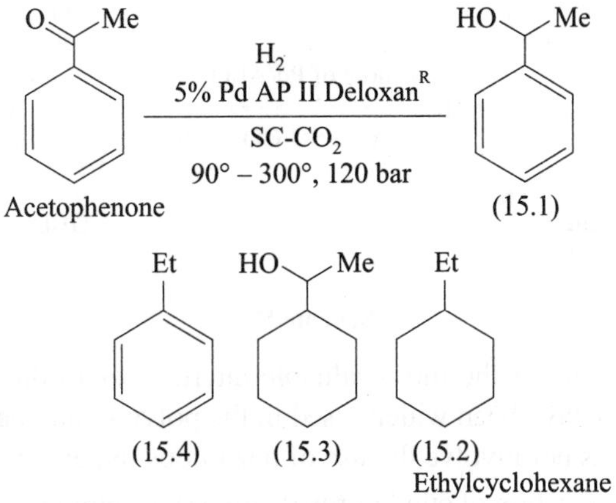

Acetophenone (15.1)

(15.4) (15.3) (15.2)
Ethylcyclohexane

Scheme 15

The selective hydrogenation (as in Scheme 15) has been achieved[23] in a number of organic compounds including aromatic and aliphatic alcohols, aldehydes, ketones, nitro-compounds, amines, oximes, olefins and acetylenes.

Dehydroisophytol, a propargylic alcohol could be reduced to the corresponding alkenol, isophytol (Scheme 16) by using the glassy alloy, Pd_{81} Si_{19} supported on Pd/SiO_2 as catalyst[24]. It has been shown that $Pd_{81}Si_{19}$ exhibited more than 50 times higher turn over frequency than a conventional silica-supported palladium catalyst under similar conditions. Selectivity to isophytol was 100 per cent at low conversion and declined to 77 per cent at about 70 per cent conversion due to over hydrogenation. The combined application of a glassy Palladium – Silicon alloy together with SC – CO_2 is promising for this type of Lindlar reactions.

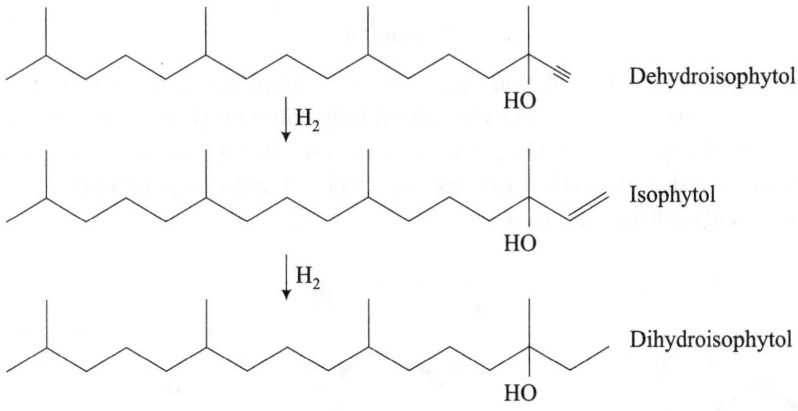

Dehydroisophytol

Isophytol

Dihydroisophytol

Scheme 16

Hydrogenation of maleic anhydride with hydrogen in presence of Pd/Al_2O_3 using SC – CO_2 as solvent at 200° gives γ-butyolactone (GBL) (Scheme 17)[25].

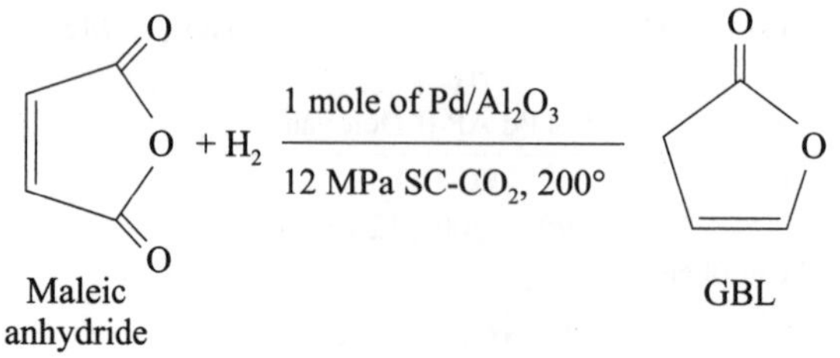

Maleic
anhydride

GBL

Scheme 17

The γ-butyolactone is one of the most valuable alternatives to the environmentally harmful chlorinated solvents, which have been widely used in the polymer and paint industry[26]. The above procedure (Scheme 17) does not involve the use of hazardous materials.

The asymmetric hydrogenation of ethyl pyruvate give (R) – ethyl lactate (Scheme 18)[27] using a heterogeneous catalyst system. In this case, the enantioselectivity is derived from a chiral cinchonidine modifier which is absorbed on the surface of supported platinum. However, there was a strong catalyst deactivation in the enantioselective hydrogenation in SC – CO_2 due to CO poising of the Pt following the reduction CO_2 to CO on the catalyst surface. This problem was overcome by using SC ethane.

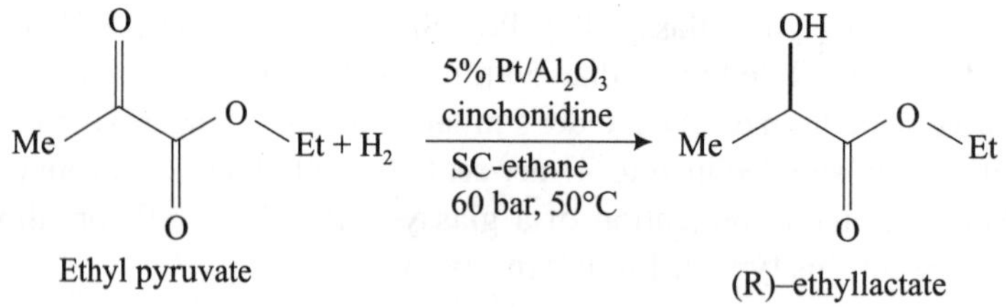

Ethyl pyruvate

(R)–ethyllactate

Scheme 18

The enantioselective hydrogenation of prochiral α-enamidies in SC – CO_2 using a catanoic rhodium species (A), which incorporates the chiral bidentate DuPHOS ligand (B) and tetrakis bis (trifluoromethyl) phenyl borate (BARF) counter ion (C) (Scheme 19) gives very high enantioselectivities with low catalyst loading (0.2 mol %) and comparable to those achieved in conventional solvents (methanol, hexane)[28].

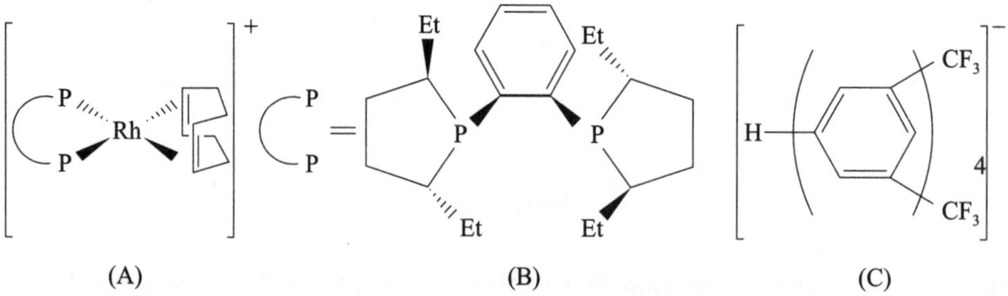

(A)   (B)   (C)

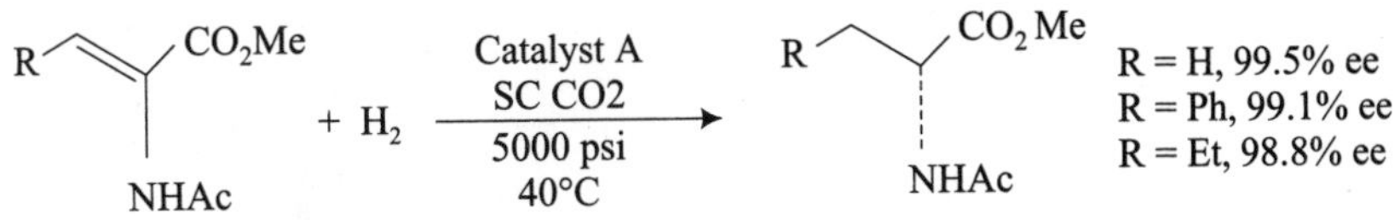

Scheme 19

The asymmetric hydrogenation of β, β-disubstituted enamide (20.1) under similar condition gave the valine derivative (20.2) (Scheme 20)[27] in 85% ee.

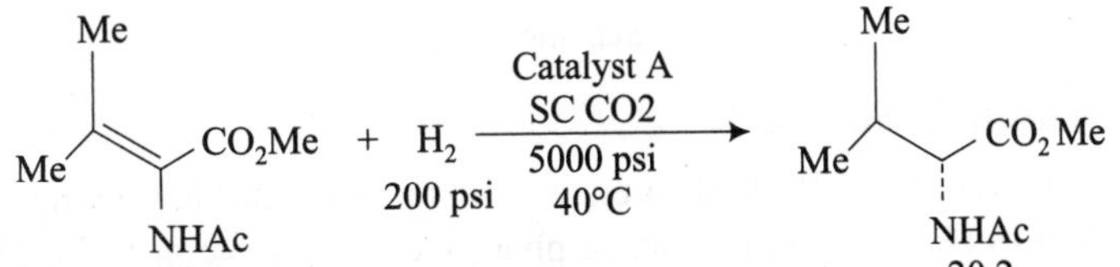

Scheme 20

Hydrogenation of Tiglic acid gives (S) 2-methyl butanoic acid in 99 per cent yield with an 81 per cent ee (Scheme 21) catalysed by ruthenium complex (D) containing the partially hydrogenated BINAP ligand which increased solubility in SC – CO_2 over the fully aromatic version[29]. This conversion and selectivity is comparable to the best obtained in conventional organic solvent.

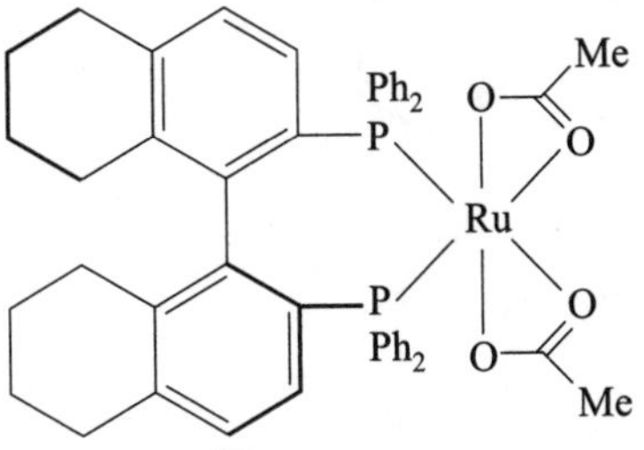

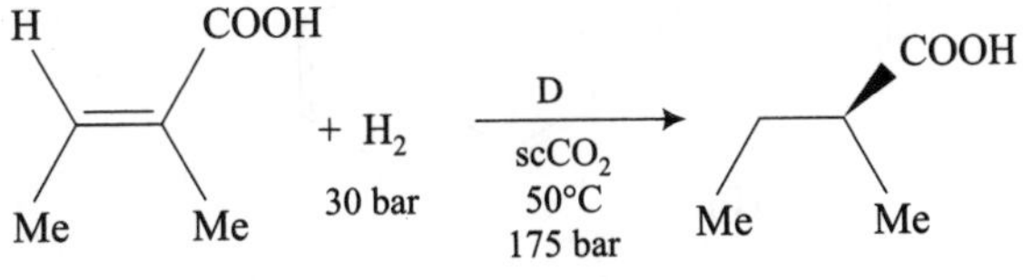

Tiglic acid

Scheme 21

Enantroselective hydrogenation of prochiral imines (22.1) ulitised the cationic iridium (I) complexes with chiral phosphinodihydrooxazole modified with perfluoroalkyl groups for increased CO_2 – philicity[30]. The product obtained was (R) – N – phenyl – 1 – phenylethylamine (22.2) in quantitative yield with an 81 per cent i.e. using 0.078 mol % of catalyst (Scheme 22).

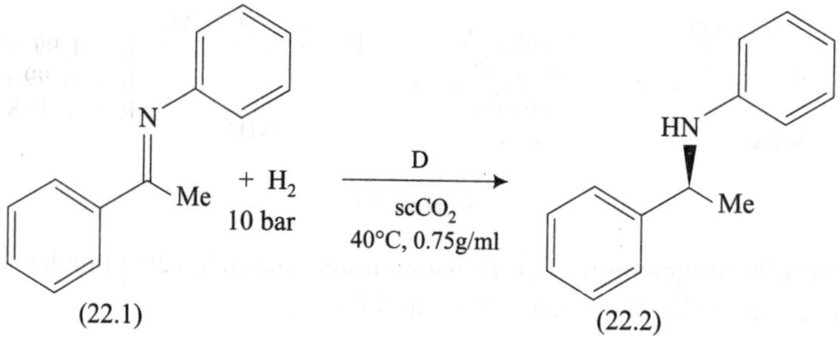

(22.1)   (22.2)

Scheme 22

4.II   Hydroformylation in SC – CO$_2$

Hydroformylation of styrene with hydrogen and carbon monoxide using Rh (CO$_2$) (acac) and (R$_1$S) – BINAPHOS (E) as ligand in dense phase CO$_2$[31,32] gave at 60° (with CO$_2$ density of 0.48 g/ml, close to the critical density) the branced product (A) in major amount along with minor achiral regioisomer (B) (Scheme 23).

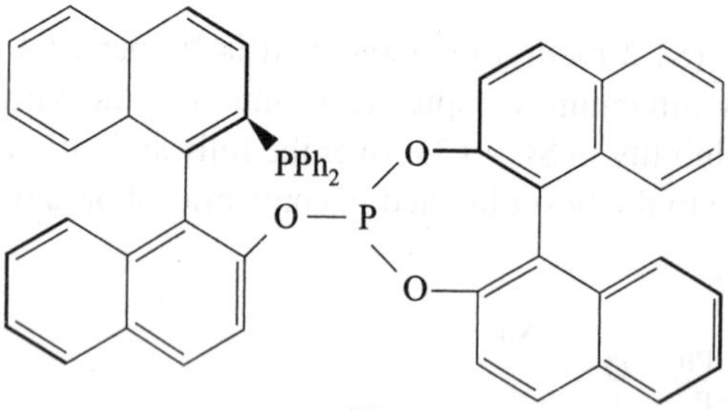

(E)

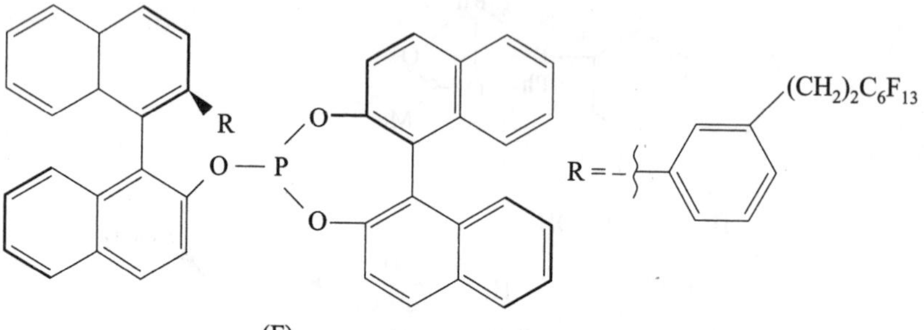

(F)

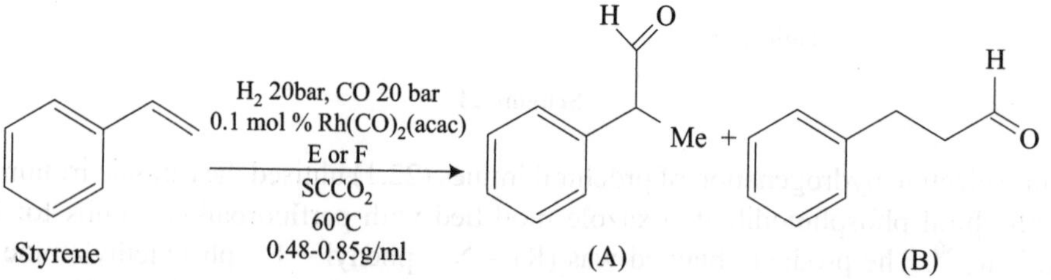

Styrene   (A)   (B)

Scheme 23

Though acrylates are amongest the least reactive olefins towards hydroformylation, but in SC – CO$_2$, the reaction is rapid and regoselective (Scheme 24)[33]. In this case the catalyst used is [Rh(acac) (CO)$_2$] and the fluoroalkylated phosphine ligand P(p – C$_6$H$_4$C$_6$F$_{13}$)$_3$.

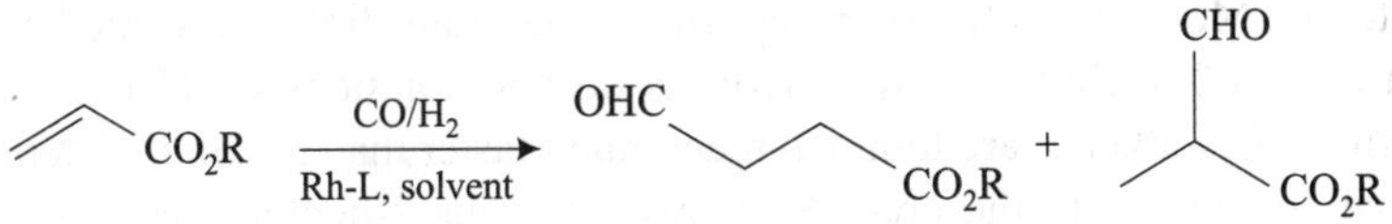

Scheme 24

4.12 Oxidations in SC – CO$_2$

The high solubility of oxygen in SC – CO$_2$ offers rate benefits for oxidations as in the case of hydrogenation and hydroformylation. This medium (i.e., oxygen dissolved in SC – CO$_2$) is particularly useful for the oxidation of weakly polar, water insoluble alcohols, due to the low polarity of SC – CO$_2$. Oxidation of alcohols to carbonyl compounds in SC – CO$_2$ has been shown to proceed with high selectivity at a high rate[34]. The oxidations were performed in a continuous fixed-bed reactor over a promoted noble metal catalyst (4% Pd, 1% Pt, 5% Bi/C). Primary alcohols could be converted to aldehydes using the above procedure. Benzyl alcohol and related substrates could be oxidised to the corresponding aldehydes with >99% selectivity.

For transition metal catalysed epoxidations with oxygen, an aldehyde was used as a sacrificial oxygen transfer agent. Such reactions occur efficiently[35] in SC – CO$_2$. Expoxidation of internal double bond could be achieved without the addition of metal catalyst. Thus, there is quantitative conversion of cis – cyclooctene into expoxycyclooctane (99% ee) (Scheme 25). In this case use of 2-propinaldehyde gave better results. Under similar conditions, cyclohexene and trans-3-hexene were quantitatively converted to epoxy cyclohexane (91% selectivity) and trans-3-epoxyhexane (>99% selectivity) respectively (Scheme 25).

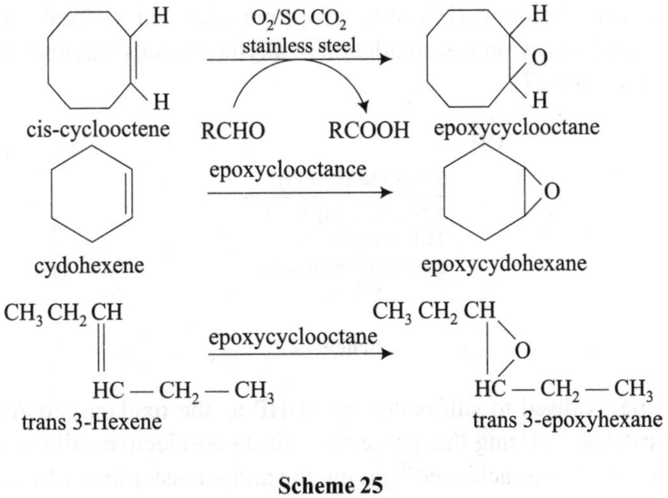

Scheme 25

The above epoxidations (Scheme 25) is catalysed by the stainless steel reactor which is expected to facililate the initial formation of acylperoxy radicals, allowing the oxidation to occur via a non-catalytic radical path way.

Epoxidation of alkenes has also been effected[36] in SC – CO_2 using tert-butyl hydroperoxide (TBHP) and catalytic $Mo(CO)_6$. It has been reported[36] that trans diols are formed by using aqueous TBHP solution (70 wt %). However, if anhydrous decane solutions of TBHP are used then the epoxide was formed. Cis-alkenes are found to react much faster than the trans-alkenes. Cyclooctene gave quantitative conversion to the epoxide. However, trans-2-heptene or trans-stilbene did not react. A number of allylic alcohols were epoxidised with aq. TBHP in SC – CO_2 using a salen catalyst[37] (G). Good diastereoselectivity for the erythro product was observed for alkenes with secondary alcohols (Scheme 26).

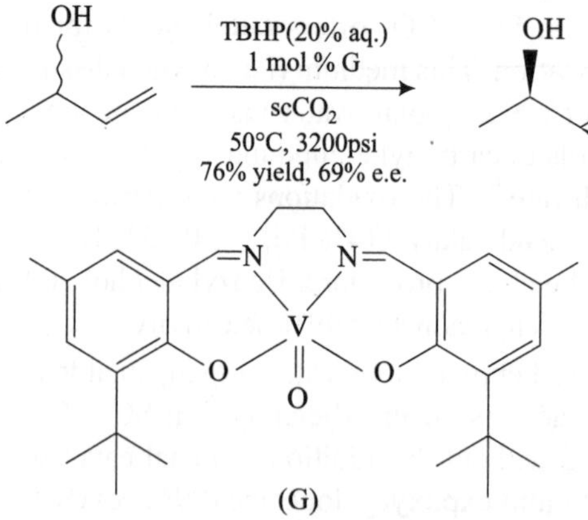

Scheme 26

Oxidations have also been carried out in liquid CO_2 as the solvent[38]. Thus epoxidation of allylic alcohols by anhydrous TBHP and catalytic oxovanadium (V) tri (isopropoxide) was effected in liquid CO_2 at 25°. Using titanium (IV) tetra (isopropoxide) and a chiral diisopropyl-L-tartrate (DIPT) ligand, the sharpless asymmetric oxidation of allylic alcohols was also shown to be effective at 0° in liquid CO_2 (Scheme 27).

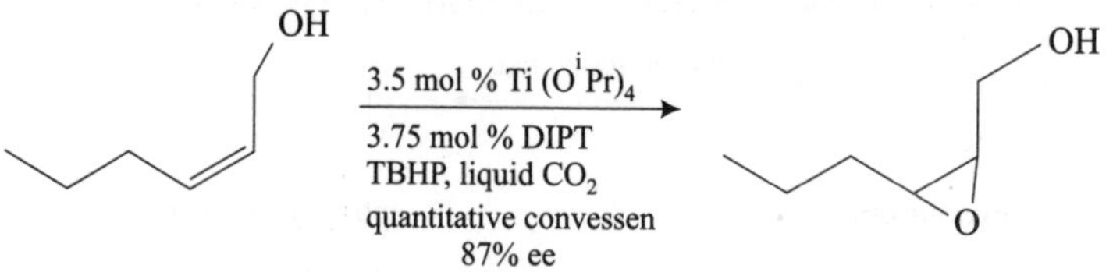

Scheme 27

Sulfides could be oxidised to sulfoxides by TBHP as the oxidant and Amberlyst™ 15 as a hetrogeneous acid catalyst[39]. Using this procedure, diastereoselective sulfoxidation of cystein derivative (28.1) in SC – CO_2 was achieved[40] giving the anti – diasteromer (28.2) as the sole product

(Scheme 28). Oxidation in conventional solvents (toluere and dichloromethane) showed no diastereoselectivity.

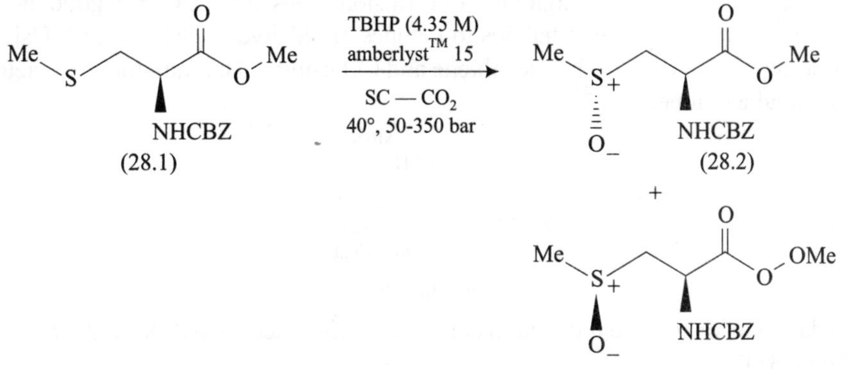

Scheme 28

An interesting epoxidation reagant is peroxycarbonic acid, which is obtained[48] in situ from H_2O_2 and CO_2. Thus the epoxidation of cyclohexene and 3-cyclohexe-1-carboxylate sodium salt in biphasic system comprising of a SC – CO_2/olefins phase and an aqueous H_2O_2 phase to yield the corresponding epoxides and diols (Scheme 29). The yield of the epoxide was improved by the addition of DMF to increase the aqueous solubility of the olefins, suggesting that epoxidation occurs in the aqueous phase. Epoxidation of 3-cyclohexen-1-carboxylate sodium salt gave 89 per cent yield of the epoxide. This show the utility of this process for use for water-soluble alkenes.

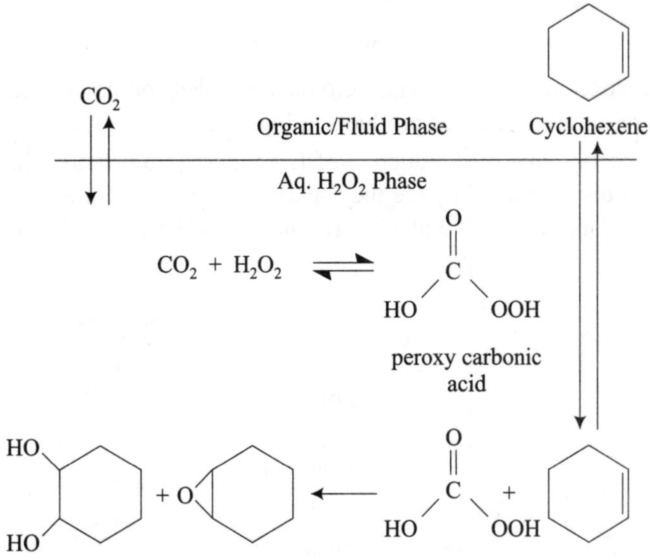

Scheme 29

H_2O_2 has also been used as a primary oxidant for olefin epoxidation in SC – CO_2 using mananganese 5, 10, 15, 20-tetrakis (2′, 6′-dichlorophenyl) porphyrinate as catalyst and hexafluoro-acetone hydrate (HFAH) as CO catalyst in the presence of 4-t-butyl pyridine[42].

4.13 Radical Reactions in SC – CO₂

SC – CO₂ offer potential benefits for radical processes. This is because SC – CO₂ is a low density fluid with low viscosity resulting in high rates of diffusion. Thus, SC – CO₂ is a good medium[43] for free radical carbonylation of organic halides to ketones or aldehydes (Scheme 30). Using a silane mediated carbonylation of an alkyl halide, alkene and CO using AlBN initiator gave yields comparable to those obtained in benzene[44].

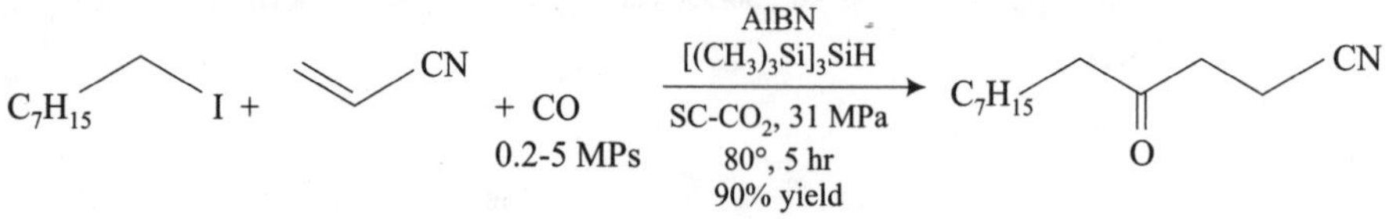

Scheme 30

Bromo adamantane could be reduced to adamantane (initiated by AlBN) under SC – CO₂ conditions (Scheme 31)[45].

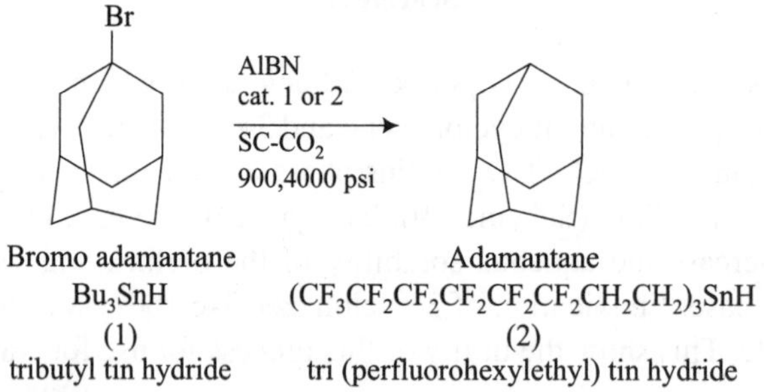

Bromo adamantane   Adamantane
Bu₃SnH $(CF_3CF_2CF_2CF_2CF_2CF_2CH_2CH_2)_3SnH$
(1)   (2)
tributyl tin hydride   tri (perfluorohexylethyl) tin hydride

Scheme 31

Using the above procedure (Scheme 31), steroidal bromides, iodides and selenides with (1) and (2) also gave the corresponding reduced products in high yields (85-95%).

Another radical reaction involved reduction of 1, 1-diphenyl-6-bromo-1-hexene (32.1) with tri (perfluoro hexylethyl) tin hydride (2) gave the 5-exo product (32.2) in 87% yield (Scheme 32). Similar reduction of aryl iodide (32.3) with (2) gave the cyclised product (32.4) in quantitative yield (Scheme 32).

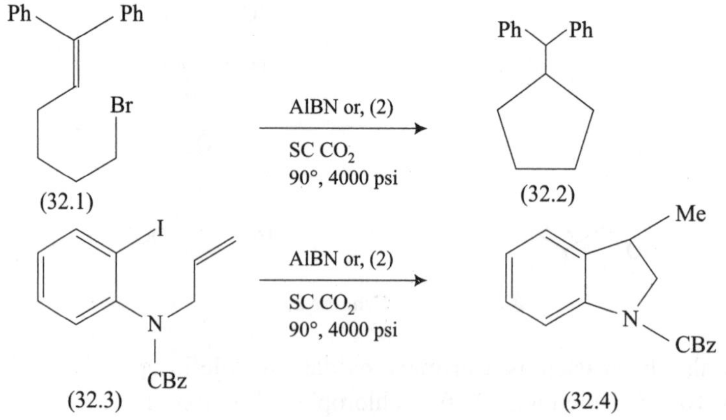

Scheme 32

4.14 Acid-Catalysed Reactions

The acid-catalysed reactions involving dehydration of alcohols in SC – CO_2 was investigated [46]. Thus, dehydration of 1, 4-butanediol gave THF (Scheme 33).

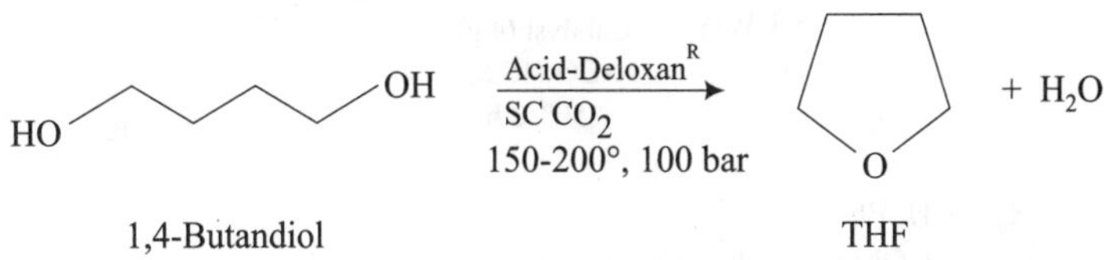

Scheme 33

A number of Lewis acid catalysed alkylation reactions have been conducted in SC – CO_2; these are aided by the addition of poly(ethylene glycol) (PEG) derivatives. This includes the Mannich and aldol reactions of silyl enolates with aldehydes and imines in SC – CO_2 (Scheme 34) [12b, 47]. In these reactions, PEGs act as surfactants and form collodial dispersions in SC – CO_2, manifested as emulsions, and can be shown to accelerate reactions. In the case of scandium catalysed aldol reactions of silyl enolates with aldehydes, poly (ethylene glycol) demethyl elter [PEG $(OMe)_2$, average MW = 500) was found to be more effective than PEG itself [47].

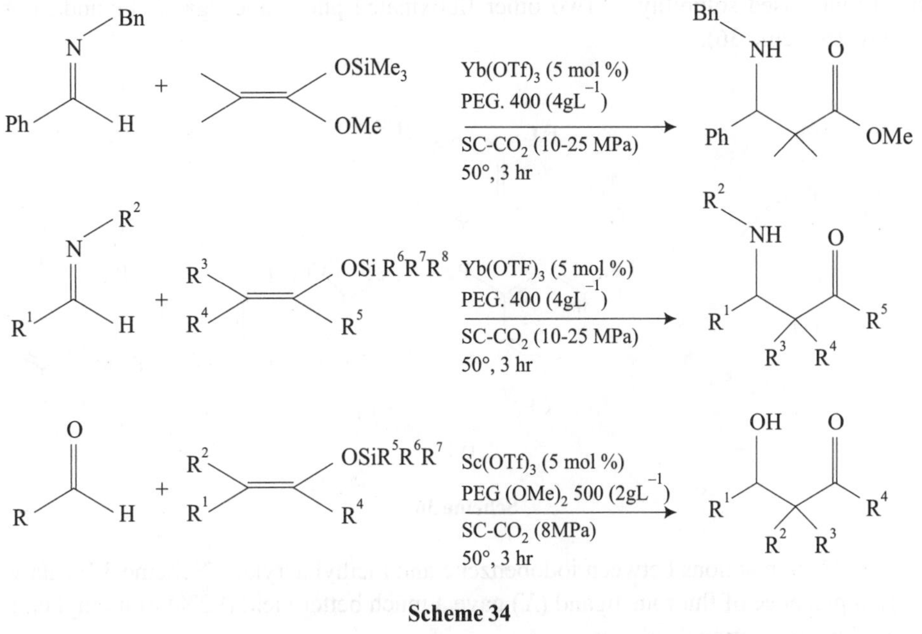

Scheme 34

An alternative additive, 1-dodecycloxy-4-heptadecafluorooctylbenzene was reported [48] to work as an efficient surfactant to accelerate aldol, Mannich and Friedel-Crafts alkylation of indoles in SC – CO_2 (Scheme – 35). The additive incorporated a CO_2 – philic unit (perfluoroalkyl chain), and a lipophilic unit (alkyl chain) in the same molecule.

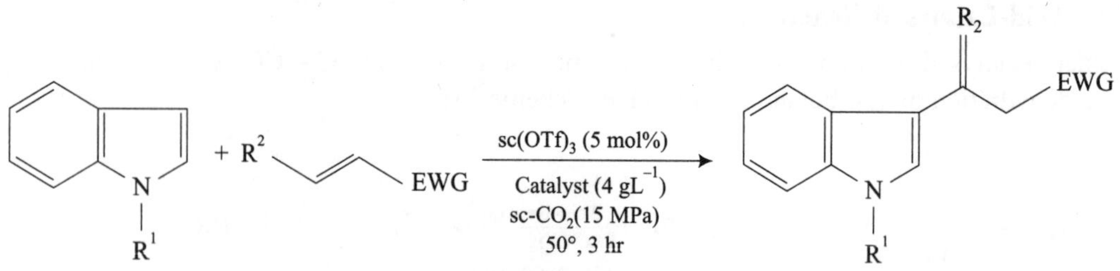

$$R_2 = H, Ph$$
$$EWG_3 = COMe, COPh, NO_2$$
$$Catalyst = 1\text{-dodecyloxy-4-}$$
$$heptadecafluorooctyl\ benzene$$

Scheme 35

4.15   Coupling Reactions

A number od palladium catalysed coupling reactions have been reported[39] in SC – CO$_2$. The main problem in these coupling reactions in the low solubility of phosphine ligands (e.g., PPh$_3$) [which is generally used in conjugation with palladium catalyst such as Pd (OAc)$_2$] in SC – CO$_2$. This draw back in overcome by using a fluorinated phosphine ligand (X), to give a palladium complex which dramatically increased solubility[49]. Two other fluoxinated phosphine ligands (*y* and *z*) are also shown below (Scheme 36).

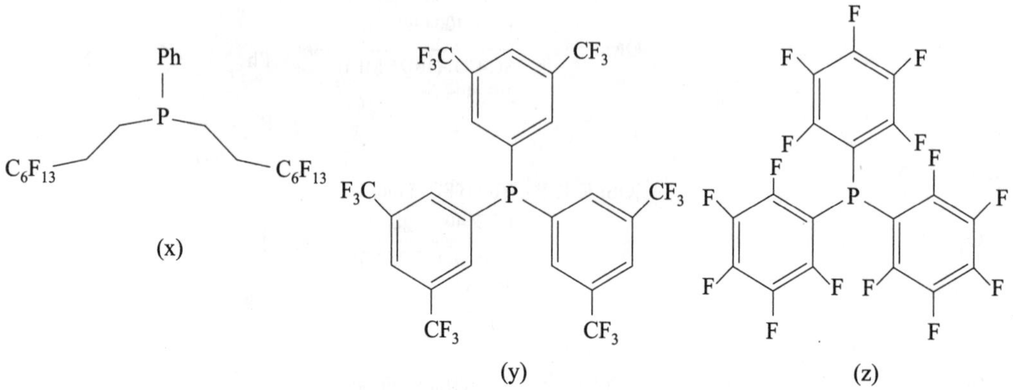

Scheme 36

   Thus, the Heck reactions between iodobenzene and methyl acrylate (Scheme 37) catalysed by Pd (OAc)$_2$ in presence of fluorous ligand (*X*) gave a much better yield (92%) of methyl cinnamate than reported in conventional solvent.

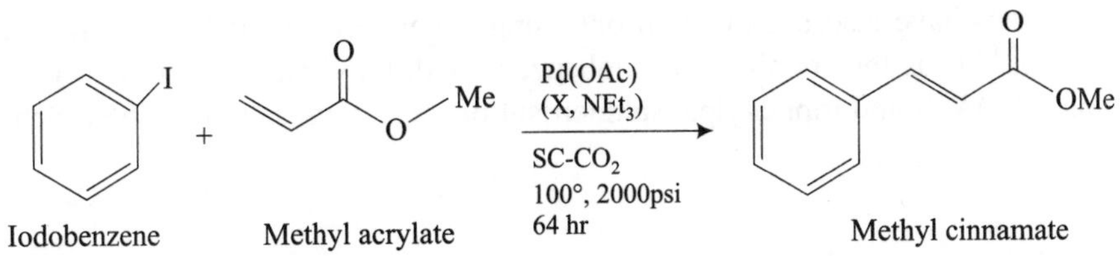

Scheme 37

Examples of other intermolecular Heck reactions, intramolecular Heck reactions, Suzuki and sonogashira couplings were also reported[50] giving better yields as compared to those obtained in conventional organic solvents. Heck and Still coupling reactions have also been reported in SC – CO_2 using the fluorinated ligands (y) and (z).

Still coupling mediated by fluorous tagged phosphines (PTP – I and PTP – II) has been achieved[51] (Scheme 38) in SC – CO_2 using $(nBu)_4NCl$ as catalyst.

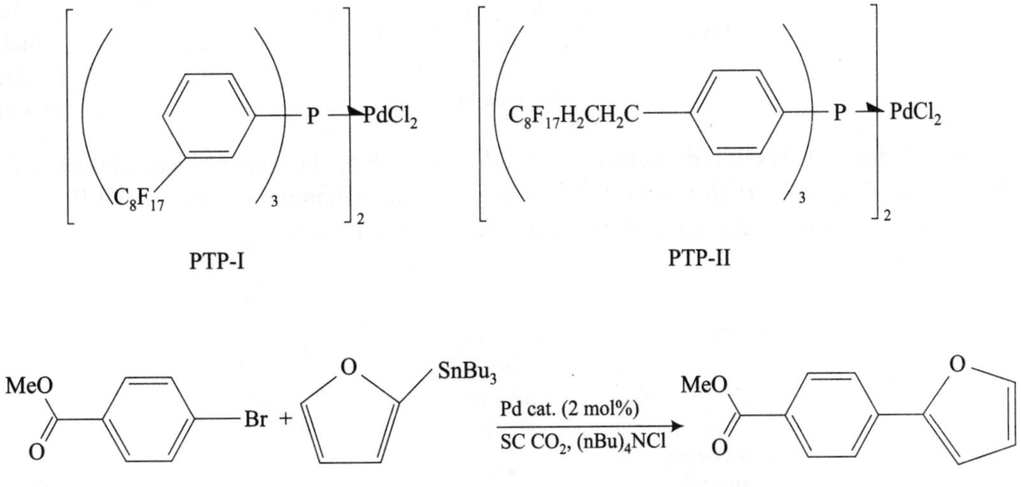

PTP-I   PTP-II

Scheme 38

Pd-catalysed biaryl formation by the homocoupling of iodobenzene in SC – CO_2 has also been achieved (Scheme 39)[52].

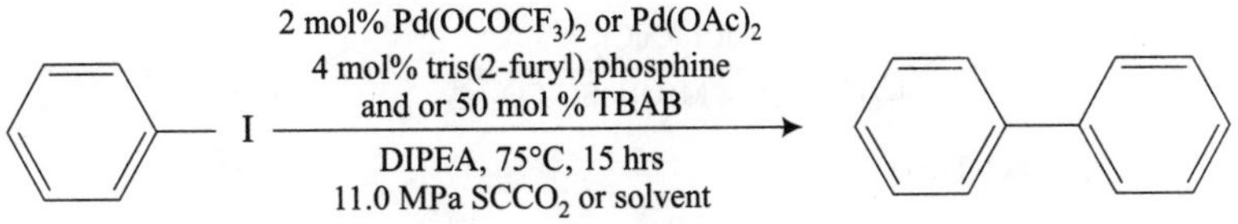

Scheme 39

Heck reactions have also been carried out using water-soluble catalysts in $SC - CO_2$/water biphasic system[53]. Thus the coupling of iodobenzene with butyl acrylate in $SC - CO_2$ was performed using $Pd(OAc)_2$ and triphenylphosphinetrisulfonate sodium salt (TPPTSS) (Scheme 40).

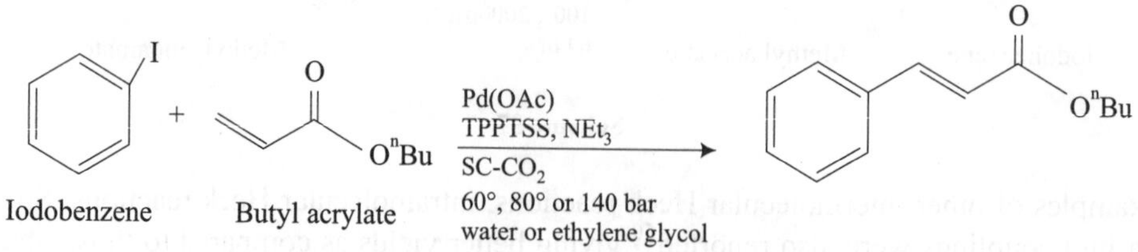

Scheme 40

Enhanced selectivity in the Mizoroki-Heck arylation reaction of ethylene has been observed in a $SC - CO_2$ – liquid bibhasic system (Scheme 41)[54]. The product obtained is exclusively the styrene derivative.

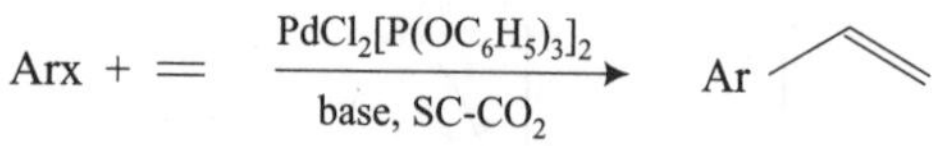

Scheme 41

The palladium catalysed carbonylation of 2-iodobenzyl alcohol in supercritical mixture of CO_2 (20MPa) and CO (1MPa) (Scheme 41a)[44,55]. In this case the palladium complex $PdCl_2[P(OEt)_3]_2$ was used as catalyst in the presence of triethylamine to give phthalide.

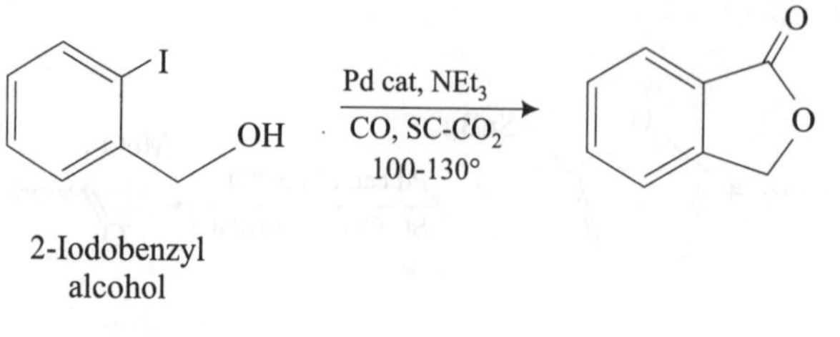

Scheme 41a

Wacker reaction of oct-1-ene in $SC - CO_2$ using methanol as cosolvent and $PdCl_2/CuCl_2$ as catalyst in presence of oxygen gives the ketone in 91 per cent yield (Scheme 42)[56].

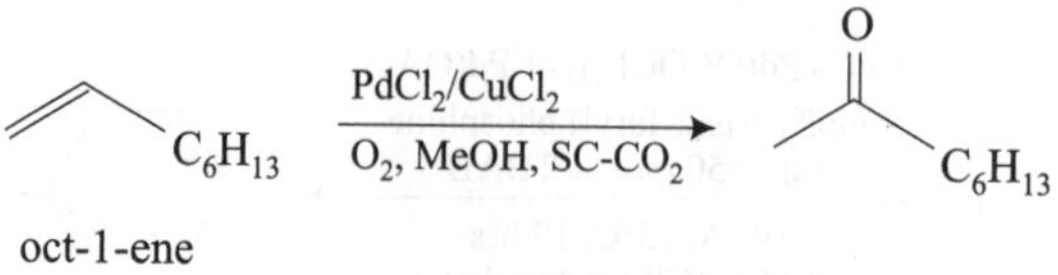

Scheme 42

4.16 Stereochemical Control in Reactions Using SC – CO₂

An important feature during development of new reactions is to allow a high degree of stereochemical control during formation of the product. Some reactions like Sc(OTf)₃ – catalysed Diel-Alder Reaction of n-Butyl acrylate with cyclopentadine in SC – CO₂ (see Section 4.5) and oxidation reactions particularly oxidation of sulfides to sulfoxides (see Section 4.12) have already been discussed.

A typical reaction in which stereochemical control is observed by using SC – CO₂ is the well known Henry reaction, which is a primary useful carbon-carbon bond forming raection giving highly functionalised products of considerably synthetic utility[57]. In the Henary reaction of p-cyanobenzaldehyde with 1-nirtopropane in SC – CO₂ in presence of Et₃N, the product obtained[58] was the syn isomer; a mixture of syn and anti isomer is obtained in conventional Henary reaction (Scheme 43).

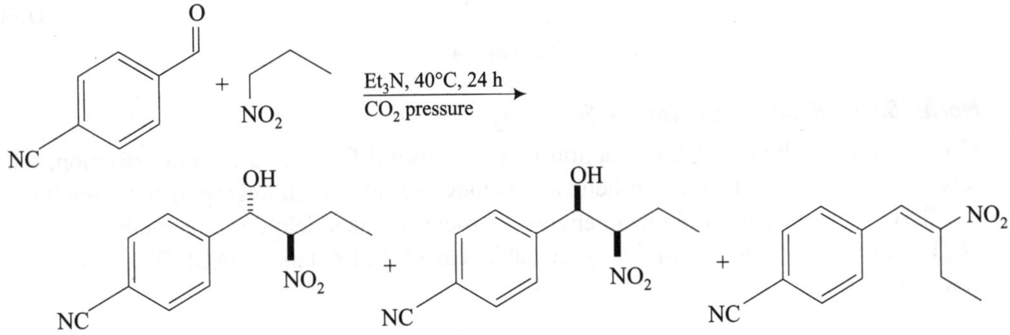

Scheme 43

One of the best reactions to illustrate the potential for stereoselectivity is asymmetric cyclopropanation (Scheme 44)[59]. Thus, the reaction of styrene and ethyl diazoacetate give trans-cyclopropane (Scheme 44).

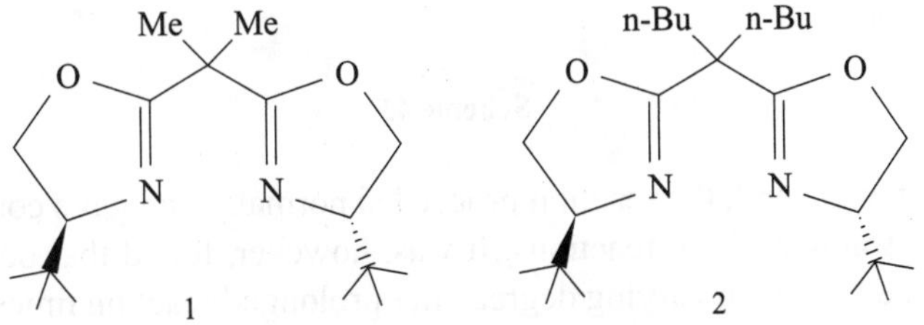

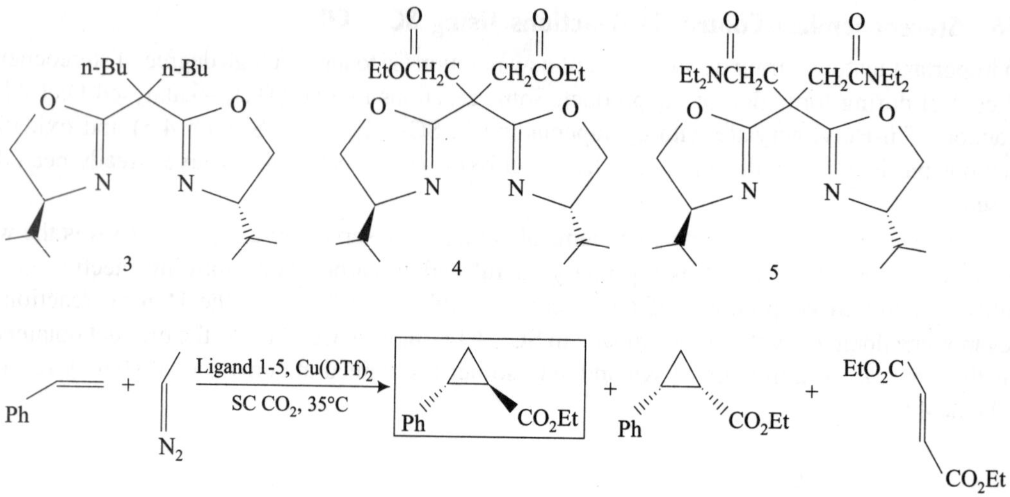

Scheme 44

The Morita-Baylis-Hillman reaction in SC – CO₂

The Morita-Baylis-Hillman (MBH) reaction is a very useful C-C bond forming reaction, whose products are particularly versatile synthetically as they contain a high degree of functionality[60]. A simple MBH reaction of p-nitrobenzaldehyde or p-cyanobenzaldehyde with methyl acrylate in SC – CO₂ with the commonly used 1, 4-diazabicyclo [2.2.2] octane (DABCO) as catalyst[61] is shown in Scheme 45.

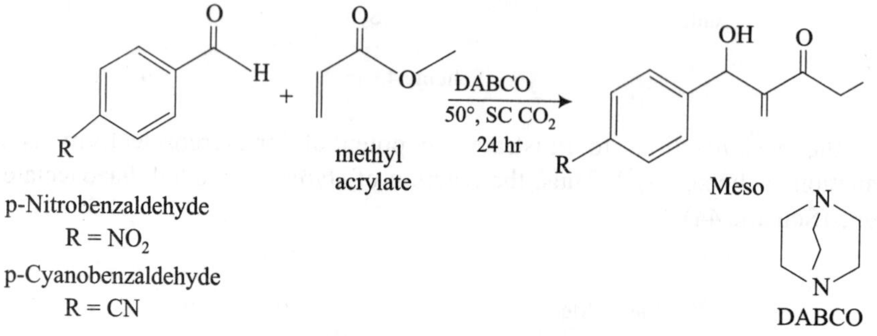

Scheme 45

It was found that in general, the reaction proceeded normally and gave conversions better than those in comparable solution-phase reactions. It was, however, found that occasionally, unanticipated byproducts were formed to varying degree after prolonged reaction times. These were identified as symmetrical diamers of the initial MBH reaction products (Scheme 46).

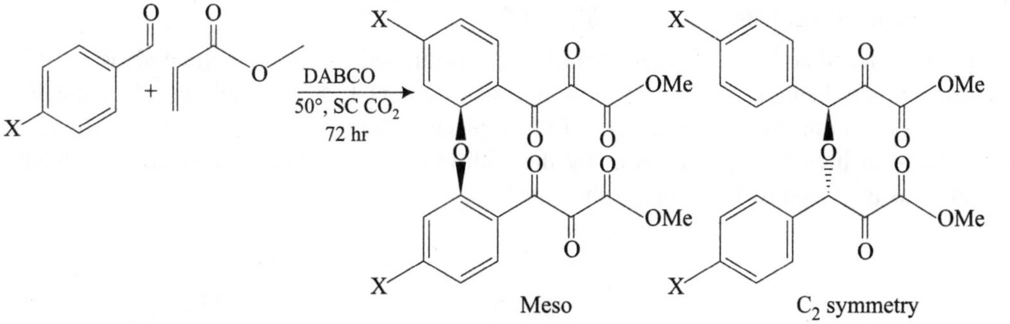

Scheme 46

The above dimerisation (Scheme 46) was novel, but it was of limited synthetic utility. Synthesis of unsymmetrical ethers by getting the initial MBH products to react with another alcohol will be more useful. Thus, the reaction of an aldehyde with methyl acrylate and appropriately substituted benzyl alcohol in SC – CO_2 gave the formation of unsymmetrical ether (Scheme 47). In this reactions only alcohols which are sparingly soluble in SC – CO_2 (e.g., p-nitrobenzyl alcohol) gave very good yield[43,61].

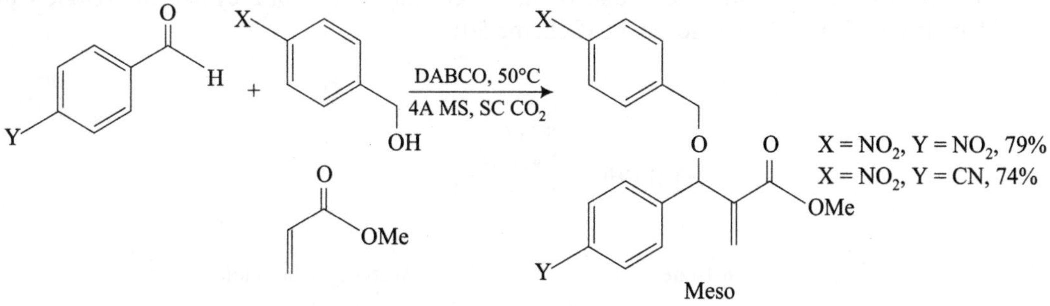

Scheme 47

In the above procedure (Scheme 47), SC – CO_2 soluble alcohols can be used by carrying out neat MBH reaction under an atmosphere of supercritical CO_2, i.e., just gaseous CO_2 above the neat reaction[43]. Thus unsymmetrical ethers were obtained in 67% yield for allyl alcohol, methylacrylate and p-nitrobenzaldehyde (Scheme 48) using unreactive aldehyde like benzaldehyde in the above reaction gave 58% yield of the product.

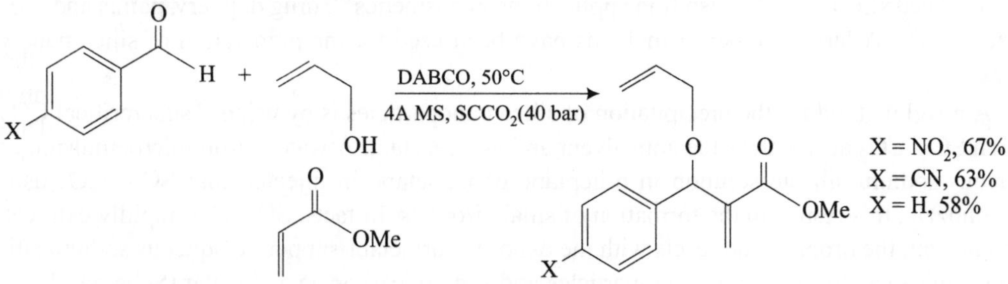

Scheme 48

4.17 Photochemical Reactions in SC – CO_2

The photo-induced addition of aldehydes to α, β-unsaturated carboxyl compounds is an effective, 'environmentally benign' method for the synthesis of 2-acyl-1, 4-hydroquinone (Scheme 49). The process has been improved by using SC – CO_2 in place of the usual solvent benzene. Higher yields are obtained at high CO_2 pressures or by the addition of 5% t-butyl alcohol as co-solvent. The reaction was mediated by using benzophenone[62].

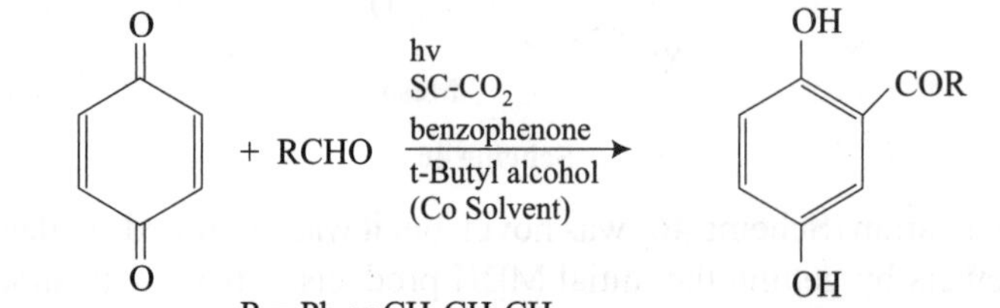

R = Ph or $CH_2CH_2CH_3$

p-Benzoquinone 2-Acyl-1,4-hydroquinone

Scheme 49

In a similar way, benzophenone mediated photochemical reaction of 2-cyclohexen-1-one with acetaldehyde give 3-acetyl cyclohexanone (Scheme 50).

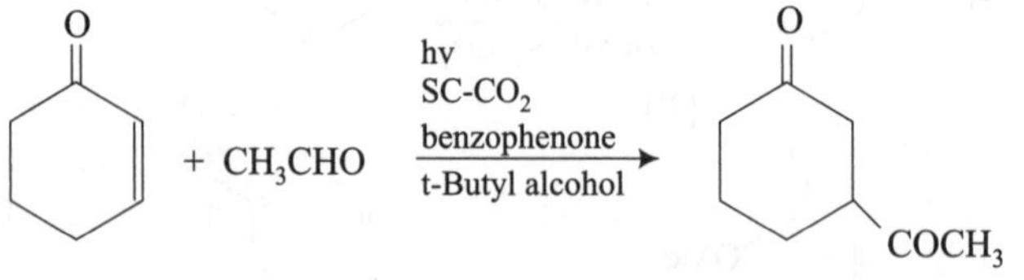

2-cyclohexen-1-one 3-Acetyl cyclohexanone

Scheme 50

4.18 Formation of Silica Nanoparticles using SC – CO_2 and Water in Oil Microemulsions

Silica particles are well known for their excellent abrasive, optical, electrical and thermal properties. They are also used as catalysts or catalyst supports, insulating materials, stiffening or binding agents for fibrous or granular materials and polishing and antisticking or antisoiling agents[63]. Encapsulated silica particles also find applications in cosmetics[64], drug delivery, paints and coating of surfaces[65]. A large number of methods have been used for the preparation of silica nano-particles.

A novel method for the precipitation of silica nanoparticles is by using[66] supercritical CO_2, in which SC – CO_2 acts both as the antisolvent and as a reactant. A water-in-oil microemulsion of an aqueous sodium silicate solution in n-heptane of isooctane in injected into SC – CO_2 using a micronozzle; this results in the formation of small droplets. In facts, SC – CO_2 rapidly extracts the solvent from the droplets and reacts with the exposed surfactant-supported aqueous sodium silicate reverse micelles, forming silica nanoparticles and sodium carbonate and water (Scheme 51).

$$2NaOH. SiO_2 + CO_2 \longrightarrow Na_2CO_3 + 2SiO_2 + H_2O$$
(in n-heptane)

Scheme 51

The precipitated silica nanoparticles are washed with water and the surfactant and sodium carbonate free particles are obtained using ultrafiltration. By this procedure silica nanoparticles having sizes in the range 20-800 nm are obtained. In fact, silica nanoparticles of adjustable size can be produced using supercritical or gaseous CO_2.

4.19 Miscellaneous Applications

4.19.1 Synthesis of 2-pyrones

The coupling of two alkyne molecules with CO_2 in the presence of nickel gives 2-pyrones. In SC – CO_2, a catalyst generated from $Ni(cod)_2$ and 1, 4-diphenyl phosphino butane [$Ph_2 P(CH_2)_4 PPh_2$] combines with 3-hexyne and CO_2 to form tetraethyl-2-pyrone (Scheme 52)[67,68].

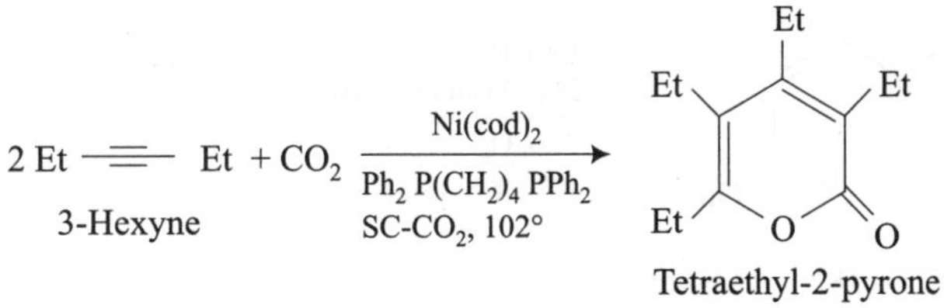

Scheme 52

4.19.2 Pauson-Khand reaction

The CO-cyclisation of an alkyne with an alkene and carbon monoxide leading to the formation of cyclopentanones is known as Pauson-Khand reaction; it is carried out in SC – CO_2 using dicobalt octacarbonyl as catalyst[69]. Thus, the intramolecular reaction of enyne gave 85% of cyclised product (Scheme 53).

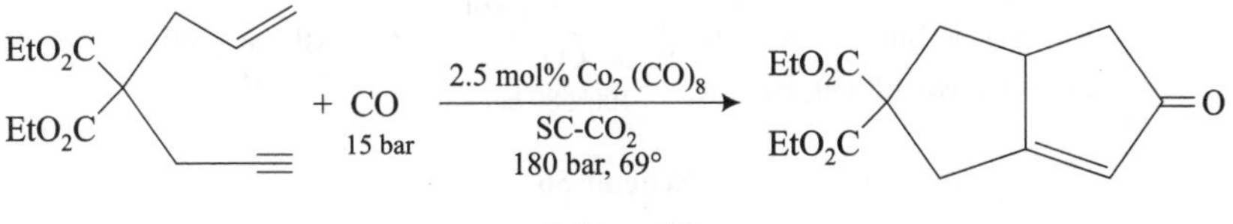

Scheme 53

The above reaction was also successful for a number of substituted enynes. An intermolecular Pauson-Khand reaction was shown to occur with phenyl acetylene coupled to an excess of norbornadiene to give the exo product in 87 per cent yield (Scheme 54).

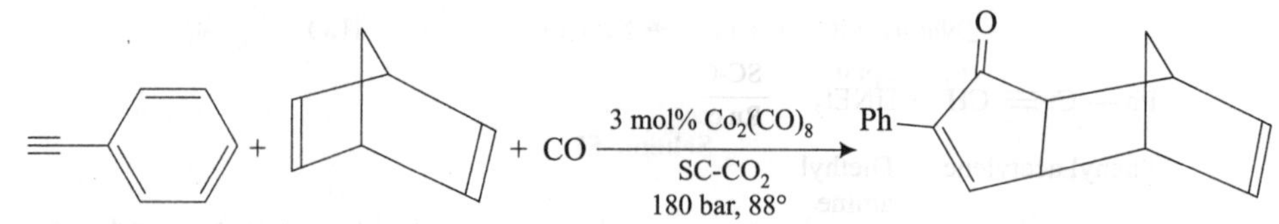

Phenyl   Nonbornadiene   exo product only
acetylene

Scheme 54

4.19.3 Hydroboration of Styrene

The rhodium catalysed hydroboration of styrene with catecholborane (HbCat), rhodium catalyst precursor (A) and phosphorous ligand (B) gave a quantitative conversion in SC – CO$_2$ (Scheme 55)[70]. The catalytic reaction is homogeneous and exhibits higher rates and regioselectivity compared with the equivalent reaction performed in perfluoromethylcyclohexane or THF solvents.

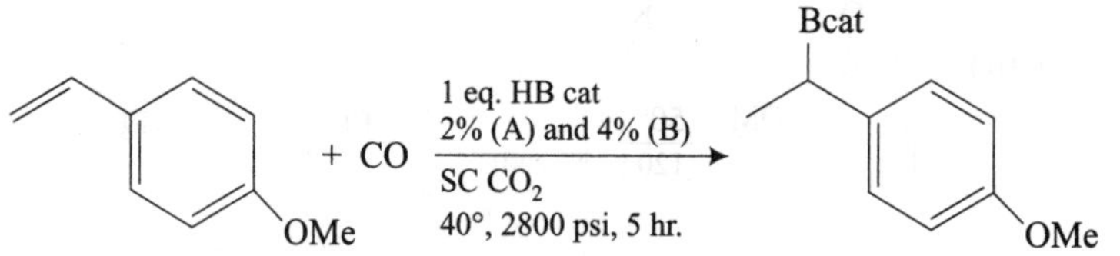

A = (hfacac) Rh (cyclooctene)$_2$
B = cy$_2$P(CH$_2$CH$_2$C$_6$H$_{13}$)

Scheme 55

4.19.4 Carbamate Synthesis

The reaction of potassium carbonate and an ammonium salt catalyst with a number of primary and secondary aliphalic as well as aromatic amines reacted with butyl chloride in SC – CO$_2$ to give the corresponding carbamate in 72-90% yield (Scheme 56)[71].

$$RR' NH + BuCl + K_2CO_3 \xrightarrow[\substack{SC\text{-}CO_2 \\ 100°, 80 \text{ bar } 2 \text{ hr}}]{10\% \, Bu_4 \, NBr} RR' NCOOBu \quad 72\text{-}90\%$$
$$PR' = H, Me, Et, Bu, Bn, Ph$$

Scheme 56

In the above synthesis (Scheme 56) SC – CO$_2$ acted as the reaction media and carbonyl source for the production of carbamates from amines. Use of potassium phosphate in place of potassium carbonate demonstrated that the carbonyl source was CO$_2$ and not the carbonate. This novel procedure is an attractive catalytic one-pot alternative to the use of phosgene in unethane synthesis.

In a related process, Vinyl carbamates were synthesised using SC – CO$_2$, secondary amines and terminal alkynes in pressure of Ru catalyst (A) (Scheme 57)[72].

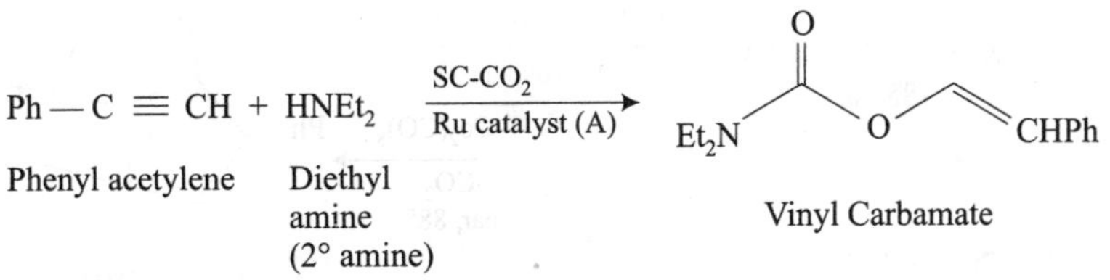
Ph — C ≡ CH + HNEt2
SC-CO2
Ru catalyst (A)
O
Et2N
O
CHPh
Phenyl acetylene
Diethyl amine (2° amine)
Vinyl Carbamate

Scheme 57

4.19.5 The Baylis-Hillman Reaction

The Balis-Hillman reaction has been carried out in SC – CO_2 and gives better conversion and reaction rates as compared to solution phase reactions (Scheme 58)[73]. In case, the reaction is carried out in presence of an alcohol, the major product is an ether resulting from a 3-component coupling reaction, which occurs only in presence of SC – CO_2.

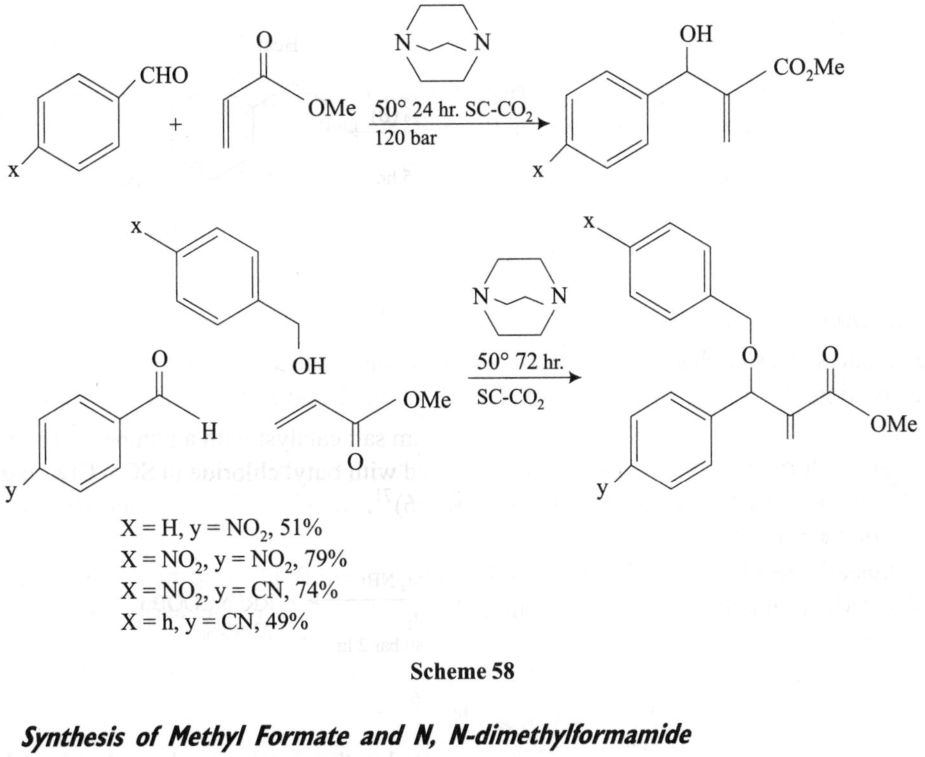
CHO
x
O
OMe
N
N
50° 24 hr. SC-CO2
120 bar
OH
CO2Me
x
X
OH
O
H
y
OMe
O
50° 72 hr.
SC-CO2
X
O
O
OMe
y

X = H, y = NO_2, 51%
X = NO_2, y = NO_2, 79%
X = NO_2, y = CN, 74%
X = h, y = CN, 49%

Scheme 58

4.19.6 Synthesis of Methyl Formate and N, N-dimethylformamide

The hydrogenation of CO_2 under super critical conditions in the presence of methanol and dimethylamine has resulted in a very efficient synthesis of methylformate[74] and N, N- dimethylformamide[75] (Scheme 59).

$$\text{SC-CO}_2 + \text{H}_2 + \text{MeOH} \xrightarrow[\substack{\text{SC-CO}_2 \text{ (Total 210 bar)} \\ \text{Et}_3\text{N, 80°}}]{\text{cat. RuCl}_2[\text{P(CH}_3)_3]_4} \underset{\substack{\text{methyl} \\ \text{formate}}}{\text{HCOOMe} + \text{H}_2\text{O}}$$

(85 bar)

$$\text{SC-CO}_2 + \text{H}_2 + \text{Me}_2\text{NH} \xrightarrow[\substack{\text{SC-CO}_2 \text{ (Total 210 bar)} \\ 100°}]{\text{cat. RuCl}_2[\text{P(CH}_3)_3]_4} \underset{\substack{\text{N,N-Dimethyl} \\ \text{formamide}}}{\text{HCONMe}_2 + \text{H}_2\text{O}}$$

(85 bar)

Scheme 59

4.19.7 Electrochemical Carboxylation of Organic halides using SC – CO₂: Synthesis of Ibuprofen

Electrochemical carboxylation of an benzylic chloride is prompted under super critical condition – the halogen is converted into COOH. This procedure is applied to the synthesis of Ibuprofin (Scheme 60)[76].

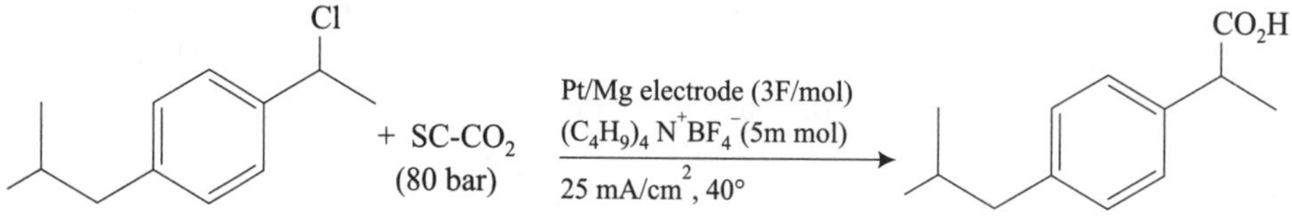

Scheme 60

4.19.8 Biotransformations in SC – CO₂

A large numbers of examples exist in literature[39] using enzymatic catalysis in SC – CO₂ and performing reactions involving hydrolysis, oxidations, esterifications and trans-esterification reactions.

Hydrolytic formation of p-nitrophenol from disodium p-nitrophenylphosphate has been achieved[77] by the enzyme alkaline phosphatase EC 3.1.3.1 in SC – CO₂ at 35° and 100 bar, with a 0.1 vol. % of water concentration.

The kinectic resolution of racemic 3-(4-methoxyphenyl) glycidic acid methyl ester by immobilised Mucor miehei liphase (Lipozyme 1M 20) in SC – CO₂ (Scheme 61)[78] at a conversion of 53% after 5 hr.

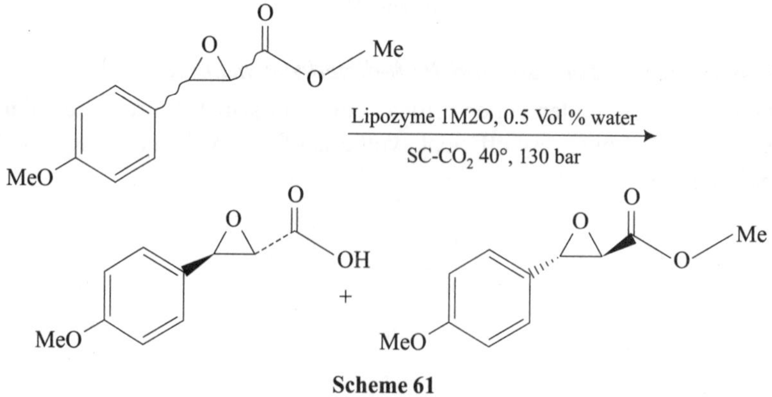

Scheme 61

Transesterification of N-acetyl -L-phenlalanine chloroethyl ester with ethanol catalysed by Subitism Carlsberg (Scheme 62)[79] gave quantitative conversion after 45 min with 2.5 vol % ethanol in $SC - CO_2$.

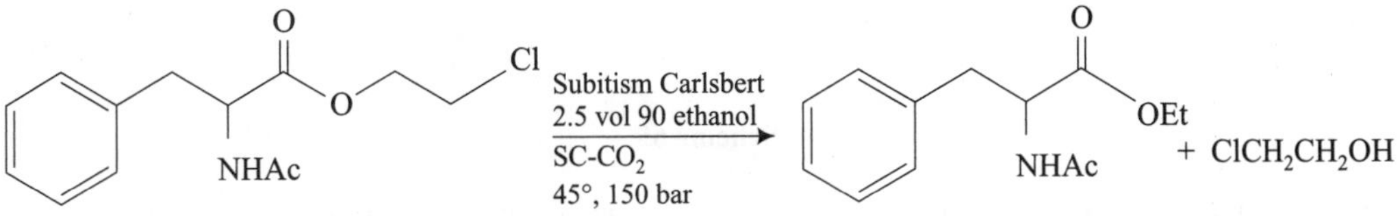

N-Acetyl-l-phenylalanine Chloroethyl ester

Scheme 62

The Lipid – Coated β-D-galactosidase (LCE) (prepared from Bacillus circulans)[80] effected trans acetalisation of 1-O-p- nitrophenyl-β-D-galactopyranoside with 5-phenylpentan-1-ol in SC – CO_2 (40°, 150 bar). The reaction was 25 fold faster in SC – CO_2 tham in isopropyl ether producing the trans acetalisation product after 3 hrs. (Scheme 63).

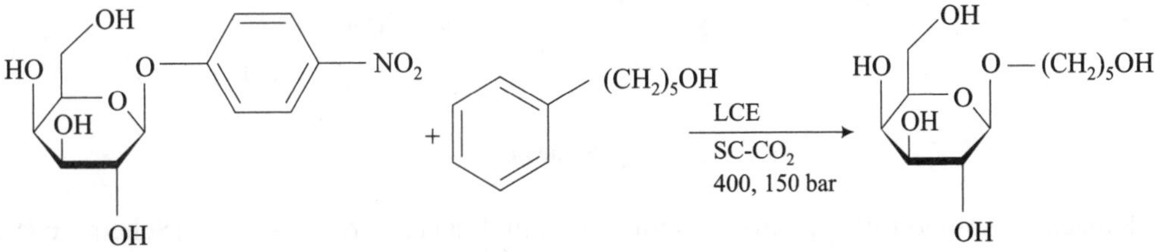

1-O-p-nitrophenyl
-β-D-galactopyranoside

5-Phenylpentan-1-ol

Scheme 63

The enzymatic esterification of lauric with glyceride at 40° using an alternative LCE prepared from Rhizopus delemar, proceeded much faster in SC – CO_2 (200 bar) than in benzene at atmospheric pressure (Scheme 64)[81]. In SC – CO_2 di and tri-glycerides were produced in 90% yield after 3 hrs.

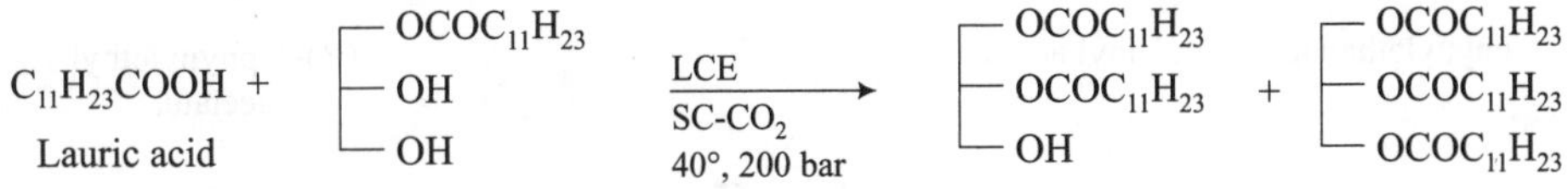

Scheme 64

The rate of esterification of n-valeric acid with citronellol in SC – CO_2 at 35° using the enzyme Cyclindracea lipase (CCL) showed a dramatic pressure dependence around critical pressure (Scheme 65)[82]. It was believed that the mechanism of this esterification in SC – CO_2 involved CO_2 interaction with and activating the enzymes in a Lewis acidic manner.

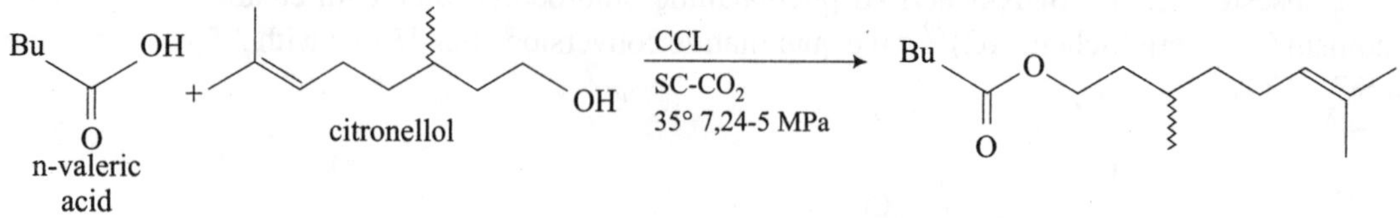

Scheme 65

In a similar way cylindracea lipase (CCL) catalysed esterification of oleic acid with citronellol in $SC-CO_2$ gave 3, 7-dimethyl-6-octenyl ester (Scheme 66). The stereochemistry exhibited a similar pressure dependence as in the case of n-valeric acid.

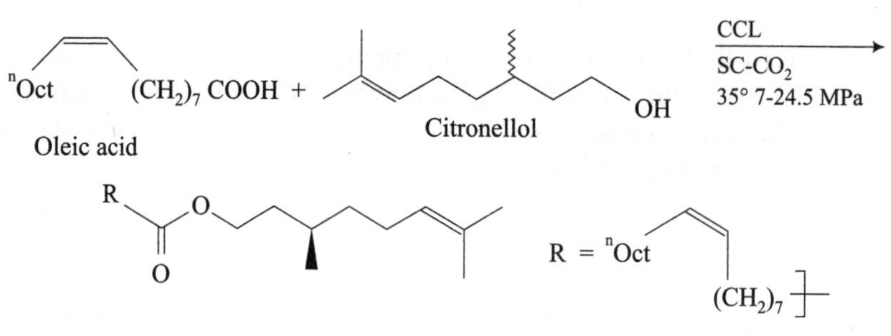

Scheme 66

Kinectic resolution of 1-phenylethanol with Vinyl acetate in $SC-CO_2$ (Scheme 67) using Novozym (Ec 3.1.1.3) from canadida antarcitica B gave[83] (R)-1-phenylethylacetate (>99% ee, 50% conversion).

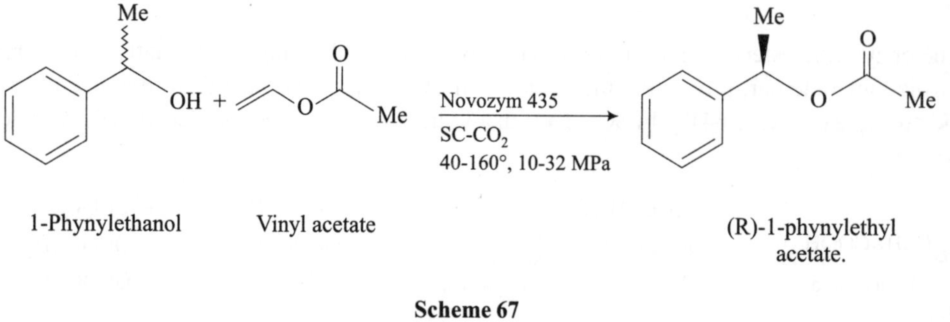

Scheme 67

A related resolution of 1-(p-chlorophenyl)-2, 2, 2-trifluoroethanol under similar conditions has also been reported[84].

A enentioselective acetylation of a number of racemic alcohols, e.g., trans-3-perten-2-ol using an immobilised lipase (Pseudomonas sp. from Aman op) in $SC-CO_2$ has been reported[85] (Scheme 68). There was 50% conversion after 250 min at 40° compared with the rate in toluene where <20% conversion is achieved in the same time. The enentioselectivity was also higher in $SC-CO_2$.

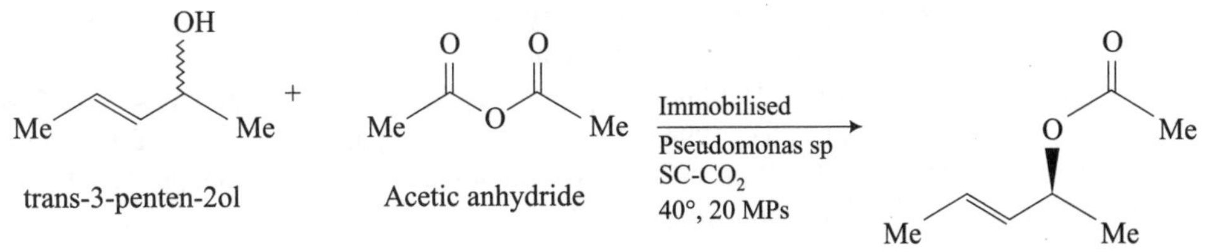

Scheme 68

Pyrrole was successfully converted to pyrrole-2-carboxylic acid in SC – CO_2 using cells of Bacillus megaterium PYR 2910 to catalyse the fixation of CO_2[86]. In this case, the reaction was conducted (Scheme 69) by adding CO_2 (10 MPa) to the system at 40° to give a moderate yield in 1 hr (54%).

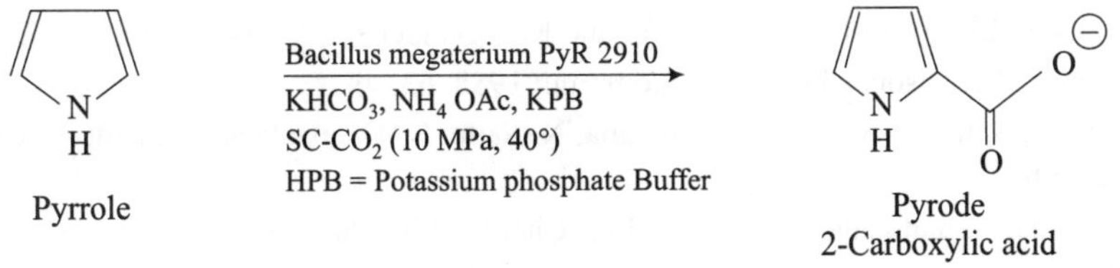

Scheme 69

A number of biotransformations have also been performed in ionic liquids (see chapter 7, section 8) see also chapter 4.

4.19.9 Polymerisation in super critical CO₂

Super critical CO_2 has been successfully used[87] as solvent in various type of polymerisations. These include free radical solution polymerisation, Emulsion polymerisation, suspension polymerisation, heterogeneous polymerisations, chain polymerisation, condensation polymerisation etc.

5 CONCLUSION

Super Critical CO_2 is emerging as a medium for carrying out different types of reactions. It has been used as a medium for hydrogenations, hydroformylations, oxidations, radical reactions, acid – catalysed reactions, coupling reactions, for stereochemical control in reactions, Photochemical reactions. Besides these applications SC – CO_2 has also been used in a number of other reactions like polymerisation and enzymatic transformations.

Refrences

1. G. Gore, Proc. R. Soc. London., 1861, 11, 85-86.
2. P.T. Anatas, P.T. Warner and J.C. Warner, Green Chemistry, Theory and practice, Oxford University Press, Oxford, 1998 and the references cited there in.
3. M. McHugh and V. Krukonis, Supercritical Fluid Extraction, Principles and Practice, Butterworths: Boston 1986, pp. 1-11.
4. K.P. Johnston, in Supercritical Fluid Science and Technology, K.P. Johnston and J.M.L. Penninger, Eds., American Chemical Society, Washington DC., 1989, pp. 1-12.

4a. P.T. Anastas and John C. Warner, Green Chemistry Theory and Practice, Oxford University Press, 1998 page 104-105 and the references cited there in.

5. J.R. Combes, Z. Guan and J.M. DeSimone, Macromolecules 1994, 27, page 865 – 7; Z. Guan and J.M. DeSimone, Macromolecules, 1994, **27**, page 5527 – 32; J.M. DeSimone, E.F. Maury, Y.Z. Menceloglu, J.B. McClain, T.J. Romack and J.R. Combes, Science, 1994, **265**, pp. 356-9.

5a. A.L. Cooper, J. Mater. Chem, 2000, **10**, 207.

5b. J.M. Tanko, R.H. Mas and N.K. Suleman, I. Am. Chem. Soc. 1990, **112**, 5557; J.M. Tanko, N.K. Suleman, G.A. Hulvey, A. Park and J.E. Powers, J. Am. Chem. Soc., 1993, **115**, 4520 – 26; J.M. Tanko and N.K. Suleman, J. Am. Chem. Soc; 1994, **116**, 5162 – 6; J.M. Tanko and J.F. Blackert, Science, 1994, **263**, 203-5.

6. J.M. Tanko and M. Sadeghipour, Angew. Chem. Int. Ed., 1999, **38**, 159-161.

7. J.W. Tester, R.L. Danheiser, R.D. Weintstein, A. Renslu, J.D. Taylor and J. I. Steinfeld, Supercritical Fluids as solvent Replacements in chemical synthesis in Green chemical synthesis, American Chemical Society, 2000; P. T. Anastas, L.G. Heime and T.C. Williansons, Editors.

8. A.R. Renslo, R.D. Weinstein, J.W. Tester and R.L. Danherisel, J. Org. Chem., 1997, **62**, 4530.

9. S. Kim an K.P. Johnson, Chem. Eng. Commun; 1988, **63**, 49.

10. Y. Ikushima, S. Ito, T. Anaso, T. Yokoyama, N. Saito, K. Hatakeda and T. Goto, J. Chem. Eng, Jpn. 1996, **23**, 96.

11. Y.I. Kushima, N. Saito and M. Arai, J. Phys. Chem., 1992, **96**, 2293.

12. R.D. Weinstein, A.R. Renslo, R.L. Danheiser and J.W. Tester, J. Phy. Chem. B. 1999, **103(15)**, 2878-2887.

12a. R.S. Oakes, T.J. Happenstall, N.Shezad, A.A. Clifford and C.M. Rayner, Chem. Commun., 1999, 1459.

12b. J. Matsuo. T. Tsuchiya, K. Odashima and S. Kobayashi, Chem. Lett., 2000, 178.

12c. R.D. Weinstein, A.R. Renslo, R.L. Danheiser and J.W. Tester, J. Phys. Chem. B., 1999, **103**, 2878.

13. A.R. Renslo, R.D. Weinstein, J.W. Tester and R.L. Danheiser, J. Org. Chem., 1997, **62**, 4530.

14. R.D. Weinstein, A.R. Renslo, R.L. Danheiser, J.G. Harris and J.W. Tester, J. Phys. Chem. 1966, **100**, 12337.

15. C.A. Eckert, Ann. Rev. Phys. Chem. 1972, **23**, 239.

16. C.A. Eckerts, C.K. Hsieh, M.A. Fox and K.P. Johnston, J. Am. Chem. Soc., 1989, **111**, 2662.

17. K.P. Johnston, K.l. Harrison, M.J. Clarke, S.M. Howdle, M.P. Heitz, F.V. Bright, C. Carlier and T.W. Randolph, Science, 1996, **271**, 624.

18. J.M. Desimone, Z. Guan and C.S. Elsbernd, Science, 1992, **257**, 945.

19. M.J. Burk, S. Feng, M.G. Gross and W. Tumas, J. Am. Chem. Soc., 1995, **117**, 8277.

19a. M. Hitzler, F.R. Smail, S.K. Ross and M. Poliakoff, J. Chem. Soc. Chem. Commun., 1998, 359.

20. P.G. Jessop, T. Ikaviya and R. Noyoro, Chem. Rev., 1999, **99**, 475.

21. A. Baiker, Chem. Rev., 1999, **99**, 453.

22. M.G. Hitzler and M. Poliakoff, J. Chem. Soc. Chem. Commun., 1997, 1667.

23. M.G. Hitzler, F.R. Smail, S.K. Ross and M. Poliakoff, Org. Proc. Res. and Dev., 1998, **2**, 137.

24. R. Tschan, R. Wandeler, M. Schneider, M. Burgener, M. Schubert and A. Baiker, Applied Catalisis A: General, 2002, **223**, 173.

25. U.R. Pillai and E. Sahle – Demessi, Chem. Commun. 2002, 422.

26. N. Harris and M.W. Tuck, Hydrocarbon Processing, International Edition, 1990, **69**, 79.

27. B. Minder, T. Mallat, K.H. Picket, R. Steiner and A. Baker., Cat. Lett., 1995, **34**, 1.

28. M.J. Burk, S. Feng, M.F. Gross and W. Tumas, J. Am. Chem. Soc., 1995, **117**, 8277.

29. J. Xiao, S.C.A. Nefkens, P.G. Jessop, T. Ikariya and R. Neyori, Tetrahedron Lett., 1996, **37**, 2813.

30. S. Kainz, A. Brinkmann, W. Leitner and A. Pfaltz, J. Am. Chem. Soc., 1999, **121**, 6421.

31. S. Kainz and W. Leitner, Catalysis Letter, 1998, **55**, 223.

32. G. Francio and W. Leitner, Chem. Commun., 1999, 1663.

33. Y. Hu, W. Chen, A.M.B. Osuna, J. Xiao, M.M. Stuart and E. Hope, Chem. Commun., 2001, 725.

34. G. Jerner, D. Sueur, T. Mallat and A. Baiker, Chem. Commun., 2000, 2247.

35. F. Locker and W. Leitner, Chem. Eur, J, 2000, **6**, 2011.

36. G.R. Hass and J.W. Kolis, Organometallics, 1998, **17**, 4454.

37. G.R. Hass and J.W. Kolis, Tetrahedron Lett., 1998, **39**, 5923.

38. D.R. Pesiri, D.K. Morita, W. Glaze and W. Tumas, J. Chem. Soc. Chem. Commun., 1998, 1015.

39. D. Clarke, M.A. Ali, A.A. Clifford, A. Parratt, P. Rose, D. Schwinn, W. Bannwarth and C.M. Rayner Current topics in medicinal chemistry, 2004, **4**, 729 and the references cited there in.

40. R.S. Oakes, A.A. Clifford, K.D. Bartle, M. Thornton – Pett and C.M. Rayner, J. Chem. Soc. Chem. Commun., 1999, 247.

41. S.A. Nolen, J. Lu, J.S. Broun, P. Pollet, B.C. Eason, K.N. Griffith, R. Glasar, D. Bush, D.R. Lamb, C.L. Liotta, C.A. Eckert, G.F. Thiele and K.A. Batels, Ind. Eng. Chem. Res., 2002, **41**, 316.

42. S. Campestrini and U. Tonellato, Adv. Synth. Catal., 2001, **343**, 819.

43. I. Ryu and N. Sonada, Angew. Chem. Int. Ed. Engl., 1996, **35**, 1051.

44. T. Ikariya, Y. Kayaki, Y. Kishimoto and Y. Noguchi, Progress in Nuclear Energy., 2000, **37**, 420.

45. S. Halida, M.S. Super, E.J. Beckman and D.P. Curran, J. Am. Chem. Soc., 1997, **119**, 7406.

46. W.K. Gray, F.R. Smail, M.G. Hitzler, S.K. Ross and M. Poliakoff, J. Am. Chem. Soc., 1999, **121**, 10711.

47. I. Komoto and S. Kobayashi, Chem. Commun., 2001, 1842.

48. I. Komoto and S. Kobayashi, Organic Letters, 2002, **4**, 1115.

49. M.A. Carroll and A.B. Holmes, J. Chem. Soc. Chem. Commun., 1998, 1395.

50. D.K. Morita, D.R. Pesiri, S.A. David, W.H. Glaze and W. Tumas, J. Chem. Soc. Chem. Commun., 1998, 1397.

51. S. Schneider and W. Bannwarth, Angew. Chem. Int. Edn., 2000, **39**, 4142.

52. N. Shezad, A.A. Clifford and C.M. Rayner, Green Chemistry, 2002, **4**, 64.

53. B.M. Bhanage, Y. Ikushima, M. Shirai and M. Arai, Tetrahedron Lett., 1999, **40**, 6427.

54. Y. Kayaki, Y. Noguchi and T. Ikariya, Chem. Commun., 2000, 2245.

55. Y. Kayaki, Y. Noguchi, S. Iwasw, T. Ikariya and R. Noyori, J. Chem. Soc. Chem. Commun., 1999, 1235.

56. H. Jiang, L. Jia and J. Li, Green chemistry, 2000, **2**, 161.

57. F. Luzzio, Tetrahedron, 2001, **57**, 915.

58. C.M. Rayner, Organic process research and development, 2007, **11**, 121 and the references cited there in.

59. D.A. Evans, K.A. Woerpel, M.M. Hinman and M. M. Faul, J. Am. Chem. Soc., 1991, **113**, 726.

60. D. Basavaiah, A.J. Rao and T. Satyanarayana, Chem. Rev., 2003, **103**, 811.

61. P.M. Rose, A.A. Clifford and C. M. Rayner. Chem. Commun., 2002, 968.

62. R. Pacut, M.L. Grimm, G.A. Kraus and J.M. Tanko, Tetrehedron Lett., 2001, **42**, 1415.

63. R.K. Iler. The chemistry of silica: solubility, polymerisation, colloidal and surface properties and Biochemistry, Wiley, New York, 1979.

64. R. Laingner, Am. Perfum. Cosmet, 1966, **81(10)**, 51.

65. M.J. Marquisee and L.S. Sandell, U.S. Patent 4, 132, 560; 1979.

66. P. Chattopadhyay and R.B. Gupta, Ind. Eng. Chem. Res., 2003, **42**, 465.

67. M.T. Reetz, W. Konen and T. Strack, Chimica, 1993, **47**, 493.

68. P.G. Jessop and W. Leitner. Chemical synthesis using super critical Fluids, Wiley – VCH, Washington 1999.

69. N. Jeong, S.H. Hwang, Y.W. Lee and J.S. Lim, J. Am. Chem. Soc., 1997, **119**, 10549.

70. C.A.G. Carter, R.T. Baker, S.P. Nolan and W. Tumas, Chem. Commun., 2000, 347.

71. M. Yoshida, N. Hava and S. Okuyama, Chem. Commun., 2000, 151.

72. M. Rohr, C. Geyer, R. Wandeler, M. Schneider, A. Murphy and A. Baiker, Green chemistry, 2001, **3**, 123.

73. P.M. Rose, A.A. Clifford and C.M. Rayner, Chem. Commun., 2002, 968.

74. P.G. Jessop, Y. Hsiao, T. Ikariya and R. Nogori, J. Am. Chem. Soc., 1996, **118**, 344.

75. P.G. Jessop, Y. Hsiao, T. Ikariya and R. Nogori, J. Am. Chem. Soc., 1994, **116**, 8851.

76. A. Sasaki, H. Kudoh, H. Senboku and M. Kokuda, In Novel Trends in Electrochemical Synthesis, S. Torii Ed.: Springer-Verlag, Tokyo, 1998.

77. T.W. Randolph, H.W. Blanch, J.M. Prausnitz and C.R. Wilke, Biotech. Lett., 1985, **7**, 325.

78. M. Rantakyla, M. Alkio and O. Aaltonen, Biotech. Lett., 1996, **18**, 1089.

79. P. Pasta, G. Mazzola, G. Carrea and S. Riva, Biotech. Lett., 1989, **11**, 643.

80. T. Mori and Y. Okahata, J. Chem. Soc. Chem. Commun., 1988, 2215.

81. T. Mori, A. Kobayashi and Y. Okahata, Chem. Lett., 1998, 921.

82. Y. Ikshima, N. Saito, K. Hatakeda and O. Sato, Chem. Eng. Sci., 1996, **51**, 2817.

83. A. Overmeyer, S. Schrader – Lippelt, V. Kasche and G. Brunner, Biotech, Lett., 1999, **21**, 65.

84. T. Matsuda, R. Kanamaru, K. Watanabe, T. Harada and K. Nakamura, Tetrahedron Lett., 2001, **42**, 8319.

85. E. Cernia, C. Palocci, F. Gaparrini, D. Misti and N. Fagnano, J. Mol. Cat., 1994, **89**, L11.

86. T. Matsuda, Y. Ohashi, T. Haranda, R. Yanagihare, T. Nagasawa and K. Nakamura, Chem. Commun., 2001, 2194.

87. E.J. Beckman, J. Supercritical Fluids, 2003, **28(1)**, 1 and the references cited there in.

Organic Synthesis using Carbon Dioxide

6

I INTRODUCTION

Carbon dioxide has the advantage of being nontoxic, abundant and is an environmentally benin chemical. It is one of the most important green house gas. It is consumed to a large extent in the well known photosynthesis or production of synthetic gas by reforming natural gas with CO_2. The consumption of CO_2 (green house gas) for useful purpose has been explored[1].

Carbon dioxide has a strong affinity towards nuclecophiles and electron-donating reagents; this is due to electron deficiency of the carbonyl carbon. It is in fact anhydrous carbonic acid and reacts with basic compounds. For example, organometallic reagents such as grignard reagent react with CO_2 even at low temperature. Also water, alkoxides and amines add to CO_2 to produce compounds with a carboxyl or carboxylate group. These species react with electrophiles leading to the formation of organic carbonates and carbamates.

2 SYNTHETIC APPLICATION OF CARBON DIOXIDE

2.I Synthesis of Dimethyl Carbonate

Dimethyl carbonate is a useful intermediate for manufacturing polycarbonates, which are extensively used engineering plastics. The current annual production of polycarbonates in two million tons world wide with annual increase of $5 - 10\%$. More than $80 - 90\%$ of polycarbonates are currently synthesised by the phosgene process (Scheme 1).

$$2\ ROH\ +\ \underset{Cl}{\overset{O}{\|}}\underset{Cl}{\diagdown}\ \longrightarrow\ R\diagdown O\underset{\|}{\overset{O}{C}}O\diagup R\ +\ 2\ HCl$$

Dialkyl carbonate

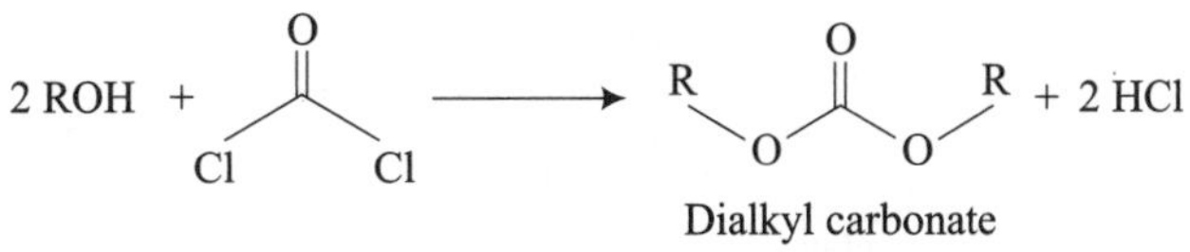

Scheme 1

The major drawbacks of the phosgene process (Scheme 1) are the high toxicrty of phosgene and the disposal the by product (HCl). However, substituting phosgene with CO_2 would drastically reduce environmental concerns (Scheme 2), as the byproduct is only water.

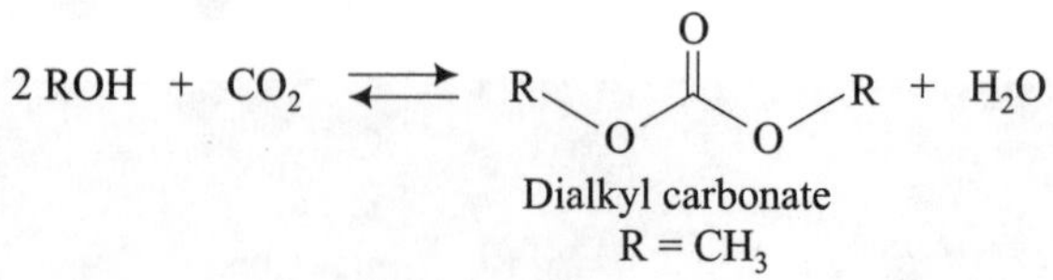

$$2\,ROH + CO_2 \rightleftharpoons \underset{\substack{\text{Dialkyl carbonate}\\ R = CH_3}}{R\text{-}O\text{-}\overset{\overset{\displaystyle O}{\|}}{C}\text{-}O\text{-}R} + H_2O$$

Scheme 2

In order to get better yields, the formed water must be removed from the reaction mixture or increase the CO_2 concentration by pressurizing CO_2. A number of procedures are avaclable for removed of water. One such procedure is recycling of ketal as a dehydrating agent. Thus the reaction of methyl alcohol with carbon dioxide in presence acetone ketal using $Bu_2Sn(OMe)_2$ and $RNH_3(OTf)$ as catalyst gives dimethyl carbonate (Scheme 3)[4].

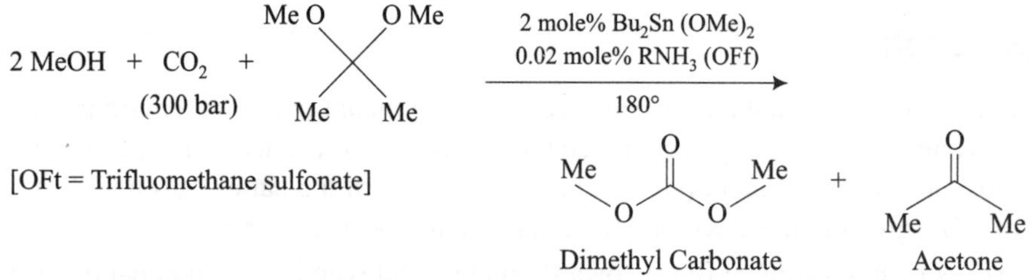

[OFt = Trifluomethane sulfonate]

Scheme 3

The formed acetone is again converted into ketal and reused.

2.2 Synthetic of Cyclic Carbonates

Cyclic carbonates are useful intermedials for the synthesis of polycarbonate (as in the case of linear carbonates). Oxiranes and oxetans undergo cydisation to give five and six membered ring carbonates (Scheme 4).

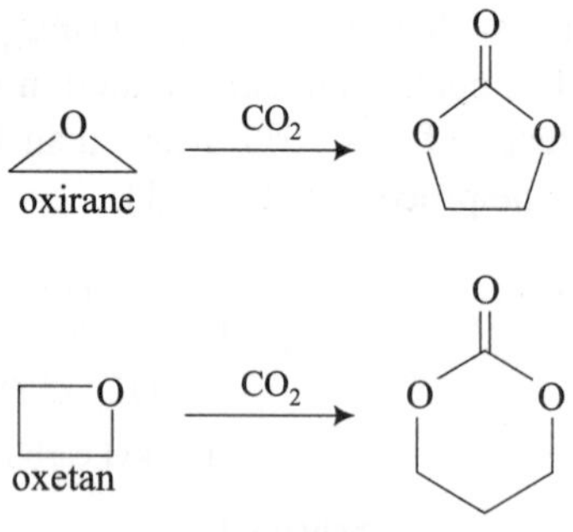

Scheme 4

The production of five membered cyclic carbonates from CO_2 is an industrial process[5]. A number of homogeneous catalysts for cyclic carbonate synthesis from oxiranes and CO_2 have been used[1].

Nb.–Catalysed oxidative carboxylation of olefins to give cyclic carbonate has been reported (Scheme 5)[6].

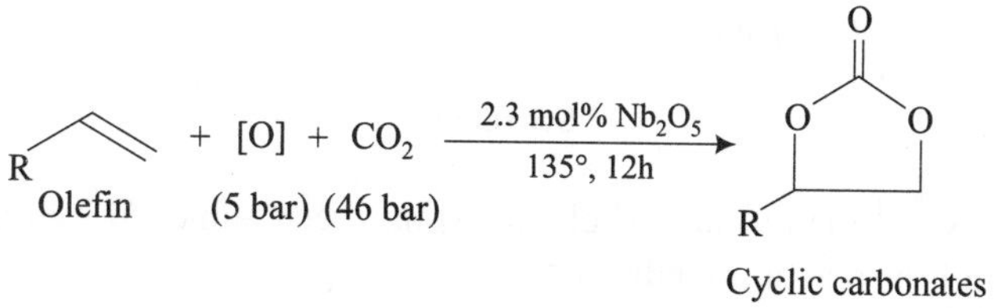

Scheme 5

Cyclic carbonates have also been prepared[7-9] by the reaction of 1,2-diols using CeO_2-ZrO_2 or Bu_2SnO as catalyst (Scheme 6)

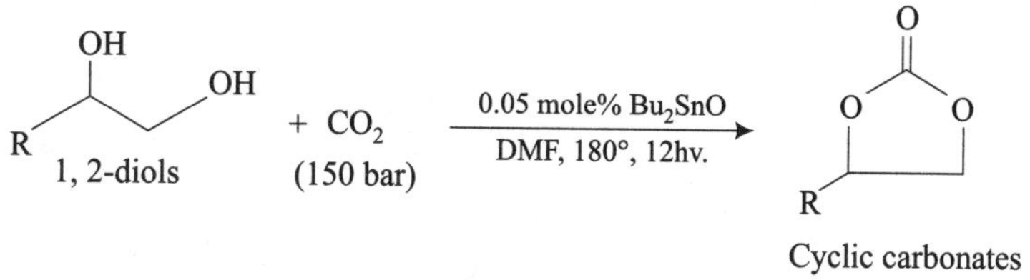

Scheme 6

2.3   Alternating Polymensation of Oxiranes and CO_2

The alternating copolymerisation (Scheme 7) uses the same reaction as in the synthesis of five membered cyclic carbonates (see Scheme 4). However polymers are kinetic products while cyclic carbonates are thermodynamic products[10].

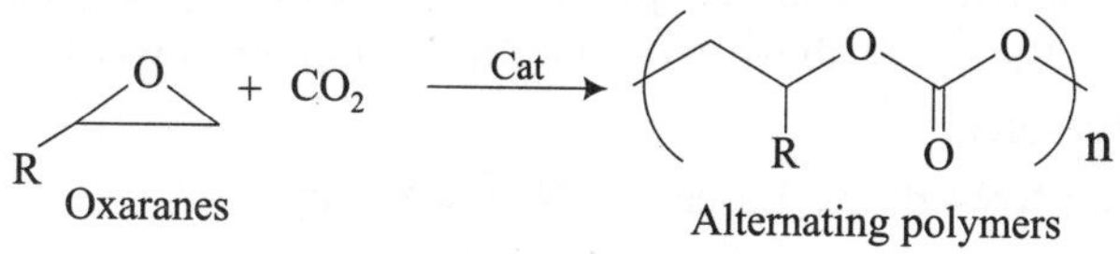

Scheme 7

A number of catalysts[1] have been used for the alternating polymerization. The alternative polymers are expected to be a substitute for polystyrene. The polymers are have low oxygen permeability, biodegradability and complete thermal depolymerisation to give cyclic carbonates. The aliphatic alternating polymers produced by the above reaction (Scheme 7) are manufactured on a commercial scale in China[11].

2.4   Synthesis of Urea and Urethane Derivatives

As already stated carbon dioxide reactily reacts with nucleophiles. For example urea is manutactured by the reaction of CO_2 with ammonia[12-14] (Scheme 8).

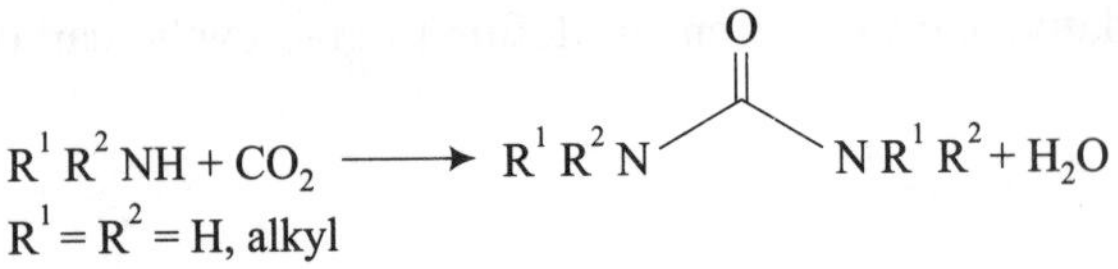

$$R^1 R^2 NH + CO_2 \longrightarrow R^1 R^2 N \overset{\overset{O}{\|}}{\diagup\!\!\!\diagdown} N R^1 R^2 + H_2O$$
$$R^1 = R^2 = H,\ alkyl$$

Scheme 8

The synthises of N, N^1-dialkyl urea (Scheme 8) has been achieved by removing water using hydrophilic ionic liquids as reaction medium[12].

In another report[14a], both symmetrical and asymmetrical urea derivatives have been prepared in good yield directly form CO_2 and amines using Cs^+ base catalyst and N – methyl pyrrolidone as the solvent (Scheme 8a)

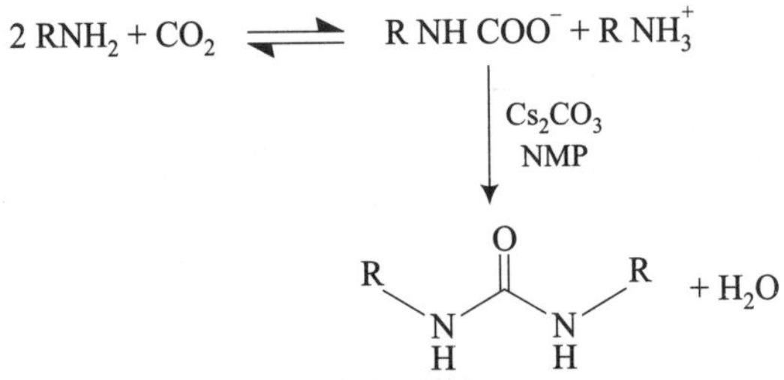

$$2\ RNH_2 + CO_2 \rightleftharpoons R\ NH\ COO^- + R\ NH_3^+$$

$$\downarrow \begin{array}{c} Cs_2CO_3 \\ NMP \end{array}$$

$$R \diagdown \overset{\overset{O}{\|}}{\underset{\underset{H}{N}}{}}\overset{}{\underset{\underset{H}{N}}{}} \diagup R \quad + H_2O$$

urea derivatives

Scheme 8a

The used catalyst were able to convert both linear and branced aliphatic amines to their corresponding urea derivatives in the absence to any dehydrating agent. The catalyst can be recovered and reused without any activity loss and the products could be easily isolated from the solution by precipitation with water. Using the above procedure following ureas were prepared:

N, N'– di(2 – heptyl) urea;

N, N'– dibutyl urea ; NN'– dihexyl urea ; N, N' diheptyl urea;

N, N'– dioctyl urea; N, N'– debenzyl urea; N, N'– di (t – butyl) urea;

N – Butyl – N'– methylbutyl urea; N – hexyl – N'– methyl urea;

N – 2 – heptyl – N' – methylbutyl urea and N – octyl – N' – methylbutyl urea.

Secondary or primary amines react with CO_2 to give carbonic acids (Scheme 9)[15]

$$R^1 R^2 NH + CO_2 \underset{\longleftarrow}{\longrightarrow} \underset{Carbonic\ acid}{R^1 R^2 N\ CO_2H} \xrightarrow{base} [R^1 R^2 NCO_2]^- [(base)H]^+$$
$$1°\ or\ 2°\ amine$$

Scheme 9

The reaction of insitu generated carbonic acids (as in Scheme 9) with electrophiles such as organic halides result in the formation of urethanes (carbamates) (Scheme 10).

$$RNH_2 + CO_2 + R^1X + base \rightarrow R\ NH\ CO_2\ R^1 + HX\ (base)$$
Urethane (carbamates)

Scheme 10

A number of homogeneous and heterogeneous catalysts are used to synthesise urethanes[16-21].

In the above procedure (Scheme 10), if organic halides are replaced by alcohols, then the product $(H - X)$ becomes water; the process is environmentally friendly (Scheme 10a)[22,23].

$$RNH_2 + CO_2 + R^1 - OH \rightarrow RNHCO_2\ R^1 + H_2O$$
Urethane

Scheme 10a

The water formed in the reaction (Scheme 10a) must be removed for better yield. It is best to carry out the dehydration (Scheme 11) using ketals[24] (as in Scheme 3).

Scheme 11

The urethane obtained by any of the Schemes 10 – 11 on heating give isocyanates (Scheme 12).

$$R\ NH\ CO_2\ R^1 \xrightarrow{\Delta} R - N = C = O + R^1OH$$
Urethane · · · · · · · · · · Isocyanate

Scheme 12

Intermolecular nucleophilic attack to nitriles result in the formation of quinazolines[25-27] (Scheme 13). The rate of the reaction is enhanced by the addition of DBU under supercritical conditions like oxirenes, the corresponding nitrogen analogues (aziridine) react with CO_2 without any catalyst to give nitrogen-containing five membered ring (oxazolidinones)[28-32] (Scheme 14). The presence of various compounds like alkali metal salts, quaternary ammonium salts and chromium salen complex promote the reaction[33-37].

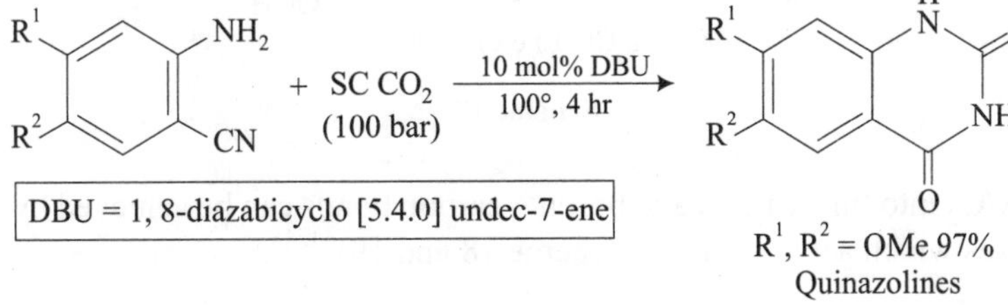

DBU = 1, 8-diazabicyclo [5.4.0] undec-7-ene

$R^1, R^2 = OMe\ 97\%$
Quinazolines

Scheme 13

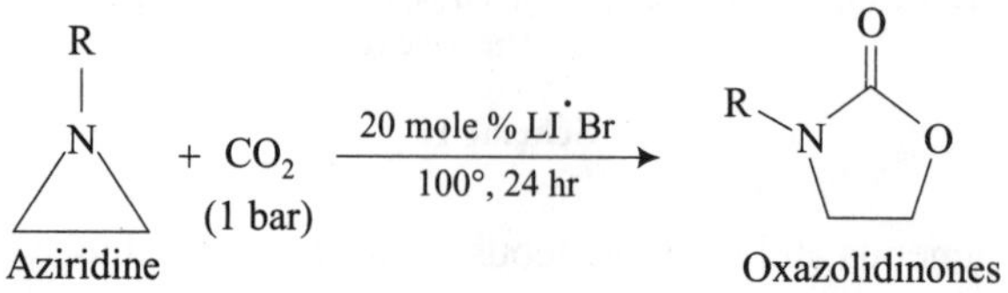

Scheme 14

Ring-opening polymensation of aziridines under supercritical conditions yield polyurethanes (Scheme –15). The resulting polymer undergoes a phase change depending on the pH and temperature[33].

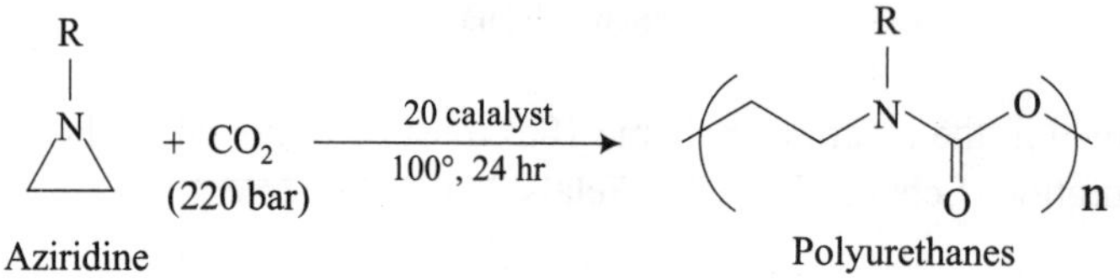

Scheme 15

The reaction of 1, 2 aminoalcohols with CO_2 produces five membered urethanes (oxazolidinones), the conversion is poor without dehydrating agent (Scheme 16)[38].

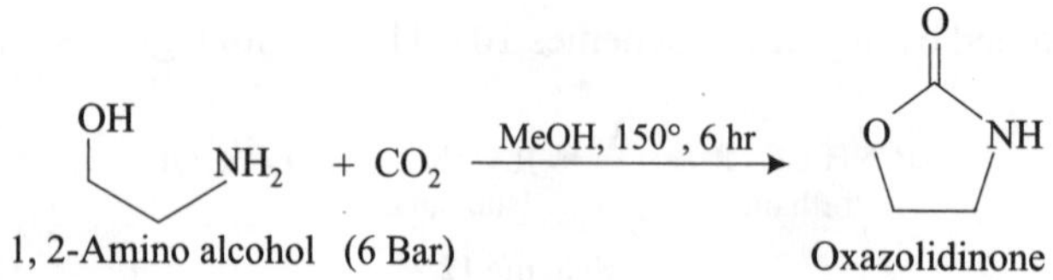

Scheme 16

2.5 Synthesis of Carboxylic Acids

A number of carbon nucleophiles like grignard reagents, alkyl lithium, active methylene compounds and metal enolates attack CO_2 under mild conditions to yield carboxylic acids (Scheme 17)[39-43].

$$R — MX + CO_2 \longrightarrow \xrightarrow{H^+} R — COOH$$
$$(M = Mg, Zn, Cu, Li \text{ etc})$$

Scheme 17

Insertion of CO_2 into tin – carbon and boron – carbon bonds can be achieved by palladium and rhodium complexes which act as catalyst (Scheme 18 and 19)[44, 45].

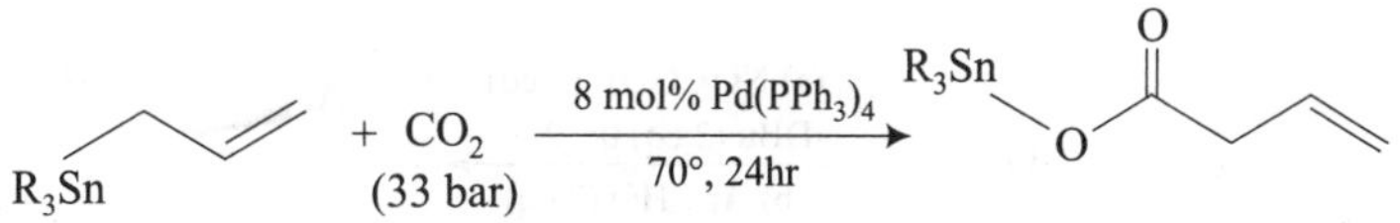

Scheme 18

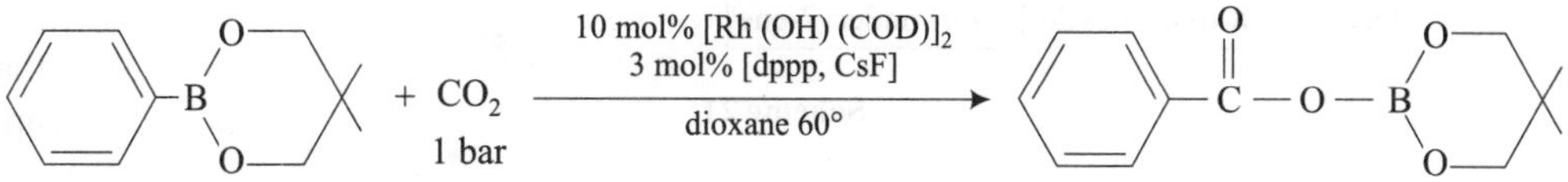

| dppp = 1,3-bis (diphenylphospino) propane |
| COD = 1,5-cyclooctadiene |

Scheme 19

Acrylic acid is a typical α, β-unsaturated carboxylic acid and is consumed on a industrial scale as a raw material for water-absorbing polymers. Conventionally, acrylic acid is produced by oxidation of propylene via acrolein. A convenient synthesis is from ethylene and CO_2 (Scheme 20) using an molybdenum complex as a cartelist[46-48].

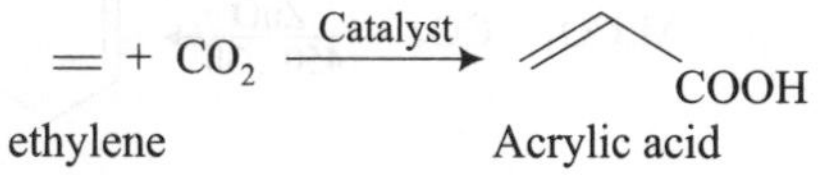

Scheme 20

Various substitute acrylic acide have been synthesised[49] from acetylene, butadiene and allene (Scheme 21). In many case, DBU promotes the reaction.

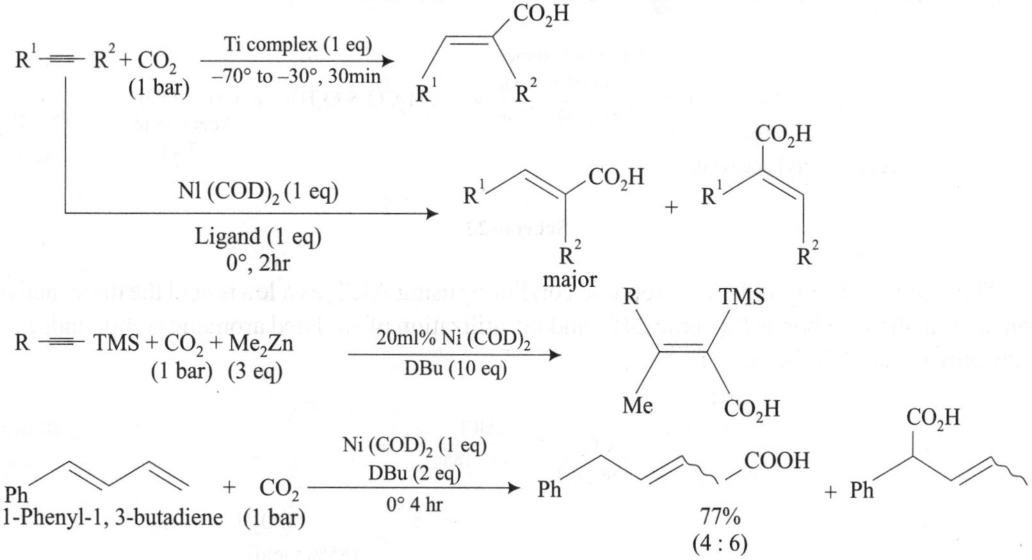

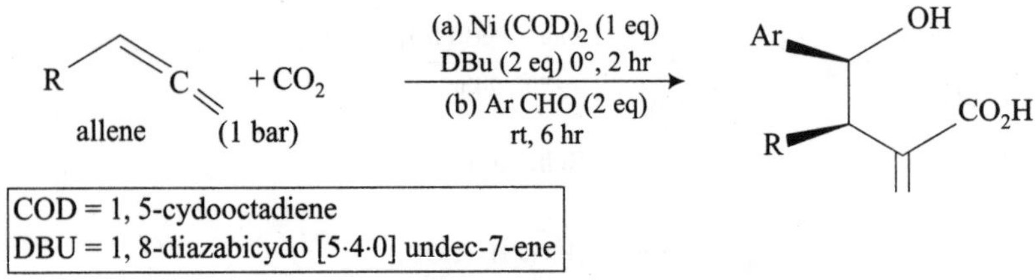

COD = 1, 5-cydooctadiene
DBU = 1, 8-diazabicydo [5·4·0] undec-7-ene

Scheme 21

Carboxylation with CO_2 can be carried out under either basic (Scheme 22) conditions[54,57] or acidic conditions. p–Hydroxy benzoic acid (Scheme 22) is one of the few chemicals that is industrially produced using CO_2 (Kolbe-Schmidt reaction)[54-56].

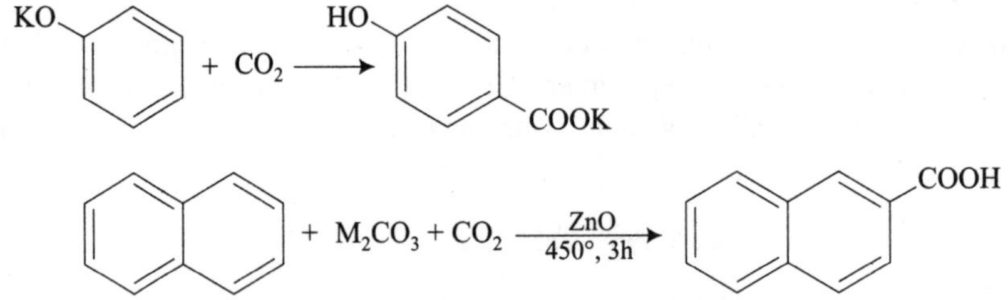

Scheme 22

The formation of naphthoic acid from naphthaline is a Henkel-type reaction[57].

Methane can be oxidised with CO_2 in presence of vanadium or palladium catalyzed reaction using an oxidizing agents like $K_2S_2O_8$ to give acetic acid (Scheme 23)[58,59].

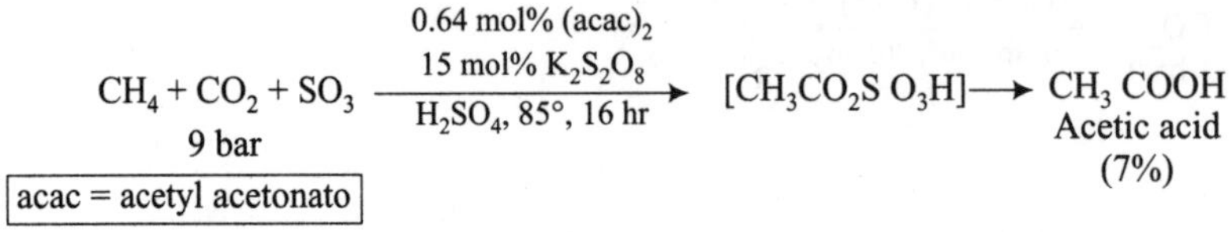

Scheme 23

The reaction of CO_2 under electrophilic conditions using $AlCl_3$ as a lewis acid the direct activation of aromatic C-H bonds (Scheme 24)[60] and the utilization of silylated aromatic compounds have been demonstrated (Scheme 25)[61,62].

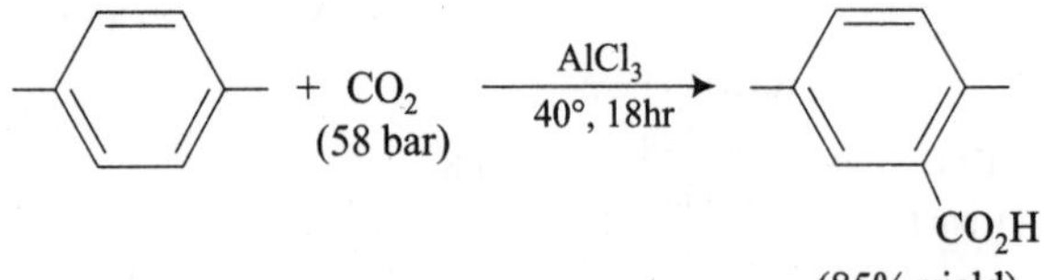

Scheme 24

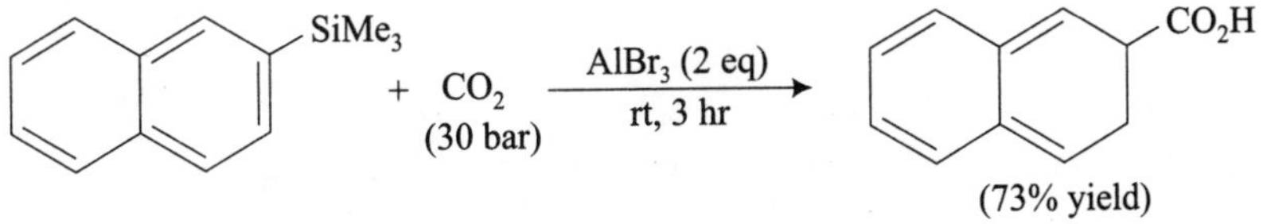

Scheme 25

Carboxylic acid can also be produced by metal calaysed reactions of organic halides, CO_2 and H_2 (Scheme 26)[63-65].

$$CH_3I + CO_2 + H_2 \xrightarrow[150°, 24\ hr]{\substack{1\ mol\% \\ [Rh_3(CO)_{12}]\ 10(Co_2(Co)_8]}} CH_3COOH$$

(20 bar) (20 bar)

Scheme 26

The reaction of olefins with CO_2 under acidic conditions give propionic acid[66] (Scheme 27). However, the details are unknown.

$$CH_2 = CH_2 + CO_2 \xrightarrow[\substack{4\ mol\%\ HBr \\ 180°, 12\ hr}]{\substack{0.04\ mol\% \\ Rh\ (PPh_3)Cl}} CH_3CH_2COOH + Et\ OH$$

(140 bar) 38%   15%

Scheme 27

2.6 Synthesis of Esters

Eslers are synthesised by the reaction of various unsaturated compounds with CO_2. For example polymerisation of vinyl ethers under CO_2 in the presence of aluminium compounds yield polymers that incorporate CO_2 into the chain (Scheme 28). The yields of these polymers are low and need further improvement[67-69].

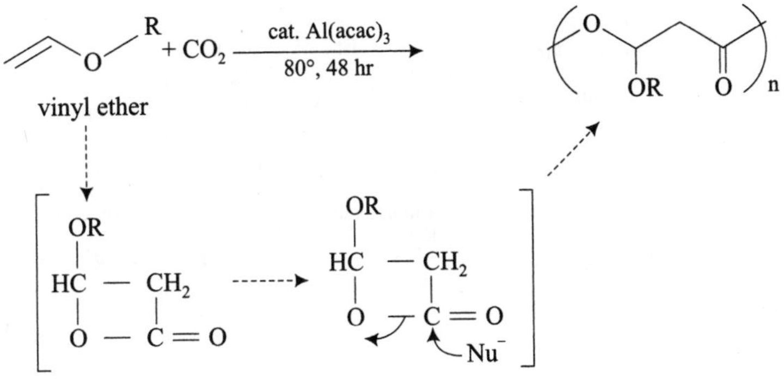

Scheme 28

A similar CO_2 incorporation has been reported for the polymerization of a three-component system, which contain a phosphorus compound (Scheme 29)[70].

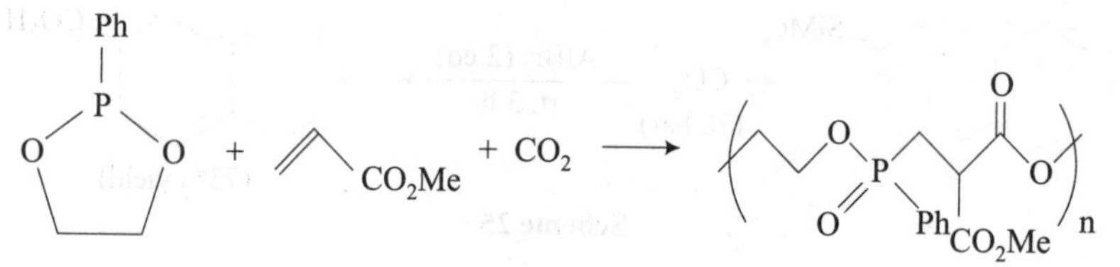

Scheme 29

2.7 Synthesis of Lactones

Lactones are obtained by the reaction of CO_2 with unsaturated compounds like dienes[71-73] allenes[74], acetylenes[75-76] and diyness[77-84] (Scheme 30).

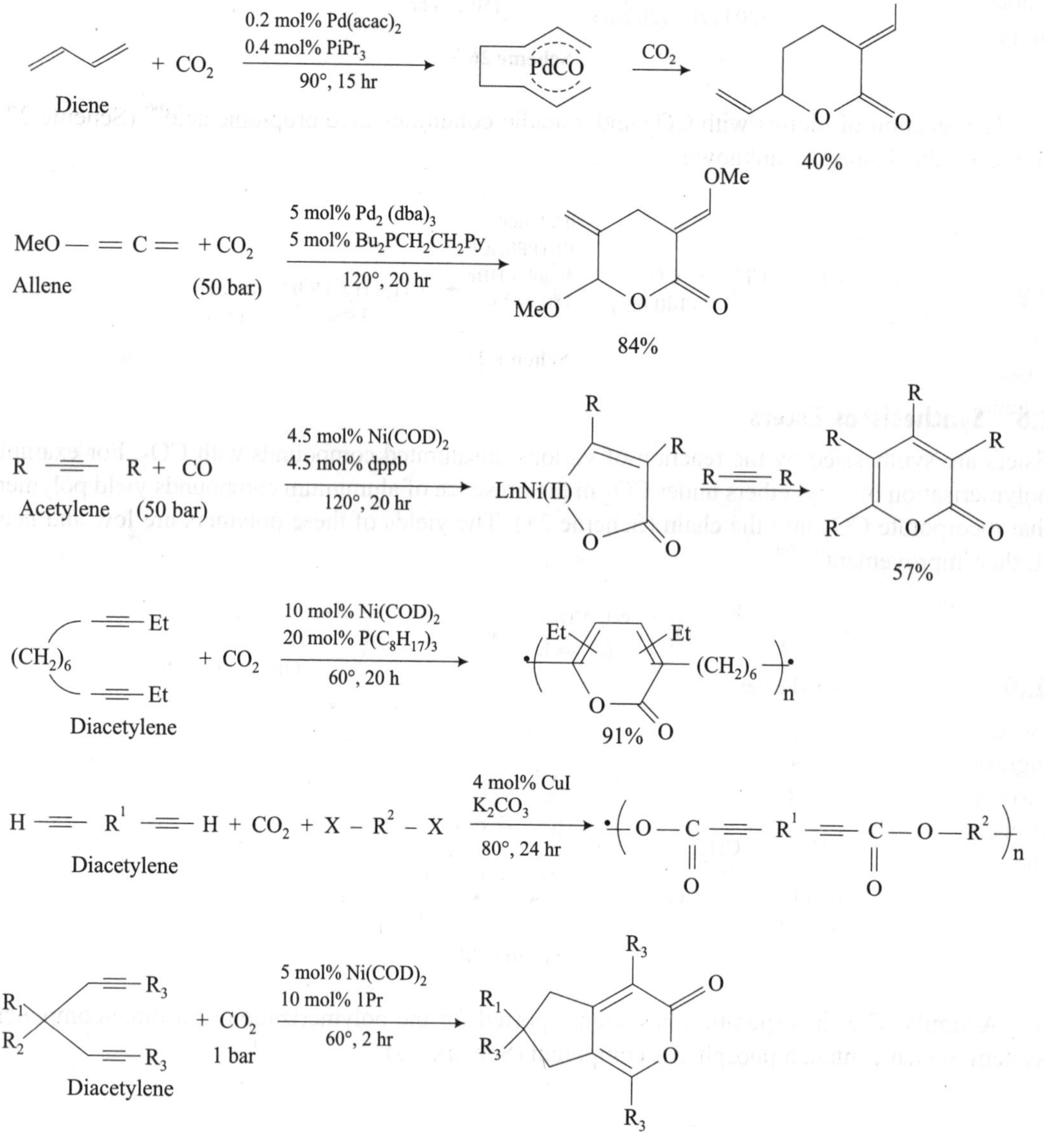

1Pr =

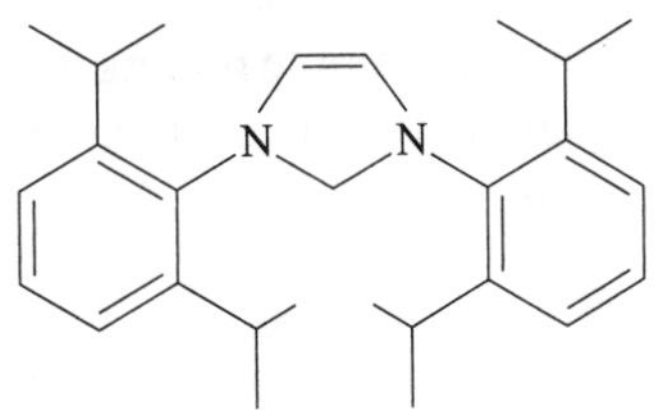

Scheme 30

2.8 Hydroformylation

Under high pressure of CO_2 and hydrogen, alkenes are hydroformylated to yield alcohol in presence of a ruthenium complex (Scheme 31)[85].

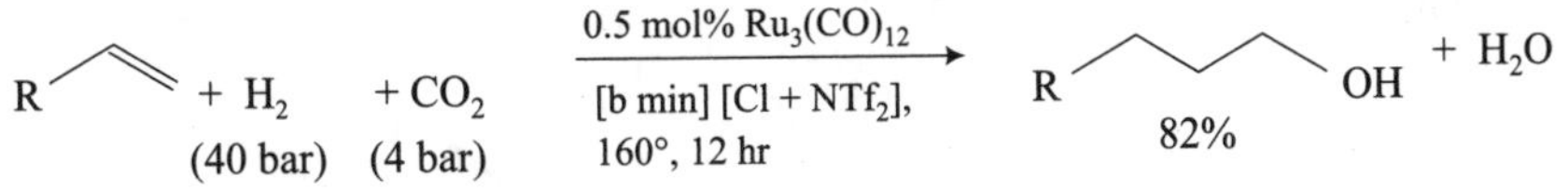

$$R\diagup + H_2 \quad + CO_2 \xrightarrow[\substack{[b\ min]\ [Cl+NTf_2],\\ 160°,\ 12\ hr}]{0.5\ mol\%\ Ru_3(CO)_{12}} R\diagup\diagdown\diagup OH \quad + H_2O$$

(40 bar) (4 bar) 82%

Scheme 31

2.9 Homologation

Homologation of alcohol using CO_2 is reported in presence of hydrogen (Scheme 32). In this case, as in the case of hydroformylation, carbon monoxide generated from CO_2 will be the real reactant[86,87].

$$MeOH + H_2 \quad + CO_2 \xrightarrow[\substack{NMP,\ 200°,\ 15\ hr}]{\substack{1\ mol\%\ Ru_3(CO)_{12}\\ 1.5\ mol\%\ Co_2(Co)_8\\ 50\ mol\%\ KI}} EtOH + H_2O$$

(100 bar) (20 bar)   10%
   rt   rt

Scheme 32

2.10 Use of Carbonic Acid as Acid Catalyzed Hydrolysis of Ketals, Acetals and Epoxides

A number of chemical reaction are acid catalysed. However such reaction on a large scale gnerate significant amount of acid waste which requires neutralisation and or disposal. A solution of carbon dioxide in water under increased pressure is mildly acid, due to the formation of carbonic acid (Scheme 33) and should be capable of catalyzing a number of reaction. Simple pressure release at the end the reaction raises the PH back to the levels which requires minimal neutralisation[88].

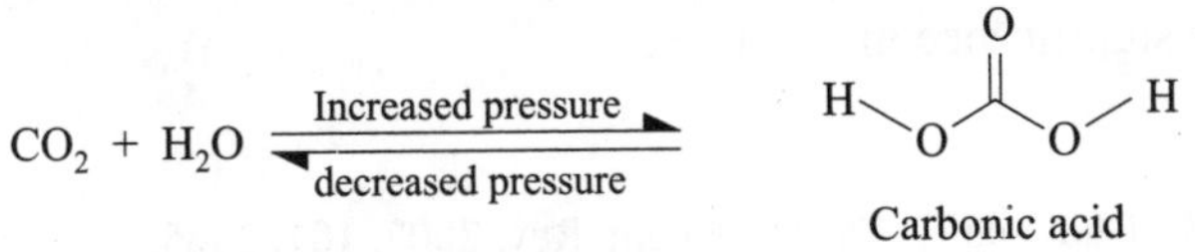

$$CO_2 + H_2O \underset{\text{decreased pressure}}{\overset{\text{Increased pressure}}{\rightleftarrows}}$$

Carbonic acid

Scheme 33

Some typical examples of simple transformation to illustrates carbonic acid catalyzed reactions are shown below (Scheme 34)[89]. As an example mixing a ketal with water, pressurizing with 20 bar CO_2 and heating to 65° gives quantitative yield of cyclohexanone within 4 hr. In a similar way epoxides also undergo deprotection.

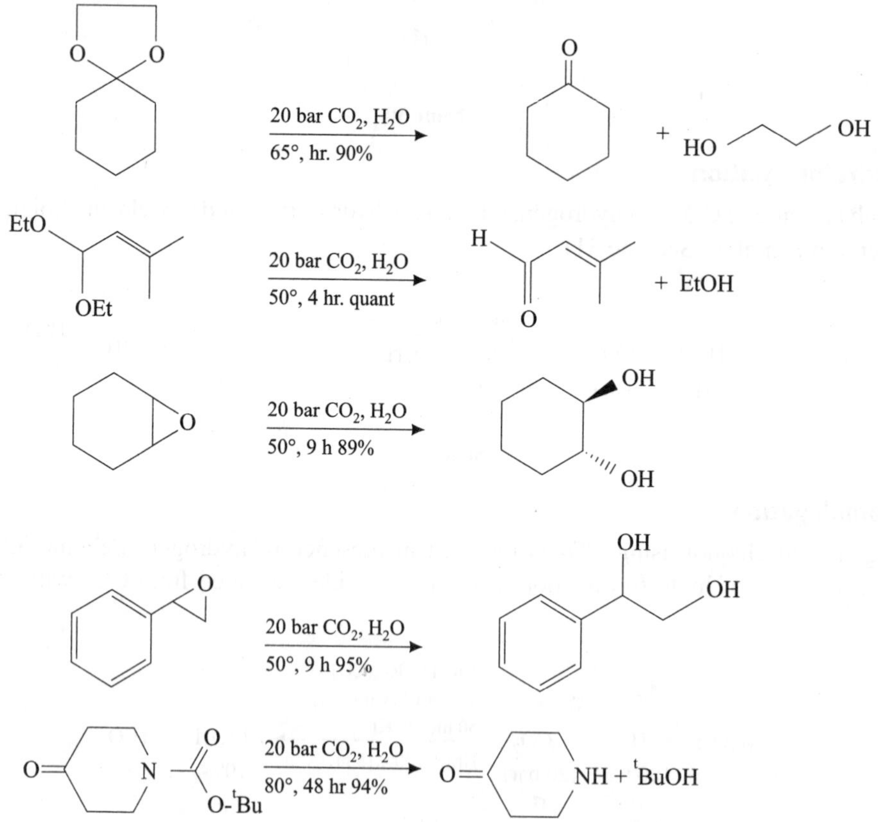

Scheme 34

3   CONCLUSION

Though a large number of chemicals can be prepared using CO_2 as a raw material but it does not necessarily help mitigate the green house effect. some of the compounds like urea, carboxylic acids, dimethyl carbonate, cyclic carbonates, alternating polymers etc are manufactured on a commercial scale. There is however, need to develop new technologies for the manufacture of other products. It is believed that the environmental aspects of many of the procedures in synthetic chemistry are going to be of greater significance in the future.

References

1. T. Sakakura, J-C. Choi and H. Yasuda, Chem. Rev. 2007, **107**, 2365.
2. M. Aresta, A. Dibenedeuo and I. Tommasi , Energy Fuels, 2001, **15**, 269.

3. M. Aresta and M.J. Galatola, Clean Prod., 1999, **7**, 181.

4. K. Kohno, J-C, Choi, H. Yasuda and T. Sakakura, 53th Symposium on organometallic chemistry, Osaka, Japan, Sept. 8-9, 2006, Kini chemical society Abstract PB 261.

5. D.J. Darenbourg and M.W. Holtcamp, Coord. Chem.. Rev., 1996, 153, 155.

6. M. Aresta and A. Dibenedetto, J. Mol. Catal. A. Chem., 2002, **182**, 399.

7. K. Tomishige, H. Yasuda , Y. Yoshida, M. Nurunnabi, B.T. li and K. Kunimori, Green. Chem., 2004, **6**, 206.

8. K. Tomishige, H. Yasuda, Y. Yoshida, M. Nurunnabi, B.T. li and K. Kunimori, Catal. Lett., 2004, **95**, 45.

9. Y. Du, D.L. Kong, H.Y. Wang, F. Cai , H.S. Tian, J.Q. Wang and L.N. He, J. Mol. Catal A: Chem., 2005, **241**, 133.

10. G.W. Coates and D.R. More, Angew. Chem. Int. Ed, 2004, **43**, 6618.

11. S. Inoue, Gendai Kagaku, 2005, 408, 42.

12. F. Shi. Y.Q. Deng, T.L. SiMa, J.J. Peng, Y.L. Gu and BT. Qiao, Angew. Chen. Int. Ed. 2003, **42**, 3257.

13. C.C. Tai, M.J. Huck, E.P. Mckoon, T. Woo and P.G. Jessop, J. Org. Chem, 2002, **67**, 9070.

14. R. Nomura, Y. Haseyawa, M. Ishrmoto, T. Toyosaki and H. Matsuda, J. Org. Chem., 1992, **57**, 7339.

14a. A. Ion, V. Parvulesu, P. Jacobs and D.D. Vos, Green Chemistry, 2007, **9**, 158.

15. D.B. Dell'Amico, F. Calderazzo, L. Labella, F. Marchetti and G. Pampaloni, Chem. Rev., 2003, **103**, 3857.

16. R.N. Salvatore, S.I. Shin, A.S. Nagle and K.W. Jung. J. Org. Chem., 2001, **66**, 1035.

17. M. Yoshida, N. Hara and S. Okuyama, Chem. Commun, 2000, 151.

18. W. McGhee, D. Riley, K. Christ, Y. Pan and B. Parnas. J. Org. Chem. 1995, **60**, 2820.

19. M. Aresta and E. Quaranta, Tetrahedron, 1992, **48**, 1515.

20. W.D. McGhee, D.P. Riley, M.E. Christ and K.M. Christ, Organometallics, 1993, **12**, 1429.

21. R. Srivastava, M.D. Manju, D. Srinivas and P. Ratnasamy, Catal. Lett, 2004, **97**, 41.

22. M. Abla, J-C. Choi and T. Sakakura, Chem. Common, 2001, 2238.

23. M. Abla, J-C. Choi and T. Sakakura, Green Chem. 2004, **6**, 524.

24. T. Sakakura, J. – C. Choi, P. Saito, T. Masuda, T. Sako, and T. Oriyama, J. Org. Chem., 1999, **64**, 4506.

25. T.J. Connolly, P. McGarry and S. Sakhtankar, Green Chem. 2005, **7**, 586.

26. T. Mizuno and Y. Ishino, Tetrahedran, 2002, 58, 3155.

27. T. Mizuno, T. Iwai and Y. Ishino, Tetrahedron Lelt, 2004, **45**, 7073.

28. H. Kawanami. H. Matsumoto and Y. Ikushima, Chem. Lett, 2005, **34**, 60.

29. A.W. Miller and S.T. Nguyen, Org. Lett, 2004, **6**, 2301.

30. A. Sudo, Y. Morioka, F. Sanda and T. Endo, Tetrahedron Lett. 2004, **45**, 1363.

31. A. Sudo, Y. Morioka, E. Koizumi, F. Sanda and T. Endo, Tetrahedron Lett, 2003, **44**, 7889.

32. M. Shi. J.K. Jiang, Y.M. Shen, Y.S. Feng, and G.X. Lei, J. Org. Chem, 2000, **65**, 3443.

33. O. Ihata, Y. Kayaki and T. Ikariya, Chem. Commun, 2005, 2268.

34. O. Jhata, Y. Kayaki and T. Ikariya, Kobunshi, Ronbunshu, 2005, **62**, 196.

35. B. Ochiai, S. Inoul and T. Endo, J. Polym. Sce. Part A: Polym Chem, 2005, **43**, 6613.

36. O. Ihata, Y. Kayaki and T. Ikariya, Macromolecules, 2005, **38**, 6429.

37. O. Ihata, Y. Kayaki and T. Ikariya, Angew. Chem. Int. Edn, 2004, **43**, 717.

38. B.M. Bhanaga, S. Fujita, Y. Ikushima and M. Arai, Green Chem, 2003, **5**, 240.
39. N.P. Mankad, T.G. Gray, D.S. Laitar and J.P. Sadighi, Organometallics, 2004, **23**, 1191.
40. K. Chiba, H. Tagaya, S. Miura and M. Karasu, Chem. Lett, 1992, 923.
41. K. Chiba, H. Tagaya, M. Karasu, M. Ishizuka and T. Sugo, Bull. Chem. Soc. Japan, 1994, **67**, 452.
42. H. Abe and S. H. Inoue, J. Chem. Soc. Chem. Commun, 1994, 1197.
43. R.P. Quirk, J. Yin, L.J. Fetters and R.V. Kastrup, Macromolecules, 1992, **25**, 2262.
44. M. Shi and K.M. Nicholas, J. Am. Chem. Soc, 1997, **119**, 5057.
45. K. Ukai, M. Aoki, J. Takaya and N. Iwasawa, J. Am. Chem. Soc, 2006, **128**, 8706.
46. A Galindo, A. Pastor, P.J. Perez and E. Carmona, Organometallics, 1993, **12**, 4443.
47. G. Schubert and I. Papar. J. Am. Chem. Soc, 2003, **125**, 14847.
48. I. Papar, G. Schubert, I. Mayer, G. Besenyei and M. Aresta, Organometallices, 2004, **23**, 5252.
49. S. Saito, S. Nakagawa, T. Koizumi, K. Hirayama and Y. Yamamoto, J. Org. Chem. 1994, **64**, 3975.
50. Y. Six. J. Org. Chem, 2003, 1157.
51. M. Aoke, M. Kaneko, S. Izumi, K. Ukai, and N. Iwasawa, Chen. Commun 2004, 2568.
52. M. Takimoto and M. Mori. J. Am. Chem. Soc. 2001, 123, 2895.
53. M. Takimoto, M. Kawamura and M. Mori, Org. Lett, 2003, **5**, 2599.
54. Y. Kosugi, Y. Imaoka, F. Gotoh, M.A. Rahim, Y. Mutsui and K. Sakanish, Org. Biomol. Chem, 2003, **I**, 817.
55. M.A. Rahim, Y. Matsui, T. Matsuyama and Y. Kosugi, Bull. Chem. Soc. Japan, 2003, **76**, 2191.
56. A. Sclafani, L. Parlmisano and G. Farneti, Chem. Commun, 1997, 529.
57. F. Thomas, G. Garo, F. Susan (shell oil), Wo Al O1/16072.
58. M. Zerella , S. Mukhopadhyay and A.T. Bedi, Org. Lett, 2003, **5**, 3193.
59. Y. Fujiwara, Y. Taniguchi, H. Takaki, M. Kurioka, T. Jintoku and T. Kitamura, Stud. Surf. Sci. Catal. 1997, **107**, 275.
60. G.A. Olah, A. Torok, J.P. Joschek, I. Bucsi, P.M. Esleves, G. Rasul and G.K.S. Parkash. J. Am. Chem. Soc, 2002, **124**, 11379.
61. T. Hattori, Y. Suzaki and S. Miyano, Chem. Lett, 2003, **32**, 454.
62. T. Suzuki, T. Hattori, T. Okuzawa and S. Miyano. Chem. Lett, 2002, 102.
63. A. Fukuoka, N. Gctoh, N. Kobayashi, M. Hirano and S. Kumiya, Chem. Lett, 1995, 567.
64. C. Amatore, A. Jutand, F. Khalil and M. F. Nielsen, J. Am. Chem. Soc. 1992, **114**, 7076.
65. K. Osakada, R. Sato and T. Yamamoto, Organometallics, 1994, **13**, 4645.
66. A.L. Lapidus, S.D. Porozhkov and N.D. Zelinky, Proc. 9th Int. Congr. Catal, 1988, **3**, 1028.
67. C. Yokoyama, Y. Kawase, N, Shibasaki – Kitakawa, and R.L. Smith, J. Appl. Polym.2003, **89**, 3167.
68. K. Soga, S. Hosoda. Y. Tasuka and S. Ikeda, J. Polym. Sci, Polym. Lett. 1975, **13**, 265.
69. K. Soga, M. Sato S. Hosoda and S. Ikeda, J. Polym. Sci. Polym. Lett, 1975, **13**, 543.
70. T. Saegusa, S. Kobayayashi and Y. Kimura, Macromolecules, 1977, **10**, 68.
71. A. Behr and V.A. Brehme, J. Mol. Catal A: Chem., 2002, **187**, 69.
72. A. Behr and M. Heite. Chem. Ing. Tech., 2002, **72**, 58.
73. A. Behr and K.D. Juszak, J. Organomet Chem, 1983, **255**, 263.
74. T. Tsuda, T. Yamamoto and T.J. Saegusa, Organometallic Chem, 1992, **429**, C46.
75. Y. Inoue, Y. Itoh, H. Kazama and H. Hashimoto, Bull. Chem. Sec. Japan, 1980, **53**, 3329.

76. H. Hoberg, D. Schaefer, G. Burkhart, C. Kruger and M. J. Roma, J. Organometallic Chem., 1984, **266**, 203.

77. T. Tsuda, H. Yasukawa, and K. Komori, Macromolecules,1995, **28**, 1356 .

78. T. Tsuda, H. Yasukawa, H. Hokazono and Y. Kitaike, Macrormolecules, 1995, **28**, 1312.

79. T. Tsuda, and H. Hokazono, Macromolecules, 1994, **27**, 1289.

80. T. Tsuda, O. Ooi and K. Maruta, Macromolecules, 1993, **26**, 4840.

81. T. Tsuda, Y. Kitaike and O.Ooi, Macromolecules, 1993, **26**, 4956.

82. T. Tsuda, K. Maruta and Y. Kitaike, J. Am. Chem. Soc. 1992, **114**, 1498.

83. T. Tsuda and K. Maruta, Macromolecules, 1992, **25**, 6102.

84. S.C. Oi, Y. Fukue, K. Nemoto and Y. Inoue, Macromolecules, 1996, **29**, 2694.

85. K. Tomimaga, Catal. Today, 2006, **115**, 70.

86. K. Tominaga, Y. Sasaki, M. Saito, K. Hagihara and T. Watanbe, J. Mol. Catal, 1994, **89**, 51.

87. K. Tominaga, Y. Sasaki, T. Watanabe M. Saito, Stud. Surf. Sci. Catal, 1998, 114 495.

88. R.R. Weekel, J.P. Hallett, C.L. Liotta and C.A. Eckert, Top. Catal, 2006, **37**, 75.

89. D.A. Clarke, J. Anmens, C.M. Rayner, Unbublished results; See also C. M. Rayner, Organic Process Researed and Development, 2007, **11**, 121.

PART – III

Organic Synthesis using Ionic Liquids

Chapter 7

I INTRODUCTION

In ideal synthesis, the objective is to produce the desired product in 100 per cent yield and selectivity[1]. Most of the organic solvents that are used as industrial solvent are volatile organic compounds that are used in organic synthesis. The toxic and hazardous properties of many solvents, notably chlorinated hydrocarbons are responsible for serious environmental issues, such as atmospheric emission and making their use prohibitive[2-4]. Recently ionic liquids[5-15]. are emerging as novel replacement for volatile organic compounds used traditionally as industrial solvents and reduce the volatility, environmental, and human health and safely concerns that accompany exposure to organic solvents.

Ionic liquids or molten salts are in general defined as liquid electrolytes composed entirely of ions. More recently the melting point criteria has been proposed to distinguish between molten salt (high melting, highly viscous and very corroseve medium) and ionic liquids (Liquid below 100°C and relatively low visiosety").

Ionic liquids are made up of at least two components (the cation and the anion) which can vary. The ionic liquids have attractive properties for a solvent. The solvent can be designed with a particular end use in mind or to posses a particular set of properties. Hence, these are also known as 'designer solvents', their properties can be adjusted to suit the requirements of a particular process. Properties such as melting point, viscosity, density and hydrophobicity can be varied by simple changes to the structure of ions. Another important property that changes with structure is the miscibility of water in these ionic liquids. By choosing the correct ionic liquid, higher product yield can be obtained and a reduced amount of waste can be produced in a given reaction. The ionic liquids can often be recycled and this leads to reduction of the costs of the process. Also the reactions are often quicker and easier to carry out than in conventional organic solvents. Ionic liquids are good solvents for a wide range of both inorganic and organic materials. They are often composed of poorly coordinating ions, so they have the potential to be highly polar noncordinating solvents. They are also immisuble with a number of organic solvents and provide a nonaqueus, polar alternative for two phase system. Hydrophobic ionic liquids can also be used as immiscible polar phase with water. The use of ionic liquids can enhance, selectivity and stability of transition metal catalysts

Properties of ionic liquids

Room temperature ionic liquids exhibit many properties[9] which make them potentially attractive media for many organic reactions.

(i) They have essentially no vapour pressure, i.e. they do not evaporate and are easy to contain.

(ii) They possess good thermal stability and do not decompose over a large temperature range, thereby making it feasible to carry out reaction requiring high temperature conveniently in ionic liquids.

(iii) They are able to dissolve a wide range of organic, inorganic and oranometallic compounds.

(iv) They serve as good medium to solubilise gases such as H_2, CO, O_2 and CO_2 and many reaction are now being performed using ionic liquids and supercritical CO_2.

(v) The solubility of ionic liquids depends upon the nature of the cations and counter anions.

(vi) They Generally do not co-ordinate to metal complexes, enzymes and different organic substrates.

(vii) Most of the ionic liquids can be stored without decomposition for a long period of time.

(viii) They show a high degree of potential for enantioselective reactions as a significant impact on the reactiveties and selectivities due to their polar and non-coordinating properties. In addition, chiral ionic liquids have been used to control the stereoselectivity.

(ix) The viscosity of 1-alkyl-3-methyl imidazolium salts can be decreased by using hightly branched and compact alkyl chain as well as by changing the nature of anion. The viscosity decreases in the order $Cl^- > PF_6^- > BF_4^- \approx NO_3^- > NTF_2$.

2 TYPES OF IONIC LIQUIDS

Ionic liquids consist of a salt where one or both the ions are large, and the cation has a low degree of symmetry. These factors tend to reduce the lattice energy of the crystalline form of the salt, and hence lower the melting pont[16]

Ionic liquids come in two main categories, namely,

(i) Simple salts (made of a single anion and cation) For example, [EtNH$_3$][NO$_3$] is a simple salt.

(ii) Binary ionic liquid (salts where equilibrium is involved). For example mixtures of aluminium (III) chloride and 1, 3-dialkylimidazolium chloride (a binary ionic liquid system). It contained several different ionic species, and their properties and melting point depend upon the mole fraction of aluminum (III) chloride and 1, 3-dialkylimidazolium chloride present.

3 PREPARATION OF IONIC LIQUIDS

Ionic liquids mainly comprise organic cations such as tetraalkylammonium[17], tetraalkylphosphonium[18], trialkylsulphonium[19], N-alkylpyidinum[20], 1, 3,-dialkylimidazolium[21], N, N-dialkylpyrrolidinum[22], N-alkylthiazolium[23], N-alkyloxazolium[24], N, N-dialkylpyrazolium[25] and N, N-dialkytriazolium[26] (Fig. 1).

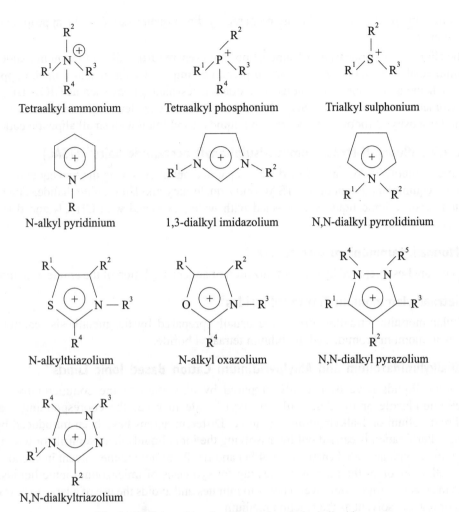

Fig. 1   Different type of organic cations in ionic liquids

The common anions which result in neutral and stoichometric ionic liquids are: BF_4^-, PF_6^-, SbF_6^-, $ZnCl_3^-$, $CuCl_2^-$, $SnCl_3^-$, $N(CF_3SO_2)_2^-$, $N(C_2F_5SO_2)_2^-$, $C(CF_3SO_2)_3^-$, $CF_3CO_2^-$, $CF_3SO_3^-$ and $MeSO_3^-$. There is another class of polynuclear anions such as $Al_2Cl_7^-$, $Al_3Cl_{10}^-$, $AuCl_7^-$, $Fe_2Cl_7^-$ and $Sb_2F_{11}^-$; the latter type of polynuclear anions are air and water sensitive.

In order to be liquid at room temperature, the cation should preferably be unsymmetrical e. g. R^1 and R^2 should be different alkyl groups in the dialkyimidazolium cation. The melting point is also influenced by the nature of the anion.

The hydrophilicity/lipophilicity of ionic liquid can be modified by a suitable choice of anion, [bmin]BF_4(bmin – 1 butyl –3- methylimidiazolium) is completely miscible with water while the PF_6 salt is largely immiscible with water. The lipophilicity of dialkylimidazolium salts or other ionic liquids can also be increased by increasing the lenth of the alkyl groups.

Room temperature ionic liquids are prepared by direct quaterisation of the appropriate amines or phosphines[27].

The aliphatic quaternary ammonium cations are prepared from alkylammonium halides which are commercially available or they can be prepared simpley by the reaction of the appropriate halogenoalkane and amine. The anions are oxidation resistant anions such as ClO_4^-, BF_4^- or PF_6^-. The asymmetric amide anion $(CF_3SO_2 - N - COCF_3)^-$ has an excellent ability to lower both melting point and viscosity of room temperature ionic liquids, combining with small aliphatic cations.

3.1 2, 2, 2-Trifluoro-N-(trifluoromethylsulphonyl) acetamide Salts[13] (TSAC)

The water insoluble TSAC salts immediately separated out after mixing the two aqueous solutions containing equimolar amount of K – TSAC and a quaternary alkylammonium halide. The resulting room temperature ionic liquid was washed with water, extracted with CH_2Cl_2 and dried under vacuum (100°C) for 24h.

3.2 Monoalkylammonium Nitrate Salts[6]

These salts are best prepared by the neutralization of aqueous solution of the amine with nitric acid.

3.3 Tetraalkylammonium Tetraalkylborides[6]

Tetralkylammonium tetraalkylborides are usually prepared by the metathesis reaction of the tetraakyl ammonium bromide and the lithium tetraakyl boride.

3.4 Dialkylimidazolium and Alkylpyridinium Cation Based Ionic Liqids[13]

These ionic liquids have been easily prepared by alkylation of the commercially available N- methylimidazole or pyridine with an alkyl halide to gives the cooresponding 1-alkyl-3-methylimidazolium or 1-alkylpyridinium halide. Different anions have been introduced by anion exchange. Purification is carried out by dissolving the ionic liquids in acetonitrile or tetrahydrofuran, treating it with activated charcoal (≥ 24 hr) and finally removing the solvent in vacuo. A more recent method involves the microwave heating for synthesis of imidazolium ionic liquids, which reduces the reaction time from several hours to minutes and avoids the use of a large excess of alkyl halides or organic solvent as the reaction medium.

3.5 Gold Nanoparticles Based on Imidazolium Cation Ionic Liquids[13]

More recently gold nanoparticles based on imidazolium cation liquids were synthesized. To an aqueous solution of $HAuCl_4$, an excess amount of $NaBH_4$ was added dropwise in the presence of 3, 3^1[disulphanylbis (hexane-1, 6-diyl) bis (1-methyl-1 H-imidazol-3-ium) dichloride. The colour of the solution immediately changed from yellow to dark red, indicating the formation of gold nanoparticles (Scheme 1).

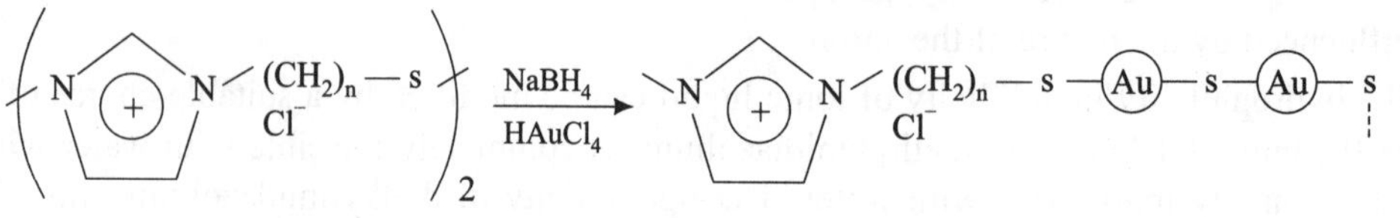

Scheme 1

These nanoparticles were further modified by reaction with various anions and it was found that the surface property of nanoparticles chanfed from hydrophilic to hydrophobic by the anion exchange. Gold nanoparticles containing Cl^- are soluble in water, while those containing PF_6^- are immiscible in water. These nanoparticles can be used as exceptionally high extinction dyes for the calorimetric sensing of anions in water via a particular aggregation process.

3.6 Ionic Liquids with Functionalised Alkyl Chains[13]

Synthesis of ionic liquids with functionalised alkyl chains also have been reported. The introduction of hydroxyl or ether functional groups in the alkyl chain considerably modifies the solubility behaviour, while modification of anion (PF_6^- or BF_4^-) does not seem to have any significant influence. The synthesis of functionalised ionic liquids required multistep procedures. These include the synthesis of a functionalised alkylating agent, followed by alkylation of amine. The desired functional group is obtained by modification of obtained salt follwed by an anion exchange reaction if required e. g. the Michael-type addition of a protonated tert. Amine or phosphine to α, β-unsaturated compounds (Scheme 2).

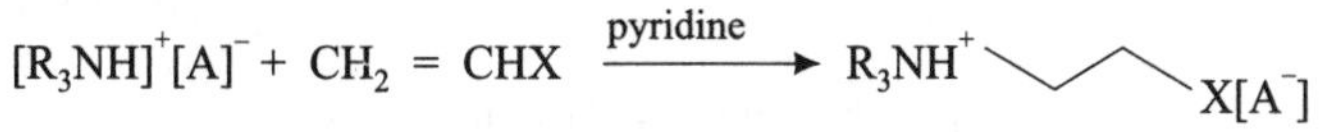

$$[R_3NH]^+[A]^- + CH_2 = CHX \xrightarrow{\text{pyridine}} R_3NH^+ \diagdown\diagup\diagdown_{X[A^-]}$$

$$A = \text{anion; } X = COOR, COCH_3, CN$$

Scheme 2

In the first step, tert. amine, N-methylimidazole or pyridine, was protonated with an acid, giving the ammonium salt, and the anion of the final ionic liquid was introduced in this step. In the second step, the protonated amine was reacted with α, β-unsaturated compound in the presence of weak and volatile base such as pyridine at 70°C for about 16 h to yield the ionic liquid.

3.7 Chiral Ionic Liquids[13]

Chiral ionic liquids have their potential application to asymmetric synthesis and optical resolution of recemates.

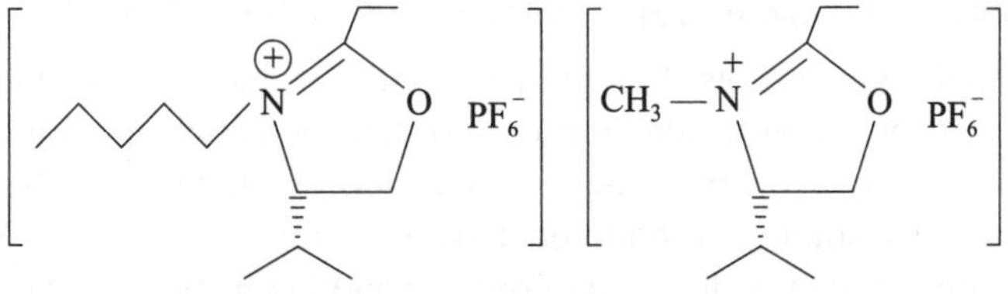

Oxazolium cation based chiral ionic liquids

The synthesis of these chiral ionic liquid required an expensive chiral alkylating agent. The oxazolinium cation based chiral ionic liquid were prepared by alkylation of the corresponding oxazoline with an alkyl bromide followed by anion exchange. Other examples of chiral ionic liquids are.

$X^- = [(CF_3SO_2)_2N]^-$

$X^- = [(CF_3SO_2)_2N]^-$

$R_1, R_2 = H, CH_3$
$X = Br, (CF_3,SO_2)_2N,$
$(C_2F_5SO_2)_2N$

Cyclophane type imidazoliums salts

3.8 Halogeno and Alkylhalogenoaluminate Ionic Liquids (Binary Ionic Liquids)

Preparation of the halogenoaluminate (III) ionic liquid is simple: an imidazolium or pyridinium halide salt is mixed directly with the appropriate aluminium (III) halide in the ratios necessary to generate the composition required. Upon mixing, an exothermic reaction occurs and the two solids melt into a liquid. The room temperature halogenoaluminate (III) ionic liquids are extremely sensitive to moisture and must be handled either in vacuo or under an inert atmosphere at all times. These ionic liquids are corrosive to many material and care must be taken in the selection of equipment. All glass apparatus is used when possible. Also, these ionic liquids reacts rapidly with water generating HCI, a toxic and irritant gas. Therefore, care is required to minimize exposure, particularly when destroying used ionic liquid.

3.9 Microwave Assisted Solvent Free Preparation of Ionic Liquids

Room temperature ionic liquids consisting predominantly of dialkyl imidazolium cations[6,21] and various anions, have received wide attention due to their potential in a variety of commererial applications such as electrochemistry[28], heavy metal ion extraction[29], phase transfer catalysts, polymensation[30] and as substitutes for traditional volatile organic solvents[31]. Most of these polar ionic salts are good solvent for a wide range of organic and inorganic material but consist of polar coordinating ions and provide a polar alternative for biphasic system. Other significant attributes of these ionic liquids include barely measuralble vapour pressure, potential for recycling, compatibility with various organic compounds and organometallic catalysts and ease of separation of products from reactions[32-35] unfortunately most of the initial preparative processes for the preparatrion of ionic liquids involve several hours of heating of alkyl halide/ organic solvent that diminish their true potential as 'greener' solvents.

Ionic liquids, being polar and ionic in character, couple to the MW irradiation very efficiently and therefore are ideal microwave absorbing candidates[36] for expediating chemical reactions[37]. An efficient preparation of 1, 3-dialkylimidazolium halides via microwave heating has been described[38] that reduces the reaction time from several hours to minutes and avoids the use of a large excess of halides/organic solvents as the reaction medium[39-41]. The efficiency of this approach has been extended to the preparation of other ionic salts bearing tetraluoroborate anion that involve exposing N, N[1]– dialkylimidazolium chloride and ammonium tetrafluoborate salt to MW irradiation (Scheme 3)[38].

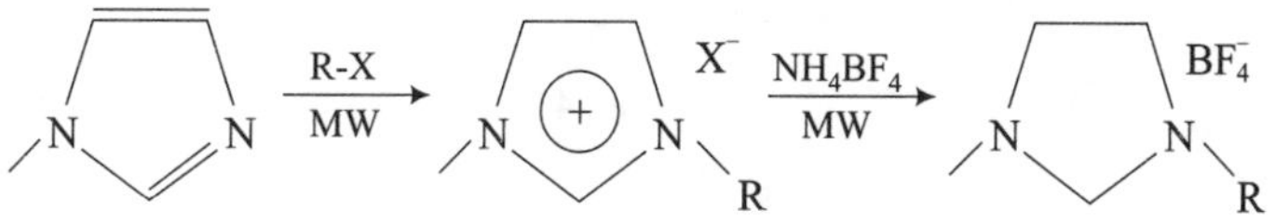

Scheme 3

The above solvent free approach requires only a few minutes of reaction time using an unmodified MW oven in contrast to several hours needed under conventional heating condition (Scheme 3)[33,42]. This process precludes to usage of volatile organic solvent, is relatively faster, efficient and eco-friendly.

An recent improvement contrasts the MW approach and involves preparation of ionic-liquids almost at room temperature under ultrasonic irradiation conditions[43]. However the surge of interest continues with this class of solvent especially under MW irradiation conditions where potential recycling of the catalyst in enhanced as demonstrated for a high-speed Heck reaction in ionic liquid media with controlled MW heating[44]. A disussion on Heck reaction forms the subject matter of a subsequent section.

3.10   Ionic Liquids with Fluorine-Containing Anions

The synthesis, characterisation and properties of alkyl – substituted ammonium, imidazolium, triazolium and pyridinum salts with a verity of fluorine – containing anions has been described[45].

3.11   Typical Preparation Routes for Ionic Liquids

The most commonly and widely used method for the preparation of ionic liquid in metatheses of a halide salt of the organic cation with a group 1 or ammonium salt containing the desired anion. Scheme 4 describes the routes for the preparation of some typical ionic liquid[51].

Recently some new categories of ionic liquids have been prepared. These include ionic liquid based or polyammonium halide salt (can be synthesis by replacing the halide ion with phosphate ion[52]. Other ionic liquids with dicyanamide anion[53] and C_2-symmrtrical imidazolium cations[54] and even deplex DNA[55] anions have also been prepared.

4   SELECTION OF A SUITABLE IONIC LIQUID FOR A PARTICULAR REACTION

Not all type of ionic liquids are suitable for all type of reaction. To give an example, imidazolium based ionic liquid should not be used with bases. This can be understood by the following reactions.

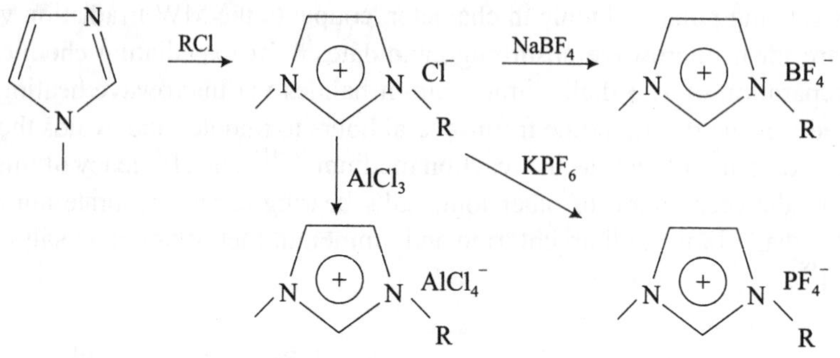

Scheme 4

4.1 Formation of N-Heterocyclic Carbenes

It is well Known that the C(2)-proton of the $1,3$-dialkylimidazolium cation is acidic and can be exchanged under mild conditions (Scheme 5)[56].

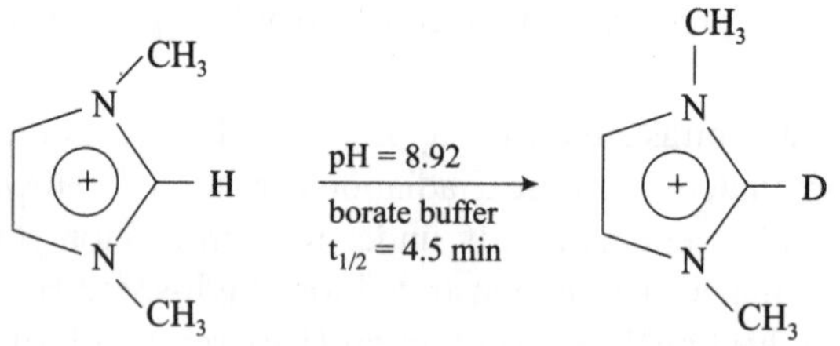

Scheme 5

A stable carbene is formed by the deprotonation of 1, 3-dialkylimidazolium cation; the carbene is strongly stabilized due to the presence of adjacent nitrogen atoms (Scheme 6)

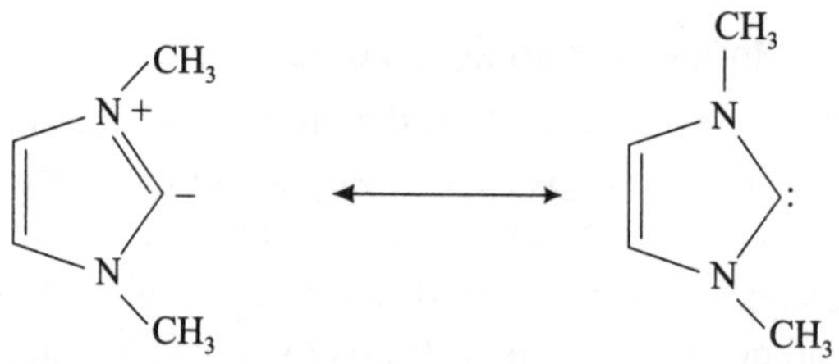

Scheme 6

A break through was achieved[57,58] by isolating and fully characterizing a stable singlet N-hetro cyclic carbene, 1, 3 –di –1- adamantylimidazol –2 –ylidene by deprotonation of an imidiazolium salt (Scheme 7)

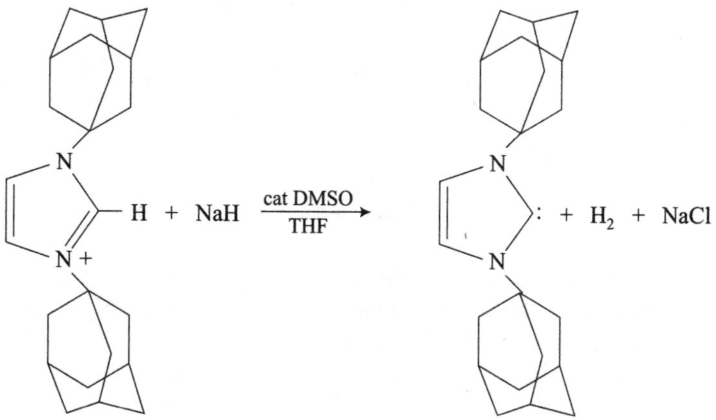

Scheme 7

The acidity of the C(2) hydrogen in 1,3-dialkyl imidazolium salts and the basicity of the resulting N-heterocyclic carbenes have significant implications in the chemistry of ionic liquids[59]. Thus it becomes obvious that imidazolium-based ionic liquids are likely to be unstable under basic conditions and due precaution must be taken in interpreting results obtained in reactions studied in such ionic liquids under basic conditions. A discussion on task-specific ionic liquids (TSILS) forms the subject matter of a subsequent section (Section 6).

4.2 The Baylis-Hillman Reaction in Ionic Liquids

This reaction generally involves a tertiary amine catalysed coupling between the α-position of an activated alkene with an aldehyde (Scheme 8)[60]. Though a number of 3° amines have been used for the above reaction, the base of choice is diazabicyclo [2. 2. 2] octane (DABCO).

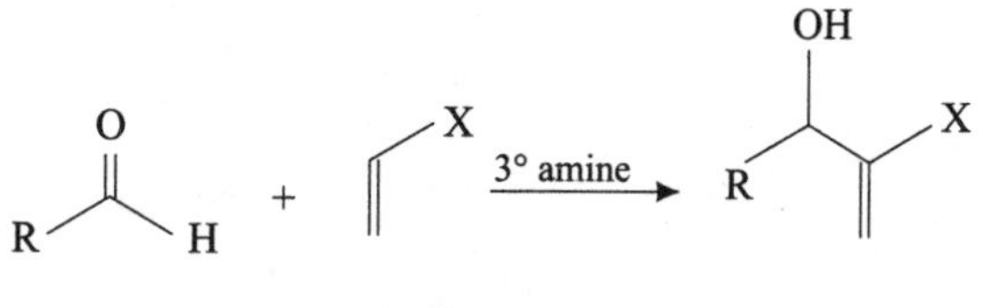

X = electron withdrawing group

Scheme 8

Though the Baylis-Hillman reaction is 100 per cent atom economical, it suffers from slow reaction rates often requiring several days for completion. Attempts to accelerate the reaction by using ultrasound[61], microwave irradiation[62] and the use of lewis acids[63] were unsuccessful. It is believed that the Baylis-Hillman reaction proceeds via an addition-elimination mechanism; the formed zwitterionic species such as (A) attacks the aldehyde to give the product (Scheme 9).

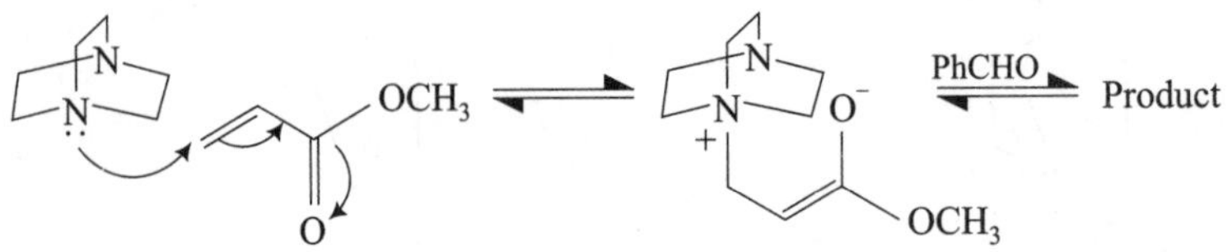

Scheme 9

The Baylis-Hillman reaction between benzaldehyde and methyl acrylate in the ionic liquid [bmim] [PF_6] was found to be 33 times faster than the reaction in CH_3CN, although only moderate yield of the desired produced was obtamed (Scheme 10)[63].

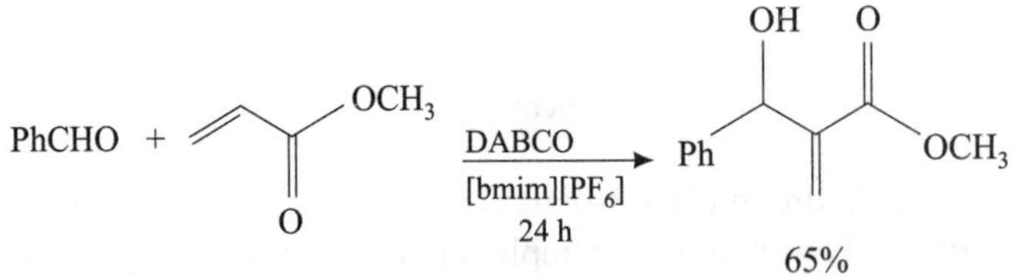

Scheme 10

It was, however, found[63] that under basic reaction conditions, the aldehyde was being consumed in a side reaction with the imidazolium cation. This accounts for low yields and also demonstrated that ionic liquids are not always inert solvents[65]. It was shown that the acidic nature of the C(2) hydrogen of the imidazolium cation was responsible for the side reaction (Scheme 11).

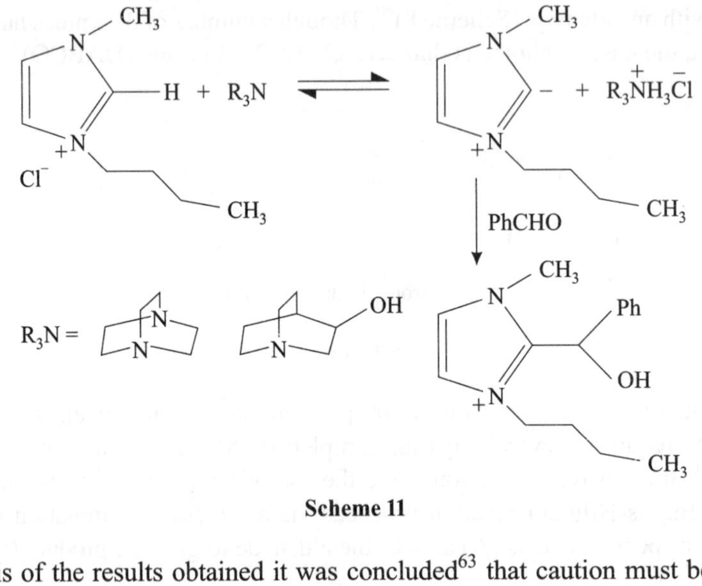

Scheme 11

On the basis of the results obtained it was concluded[63] that caution must be exercised when using ionic liquids from one reaction for another; in such a case mixture of producet were obtained.

In order to overcome the problem of low yields due to formation of side reaction product (because of the acidity of C(2) imidazolium cation), ionic liquids substituted at the 2-position were used[66]. It was found[66] that the Baylis-Hillman reaction between a variety of aldehydes and methyl acrylate proceeded smoothly in the ionic liquid [bmmin][PF$_6$], in contrast to results obtained with [bmin][PF$_6$] (Scheme 12).

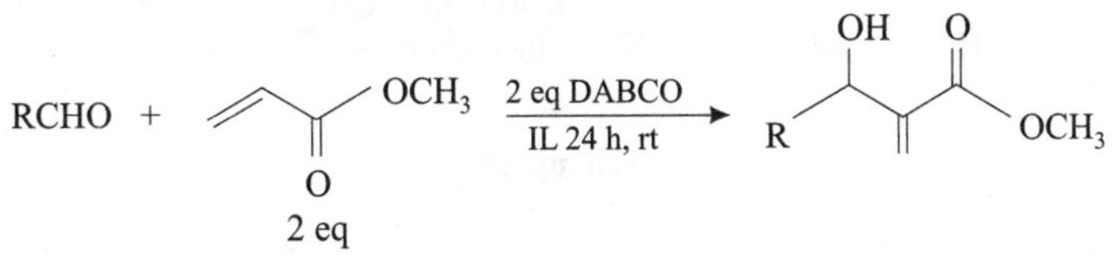

Scheme 12

The substitution at the 2-position of the imidazolium cation does prevent the side reaction in the Baylis-Hillman reaction, it has, however been found even the 2-methyl substituted imidazolium cation is not completely inert[67]. It has been found that the 2 methyl group undergoes slow proton exchange even in the presence of a weak base such as triethyl amine (Scheme 13).

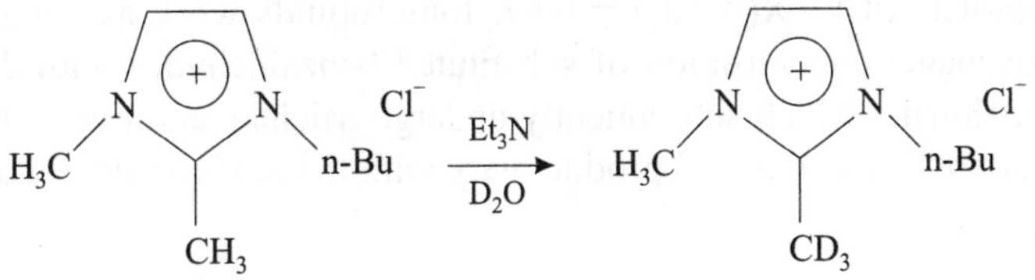

$$k = 0.04 \times 10^{-3} \, \text{min}^{-1}$$

Scheme 13

Further evidence for the acidic nature of this methyl group is obtained by the attempted methylation of the imidazolium salt with CH$_3$I in presence of NaH. The expected product from methylation of the imidazolium salt at C-2 was not even detected; instead the product was the corresponding 2-ethyl substituted imidazole (Scheme 14).

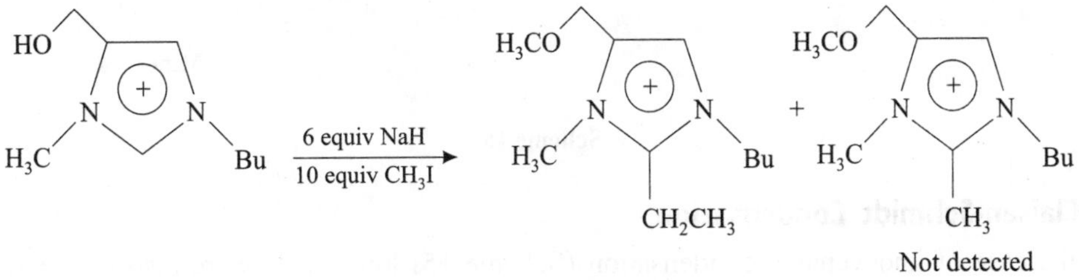

Scheme 14

4.3 The Knoevenagel Condensation

The knoevenagel condensation reaction of benzaldehyde with malonoitrile in presence of KOH dissolved in [bmim][PF$_6$] gave[68] only low yield of the styrene product (Scheme 15)

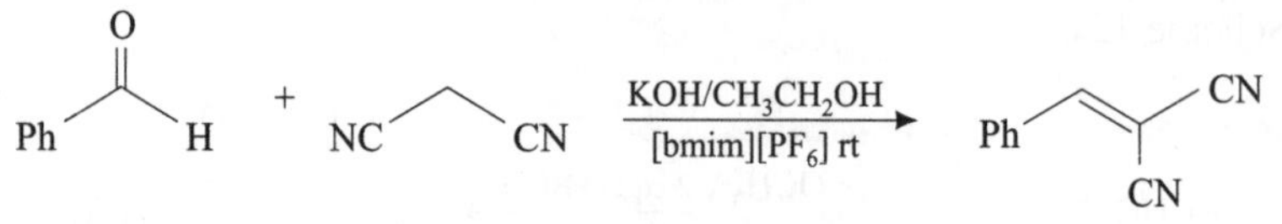

Scheme 15

The low yield in the above knoevenagel condensation was due to the solubility to the formed product (styrene derivative) in the ionic liquid. The yield improved as the substrate concentration was increased and also as the ionic liquid was reused. The ionic liquid could be reused up to five times without the need of additional base.

Kneovenagel condensation can also be carried out by using chloroaluminate ionic liquids[69], which have a variable lewis acidity such as 1-butyl-3-methylimidazolium chloroaluminate [bmim]Cl. AlCl$_3$, X(AlCl$_3$) = 0.67, were X is the molefraction and 1-butyl pyridinium chloroaluminate [bpy]Cl. AlCl$_3$, X(AlCl$_3$) = 0.67. Ionic liquids work as lewis acid catalyst and solvent in the kneovenagel condensation of substituted benzaldehydes with diethyl malonate to gives benzylidene malonate, which subsequently undergo Michael addition with diethyl malonate (Scheme 16). The extent of the Michael product vary with the lewis acidity and the molar proportion of the ionic liquids.

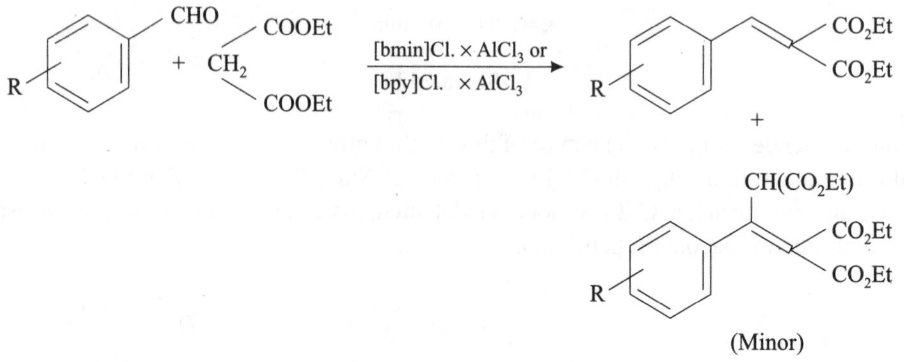

Scheme 16

4.4 Claisen-Schmidt Condensation

As in the case of knoevenagel condensation (Scheme 15) low yields were also obtained in the Claisen-Schmidt condensation between acetophenone and benzaldehyde (Scheme 17). However, in this case, ethyl benzoate was obtained as a byproduct and the base was depleted after two cycles of reuse of the ionic liquid.

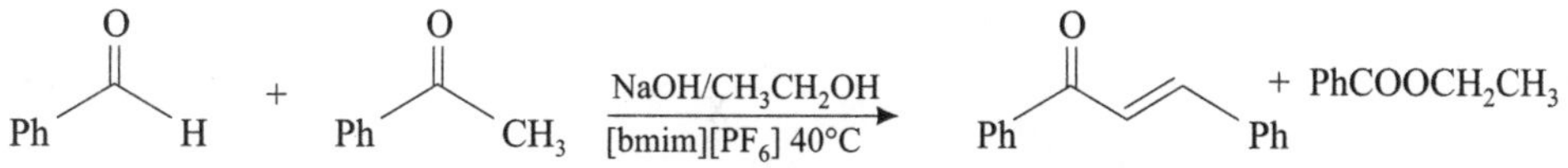

Scheme 17

In the reaction of the ionic liquid with the base in the absence of the substrates, the base was being consumed by reaction with imidiazolium cation. This reaction was more pronounced at elevated temperature and so it was less of a problem in catalytic knovenagel condensation, which was carried out at room temperature. It was also shown on the basis of controlled experiments, that the source of ethyl group was sodium ethoxide and not ethanol.

On the basis of the results obtained of was concluded that imidazolium ionic liquid are suitable under basic condition, only in a few reactions and precaution must be taken when reactions are carried out using these ionic liquids in conjunction with bases especially at higher temperatures.

4.5 The Horner-Wadsworth-Emmons Reaction in Ionic Liquids

The Horner-Wadsworth-Emmons reaction between aldehydes and phosphonoacetates in both [emim][BF$_4$] and [emin][PF$_6$] gave low yield of either of the products (Scheme 18)[70]. The low yields are due to incompatibility of imidazolium–based ionic liquids with the strongly basic reaction conditions.

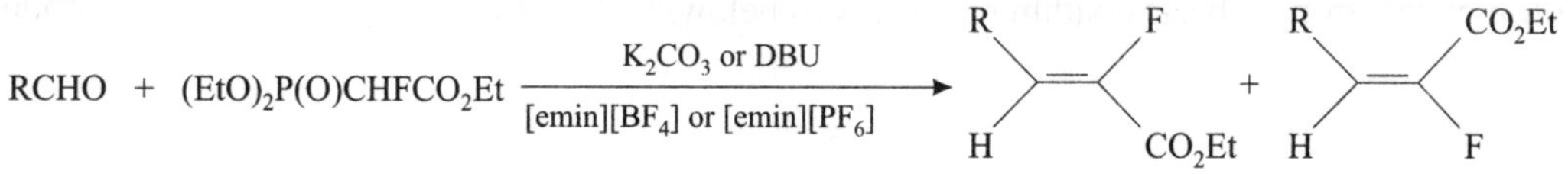

Scheme 18

The yield of the product increased considerably if the reaction be carried out in the ioic liquids 8-ethyl – 1, 8- diazabicyclo [5, 4, 0] –7-undecene trifluoromethane sulfonate (A) and 8- methyl –1, 8- diazabicyclo [5, 4, 0] –7-undecene trifluoromethane sulfonate (B) (Scheme 19).

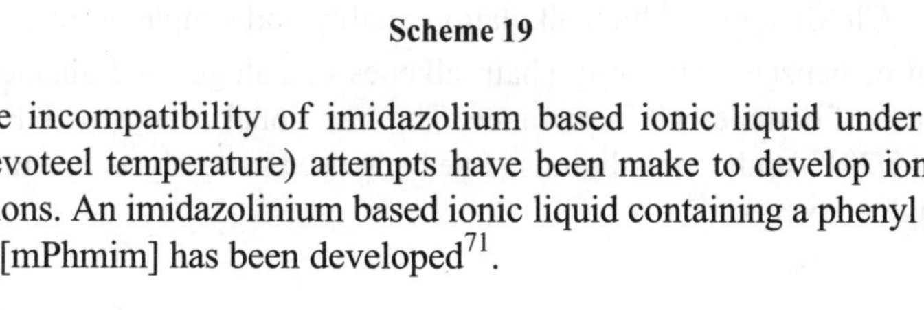

(A)   (B)

Scheme 19

In vew of the incompatibility of imidazolium based ionic liquid under basic conditions (partriularly at elevoteel temperature) attempts have been make to develop ionic liquids for use under such conditions. An imidazolinium based ionic liquid containing a phenyl group at the C (2) position [cation = [mPhmim] has been developed[71].

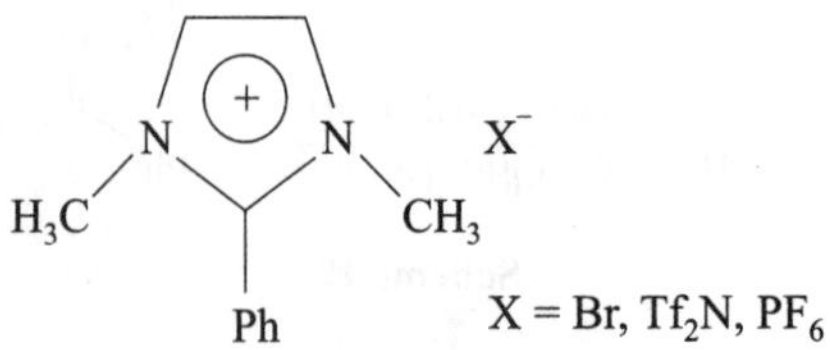

$$X = Br, Tf_2N, PF_6$$

Thus, the Baylis-Hillman reaction between methyl acrylate and a variety of aromatic aldehyles using DABCO or quinuclidinol as the base was successfully carried out in these ionic liquids. Ionic liquid[mPh mim][Tf$_2$N] was also shown to be a suitable solvent for Grignard reaction(Scheme 20). It was shown that the ionic liquid did not undergo any deprotonation under the reaction conditions.

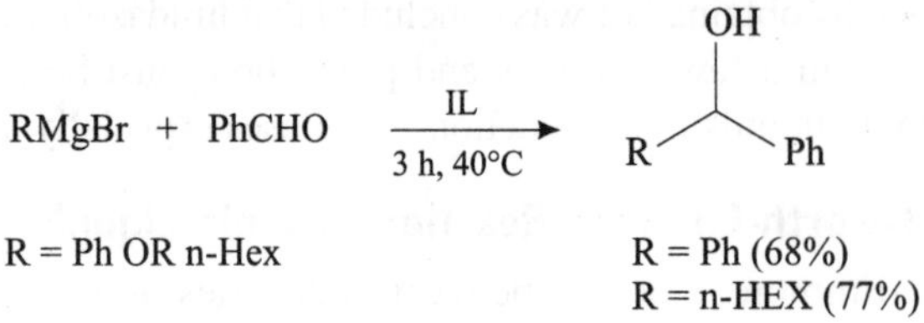

RMgBr + PhCHO $\xrightarrow[\text{3 h, 40°C}]{\text{IL}}$

R = Ph OR n-Hex

R = Ph (68%)
R = n-HEX (77%)

Scheme 20

Another phosphonium-based ionic liquid such as tetradecyl (trihexyl) phosphorium chloride for use under strongly basic conditions[72] is given below.

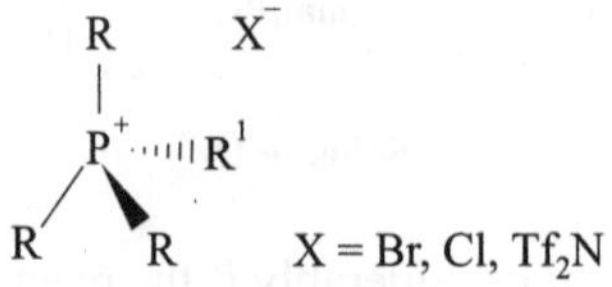

$$X = Br, Cl, Tf_2N$$

The inertness of the above ionic liquid towards reaction with bases is primarily due to the difficulty in accessing the acidic hydrogen.

5 SYNTHETIC APPLICATIONS

5.1 Alkylation

The alkylation of isobutene with 2-butene to give isooctane, which can be converted to a methoxyether for use as a fuel additive to increase octane number, is a commercially important reaction. Traitionally used catalysts for the reaction are HF or H$_2$SO$_4$ which are non green processes because of cooling and preparation problems, high operating costs and safety aspects. The use of ionic liquid [bmim] CI/AICl$_3$ give[73] high alkylation quality and simple product separation.

The alkylation of benzene with long chain alkenes or halogenated alkanes to produce liner alkylbenzenes is also of commercial importance. The traditional catalyst is HF or AICl$_3$(catalyst/olefin mole ratio = 5/20). Acidic ionic liquids have been used as catalysts in a ratio as low as about 0.004 with very high conversion[74].

An efficient alkylation of the ambident nucleophiles, indole and 2-naphthol has been carried out with simple alkyl halides at room temperature in [bmin]PF_6 using solid KOH to give exclusively N-alkyated and O-alkylated products respectively[75].

The alkylation of active methylene compounds is an important reaction for formation of C-C bonds. A room temperature ionic liquid, N-butylpyridinium tetrafluoroborate [bpy][BF_4] has been used as recyclable solvent for the alkylation of Meldrum's acid[76]. with various alkyl halides at 60-70°C in presence of triethylamine as base, exclusively dialkylated products are obtained (Scheme 21)

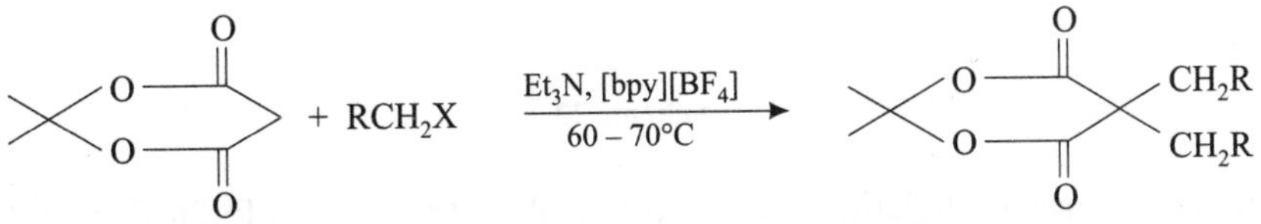

Scheme 21

5.2 Allylation

The palladium (O) catyzed allylation of methylene compound by 1,3-diphenylallyl acetate in [bmin] BF_4 proceeds smoothly with easy recycling of catalyst and solvent[77]. In ionic liquids, the stabilized intermediate may be generated in situ and is a "greener" alternative to conventional process where volatile organic solvents are frequently employed and catalyst reuse is difficult to implement.

5.3 Hydroformylation

Hydroformylation of olefins is another industrially important reaction. The reaction is carried out in aqueous –organic biphasic system catalyzed by water soluble Rh catalyst. But the use of water as polar phase limits this process to C_2-C_5 olefins due to low water solubility of higher olefins. This solubility problem is overcome by using ionic liquids containing PF_6^-, SBF_6^- and BF_4^- in an ionic liquid-organic biphasic system[78-83]. The products are separated as an organic phase and the catalyst can also be used. A small amount of catalyst leachging into organic phase causes some loss in activity after each run. These problems have been improved by varying the ligand and the ions of ionic of ionic liquids[84-86].

The platinum catalysed hydroformylation of 1-octene in chlorostannate melts in [bmim] [CI] give high n/iso selectivities[87]. The biphasic nature of the reaction enabled a very simple product isolation and leaching of the platinum catalyst into the product phase was not observed (Scheme 22)

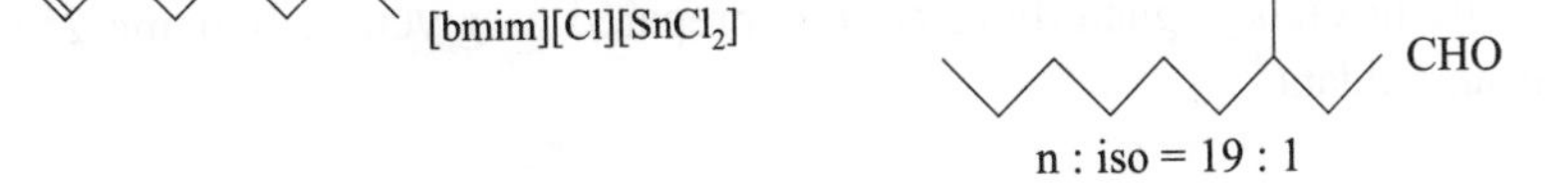

n : iso = 19 : 1

Scheme 22

5.4 Alkoxycarbonylation

Palladium catalyzed alkoxy carbonylation of aryl halides in ionic liquids[bmim] [BF_4] and [bmim][PF_6] has been reported[88]. High reactivity was observed in ionic liquids as compared to those in alcohols. High regio selectivities(99.5%) were achieved for the branched ester (Scheme 23)

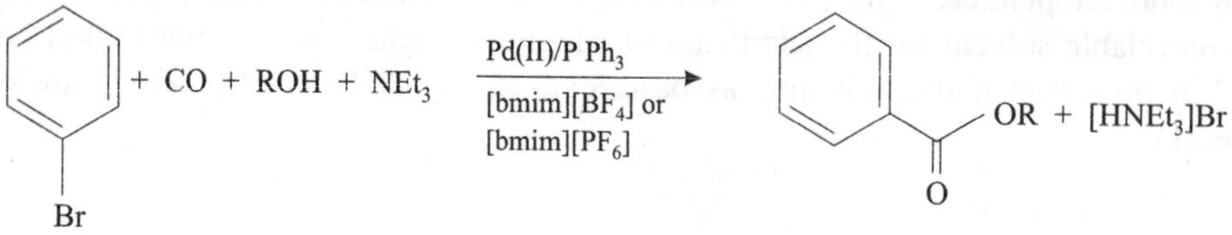

$$
\text{(C}_6\text{H}_5\text{Br)} + CO + ROH + NEt_3 \xrightarrow[\substack{\text{[bmim][BF}_4\text{] or} \\ \text{[bmim][PF}_6\text{]}}]{Pd(II)/P\,Ph_3} \text{(C}_6\text{H}_5\text{C(=O)OR)} + [HNEt_3]Br
$$

Scheme 23

The intramolecular carbonylation of alkynols catalyzed by Pd (II)/PyPh$_2$P. complex immobilized in [bmim][BF_4] or [bmim][PF_6] affored selectivity exomethylene five membered or sixmembered lactones in high yields[89].

5.5   Oxidations

5.5.1   Oxidation of alkyl groups

A number of transition metal-catalysed oxidation reactions have been performed in low-melting imidazolium and pyridinium ionic liquids. Thus ethyl benzene could be oxidised by bis (acetylacetonato) nickel immoblised in the ionic liquid [bmim][PF_6] at atmospheric presure[90]. This catalyst system is an important alternative to the heterogeneous catalyst presently used.

5.5.2   Oxidation of aldehydes

A number of aromatic aldehydes have been oxidised to the corresponding carboxylic acids using bis (acetyacetonato) nickel (II) immobilized in [bmim][BF_6] and oxygen at atmospheric pressure (Scheme 24)[91]

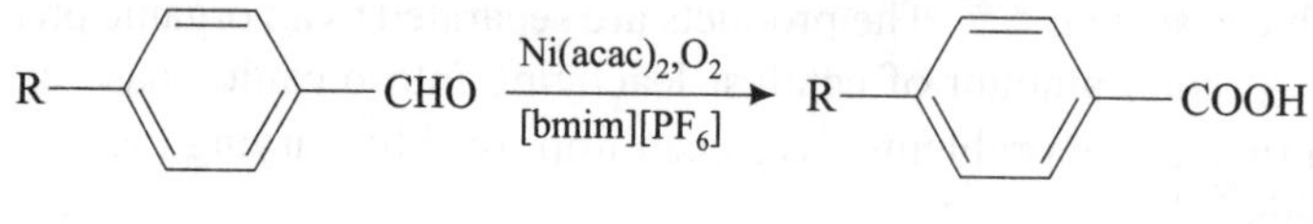

$$
R\text{—(C}_6\text{H}_4\text{)—CHO} \xrightarrow[\text{[bmim][PF}_6\text{]}]{Ni(acac)_2,O_2} R\text{—(C}_6\text{H}_4\text{)—COOH}
$$

Scheme 24

5.5.3   Oxidation of alcohols

Oxidation of alcohols to the corresponding aldehydes and ketones is an important functional group transformation in organic synthesis. Thus benzyl alcohol could be oxidised selectively to benzaldehyde in dry ionic liquids using Pb(OAc)$_2$ as a catalyst and O$_2$ as oxidant[92].

Selective oxidation of a series of substituted benzyl alcohol was carried out in a room temp. ionic liquid, cyclic hexaalkyl guanidium cation (prepared as given in Scheme 25) with sodium hypochlorite as an oxidant[93].

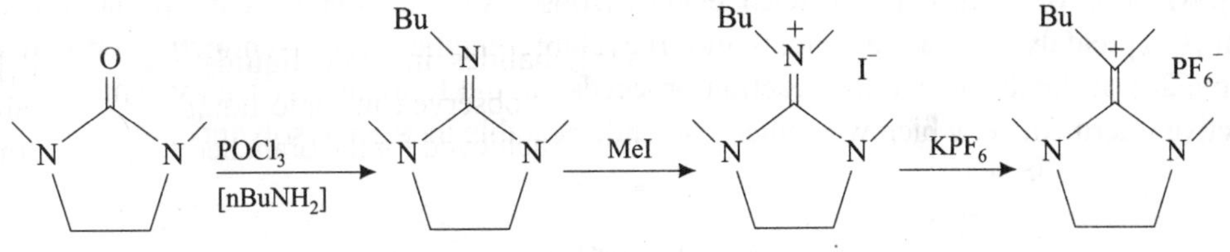

Scheme 25

The classical oxidation of alcohols promoted by tetra-N-propylammonium perruthenate has also been carried out in tetraethylammonium bromide or [bmim][BF$_4$][94]. In this case the ionic liquid was used to remove or extract excess MnO$_2$ and other associated impurities from the oxidation of codeine methyl ether to thebaine (Scheme 26)[95].

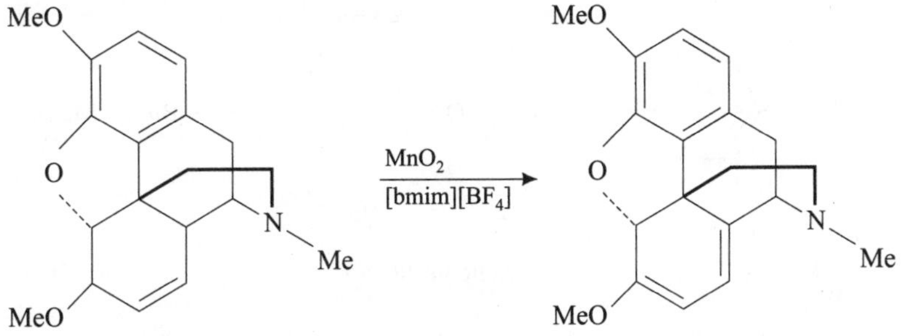

Codeine methyl ether   Thebaine

Scheme 26

The selective oxidation of primary and secondary benzlic alcohol with KMnO$_4$ in ionic give carbonyl compounds (See Section 7.24)

5.5.4 Oxidation of Oximes

A efficient and eco-friendly method for the chemoselective oxidative cleavage of oximes with H$_2$O$_2$ catalysed by phosphotungstic acid in ionic liquid at room temperature to generate the corresponding carbonyl compound in excellent yield has been developed (Scheme 27)[13].

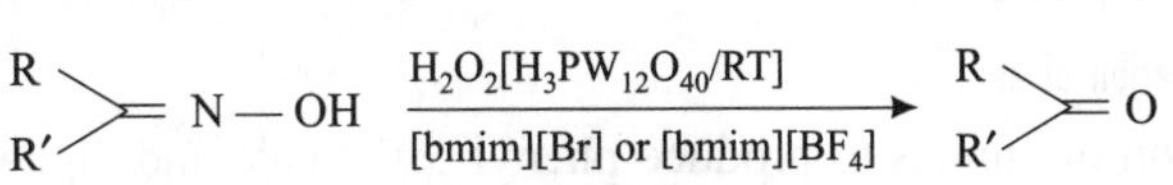

Scheme 27

5.5.5 Oxidation of olefins

5.5.5.1 Epoxidation

Alkenes and allylic alcohols could be oxidized to the corresponding epoxides in high yield[96], using a room temperature ionic liquid as the solvent, methyltrioxorhenium (MTO) as the catalyst and urea-hydrogen peroxide (UHP) as the oxidant, both of which were completely soluble in [bmim][PF$_6$] (giving a homogeneous solvent).

Epoxidation of olefins with NaOCl using Jacobsen's chiral Mn(III) salen immobilized in a [bmim][PF$_6$] catalyst is an efficient and recyclable method for asymmetric epoxidation[97] (Scheme 28). In ionic solvent, the reaction proceeds via the formation of high valent manganese-oxo active intermediate, which was otherwise undetecatable in organic solvent[98].

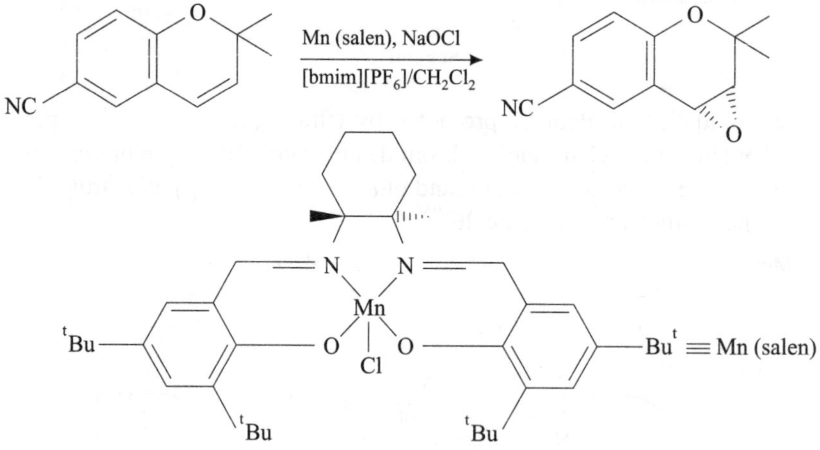

Scheme 28

Room temperature based catalysed epoxidation of electrophilic alkenes with H$_2$O$_2$ in ionic liquids as solvent has been disussed subsequently [See Section 7.23].

5.5.5.2 Asymmetric Dihydroxylation of Olefins

Osmium catalysts have been used in asymmetric dihydroxylation reactions of olefins. The high cost and toxicity of, and contamination of the product with the osmium catalyst, however, restrict the use of the asymmetric dihyroxylation reaction in industry. This problem is now overcome by making use of ionic liquids. The reaction is carried out either in biphasic [bmim][PF$_6$]/ water or monophasic [bmim] [PF$_6$]/tert. butanol system. Both procedures were applied to substrates using the chiral ligands. This method allows the recycling and reuse of the osmium ligand catalyst. The use of the supercritical carbon dioxide extraction helped in minimizing the osmium leaching from the room temperature ionic liquid phase[13].

5.5.5.3 Oxidative carbonylation of amines

Oxidative carbonylation of amines to produce phenyl carbamate and diphenyl urea has normally been achieved by alkali metal containing selenium compounds as effective catalyst[99]. The main disadvantage in this reaction is the difficulty in separating the product and the catalyst from the reaction mixture. This problem was solved by preparing ionic liquids containing anionic selenium species; these were found to show a high activity[100] for the carbonylation of aniline, at temperatures as low as 40°.

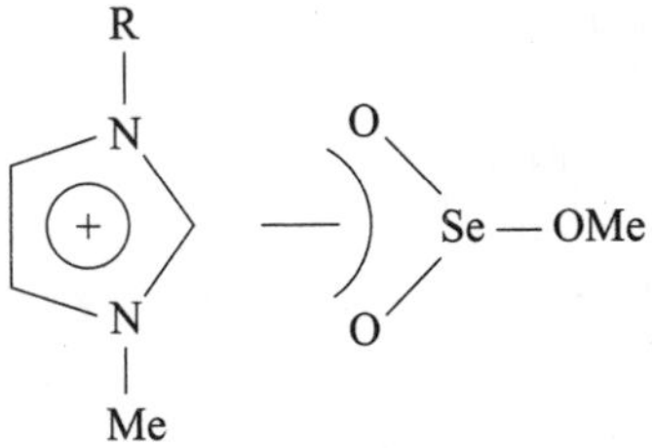

Selenium-anion based imidazolium ionic liquid

5.5.5.4 Wacker-type oxidation reactions

Wacker-Type oxidation reaction have been performed by $PdCl_2$ immobilised in [bmim][BF$_4$] and [bmim][PF$_6$] using H_2O_2 as the oxidant (Scheme 29)[101].

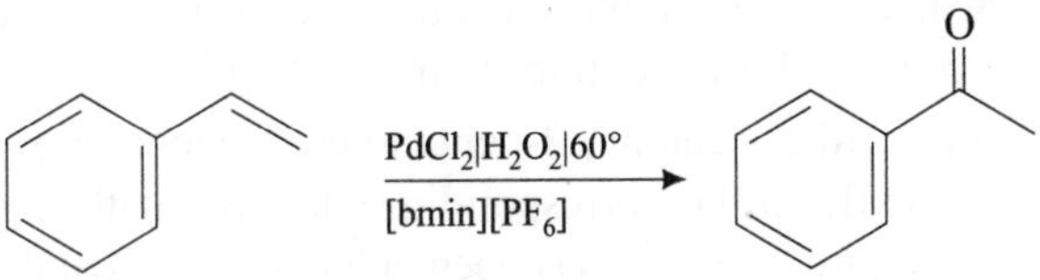

Scheme 29

5.6 Hydrogenations

Butene-1 on hydrogenation using ionic equids such as [bmim][BF$_4$], [bmim][PF$_6$] and [bmim][SbF$_6$] as solvent and using Wilkinson's catalyst (Scheme 30)[102-104] gave the reduced product.

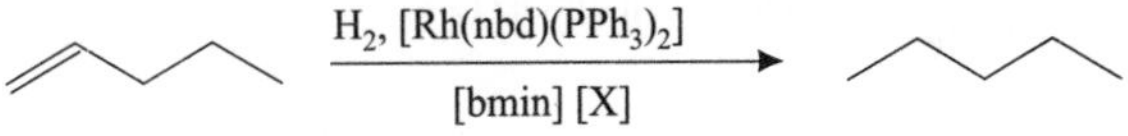

$X = BF^-_4$, PF^-_6, $Sb\ F^-_6$, nbd = norboranadeine

Scheme 30

The product obtained being not miscible with the ionic catalyst solution could be removed from the reaction mixture by simple decantation and the recovered ionic catalyst solvent was reused several times without any significant change in catalyst activity and selectivity.

A stereoselective ruthenium-catalysed hydrogenation of sorbic acide to cis–3-hexanoic acid was carried out in [bmim][PF$_6$]/MTBE (MTBE = methyl t-butyl ether) system (Scheme 31)[105].

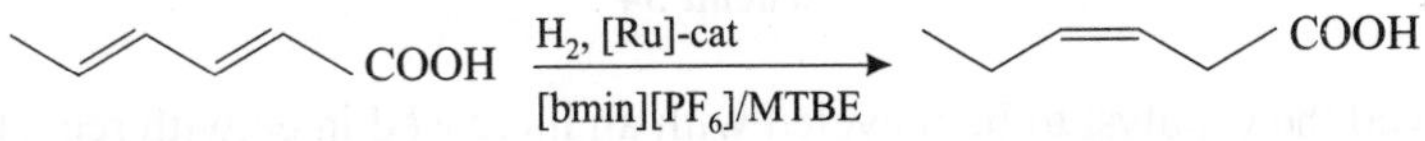

Sorbic acid   cis-3-hexanoic acid

Scheme 31

Hydrogenation of 1, 3-butadline to but-1-ene was found to be highly selective using Pd Nan particles in [C_4 mim][BF_4](Scheme 32)[106].

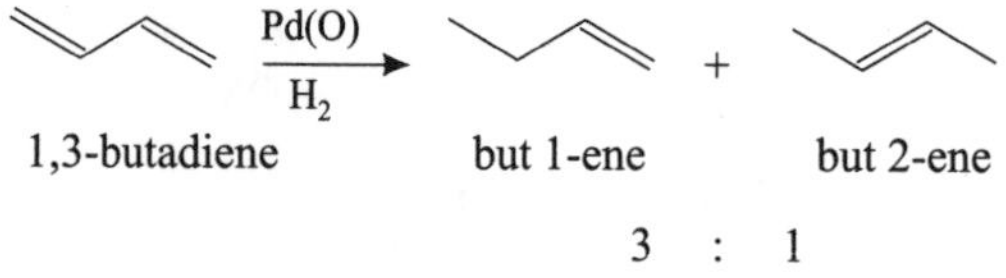

1,3-butadiene   but 1-ene   +   but 2-ene

3 : 1

Scheme 32

Phenanthroline ligand-protected palladium nanoparticles in [C_4mim][PF_6] have been shown to be very active and selective for the hydrogenation of C_6-olefins (hex-1-ene, cyclohexene, cyclohexadiene) at low temperature and low pressure of hydrogen[107]

Paladium nanoparticles, prepared frome mixture of [N_{4444}]Br, nBr_3N and $PdCl_2$ or $pd(OAc)_2$ are reported to be catalyically active for the chemoselective hydrogenation of carbon-carbon double bonds the presence of benzyloxy group in [C_4mim][PF_6][108].

Hydrogenation of ketones, like Acetone, 2-pentanone, 3-pentanone, 4-methyl-2-pentanone, cydopentanone and benzaldehyde to the corresponding alcohols with high TOFs using iridium nanoparticles stabilized by [C_4mim] [PF_6][109] has been achieved. The catalyst was prepared by the reduction of [Ir(Cod)Cl_2] in the ionic liquid and found to be recyclable catalytic system.

An enantroselective hydrogenation of α-acetamidocinnamic acid using [Rh(cod){(−) − diop}][PF_6] catalyst in the biphasic system [C_4 mim] [SbF_6]/i-PrOH was found to yield (S)-N-acetyl phenylalanine in 64% ee (Scheme 33)[110]

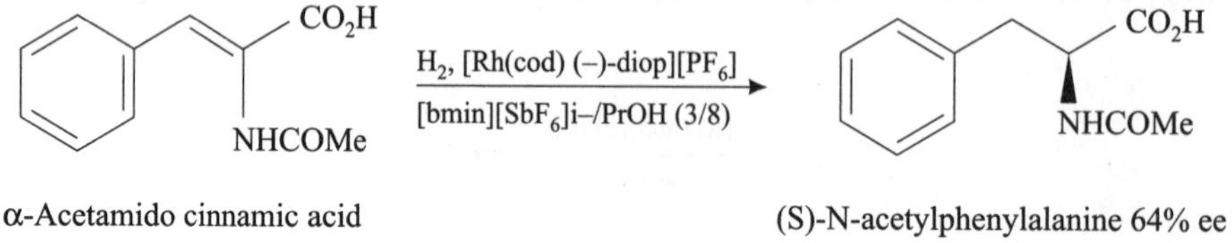

H$_2$, [Rh(cod) (−)-diop][PF_6]
[bmin][SbF_6]i–/PrOH (3/8)

α-Acetamido cinnamic acid   (S)-N-acetylphenylalanine 64% ee

Scheme 33

Hydrogenation of ethy actoacetate with the ammonium salt of 4. 4′- and 5, 5′-Rudiam BINAP in ionic liquids based on 1, 3-dialkyl imidazolium, N-alkylpyidinium and tetralkyl phosphonium cations occurred with moderate ee's (Scheme 34)[111]

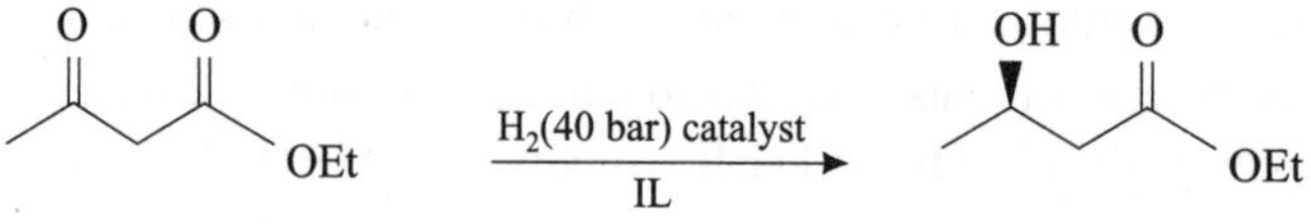

H$_2$(40 bar) catalyst
IL

Scheme 34

The 1L allowed the Catalyst to be recycled with an increased in ee with recycle number.

Halonitrobenzenes on hydrogenation with 5% Pt/c, Pd/C or Raney nickel catalyst to the corresponding Haloanilines could be achieved in $[BF_4]^-$ and $[PF_6]^-$ 1, 3-dialkylimidazolium based ionic liquids (Scheme 35)[112].

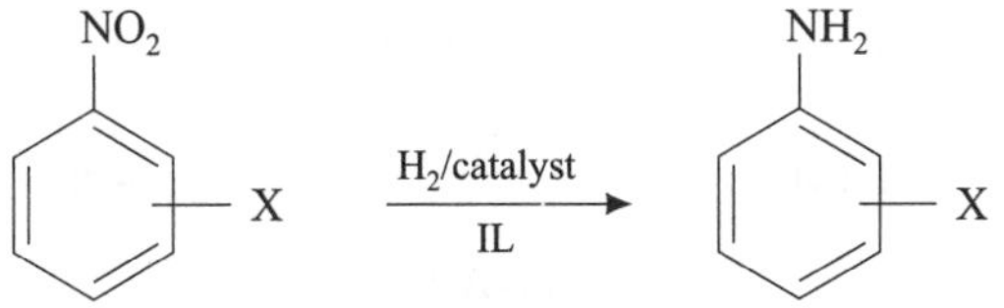

Scheme 35

The reaction of aliphatic and aromatic aldehydes with trialkylborane generally requires reaction temperature in excers of approx 150°. Ionic liquids like [b mim] $[BF_4]$ and [e mim] $[PF_6]$ can be used in trialkylborane reduction of aldehydes with enhanced rate at low temperature[113]. The organic products can be easily removed from the ionic liquid via extraction and the ionic liquid can be reused with no reduction in yield.

(For more on hydrogenation see Section 7.17.)

5.7 Carbon-carbon Bond Forming Reactions

Carbon-carbon bond formation is extremely important for synthetic organic chemist. Some of the carbon-carbon bond forming reactions like the Baylis-Hillman reaction (Section 4.2). Knoevenagel condensation (section 4.3) and the Horner-Wadsworth-Emmons reaction (Section 4.5) have already been discussed. Following are some of the other important carbon -carbon bond forming reactions.

5.7.1 Heck Reaction

The carbon-carbon coupling of an aryl or alkenyl halide with an olefin is known as the Heak reaction (Scheme 36)

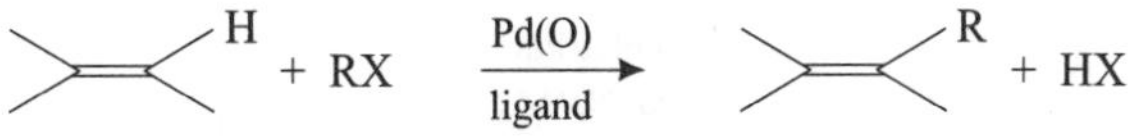

Scheme 36

Interst in the Heck reaction is due to versatility of the reaction and the relatively mild reaction condition used. In fact, Heck reaction has received a great attention in organic synthesis and in the manufacture of fine chemicals,[114, 115]. It has been found that the Heck reaction with less reactive halides (bromides and chlorides) require the use of phosphine liquids to stabilize the active palladium species. A drawback of the Heck reaction is that the palladium catalyst cannot be recovered and reused. Use of ionic liquids provide a convenient medium for the Heck reaction and also allows recyding of the catalyst[116]. In the Heck reaction of iodobenzene with ethylacrylate in both N-hexylpyidinium, [C_6py) and N, N-dialkylimidazolium based ionic liquid (Scheme 37), higher yields were obtained in the former ionic liquid then the corresponding reaction in the imidazolium salts.

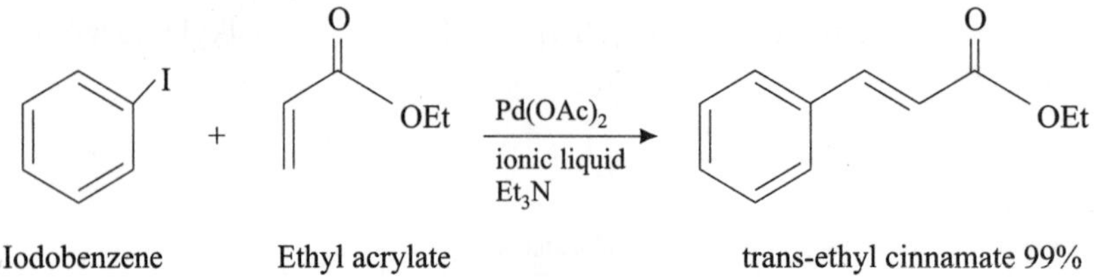

Iodobenzene   Ethyl acrylate   trans-ethyl cinnamate 99%

Scheme 37

The low yield in imidazolium ionic liquid is due to the formation of carbene (See Scheme 6) which reacts with palladium to form a mixture of palladium carbene complex.

The Heck reaction was also carried out by are reaction of aryl halides with acrylates as well as with styrene in presence of Pd (OAc)$_2$ in the ionic liquids [bmin] [BF$_4$] and [b mim][Br] (Scheme – 38)[117]

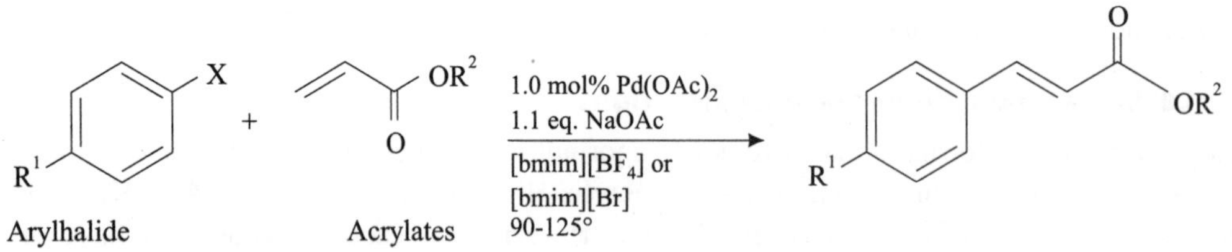

Arylhalide   Acrylates   90-125°

R^1 = H, CHO, COCH$_3$
R^2 = CH$_2$CH$_3$ OR n Bu

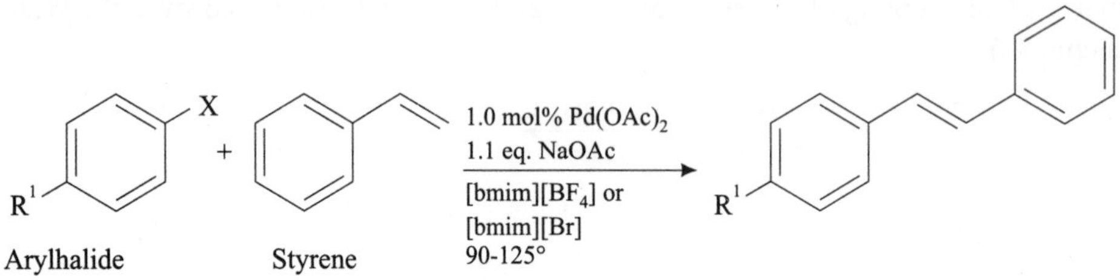

Arylhalide   Styrene   90-125°

R^1 = H, CHO, COCH$_3$

Scheme 38

Better conversion and selectivity was noted in reactions carried out in [b mim][Br]. However in both ionic liquids a homogeneous yellow solution was initially obtained, which was followed by slow precipitation of palladium black. The low yield in case of [bmim] [BF$_4$] was due to the formation of carbene intermediate which complexes with palladium to give a mixture of palladium carbene complex.

It was suggested[117] that the active catalyst in the Heck reaction is a palladium nanoparticle generated in situ from palladium-carbene species. It has also been shown[118] that solution of ammonium stabilized Pd clusters are useful catalyst for the Heck reaction. Thus, the Heck reaction between iodobenzere and n-butyl acrylate in the presence of $[N_{8.8.8.8}]$ [Br] stabilized 3nm Pd clusters to afford n-butyl cinnamate (Scheme 39).

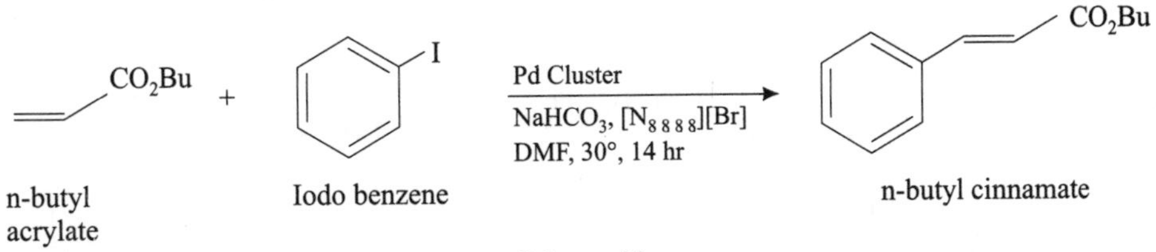

Scheme 39

5.7.2 Friedel-Craft Reaction

Friedel Craft alkylation and acylation are of great commercial importance. The conventional calayst in Friedel Craft reaction is $AlCl_3$ which gives rise to disposal and byproduct problems. The use of ionic liquid [e mim] $Cl-AlCl_3$ in place of solid $AlCl_3$ enhances the reaction rates and selectivity[119-125] and also it a solvent for the reaction. These reaction worked efficiently giving the slereoelectronically favored products. In acetyation reaction of naphthalene, the major product was the thermodynamically, unfavoured 1- isomer.

Friedel Craft alkylation of aromatic compounds with alkenes using Sc $(OTf)_3$ – ionic liquid system giving the benefits of simple procedure, easy recovery and reuse of catalyst, contributing to the development of environmentally benign and waste free process[126].

Some interesting examples of Fridel Craft reaction have been discussed subsequently (see sections 7.15, 7.16 and 7.20).

5.7.3 Diels-Alder Reaction

The great usefulness of Diels-Alder reaction lies in its high yield and high stereospecificity. Use of ionic liquids such as [bmim][BF$_4$], [bmin][ClO$_4$], [emin][CF$_3$SO$_3$] and [emin][PF$_6$] for Diels-Alder reaction between cyclopentadiene and methyl acrylate result in rate enhancement, high yields and strong endoseclectivities (Scheme 40)[127, 128].

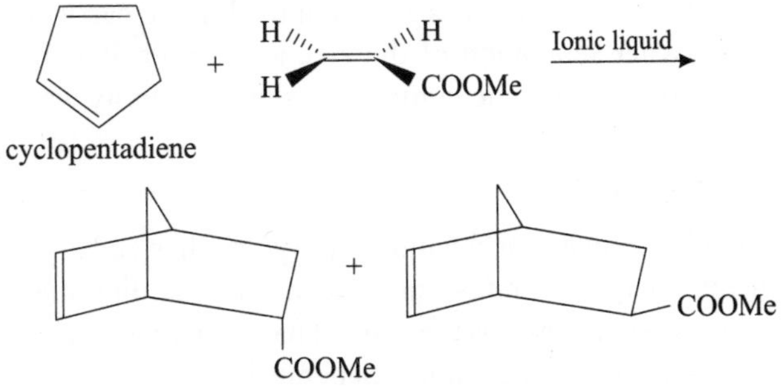

Scheme 40

5.7.4 *Aldol Condensation*

The self-condensation reaction of propanal to form 2-methylpent 2-enal has been carried out in non-coordinating imidazolium ionic liquid[129]. The reaction proceeded through an aldol intermediate and produced unsat'd aldehyde under the reaction condition (Scheme 41). In aldol condensation highest product selectivity was found for [bmim][PF$_6$].

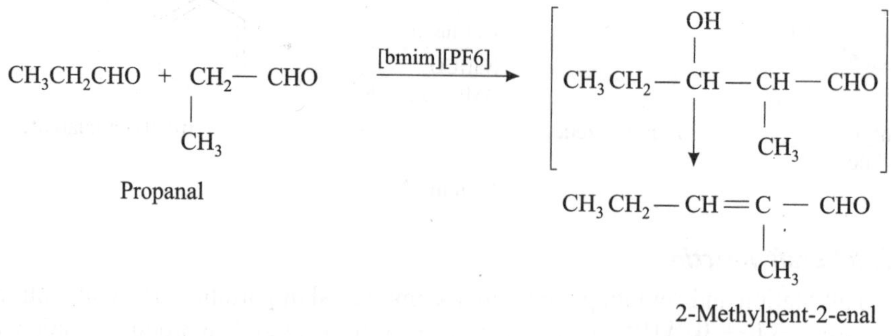

$$CH_3CH_2CHO \ + \ CH_2—CHO \xrightarrow{\text{[bmim][PF6]}}$$

(with CH$_3$ below the CH$_2$)

Propanal

$$\begin{bmatrix} & & & & OH \\ & & & & | \\ CH_3\,CH_2—CH—CH—CHO \\ & & & | \\ & & & CH_3 \end{bmatrix}$$

$$CH_3\,CH_2—CH=C—CHO$$
(with CH$_3$ below C)

2-Methylpent-2-enal

Scheme 41

The proline-catalysed asymmetric direct aldol reaction of different aromatic aldehydes with acetone and other ketones in the ionic liquid [bmim][PF$_6$] gave good yield of the aldol producet with reasonable enantioselectivies (Scheme 42)[130].

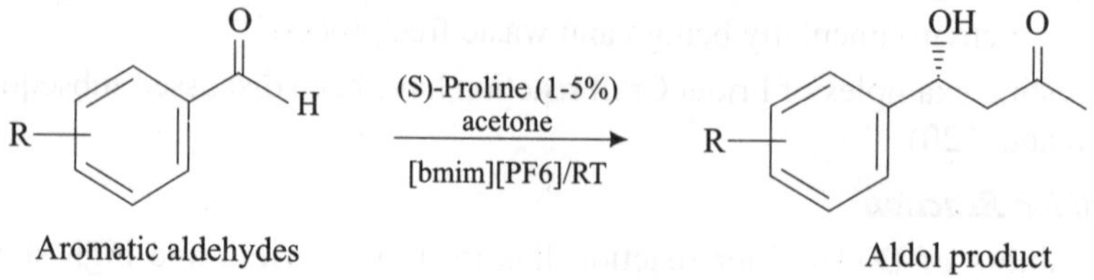

Aromatic aldehydes

(S)-Proline (1-5%)
acetone
[bmim][PF6]/RT

Aldol product

Scheme 42

5.7.5 *Wittig reaction*

The wittig reaction is the most popular method for C = C bond formation with high stereo control. The ionic liquid [bmim][PF$_4$] has been used as a solvent medium to carry out Wittig reaction using stabilized ylides allowing easier separation of the alkene from Ph$_3$PO and also recycling of the solvent[131]. In the Wittig reaction using ionic liquid the E-steroselectivity was observed as in the case of organic solvents.

5.7.6 *Suzuki Coupling Reaction*

Palladium catalysted coupling between aryl halides or aryl trifaltes and aryl boronic acids is a convenient method to generate biaryls[132] and is know as Suzuki coupling reaction. The Suzuki coupling using a Pd catalyst in an ionic liquid as the solvent has been repotted[133, 134] to give an excellent yield and turnover numbers at room temperature (Scheme 43).

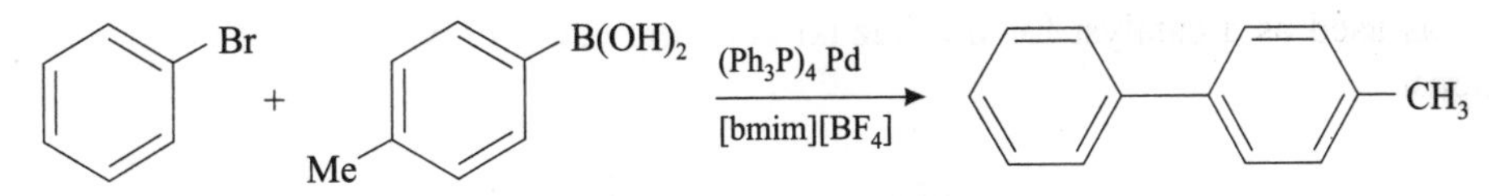

Bromobenzene   Tolyl boranic acid   p-Methyl biphenyl (92%)

Scheme 43

It was shown[135] that 1, 3-bis-(2, 4, 6-Trimethylphenyl) imidazol-2-ylidene (A) catalyzed the coupling raction between 4-chlorotoluene and phenyl boronic acid in dioxane at 80°. Since imidazol-2-ylidene carbenes are not very stable to air and moisture, the carbene ligand was generated in situ from the salt (A) using Cs_2CO_3 as the base (Scheme 44). The results suggested the involvement of N-heterocyclic carbene in Suzuki coupling.

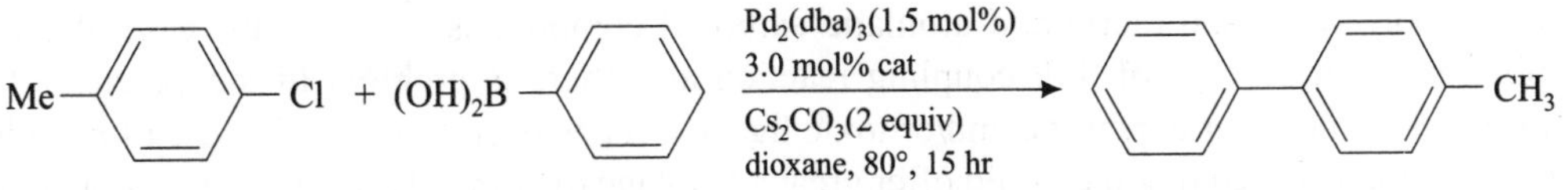

p-Chlorotoluene   Phenyl   p-Methyl biphenyl
               boronic acid

Scheme 44

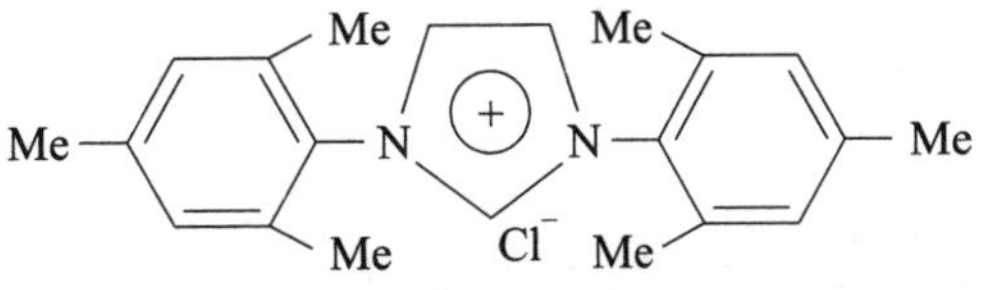

The Suzuki coupling reaction has also been carried art under mild conditions in an ionic liquid with methanol as a co solvent (necessary to solubilize the phenylboronic acid) using ultrasound[136] Scheme 45.

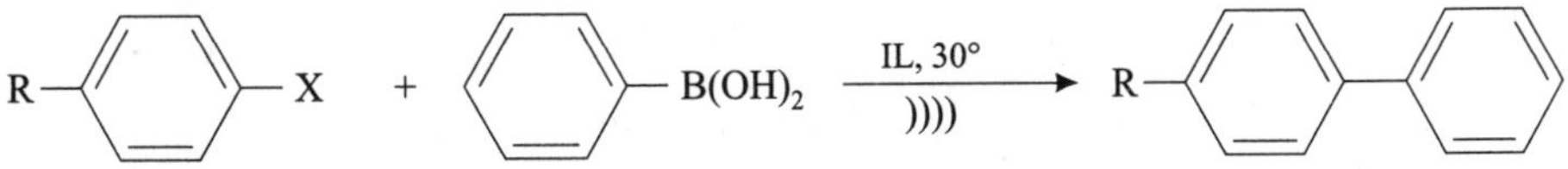

Halobenzenes   Phenyl   Substituted biphenyls
R = H, Cl, OCH_3,   boronic acid
     CH_3, NO_2
X = Br, Cl, I

Scheme 45

In the above reaction (Scheme 45) there was formation of inactive Pd black; this prevented the recycling of the catalyst. This problem was overcome by synthesing a Pd-biscarbene complex (B), which was used as a catalyst for the Suzuki coupling using only methanol under sonochemical conditions.

(B)

5.7.7   Still Coupling Reaction

The still coupling reaction is one of the most widely used in the preparation of a variety of materials including polyarenes and diaryl and aromatic carbonyl compounds[137]. As in the case of Suzuki coupling reaction, in case of Still coupling reaction also there is problem of the expense of the catalyst and the need for expensive and/or toxic ligands. It has been found[138] that use of palladium complexes immobilized in ionic liquid offer great advantage over the classical organic solvent used for Stille coupling reactions. A large number of stille coupling reactions with Pd(0) or Pd(II)catalyst procursors associated with Ph_3 As in the presence of CuI of has been developed in [b mim][BF_4] (Scheme 46)[138].

(Scheme-46)

5.7.8   Negishi Cross Coupling Reaction

The Negishi cross coupling reaction of organozinc reagents has been achieved in 1-butyl-2,3-dimethylimidazolium tetrafluoroborate ([bmim][BF_4]) ionic liquid using a novel phosphine (C) prepared by the reaction of PPh_2Cl with [b mim][PF_4] and is catalysed by palladium[139].

(C)

Better yields (70-92%) were obtained using different types of substrates; the fastest reaction was observed for aryl iodides. An additional advantage in Negishi cross coupling reaction is that ionic phase could be recycled thrice. However the yield of the product decreased in each cycle.

5.7.9 The Trost-Tsuji Coupling Reaction

This coupling reaction involved nucleophilic allylic substitution and is catalysed by Pd(0) complexes and is a convenient method to form C-C-bonds in organic synthesis. This reaction has also been preformol in ionic liquid using Pd(OAc)$_2$ – PPh$_3$/K$_2$CO$_2$ in [bmim] [BF$_4$][140] and PdCl$_2$ – TPPTS(TPPTS = triphenyl phosphine trisulphonate sodium salt) in [bmim][Cl]/cyclohexene[141] respectively (Scheme 47).

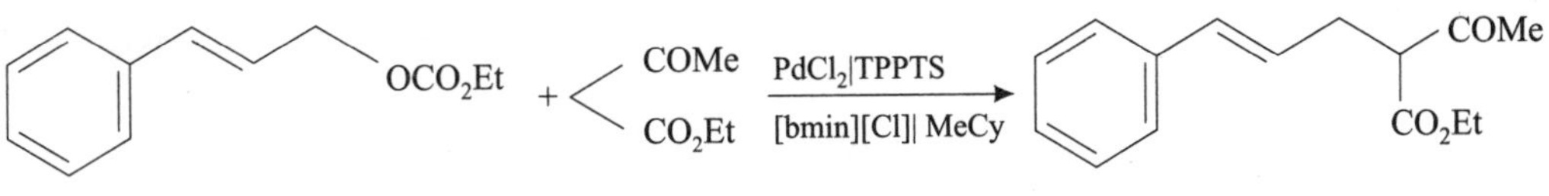

Scheme 47

5.7.10 Sakuai Reaction

α, β-Unsaturated ketones undergo the Sakuai reaction with allytrimethylsilane in presence of InCl$_3$ using, [C$_4$mim] [PF$_6$] or [C$_4$ mim][BF$_4$]as solvent (Scheme 48)[142].

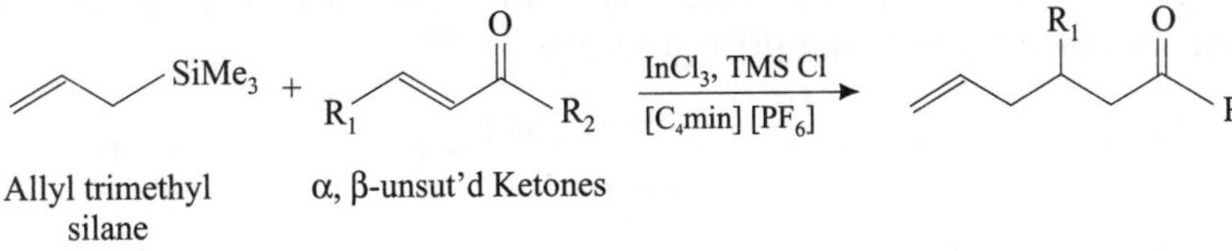

Scheme 48

5.7.11 Henry Reaction

Nitroalkanes having α-hydrogen atom undergo aldol type reaction with carbonyl compound to give β-hydroxy nitro compounds. This reaction known as Henry reaction[143], can be accelerated in chloroalumimate ionic liquids[144]. The tetra methyl guanidine (trifluoroacetate and lactate) –based ionic liquids was reported as a recyclable catalyst for Henry reaction to produce 2-nitroalcohols (Scheme 49)[145].

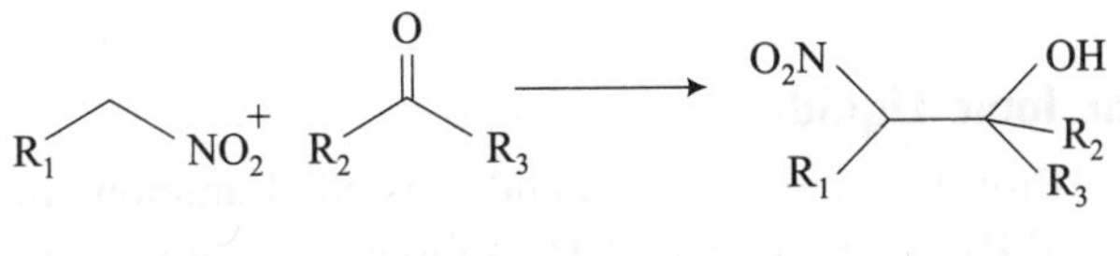

Scheme 49

5.7.12 Stetter Reaction

The reaction of aldehydes and olefins to give 1, 4-dicarbonyls is known as Stetter reaction. It is now possible to carry out the reaction in ionic liquid using Et$_3$N as catalyst (Scheme 50)[146].

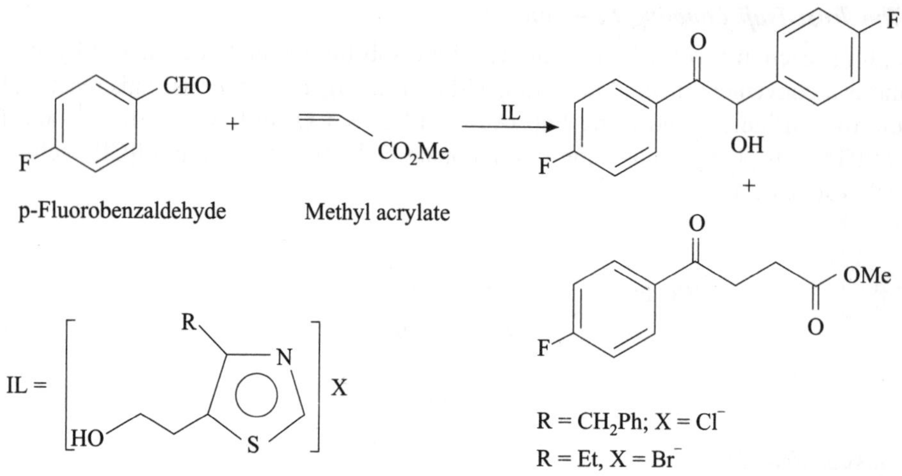

Scheme 50

5.7.13 Sonogashira Reaction

Copper and ligand free Sonogashira reaction catalysed by Pd(0) nanoparticles proceed under ultrasound irradiation in ionic liquid [bbmim][BF$_4$](Scheme 50a)[147]

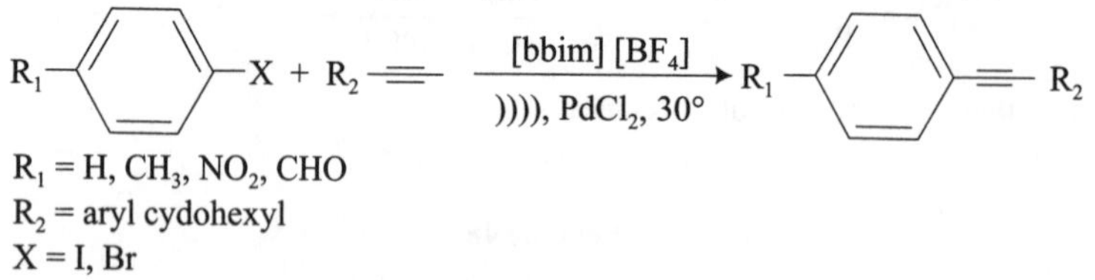

R_1 = H, CH$_3$, NO$_2$, CHO
R_2 = aryl cydohexyl
X = I, Br

Scheme 50a

6 TASK-SPECIFIC IONIC LIQUIDS (TSILs)

An increasing number of ionic liquids are being designed with a specitic activity in mind. These task-specific ionic liquids (TSILs) serve the dual role of catalyst and reaction medium. These are of two types, viz. Brønsted-acidic ionic liquids and Brønsted-basic ionic liquids. Besides the above two types of TSILs, we come across another type which is Lewis acid ionic liquids such as [cation][Cl$^-$/AlCl$_3$]

6.1 Brønsted Acidic Ionic Liquids

An early example of a Brønsted acidic ionic liquid[148] is ethyl ammonium nitrate. Subsequently acidic ionic liquids [I and II) containing an alkane sulfonic acid group covalently attached to the ionic liquid cation[149] were designed.

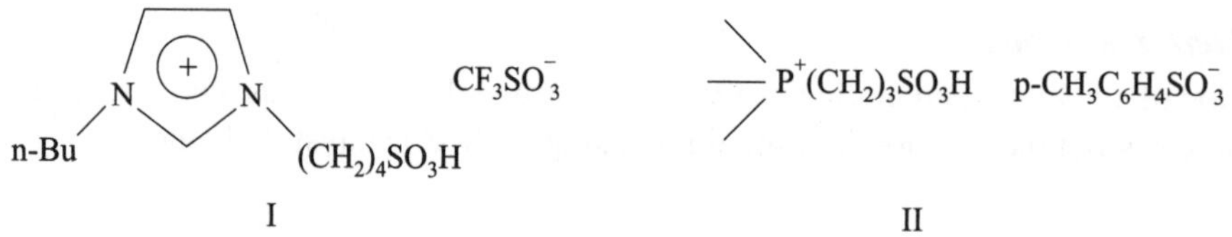

The ionic liquid (I) is a viscous liquid at room temperature while (II) is a glass-like material which becomes liquid at about 80°. These task- specific Brønsted acids exhibited behavior of typical ionic liquid. Neither of the compound (I or II) fumed or exhibited any observable vapour pressure. It has been shown that these ionic liquids (I or II) are not mere mixture of a strong acid with dissolved zwitterions.

The TSIL(II) has been used to effect a number of transformations like esterification, ether formation and the pinacol-pinacolne rearrangement (Scheme 51).

Esterification

$$CH_3(CH_2)_4 \, COOH + CH_3(CH_2)_6 \, CH_2OH \xrightarrow[22°, \, 48 \, hr]{IL \, (II)} CH_3(CH_2)_4 \, CO_2CH_2 \, (CH_2)_6 \, CH_3$$

Caproic acid   1-Octanol   n-octylcaproate
                                                                            82%

Ether formation

$$2CH_3(CH_2)_6CH_2OH \xrightarrow[22–175°, \, 2 \, hr]{IL \, (II)} [CH_3(CH_2)_6CH_2]_2O$$

1-Octanol   dioctyl ether

Pinacol-Pinacolone remanagement

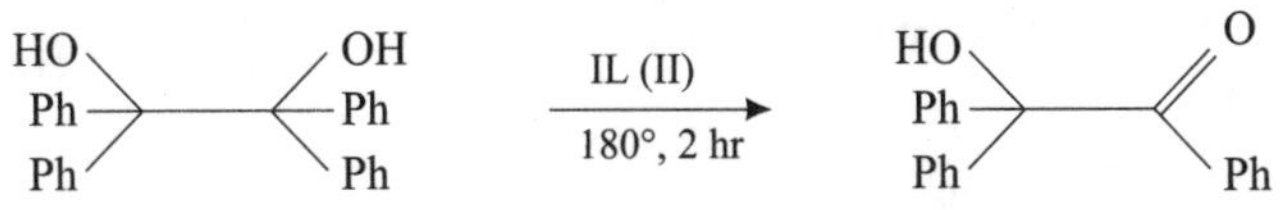

Pinacol   Pinacolone

Scheme 51

It should be noted that in contrast to the results using (II), although the conversion of 1-octanol to dioctyl ether with p-TsOH gave a better yield, but more byproducts formed. Typically, the pinacol-pinacolone rearrangement is carried out using H_2SO_4 or H_3PO_4 as catalyst. The advantage of using (II) as a catalyst for the pinacol rearrangement is that the product (Pinacolone) could be directtly distilled from the reaction mixture.

Esterification of a variety of aliphatic acids with olefins using the ionic liquid (III) has been cameed out[150].

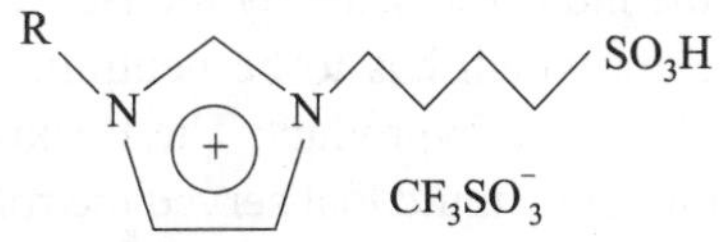

R = Me, Et, n-Bu, n-Hex
(III)

Using 3equiv. of the often in the ionic liquid (III, R = hex) (Scheme 52) best results were obtained[150].

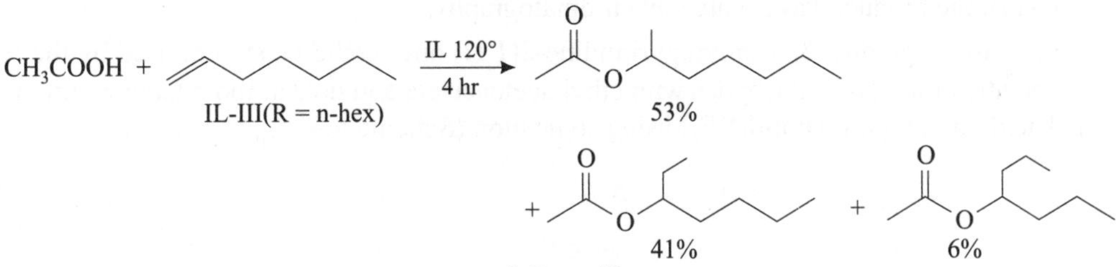

Scheme 52

In the above reaction (Scheme 52), The ester product being insoluble in the ionic liquid was separated by decantation. The excess olefin was extracted from the ionic liquid using toluene and the ionic liquid was reused aften drying under vacuum at 80°.

A large number of Brønsted –acidic ionic liquids have been synthesized[64].

A number of substituted coumarins have been synthesised via the Pechmann condensation using a brønsted-acidic ionic liquid as both catalyst and solvent (Scheme 53)[151].

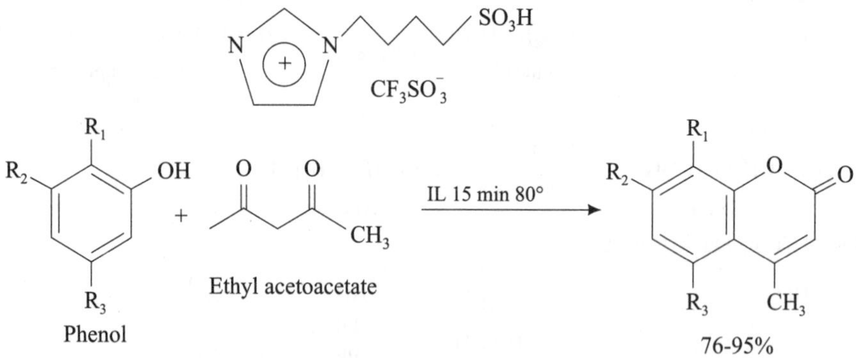

Phenol		
R$_1$	R$_2$	R$_3$
H	OH	H
H	OH	OH
H	OMe	H
MeO	OH	H
OH	OH	H
Me	H	H

Scheme 53

Caprolactam is prepared on the industrial scale by the Beckmann rearrangement of cyclohexanone oxime using corrosive oleum, which has to be neutralized using NH$_4$OH; this procedure produces large amount of (NH$_4$)$_2$ SO$_4$ as a byproduct. The Beckmann rearrangement of cyclohexanone oxime has been carried out in ionic liquid that served the role of a catalyst and also[44] reaction medium[152]. The main problem in using acidic ionic liquid is that the caprolactam product (being basic in nature) combines with the ionic liquid making the product separation impossible. It is found[152] that the use of caprolactam based ionic liquid coupled with a dynamic exchange between the caprolactam product and the ionic liquid permitted facile product isolation. Better yields were obtained when the product was isolated by chromatography.

Another useful product 3, 4-dihyropyrimidine-2(1 H) ones could be synithesised by the reaction of aromatic or aliphatic aldehydes with ethyl acetoacetate and urea at room temperature in the Brønsted acid ionic liquid [Hbim][BF$_4$] using sonication (Scheme 56)[153].

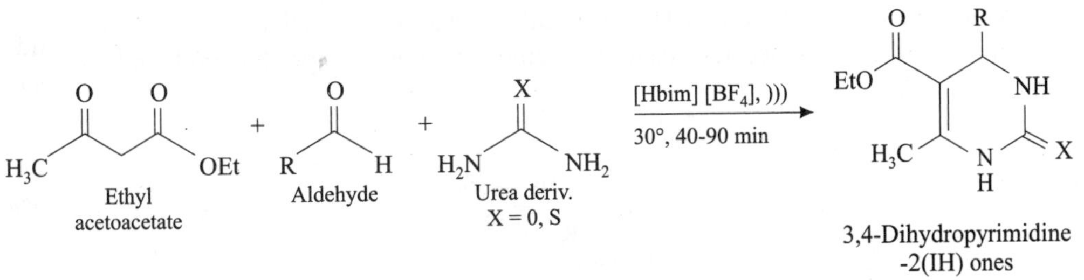

Scheme 56

The same Brønsted acidic ionic liquid [Hbim][BF$_4$] has also been used[153] for the synthesis of β-enaminones (Scheme 57).

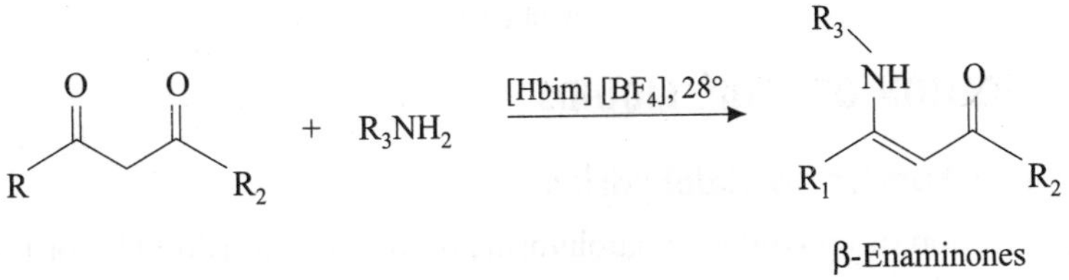

Scheme 57

A number of alcohols have been tetrahydropyranylated using Brønsted-acidic ionic liquids (Scheme 58)[154].

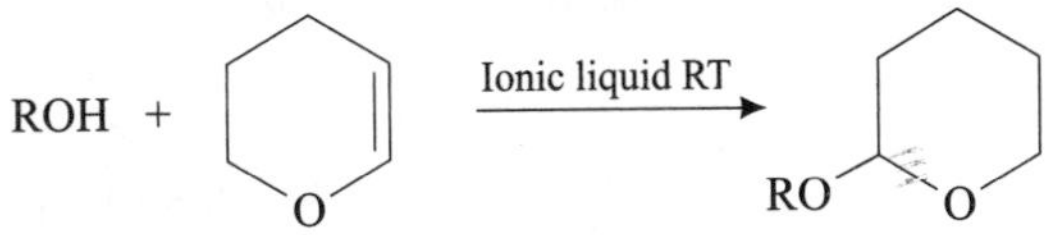

Scheme 58

6.2 Brønsted-basic Ionic Liquids

A typical example of Brønsted-basic ionic liquid is [bmim][OH]. It is used as a catalyst and reaction medium for Michael addition. This ionic liquid provides an efficient and convenient procedure for Michael addition of active methylene compound to conjugated alkenes in one step without requiring any other catalyst or an organic solvent[155]. Thus, different types of active methylene compounds underwent Michael addition with a number of α-β-unsaturated ketones, carboxylic esters and nitriles by this procedure to yield the corresponding adducts (IV) or (V) in good yield (Scheme 59)[155].

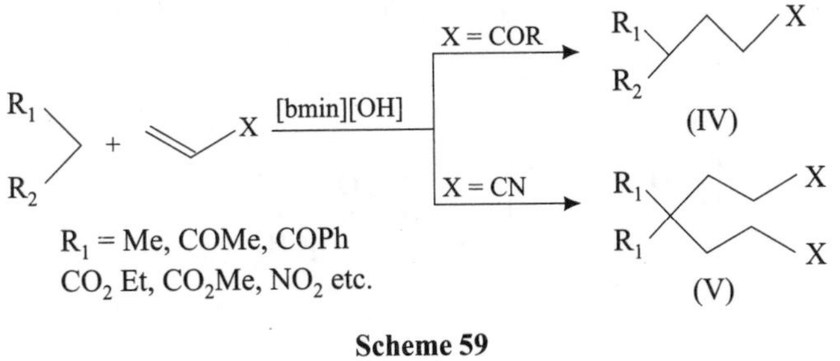

R$_1$ = Me, COMe, COPh
CO$_2$Et, CO$_2$Me, NO$_2$ etc.

Scheme 59

The same ionic liquid, [bmim] [OH] was used[156] as catalyst as well as reaction medium for the Markovnikov addition of N-hetrocycles to vinyl ethers, yielding the product under mild conditions (Scheme 60).

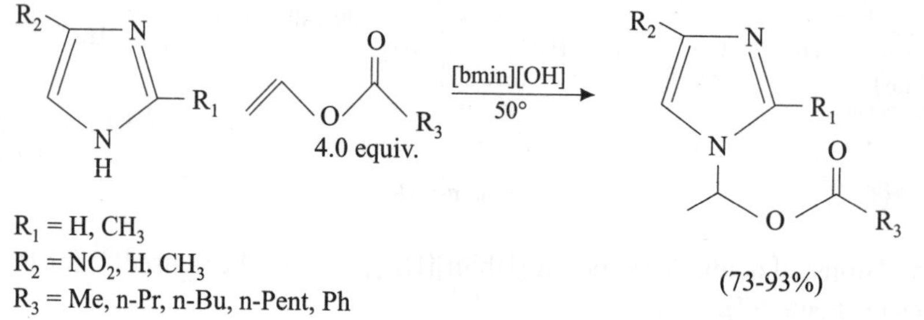
[bmin][OH]
50°
4.0 equiv.
R1 = H, CH3
R2 = NO2, H, CH3
R3 = Me, n-Pr, n-Bu, n-Pent, Ph
(73-93%)

Scheme 60

7 OTHER APPLICATION OF IONIC LIQUIDS

7.1 Conversion of Epoxies to Halohydrins

Typically, the conversion of epoxodes to halohydrins is carried out using HX or hypohalite water, which often results in the generation of byproducts. It is now possible to carry out the conversion with ionic liquids, such as (VI) (Scheme 61)[157].

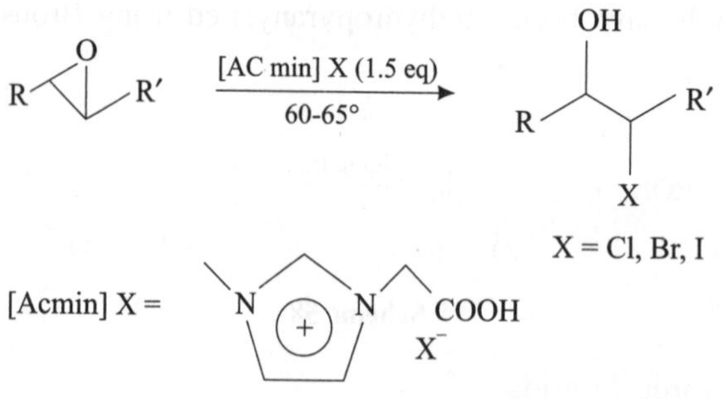
[AC min] X (1.5 eq)
60-65°
X = Cl, Br, I
[Acmin] X =
COOH

(VI)

Scheme 61

Using the above method (Scheme 61), following epoxides could be converted into the corresponding halohydrins.

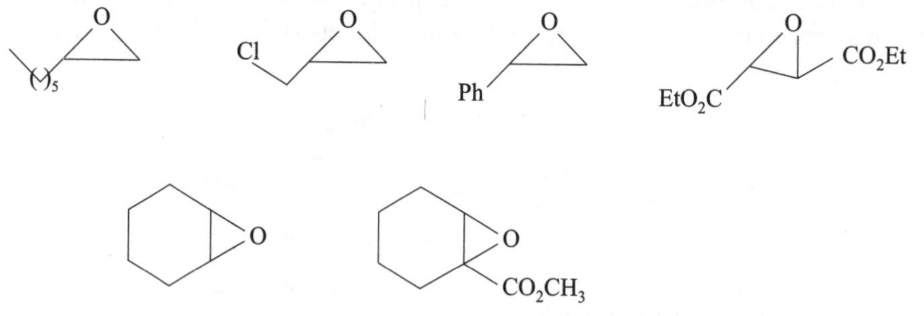
Cl
Ph
EtO2C
CO2Et
CO2CH3

However, trans strlbene epoxide did not yield the corresponding halohydrim. In this case, the epoxide underwent a rearrangement to give deoxybenzoin (Scheme 62).

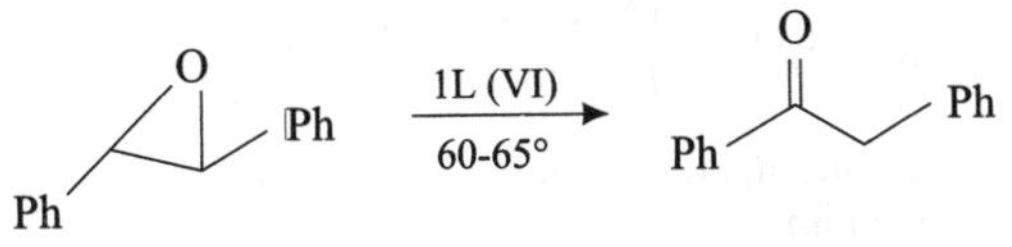

Trans stilbene epoxide

Deoxybenzoin

Scheme 62

7.2 Conversion of Oxiranes (Epoxides) into Thiiranes

Oxiranes (epoxides) could be converted into thiiranes by reacting with potassium thiocyanate in [bmim] [PF$_6$]-H$_2$O (2:1) solvent system at room temperature to produce the corresponding thiiranes in good yields (Scheme 63)[158].

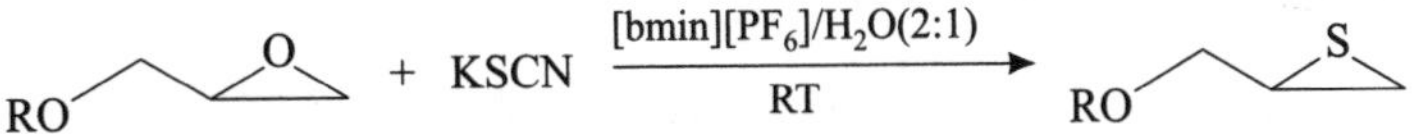

Oxiranes

thiiranes

Scheme 63

7.3 Thiocyanation of Alkyl Halides

Alkyl halides on treatment with ionic liquid [bmim][SCN] could be converted into alkyl thiocyantes at room temperature (Scheme 64)[159]. In this case the ionic liquid acted as both solvent and reactant. The ionic liquid was regenerated by the reaction of [bmim] [X] with KSCN.

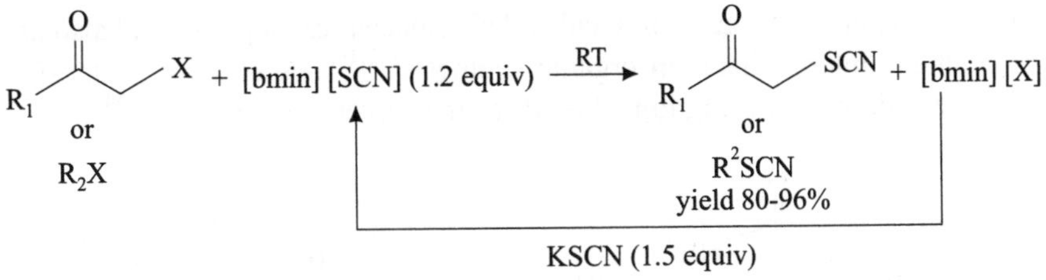

R^1 = C$_6$H$_5$, 4-BrC$_6$H$_4$, 4-ClC$_6$H$_4$, 4Me C$_6$H$_4$, 2-thenyl
R^2 = C$_6$H$_5$CH$_2$, HOC$_2$H$_4$, HOOCC$_3$H$_6$, X = Cl, Br

Scheme 64

7.4 Synthesis of Cyclic Carbonates

The reaction of epoxide with carbon dioxide in tetrahaloindate (III) based ionic liquids generated cyclic carbonates (Scheme 65)[160].

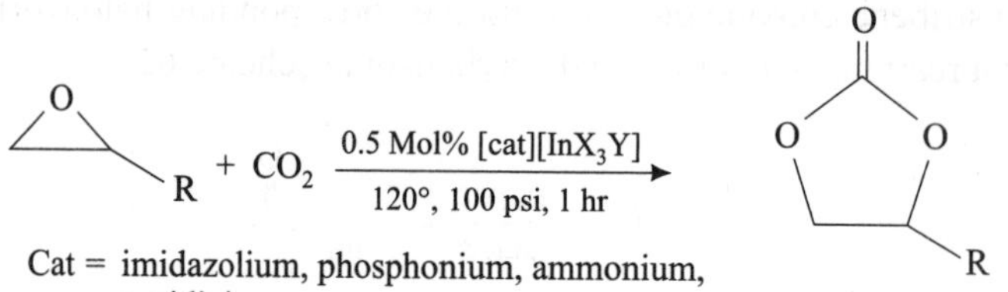

Cat = imidazolium, phosphonium, ammonium,
        pyridinium
X   = Cl, Br, I ; y = Cl, Br

Scheme 65

These thermally stable ionic liquids were synthesis by the microwave promoted reaction of indium chloride, In X_3, with a variety of ionic liquids (see also section 3.9)

7.5 Biginelli Reaction

Ionic liquids like [bmim] [PF_4] and [b mim] [PF_6] have used as catalysts for the Biginelli reaction under solvent free conditions (Scheme 66)[161]

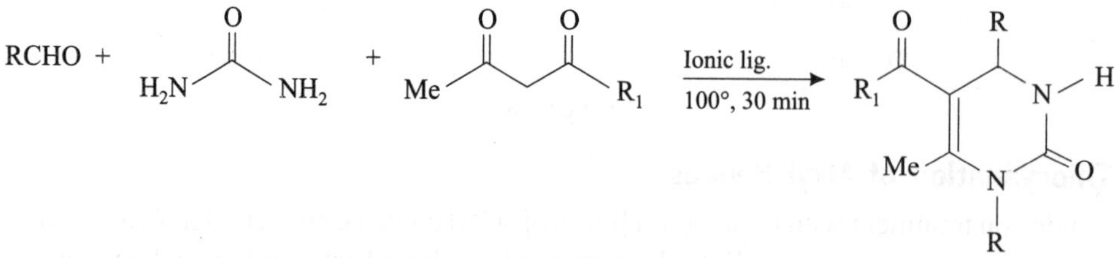

Scheme 66

7.6 Synthesis of 3-Acetyl-5-[(z)-Arylmethylidene] I, 3-Thiazolidine-2, 4-Diones

The title compounds exhibit various biological and pharmaceutical activites and also are an important calss of synthetic intermediates in organic synthesis[162,163]. A one pot synthesis of the title compounds has been deseribed using ioinc liquids as the solvent (Scheme 67)[164].

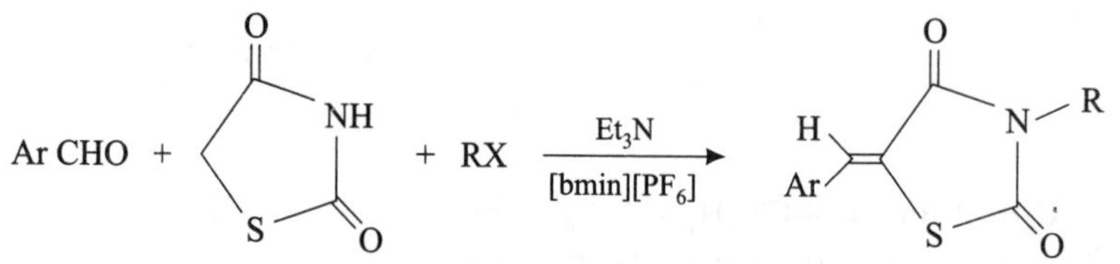

Scheme 67

7.7 Synthesis of Symmetric Urea Derivatives

N, N-disubstituted urea derivatives are important chemicals and are mainly maufactured by the reaction of phosgene on amines. An effective process for the direct synthesis and separation of symmetric urea derivatives in good yield from amines by using CO_2 in ionic liquid has been developed[165]. In this synthesis, the recyclable catalytic system consisted of an ionic liquid [bmim] [BF_4], [bmim] [PF_6] N [bmim] [Cl] and base CsOH.

7.8 Synthesis of Homoallylic Amines

Homoallylic amines are prepared from imines (which are derived in situ from aldehydes and amines) by nucleophilic addition with allylbutyl stannate in the ionic liquid [bmim] [BF$_4$]. The products are obtained in high yields with high selectivity[166]. This method is particularly useful for acid sensitive aldehydes.

7.9 Conjugate Addition of Thiols to α, β-unsaturated Ketones

The α, β-unsaturated ketones underwent addition with thiols in [bmim] [PF$_6$]/H$_2$O solvent system (2:1) to afford the corresponding Michael adducts in high yield and with excellent 1, 4-selectivity under mild and neutral conditions (Scheme 68)[167]

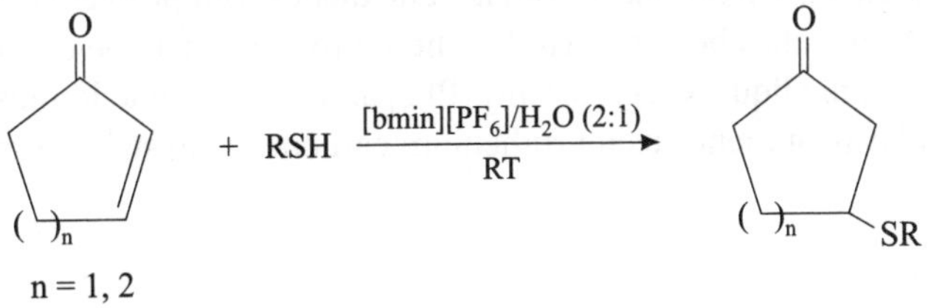

Scheme 68

The use of ionic liquid in the above reaction helped to avoid the acid or base catayyst for this conversion.

7.10 Nucleophilic Displacement Reactions

Nucleophilic displacement reaction are often carried out using phase transfer catalyst (PTC) to facilitate the reaction between the organic reactants and the inoganic salts that provide the nucleophile. However, conventional PTC uses environmentally undesirable organic solvent like methylene chloride or o-dichlorobenzene. Ionic liquids because of their bulky organic cations are well suited for the type of reaction for which PTC is effective[168]. Thus, nucleophilic fluorination of 2-(3-methanesulphanyloxypropyl) naphthalene with metal fluorides (e.g. KF.) in ionic liquid [bmim] [BF$_4$] gives the corresponding substitution product[169, 170] (Scheme 69).

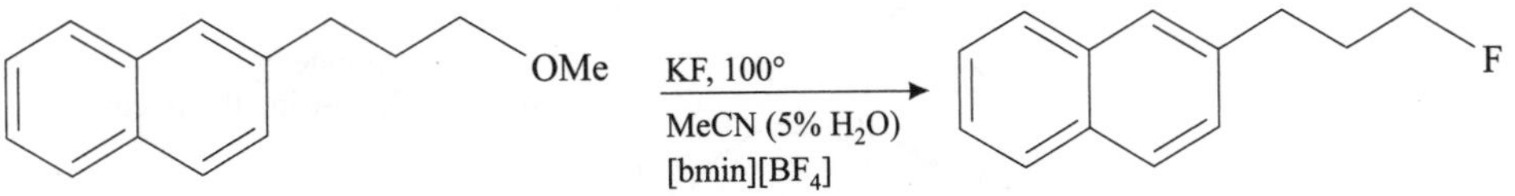

Scheme 69

The above reaction in MeCN at 100° hardly gave any produce even after 24hr., where as the same reaction in [bmim] [BF$_4$] was completed in 2 hr. The addition of water eliminated the formation of undesired alkene.

7.11 Bromination of Alkynes

Arylalkynes on bromination with bromime in [bmim] [Br] gave the anti addition product, (Scheme 70) reaction following a second order rate law. However in [bmim] [PF$_6$] mixture of syn and anti addition products were obtained and the reaction followed a second or third order rate law, depending on the structure of alkyne and the concentration of Br_2[171]

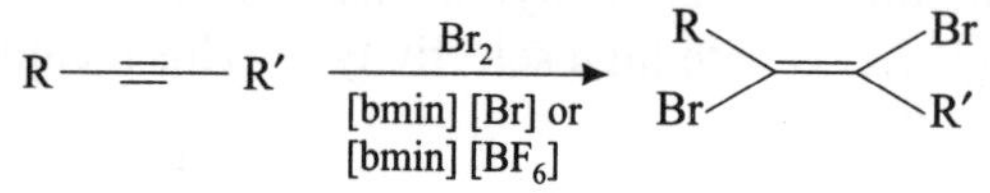

Scheme 70

7.12 Alkene Metathesis

Ruthenium catalysed ring closing metathesis is a powerful method for synthesizing heterocyclic compounds and complex natural products from acyclic dienes. But problem is recovering and recycling of the catalyst. Now, it has been shown that these problems may be overcome by using recyclable and non volatile ionic liquids e.g. [bmim] [PF$_6$] and related ionic liquids are effective media for ring closing metathesis of dienes using ruthenium carbene catalysts[172] (Scheme 71).

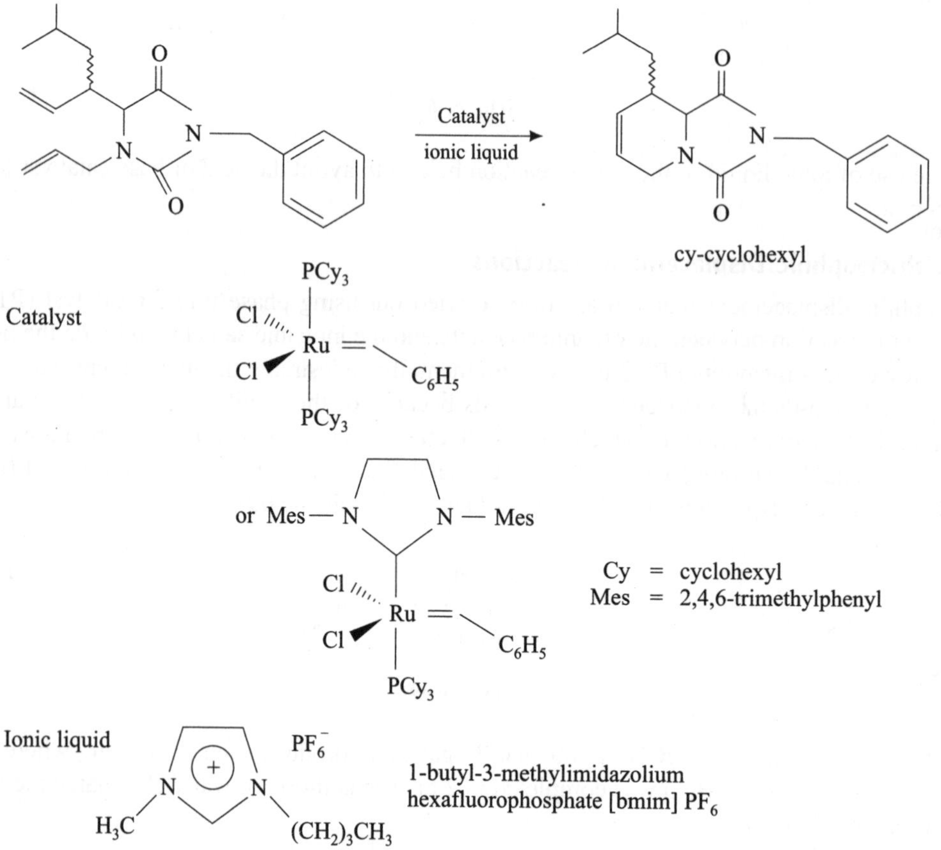

cy-cyclohexyl

Catalyst

Cy = cyclohexyl
Mes = 2,4,6-trimethylphenyl

Ionic liquid

1-butyl-3-methylimidazolium
hexafluorophosphate [bmim] PF$_6$

Scheme 71

The reaction can also be carried out in ionic liquid in the presence of cationic ruthenium allenylidene complexes[173] (Scheme 72)

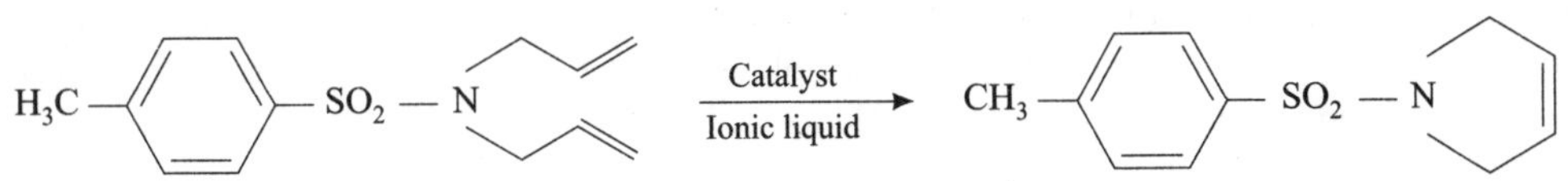

Catalyst = [(C$_6$H$_5$)$_2$ C = C = C = RuCl (PCy$_3$) (p-cymene) X$^-$
X = PF$_6$ or CF$_3$ or CF$_3$SO$_3$, Cy = cyclohexyl ionic liquid-[bmim] PF$_6$

Scheme 72

7.13 Electrophilic Nitration of Aromatics

Electrophilic nitration of aromatics is a fundamental reaction, whose products are key organic intermediates or energetic material. The major problem with the existing process is disposal and regeneration of the used acids. The use of ionic liquids based on [emim] and [bmim] cations[174], is a useful alternative to calssical nitration route due to easier product isolation and the recovery of the ionic liquid solvent, and because it avoids problems associced with netralization of large quantities of strong acid.

7.14 Carbon-Oxygen Bond Formation

The synthesis of diaryl ethers from aryl halides and phenols in presence of base, catalysed by CuCl immobilised in [bmim] [BF$_4$] (Scheme 73) produces high yield[13] of the diayl ethers as compared to those obtained in conventional solvent as DMF.

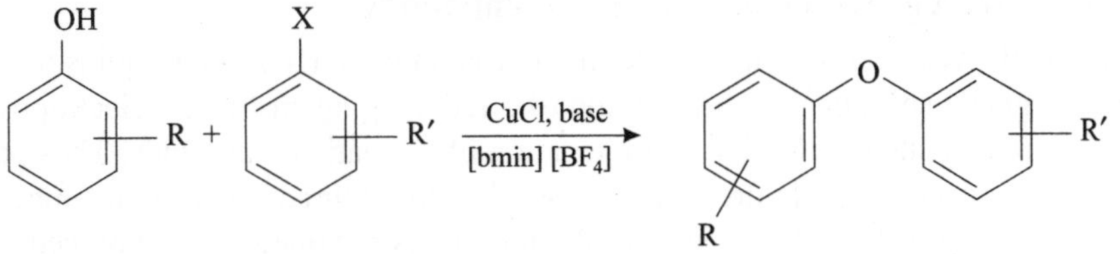

Scheme 73

7.15 Synthesis of 1-Acetylnaphtholene

Acetylation of naphthaline in chloroaluminate ionic liquid gives 89% of 1-acetyl naphthalene (Scheme 74)[175].

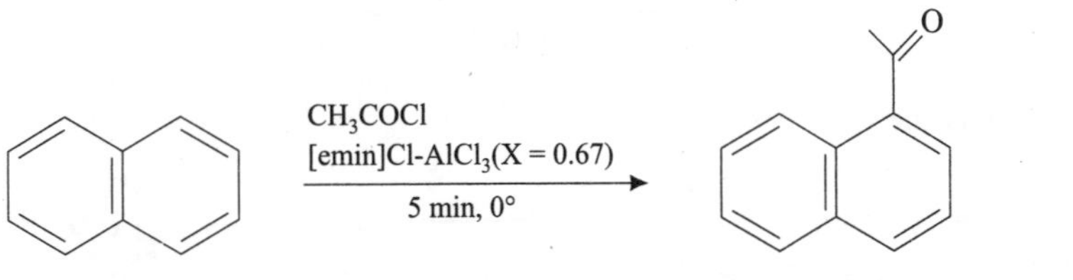

Naphthalene   1-Acetyl naphthalene (89%)

Scheme 74

7.16   Synthesis of Tonalid and Traseolide

Todalid (5-acetyl-1, 1, 2, 6-tetramethyl-3-isopropylindane) and Traseolide (6-acetyl-1, 1, 2, 4, 4, 7-hexamethyltetralin), both commercially important fragrance molecules[176] have been synthesised by the acctylation of 1, 1, 2, 6-tetramethyl-3-isoproplindane and 1, 1, 2, 4, 4, 7-hexamethyl tetralin in the ionic liquid [emin]Cl–AlCl₃(X = 0.76) (Scheme 75)[175].

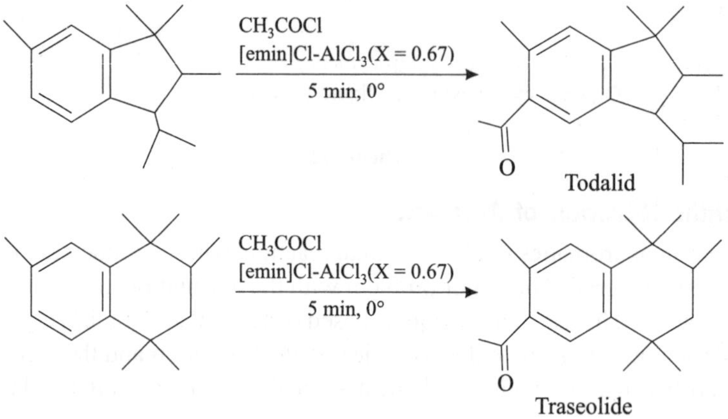

Scheme 75

The chloroaluminate (III) ionic liquids are powerful lewis acids and are prepared[176] by mixing the appropriate organic halide salt with aluminum (III) chloride, the two solids melt on mixing to form the ionic liquid. The synthesis needs inert atmosphere.

7.17   Selective Hydrogenation of Aromatic Compounds

Polycyclic aromatic hydrocarbon are soluble in chloroaluminate (III) ionic liquids to form highly coloured paramagnetic solution[177]. The addition of a reducing agent like an electropositive metal and a proton source results in selective hydrogenation of aromatic compounds. Thus perylene and anthracene can be reduced to perhydroperylene and perhydroanthracene at room temperature; only the thermodynamically more stable isomer of the product is obtained[178]. The procedure contrasts with catalytic hydrogenation reaction which need high temperature and pressure and expenseve platinum oxide catalyst and generally gives a mixture of products[179]. By monitoring carefully the reduction in the ionic liquids, a number intermediates can be isolated and the sequence of reaction in the reduction process can be determind (Scheme 76).

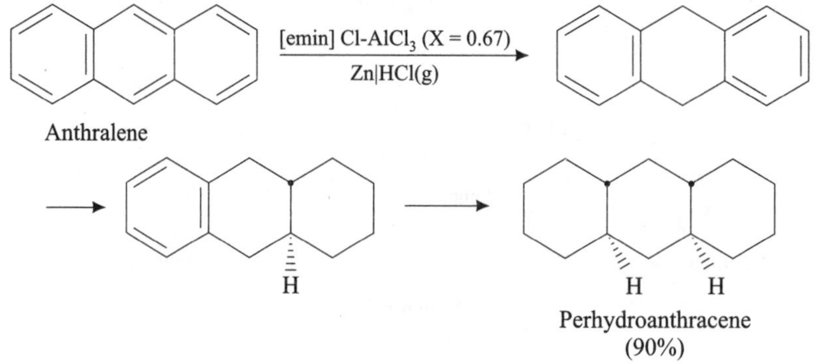

Scheme 76

7.18   Alkylation of Indole and 2-Naphthol

Indole and 2-napthol undergo alkylation on the nitrogen and oxygen atoms, respectively , on treatment with a haloalkane and base (Usually NaOH or KOH) in [bmim] [PF$_6$][180]. The main advantage of using ionic liquid is that the products of the reaction can be extracted by an organic solvent such as toluene, leaving behind the ionic liquid. The byproduct of the reaction is sodium or potassium halide; this can be extracted with water and the ionic liquid can be used again.

7.19   Methylene Insertion Reactions

Methylene insertion reactions can be carried out in ionic liquids such as [bmin] [PF$_6$] or [bmin] [PF$_4$]. Thus the reaction of naphthalene 2-aldehyde with sulfonium ylids (prepared by the reaction of alkyl halides with sulfides) gives the methylene insertion product (Scheme 77)[176]. The reaction works equally well with preformed sulfonium salts. Alternatively, dialkyl sulfides and methyl iodide can be used.

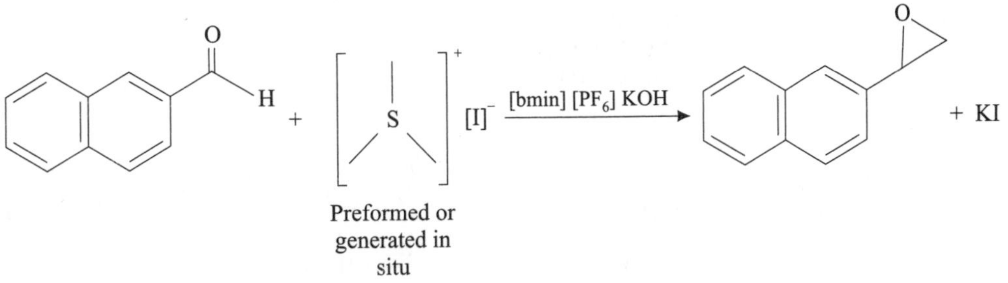

Preformed or
generated in
situ

Scheme 77

By using a chiral sulfide such as 2R, 5S-tetrahydrothiophene, it is possible to carry out asymmetric methylene insertion reaction. In this case, the product (stilbene oxide) obtained can be extracted from the reaction mixture with solvent. The byproduct (potassium halide) can be extracted from the ionic liquid with water. The ionic liquid containing the chiral catalyst is dried and reused[181] (Scheme 78).

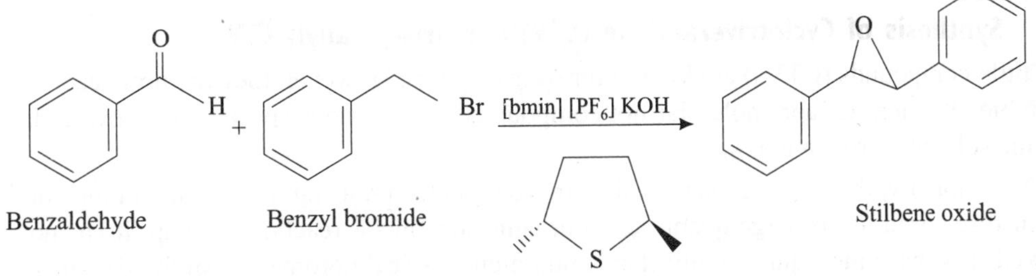

Benzaldehyde   Benzyl bromide   Stilbene oxide

Scheme 78

7.20 Synthesis of Pravadoline

Pravadoline an important pharmaeutical was synthesized using ionic liquid and a combination of Friedel crafts reaction and a nuclophilic displacement reaction. Thus the alkylation of 2 – methylindole with 1 – (N – morpholine) – 2 – chloroethane in ionic liquid, 1 – butyl – 2, 3 – dimethylimidazolium hexaflurophosphate ([bd mim] [PF$_6$]) and KOH as base. The alkylated product obtained in 99% yield), on Friedel crafts acylation in chloroaluminate (III) ionic liquid at 0° give the required pravadoline (Scheme 79)[181].

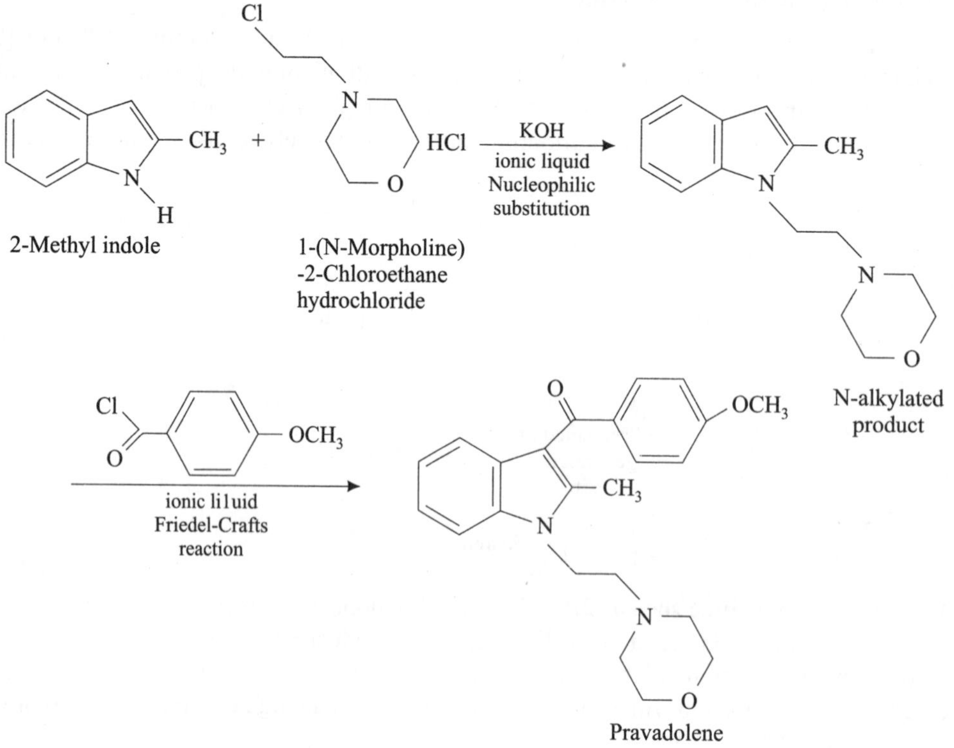

2-Methyl indole

1-(N-Morpholine)
-2-Chloroethane
hydrochloride

N-alkylated
product

Pravadolene

Scheme 79

7.21 Synthesis of Cyclotriveratylene (CTV) and Tris-(O-allyl) CTV

The tittle compounds (CTVs) are known for over 80 years. However, they are now receiving considerable attention as supramoleurlar hot compounds[182] for various species from low molar mass organic solvents through to C$_{60}$.

Traditionally, the CTV, are synthsed from Veratyl alcohol using harsh dehydrating conditions and also required use of large quantities of organic solvent for reaction workup. It has now been showed that the ionic liquid tributyl hexlammonium bis (trifluoromethyl sulfonyl) amide (N$_{6444}$ Imide) is a safe, non – volatile reaction medium that can be recycled[183]. In this procedure, extensive recyrstallisation or chromatographic separations are avoided.

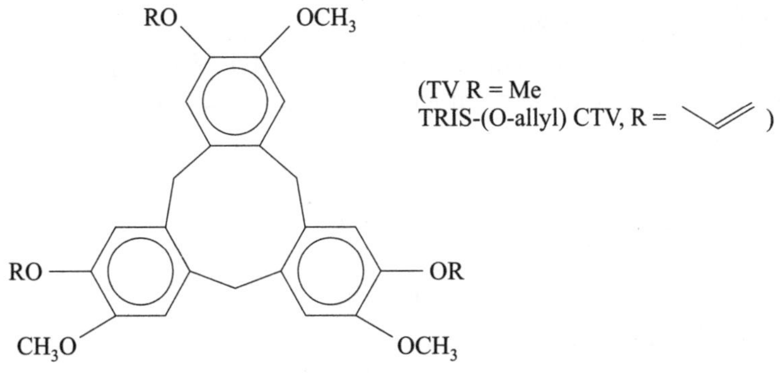

(TV R = Me
TRIS-(O-allyl) CTV, R = ⟍⟋)

7.22 Cycloaddition of Carbon Dioxide to Propylene Oxide Catalysed by Ionic Liquids

Cydoaddition ot CO_2 to propylene oxide to give five membered cyclic carbonate using ionic liquids based on [bmim]$^+$ and [bpy]$^+$. It is found[184] that the ionic liquid [bmim] [BF$_4$] is to best catalystic medium for the reaction. The resulting cyclic carbonate can be separated from the ionic liquid by simple distillation, and the ionic liquid catalyst can be reused.

7.23 Epoxidation of Electrophilic Alkenes in Ionic Liquids

A efficient procedure for epoxidation of electrophilic alkens in ionic liquids, [bmim] [PF$_6$], [Bmim] [PF$_4$] as solvent by using aqueous solution of H_2O_2 in the presence of base catalyst has been reported (Scheme 80)[185].

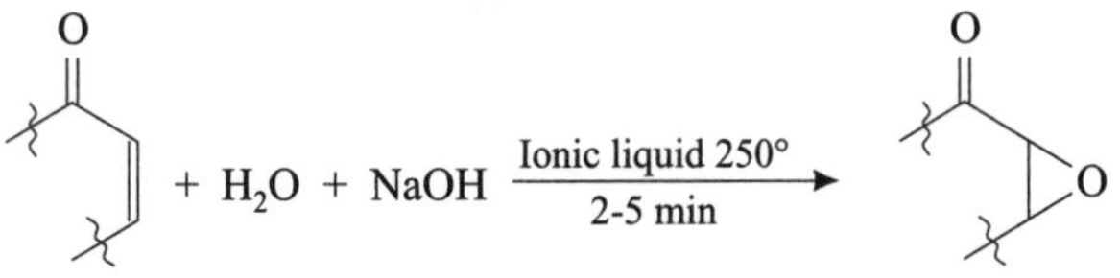

Scheme 80

Using the above procedure, following alkenes were converted into epoxodes,

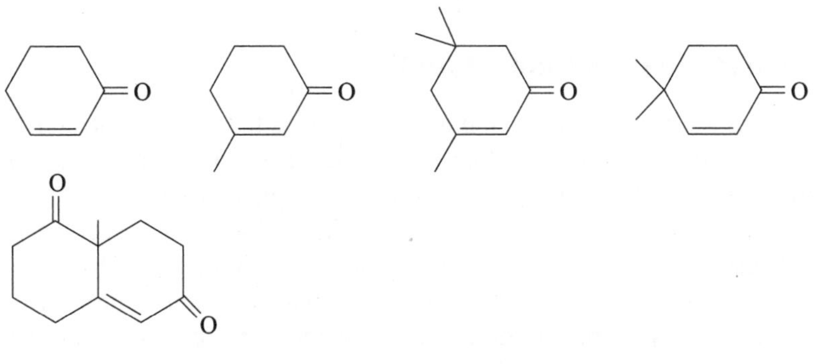

7.24 Oxidation of Benzylic Alcohols to Carbonyl Compounds with KMnO₄ in Ionic Liquids

The oxidation of benzyl alcohol with $KMnO_4$ in 1-butyl -3-methylimidazolium tetrafluoroborate [bmim] [BF₄] ionic liquid at room temperature gave benzaldehyde in 90% yield in 1 hr (Scheme 81)[186].

$$C_6H_5CH_2OH \xrightarrow[\substack{[bmin][BF_4] \\ 1\ hr.\ R.T.}]{KMnO_4} C_6H_5CHO \atop 90\%$$

Scheme 81

Following alcohols were oxidized

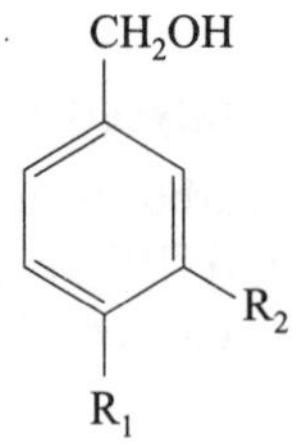

R₁	R₂
H	H
OCH₃	H
Cl	H
NO₂	H
CH₃	H
OCH₃	OCH₃

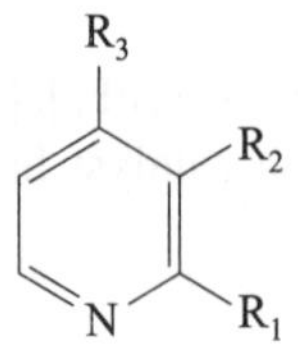

R₁	R₂	R₃
CH₂OH	H	H
H	CH₂OH	H
H	H	CH₂OH

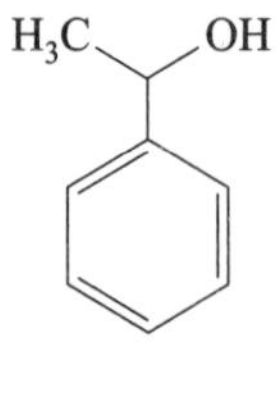

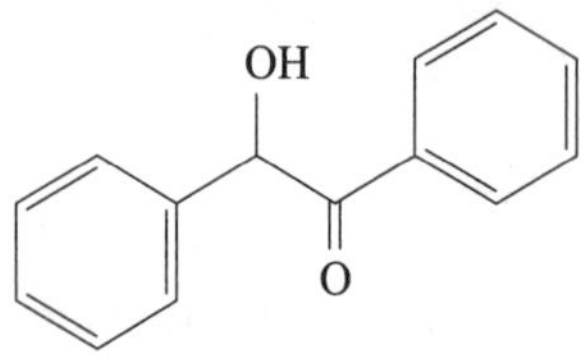

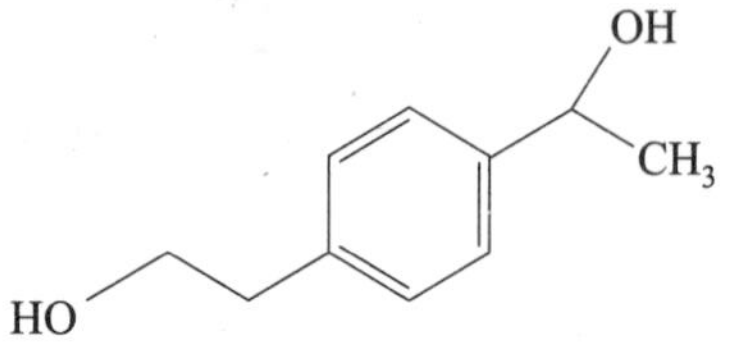

8 BIOTRANSFORMATIONS IN IONIC LIQUIDS

Most of the enzymes tolerate aquous ionic liquid mixtures as the reaction medium. In fact, there is hardly an ionic liquid that is not tolerated by an enzyme. The general impression is that the ionic liquids are tolerated to higher concentrations than water miscible molecular solvents. In ionic liquids activites of the enzymes are comparable or higher than those observed in conventional solvents. Also, enhanced thermal and operational stabilities have been observed. Regio and or enantioselectives have also been observed in many cases. The retention of the activity of enzymes in ionic liquids present a very promising green alternative to organic solvent for enzyme catalysed reactions. Following are given some of the important biotransformations in ionic liquid.

8.1   Synthesis of Z-Aspartame

Z-Aspartame, a precursor to the artificial sweetener, aspartame, has been synthesized by the reaction of carbobezoxy-L-aseparate and L-phenylalanine methyl ester. Z is a protecting group that is later removed. By using [bmim] [PF$_6$] containing 5 per cent by volume of the water. The reaction is catalysed by thermolysin, a proteolytic enzyme (Scheme 82)[187]. The yield was 95 per cent which is similar to that reported for enzymatic aspartame synthesis in organic solvent with low water content. The enzyme, thermolysin exhibited excellent stability in the ionic liquid.

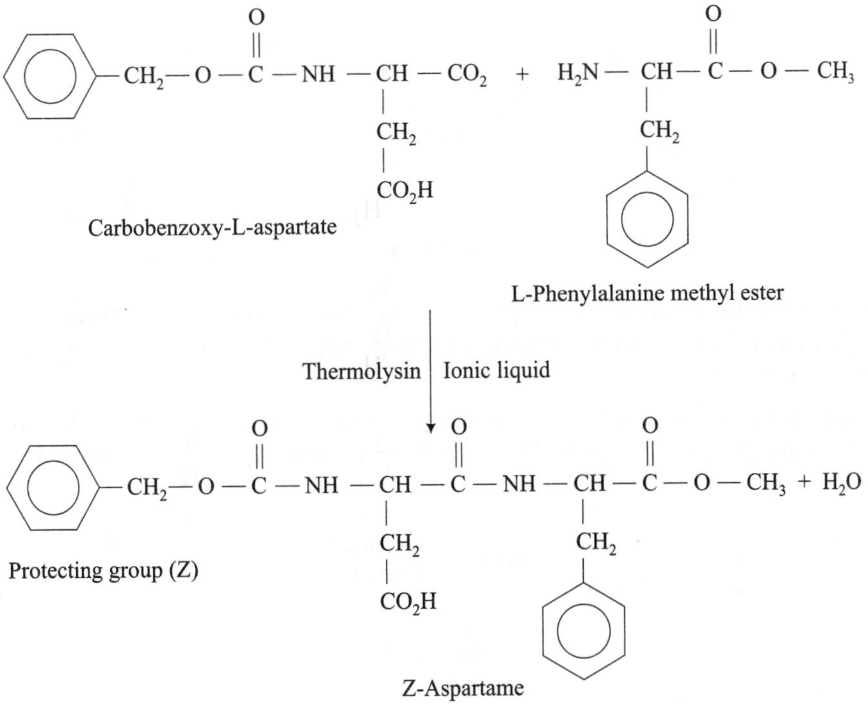

Scheme 82

8.2   Conversion of l, 3-Dicyanobenzene to 3-Cyanobenzamide and 3-Cyanobenzoic Acid

The reaction of 1, 3-dicyanobenzone with nitrile hydratase from Rhodocococus 313 give 3-cyanobenzamide and 3-cyanobenzoic acid. The transformation[188] was carried out in biphasic water-[bmim] [PF$_6$] system. It is found that the enzyme is not active in [bmim] [PF$_6$] and the ionic liquid serves only as a reservoir for the substrate. The Rhodococcus R312 remains in the aqueous phase, where the reaction takes place; the ionic liquid only dissolved concentrations of substrate above the aqueous solubility limit, which than partitions into the aqueous phase.

8.3   Transesterification Reactions

Transesterification could be carried out using candida antarctica lipase B(CaLB) either as free enzyme (SP525) or in an immobilized form (NOVOZYM 435) in ionic liquid [bmim] [BF$_4$] or [bmim] [PF$_6$] in the absence of added water[189] (Scheme 83).

$$R^1CO_2Et + R^2OH \xrightarrow[\text{or [bmin][BF}_4\text{] 40°}]{\text{Cal. B [bmin][PF}_6\text{]}} R^1CO_2R^2 + EtOH$$

Scheme 83

Transesterification at N acetyl-L-phenyl alanine ethyl ester with 1-propanol in [bmim] [PF$_6$] and 1-octyl-3-methylimidazolium hexafluorophosphate [Omim] [PF$_6$] could be carried out using α-chymotrypsin-catalysed enzyme[190] (Scheme 84).

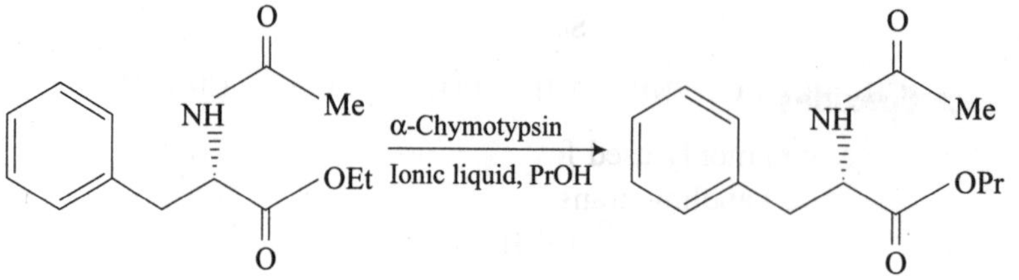

Scheme 84

In the above transesterification, the presence of certain amount at water was necessary. The transesterification activity of α-chymotypsin in [Omim] [PF$_6$] increased by co-lyophilisation with polyethylene glyere (PEG).

The transesterification of ethyl butanuate with butan-1-ol in ionic liquid [bmim] [BF$_4$] or [bmim] [PF$_6$] gave good yield[189] of butyl butanoate with supported CALB (Scheme 85).

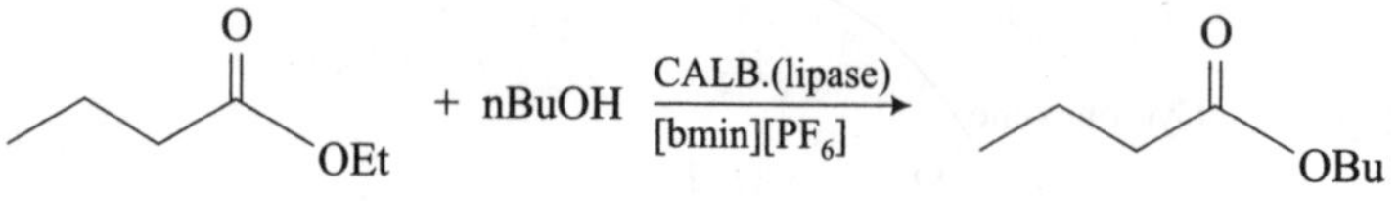

Scheme 85

The transsestirification of 2-hydroxymethyl-1,4-benzodioxane using vinyl acetate (Scheme 86) is catalysed by lipases in [bmim] [PF$_6$] and [bmim]]BF$_4$] ionic liquids[191]

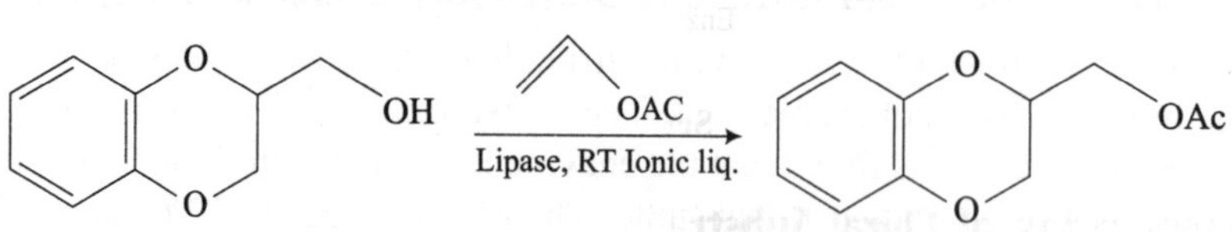

Scheme 86

For transestenfication of chiral alcohol see section 8.6

8.4 Ammoniolysis of Carboxylic Acids

Ammoniolysion of carboxylic acid, eg. Octanoic acid with ammonia in presence of NOVOZYM 435 at 40° in [bmim] [BF$_4$] proceeded[189] to completion in 4 days (Scheme 87).

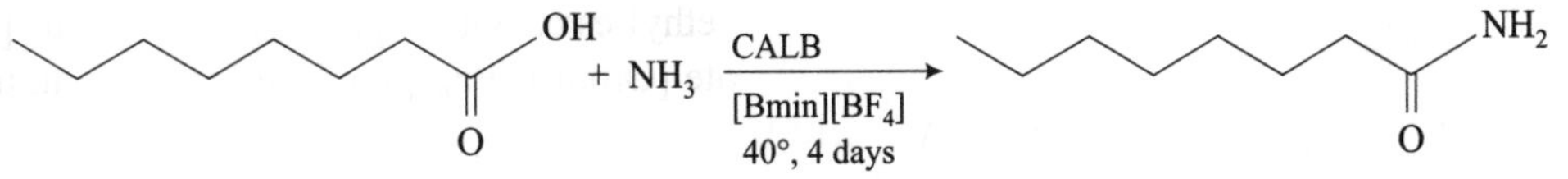

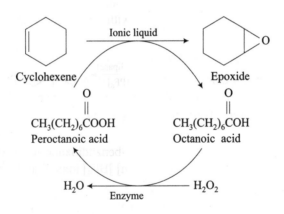

Scheme 87

8.5 Synthesis of Epoxides

Peroxycarboxylic acids are commonly used for the preparation of epoxides. However, increasing restritions with respect to their handling, transport and storage are prohibitive factors for its use as an industrial chemical. It has been shown[192] that it is feasible to generate peroxy carboxylic acid by lipase-catalysted perhydrolysis of the corresponding carboxylic acids. It is now possible to perform this reaction in an ionic liquid[189]. Thus epoxidation of cyclohexene by peroctanoic acid, generated in situ by Novozym435 catalysed reaction of octanoic acid by commonly available 60 per cent aqueous H$_2$O$_2$ in [bmim] [BF$_4$]. The product obtained is cyclohexane epoxide in 83 per cent yield in 24hr. (Scheme 88).

Scheme 88

8.6 Transestenfication of Chiral Substrates

Transesterification of chiral substrates in ionic liquids has been studied, with a view to ascertain the effect of ionic liquid media on enantio selectivites of the transformations. Thus, the kinitic resolution of 1-phenylethanol (Scheme 89) has been investigated with nine different lipases in ten different ionic liquids.

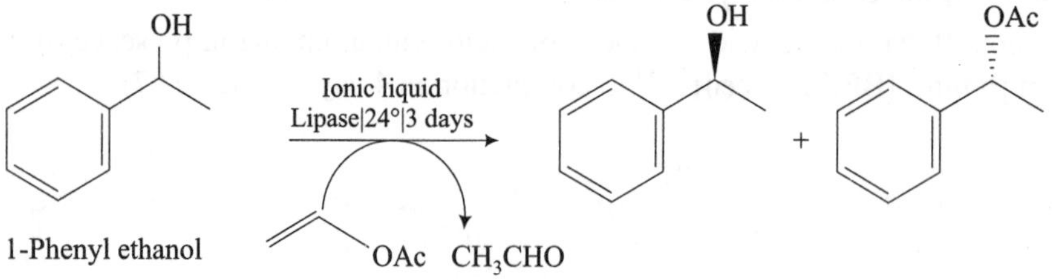

Scheme 89

Improved enantroselectivites were observed in the above reaction[193]. which can also be viewed as kinetic resolution of 1-phenylethanol. In a similar way the transesterification of chiral allylic alcohol was sturdied (Scheme 90)[194].

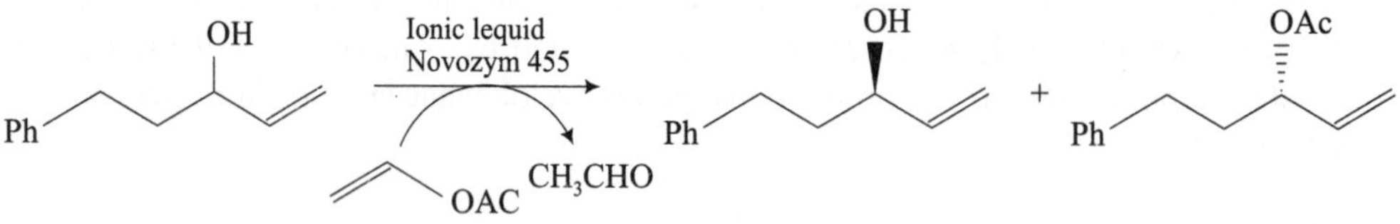

Scheme 90

Best results were obtained in [bmim] [BF$_4$] and [bmim] [PF$_6$].

Transesterification of several chiral alcohol catalysed by caLB and PCL in [emim] [BF$_4$] and [bmim] [PF$_6$] were studeed (Scheme 91). Markedly enhanced enantioselectivities were observed compared with the same reaction performed in THF or tolure[195]

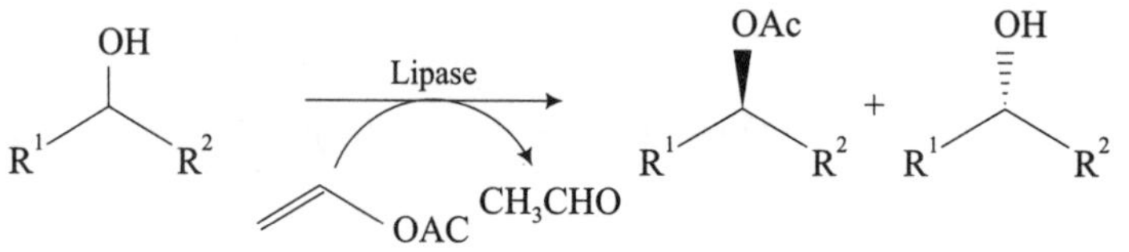

Scheme 91

8.7 Synthesis of Geranyl Acetate

Geranyl acetate, the natural fragrance is produced by the esterification of commonly available geraniol (3, 7-dimethyl-2, 6-octadien-1-ol). The esterification is done in presence of a lipase, immobilized CaLB (Novozym 435) in [BMIm] [PF$_6$] (Scheme 92)[196].

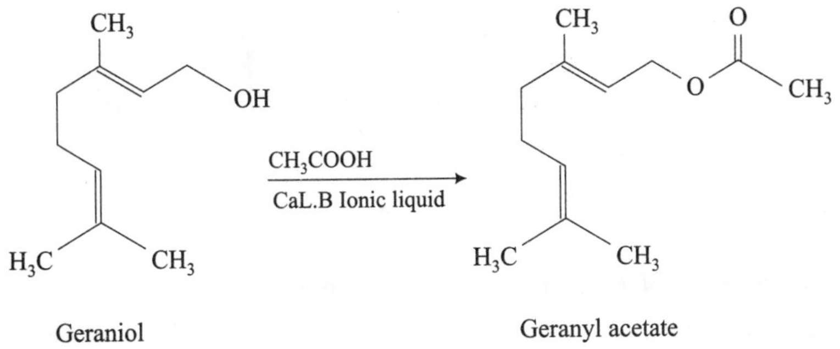

Geraniol   Geranyl acetate

Scheme 92

8.8   Transesterification of Glucose and L-Ascorbic Acid

The CaLB-catalysed esterfication of glucose with vinyl acetate in the ionic liquid [EMIm] [BF$_4$] was completely selective. The symthesis of long chain fatty acid esters of carbohydrates in more demanding due to their potential useful and fully green nonionic surfactants. Though glucose did not react with vinyl laurate in pure ionic liquid but in biphasic tert-butyl alcohol-[BMIm] [PF$_6$], glucose could be acetylated by the vinyl esters of C$_{12}$ – C$_{16}$ fatty acids. Best results were obtained with CaLB[197]. The esterification of glucose with palmitic acid has been effected in tert-butyl alcohol [BMIm] [PE$_6$] medium[198], the latter estrificatione is important in industrial context.

L-Ascorbic acid could be esterified with palmitic acid in presence of cal B, in [BMIm] [BF$_4$] and other similarly related ionic liquids (Scheme 93)[199, 200].

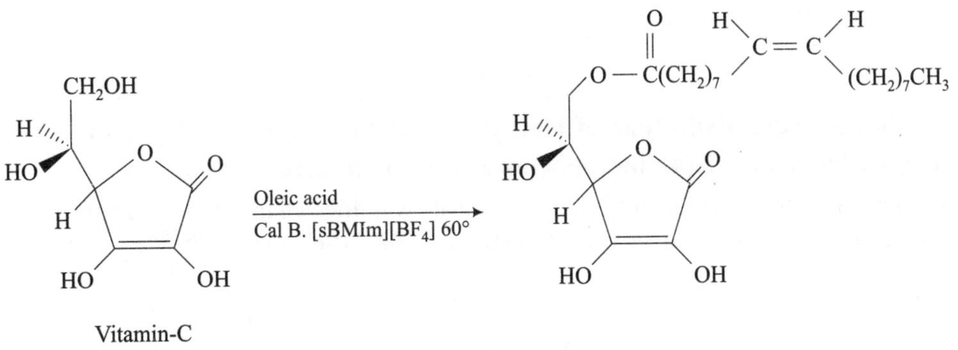

Vitamin-C

Scheme 94

8.9   Enantioselective Hydrolysis of a Prochiral Malonic Ester

The enantioselective hydrolysis of a prochiral malic ester in presence of pig liver esterase (PLE) in presence of trace amount of ionic liquids gave the carboxlic acid. Addition of 10% of a cosolvent like isopropyl alcohol improved the yields (Scheme 95)[201].

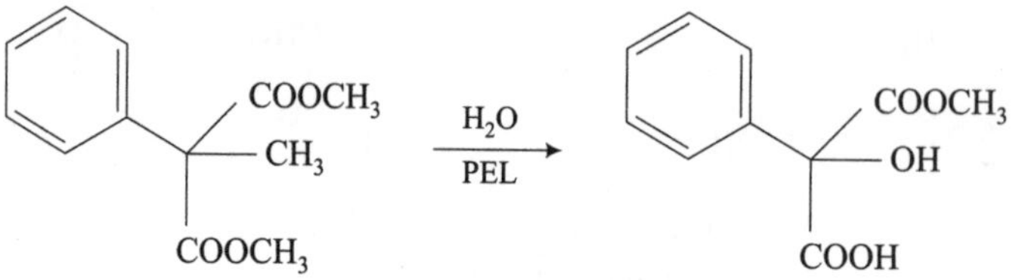

Scheme 95

8.10 Kinetic Resolution of N-Acetyl-α-Amino Acid Esters

The enantioselectivity of PPL in the kinitic resolution of a number of N-acetyl-α-amino esters improved by using an an ionic liquid as cosolvent (Scheme 96)[202].

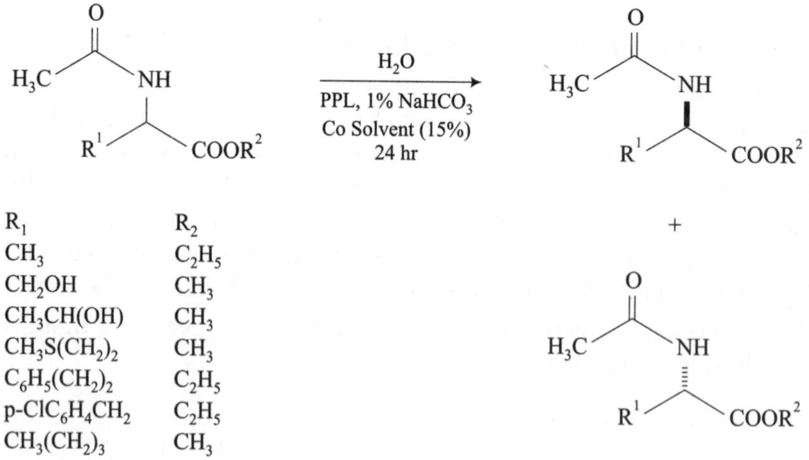

R_1	R_2
CH_3	C_2H_5
CH_2OH	CH_3
$CH_3CH(OH)$	CH_3
$CH_3S(CH_2)_2$	CH_3
$C_6H_5(CH_2)_2$	C_2H_5
p-ClC$_6$H$_4$CH$_2$	C_2H_5
$CH_3(CH_2)_3$	CH_3

Scheme 96

8.11 Enantioselective Hydrolysis of Methyl Phenyl Glycinate and Naproxen Methyl Ester and 2-(4-Chlorophenoxy) Porpoinic Ester

Enantroselective hydrolysis of methyl phenyl glycinate was effected in the presence of cal B. The E ratio was 12, which improved to 34 with 20% [Bmim] [BF$_4$] (Scheme 97)[203, 204].

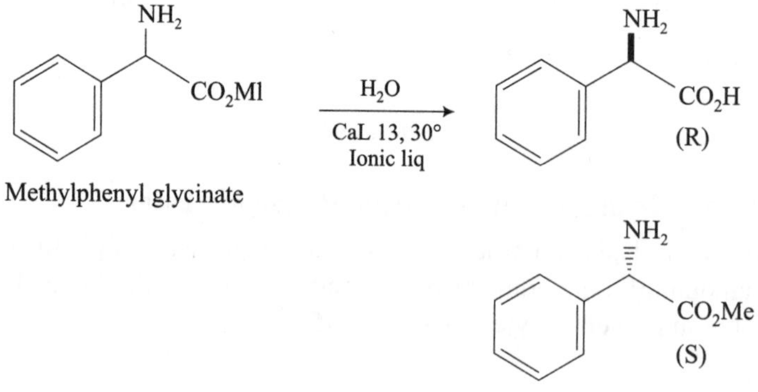

Methylphenyl glycinate

Scheme 97

The enantroselective hydrolysis of naproxen methyl ester to gives (S)-naproxen is important since the latter is a pharmaceutically active enantiomer. The reaction was performed in presence of CrL, which has the desired enantiopreference in a number of ionic liquids that contained [MBIm] [HMIm] cations and anions like [PF$_6$], [BF$_4$] and [HpSO$_4$] (Scheme 98)[205].

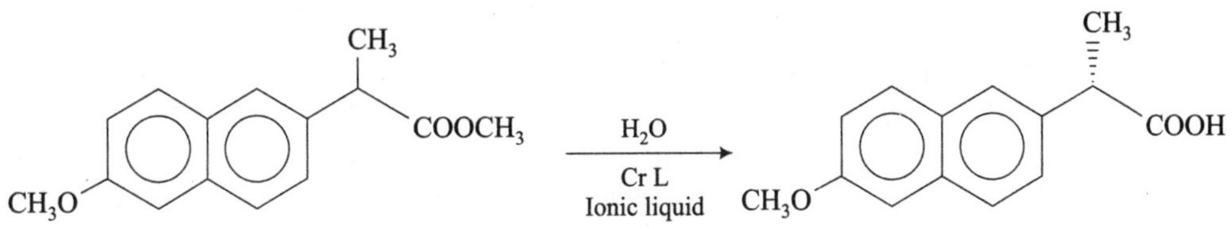

Naproxen methyl ester   S-Naproxen

Scheme 98

The enantioselective hydrolysis of 2-(4-chlorophenoxy) propionic ester in presence of CrL was successful in ionic liquid [BMIm] [BF$_4$] (Scheme 99)[206].

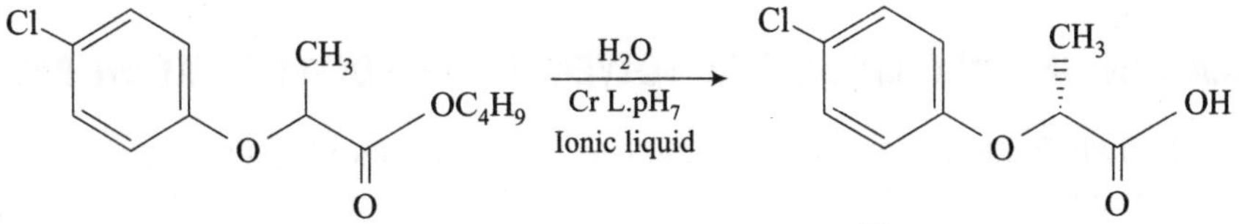

2-(4-Chlorophenoxy)   (R)
propionic ester   2-(4-Chlorophenoxy)
                             propionic acid

Scheme 99

8.12 Enantroselective Esterification of Ibuprofen and 2-Substituted Propanoic Acids

The esterification of ibuprofen with butyl alcohol into the (S)-ester in the presence of CrL took place with modest enantioselectivity (E = 13) when the reaction was carried out in isooctane. However the enantroselectivity increased to 24 in [BMIm][PF$_6$] (Scheme 100)[207,208].

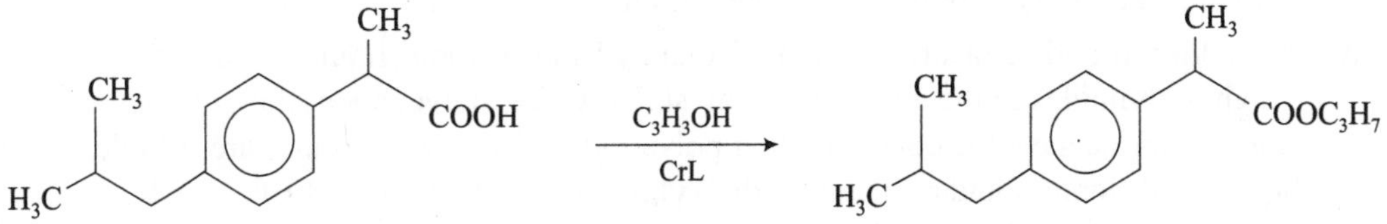

Ibuprofen   (S)-ester

Scheme 100

8.13 Enantioselective Aminolysis of Methyl Mandelate

Enantioselective aminolysis of methyl mandelate with CaLB in conventional media will modest E ratios, which became near quantitative when 20% [BMIm][BF$_4$] was added to the medium[209] (Scheme 101).

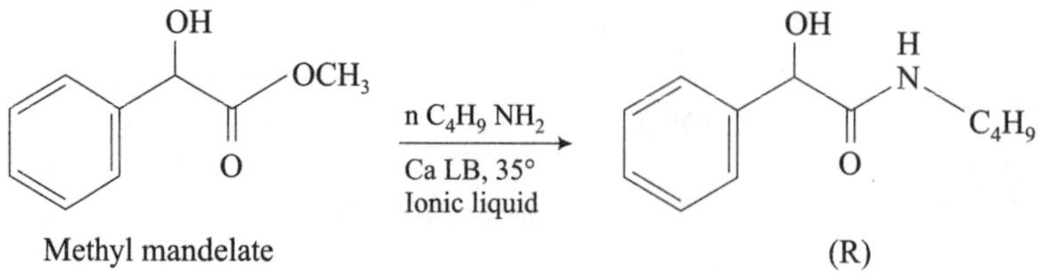

Scheme 101

It was found[209] that changing the medium from tert-butyl alcohol to chloroform switched the enantiomeric preference of CaLB from (R) into S.

The above biotransformations have been catalysed with lipases and Estereses in ionic liquid medium. However, a number biotransformations can be catalysed by Proteases and Redox enzyme systems[210]

9 APPLICATION OF IONIC LIQUIDS AS SOLVENTS FOR POLYMERIZATION PROCESSES

It is very well known that ionic liquids are organic salts that are liquid at ambient temperature. They are non-vlatite, highly polar solvent that dissolve several organic, inorganic and metaloorganic compounds. The use of ionic liquids for organic synthesis has been discussed. It has been shown that the ionic liquid can be advantageously used also for polymer synthesis[211]. Some representative examples of polymenisation in ionic liquid are given below.

(i) Ethylene can be polymenrised using relatively mild conditions (1050 mbar at temperature from-10 to 10°) with diiminenickel catalyst in the ionic liquid [bmim] [AlCl$_4$][212].

(ii) Phenylacetylene was polymenrised in high yield in [bmim] [BF$_4$] with Rh(I) catalyst. By this processure polymers having molecular weight up to 2 × 10^5 were obtained and the solution of the liquid was reused without any significant loss of ionic activity[213].

(iii) The palladium-catalysed copolymerisation of styrene and CO in an ionic liquid solvent, 1-hexyl pyridinum bis (trifluromethylsulfonyl) imide gave improved yields than in typical solvent . The catalyst solution could be reused[214,215].

(iv) Polyaddition and tetracarboxylic acid dianhydride in ionic liquid gave high molecular weight polyimides in the absence a catalyst. However, polycondensation of diamines with diacyl chloride gave the corresponding polyamides. These polyamides are soluble in ionic liquid used (ionic liquids cantaining dialkylimidazolium cation and BF$_4$ (CF$_3$SO$_2$)$_2$ N$^-$, or Br$^-$ anion were used during the polycondensation process[216].

(v) Electrochemical polymensation: Ionic liquid are a suitable reaction media for electro chemical polymerisation processes Thus, benzene and other aromatic hydrocarbon on anodic polymensation in chloroaluminate ionic liquid yield highly conducting films[217]. Also, poly (p-phenylene) was also obtained by oxidative dehydropolycondunsation of benzene in ionic liquid[218]. Electro chemical polymensation was also used for the synthesis of other conducting polymers including polythiophene and substituted polythiophenes[219] and polypyrole[220]. Electrochemical synthesis of inherently conducting polymers such as polypyrrole is traditionally performed in a molecular solvent/electrolytic system such as acetonitrile/lithium perchlorate. It has now been possible to carry out the synthesis in ionic liquids, 1-butyl-3-methylimidazolium hexafluorophosphate, 1-ethyl-3-methylimidazolium bis (trifluoromethane sulfonyl) amide and N, N-butylmethylpyrrolidinum bis (trifluoromethane sulfonyl) amide as growth medium and as electrolyte for the electro-chemical cycling of polypyrrles[220a].

(vi) Enzymatic polymerisation: Polymerisation of ε-caprolactone and polycondensation of aliphatic diesters with 1, 4-butanediol in [bmim] [PF_6] and [bmim] [BF_4] catalysed by lipase gave the corresponding polyesters in 97% for polymerisation and 72% for polycondensation[221]. The above polymensation showed high activity of enzymes in the synthesis of low molecular weight esters and amides conducted in ionic liquids[222]

(vii) High molecular weight polyisobutylene (M_w up to 5×10^5 at 40° in 1-methyl-3-ethyl imidazolium tetrachloroaluminate ionic liquid) was obtained[223].

(viii) Zieglar-Natta polymensation of ethylene[212,224-226] and metathesis polymerisation of acidic dienes[227,228].

(ix) Reverse atoms transfer radical polymerisation (ATRP) of methyl methacrylate (MMA) employing 2, 2-azobisisobutyronitrile (AIBN) |$CuCl_2$| bipyridine (bcpy) as the initating system at 80° was performed in two ionic liquids 1-butyl-3-methylimidazolium fluroborate ([C_4min] [BF_4] and 1-dodecyl-3-methylimidazoliumtetrafluoroborate ([C_{12}min][BF_4]). The resultant polymers and the catalysts were easily isolated and the ionic liquid could be recovered and reused with simple treatment[229].

(x) The room temperature ionic liquid, 1-methyl-3-methylimidazolium hexafluoro-phosphate, [C_4min] [PF_6] was found to be an efficient plasticizer[230] for poly (methyl methacrylate) prepared by in situ radical polymerisations in the ionic liquid medium. The polymers obtinined has physical characteristics comparable with those cantaing traditional plasticizers and retain thermal stability.

(xi) Block copolymers of styrene and methyl methacrylate (MMA) have been made[231] by the sequential addition of the monomers in the room temperature ionic liquid [C_4mim] [PF_6] using BPO as the initiator. The formed polymers could be easily separated from the reaction medium followed by working with methanol due to their poor solubility in [C_4mim] [PF_6].

(xii) Free radical polymensation of methyl methacrytale (MMA) and styrene using conventional organic initiators in the room temperature ionic liquids, 1-butyl-3-methylimidazolium hexafluorophosphate ([C_4min] [PF_6]) is rapid[232]. The polymer produced is of high molecular weights up to $10 \times$ higher than from benzene. In this case, both the polymensation and isolation of the products were achieved without using VOCs; this gives economic and environmental advantage.

(xiii) The cationic polymerization of styrene in room temperature ionic liquid under mild reaction cmditions and using mild acid catalyst (e.g., orgonoborate acids) to obtaihn polymers of narrow polydisperity[233].

10 CONCLUSION

Since the properties and behavior of ionic liquids can be adjusted to suit an individual reaction type, they can truly be described as designer solvents. There are a very large number of simple and complex ionic liquids which can be synthesized. However, selecting the best system for a particular process is a real problem and challenge. The ionic liquids have huge potential for the various pharmaceutical industries, since its use makes the process green. A large number of synthetic applications of ionic liquids have been described.

Ionic liquids have obvious potential as reaction media for biotransformations of highly polar substanges, such as (poly) saccharides, which cannot be performed in water due to equilibrium limitations.

During the recent few years there has been an increasing number of reports concerning application of ionic liquids as solvent for different polymensation processes.

References

1. For a recent review of solventless reactions, see : G.W.V. cave C.L. Raston and J.L. Scott, Chem. Commum, 2001, 2159.

2. V.K. Ahluwalra and Sunita Malhotra, Environmental Science, Ane Books, India, 2006, and the references cited there in.

3. V.K. Ahluwalia, Environmental Chemistry, Ane Books, India, 2008 and the references cited there in.

4. V.K. Ahluwalia and M. Kidwai, New trends in Green Chemistry. Anamaya, 2006 and the references cited therein.

5. P. Wassercheid and W. Keim, Angew. Chem. Int. Ecl 2000, **39**, 3772.

6. T. Weltan, Chem. Rev, 1999, **99**, 2071.

7. H. Olivier-Boutbigu and L. Monga. J. Mol. Catal. A : Chem. 2002, **182**, 419.

8. D. Zhao, W. Wu and Y. Kou, Min. E. Catal. Today, 2002, **74**, 157.

9. R. Sheldon, Chem. Commum, 2001, 2399.

10. J.D. Holbrey and K.R. Seddon, Clean Produicls processes, 1999, **1**, 223.

11. B.S. Chhikara, A.K. Mishra and V. Tandon, Hetrocycles, 2004, **5**, 1057.

12. L. Dupont, R.F. Desouza, Chem. Rev. 2002, **102**, 3667.

13. N. Jain, A. Kumar, S. Chauhan and S.M.S. Chauhan, Tetrahedron, 2005, **61(5)**, 1015.

14. V.K. Ahluwalia and Renu Aggarwal, Organic synthesis; Special Techniques, Narosa Publishing House, 2006, page 195 and the reference cited there in.

15. M.J. Earle and K.R. Seddon, Pune Apple Chem, 2007, **72(7)**, 1391.

16. K.R. Seddon. In molten salt Forum: Proceeding of 5*th* International conference on molten salt Chemistry and Technology, Vol. 5-6, H. Wendt (Ed) pp. 53-62 (1998).

17. J. Sun, M. Forsyth and D.R. Mac Farlane, J. Phy. Chem. 1998, 102, 8558.

18. H.S. Kim, Y.J. Kim, J.Y. Bae, S.L. Kim, M.S. Lah and C.S. Chin, Organometallics, 2003, **22**, 2498.

19. K. Mujatake, K. Yamamoto, K. Endo and E. Tsuchida, J. Org. Chem, 1998, **63**, 7522.

20. S. Tait and R.A. Osteryoung, Inorg. Chem. 1984, **23**, 4352.

21. P. Bonhote, A.P. Dias, K. Papageorgiou, K. Kalyanasundaram, and M. Gratzel, Inorg. Chem, 1996, **35**, 1168.

22. D.R. Mac-Farlane, P. Meakin, J. Sun, N. Amini and M. Forsyth, J. phy. Chem. B 1999, **103**, 4164.

23. J.H. Davis and K. Forrester, Tetrahedron Lelt, 1999, **40**, 1621.

24. N. Tomoharu. Sanyo Chem. Ind. Ltd. JP11273734, 1999.

25. G.J.C. Manmantov and J.D.J. Dunstan, Electrochemical syms Inc. K. S. Patent 5552241, 1996.

26. B.B. Vestergaard, N.J.I. Petrushina, H.A. Hjuler. R.W. Berg and M. Begtrup, J. Electrochem soc., 1993, **140**, 3108.

27. P.J. Dyson. M.C. Grossel, N. Srinivason, T. Vini, T. Welton, D.J. Williams S, A.P.J. White and T. Zigras, J. Chem. Soc. Dalton Trans. 1997, 3465.

28. J.S. Wilkes, J.A. Levinsky, R.A. Wilson and C.L. Hussey, Inorg. Chem., 1982, **21**, 1263.

29. A.E. Visser, R.P. Swatloski, W.M. Reichert, R.D. Rogers, R. Mayton, S. Sheff, A. Wierzbicki and J. H. Davis, Jr, Chem, Commun, 2001, 135.

30. A.J. Carmichael, D.M. Haddleton, S.A.F. Bon K.R. Seddon, Chem. Commun, 2000, 1237.

31. J.S. Wilkes and M.J. Zaworotko, J. Chem. Soc. Chem. Commun, 1992, 965.

32. J.D. Holbrey and K.R. Seddon, Clean Products and Processes, 1999, **1**, 223.

33. J.G. Huddleston, H.D. Willauer, R.P. Swatloski. A.E. Visser and R.D. Rogers, Chem. Commum., 1998, 1765.

34. M. Freemantle, Chem. Eng. News, January 21, 2001.

35. J.G. Huddleston, A.E. Visser, M.W. Reichert, H.D. Willauer, G.A. Brocker and R.D. Koggers. Green Chem., 2001, **3**, 156.

36. N.E. Leadbeater and H.M. Trenius, J. Org. Chem., 2002, **67**, 3145.

37. E. Vander Eycken, P. Appukkuttan, W. De Borggraeve W. Dechaen, D. Dallinger and C.O. Kappe. J. Org. Chem, 2002, **67**, 7904.

38. N.V. Namboodiri and R.S. Varma, Tetrahedron Lett. 2002, **43**, 5381.

39. R.S. Varma and V.N. Namboodiri, Chem. Commun, 2001, 643.

40. R.S. Varma and V.N. Namboodiri, Pure Applied Chem., 2001, **73**, 1307.

41. V.N. Namboodri and R.S. Varma, Chem. Commun, 2002, 342.

42. P. Volker, W. Bohm and W.A. Herrmann, Chem. Eur. 2000, **6**, 1017.

43. V.N. Namboodri and R.S. Varma, Org. Lett. 2002, **4**, 3161.

44. K.S.A. Vallim, P. Emilsson, M. Larhed and A. Hallberg. J. Org. Chem, 2002, **67**, 6243.

45. X. Hong, R. Varma and J.M. Shreive, J. Fluorine Chemistry, 2006, **127**, 159 and the reference cited there in.

46. A.S. Larsen J.D. Holbrey, F.S. Tam and C.A. Reed, J. Am. Chem Soc. 2000, **30**, 7264.

47. C.L. Hussey. Adv. Molten Salt Chem. 1983, **5**, 185.

48. J.S. Wilkes, R.A. Levisky, R.A. Wilson and C.L. Hussey, Inorg. Chem., 1982, **21**, 1263.

49. J. Fuller, R.T. Carlin. H.C. De long and D. Haworth, J. Chem. Soc. Chem. Comum, 1994, 299.

50. J. Fuller, R.T. Carlin and R.A. Osteryoung, J. Electrochemical Soc, 1997, **144**, 3881.

51. D. Zhao, M. Wu, Y. Kou and E. Min, Catalysis Today, 2002, **74**, 157 and the reference cited there in.

52. S.I. Lall, D. Mancheno, S. Castro, V. Behaj, J. I. Cohen and R. Engel, Chem. Commum, 2000, 2413.

53. D.R. MacFarlane, J. Golding, S. Forsyth, M. Forsyth and G.B. Deacon, Chem. Commun, 2001, 1430.

54. S.V. Dzyuba and R.A. Bartsch, Chem. Commun. 2001, 1466.

55. AM. Leone, S.C. Weatherly, M.E. Williams, H.H. Thorp and R.W. Murray, J. Am. Chem. Soc., 2001, **123**, 218.

56. R.A. Olofson, W.R. Thompson and J.S. Michelaman, J. Am. Chem. Soc., 1964, **86**, 1865.

57. A.J. Arduengo, III, R.L. Harlow and M.K. Klini, J. Am. Chem. Soc., 1990, **113**, 361.

58. A.J. Anduengo, III, Acc. Chem. Res, 1999, **32**, 913.

59. J.P. Canal, T. Rammtal, D.A. Dickie and J.A.C. Clyburne, Chem. Commun, 2006, 1809.

60. D. Basavaiah, P.D. Rao and R.S. Hyma, Tetrahetron, 1996, **52**, 8001.

61. G.H.P. Roos and P. Rampersadh, Synth. Commun, 1993, **23**, 1261.

62. M.K. Kundu, S.B. Makherjee, N. Balu, R. Padmakumar and S. Bhat, Synlett, 1994, 444.

63. V.K. Aggarwal, A. Mereu, G.J. Tarver and R. Mc Cague, J. Org. Chem., 1998, **63**, 7183.

64. S. Chowdhury, R.S. Mohan and J.L. Scott, Tetrahedron, 2007, 2363 and the reference cited there in.

65. A.K. Agarwal, I. Emme and A. Mereu, Chem. Commun., 2002, 1612.

66. J-C. Hsu, Y-H. Yen and Y-H. Chu, Tetrahedron Lett, 2004, **45**, 4673.

67. S.T. Handy and M. Okello, J. Org. Chem., 2005, **70**, 1915.

68. P. Formentin, H. Garcia and A. Leyva, J. Mol. Catal. A: Chem. 2004, **214**, 137.

69. J.R. Harjani, S.J. Nara and M.M. Salunkhe, Tetrahedron Lett, 2002, **43**, 1127.

70. T. Kitazume and G. Tanaka, J. Fluorine Chem, 2000, **106**, 211.

71. V. Jurcik and R. Wilhelm, Green Chem. , 2002, **7**, 844.

72. T. Ramnial, D.D. Ino and J.A.C. Clyburne, Chem. Commun, 2005, 325.

73. Y. Chauvin, H. Hirschaurer and J. Olivier, Mol. Catal. 1994, **92**, 155.

74. F.G. Sherif, World Patent Wo, 1998, 98/03454.

75. M.J. Earle, P.B. McCormae, and K.R. Seddon, Chem. Commun, 1998, 2245.

76. C. Su, Z-C. Chen. And Q-G. Zheng, Synth. Commun, 2003, **33**, 2817.

77. W. Chen, L. Xu, C. Chatterton and J. Xiao. Chem. Commun. 1999, 1247.

78. Y. Chauvin, L. Mussmann and H. Olivier, Chem. Int. Ed. Engl., 1995, **34**, 2698.

79. W. Keim, D. Vogt, H. Waffenschmidt and P. Wasserscheid, J. Catal., 1999, **186**, 481.

80. N. Karodia, S. Guise, C. Newlands, and J.A. Andreson. Chem. Commun, 1998, 2341.

81. H. Bahrmann, U.S. Patent, 2000, US 602 5529.

82. Y. Chauvin, H. Mussmann and H. Olivier, U. S. patent, 1998, US 5874638.

83. J. Fuller, A.C. Breda and R.T. Carlin, J. Electro. Chem. Soc. 1997, **144**, 67.

84. F. Favre, H. Olivier-Boubigou, D. Commereue and L. Saussine, Chem. Commun, 2001, 1360.

85. P. Wassercheid, H. Waffenschmidt, P. Machnetzki, K.W. Kottsieper and O. Stelzer, Chem. Commun, 2001, 451; H. Waffenschmidt, P. Wasserscheid, Organomitallics, 2000, **19**, 3818.

86. Q.F. Leconte and M. Basset, J. Mol. Catal. 1986, **36**, 13.

87. H. Waffenschmidt and P. Wasserscheid, J. Mol. Catal. A : Chem. 2000, **164**, 61.

88. E. Mizushima, J. Hayashi and M. Tanaka, Green Chem., 2001, **3**, 76.

89. C.S. Consortic, G. Ebeling and J. Dupont, Tetrahedron Lett, 2002, 753.

90. R. Alcantara, L. Canoria, P. Guilhermo-Joao and J.P. Perez- Mendo, Appl. Catal. A. 2001, **218**, 269.

91. J. Howarth, Tetrahedron Lett., 2000, **41**, 6627.

92. K.R. Seddon and A. Stank, Green. Chem., 2002, **4**, 119.

93. H. Xie, S. Zhang and H. Duan, Tetrahedron Lett., 2004, **45**, 2015.

94. S.V. Ley, C. Ramarao and M.D. Smith, Chem. Commun, 2001, 2278.

95. R.D. Singer and P. Scammells, Tetrahedron Lett., 2001, **42**, 6831.

96. G.S. Owens and M.M. Abu-Omar, Chem. Commun, 2000, 1165.

97. C.E. Song and E.J. Roh, Chem. Commun, 2000, 837.

98. L. Gallion and F. Bedioui, Chem. Commun, 2001, 1458.

99. H.S. Kim, Y.J. Kim, S.D. Lee and C.S.J. Chin. Catal, 1999, **184**, 526.

100. H.S. Kim, Y.L. Kim, H. Lee, K.Y. Park, C. Lee and C.S. Chin, Angew. Chem. Int. Ed. Ed. Engl., 2002, **41**, 4300.

101. R.S. Varma, E. Shale-Demessie and U.R. Pillai, Green Chem, 2002, 170.

102. Y. Chauvin, L. Mussmann and H. Olivier, Angew. Chem. Int. Ed. Engl, 1955, **34**, 2698.

103. P.A.Z. Suarez, J.E.L. Dulles, S. Einloft, R.F. De Souza and J. Dupont, Polyhydron, 1996, **15**, 1217.

104. P.A.Z. Suarez, J.E.L. Dulles, S. Einloft, R.F. De Souza and J. Dupont, J. Inorg. Chim. Acta, 1997, **255**, 207.

105. S. Steines, B. Orieben-Holscher and P. Wasserscheed, J. Prakt. Chem. 2000, **342**, 348.

106. A.P. Umpierre, G. Machado, G.H. Fecher. J. Morais and J. Dupont, Adv. Synth Catal., 2005, **347**, 1404.

107. J. Huang, T. Jiang, B. Han, H. Gao, Y. Chang. G. Zhao and W. Wu Chem. Commun, 2003, 1654.

108. J. Le Bras, D. K. Mukerjee, S. Gonzalez, M. Tristany B. Ganchegui, M. Moreno-Manas, R. Pleixats, F. Herin and J. Muzart, New J. Chem., 2004, **28**, 1550.

109. G.S. Fonseca, J.D. Scholten and J. Dupont, Synlett, 2004, 1525.

110. S. Guernik, A. Wolfson, M. Herskowitz, N. Greenspoon and S. Geresh, Chem. Commun, 2001, 2314; A. Wolfson, I.F.J. Vankelecom and P.A. Jacobs, Organomet, Chem, 2005, **690**, 3558.

111. M. Berthod, J.M. Joerger, G. Mignani, M. Vaultier and M. Lemaire, Tetrahedron Asymmetry, 2004, **15**, 2219.

112. D-Q. Xu, Z-Y. Hu, W.-W. Li, S-P. Luo and Z. – y. Xu, J. Mol. Catal A, 2005, **235**, 137.

113. G.W. Kobalka and R.R. Malladi, Chem. Commun, 2000, 219.

114. I.P. Beletskaya and A.V. Cheprakov, Chem. Rev, 2000, **100**, 3009.

115. R.F. Heck. J. Am. Chem. Soc. 1968, **90**, 5518.

116. A. Carmichacl, M.J. Earle, I.D. Holbrey, P.B. McCormac and K.R. Seddon, Org. Lett., 1999, **1**, 997.

117. L. Xu, W. Chen and J. Xiao, Organometallics, 2000, **19**, 1123.

118. M.T. Reetz, R. Breinbauer and K. Wanninger, Tetrahedron Lett, 1996, **37**, 4499.

119. A.K. Boon, J.A. Levisky, J.L. Pflug and J.S. Wilkes, J. Org. Chem. 1986, **51**, 480.

120. A. Stark, B.L. MaClean and R.D. Singer, J. Chem. Soe, Dalton Trans, 1999, 63.

121. C.W. Lee, Tetrahedron Lett., 1999, **40**, 2461.

122. E. Ota, J. Electrochem. Soc., 1987, **134**, 512.

123. J.A. Boon, S.W. Lander, J.A. Levisky, J.L. Pflug, L.M. Skrzynecki-Cooke and J.S. Wilkers, J. Electrochem. Soc, 1987, **134**, 501.

124. S. Kobayashi, J. Synth. Org. Chem. 1955, **53**, 370.

125. C.J. Adams, M.J. Earle, G. Roberts and K. Seddon, Chem. Commun, 1998, 2097.

126. C.E. Song, W.H. Shim, E.J. Roh. And J.H. Chori, Chem. Commun, 2000, 1695.

127. T. Fisher, T. Sethi, T. Welton and J. Woolf, Tetrahedron Lett, 1999, **40**, 793.

128. M.J. Earle, P.B. McMormae and K.R. Seddon, Green Chem, 1999, **1**, 23.

129. C.P. Mchnert, N.C. Dispenziere and R.A. Cook. Chem. Commun., 2006, 1610.

130. P. Kotrusz, I. Kmentova, B. Gotov, S. Toma and E. Solcaniova, Chem. Commun. 2002, 2510.

131. Le Boulaire and R. Gree. Chem. Commun. 2000, 2195.

132. N. Miyaura and A Suzuki, Chem. Rev, 1995, **95**, 2457. A. Suzuki, J. Organomet. Chem. 1999, 576, 147.

133. T. Welton, P.J. Smith and C.J. Mathew, 221*st* American Chemical Society National meeting, 1EC – 311, 2001.

134. C.J. Mathew, P.J. Smith and T. Welton, Chem. Commun 2000, 1249.

135. C. Zhang, J. Huang, M.L. Trudell and S.P. Nolan, J. Org. Chem, 1999, **64**, 3804.

136. R. Rajgopal, D.V. Jarikote and K.V. Srinivasan, Chem. Commun. 2002, 616.

137. M. Kosugi and K. Fugami, J. Oranomet. Chem., 2002, 653, 50.

138. S.T. Handy and X. Zhang, Org. Lett, 2001, **3**, 233.

139. J. Sirtieix, M. Ossberger, B. Betzemeier and P. Knochel, Synlett, 2000, 1613.

140. W. Chen, L. Xu, C. Chatterton and J. Xiao. Chem. Commun, 1999, 1247.

141. C. de Bellefon, E. Pollet and P. Grenouillet, J. Mol. Catal A. Chem. 1999, **145**, 121.

142. J. Howarth, P. James and J. Dai, J. Mol. Catal. A. 2004, **214**, 143.

143. H. Henry, Compt. Rend, 1895, 120, 1265; J. Kamlet, U.S. Pat. 2, 151, 517 (1939); CA, 1939, **33**, 5001; B. Hass and E. F. Riley Chem Rev, 1943, **32**, 406.

144. A. Kumar and S.S. Pawar, J. Mol. Catal. A. 2005, **235**, 244.

145. T. Jiang, H. Gao, B. Han, G. Zhao, Y. Chang, W. Wu, L. Gao and G. Yang, Tetrahedron Lett. 2004, **45**, 2699.

146. S. Anjaiah, S. Chandrasekhar and R. Gree, Adv. Synth. Catal. 2004, **346**, 1329.

147. A.R. Gholap, K. Venkatesan, R. Pasricha, T. Daniel, R. Lahoti and K.V. Srinivasan, J. Org. Chem., 2005, **70**, 4869.

148. S. Sugden, and H. Wilkins. J. Chen. Soc, 1929, 1291.

149. A. Cole, J.L. Jensen, I. Ntai, K.L.T. Tran, K.J. Weaver, D.C. Forbes and J.H. Davis, J. Am. Chem. Soc, 2002, **124**, 5962.

150. Y. Gu, F. Shi and Y.J. Deng, J. Mol. Catal. A: Chem. 2004, **212**, 71.

151. Y. Gu, J. Zhang, Z. Duan and Y. Deng. Adv. Syth. Catal. 2005, **347**, 512.

152. S. Guo, Z. Du, S. Zhang, D. Li, Z. Li, and Y. Deng. Green Chem. 2006, **8**, 296.

153. A.R. Gholap, N.S. Chakor , T. Daniel, R.J. Lahoti and K.V. Srinivasan, J. Mol. Catal, A: Chem. 2006, **245**, 37.

154. Z. Duan, Y. Gu and Y. Deng. Synth. Commun. 2005, **35**, 1939.

155. B.C. Ranu and S. Banerjee, Org. Lett, 2005, **7**, 3049.

156. J.-M. Xu, K.-B. Liu, W.-B. Wu, C. Qian, Q. Wu and X-F Lin, J. Org. Chem, 2006, **71**, 3991.

157. B.C. Ranu and S. Banerjee, J. Org. Chem., 2005, **70**, 4517.

158. J.S. Yadav, B.V.S. Reddy, C.R. Reddy and K. Rajasekhar, J. Org. Chem, 2003, **68**, 2525.

159. A. Kamal and G. Chouhan, Tetrahedron Lett, 2005, **46**, 1489.

160. Y.J. Kim and R.S. Varma, J. Org. Chem, 2005, **70**, 7882.

161. J. Penj and Y. Deng, Tetrahedron Lett, 2001, **42**, 5917.

162. E.B. Grant, D. Guiadeen, E.Z. Baum and B.D. Foleno, Biorg. Med. Chem. Lelt, 2000, **10**, 2179.

163. R.G. Giles, N.J. Lewis, J.K. Quick, M.J. Sasse, M.W.J. Urquhart and L. Youssef, Tetrahedron, 2000, **56**, 4531.

164. D.-H. Yang, Z.-C. Chen, S.-Y. Chen and Q.-G. Zheng, Synthesis, 2003, **12**, 1891.

165. F. Shi, Y. Deng, T. SiMa, J. Peng, Y. Gu and B. Qiau, Angew. Chem.Int Ed. 2003, **42**, 3257.

166. J.S. Yadav , B.V.S. Reddy and A.K. Raju, Synthesis, 2003, **6**, 6883.

167. J.S. Yadav, B.V.S. Reddy and G. Baishya, J. Org. Chem, 2003, **68**, 7098.

168. C. Wheeler, K.N. West, C.L. Liotta, C.A. Eckert, Chem. Commun. 2001, 887.

169. D.W. Kim, C.E. Soong and C.Y.J. Chi, Am. Chem. Soc, 2002, **124**, 10278.

170. M.R.C. Gerstenberger and A. Hass, Angew. Chem. Int. Ed. 1981, **20**, 647.

171. C. Chippl, V. Conte, Pioraccini. Eur. J. Org. Chem, 2002, 2831.

172. Org. Lett, 2001, **3**, 3785.

173. Chem. Commun, 2002, 146.

174. K.K. Laali and V.S. Gettwert, J. Org. Chem. 2001, **66**, 55.

175. C.J. Adams, M.J. Earle, G. Roberts and K.R. Seddon, Chem. Commun 1998, 2097.

176. M.J. Earle and K.K. Seddon, Pure Appl. Chem. 2000, **72**, 1391 and the references cited there in.

177. P. Tarakeshwar, J.Y. Lee and S. Kim, J. Phys. Chem. A 1998, **102**, 2253.

178. C.J. adams, M.J. Earle and K.R. Seddon, Chem. Commun, 1999, 1043.

179. D.K. Dalling and D.M. Grant, J. Am. Chem. Soc, 1974, **96**, 1827.

180. M.J. Earle, P.B. McCormac and K. R. Seddon, Chem. Commun, 1998, 2245.

181. M.R. Bell, T.E. Dambra, V. Kumar, M.A. Eissenstat, J.L. Herrmann, J.R. Wetzel, D. Rosi, R.E. Philion, S.J. Daum. D.J. Hlasta, R.K. Kullnig, J.H. Ackerman, D.R. Haubrich, D.A. Luttinger, E.R. Baiziman, M.S. Miller and J. Ward, J. Med. Chem. 1991, **34**, 1099.

182. D. Zhao, M. Wu, Y. Kou and E. Min, Catalyst today, 2002, **74**, 157 and the reference cited there in.

183. J.L. Scot, C.L. MacForlane, C.L. Raston and C.M. Teoh. Green Chem, 2000, **2**, 123.

184. J.J. Peng and Y.Q. Deng, New J. Chem., 2001, **25**, 639.

185. O. Bortolini, V. Conte, C. Chiappe, G. Fantin, M. Fogagnolo and S. Maietti, Green Chemistry, 2002, **4**, 94.

186. A. Kumar, N. Jain and S.M.S. Chauhan, Synthetic Communication, 2004, **34**, 2835.

187. M. Erbeldinger, A.J. Mesiano and A.J. Russell, Biotechnol. Prog. 2000, **16**, 1129.

188. S.H. Schöfer, N. Kaftzik, P. Wasserscheid and U. Kragl, Chem. Commun, 2001, 425

189. R.M. Lau, F. Van Rantwijk, K.R. Seddon and R.A. Sheldon, Org, Lett, 2002, **2**, 4189.

190. J.A. Laszlo and D.L. Compton, Biotechnol. Bioeng. 2001, **75**, 181.

191. S.J. Nara, J.R. Harjani and M.M. Salunkhe, Tetrahedron Lett, 2002, **43**, 2979.

192. F. Björkling, S.E. Godtfredsen and O. Kirk, J. Chem. Soc. Chem. Commun, 1990, 1303; F. Björkling, H. Frykman, S.E. Godtfredsen and O. Kirk, Tetrahedron, 1992, **48**, 4587.

193. S.H. Schöfer, N. Kafzik, P. Wasserscheid and U. Kragl, Chem. Commun, 2001, 425.

194. T. Itoh, E. Akasaki, K. Kudo and S. Shirakami, Chem. Lett, 2001, 263.

195. K.-W. Kim, B. Song, M.-Y. Choi and M.-Kim. Org. Lett. 2001, **10**, 1507.

196. D. Bdrahona, P.H. Pfromm and M.C. Rezac, Biotechnol. Bioeng. 2006, **93**, 318.

197. F. Ganske and U.T. Borncheuer, Mol. Catal, B: Enzym. 2005, **36**, 40.

198. F. Ganske and U.T. Borncheuer, Org. Lett, 2005, **7**, 3097.

199. S. Park, F. Vilkund, K. Hult and R.J. Kazlauskas in Ionic liquids as green solvent. ACS Symposium series Vol. 856 Amencan Chemical Society, Waghington, DC 2003, P 225.

200. S. Park, F. Viklund and R.J. Kuzluskas, Green. Chem, 2003, **5**, 715.

201. S. Waltert, K. Drauz, I. Grayson, H. Gröger, P. Dominguez de Maria and C. Bolm, Green Chem., 2005, **7**, 602.
202. S.V. Malhotra and H. Zhao, Chirality, 2005, **17**, S 240.
203. Y.-Y. Liu, W.-Y. Lou, M.-H. Zong, R. Xu, X. Hong are H. Wu, Biocatal. Transform., 2005, **23**, 89.
204. W.-Y. Lou, M.-H. Zong, Y.-Y. Liu and J.-F. Wang. Biotechnol. 2006, **125**, 64.
205. J.-Y. Xin, Y.-J. Zhao, G.-L. Zhao, Y. Zheng, X.-S. Ma, C.-G. Xia and S.-B. Li, Biocatal. Biotransform, 2005, **23**, 353.
206. S.S. Mohile, M.K. Potdar, J.R. Harjani, S.J. Nara, and M.M. Salunkhe, J. Mol. Catal, B. Enzym, 2004, **30**, 185.
207. O. Ubert, J. Fráter, K. Bélafi – Bakó and L. Gubicza, J. Mol. Catal. B. Enzym. 2004, **31**, 39.
208. H. Yu, J. Wu and C. B. Ching, Chirality, 2005, **17**, 16.
209. C. Polisäo and M.G. Nascimento, Tetradron Asymmetry 2006 , **17**, 428.
210. F. Van Rantwijk and R.A. Shedon, Chem. Rev. 2007, **107**, 2757 and the references cited there in.
211. P. Kubisa, Progress in Polymer Science, 2004, **29**, 3.
212. M.F. Pinheiro, R.S. Mauler and R.F. de Souza, Macromol Rapid Commun., 2001, **22**, 425.
213. P. Mastrorilli , C.F. Nobile, V. Gallo, G.P. Suranna and G. Farinola, J. Mol. Catal A. Chem. 2002, **184**, 73.
214. C. Hardacre, J.D. Holbrev, S.P. Katdane and K.R. Seddon, Green Chem, 2002, **4**, 143.
215. M.A. Klingshirn, G.A. Broker, J.D. Holbrey, K.H. Shoughnessy and R. D. Rogers, Chem. Commumication, 2002, 1394.
216. Y.S. Vygodskii, E.I. Lozinskaya and A.S. Shaplov, Macromol Rapid Commun., 2002, **23**, 676.
217. D.C. Trivedi, J. Chem. Soc. Chem. Commun, 1989, 544.
218. V.M. Kobryanskii and S.A. Arnautov, J. Chem. Soe. Chem. Commun, 1992, 720.
219. L. Janiszewska and R.A. Osteryoung, J. Electrochem. Soc, 1987, **134**, 2787.
220. P.G. Pickuo and R.A. Osteryoung, J. Electrochem., 1985, 195, 271, 88.
220a. J.M. Prongle, J. Efthimiadis, P.C. Howlett, J. Efthemiadis D.R. MacFarlane, A.B. Chaplin, S.M. Hall, D.L. Officer, G.G. Wallace and M. Foryth, Polymer, 2004, **45**, 1447.
221. H. Uyama, T. Takamoto and S. Kobayashi, Polyn. J. 2002, **24**, 92.
222. R.M. Lau, F. Van Rantwik, K.R. Seddon and R.O. Sheldon, Org. Lett, 2000, **2**, 4189.
223. V. Murphy, WOO, 032, 658:2000.
224. R.T. Carlim, R.A. Ostervoune, J.S. Wilkes and J. Rovane, Inorg. Chem., 1990, **29**, 3003.
225. R.T. Carlin and J.S. Wilkes, J. Mol. Catal, 1990, **63**, 125.
226. P. Wasserscheid, C.M. Gordan, C. Hilgers, M.J. Muldoon and I.R. Dunkim, Chem, Commun, 2001, 1186.
227. A. Frstner, Angew. Chem. Int. Ed. Engl. 2000, **39**, 3012.
228. M.R. Buchmeiser, Chem. Rev., 2000, **100**, 1565.
229. H. Ma, X. Wan, X. Chen and Qi – Feng Zhou, Polymer, 2003, **44**, 5311.
230. M.P. Scott, C.S. Brazel, M.G. Benton , J.W. Mays, J.D. Holbrey and R.D. Rogers, Chem. Commun, 2002, 1370.
231. H. Zhang. K. Hong and J.M. Mays, Macromolecules 2002, **35**, 5738.
232. K. Hong, H. Zhang, J.M. Mays, Ann E. Visser, C.S. Brazel, J.D. Holbreg, W.M. Reichert and R.D. Rogers. Chem. Commun, 2002, 1368.
233. R. Vijaraghavan and D.R. MacForlane, Chem. Commun, 2004, 700.

PART – IV

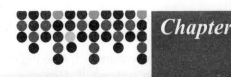

Polyethylene Glycol and its Solutions as Green Reaction Medium of Future

Chapter 8

I INTRODUCTION

The development of non-hazardous solvents is one of the several goals of green chemistry[1]. There are many advantages of replacing volatile organic compounds (VOCs) with water or various types of aqueous solutions. The most obvious advantages are low cost, reduced flammability, reduced toxicity and the most important are reduced environmental risk due to discharge of the various by products. The most commonly used VOC solvent alternatives include, water, super critical fluids and ionic liquids.

The low solubility of organic reactants and their intermediates is the main limitations to the widespread use of water as a reaction solvent. It has been found that polyethylene glycol (PEG) solutions are a better alternative[2]. It is believed[2] that polyethylene glycol may prove to be a green reaction medium of the future.

2 CHARACTERISTICS OF PEG

Polyethylene glycol, PEG, $HO - (CH_2CH_2O)_n - H$, is available in a variety of molecular weights (200 to tens of thousands). At ambient temperature PEG – water solution and hygroscopic polymer is a colourness viscous liquid of molecular weight < 600 and a waxy white solid of molecular weight > 800[3]. The numerical designation of PEG indicates the number of average molecular weight (e.g. PEG – 2000). Liquid PEG is miscible with water in all proportions and solid PEG is highly soluble in water. For example, PEG – 2000 is soluble to the extent of 60 per cent in water at 20°. Lower molecular weight PEG can be used as solvents with or without the addition of water.

PEG has a number of benign characteristics, which are useful in bioseparations[4]. According to US FDA, PEG is recognised as safe and is approved for internal consumption[5,6]. PEG is very weakly immunogenic, a factor due to which it is used by the drug companies[7-10]. Aqueous solutions of PEG are biocompatible and are used in tissue culture media for the preservation[4] of organs.

The low molecular weight PEGs (unlike VOCs) are non-volatile. The requirement of industry standard for selection of alternative solvents to VOC's are met, since the vapour density for low molecular weight PEG is greater than 1 relative to air according to available MS DS data[11]. Another advantage of PEG is that it has low flammability and is biodegrable. Besides, PEG is stable to acid, base and high temperature[12-15]. Also PEG is not effected by O_2, H_2O_2, high oxidation systems[16] and $NaBH_4$ reduction system[17,18]. However, partial oxidation of PEG terminal – CH_2OH group to COOH may occur in such systems as $H_2O_2 - Na_2WO_4$[13]. PEG can also be recovered from aqueous solution by extraction with a suitable solvent or by distillation of water or solvent[19]. Due to this PEG can be recovered and recycled.

3 USE OF PEG IN ORGANIC REACTIONS

PEG has been successfully used in a number of organic reactions. Following are seven some of such reactions.

3.I Substitution Reactions

Following are given some examples of substitution reactions performed using liquid PEG as the solvent.

(i) The reaction of alkyl halides of the type RCH_2Br with nucleophiles like CH_3COO^-, I^- and CN^- in PEG 400 give[20] the corresponding substituted products (Scheme 1).

$$R\ CH_2\ Br\ +\ CH_3COO^- \xrightarrow{\text{PEG-400}} R\ \text{-}CH_2OCOCH_3$$

$$R\ CH_2\ Br\ +\ I^- \xrightarrow{\text{PEG-400}} R\ CH_2I$$

$$R\ CH_2\ Br\ +\ CN^- \xrightarrow{\text{PEG-400}} R\ CH_2CN$$

$$R = C_6H_5,\ C_3H_7\ \text{etc.}$$

Scheme 1

(ii) Potassium thioacetate in PEG – 400 has been used as a nucleophilic reagant to substitute alkyl halides of the type R_1– $CHXR_2$ to give[21] the products in 92-98% yield (Scheme 2).

$$R_1 - CHX - R_2\ +\ CH_3COS^- \xrightarrow{\text{PEG-400}} R_1 - CH - R_2$$

$$R_1 = C_6H_5,\ C_7H_{15},\ C_9H_{10}$$
$$R_2 = H,\ CH_3$$
$$X = Cl,\ Br,\ I$$

$$SCOCH_3$$

Scheme 2

(iii) The reaction of tert. butyl chloride with H_2O in PEG-300 gives[22] tert. butyl alcohol (Scheme 3).

$$(CH_3)_3\ CCl\ +\ H_2O \xrightarrow{\text{PEG-300}} (CH_3)_3\ COH$$

Scheme 3

(iv) The reaction of 1-chloro-2-methylpropene with H_2O in PEG-425 gave[23] a mixture of alcohols (Scheme 4).

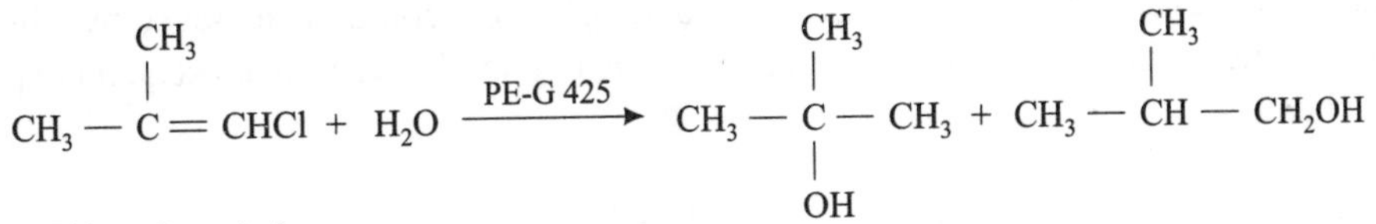

CH$_3$ — C = CHCl + H$_2$O $\xrightarrow{\text{PE-G 425}}$ CH$_3$ — C — CH$_3$ + CH$_3$ — CH — CH$_2$OH

1-Chloro-2-methyl propene

Scheme 4

(v) The Diel-Alder reaction of 2, 3-dimethyl – 1, 3-butadiene with acrolein gave[22] the adduct in good yield (Scheme 5).

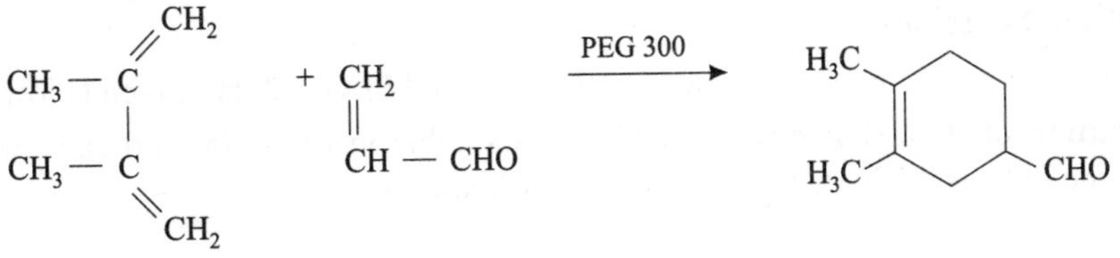

$\xrightarrow{\text{PEG 300}}$

2,3-Dimethyl   Acrolein   Adduct
1,3-butadiene

Scheme 5

In the above reaction, the yield was 14 fold in comparison to the reaction carried out in methanol. However, The Diel-Alder reaction of 2, 3-dimethy-1, 3-butadiene with nitroso-benzene in PEG-300 showed a 3.3 fold increase compared to the same reaction in dichloro-methane.

(vi) The diazotization of aryl amines followed by Sandmeyer reaction gave halogeno arenes and cyanoarenes. The reaction could be carried out even in 10 mM dilute substrate acid is comparable with these reactions in various organic solvents (e.g. Xylene, DMSO and THF) giving high yields only in high concentrations of the substrate ($\geq$73 mm)[24]. The usual aqueous Sandmiger reaction reported in organic synthesis gave very poor yields[24] (Scheme 6).

Ar NH$_2$ $\xrightarrow[\substack{\text{2) Sand meyers Reaction} \\ \text{X or CN}^-}]{\text{1) Diazotization}}$ ArX or ArCN

Ar = C$_6$H$_5$,
p-OCH$_3$C$_6$H$_4^-$
o-CH$_3$OC$_6$H$_4^-$
m-CH$_3$OC$_6$H$_4^-$

Scheme 6

(vii) Heck coupling reaction could be performed using molten liquid PEG – 2000 at 80°. The yield of the product was good[25]; the reaction rate, yield and regio and stereo selectivies in this solvent system are comparable with the conventional organic solvents like DMF, DMSO, CH$_3$CN or ionic liquid, 1-butyl-3-methylimidazolium tetrafluoroborate. In this case, the recyclability of both PEG-2000 and Pd(OAc)$_2$ could be achieved by ether extraction of the product. The higher yield can also be obtained after four subsequent experiments (Scheme 7).

$$R \!-\! C_6H_5 \, Br \; + \; CH_2 = CHX \qquad \xrightarrow[\text{(Pd(OAc)}_2 \text{ Catalyst)}]{\text{PEG-2000}} \qquad RC_6H_4 \!-\! CH = CHX$$

R = Cl, OCH$_3$ X = C$_6$H$_5$, CO$_2$Et

Scheme 7

The Heck coupling reaction form the subject matter of a subsequent section (see section 8)

3.2   Oxidation Reactions

Some of the oxidation reactions conducted in PEG-200 and PEG-400 are given below.

(i) **Oxidation of Benzyl Bromide**. K$_2$Cr$_2$O$_7$ is soluble in PEG-400 and can oxidize benzyl bromide to benzaldehyde in good yield[19] (Scheme 8).

$$C_6H_5CH_2Br \qquad \xrightarrow[\text{Oxidation}]{K_2Cr_2O_7/\text{PEG-400}} \qquad C_6H_5CHO$$

Benzyl bromide   Benzaldehide

Scheme 8

The above oxidation is similar to the raection of Na$_2$Cr$_2$O$_7$ in hexamethyl phosphoramide (HMPA) and Crown ether using the same substrate.

(ii) **Dihydroxylation of olefins**. Using PEG-400 as solvent and osmium tetraoxide as catalyst[26] gives high yield of diols (Scheme 9).

$$C_6H_5CH = CHC_6H_5 \qquad \xrightarrow[\substack{\text{Catalysed by OsO}_4 \\ \text{PEG-400 (2-4 hr)}}]{\text{N-Methylmorpholine (NMO)}} \qquad C_6H_5CH \!-\! \underset{\underset{OH}{|}}{CH} \!-\! \underset{\underset{OH}{|}}{CH} \!-\! C_6H_5$$

Scheme 9

In the above reaction, the PEG-400 and OsO$_4$ could be recused by extraction of the product diols using ether. More than 90% yield was obtained even after five cycles. Also, the reaction was suitable for asummetric dihydroxylation (Sharpless reaction) with high yields and good enantioselectivity. This oxidation procedures forms the subject matter of a subsequent section (see section 7).

3.3   Reduction Reactions

(i) In PEG-400, carboxyl compounds could be reduced by NaBH$_4$ more conveniently and efficiently than by the slow reaction in THF[19] (Scheme 10).

$$CH_3COC_6H_{13} \; + \; NaBH_4 \qquad \xrightarrow{\text{PEG-400}} \qquad CH_3CHOH \, C_6H_{13}$$

Scheme 10

(ii) The reduction of alkyl and aryl esters to the corresponding alcohol by $NaBH_4$ in PEG-400 was enhanced. These alkyl and aryl esters are considered inert towards reduction in other organic solvents[27] (Scheme 11).

$$R — COOR' \quad + \quad NaBH_4 \quad \xrightarrow{\text{PEG-400}} \quad R — CH_2OH$$

R = alkyl, aryl
R' = CH_3, C_2H_5

Scheme 11

(iii) The reduction of halides of the type R-CHX-R' by $NaBH_4$ in PEG-400 is comparable[28] to that in other polar protic solvents like DMSO, HMPA and DMF (Scheme 12).

$$R — CHX — R' \quad + \quad NaBH_4 \quad \xrightarrow{\text{PEG-400}} \quad R — CH_2 — R'$$

R = alkyl, aryl
X = Cl, Br, I
R' = H, CH_3, C_4H_9

Scheme 12

(iv) The reduction of acyl chloride can be conveniently effected in PEG-400 as a substitute for inert solvent dioxane[28] (Scheme 13).

$$R — COCl \quad + \quad NaBH_4 \quad \xrightarrow{\text{PEG-400}} \quad R — COH$$

R = C_6H_5, p-BrC_6H_4

Scheme 13

(v) The partial reduction of triple bonds in alkynes to cis-olefins has been achieved[29] by Lindlar's catalyst, Pd-$CaCO_3$ poisoned with PbO in presence of PEG-400. The PEG and the catalyst could be used a number of times (3-5) without loss of activity or yield.

(vi) Hydrogenation of styrene is possible[30] using waxy solid PEG-900 at 155 bar pressure in SC – CO_2 at 40°. The $RhCl(PPh_3)$ – catalysed hydrogenation of styrene to ethyl benzene in PEG – 900 at 155 bar, 55° in SC – CO_2 was conducted as a homogeneous catalyst reaction. Ethyl benzene could be extracted into SC – CO_2 and the catalyst containing PEG phase was reused[30] (Scheme 14).

$$C_6H_5CH = CH_2 \quad + \quad H_2 \quad \xrightarrow[\text{RhCl(PPh}_3)]{\text{PEG-900}} \quad C_6H_5CH_2CH_3$$

Styrene   Ethyl benzene

Scheme 14

4 PEG AS PHASE-TRANSFER CATALYST (PTC)

It is well known that PTCs are used to transport an aqueous reagent into an organic phase in an activated state, so that the reaction can proceed due to bringing the aqueous reagent and the organic substrate together[15]. PEG has the ability to serve as a PTC because the polyethylene oxide chain can form complexes with metal cations similar to Crown ethers[31]. In order to maintain electroneutrality, such PEG – metal cation complexes must bring an equivalent anion into the organic phase. In this way, the anion is made available for reaction with organic substrates. A number of factors affect phase catalytic activity. These include PEG molecular weight, chain end effects and the nature of the associated cations and anions.

PEGs are used as PTCs in a number of commercial processes to replace expensive and environmentally-harmful PTCs[31-35]. Of the commonly used PTCs, lintar PEGs are much cheaper than analogous macrocyclic Crown ethers and Cryptands[36]. PEGs are also comparatively more stable at high temperature upto 150-200° and show higher stability to acidic and basic conditions than quaternary onium salts[15].

Following are given some of the examples in which PEGs have been used as Phase Transfer Catalysts.

4.1 Williamson Ether Synthesis

Williamson Ether synthesis is an important nucleophilic substitution reaction (S_N2) and involves the synthesis of ether using alkyl halides and an alkoxide in an alcoholic solution (Scheme 15).

$$R - OH + R'X \xrightarrow{\text{PEG}} R - O - R'$$

Scheme 15

The yield of decan-1-ol during etherification in using PEG-2000 as PTC is 84%, which is comparable to that found by using 18-Croun-6 and higher than 72% yield found using kryptofix 222 (cryptand)[37-39] (Scheme 16).

$$C_{10}H_{21}OH + C_4H_9X \xrightarrow{\text{PEG - 300–2000}} C_{10}H_{21} - O - C_4H_9$$

$$X = Cl, Br, I$$

Scheme 16

The crown ethers and cryptand are expensive and may constitute toxins or irritants[37].

4.2 Substitution Reactions Using PEGs as PTC

PEGs have been used as PTC in nucleophilic substitution reactions. The common anionic nucleophilic reagents which have been used are hydroxides, halides, sulfides, cyanides, cyanamides, carboxylates etc. Thus, the synthesis of 1, 4-phenylenedioxydiacetic acids and aryl 1,4-phenylenedioxydiacetate has been achieved[40] by using PEG-400 as PTC in good yields under mild conditions (Scheme 17).

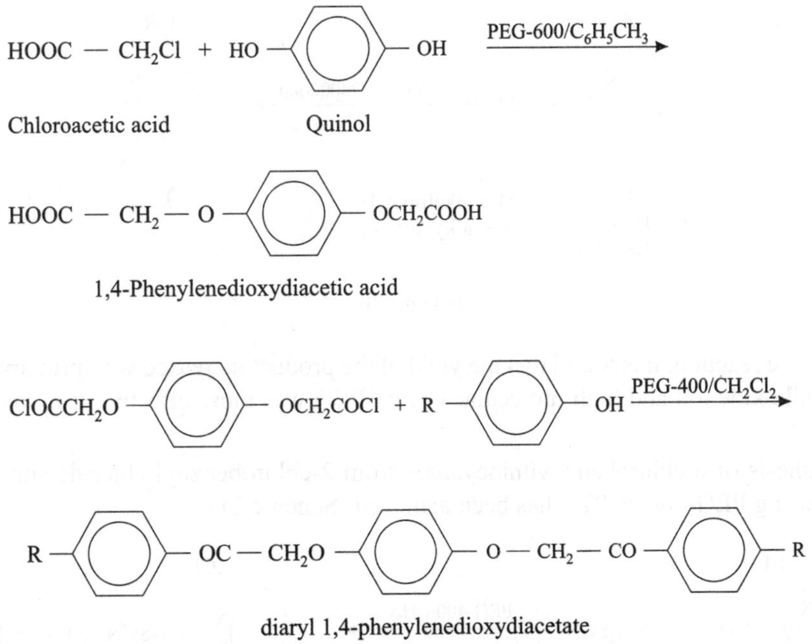

HOOC — CH$_2$Cl + HO —⟨◯⟩— OH $\xrightarrow{\text{PEG-600/C}_6\text{H}_5\text{CH}_3}$

Chloroacetic acid   Quinol

HOOC — CH$_2$ — O —⟨◯⟩— OCH$_2$COOH

1,4-Phenylenedioxydiacetic acid

ClOCCH$_2$O —⟨◯⟩— OCH$_2$COCl + R —⟨◯⟩— OH $\xrightarrow{\text{PEG-400/CH}_2\text{Cl}_2}$

R —⟨◯⟩— OC — CH$_2$O —⟨◯⟩— O — CH$_2$ — CO —⟨◯⟩— R

diaryl 1,4-phenylenedioxydiacetate

Scheme 17

PEG as PTC has been employed in a SC – CO$_2$ solvent to convert benzyl chloride with potassium cyanide to form phenylacetonitrile, although the yield is lower than a similar reaction using tetraheptylammonium cyanide. However, use of PEG as PTC is a beginning of a low cost, green reaction process[41] (Scheme 18).

C$_6$H$_5$CH$_2$Cl + KCN $\xrightarrow{\text{PEG/SC-CO}_2}$ C$_6$H$_5$CH$_2$CN

Benzyl chloride   Phenyl acetonitrile

Scheme 18

Use of potassium sulphocyanide in the above reaction gives the corresponding sulphocyanide (Scheme 19).

C$_6$H$_5$CH$_2$Cl + KSCN $\xrightarrow{\text{PEG/SC-CO}_2}$ C$_6$H$_5$ — CH$_2$SCN

Scheme 19

The reaction of mono and di-halobenzenes with alkoxide ions give[42] monoalkybenzenes (Scheme 20).

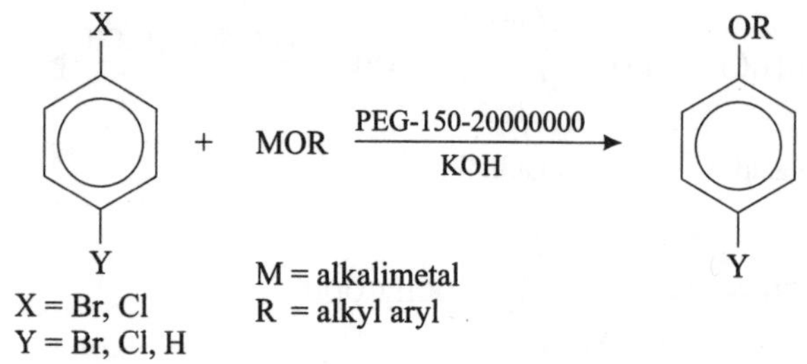

Scheme 20

In the above reaction, it is found that the yield of the product increased with primary, secondary and tertiary alkoxide ion and high molecular weight PEG was more effective than low molecular weight PEG.

The synthesis of o-chlorobenzoylthiocyanate from 2-chlorobenzoyl chloride and ammonium thiocyanate using PEG-400 as PTC has been achieved (Scheme 21).

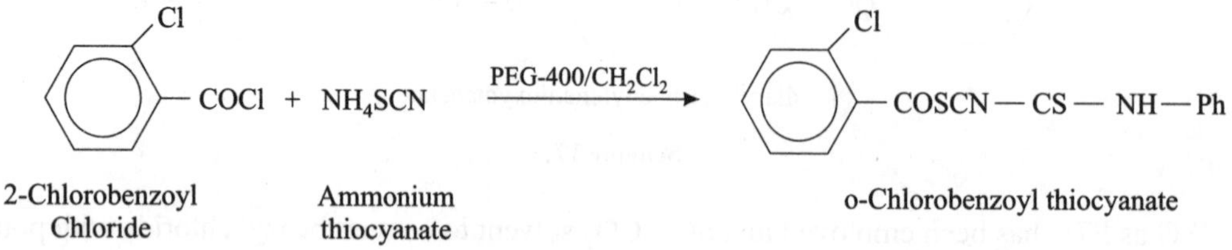

Scheme 21

The above synthesis is more effective than most quaternary ammonium salts and Crown ethers[42a].

n-Alkylations of different types of amines by alkyl halides using PEG-350 methyl ether has been effected (Scheme 22).

$$R - NH_2 + R'I \xrightarrow{\text{PEG-350 methyl ether}} R - NH - R'$$

Scheme 22

The above N-alkylation is enhanced in presence of ultrasound[43]. In all these reactions the cost of PEG is an important factor[44].

4.3   Oxidation Reactions Using PEG as PTC

PEG has been used with success in many oxidation reactions. Thus benzylalcohol on oxidation with potassium hypochloride in PEG-6000 and ethyl acetate yields[45] benzaldehyde (Scheme 23).

$$C_6H_5CH_2OH + KOCl \xrightarrow{\text{PEG-6000/CH}_3\text{COOC}_2\text{H}_5} C_6H_5CHO$$

Benzyl alcohol   Benzaldehyde

Scheme 23

The cobalt catalysed carbonylation of benzyl halides using PEG-400 proved to be much cheaper than that using quaternary ammonium salts or Crown ethers[46] (Scheme 24).

$$R - C_6H_4 - CH_2X \xrightarrow[\substack{PEG-400 \\ 2-CH_3 C_4H_9OH}]{Air/Co_2(CO)_8} R - C_6H_4 - CHO$$

$$X = Cl \text{ or } Br$$

Scheme 24

Ultrasound assisted base catalysed oxidation of alkylnitrobenzene using PEG as PTC gave[47] p-nitro benzoic acid (Scheme 25).

$$O_2N - \langle \text{ring} \rangle - CH_3 \xrightarrow[O_2]{PEG-400|C_6H_5CH_3|KOH} O_2N - \langle \text{ring} \rangle - COOH$$

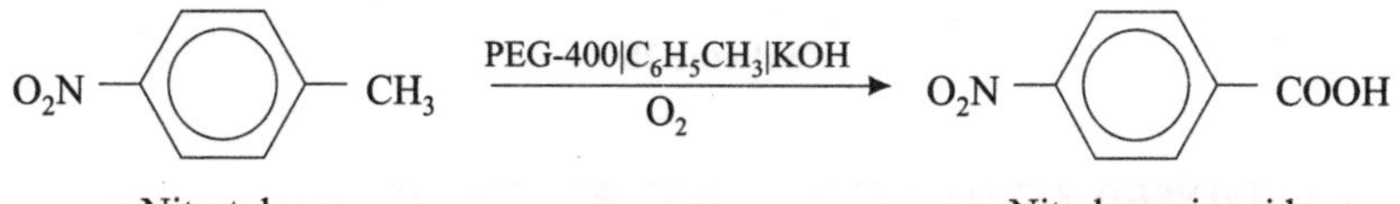

p-Nitrotoluene   p-Nitrobenzoic acid

Scheme 25

Iodoarenes and Iodoalkanes an oxidation with oxygen in PEG-400 and inexpensive $CoCl_2$ in $KCN - BF_3 \cdot Et_2O - FeCl_2$ gave[48] carboxylic acids. The reaction conditions in the above oxidation are milder compared to the use of a platinum catalyst[48] (Scheme 26).

$$\begin{array}{c} RI \\ R = H_3C - C_6H_4\, CH_3(CH_2)_n \end{array} \xrightarrow[\substack{PEG-400|KCN|KOH}]{air/CoCl_2} RCOOH$$

Scheme 26

Oxidation of diphenyl methane with oxygen and PEG-6000 gave[49] benzophenone.

4.4 Reductions Using PEG as PTC

The reduction of ketones and aldehydes can be effected[17,18,50] with PEG and $NaBH_4$ and PEG-$NaBH_4$ complexes (Scheme 27).

$$R\, COR' \quad + \quad NaBH_4 \xrightarrow{PEG-400/C_6H_6} R\, CH\,(OH)\, R'$$

$$R = C_6H_5, C_6H_5CH_2$$
$$R' = CH_3, C_6H_5$$

Scheme 27

It is found that free PEG can catalyze[50] reduction of ketones by $NaBH_4$. However, PEG − $NaBH_4$ derivative can selectively reduce aldehydes in the presence of ketones without concurrent reduction of ketone group[17].

PEG-6000 in benzene is found to be more effective than using Crown ether or quaternary ammonium salts for base catalysed autoxidation of picoline[17].

The conversion of aldehydes to homologous acids by a simple two step process using PEG is considered more practical than the usual conversion of p-anisaldehyde to p-methoxyphenylacetic acid [51] (Scheme 28).

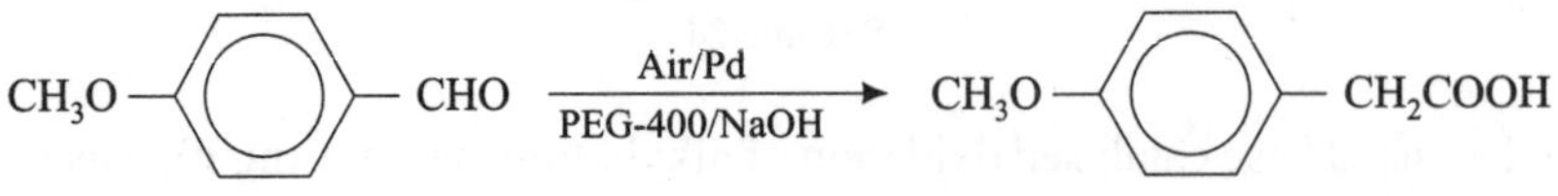

$$CH_3O-\langle C_6H_4 \rangle-CHO \xrightarrow[\text{PEG-400/NaOH}]{\text{Air/Pd}} CH_3O-\langle C_6H_4 \rangle-CH_2COOH$$

Anisaldehyde   p-Methoxy phenylacetic acid

Scheme 28

5 L-PROLINE CATALYSED ASYMMETRIC ALDOL REACTIONS

Aldol condensation is known to be very effective in C-C bond forming process and is used widely in organic synthesis. Usually aldehydes containing α-hydrogen atom undergo aldol condensation to give β-hydroxy aldehydes called aldol (Scheme 29).

$$CH_3CHO + CH_3CHO \xrightarrow{\text{NaOH}} CH_3-\underset{\underset{\text{OH}}{|}}{CH}-CH_2-CHO$$

Scheme 29

Aldol condensation is also known to take place between an aldehyde and a ketone. In this reaction called crossed aldol condensation or Claisen-Schmidt reaction, the formed aldol undergoes elimination of water to give the product (Scheme 30).

$$C_6H_5CHO + CH_3COCH_3 \xrightarrow[\Delta \ H_2O]{10\% \ NaOH} C_6H_5CH=CHCOCH_3$$

Benzaldehyde   Acetene   Benzylideneacetone

Scheme 30

Asymmetric version of aldol condensation[52-58] has been utilised for enantioselective C-bond forming. This is the prime objective in organic synthesis. Such reactions have also been attempted using a recyclable ionic liquid as solvent[59], buffered aqueous media or aqueous micelles[61].

L-Proline catalysed direct asymmetric aldol reaction of acetone with various aromatic and aliphatic aldehydes in PEG-400 has been reported[62] to give asymmetric aldol products (Scheme 31).

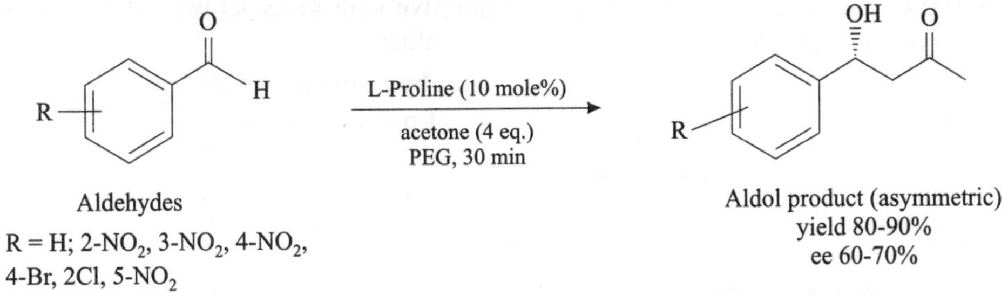

Scheme 31

The aliphatic aldehydes, isobutyraldehyde and cyclohexane carboxaldehyde have also been used as substractes[62] and asymmetric aldol products obtained in 90 and 65 per cent yield respectively. Also high enantioselectivity (about 84%) was obtained for the reaction of isobutyraldehyde with acetone (Scheme 32).

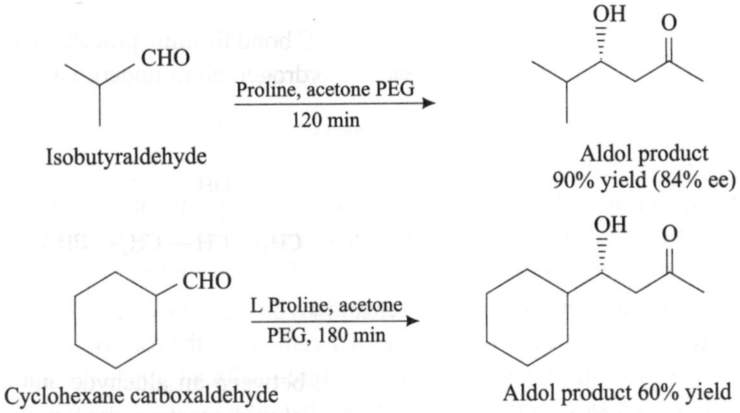

Scheme 32

The above asymmetric aldol reactions are green reactions[62], since PEG (a biologically compatible product) is used as a solvent, which is much cheaper ($43/kg) compared io ionic liquids ($1200-2400/kg) and L-proline is required in small concentration. Besides the catalyst, solvent can be recycled for about ten runs without loosing any of the characteristics.

6 L-PROLINE CATALYSED ASYMMETRIC TRANSFER ALDOL REACTION

Transfer aldol reaction involves the reaction of aldehydes with diacetone alcohol (as a source of ketone, acetone) in presence of alkoxides. In these reactions Aldol-Tischeno reaction in competitive to get mono protected 1, 3-diols and in a few cases normal products were observed[63]. It has now been possible to use[62] L-Proline as catalyst for asymmetric transfer aldol reaction. Thus, the reaction of 4-nitrobenzaldehyde and diacetone alcohol in the presence of L-Proline (30 mole %) in DMSO afforded the corresponding β-hydroxy ketone in 86 per cent yield and 71 per cent ee. No difference in yield was observed even after increasing the concentration of catalyst to 100 mole per cent. Using PEG – 400 as the solvent only lowered the yield and ee compared to the standard solvent (DMSO) (Scheme 33). The reaction conditions were mild enough to avoid the formation of Tischeno-Addol product (A).

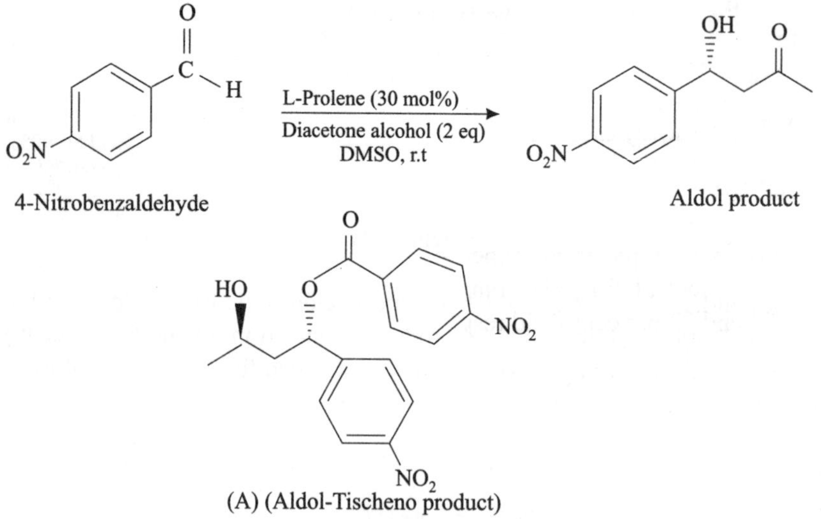

Scheme 33

In a similar way various other aldehydes such as 3-nitrobenzaldehyde, 4-bromobenzaldehyde, 2-chloro-5-nitrobenzaldehyde and 2-chlorobenzaldehyde on subjecting to this transformation gave the corresponding aldol products up to 88 per cent yield and ee's up to 71 per cent.

Transfer aldol reaction between simple benzaldehyde and diacetone alcohol gave the corresponding β-keto ester in 50 per cent yield and 57 per cent ee. In the case of anisaldehyde, the aldol product was obtained only after 5 days at room temperature with 48 per cent ee and 40 per cent yield along with the dehydrated aldol condensation product.

Amongst aliphatic aldehydes, isobutyraldehyde gave aldol product in 80 per cent yield and 84 per cent ee and cyclohexane carboxaldehyde gave the aldol product in 90 per cent yield with 86 per cent ee. A plausiable reaction mechanism involving a cyclic transition state (re-facial attack of aldehyde to proline derivative) where a retro aldol and aldol reactions are initated by the same catalyst has been proposed [62].

7   ASYMMETRIC DIHYDROXYLATION OF OLEFINS

Conventionally vicinal diols are prepared[64] by the dihydroxylation of olefins using catalytic amount at OsO_4. Even though the vicinal diols are used in pharmaceuticals and fine chemicals[65], the cost, toxicity[66] and contamination of the product with osmium restricts its use in industry.

Asymmetric dihydroxylation of olefins has been carried out[26] using catalytic amount of osmium tetraoxide and PEG-400. The ligand is efficiently recovered and recycled with good enantioselectivity. Thus, dihydroxylation of styrene and α-methyl styrene using OsO_4 (0.5 mol %) in PEG (400 MW) using N-metthyl morpholine (NMO, 1.3 eq.) as the reoxidant give 94 per cent and 97 per cent respectively of the diols (Scheme 34).

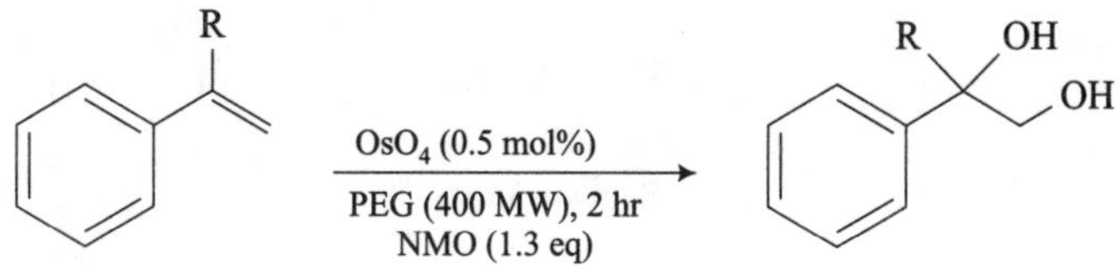

Styrene R = H
α-Methylstyrene R = Me

Diol R = H 94%
Diol R = CH_3 97%

Scheme 34

Other olefins, for example, trans-stilbene produced 1, 2-diphenyl-1, 2-ethane diol in 95 per cent yield. Electron deficient olefins, viz. trans-ethylcinnamate and ethyl 4-methoxy cinnamate produced diols in 93 and 92 per cent yield respectively (Scheme 35).

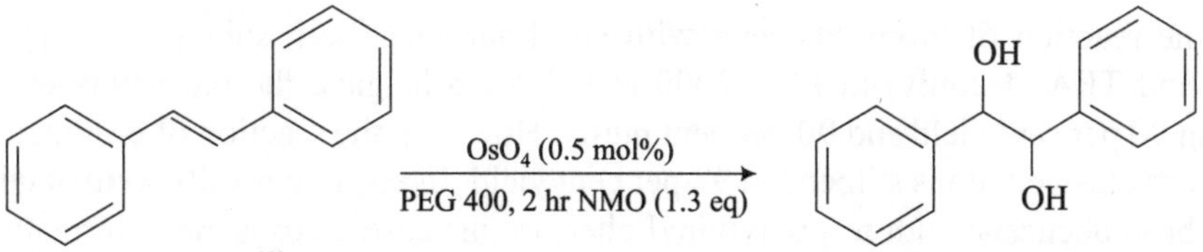

trans stilbene

1,2-Diphenyl-1,2-ethane diol (95%)

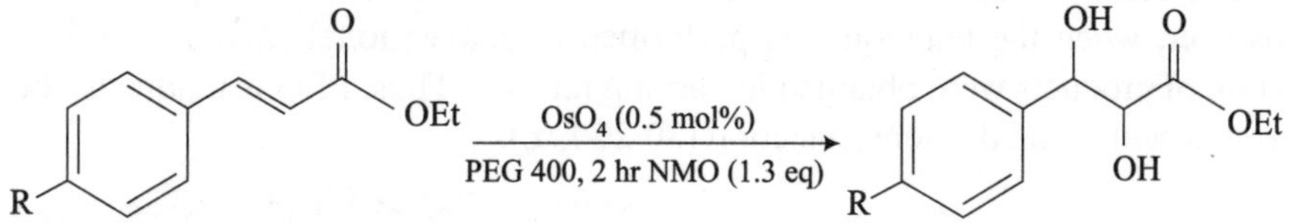

Trans ethyl cinnamate R= H
4-methoxy trans ethyl cinnamate R= OMe

92-93%

Scheme 35

Some other olefins which produced diols on oxidation with OsO_4/PEG/NMO are given below (Scheme 36).

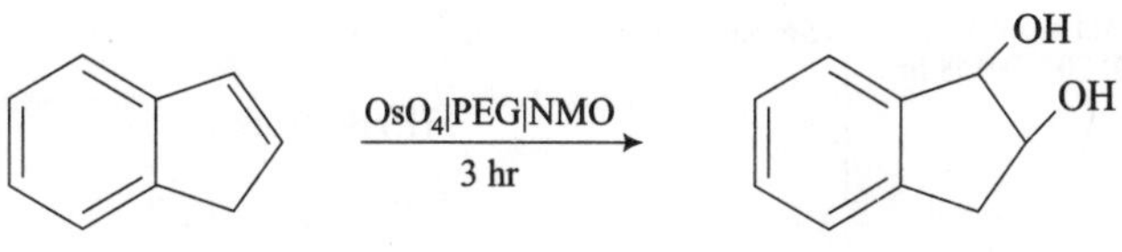

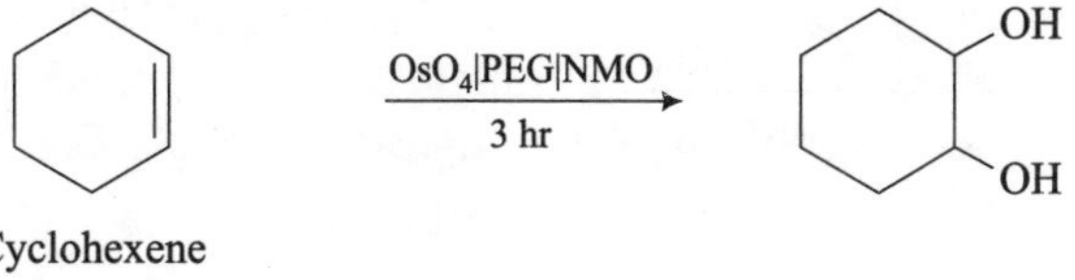

Cyclohexene

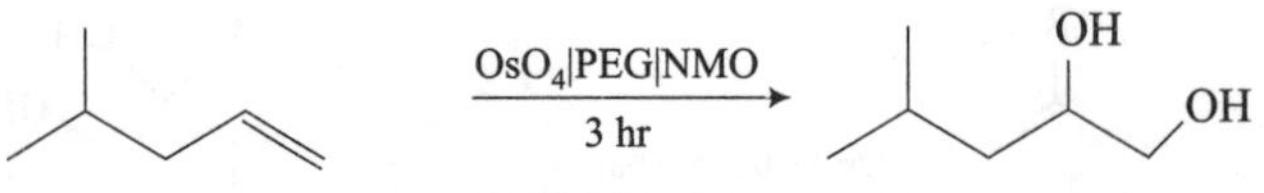

Scheme 36

In all the above cases, the catalyst and PEG were recovered and recycled. The asymmetric dihydroxylation of olefins according to the Sharpless procedure took longer time (up to 24 hr).

8 REGIOSELECTIVE HECK REACTION

PEG having molecular weight 2000 (or lower) has been used[25] as an efficient reaction medium for Pd – catalyzed C – C bond formations, namely the Heck reaction[67,68]. This transformation[25] is more rapid and high yielding; the catalyst is easily recycled with high efficiency. The stereo – and regioselectives are also different from those with conventional solvents and ionic liquids[69].

Thus, the reaction of bromobenzene with ethyl acrylate (both substrates 1 : 1), Pd(OAc)$_2$ (3 mol %) and TEA (1 equiv) in PEG 2000 at 80° for 8 hr gave the clean formation of ethyl cinnamate in 90 per cent yield and 90 per cent purity. However, the reaction of bromobenzene with styrene gave exclusively trans stilbene in 93 per cent yield. Interesting results were obtained by the reaction of bromobenzene with n – butylvinyl elter; in this case there is clean formation of butyl styryl ether with exclusive attack of aryl palladium species at the β-carbon of butyl vinyl elher (Scheme 37). The results obtained are different than when the reaction was performed in ionic liquids[69]. However, when the reaction was performed in conventional solvents (DMF, DMSO, CH$_3$CN) mixture of products were obtained in varying ratios[70]. Thus, PEG is unique is obtaining a single regioisomer with good diastereoselection (80/20 E/Z).

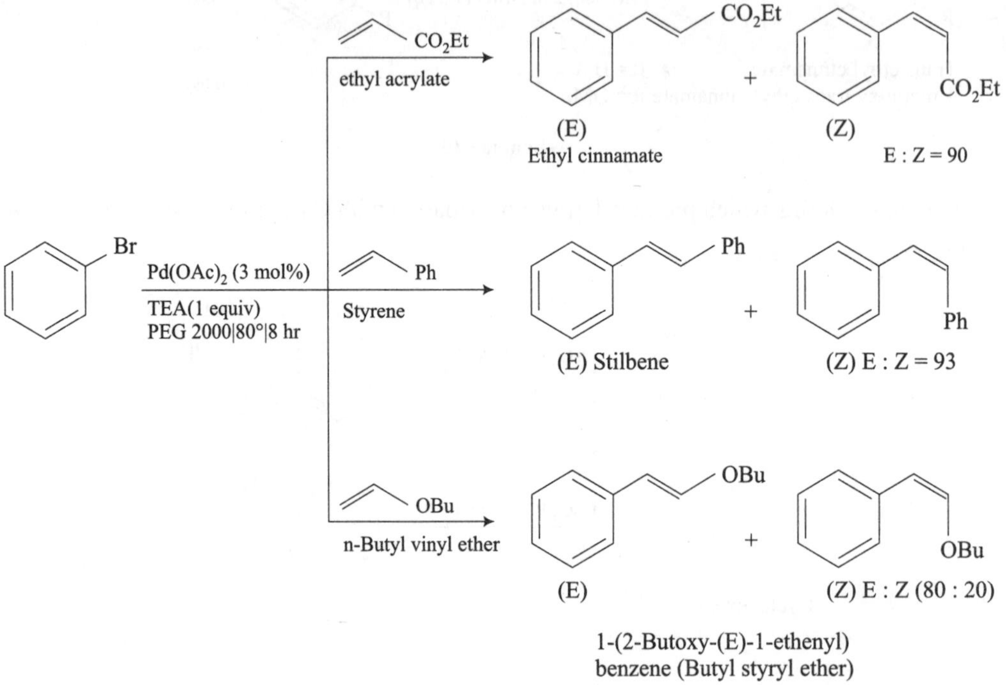

Scheme 37

The Heck reaction of 4-bromoanisole with all the three olefins, vig. ethyl acrylate, styrene and n-butyl vinyl ether gave excellent regio and stereoselectivies of 4-methoxy ethyl cinnamate (E:Z 91), 4-methoxy stilbene (E:Z 85) and 1-(2-butoxy-(E)-1-ethenyl-4-methoxybenzene (butyl p-bromostyryl ether) (E:Z/70:30) respectively. The Heck reaction of 4-chlorobromobenzene with butyl vinyl elter, there is exclusive formation of E-geometrical olefin. On the basis of the results obtained it was concluded[25] that electronic factors in the aryl system control the geometry of the olefins to a certain extent; the other olefines, viz. styrene and ethyl acrylate behaved normally.

The Heck reaction of 3, 4-methylenedioxy benzene with butyl vinyl ether yielded a single regioisomer (β-attack) with 75 per cent diastereoselectivity of the E isomer. In all the cases cited above, no additional PTC was added as was required in earlier reports[71]. In fact PEG besides being an efficient solvent medium, also acted as a PTC for smooth C-C bond formation.

9 BAYLIS-HILLMAN REACTION

Baylis-Hillman reaction[72] involves the reaction of an aldehyde and electron deficient olefins resulting in a new C-C bond formation. The products obtained are used as synthons for other synthesis[73]. The main draw back is low yields of the products, requirement of high concentration of catalyst and long reaction times (some times up to a week for less than 50 per cent conversion). It is found that the reaction is also inert to enones, α, β-substituted aldehydes and hindered aldehydes.

PEG-400 has been used[74] as a rapid and recyclable reaction medium for the Baylis-Hillman reaction [using the conventional basic catalyst DABCO (20 mole per cent)] between unreactive aldehydes and activated olefins. Thus, the reaction of benzaldehyde, ethyl acrylate and DABCO (20 mol per cent) in PEG 400 at room temperature for 2 hr gave the Baylis-Hillmann product in 92 per cent yield. Similar reaction of benzaldehyde with acrylonitrile or methyl vinyl ketone and DABCO in PEG gave similar products (Scheme 38).

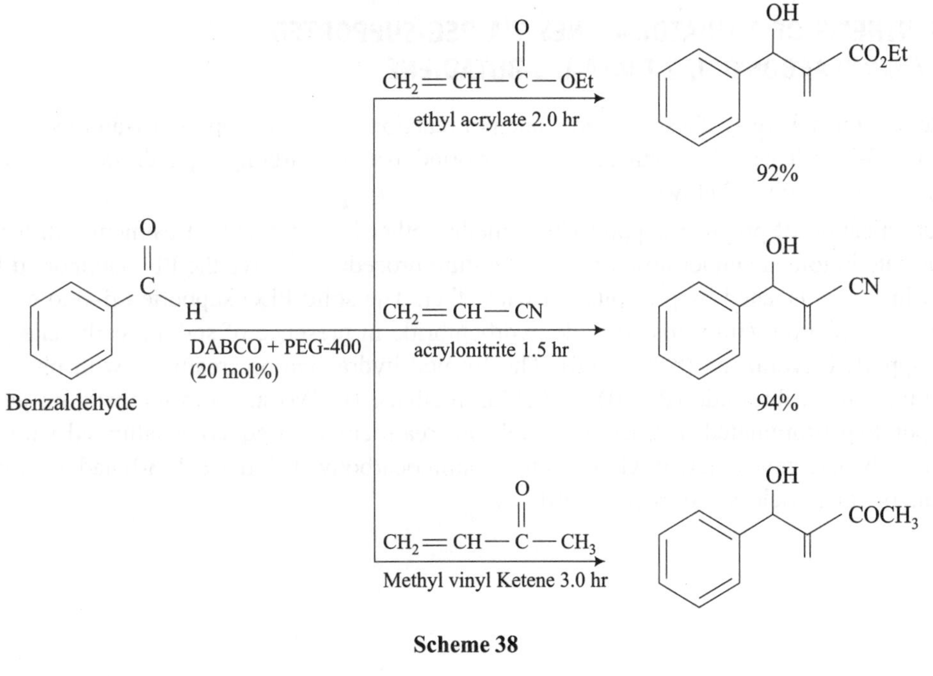

Scheme 38

The above procedure represents as improvement on earlier methods with respect to reaction time, concn., catalyst and yields.

4-Nitrobenzaldehyde reacted with ethyl acrylate and acetonitrile giving the expected product in 90% and 93% respectively after 2 hr. 4-Fluorobenzaldehyde reacted much faster forming the expected product in 4 hr; the same reaction took over 60 hr. using triethylamine (Scheme 39).

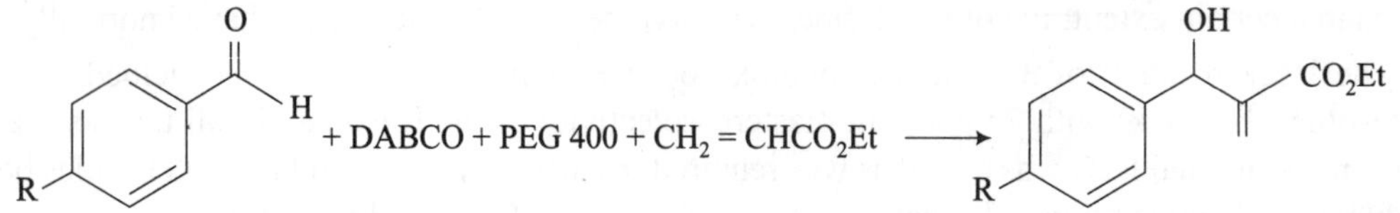

4-Nitrobenzaldehyde   R = NO$_2$
4-Fluorobenzaldehyde R = F

89-96%

Scheme 39

Some other aldehydes like 2-chloro-5-nitrobenzaldehyde, 2-furaldehyde and 2-thiophene-carboxaldehyde showed similar results. However, the yield was considerably reduced for the reaction between 4-methoxybenzaldehyde and ethylacrylate. Aliphatic aldehydes like 3-phenyl-proponal (C$_6$H$_5$CH$_2$CHCHO), isobutyraldehyde ((CH$_3$)$_2$ CHCHO) and hexanal ($\sim\sim$CHO) also underwent the Baylis-Hillman reaction with activated olefins (viz. acrylonitrile and ethyl acrylate) in 75%, 86% and 80% yields respectively. Also formaldehyde and trans-cinnamaldehyde reacted with acrylates in PEG to provide good yields of the expected products.

The Baylis-Hillman reaction (as described above) is one of the very few reactions where in there is 100% atom economy.

I0   SYNTHESIS OF 2-THIAZOL-4-ONES VIA PEG-SUPPORTED I-AMINOCARBONYL I, 2-DIAZA-I, 3-BUTADIENE

2-Thiazol-4-ones were synthesised[77] in a one pot reaction via PEG-supported 1-aminocarbonyl 1, 2-diaza-1, 3-butadiene. The required PEG-supported 1-aminocarbonyl 1, 2-diaza-1, 3-butadiene was prepared[77] as given below.

Esterification of polymer support (PEG methyl ether MW 5000) by treatment will tert.butyl acetoacetate in toluene under reflux as per literature procedure [78] gave the PEG-supported β-keto ester, which was isolated by precipitation with ether. The solid PEG-supported β-keto ester thus obtained on reaction with semicarbazide hydrochloride in presence of sodium carbonate yielded PEG-supported hydrazone (89% yield). The formed hydrazone on treatment with phenyltrim-ethylammonium tribromide (PTAB) in dichloromethane (DCM) at room temperature gave the corresponding brominated hydrazone, which on treatment with aqueous saturated solution of sodium carbonate gave a new PEG-supported 1-aminocarbonyl 1, 2-diaza-1, 3-butadiene (isolated by addn. of ether, yield 82%) (Scheme 40).

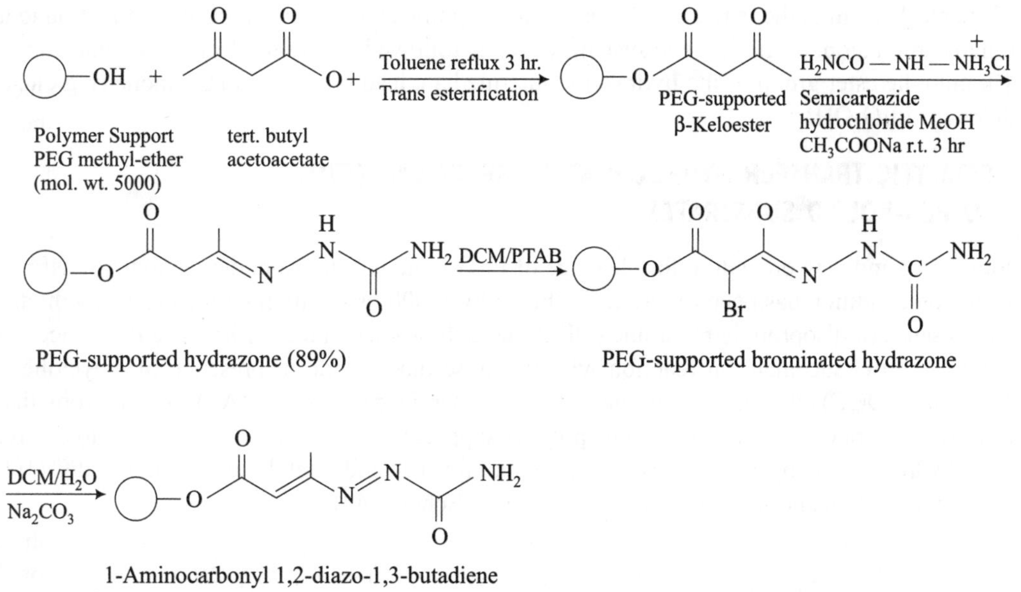

PEG-supported hydrazone (89%)

PEG-supported brominated hydrazone

1-Aminocarbonyl 1,2-diazo-1,3-butadiene

Scheme 40

The 1-aminocarbonyl 1, 2-diaza-1, 3-butadiene on treatment with various substituted thioamides in dichloromethane/methanol at room temperature gave the required 2-thiazolin-4-ones (with E configuration) (Scheme 41)

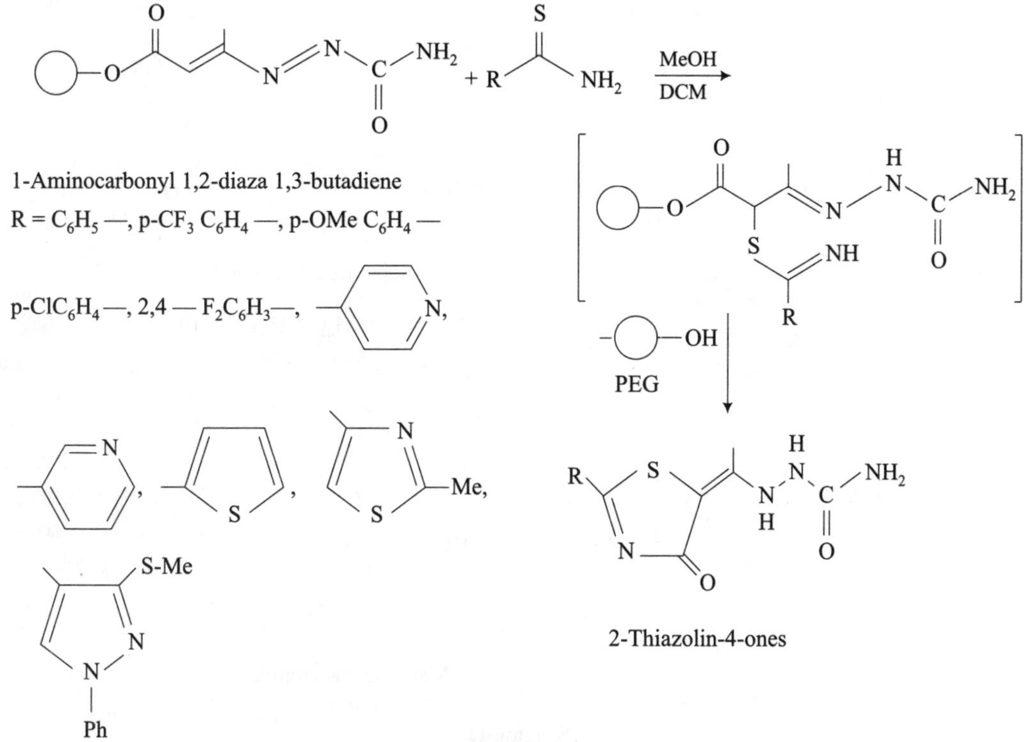

1-Aminocarbonyl 1,2-diaza 1,3-butadiene

$R = C_6H_5$ —, p-CF_3 C_6H_4 —, p-OMe C_6H_4 —

p-ClC$_6$H$_4$—, 2,4 — F$_2$C$_6$H$_3$—,

2-Thiazolin-4-ones

Scheme 41

The mechanism of the reaction[77] is the SH nucleophilic attack of the thiolomido function to the terminal carbon atom of the azo-ene system, which is followed by intramolecular NH nucleophilic attack onto the ester group of the hydrazonic intermediate leading to the thiazolinone ring closure with loss of PEG-OH.

II CATALYTIC TRANSFER HYDROGENATION REACTIONS (CTH) TO PEG-BOUND SUBSTRATES

A convenient and new procedure for cleavage of PEG-bond substrates under catalytic transfer hydrogenation condition has been reported[79]. Thus, PEG-5000 on refluxing with succinic anhydride in the presence of disopropylethylamine (DIEA) in dichloromethane for 1 hr. gave PEG-succinate. The formad PEG-succinate on reaction with mannose diacetonide in presence of dicyclohexyl-carbodiimide (DCC) and catalytic amount of dimethylaminopyridne (DMAP) in dichloromethane gave polymer-supported diacetonide. The polymersupported diacetonide on subjecting to catalytic transfer hydrogenation by refluxing with ammonium formate and a catalytic amount of Pd/C (10%) in methanol gave mannose diacetonide in 86% yield (Scheme 42).

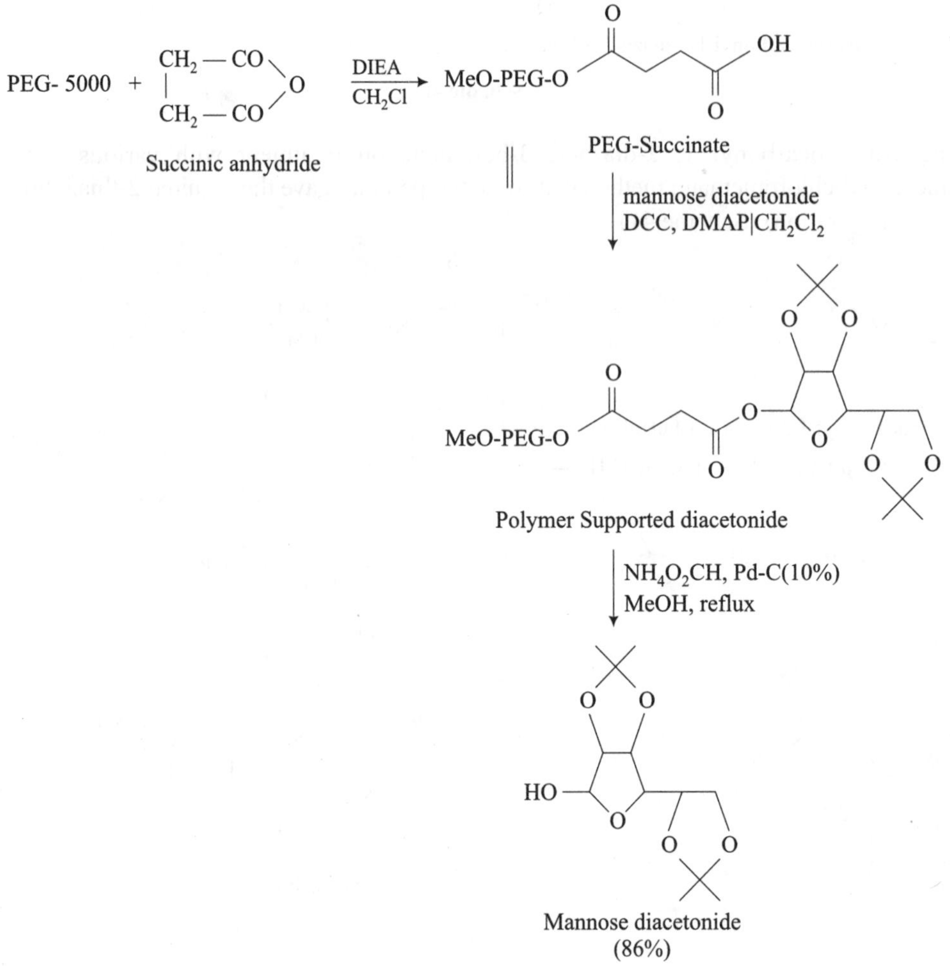

Scheme 42

A number of substrates with –OH functions were anchored to PEG through succinyl ester linkages and subjected to catalytic transfer hydrogenation (CTH) (as in the above case). The cleavage products were isolated from the solvent after precipitation of PEG by addition of diethyl ether. Following are given the substrates and the products obtained on catalytic transfer hydrogenation. (Scheme 43).

Substrate	Product

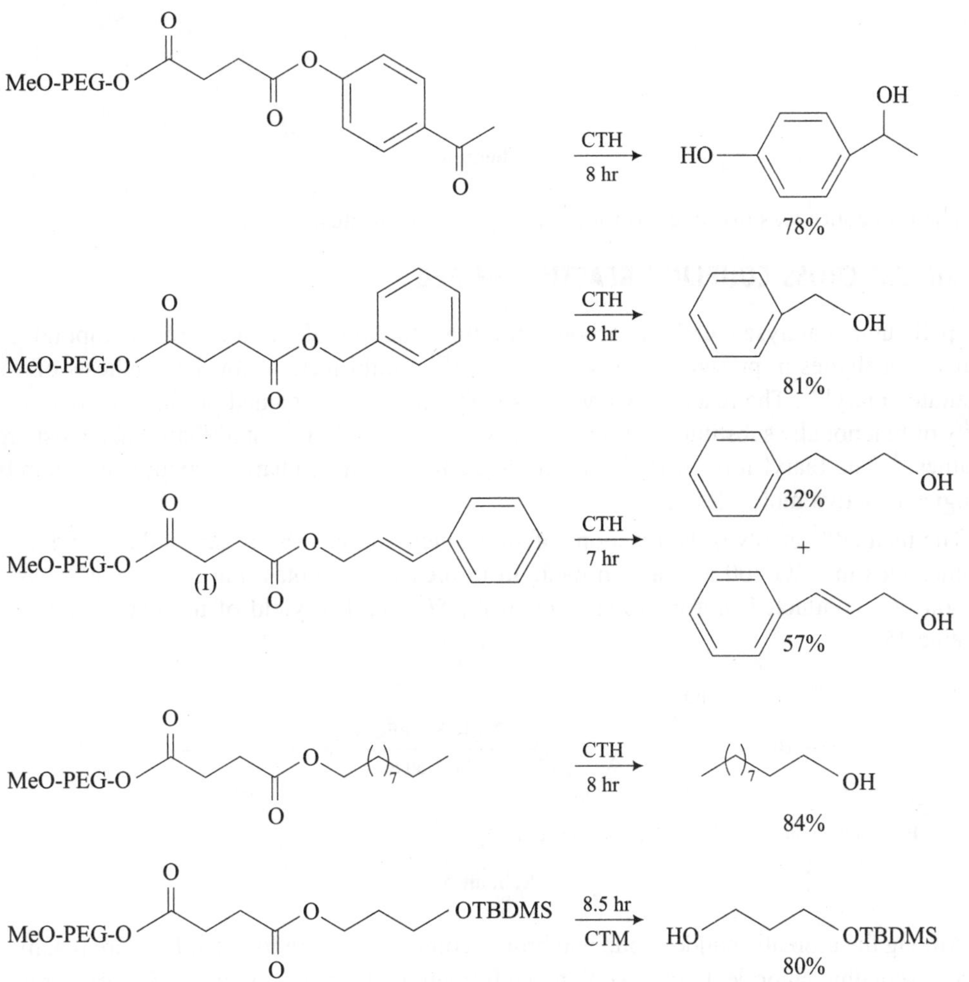

Scheme 43

It was found that unsaturated substrates like (I) underwent partial or complete hydrogenation. The above procedure was also suitable for base-sensitive substrate, 6-hydroxycoumarin, (II) which was found to retain its lactone structure but showed partial reduction of the double bond (Scheme 44).

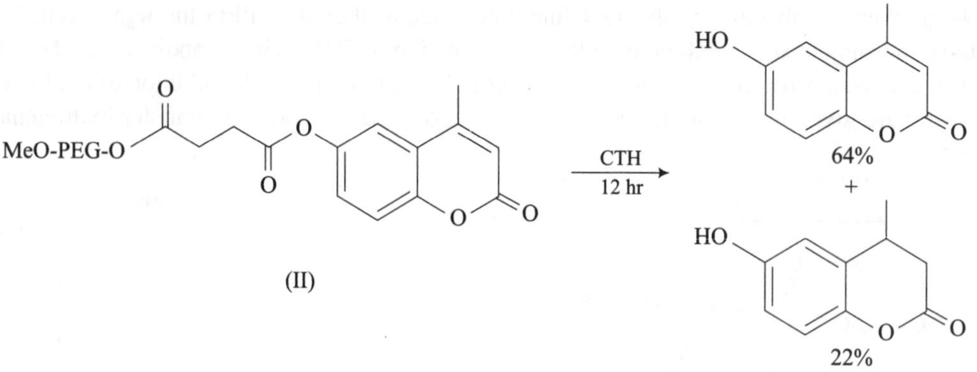

Scheme 44

The procedure was useful even for acid sensitive substrates.

12 SUZUKI CROSS-COUPLING REACTION IN PEG

The palladium catalysed carbon-carbon coupling reaction of organoboron compounds with aromatic aldehydes in presence of a base provides[80] a mild method for the synthesis of various substituted biaryl[81]. The reaction, known as suzuki reaction has gained prominance due to availability of functionally substituted boronic acids, which are environmentally safer than most organometallics[82]. The biaryl formed in this reaction are important as pharmacophores in a number of biologically active molecules[83].

The method[80] involves the reactions of substituted aromatic bromides/ iodides and aromatic boronic acids in PEG-400 as reaction medium in presence of potassium fluoride as a base. The reaction was conducted in a microwave oven for 50 sec. The yield of the biarys was 55-81% (Scheme 45).

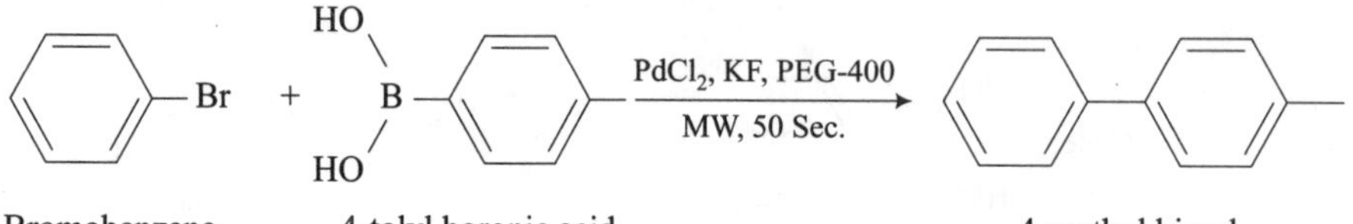

Bromobenzene   4-tolyl boronic acid   4-methyl biaryl

Scheme 45

Among the aromatic halides, iodo and bromo compounds were found to be more reactive than the corresponding chloride. In this reaction, the formation of a small amount (<5%) of symmetrical biaryls occurs due to the self-coupling of boronic acids[84].

The aliphatic halides, 1-butyl iodide, did not undergo reaction under the above conditions. The reaction, however, could be conducted in 15 min using an oil bath (100°) with similar yields. It is generally found that the use of microwave oven is very convenient and clean. The microwave approach could be adapted for the parallel synthesis to generate a library of compounds[85].

The synthesis of biaryls (74-92% yield) by the Suzuki coupling reaction was conducted[80] using a variety of aromatic halides (as given below) and reacting with 4-tolylboronic acid.

	R	R'
	Br	Me
	Br	CHO
	Br	OMe
	Br	COMe
	I	Me
	I	OMe
	I	NO_2
	I	F
	I	

R—⟨Aromatic halide⟩—R'

The Suzuki reaction of bromobenzene was conducted with a variety of substituted boronic acids (given below)

It was found that the yield of the biaryls increased by the presence of electron withdrawing substituents.

13   SYNTHESIS OF AZO COMPOUNDS USING PEG

Azo compounds are known to be utilized as dyes, analytical reagents and as materials for non-linear optics and for storage optic information in laser dishes[86]. These are found to possen photoelectric properties[87] and have played a significant role in the development of mechanistic and synthetic organic chemistry[88]. A number of methods have been used[89] for the synthesis of azo compounds. In most of the methods evolution of large amounts of nitrogen oxide causes air pollution; also control of the reaction temperature is a major cost factor in industrialised manufacturing.

A green route for the synthesis of azo compounds has been developed[90]. It absorps NO_2 in PEG-400 to form an adduct PEG NO_2. The absorption efficiency of NO_2 (determined by Griess-Saltzan method[91]) was found to about 97 per cent. The concentration of NO_2 in PEG was found to be 10.53 mmol; this was determined by reacting the adduct (PEG NO_2) with excess of aqueous sodium hydroxide and then back titrating with hydrochloric acid[92]. The resulting absorbent product, proved to be a very efficient, clean and moderate oxidant (Scheme 46).

$$PEG \ + \ NO_2 \longrightarrow PEG. \ NO_2$$

Scheme 46

The absorbent product (PEG NO_2) can convert hydrozo derivatives to the corresponding azo compounds. The spent PEG can be recovered and recycled after the oxidation process (Scheme 47).

$$R^1 NHNH \ R^2 \ + \ PEG \ NO_2 \ \xrightarrow{\text{20-30 min}} \ R^1 N = N \ R^2 \ + \ N_2$$

Hydrazo deriv

azo compound
75-80%

$R = R' = Me \ C_6 \ H_4\text{-};$
$R = m\text{-}Me \ C_6H_4\text{-};$
$R' = p\text{-}Cl \ C_6H_4\text{-}$

Scheme 47

This is a convenient method of transformation of –NH–NH– to –N = N– by PEG NO_2.

Following are some more examples of transformation of other substrates into N = N compounds (Scheme 48).

$$R - NHCONHNH - R' \ \xrightarrow[\text{25 min}]{PEG. \ NO_2} \ R\text{-}NH \ CON = N - R^1$$

80–95%

R	R'
p-FC$_6$H$_4$-	C$_6$H$_5$
m-ClC$_6$H$_4$	p-Me C$_6$H$_4$
p-ClC$_6$H$_4$	C$_6$H$_5$
p-BrC$_6$H$_4$	C$_6$H$_5$
p-MeC$_6$H$_4$-	C$_6$H$_5$

Scheme 48

Two other examples of compounds containing NH – NH in a heterocyclic rings are as follows. (Scheme 49)

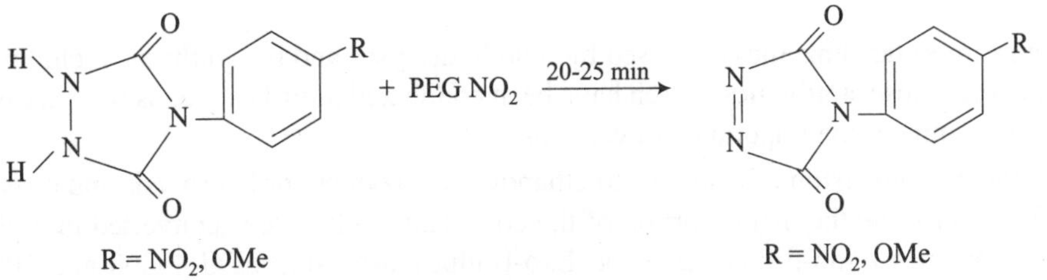

Scheme 49

The above procedure brings together a new form of NO_2 capture by PEG-400 and the application of the formed PEG NO_2 as an oxidant for the oxidation of hydrazo derivatives to the corresponding azo compounds.

14 OXIDATION OF CYCLOHEXENE TO ADIPIC ACID IN POLYETHYLENE GLYCOL BASED AQUEOUS BIPHASIC SYSTEM USING SODIUM TUNGSTATE AND HYDROGEN PEROXIDE

Adipic acid is an important intermediate in the manufacture of nylon-6, 6. At present, most industrial adipic acid production uses nitric acid oxidation of cyclohexanol or cyclohexene or both[93]. In these processes, the emission of N_2O is a considerable source of NOx environmental pollution. Environmentally benign oxidation methods were developed; there were based on catalytic oxidation of cyclohexene with concentrated aqueous hydrogen peroxide. Subsequently the effectiveness of catalytic oxidation of cyclohexene with hydrogen peroxide and sodium tungstate in the presence of $[CH_3(nC_8H_{17})_3N]HSO_4$ as a PTC was described[94]. Adipic acid was also synthesised by direct oxidation of cyclohexane with H_2O_2 over peroxytungstateorganic complex catalyst[95].

An elegant, environmentally benin synthesis of Adipic acid from cyclohexene in polyethylene glycol based aqueous biphasic system using sodium tungstate and hydrogen peroxide has been reported[96] (Scheme 50).

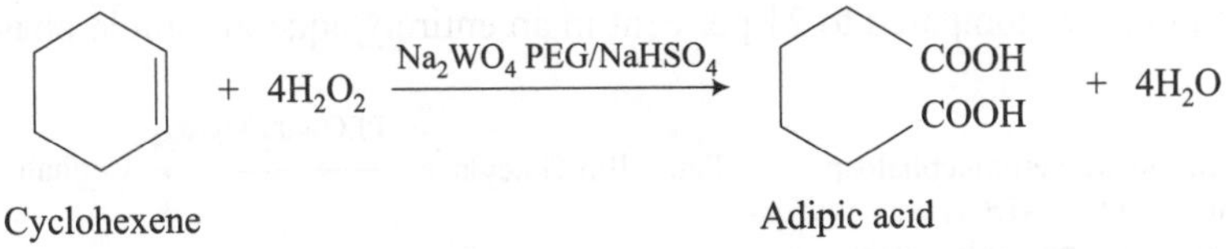

Cyclohexene   Adipic acid

Scheme 50

Both PEG and PEG/salt ABS can be considered as potentially important green solvent systems with markedly reduced hazards to health compared to many aqueous/organic biphasic systems incorporating volatile organic components[97]. In fact PGE/NaHSO$_4$ was found[96] to be the only ABS in which the reaction took place.

15 ENZYMATIC REACTIONS

A number of important enzymes catalysed bioman hydrolyses and biosynthesis, including process applicable to cellulose, antibiotics, starch have been conducted in PEG aqueous two phase systems. Following are some of the important conversions.

(i) In the bioconversion of cellulose to ethanol, the enzymes for hydrolysis and enzyme recycling constitute the major portion of the cost. Thus, cellulose is converted into glucose by the enzymes Endo-β-glucanase and Exo-β-glucanase using PEG-40000 and 200000 and Dextrin (Scheme 51)[98-104].

Cellulose + Endo-β-glucanase $\xrightarrow[\text{(MW} = 1,4,11,50,200 \times 10^4)]{\text{PEG-40,000; 200000 Dextran}}$ Glucose

$(C_6H_{10}O_5)$ Exo-βO-glucanase $(C_6H_{12}O_6)$

Scheme 51

(ii) The conversion of starch or native starch to glucose has been accomplished[104-107] using the enzymes α-amylase; glucoamylase and Amyloglucosidase in PEG-6000, 20000 and Dextran (M.W. $= 5.7 \times 10^4$). A continuous stream of glucose could be produced and PEG, Dextran and the starch degrading enzymes could be recycled (Scheme 52).

Starch + α-Amylase; $\xrightarrow[\text{Dextran (M.W.} = 5\text{-}7 \times 10^4)]{\text{PEG-6000, 20000}}$ Maltose + glucose

or   Glucoamylase;

Native   Amyloglucosidase

starch

Scheme 52

(iii) Cephalexin has been synthesised[108,109] in ABS by using penicillen G acylase (PGA) as catalyst and 7-amino-deacetoxicephalosoporanic acid (7-ADCA) and phenyl glycine methyl ester (PGME) as substrate (Scheme 53). A yield of 60 per cent of cephalexin was obtained in ABS compared to 21 per cent in an entirety aqueous single phase reaction[108].

7-Amino-deacetoxicephalosp + Penicillin G acylase $\xrightarrow{\text{PEG-400 MgSO}_4}$ Cephalexin
oranic acid (7-ADCA)
Phenyl glycine methyl ester
(PGM)

Scheme 53

16 SYNTHESIS OF 2-AMINO-2-CHROMENES

2-Amino-2-chromenes were synthesised by a nano-sized magnesium oxide catalysed three component condensation reaction of aldehyde, malononitrile and α-naphthol in PEG-H_2O. The chromenes were obtained in high yields at room temperature (Scheme 53a). The attractive feature of this protocol are the simple experimental procedure, use of benign reaction solvents, cost effectiveness, the recyclability of catalyst and its adaptability for the synthesis of diverse set of 2-amino-2-chromenes[110].

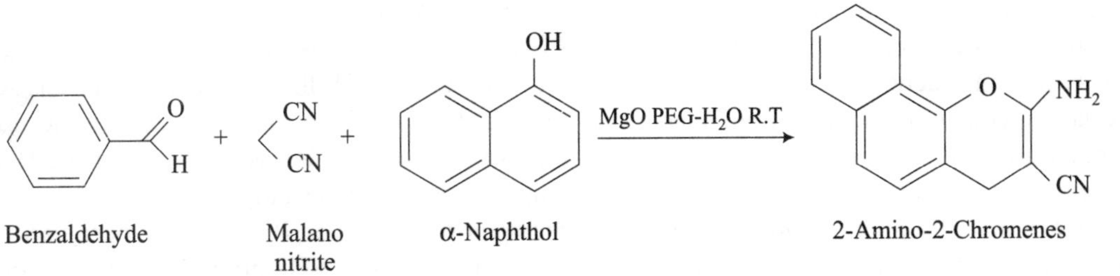

Benzaldehyde   Malano   α-Naphthol   2-Amino-2-Chromenes
                nitrite

Scheme 53a

I7   DECARBOXYLATION OF CINNAMIC ACID

Decarboxylation of substituted α-phenyl cinnamic acid derivatives has been achieved[111] using catalytic amount of methylimidazole and aqueous $NaHCO_3$ in PEG under MW irradiation to give the corresponding para/ortho hydroxylated (E) stilbenes in a mild and efficient manner (Scheme 54).

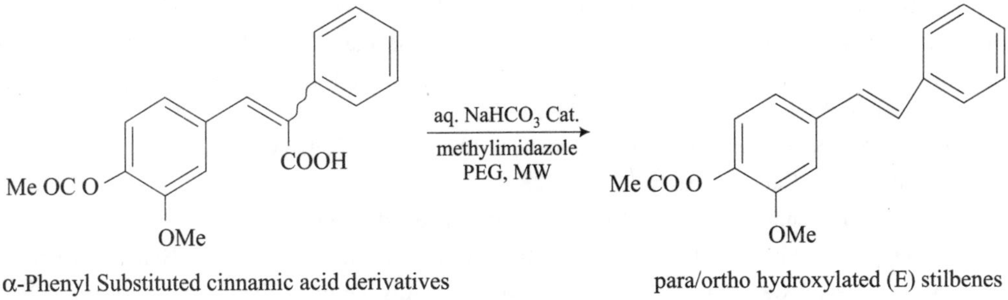

α-Phenyl Substituted cinnamic acid derivatives   para/ortho hydroxylated (E) stilbenes

Scheme 54

The critical role of water in the above reaction in facilitating the decarboxylation imparts an interesting facet to the synthetic utility of water (PEG – H_2O) mediated organic transformations. This procedure provides a clean alternative to the hitherto indispensable multistep approaches involving toxic quinoline and a copper salt combination as the common decarboxylating agent[111]. It may be appropriate to mention here that decarboxylations has also been achieved using SC – H_2O without any catalyst (see Chapter 2, Section 2).

A number of acid catalysed alkylation reactions conducted in SC – CO_2 are aided by the addition of poly (ethylene glycol) (PEG) derivatives (For details chapter 5, section 4.14).

18 CONCLUSION

Polyethylene glycol (PEG) and its aqueous solutions have been used in many different types of reaction systems. The special feature of PEGs is their low toxicity, low volatility and biodegradability and relatively low cost as a bulk commodity chemical. Also, aqueous PEG solutions are good substitutes for expensive and often toxic PTCs. PEG finds use in substitution reactions, oxidation and reduction reactions. As PTC, the PEG's have been used in Williamson ether synthesis and oxidation reduction reactions. PEG's have also been used in L-Proline catalysed asymmetric aldol condensation. It is also used in asymmetric dihydroxylation of olefins. Regioselective Heck reaction, Baylis-Hillman reaction, Suzuki cross coupling reaction and catalytic transfer hydrogenation reaction to PEG-bound substrates have also been reported. Besides, PEG has also been used for absorbing NO_2; the adduct finds application for conversion of –NH–NH– group to –N = N– group. The conversion cyclohexene to adipic acid is worth mentioning. Finally PEG has been used in a number of enzymatic transformations.

References

1. P.T. Anastas, in Clean Solvents, Alternative media for chemical reactions and Processing. ed. M.A. Abraham and L. Moens, ACS Symposium series 819, American Chemical Society, Washington DC., 2002, P. I.

2. J.I. Chin, S.K. Spear, J.G. Huddleston and R.D. Rogers, Green Chemistry, 2005, **7**, 64-82 and the references cited there in.

3. F.E. Bailey, Jr. and J.V. Koleske, Poly (Ethylene oxide), Academic Press, New York, 1976.

4. P.A. Albertsson, Partition of cell particles and Macromolecules, Wiley, New York, 3rd., edn., 1986.

5. J.M. Harris in Polyethylene glycol chemistry, Biochemical and Biomedical applications, ed. JM. Harris, Plenium Press, New York and London, 1992, p. 7.

6. D.A. Herold, K. Keil and D.E. Bruns, Biochem. Pharmacol; 1989, **38**, 73.

7. M.G. Peglation, Cancer Treat Rev., 2002, **28**, 13.

8. D. Bhadra, P. Bhadra, P. Jain and N.K. Jain, Pharmazie, 2002, **57**, 5.

9. G.E. Francis, D. Fisher, C. Delgado, F. Marlik, A. Gardiner and D. Neale, Int, J. Hematol, 1998, **68**, 1.

10. F.M. Veronise, P. Caloceti, O. Schiavon and M. Sergi, Adv. Drug. Delivery Rev., 2002, **54**, 581.

11. Carbowax PEG-2000 MSDS of Canadian Center for Occupational Health and Safety (CCOHS) Record number 22426725, Oct. 2002, http.//www. safety, Vanderbilt, edu/pdf/hcs_msds/carbowax PEG 200.pdf.

12. Z. Guo, M. Li., H.D. Willauer, J.G. Huddleston. G.C. April and R.D. Rogers, Ind. Eng. Chem. Res., 2002, **41**, 2535.

13. J. Chen, S.K. Spear, J.G. Huddleston, J.H. Holbrey, R.P. Swatloski and R.D. Rogers, Ind. Eng. Chem. Res., 2004, **43**, 5358.

14. J. Chen, S.K. Spear, J.G. Huddleston, J.H. Holbrey and R.D. Rogers, J. Chromatogr. B: Biomed. Appl. 2004, 807, 145.

15. S.D. Naik and L.K. Doraiswamy, AlchEJ. 1998, **44**, 612.

16. A. Haimov and R. Neumann, Chem. Commun., 2002, 867.

17. J.R. Blanton, Synth. Commun., 1977, **27**, 2093.

18. J.R. Blanton, React. Funct. Polym., 1997, **33**, 61.

19. E. Santaniello, A. Manzocchi and P. Sozzani, Tetrahedron Lett., 1979, **20**, 4581.

20. E. Santaniello, in Crown ethers and phase transfer catalysis in Polymer Science, ed. L.J. Mathias and C.E. Carraher, Jr., Plenum, New York, 1984, p. 397.

21. P. Ferravoski, A. Fiecchi, P. Grisenti, E. Santaniello and S. Trave, Synth. Commun. 1987, **17**, 1569.

22. N.F. Leininger, R. Clontz, J.L. Gainer and D.V. Kirwan in Clean Solvents, Alternative Media for Chemical Reactions and Processing, ed. M.A. Abraham and L. Moens, ACS sympossium series 819, American Chemical Society, Washington DC., 2002, p. 208.

23. N.F. Leininger, J.L. Gainer and D.J. Kirwan, AICHEJ, 2004, **50**, 511.

24. N. Suzuki, T. Azuma, Y. Kaneko, Y. Izawa, H. Tamioka and N. Nomoto, J. Chem. Soc., Perkin Trans. I., 1987, 645.

25. S. Chandrasekhar, Ch. Narsihmulu, S.S. Sultana and N.R. Reddy, Org. Lett., 2002, 4399.

26. S. Chandrasekhar, Ch. Narsihmulu, S.S. Sultana and N.R. Reddy, Chem. Commun., 2003, 1716.

27. E. Santaniello, P. Ferraboschi and P. Sozzani, J. Org. Chem., 1981, **46**, 4584.

28. E. Santaniello, A. Fiecchi, A. Manzocchi and P. Ferraboschi, J. Org. Chem., 1983, **48**, 3074.

29. S. Chandrasekhar, Ch. Narsihmulu, G. Chandrashekar and T. Shyamsunder, Tetrahedron Lett., 2004, **45**, 2421.

30. D.J. Heldebrant and P.G. Jessop, J. Am. Chem. Soc., 2003, **125**, 5600.

31. G.E. Totten, N.A. Clinton and P.L. Matlock, J. Macromol. Sci. Rev. Nacromol. Chem. Phys., 1998, **C38**, 77.

32. G.E. Totten and N.A. Clinton, J. Macromol. Sci. Rev. Macromol. Chem. Phys., 1998, **C28**, 293.

33. C.M. Starks, C.L. Liotta and M. Halpern, Phase Transfer catalysts, Fundamentals, Applications and Industrial Perpectives, Chapman and Hall, New York, 1994, p. 158.

34. Phase-Transfer catalysis, Mechanism and Synthesis, ed. M. E. Halpen, ACS Symposium Series 659, American Chemical Society, Washington Dc., 1997.

35. J.M. Harris, N.H. Hundley, T.G. Shannon and E.C. Struck in Croun ethers and Phase transfer catalysts in Polymer science, ed. L.J. Mathias and C.E. Carraher, Jr., Plenum Press, New York, 1984, p. 371.

36. C.B. Dartt and M.E. Davis, Ind. Eng. Chem. Res., 1994, **33**, 2887.

37. B. Abribat, Y. Le Bigot and A. Gaset, Synth. Commun., 1994, **24**, 2091.

38. B. Abribat, Y. Le Bigot and A. Gaset, Tetrahedron, 1996, **52**, 8245.

39. B. Abribat and Y. Le Bigot, Tetrahedron, 1997, **53**, 2119.

40. T.B. Wei, J.C. Chen, X.C. Wang, Y.M. Zhang and L.L. Wang, Synth. Commun., 1996, **26**, 1447.

41. K. Chandler, C.W. Culp, D.R. Lamb, C.l. Liotta and C.A. Eckert, Ind. Eng. Chem. Res., 1998, **37**, 3252.

42. R. Neumann and Y. Sasson, Tetrahedron, 1983, **39**, 3437.

42a. Y.M. Zhang, T.B. Wei and L.L. Wang, Synth. Commun., 1997, **27**, 751.

43. R.S. Davidson, A.M. Patel, A. Safdar and D. Thornthwaite, Tetrahedron Lett., 1983, **24**, 5907.

44. R.A. Bartsch and I.W. Wang, Tetrahedron Lett., 1979, **20**, 2503.

45. D. Balasubramian, P. Sukumar and R. Chandani, Tetrahedron Lett., 1979, **20**, 3543.

46. C. Zucchi, G. Palyi, V. Galamb, E. Sámpár-Szerencsés, L. Markó, P. Li and H. Alper, Organometallics, 1996, **15**, 3222.

47. R. Neumann and Y. Sasson, Chem. Commun., 1985, 616.

48. J.T. Lee and H. Alper, Organometallics, 1990, **9**, 3064.

49. R. Neimann and Y. Sasson, J. Org. Chem., 1984, **49**, 1282.

50. B.G. Zupancic and M. Kolalj, Synth. Commun., 1982, **12**, 881.

51. P. Li and H. Alpert, J. Org. Chem., 1986, **51**, 4354.

52. N. Yoshikawa, N. Kumagai, S. Matsunaga, G. Moll, T. Ohshima, T. Suzuki and M. Shibasaki, J. Am. Chem. Soc., 2001, **123**, 2466; M.A.Y. Yamada and M. Shibasaki, Tetrahedron Lett., 1998, **39**, 5561.

53. B.M. Trost and H. Ito, J. Am. Chem. Soc., 2000, **122**, 12003.

54. A. Bogevig, N. Kumaragurubaran and K.A. Jorgensen, Chem. Commun. 2002, 620.

55. A.B. Northrup and D.W.C. Mac Millan, J. Am. Chem. Soc., 2002, **124**, 6798.

56. B. List, R.A. Lerner and C.F. Barbas, J. Am. Chem. Soc., 2000, **122**, 2395.

57. A. Cordova, W. Notz and C.F. Barbas, J. Org. Chem., 2002, **67**, 301.

58. A. Cordova, Tetrahedron Lett., 2004, **45**, 3949.

59. P. Kotruzp, I. Kmentova, B. Gotov, S. Toma and E. Solcaniova, Chem. Commun., 2002, 2510.

60. A. Gordova, W. Notz and C.F. Barbas, Chem. Commun., 2002, 3024; A.I. Nyberg, A. Usano and P.M. Pihko, Synlett. 2004, 1891; A. Hartikka and P.I. Arvidsson, Tetrahedron Asymmetrt, 2004, **15**, 1831; Y.-Y. Peng, Q.P. Ding, Z. Li, P.G. Wang and J.P. Cheng, Tetrahedron Lett., 2003, **44**, 3871; Y. Hayashi, W. Tsuboi, M. Shaji and N. Suzuki, Tetrahedron Lett., 2004, **45**, 4353; Y. Wu, W. Shao, C. Zhang, Z. Huang, J. Cai and Q. Deng, Helv. Chem. acta, 2004, **87**, 1377.

61. T. Darbre and M. Machuqueiro, Chem. Commun, 2003, 1090.

62. S. Chandrasekher, N. Ramakrishna Reddy, S. Shameem Sultana, Ch. Narsihmulu and K. Venkatram Reddy, Tetrahedron Lett., 2006, 338.

63. S. Chandrasekher, Ch. Narsihmulu, N.R. Reddy and S.S. Sultana, Chem. Commun, 2004, 2450.

64. M. Schroder, Chem. Rev., 1980, **80**, 187.

65. E.J. Corey and J.P. Dittami, J. Am. Chem. Soc., 1985, **107**, 256; X. Lu, Z. Xu and G. Yang, Org. Process Res. Dev., 2000, **4**, 575, L. Ahrgren and L. Sutin, Org. Process Res. Dev., 1997, **1**, 425; Z.-M. Wang and K.B. Sharpless, J. Org. Chem., 1994, **59**, 8302.

66. C.R. Hammand, in CRC Handbook of Chemistry and Physics, 81st edn, D.R. Lide, ed., CRC Press, Boca Raton, Fl. pp. 4.

67. H.A. Dick and R.F. Heck, J. Org. Chem., 1975, **40**, 1083; T. Jeffery, Chem. Commun. 1984, 1287; A. De Meijere and F.E. Meyer, Angew. Chem. Int. Ed., 1994, **33**, 2379; G.T. Grisp, F.E. Meyer, Angew. Chem. Int. Ed., 1994, **33**, 2378; G.T. Grisp. Chem. Soc. Rev., 1998, **27**, 427; I.P. Beletskaya and A.V. Cheprakov, Chem. Rev., 200, 100, 3009.

68. D.E. Kaufmann, M. Nouroozian and H. Henze, Synlett, 1996, 1091; A.J. Carmichael, M.J. Earle, J.D. Holbry, P.M. McComac and K.K. Seddon, Org. Lett., 1997, **1**, 997; L. Xu, W. Chen and J. Xiao, Organometallics, 2000, **19**, 1123; H. Hagiwara, Y. Shimizu, T. Hoshi, T. Suzuki, M. Ando, K. Ohkubo and C. Yokoyama, Tetrahedron Lett., 2001, **42**, 4349; R.R. Deshmukh, R. Rajagopal and K.V. Srinivasn, Chem. Commun., 2001, 1544.

69. L. Xu, W. Chen, I. Ross and J. Xiao, Org. Lett., 2001, **3**, 293.

70. W. Cabri, I. Condiani, A. Bedeschi and S. Penco, J. Org. Chem. 1992, **57**, 1481; W. Cabri, I. Candiani and A. Bedeschi, J. Org. Chem., 1993, **58**, 7421; W. Cabri and I. Candiani, Acc. Chem. Res., 1995, **28**, 2; M. Larhed and A. Hallberg, J. Org. Chem., 1997, **62**, 7858.

71. D. Morales-Morales, R. Redon, C. Yung and C.M. Jensen, Chem. Commun., 2000, 1619; C. Dai and G.C. Fu., I. Am. Chem. Soc., 2001, **123**, 2719.

72. A.B. Baylis and M.E.D. Hillman, German Patent, 2, 155, 113, 1972 (Chem. Abstr. 1972, **77**, 34174q); S.E. Drewes and G.H.P. Rooos, Tetrahedron Lett., 1988, **44**, 4653; D. Basavaiah, P.D. Rao and R.S. Hyma, Tetrahedron, 1996, **52**, 8001; P. Langer, Angew. Chem., Int. Ed. 2000, **39**, 3049.

73. D. Basavaiah, A.J. Rao and T. Satyanarayana, Chem. Rev., 2003, **103**, 811.

74. S. Chandrasekher, Ch. Narsihmulu, B. Saritha and S.S. Sultana, Tetrahedron Lett., 2004, **45**, 5865.

75. J.N. Rosa, A.M. Afonso and A.G. Santos, Tetrahedron Lett., 2001, **57**, 4189.

76. B.M. Trost, Science, 1991, **254**, 1471.

77. O.A. Attanasi, L. De. Crescentini, G. Favi, P. Filippone, S. Lillini, F. Mantellini and S. Santeusania, Organic Letters, 2005, **7**, 2469.

78. J.S. Witzeman and W.D. Nottingham, J. Org. Chem., 1991, **56**, 1713.

79. H.M.S. Kumar, P. Chakravartthy, S.D. Sawant, P.P. Singh, M.S. Rao and J.S. Yadav, Tetrahedron Lett., 2005, **46**, 3591.

80. V.V. Namboodiri and R.S. Varma, Green Chemistry, 2001, **3**, 146.

81. N. Miyaura and A. Suzuki, Chem. Rev., 1995, **95**, 2457; T. Ishiyama, H. Kizaki, T. Hayashi, A. Suzuki and N. Miyaura, J. Org. Chem., 1998, **63**, 4726; A.R. Martin and Y. Yang, Acta Chem. Scand., 1993, **47**, 221.

82. A. Suzuki, J. Organomet. Chem., 1999, **576**, 147.

83. Y.F. Hallock, K.P. Manfredi, J.W. Blunt, J.H. Cardellina, M. Schaffer, K.P. Gulden, G. Bringman, A.Y. Lee, J. Clandy, G. Francois and M.R. Boyd, J. Org. Chem., 1994, **59**, 6349.

84. M. Moreno-Manas, M. Perez and R. Pleixats, J. Org. Chem., 1996, **61**, 2346.

85. R.S. Varma and D. Kumar, Tetrahedron Lett., 1999, **40**, 7665; C.O. Kappe, D. Kumar and R.S. Varma, Synthesis, 1999, 1799.

86. H.W. Russ and H. Tappe, Eur. Pat. Appl; Ep, 629, 667, 1994; T. Ikeda and O. Tsutumi, Science, 1995, **268**, 1873; X.J. Peng anf J.D. Yang, Chin, Image Sci. Practice, 1998, **4**, 5.

87. Z.F. Liu, K. Hashimoto and A. Fujishima, Nature, 1990, **347**, 658.

88. R.D. Little and M.G. Venegas, J. Org. Chem., 1978, **43**, 2921; A.B. Hashim, A.J. Elie and C. Noel, Tetrahedron Lett., 1996, **37**, 2951.

89. R.G. Anderson and G. Nickless, Anal. Chim. Acta, 1967, **39**, 469; E. Kiss, Anal. Chem. Acta, 1973, **66**, 85.

90. R.Z. Qiao, Y. Zhang, X.P. Hui, P.F. Xu, Z.Y. Zhang, X.Y. Wang and Y.L. Wang, Green Chem., 2001, **3**, 186.

91. R.W. Boubel, Foundation of Air Pollution, Academic Press, Inc., New York, 2nd edn., 1982, p. 765.

92. Q.Z. Zhang, R.Z. Qiao and S.S. Zhang, Hua Xue Tong Bao (China), 1994, **4**, 55.

93. D.D. Davis and D.R. Kemp, Adipic and In Kirk-Othmer Encyclopedia of Chemical Technology, J.I. Kroschwiz and M. Howe-Grant, Eds, Wiley; New York 1991, Vol 1, p. 466.

94. K. Sato, M. Aoki and R. Noyori, Green Route to Adipic Acid, Direct Oxidation of Cyclohexenes with 30 percent Hydrogen Peroxide, Science 1998, **281**, 1646.

95. Y. Deng, Z. Ma, K. Wang and J. Chen, Clean synthesis of Adipic acid by direct oxidation of cyclohexene with H_2O_2 over Peroxytungstate-organic complex cataltsts, Green Chem, 1999, **1**, 275.

96. J. Chin, S.K. Spear, J.G. Huddleston, J.D. Holbrey, R.P. Swatloski and R.D. Rogers, Ind. Eng. Chem. Res., 2004, **43**, 5358.

97. P.T. Anastas, Green Chemistry as applied to Solvents. In clean solvents, Alternative Media for Chemical reactions and Processing, M.A. Abraham and L. Moens Eds., American Chemical Society, Washington DC, 2002, Vol. 819, p. 1.

98. T. Tjerneld, I. Persson, P.Å. Albertsson and B. Hahn-Hägerdal, Biotechnol. Bioeng., 1985, **27**, 1036.

99. T. Tjerneld, I. Persson, P. Å. Albertsson and B. Hahn-Hägerdal, Biotechnol. Bioeng., 1985, **27**, 1044.

100. I. Persson, H. Stålbrand, F. Tjerneld and B. Hahn-Hägerdal, Appl. Biochem. Biotechnol., 1992, **27**, 27.

101. C.F. Mandenius, B. Nilsson, I. Persson and F. Tjerneld, Biotechnol. Bioeng., 1988, **31**, 203.

102. T. Tjerneld, I. Persson, P.Å. Albertsson and B. Hahn-Hägerdal, Biotechnol. Bioeng. Symp, 1986, **15**, 419.

103. T. Tjerneld, I. Persson and J.M. Lee, Biotechnol. Bioeng., 1991, **37**, 876.

104. A. Kondo, T. Urabe and K.J. Higashitani, J. Ferment, Bioeng., 1994, **77**, 700.

105. M. Larsson, V. Arasaratnam and B. Mattisson, Biotechnol. Bioeng., 1989, **33**, 758.

106. M. Li, J.W, Kim and T.L. Peeples, Biochem. Eng. J. 2002, **11**, 25.

107. M. Li, J.W, Kim and T.L. Peeples, Biotechnol. Eng. J. 2002, **93**, 15.

108. D.Z. Wei, J.H. Zhu and X.J. Cao, Biochem. Eng. J., 2002, **11**, 95.

109. T.J. Bartlet, R.A. Rastall, N.H. Rees, M.W. Adlard and C. Buckle, J. Chem. Technol. Biotechnol., 1992, **55**, 73.

110. D. Kumar, V.B. Reddy, B.G. Mishra, R.K. Rana, M.N. Nadagouda and R.S. Varma, Tetrahedron, 2007, **63**, 3093.

111. V. Kumar, A. Sharma, A. Sharma and A.K. Sinha, Tetrahedron, 2007, **63**, 7640.

PART – V

Organic Synthesis using Fluorous Phase Techniques

9

I INTRODUCTION

Fluorinated compounds and solvents are useful tools in synthetic organic chemistry[1]. It was only in 1994 that the concept of fluorous biphasic system (FBS) and fluorous biphasic catalysis (FBC) was invented[2]. It is based on reagents or catalysts having perfluorated carbons chains, which are soluble in perfluorated solvents as FC – 72 (a mixture of perfluorohexanes). At ambient temperature, the perflouroalkanes are very less soluble in common organic solvents resulting in the formation of biphasic mixtures. At elevated temperatures, the biphase heterogeneous mixtures becomes monophasic and a clear solution is obtained. For carrying out a reaction, the organic substrate is dissolved in an organic solvent (e.g. toluene or dichloromethane) and the fluoro-tagged catalyst or reagents dissolved in perfluoroalkanes added. At elevated temperatures the biphasic heterogeneous mixture becomes monophasic permitting the reaction to take place.

After the reaction has taken place (as indicated by TLC), the resultant liquid is cooled when the two phase are again formed. The formed product of the reaction is in the organic phase and is recovered by decantation of the upper organic phase. The catalyst remains in the lower fluorous phase and can be reused. In this procedure, the reaction time can be regulated by change of temperature.

The FBS technique can be compared with solid phase organic synthesis (SPOC, Scheme 1), which is generally used in pharmaceutical industry. Both the FBS technique and the SPOC technique offer similar opportunities for the separation of product/catalyst. However, The FBS technique seems to offer advantages over reaction on solid support. The FBS procedure is depected in Scheme 2.

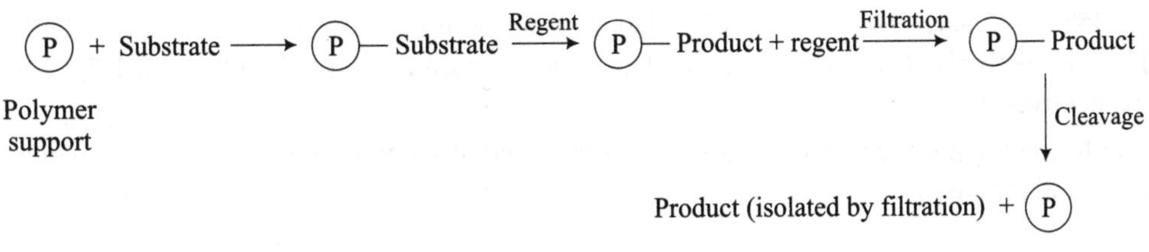

$$\boxed{P} + \text{Substrate} \longrightarrow \boxed{P}\!\!-\text{Substrate} \xrightarrow{\text{Regent}} \boxed{P}\!\!-\text{Product} + \text{regent} \xrightarrow{\text{Filtration}} \boxed{P}\!\!-\text{Product}$$

Polymer
support

$\downarrow$ Cleavage

Product (isolated by filtration) + $\boxed{P}$

Scheme 1   (SPOC-technique)

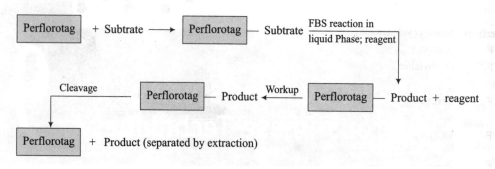

Scheme 2   (FBS-technique)

2 CHARACTERSTICS OF PERFLUOROUS LIQUIDS

Most of the common perfluorous liquids, especially perfluoroalkanes, perfluoroethers and perfluoroamines[3] exhibit unique characteristics. This makes them convenient alternatives to conventional organic solvents. Thus, the perfluoro liquids are inert against chemical treatment; this permits reactions under drastic conditions whenever necessary[4].

The boiling points of perfluorous liquids is dependent on their molar mass and so a broad range is possible. As an example, the boiling points of fluorous alkanes are usually lower than the corresponding alkanes; this is attributed to decreased Van der Waals interactions. The density of perfluorous alkanes is higher than water and most other organic molecules. The perfluorous alkanes are commercially available; these also contain isomers and small amounts of their homologous.

Gases like oxygen, carbon dioxide and hydrogen are highly soluble in perfluorocarbons. At one time, the perflourocarbons were investigated as blood transfusion survogates[5]. However, due to high volatility and risk of embolism, this area of research was curtailed. The perfluorous organic compounds are mostly used in electrical power industry as dielectric liquids and in the pharmaceutical industry as additives[6]. Perfluorinated molecules show excellent solubilities in perfluorous solvents and also in supercritical $CO_2(SC - CO_2)$[7].

As already stated, the solubility of perfluorous liquids in organic solvents is temperature dependent. At ambient, most of the combinations of an orananic and a fluorous solvent are biphasic and at higher temperature they become monophasic; lowering of the temperature will result in re- formation of the biphasic system.

Following are some commonly used and commercially available perfluorinated solvents[8,9]: perfluorohexane (C_6F_{14}), perfluoroheptane (C_7F_{16}), perfluoromethylcyclohexane (C_7F_{14}), perfluorodecalin ($C_{10}F_{18}$) and perfluorotributylamine ($C_{12}F_{27}N$). Their m.p's are of the order $-87°$, $-78°$, $-45°$, $-10°$ and $-50°$ respectively. Their boiling points are of the order $75°$, $82°$, $72°$, $142°$ and $173°$ respectively. They are all heavier than water (density $1 g/cm^3$) is 1.68, 1.73, 1.79, 1.95 and 1.88 respectively).

The following are the various solvent systems[9] used along with the temperature at which they exist in 1 and 2 phases.

Solvent system (ratio 1 : 1)	No. of phases	Temperature (°C)
Perfluoro (methyl cyclohexane)	2	−16
$CF_3C_6F_{11}$/pentane	1	r.t.
$CF_3C_6F_{11}$/Diethylelter	2	0
	1	r.t.
$CF_3C_6F_{11}$/hexane	2	0
	1	r.t.
$CF_3C_6F_{11}$/CCl$_4$	2	r.t.
	1	>27
$CF_3C_6F_{11}$/CHCl$_3$	2	r.t.
	1	>50
Perfluorodecalin/toluere	2	r.t.
	1	64
$CF_3C_6F_{11}$/benzane	2	r.t.
	1	>85
$CF_3C_6F_{11}$/toluere	2	r.t.
	1	>89
$CF_3C_6F_{11}$/chlorobenzane	2	r.t.
	1	>127

Data taken from Ref. 9

3 PHASE SWITCHING

While planning any reaction involving fluorous technique, it is most important to think about the removal of the covalently bound fluorous tag from the desired product. The method chosen should not effect the organic moiety chemically. This is called phase switching. For this mild and efficient procedures are required. One such method, commonly used is Fluorous Reversed Phase Silica Gel Aided Work Up Procedure (FRPSG)[10,11]. In this procedure, interactions between the perfluoroalkyl chains on the surface of the gel and the fluorous ponytail of the labelled molecules lead to a retardation-the principle-which could be applied to purification of a single compound or isolation of various molecules with fluorous tags of different length by HPLC (fluorous mixture synthesis, Scheme 3)[12-16].

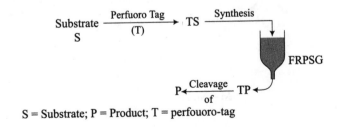

S = Substrate; P = Product; T = perfouoro-tag

Scheme 3

For filtration and extraction, organic solvent of variable polarity are applied, decreasing the polarity from polar (water, acetonitrile) via a polar organic to fluorous eluting the perfluorous tagged substance as the final fraction. This procedure was applied[12-16] to isolate perfluoro-allyl compounds, products of radical allylations of perfluoroalkyl iodides (Scheme 4)[17].

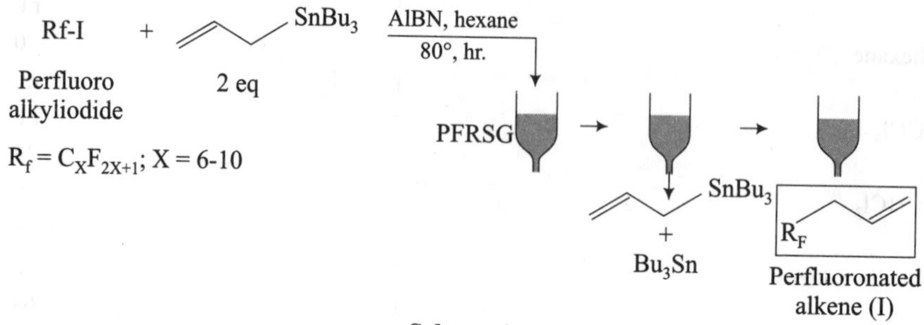

$R_f = C_X F_{2X+1}$; X = 6-10

Scheme 4

4 PERFLUORINATED CATALYSTS

A number of perfluorinated catalysts involving transition metals have been developed for use in organic synthesis involving fluorous phase techniques. Some of such catalysts are given below[1].

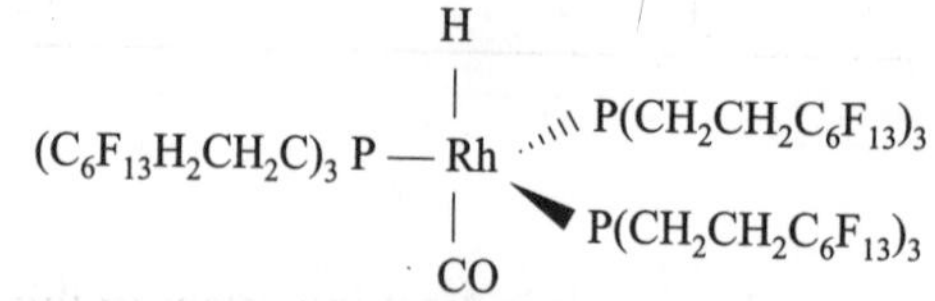

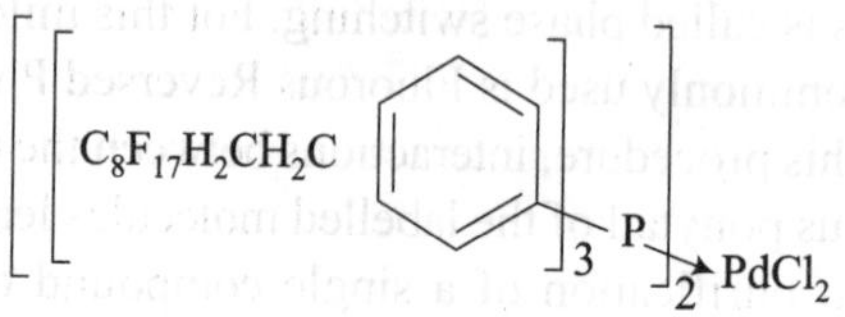

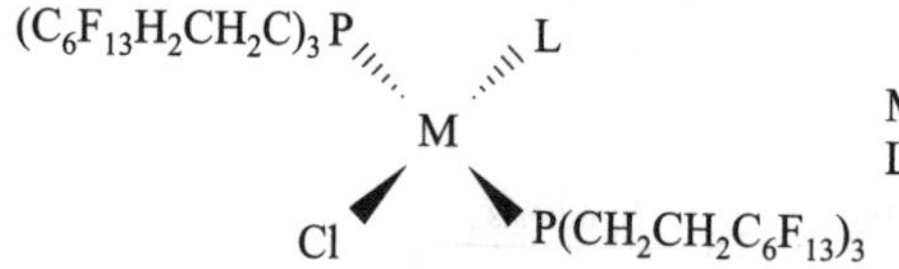

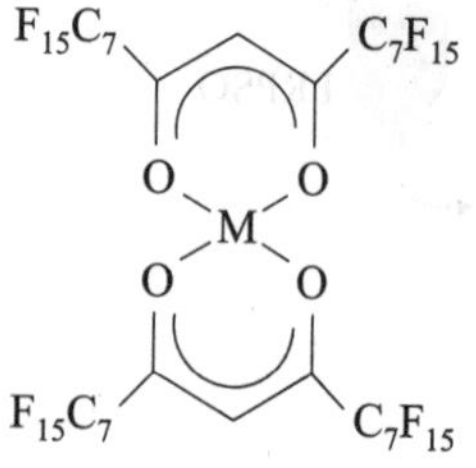

5 SOME APPLICATION OF FLUOROUS PHASE TECHNIQUES

1. Palladrium-catalysed carbon-carbon cross-coupling reactions such as Heck, Stille, Suzuki, Negishi and Sonogashira reactions[18-22] were carried out under fluorous conditions. In all these cases there is already elucidated advantage of product isolation and catalyst recovery. Now, reaction kits for Pd-catalysed carbon-carbon cross-coupling reactions in FBS are commercially available. These kits have been developed by Schneider and Bannwarth, Fluka company Lid, Buchs, Switzerland.

2. Friedel-crafts acylation was carried out in FBS applying lanthanide methides[23,24] and non-fluorous zinc chlorode was used as Friedel-Crafts catalyst in perfluorotriethylamine, which replaced highly toxic sym. tetrachloroethane[25].

3. Enantioselective alkylation of benzaldehyde in presence of chiral binaphthols and arylzinc-thiolates[26-28] was carried out.

4. Some other applications of Fluorous Phase Techniques are given below (Scheme 5).

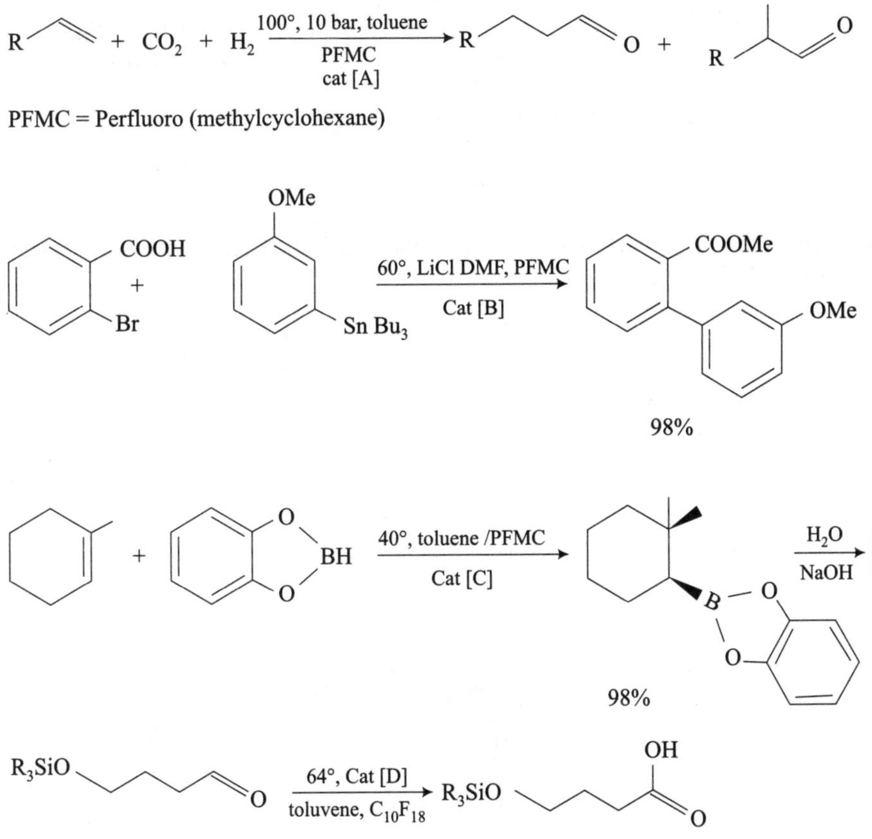

$$R \diagup\diagdown + CO_2 + H_2 \xrightarrow[\substack{PFMC \\ cat [A]}]{100°, 10 \text{ bar, toluene}} R \diagup\diagdown\diagup O + R \diagdown\diagup^O$$

PFMC = Perfluoro (methylcyclohexane)

Scheme 5

5. The reaction of an aldehyde with grignard reagent using fluorous phase technique give secondary alcohol (Scheme 6). The grignard reaction was worked up by double triphasic (fluorous/organic/aqueous) extraction comprising first a fluorous scavenging reaction of the alcohol followed by a cleavage of the perfluoro moiety by addition of CsF. Various stages/steps are shown in Scheme 6. In this procedure, recycling of the fluorous tag is not possible; this is a major disadvantage in this case.

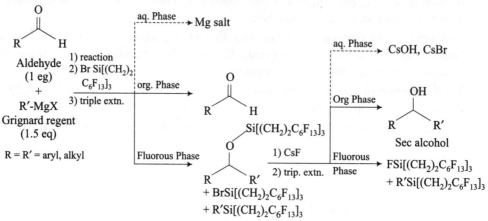

Scheme 6

6. Synthesis of tetrazoles: The reaction of perfluoro stannane linked azido with cyanides gave tetrazoles (Scheme 7)[29].

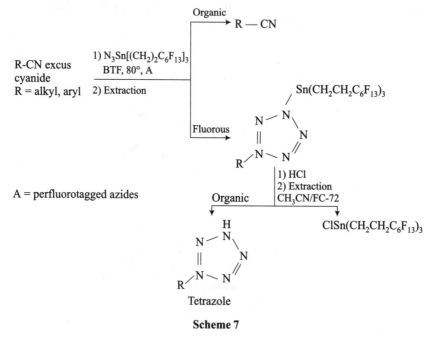

Scheme 7

7. N-Alkylation of primary and secondary amines can be achieved by reacting with excess of alkyl bromides[30,31] (Scheme 8).

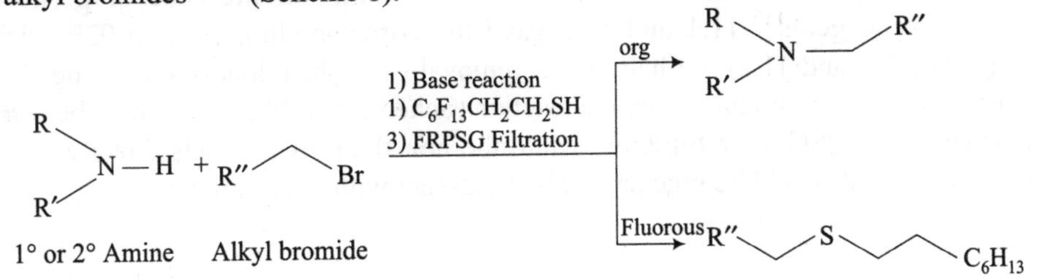

Scheme 8

8. Stille coupling has been achieved (Scheme 9) with perfluoro-tagged tin compounds[32,33].

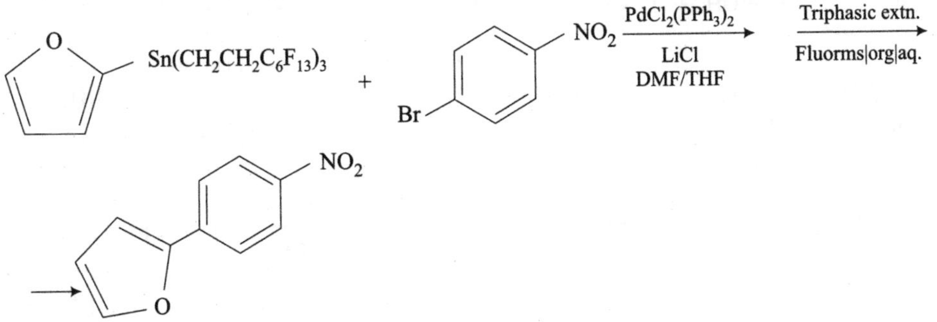

Scheme 9

9. 3H-Quinazoline-4-ones were prepared by an aza-Wittig reaction using fluorous triphenyl-phosphine (Scheme 10)[34,35].

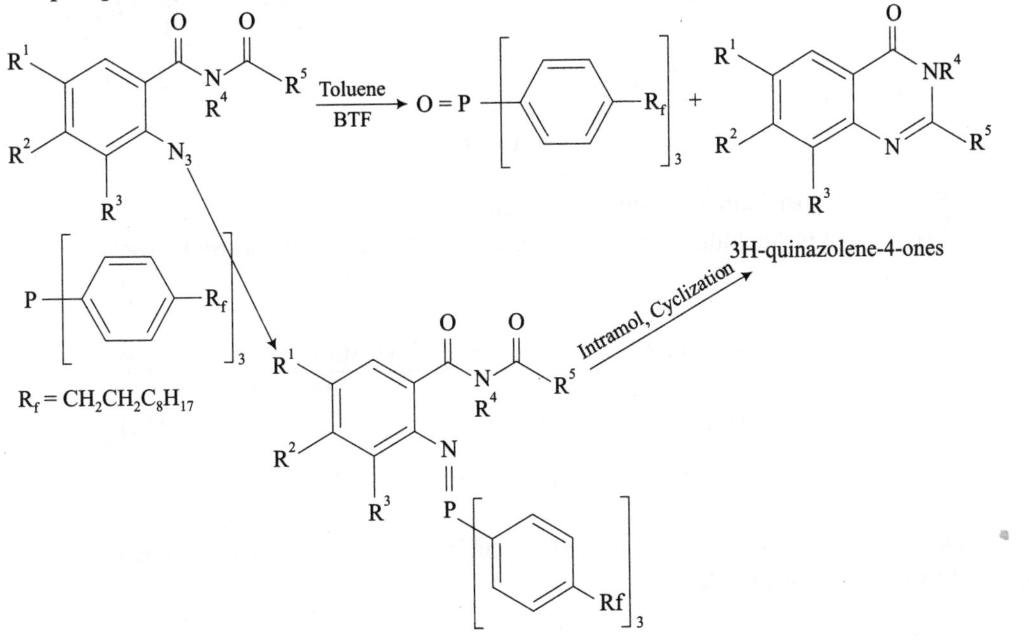

Scheme 10

10. Mitsunobu reaction with perfluorinated reagents.

    The reaction of 3,5-dinitrobenzoic acid with ethanol in presence of perfluorinated Mitsunobu reagents[36] 11.1 and 11.2 gave the corresponding ester in 92% yield. The reagents (11.1 and 11.2) are helpful for removal of triphenylphosphine oxide (11.3) and hydrazide (11.4) byproducts after the reaction (Scheme 11)[36,37]. These could be completely retained on FRPSG after filtration, while the non-fluorous products directly eluted. The original reagents could be regenerated by treatment with AlH_3 and Br_2.

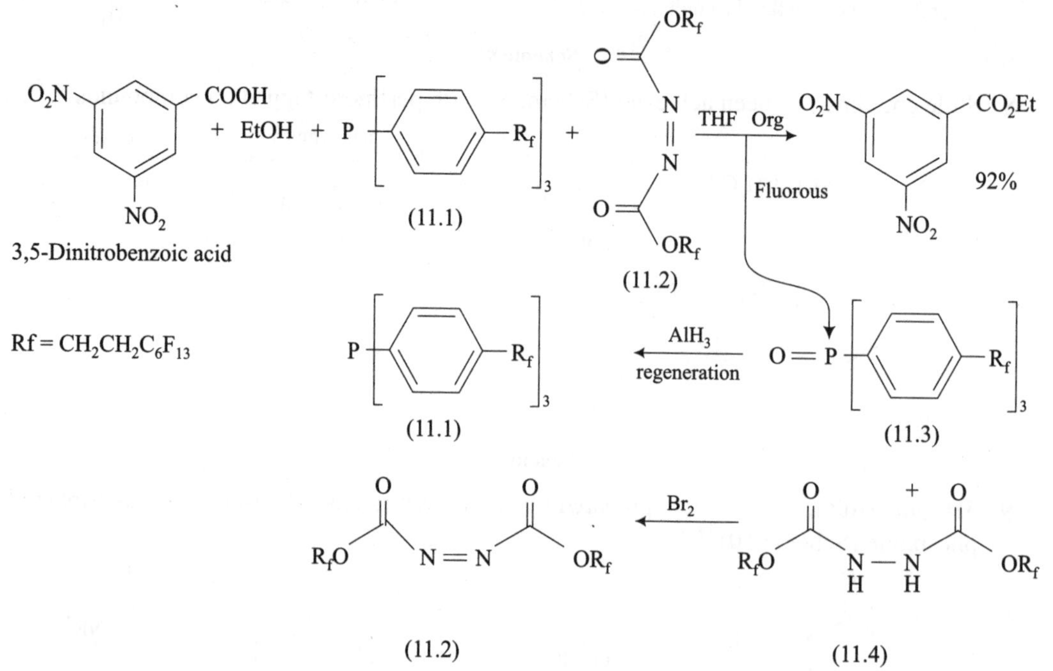

$Rf = CH_2CH_2C_6F_{13}$

Scheme 11

11. Synthesis of perfluoroalkyl sulfides and sulfoxides.

    Perfluoroalkyl sulphides (12.1) and sulfoxides (12.2) were synthesised[38] (Scheme 12)

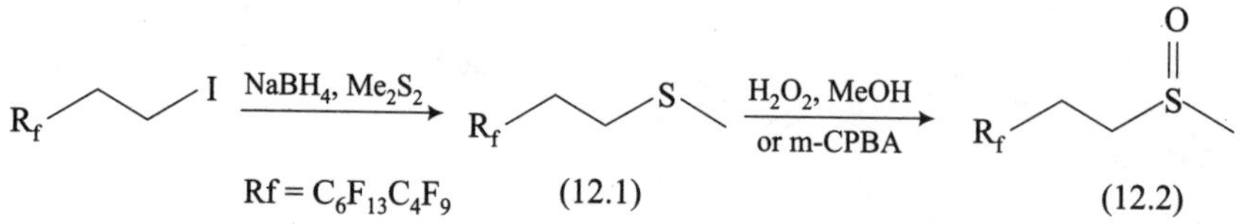

$Rf = C_6F_{13}C_4F_9$

Scheme 12

Using the sulfoxide (12.2), a number of 1° and 2° alcohols could be converted to the corresponding aldehydes and ketones.

6   CONCLUSION

Perfluorinated hydrocarbons are found to be unique solvents with interesting applications in organic synthesis. Due to their immisicibility with water and most common organic solvents, they represent a third liquid phase – the perfluorous phase. The high solubility of oxygen in the perfluorinated hydrocarbons permits some selective and efficient oxidation reactions under mild conditions. The individual components of the reaction mixtures which bear perfluoroalkyl substituents of sufficient size and number, can be selectively extracted into fluorous phase. This is the basis of the so-called fluorous synthesis.

References

1. D. Clarke, M.A. Ali, A.A. Cliford, A. Parratt, P. Rose, D. Schwinn, W. Bannwarth and C.M. Rayner, *Current Topics in Medicinal Chemistry*, 2004, **4**, 729.
2. I.T. Horvath and J.R. Abai, Science, 1994, **266**, 72.
3. P.L. Nostro, *Adv. Colloid Interface Sci.*, 1995, **56**, 245.
4. W. Keim, M. Vogt, P. Wasserscheid and B. Driessen-Holscher, *J., Mol. Catalysis A. Chemical*, 1999, **139**, 171.
5. T.H. Maigh, Science, 1979, **206**, 205; J.G. Riess and M.L. Blanc, Pure Appl. Chem., 1982, **54**, 2383.
6. G. Sandford, Phil. Trans. R. Soc. London. A, 2000, **358**, 455.
7. T. Osswald, S. Schneider, S. Wang, W. Bannwarth and W. Stille, Tetrahedron Lett., 2001, 42, 2965; S. Kainz, D. Koch, W. Baimann and W. Leitner, Angew. Chem. Int. Ed., 1997, **36**, 1628.
8. B. Betzemeier and P. Kochil, Top. Curr. Chem., 1999, **206**, 61.
9. L.P. Barthel-Rosa and J.A. Gladysz, Coord. Chem. Rev., 1999, Pages 190, 587.
10. C.C. Tzschucke, C. Markert, H. Glatz and W. Bannwarth, Angew. Chem. Int. Ed., 2002, **41**, 4500.
11. S. Kainz, Z. Luo, D.P. Curran and W. Leithner, Synthesis, 1998, 1425.
12. D.P. Curran and Z. Luo, J. Am. Chem. Soc., 1999, **121**, 9069.
13. Q. Zhang, Z. Luo and D.P. Curran, J. Org. Chem., 2000, **65**, 8866.
14. D.P. Curran and S. Hadida, J. Am. Chem. Soc., 1996, **118**, 2531.
15. D.P. Curran and T. Oderaotoshi, Tetrahedron, 2001, **57**, 5243.
16. Z. Luo, Q. Zhang, Y. Oderaotoshi and D.P. Curran, Science, 2001, **291**, 1766.
17. I. Ryu, S. Kreimerman, T. Niguma, S. Minakata, M. Somatsu, Z. Lou and D.P. Curran, Tetrahedron Lett., 2001, **42**, 947.
18. J. Monineau, G. Pozzi, S. Quici and D. Sinou, Tetrahedron Lett., 1999, **40**, 7683.
19. B. Betzemeier and P. Knochel, Angew. Chem. Int. Edn., 1997, **36**, 2623.
20. S. Schneider and W. Bannwarth, Angew. Chem. Int. Edn., 2000, **39**, 4142.
21. S. Schneider and W. Bannwarth, Helv. Chim. Acta, 2001, **84**, 735.
22. C. Markert and W. Bannwarth, Hel. Chim, Acta, 2002, **85**, 1877.
23. A.G.M. Barrett, D.C. Braddock, D. Catterick, D. Chadwick, J.P. Henschke and R.M. Mckinnell, Synlett, 2000, 847.
24. K. Mikami, Y. Mikami, Y. Matsumoto, J. Nishikido, F. Yamamoto and H. Nakajima, Tetrahedron Lett., 2001, **42**, 289.
25. T. Kitazume, J. Fluorine Chem., 2000, **105**, 265.

26. H. Kleijn, E. Rijnberg, J.T.B.H. Jastrzebski and G.V. Koten, Org. Lett., 1999, **I**, 853.

27. Y. Nakanura, S. Tekeuchi, Y. Ohgo and D.P. Curran, Tetrahedron, 2000, **56**, 351.

28. Y. Tian and K.S. Chan, Tetrahedron Lett., 2000, **41**, 8813.

29. D.P. Curran, Angew. Chem. Int. Ed., 1998, **37**, 1175.

30. M.W. Creswell, G.L. Bolton, G. Hodges and M. Meppen, Tetrahedron, 1998, **54**, 3983.

31. B. Linclau, A.K. Singh and D.P. Curran, J. Org. Chem., 1999, **64**, 2835.

32. M. Hoshino, P. Degenkolb and D.P. Curran, J. Org. Chem., 1997, **62**, 8341.

33. J.K. Still, Angew. Chem. Int. Ed. Engl., 1986, **25**, 508.

34. P. Molina and M.J. Vilaplane, Synthesis, 1994, 1197.

35. S. Barthemy, S. Schneider and W. Bannwarth, Tetrahedron Lett., 2002, **43**, 807.

36. S. Dandapani and D.P. Curran, Tetrahedron, 2002, **58**, 3855.

37. O. Mitsunobu, M. Yamada and T. Mukaiyama, Bull. Chem. Soc. Jpn., 1967, **40**, 935.

38. D. Crich and S. Neelamkavi, Tetrahedron, 2002, **58**, 3865.

Index